THE
DVD
STACK

April 2009

David,

A small thankyou for all
your hard work & patience
in taking the photographs
at our wedding. It really
was most appreciated and
we have some fantastic
pictures to remember the
day.

Much love

Andy, Taz
(& Piper)

x

THE DVD STACK 2

THE ESSENTIAL GUIDE TO THE WORLD'S BEST DVDS

EDITED BY
NICK BRADSHAW & TIM ROBEY

CANONGATE
Edinburgh · New York · Melbourne

First published in Great Britain in 2007 by
Canongate Books Ltd, 14 High Street,
Edinburgh EH1 1TE

1

British Library Cataloguing-in-Publication Data
A catalogue record for this book is available on
request from the British Library

ISBN 978 1 84767 004 5

Typeset by Palimpsest Book Production Ltd,
Grangemouth, Stirlingshire
Printed and bound in Great Britain by Creative Print and Design Ltd,
Ebbw Vale, Wales

www.canongate.net

Contributors

Manish Agarwal
Vera Brunner-Sung
Tom Charity
Ian Christie
James Clasper
Jonathan Clements
Simon Cropper
Nick Davis
Gareth Evans
Dan Franklin
Toby Frost
Nick Funnell
Ryan Gilbey
Arwa Haider
Ian Haydn Smith
Larushka Ivan-Zadeh
Geoffrey Macnab
Demetrios Matheou
Dominic Maxwell
Sophie Mayer
Mike McCahill
Hannah McGill
Isabelle McNeill
Andy Miller
Henry K Miller
Mark Monahan
Fiona Mountford
Joe Perkins
Mark Pilkington
Rebekah Polding
Jonathan Rafman
Andy Richards
SF Said
Sukhdev Sandhu
Adam Strevens
Maxie Szalwinska
Paul Tickell
Peter Vásáry
Ben Walters
Peter Watts

CONTENTS

PREFACE

The world of DVD gets ever shinier, happier and more complicated, year on year. There has never been a better moment to build a film collection than right now, because there's never been a medium offering such high-quality home viewing, and such a comprehensive range of titles, this affordably. And the situation keeps getting better: the last 12 months have brought in a deluge of new box sets, remasterings, special editions and movies arriving on disc for the first time.

In our aim to provide as up-to-date as possible a template for DVD libraries everywhere, we've added some 100 completely new entries for this edition, deleted a handful, and revised around 50 to keep up with the curve. If an entry from *The DVD Stack 1* now comes on a Region 0 double-disc edition with unmissable outtakes and a director's commentary, it's in here. If they've spruced up the visuals for its twenty-fifth anniversary, that's in here too.

The other bonus of an expanded list has been the scope it's given us for beefing up our overview of world cinema. Having frugally rationed out a lot of our choices by director (*Nashville* for Altman, say, and *Some Like it Hot* for Billy Wilder) we've enjoyed the chance to splash out a bit (with *The Company* and *Sunset Boulevard*). Significant gaps (William Wyler, Max Ophüls, Louis Malle) have been plugged. And while we might have baulked at considering *Labyrinth* or *The Cell* completely essential inclusions the first time around, we don't now.

With the rival hi-def formats locking heads and looking unconvincing to all but the most specialist (and loaded) consumer, DVD is truly in its heyday. It is the moment to capitalise, to pounce, to put up more shelves. And to go out on a limb, not just rectifying the absence of *Jaws* or *Apocalypse Now* from your living room, but taking a punt, perhaps, on the Argentinian masterpiece *La Niña Santa*, the vintage experimental films of Maya Deren, or the neglected comic gem that is – yes – *MouseHunt*.

All are featured, and the presentations are as deluxe, for the most part, as DVD knows how to make them. Take a browse . . .

TIM ROBEY, JUNE 2007

INTRODUCTION

> 'Movies are dead'
> — Susan Sontag, *New York Times*, 1996

> 'It has never been a better time to be a film fan'
> — Gary Tooze, *DVDBeaver.com*, 2005

In the beginning God created 120-millimetre optical discs. And the discs were blank; and worn-out VHS tape was upon the face of the television. And God said, Let there be encoded MPEG-2 compressed video, and two to six channels of AC3 sound. And a 650-nanometer red laser moved upon the face of the discs.

And God said, Let there be popcorn: and the disc was spun. And God saw that the first film was *Twister*, and it was not so good. But it shone bright and was loud. And God listened to tales of how Jan de Bont created the blustering wind from the void. And the evening and morning were the first day.

And men from the Americas came to God and said, Lord, our analogue television system uses the standards laid down by the National Television Systems Committee in 1941 and 1953, in which there are fewer lines of picture resolution than in the lands of Phase Alternating Line, and a different refresh rate, according to the electrical current frequency of our land. And God divided the PAL discs from the NTSC discs, and formatted the NTSC discs to play 720x480 pixels at 29.97 frames per second, and the PAL discs to play 720x576 pixels at 25 frames per second. And the evening and morning were the second day.

And men from Digital Theater Systems, Inc came to God and said, Lord, our multi-channel surround-sound format is richer and more life-like than Dolby's AC3. And God added DTS alongside the AC3 encoding, on discs where there was spare bit-space and a likely market. And the evening and morning were the third day.

And the masters of Jan de Bont came to God and said, Lord, the devil may take digital copies of *Twister*, and beguile our customers therewith, unless we can place a flaming sword at the gate of the digital bit-stream, to keep the way of the river of revenue. And God added Content Scrambling System encryption coding, and gave the masters of de Bont the power to licence the software key.

And those masters again came before God and said, Lord, we would sell *Twister* to the Kenites before we sell it to the Kennizites, and to the Kadmonites before the Hittites; and the Perizzites should wait the longest to buy our produce: for so suiteth our business model. And God granted them a system of region coding, so that the world would be as six. And the evening and morning were the fourth day.

And the cinematographer of Jan de Bont and his brethren came before God and said, Lord, our eyes are opened wide by the wonders of the world, and we no longer shoot in the television ratio of 4:3, but rather in widescreen 16:9, yeah, even up to the CinemaScope ratio called 2.35:1 which is actually 2.39:1, for this is suitable for filming serpents and coffins. But if we must still encode our picture onto discs in that old ratio that was first born, then we must also record black bars above and below to preserve our picture format, lest the masters of Jan de Bont and the broadcasters of television make us chop the sides off our images. And yet those black bars will waste valuable lines of resolution, and make the effective picture smaller. And we would rather make larger movies like *The Robe*. And God pondered, and developed anamorphic enhancement for widescreen television, so that a horizontally squeezed picture on the disc could be re-stretched on the screen.

And the evening and morning were the fifth day.

And the masters of Jan de Bont again came before God and said, Lord, the manufacturers of DVD players are our enemies: for they make machines which play discs from all regions, and disregard our region coding. And God wondered if it was the seventh day yet; but he added Region Coding Enhancement to certain discs, which would not play in open-coded and many older players. And the evening and morning were the sixth day.

And on the seventh day God put his feet up. But yet came forth the manufacturers of discs from the lands of PAL, saying, Lord, films shot at 24 frames per second run 4 per cent faster when we transfer them to disc at PAL speed; and the pitch of their soundtracks rises almost a semi-tone. Where can we find digital signal processing techniques that will again lower the pitch without introducing audio smearing?

And their cousins in the lands of NTSC joined them saying, Lord, when we take our digital transfers of films' prints from PAL video sources, which might be cheaper than making our own transfers, we introduce surplus and blended video fields, which wastes disc space, and causes double-exposure ghosting on still-frame images. How may we silence the critics who would cavil?

And God considered these details, and said, Devil, get thee out. For thou hast sown great confusion in the living-rooms of the world.

And Satan came forth, saying, Wouldst thou like to see my new

405-nanometer blue laser technology? I have made two rival high-definition formats to replace thy DVDs. How about a format war?

Susan Sontag mourned the decay of cinephilia, defined as an attentive (and tasteful) surrender to the awe-inspiring cinema image – impossible, she argued, in a living-room or bedroom. Others would argue that mystic rituals of spectatorship remain possible in private; even, indeed, that concentrated communion might be easier in isolation than amongst the theatre's distraction-seeking masses. Others again might suggest that the movies have always been as much about appropriation as self-abnegation: as with pop music, you surround yourself with the films you love. Stacking DVDs to the ceiling merely literalises the process.

The Best Making-ofs

Buenos Aires Zero Degrees (on *Happy Together*)
The Hamster Factor (on *Twelve Monkeys*)
Shadowing the Third Man (on *The Third Man*)
Terror Takes Shape (on *The Thing*)
10 on *Ten* (on *Ten*)

What seems most true is that, as screen types and sizes proliferate, turning our phones, fridges, transport and billboards into virtual windows, moving imagery will continue to multiply and mutate; Sontag's One True Cinema may become a museum phenomenon, but that does not necessarily leave the entirety of the movie culture that survives it as its binary opposite, banal and disposable.

Peer closely into a DVD and, unlike in a frame of film, you won't see a miniature of Godard's 'truth 24 times a second', merely a rainbow reflection; digital video removes us from the moving image as well as bringing it closer home. (The likes of Len Lye and Stan Brakhage would not have found great joy trying to scratch artful animating patterns into the surface of a disc.)

Nevertheless, this is now the medium we are consigning most of our movie culture to, its convenience, accessibility and longevity prevailing over qualitative concerns about the loss of organic celluloid photographic resolution. DV is non-degradable (except by the attrition of technological innovation), easily distributable (by post or by telecom), privatisable (which suits both the capitalists and collectors) and endlessly reproducible (which spooks them both). As for DVDs, in particular, do we need to remind ourselves of their gains on videotape? Double the video resolution; multi-linearity (extras, and multiple edits, soundtrack and subtitle options); chapter markings and instant track access; slimmer packaging; and, while they may scratch, they don't twist or snap.

DVD doesn't officially stand for anything – its inventors couldn't agree on whether they preferred 'Digital Video Disc' or 'Digital Versatile Disc'. In this book, we're not too interested in data-storage DVDs, multi-channel DVD-Audio albums or PlayStation games; we're surveying DVD as the new medium of film repertory (ie a repository for the cinema repertoire). While the world's remaining repertory theatres do a valiant job of circulating and showcasing 110 years of celluloid history, they're a rare breed, permanently tilting against the deterioration of prints. Budding students of film must nowadays make their exploratory forays in large part on video; fans and historians must feed their movie monkeys in bytes.

> ## The Best Extras
>
> *Andrei Rublev*
> *Clerks*
> *The Corporation*
> *DodgeBall: A True Underdog Story*
> *Dr. Strangelove*
> *Eternal Sunshine of the Spotless Mind*
> *The Matrix*
> *Monty Python and the Holy Grail*
> *The Royal Tenenbaums*
> *A Streetcar Named Desire*
> *The Terminator*
> *The Texas Chainsaw Massacre*
> *The Battle of Algiers*
> *The Wicker Man*
> *Children of Men*

DVD is also a medium that has its own particular qualities (setting aside the question of its audio and visual characteristics). 'Extras' like commentary tracks, interviews, making-of featurettes and supplementary short films may offer added value, but they can also serve as annotations and appendices to the main feature, providing context and critical interpretations. DVD producers are still learning the art of these extras, some faster than others. Equally, criticism needs to broaden its sights to encompass these new aspects of movie appreciation. Certainly, there are some DVDs so stuffed with creative extras that the centre no longer holds: the notion of the unified 'film', artistically above and apart from its surrounding DVD aperçus, no longer holds water. (See *DodgeBall* and *Fight Club* for particular illustration of this point.)

This tome, then, is aimed as a guidebook for those revisiting old familiars in the digital medium anew, as much as for those hunting the treasures of cinema afresh. We also hope it hosts some new voices and perspectives on some of those old favourites (speaking of both films and filmmakers). The science behind our choice of 350-odd titles is subject to strict commercial confidentiality, not to mention several pending patents, but suffice it to say we've striven for a mix of the canonical and eclectic, representing both the best of cinema and the best of DVD. Insofar as the sales catalogues are now bewilderingly vast, we've tried to suggest some essential viewing; insofar as all the best-of film polls you've ever seen become blinkered by aggregation and the limits of their polling constituencies, we've tried to throw in some alternatives, and let our writers follow their idiosyncrasies.

Thus some titles are here as exemplars of the DVD form (see *Directors Commentary* for the most piquant example), some despite their current DVD presentation. Wong Kar-Wai's *In the Mood for Love* has fared much better by various digital publishers than his relatively underrated *Happy Together* – but you already know how great the former is, right? We hear different voices singing the praises of both Chaplin and Keaton. They can't both be right – but here they both are. And for every Ozu there's a *Wizard of Oz*; for every *Un Chien Andalou*, a *Gremlins*.

The Best Movies About Movies

Bowfinger
David Holzman's Diary
Directors Commentary
Histoire(s) du Cinéma
Man with a Movie Camera
Le Mépris (Contempt)
Mulholland Drive
Onde Jaz O Teu Sorriso? (Where Does Your Hidden Smile Lie?)
A Personal Journey with Martin Scorsese through American Movies
Sherlock Junior (in The Buster Keaton Collection)
Sunset Boulevard
Visions of Light

Just as DVD extends the parameters of film appreciation, so we've stretched the definition of the term 'movie'. We've included short films (the original film form): *Un Chien Andalou, Avant Garde: Experimental Cinema of the '20s and '30s,* and compilations dedicated to Norman McLaren, Maya Deren, Kenneth Anger, Stan Brakhage, Jan Svankmajer, Margaret Tait, the Brothers Quay and British short films; we've also included similar round-ups of non-feature work by Spike Jonze and Chris Cunningham, which centre on their music videos. We've excluded serials and television work (with the exception of *Directors Commentary*) – although, as argued, *Kill Bill* might best be viewed in the mode of a Saturday morning serial. We also broke that rule for Lars von Trier's haunted hospital drama *The Kingdom* (*I* and *II*), in the spirit of von Trier's own ad lib approach to guidelines. *A Personal Journey with Martin Scorsese through American Movies* could also be described as a made-for-television rather than a feature documentary; it's in here because, as much as *Directors Commentary*, it's 'meta'.

No doubt we've made some mistakes, of omission and commission. Where are Griffith, Vidor, Warhol, Mike Leigh? There should be 25 more Renoirs. The list tilts towards Western filmmaking – pretty much half the book are American films – and it's skewed towards the modern; these are functions both of pet favouritism, likely that of most readers as much as our writers, and of the bias of DVD production (and English subtitles were a prerequisite). Certain tech-savvy modern auteurs – I'm thinking David Fincher – are also far more likely to have a hand in producing feature-rich DVDs – and, perhaps, to appeal to similarly geeky DVD-philes.

A list of the directors on whom we've doubled up perhaps encapsulates our coverage: we've included two entries for each of the following (deep breath): Luis Buñuel, Howard Hawks, Victor Fleming, Robert Bresson, Douglas Sirk, Billy Wilder, Elia Kazan, Orson Welles, Akira Kurosawa, Alfred Hitchcock, Robert Aldrich, Michelangelo Antonioni, Jean-Luc Godard, Eric Rohmer, Sam Peckinpah, Stanley Kubrick, Francis Ford Coppola, Robert Altman, Bernardo Bertolucci, Rainer Werner Fassbinder, Nic Roeg, Brian De Palma, Terry Gilliam, David Lynch, David Cronenberg, Lars von Trier, John McTiernan, the Coen brothers, Michael Mann, Ang Lee, Todd Haynes, Richard Linklater, Alfonso Cuáron and Paul Greengrass. (Yep, all men.) And if you factor in the directors represented in the *Alien Quadrilogy* box set you'd also have two by James Cameron and three by David Fincher, joining the trio of films by Michael Powell, Ingmar Bergman and Steven Spielberg and the quartet by Martin Scorsese.

On the other hand, younger generations of film fans will espy only one title by Ridley Scott. *Blade Runner* has been in DVD limbo for several years, licensing wrangles following on from a less than splendid release of Scott's 1992 Director's Cut in the early days of DVD. Warners finally released a limited edition remaster of that particular cut in late 2006, but we're still waiting on Scott's 'Final Cut', which promises a new digital print, reworked special effects (see our *Empire Strikes Back* review for a discussion of whether this particular promise isn't more of a threat), and remastered digital surround sound. At the time of writing, the studio plans to promote this cut with a theatrical (re)release, followed by a multi-disc DVD and HD-DVD special edition featuring the two original cuts (American and international), the remastered Director's Cut, and the new Final Cut. Gulp.

Most Wanted

Unavailable

Shohei Imamura's Palme d'Or winner *The Ballad of Narayama*
FW Murnau's long-lost *City Girl*
Walerian Borowczyk's **surrealist short animations**
Wang Xiaoshuai's Sixth Generation underground *The Days*
  ('*Dongchun de Rizi*')
Abbas Kiarostami's breakthrough **Koker Trilogy** (*Where Is My
  Friend's House?*; *And Life Goes On . . .*; *Through the Olive Trees*)
More **Ken Loach**!
Len Lye's **complete animation**
Jean Eustache's epic *nouvelle vague* epitaph *La Maman et la Putain*
  (*The Mother and the Whore*)
Victor Erice's *The Quince Tree Sun*
Max Ophüls's *La Ronde*
Chen Kaige's mould-breaking early features *Yellow Earth* and *King
  of the Children*

Better editions required

Errol Morris's eccentric masterpiece *Fast, Cheap and Out of Control*
Albert Lewin's Technicolor fantasia *Pandora and the Flying
  Dutchman*
Apichatpong Weerasethakul's *Tropical Malady*

Coming soon (we're promised) . . .

Ridley Scott's *Blade Runner: Final Cut*
The Charles Burnett Collection (including *Killer of Sheep* and *My
  Brother's Wedding*)
Terence Davies' *Distant Voices, Still Lives*
Disney's *The Jungle Book*
Frantisek Vlácil's *Marketa Lazarová*
Jean-Marie Straub and Danièle Huillet's *Moses and Aaron*
Abel Gance's *Napoleon*

Last year we were also crossing our fingers for long-promised DVDs of Godard's mammoth 1998 video meditation *Histoire(s) du Cinéma* from Gaumont in France, and Charles Burnett's 1977 neorealist Watts ghetto rapture *Killer of Sheep* from Milestone in the US. The Godard finally came out, and is in here. *Killer of Sheep* got a full-blown 30th-anniversary restoration, and belated music-rights clearance, and is making its way from an international theatrical release onto DVD as part of a collected Charles Burnett box set this autumn.

Disney is another story. Hardly a company to believe in gifting the culture its heritage, Disney sticks to a business plan whereby it releases its cartoon classics in strictly limited time-frames, thus giving them an artificial rarity value. We thought it might be nice to include, say, *Snow White*, *Pinocchio*, *The Jungle Book* or even *Beauty and the Beast*, some of which have previously appeared (and are often still available from secondary vendors) in lavishly festooned collector's and 'platinum' edition box sets. But the next scheduled DVD appearance of *Beauty and the Beast*, for instance, is now 2012. (*The Jungle Book* is due out in October 2007 in a limited 'Platinum Edition'.)

One last point. Could the makers of *Final Destination 2* please record a commentary track for *Ai No Corrida*? That could be glorious.

Boring technical overview

This book took us into some dark places. We're grateful to DVD Beaver (*dvdbeaver.com*) for its meticulous technical comparisons of many DVDs (with screen captures!) and discussions of the myriad ways in which DVD producers can fall astray. Rewind (*dvdcompare.net*) hosts an invaluable comparative database of technical specifications and extras on different DVD editions. DVD Verdict (*dvdverdict.com*) and DVD Times (*dvdtimes.co.uk*) are also excellent news and review sites that critique DVDs as well as the films on them.

All of this assumes that you care about the quality of the DVDs you buy. (If not, this book isn't for you.) Unfortunately, the complexities of DVD technology would make geeks out of all of us.

The most outrageous obstacle DVD buyers face is an entirely artificial one: the imposition of the Hollywood studios' **Region Coding** system which attempts to divide the world into six separate markets, presumably in descending order of privilege (North America and Canada; Europe, Japan, the Middle East and South Africa; South-East Asia; South America and Australia; the rest of Africa and Asia; and China). A disc sold in one region is meant to be unplayable in machines in a different region: the idea is to allow the studios to maintain control over differential DVD release dates, content and prices, regardless that this flies in the face of the modern mantra of free (let alone fair) trade and competition.

Besides pissing off travellers and professional migrants who might need to watch discs from different regions on their laptops, this would also stop collectors from buying titles released in regions other than their own; thankfully, the system has largely been a failure. Multi-region DVD players, usually hacked by the vendor before sale to disable the region-enforcement hardware, are easy purchases; several DVD publishers code their discs as Region 0 (all regions); and the authorities in Australia and New Zealand have ruled against region coding as a violation of competition law. Of the two rival formats designated to succeed DVD, HD-DVD has abondoned region coding altogether, while Blu-Ray has reduced the divisions to three (the Americas and South-East Asia, Europe, Africa and Australasia, and central Asia), albeit with reinforced digital locks.

Then there's the **PAL/NTSC** divide, born of the different electricity frequencies in Europe and America. Most European televisions happily play NTSC signals; North American televisions more rarely play PAL. (Front projectors, plasma and LCD screens, including computer monitors, are even more adaptable.) Come the era of High Definition, rival standards will only affect broadcast transmission signals, not the recorded information on HD discs, which should, in technical terms, become universally standardised.

What does that mean for international DVD buyers? PAL pictures are higher resolution; NTSC have a faster (better) refresh rate, although most modern PAL TV sets double the scanning frequency to 100Hz to remove noticeable flicker. The two standards also produce different side-effects when transferring movies shot on film at 24 frames per second. **PAL Speed-up** describes the process of copying cinema frames directly to PAL video frames; in effect, the film is made to run at 25 rather than 24 frames per second. You may or may not be bothered that the resulting video runs 4 per cent faster than at the cinema, but certainly those with perfect pitch can hear the audio rise nearly a semi-tone, which also affects the timbre of sound. Digital signal processors can be used to shift the pitch back down, although not without compromising the sound to a degree.

NTSC avoids this with a system to distribute film's 24 frames per second evenly across the video signal's 30. Known as **3:2 pulldown**, this introduces its own problems on traditional cathode ray tube televisions, which split the video frames into interlaced 'fields', or half-frames, fired in turn on the odd and even lines of resolution (another antique solution, in this case to reduce flicker on slower displays). In effect, the 3:2

pulldown equation recomposes some video frames from two consecutive film frames. When there's pronounced movement across those frames, their overlap causes visual quirks — '**interlacing artefacts**' — that include 'ghosting' (overlapping images on cuts), 'combing' (jagged edges, when half the image moves before the other half) and line twitter (flickering fine horizontal lines). (DVD resolution is normally deliberately limited to preempt the latter.)

These foibles are usually introduced in the playback, rather than encoded onto the disc, and modern 'progressive scan' DVD players can skip the interlacing, sending full clean frames to a display, albeit at the cost of slight judder on smooth movements. There's an exception, though: NTSC videos recorded from PAL transfers of film sources encode the extra interlaced fields right into their source code, wasting disc space as well as making the artefacts indelible. NTSC DVD producers who rely on PAL transfers get low marks.

Elsewhere, too, good DVD presentation is a matter of due diligence.

Between the advent of widescreen televisions and our better education about differences of **aspect ratio** (the proportions of a screen), DVDs certainly do a better job of preserving films' original framing than in the early days of VHS; panning-and-scanning (truncating the sides of a widescreen image to fit the 4:3 ratio of old-fashioned TV screens) is now mercifully rare, although some American DVDs still offer it as an option (usually called 'full screen'). Some publishers are wont to make minor trims from the sides of film prints, for reasons best known to themselves. There's also the technology variously labelled as 'anamorphic enhancement' or 'enhancement for 16:9 widescreen' (as opposed to 'letterboxed'), which squeezes the widescreen picture into the available disc space, without wasting resolution on black bars; the display unpacks it again. Older academy ratio (4:3) films, of course, require 'pillarboxing', or framing between vertical black bars, to maintain their dimensions on a widescreen display.

There's also some minor controversy surrounding the recent practice of **black-windowboxing** a DVD's entire image (horizontally and vertically) to compensate for 'TV overscan', whereby older televisions deliberately zoom in on an image and crop the edges to boost the picture stability. Opponents argue that this is a regressive policy, designed for older hardware that will likely become obsolete sooner than your DVD collection (or so you'd hope). As the folks at DVD Beaver point out, flaws (in this case, reduced picture resolution) that may seem minor on current set-ups will be more pronounced on the more demanding High Definition screens of the future.

A **high-quality transfer** from a clean or restored negative is of course ideal. Digital noise reduction attempts to remove scratches, spots and other debris from the image; image enhancement, often aiming to present a cleaner-looking image and sharper contours, tends to efface finer textural details and produce chiselled outlines around subjects and haloes around light sources. Similarly, contrast boosting risks blowing out whites and polarising tones. **Subtitles** shouldn't be burnt into the recorded image; DVDs are capable of storing them separately, to be toggled on or off (although that explains why DVD subtitles have their jagged bitmapping rather than the smoothness of film subtitles).

The Best Sound

Apocalypse Now – The Complete Dossier
Kill Bill
Lord of the Rings – The Fellowship of the Ring
Once Upon a Time in the West
Solaris

Some sound connoisseurs prefer **DTS** surround-soundtracks to the lower-bitrate **Dolby Digital**. Their availability is more common on American DVDs; European and other discs often sacrifice them to make way for multiple subtitle tracks (*Toy Story* is one example). Purists might also take issue with the fashion for remastering old films' soundtracks in more modern surround formats, rendering them somewhat anachronistic. Musicals aside, it's usually rare that the practise actually revises the sound substantially, except in cases where such directors as Steven Spielberg, George Lucas and Robert Zemeckis have been able to retinker with their old pop hits. There are also examples of discs (see *Sunrise*, *The Umbrellas of Cherbourg*, *Vertigo*) that offer original mono soundtracks alongside spruce new speaker workouts.

Finally, there's the question of the **cut** of the original movie itself. Director's cuts, extended versions and 'unrated' special editions have helped drive the DVD boom, but there are still many examples of films that are censored, either by bodies such as the Board of British Film

Classification (see *Strange Days*, *Lilo and Stitch*) or by producers and studios looking for a lower age rating or a trimmer running time. Some older films can be reassembled into a best-guess assembly (*L'Atalante*, *The Passion of Joan of Arc*, *The Big Red One*); some remain broken-backed for all their restorers' diligent archaeology (*A Star is Born*). And even the directors of *Andrei Rublev* and *The Shining* left us with multiple versions of those movies. It gets messy (*Manhunter*). But hell, so does the world. And if spotlessness is next to Godliness in the garden of the digital, the one true eternally shiny DVD is surely spinning where Pope's 'unfading rose of Eden blooms'.

NICK BRADSHAW, 2006 and 2007

The Very Best DVDs

Casablanca
Fanny and Alexander
Fight Club
Jaws
The Work of Director Spike Jonze
King Kong (1933)
Man with a Movie Camera
Oldboy
Pandora's Box
Seven Samurai
Singin' in the Rain
Sunrise
The Third Man
This is Spinal Tap
Timecode
24 Hour Party People
The Complete Shorts Films of Jan Svankmajer
Vertigo
The Jean Vigo Collection

The Best Box Sets

The Aliens Quadrilogy
The Back to the Future Trilogy
John Cassavetes: Five Films
The Film Noir Classic Collection, Vol 1
The Buster Keaton Collection
The Marx Brothers Silver Screen Collection
Norman McLaren: The Masters Edition
Mikio Naruse Volume One
Eric Rohmer's Six Moral Tales
The John Wayne John Ford Film Collection

The Adjuster

(Canada, 1991)

Director: Atom Egoyan
Label: Network (UK)
Region: 2 (PAL)
Discs: 1

THE FILM

An experiment: you cut up scenes from *The Adjuster*, Atom Egoyan's movie about sexual perversity and arson in Ontario, and *Exotica*, his strip-club-set follow-up to this last, and splice them together. You then show them to somebody who knows Egoyan's stuff only from his earlier *Family Viewing* or *Speaking Parts*. Will that person realise that s/he is watching an edited compilation rather than a single movie? Probably not, we're guessing. If there's one thing that binds those of Egoyan's films which he wrote himself, it's the fact that (a) they share an identical concern with the phenomenology of the recorded image and the idea of erotic performance as communicational device, and (b) their deracinated individual sequences together make no sense until the final shot.

Cut from Toronto-based Armenian film censor Héra (Arsinée Khanjian) in *The Adjuster* secretly taping porn (in order, we learn over time, that her monoglot immigrant sister can piece together the hours in her day) to Bruce Greenwood's character in *Exotica* stalking a young lap-dancer (thus to see, it transpires, how his murdered daughter might have grown up), and the effect would be no more discombobulating than any of the Robert Lepage-like jumps from scene to scene within either movie. With as much authorial coherence thus *between* his films as *within* them, Egoyan's individual movies are pretty slippery things to evaluate. It's worth making a special plea for *The Adjuster*, though, as something far stranger than any of his later work, with a terrifying performance from Maury Chaykin as a twitchy millionaire knocking on the door: after seeing this, *MouseHunt* will never look the same. Try to avoid assuming *anything*, meanwhile, and you may just escape being caught out by the near-*Sixth Sense* ending, as another house burns on the prairie and you realise that Canada is a very empty country indeed.

THE DISC

Network have updated their earlier R2 edition with digital remastering and a director's commentary. The film's trailer, still included, is well worth watching as an illustration of how resistant Egoyan's early filmmaking style is to narrative – or even atmospheric – summary: the film's sphinx-like performances appear merely stilted, and there's not a single dramatically loaded line or outburst of action as usually dredged up to sell even the most rarefied piece of art-house. After the clear difficulty of marketing *The Adjuster*, you understand why Egoyan's producers subsequently opted – notoriously, ludicrously – to push *Exotica* as soft-core porn. (PETER VÁSÁRY)

A.I. Artificial Intelligence

(USA, 2001)

Director: Steven Spielberg
Label: DreamWorks (US)
Region: 1 (NTSC)
Discs: 2

THE FILM

Saving Private Ryan, Steven Spielberg's previous film, quickly dulled the pain of its horrifying first act with predictably brassy patriotism and comfy Tom Hanks. Quite by contrast, *A.I. Artificial Intelligence* starts with a quietly unsettling prologue about rising waters and epidemic famine, then plunks us into an onyx lecture hall with mealy, implosive William Hurt. Reassurance never arrives. Thus, global climate change, more than a context for *A.I.*'s plot, furnishes an apt metaphor for the drastic rupture it marked from Spielberg's previous decade of work. The end result, far from cataclysmic, may well be the director's most fearlessly creative movie, ambitiously stranding Haley Joel Osment's intensely sympathetic robot-protagonist within a frigid millennial vision, and filtering it all through a boldly arrhythmic narrative.

John Williams' score keeps wondrous pace with all the hairpin turns and restless flows of the story, allowing him, like his director, to reinvent his style, largely by scuttling his usual recipes. Not everything works – the Flesh Fair stalls rather badly, and Jude Law's Gigolo Joe is a rattletrap of concepts and functions, never a character. Still, many seeming 'errors', like the serial endings and the dewy mom-worship, reveal their layers and rationales on repeat viewings, finally proving crucial to the film's dark maze of ironies. Subsequent Spielberg films, particularly *Minority Report* and *War of the Worlds*, offer simpler, shakier retreads of similar idioms and images, but *A.I.* holds up as a modern landmark.

THE DISCS

A.I. tests the limits of filmmaking on so many levels that the DVD fully warrants its dozen or so behind-the-scenes featurettes. Name an Oscar category, and you'll find it helpfully explained for you here: Osment and Law say what actors always say on these occasions (give or take Osment's uncanny habit of referring to himself as 'we'), but Gary Rydstrom anatomizes the sound design with real eloquence, Williams opens our ears to the details and movements of his score, Stan Winston explains the logic of casting multiple amputees in key Mecha roles, and the design, makeup, photography, costume, blue-screen and robotics artists offer their own revealing testimonies. The 'Creating *A.I.*' short documentary on the first disc offers a clear, concise genealogy of Kubrick's involvement and Spielberg's inheritance, and though some of these on-set accounts betray a sentimental plumminess which the film determinedly avoids, the information is well worth the occasionally fulsome tone. (The multilingual R2 disc crams on ten different subtitle tracks rather than the R1's optional DTS.) (NICK DAVIS)

Ai No Corrida

(Japan, 1976)

Director: Nagisa Oshima
Label: Arte (France)
Region: 2 (PAL)
Discs: 1

ENGLISH TITLE: *In the Realm of the Senses*

THE FILM

Even the dopiest buff has heard of the unfaked sex and gruesome finale in Nagisa Oshima's widely censured and censored *Ai No Corrida*, but the biggest shock for the first-time viewer is to find in the fog of scandal such a beautiful, unhysterical and honourable film. It's based on real events in the life of Sada Abe (Eiko Matsuda), a prostitute-turned-maid whose energetic affair with her employer Kichizo (Tatsuya Fuji) ended in 1936 when she accidentally killed him during sex, then cut off his genitals. Four decades later, the politically and intellectually zealous Oshima was keen to dynamite the self-restraint of post-war Japan, and the whole point of the graphic sex was to shock.

That said, arguments about *Ai No Corrida*'s political content have been heavily overstated: the film ends shortly after Kichizo's death, whereas a political programme would have been better served by an account of the trial that followed Sada's arrest. Instead, the qualities that linger after the credits have rolled are the love story's intimacy and tenderness, the wholesome shamelessness of the lovers' games. As for the hardcore stuff, it all adds up to no more than two minutes, and none of the sex – simulated or otherwise – is sleazy or gratuitous. (Interesting, too, to note the film's reversal of the usual sex dynamic, with Sada quickly assuming the dominant role.) When the film was released 'uncut' in Japan in 2000, the male nudity was still prudishly censored: Oshima said that such treatment made his pure film dirty.

THE DISC

Arte's disc, put out under the French title *L'Empire des Sens*, is the only release that presents the film in its correct 1.66:1 aspect ratio. It's also the best for extras, though the subtitling is in French only. The film can be watched in its 105-minute video cut (the trimming is of dialogue scenes, and has nothing to do with censorship) or, with some industry, the 111-minute theatrical edit: shortened scenes are flagged *in situ* by the appearance of a red dot in the corner of the screen, and a touch on the remote control plays them at their full length. A droll and informative 38-minute suite of interviews with crew and production personnel – but not director or cast – remembers the film's legal and casting difficulties and Oshima's artistic intentions; a booklet contains a background essay and an interview with the director. Fox Lorber (R1) and Nouveaux Pictures (R2) have released the video edit with English subtitles, but in scruffier transfers and without notable extras; both obscure or remove the scene in which a small boy has his penis pulled. (SIMON CROPPER)

Airplane!

(USA, 1980)

Directors: Listed below
Label: Paramount (USA)
Region: 1 (NTSC)
Discs: 1

DIRECTORS: Jim Abrahams, David Zucker and Jerry Zucker

THE FILM

There are many kinds of comedy. There's slapstick, screwball and satire. There's romantic comedy, black comedy and gross-out comedy. There's farce, sketch and tragicom. And then there's *Airplane!*. When it comes to pure gags-per-minute saturation comedy, there's not a film to touch Jim Abrahams and the Zucker brothers' rapid-fire, farfetched, freewheeling and brazenly entertaining disaster spoof. The initial inspiration was the long-forgotten *Zero Hour*, a '50s B-movie that the writers caught on late-night TV, in which the pilot of a commercial liner is incapacitated by some dodgy fish, forcing a flaky former Army pilot and ground crew with serious personal problems to take control.

Abrahams-Zucker filched the plot wholesale, leaving much of the original dialogue in place and enhancing the ridiculousness by opening up the spoof to take in other disaster movies (including the dismally melodramatic *Airport* series), while lacing the material with some of the most seriously delivered stupid gags, non-sequiturs and one-liners ever committed to celluloid. Few comic writers could take such delight in – and extract so much humour from – the delicious simplicity of the often very literal gags employed by the Abrahams-Zucker team. They followed this up with the Cold War/Elvis spoofing *Top Secret!*, before hitting gold with the *Naked Gun* series, which swung on the straight bat of Leslie Nielsen, who had thought he was a serious actor until he discovered his comic muse in *Airplane!*. No bad thing, surely?

THE DISC

'Don't call me Shirley' is the catchphrase-riffing title of this special edition, which shows its class from the go with an impeccably designed interactive menu (there's also an inlay card that allows you to send off for your own inflatable autopilot). There are multiple versions of the movie: one with excellent commentary from the writer-directors, one with a pop-up Trivia Track (boxes that helpfully point out jokes you may have missed, or which of the members of the extended Zucker family acted as extras in any given scene), and finally the Long Haul Version, featuring 10–15 minutes of deleted scenes. Unfortunately you can't view the deleted scenes separately from this aptly titled last, which also interrupts the film for interviews with the cast and crew, somewhat distractingly for a comedy so reliant on its frenetic pace. Sound and vision are impeccable, even if the Dolby Digital 5.1 sound is slightly under-used. (PETER WATTS)

Akira

(Japan, 1988) Signature Series

Director: Katsuhiro Otomo
Label: Geneon-Pioneer (USA)
Region: 1 (NTSC)
Discs: 2

THE FILM

Akira ignited the 1990s boom in Japanese animation, and with it the mistaken belief that all anime was cyberpunk sci-fi. Much dross indeed followed, but this was the original diamond. Remembered chiefly for its ultra-violent, first-reel motorcycle chase through a sprawling future metropolis, with groundbreaking artificial lens-flares, light trails and glare effects, *Akira* conceals beneath its psychic combat and casual brutality a complex political thriller. A corrupt government official hires terrorists to incite urban unrest, and military scientists try to keep a lid on a weapon of mass destruction – but our viewpoint, as in *Ghost in the Shell*, is not that of the boffins, politicians and military men, but of baffled outsiders – in this case, a teenage biker gang.

Like all the best teen anime, *Akira* inflates pubertal angst to the point where it really is the end of the world – resentful underdog Tetsuo develops powers of his own, but uses them to act out his deep-seated envy of his friend and rival Kaneda, until his growing pains almost engulf the film.

THE DISCS

With few substantial extras beyond the 50-minute Production Report lifted from the VHS and LaserDisc editions, *Akira* on DVD favours the audio nerd, with R1 editions offering Japanese on Dolby 2.0, a DTS edition and Dolby 5.1, optimised for THX.

Beware all cheap discs with a twentieth-century release date. Versions post-2001 utilise a multi-million-dollar clean-up from Geneon that made the film as good as new. Geneon also replaced the former US dub from Streamline with a superior translation and English audio track, and added a 30-minute catch-up interview with creator Katsuhiro Otomo, whose career has been eternally overshadowed by the blockbuster success of his feature anime directorial debut.

Manga Entertainment in the UK has largely ported the US versions – using the Geneon remaster in two releases since 2002, including a disappointing 'Ultimate Edition'. UK extras are bungled, amounting to a pointless 'bonus' of the old dub version and a silly interactive feature, seemingly cobbled together to justify a rash promise that the British version would have something to distinguish it. It also has 'dubtitles' – subtitles that translate the English audio, not the original Japanese. Readers should not be surprised if a new edition in 2008 supersedes these versions, either in recognition of the movie's twentieth anniversary, or the original comic's twenty-fifth. (JONATHAN CLEMENTS)

The Alien Quadrilogy

(USA, 1979/1986/1992/1997)

Directors: Listed below
Label: 20th Century Fox (all territories)
Region: Any
Discs: 9

FILM TITLES: Alien, Aliens, Alien³, Alien: Resurrection

DIRECTORS: Ridley Scott, James Cameron, David Fincher, Jean-Pierre Jeunet

THE FILMS

This hefty nine-disc box set charts the progress of HR Giger's magnificent beast in its first four representations: from the Lovecraftian elder god of *Alien*, through the Vietcong-style giant ants of *Aliens* and the medieval demon of *Alien³*, to the cartoony action of Jean-Pierre Jeunet's *Alien: Resurrection*.

It is a story of slow decline. Ridley Scott's *Alien* is a masterpiece, better even than his superb *Blade Runner*, and remains intelligent, accessible and oddly elegant. In *Aliens* James Cameron retains the excitement he brought to *The Terminator* against the expansive backdrop of hapless soldiers trapped in a corrupt, profiteering world. *Alien³* appears not the confused result of studio politics so much as flawed filmmaking: it is a curio, and works best as a hint of the talent David Fincher would bring to later films. *Alien: Resurrection* is by far the weakest: slick with CGI and set 300 years after the other films, it looks like the sort of generic science-fiction that thrills nerds and puts off casual viewers. Tellingly, it is the effects rather than the performances or script that stand out – the aborted Ripley clones and the swimming aliens being, indeed, two of the finest moments in any of the films.

THE DISCS

The extras are almost too expansive – all five discs and more of them. Picture and sound quality are excellent, especially on *Alien*, given its age and the continual engine hum through the film. The extras decline in interest along with the quality of the films, but there are some real highlights. All four features come with full commentaries with cast, crew and production team, but Scott's comments on *Alien* are particularly fascinating, as are the production documentaries, and the cast commentary for *Aliens* is both revealing and fun. Bill Paxton (Hudson) is reliably entertaining, and Jenette Goldstein (Vasquez) admits that she hardly knew how to fire a gun.

Pre- and post-production featurettes suggest the story of *Alien³*'s troubled birth is at least as interesting as the film itself. Vincent Ward's bizarre vision of a planet made of wood stands out among a wide and sometimes surprisingly honest selection of extras. Amongst its many design and animation features, *Alien: Resurrection* includes a first-draft screenplay from Joss *Buffy* Whedon, an interesting comparison to his later science-fiction work. There are a tangle of special and collector's editions of the individual films, often with as good picture and sound, if you can't be doing with the mass of this set, but you can certainly pick it up without great expense. (TOBY FROST)

Ali: Fear Eats the Soul

(Germany, 1974)

Director: Rainer Werner Fassbinder
Label: Criterion Collection (USA)
Region: 1 (NTSC)
Discs: 2

THE FILM

Plain, widowed Emmi (Brigitte Mira), no longer middle-aged, dodges a rainstorm one night by dropping into a bar run by tough-looking Barbara (Barbara Valentin). One of Barbara's handful of patrons, a young, roughly handsome Moroccan immigrant named Ali (El Hedi ben Salem), joins Emmi at her table, then invites her to dance beneath the garish lights at the cavernous back of the bar. It isn't long before she invites him home and, almost as briskly, the couple are married, drawing the bemusement of Ali's friends, the embarrassed fury of Emmi's children, the ostracism of her co-workers and the salacious curiosity of her neighbours.

Eventually, the film's plot and tone make good on its opening shot of water pooling in a gutter: the romance stalls, its foundations are questioned and a world of bigots (or 'swine', in the movie's parlance) appears for a while to win the day. Still, for all of Fassbinder's habitual pessimism, the coda offers complex surprises, and the entire film is deeply emotional, eminently accessible and poignantly sympathetic to its tragi-comic, perfectly rendered leads (and this without consigning the supporting cast to simple stereotypes). Fassbinder reflects his admiration for the Douglas Sirk of *All That Heaven Allows*, but he has clearly absorbed the feelings of those movies instead of merely studying their constructions. Adapting Sirk's florid expressionism into his own distinctive network of charged gazes, distant but revealing angles, banal spaces and socioeconomic commentary, Fassbinder achieves his most humane and ardent film, a miracle of political smarts and harsh social critique wedded to heartbreaking clarity and compassion.

THE DISCS

Rarely has such greatness emerged in such haste: *Ali* was filmed in 16 days, with a mere four weeks between the first rehearsal and the master print. Actress Brigitte Mira and editor Thea Eymèsz shed a welcome light on the story's origins and their prolific director's preferred style of working. Two liner-notes essays and a filmed interview with director Todd Haynes (who reworked the same basic story for *Far from Heaven*) are eloquent, if a bit repetitious, and a 1976 BBC segment about the New German Cinema is as eager to trash the preceding decades of German film as to hail the arrival of new talents. Still, the real glory of the two-disc set is the film itself, sharply and colourfully restored and furnished with savvy, updated subtitles. (The German R2 DVD from E-M-S features longer interviews with the actors and a feature profiling Fassbinder, but none of these are equipped with English translations.)
(NICK DAVIS)

All About Eve

(USA, 1950)

Director: Joseph L Mankiewicz
Label: 20th Century Fox (all territories)
Region: Any
Discs: 1

THE FILM

'Fasten your seat belts. It's going to be a bumpy night,' snaps Bette Davis in Joseph L Mankiewicz's bitchy Broadway satire *All About Eve*. The turbulence begins when aspiring actress Eve Harrington (Anne Baxter) waltzes into the dressing room of ageing star Margo Channing (Davis) with a story so pitiful she's hired as her personal assistant. But it's soon clear that Eve is merely conniving to use Margo's circle of friends to advance her career.

Garlanded with multiple Oscars, including Best Picture, back in the day, *All About Eve* still glows white hot with sharp, flashy dialogue and cast chemistry that sizzles. Davis is at her firecracker best, while Baxter is scintillatingly catty – her caustic performance prompted critic Andrew Sarris to call her one of those women who 'shine with special brilliance from midnight to five o'clock in the morning of the soul'.

But it's the bilious humour that gives the movie its snap. A Restoration comedy set in theatreland, *All About Eve* was Hollywood's shot across the bow after years of poison plays about the film industry. Acidulous humour drips from Mankiewicz's pen. Pity poor Marilyn Monroe, introduced by George Sanders' sneering theatre critic Addison DeWitt as 'a graduate of the Copacabana school of dramatic art'.

THE DISCS

All About Eve is famously barbed – as are the two commentaries included on Fox's new edition. Introducing himself as the author of one book about the movie, Kenneth Geist says he was moved to write a second 20 years later after receiving a copy of Sam Staggs' *All About 'All About Eve'*, which he thought awful. Did Geist know that Staggs would be providing the second commentary? Seconds later, Geist mocks Celeste Holm's decision to accept the Sara Siddons Award two years after making *All About Eve*, seemingly oblivious to Holm's role on the commentary track, too. No matter: it's clearly Geist's riff on 'bitch virtuosity', Mankiewicz's explanation for why Baxter got the nod to play Eve.

Indeed, as Geist explains, casting was crucial in *All About Eve*, one of those classic movies where art imitates life, and vice versa. The off-screen rivalry between Joe Mankiewicz and his screenwriter brother Herman, co-writer of *Citizen Kane* mirrored the onscreen feud between Eve and Margo. And Bette Davis's fears about the twilight of her career are echoed by Margo's gnawing self-doubt. Davis later said that the movie saved her from oblivion, that it was her resurrection. 'You're maudlin and full of self-pity. You're magnificent!' the snarky DeWitt tells Margo. He could have meant Davis too. (JAMES CLASPER)

All That Heaven Allows

(USA, 1955)

Director: Douglas Sirk
Label: Criterion Collection (USA)
Region: 0 (NTSC)
Discs: 1

THE FILM

These days filmmakers as varied as Haynes, Almodóvar and Ozon fall over themselves to pay tribute to Douglas Sirk's 1950s weepies, once considered the purview of incurable, dewy-eyed sentimentalists (read: women). Anyone sitting down to a Sirk picture hoping for a banquet of Technicolor Hollywood kitsch won't be disappointed, but his unabashedly emotional masterpieces – *All That Heaven Allows*, *Written on the Wind*, **Imitation of Life** – are impossible to watch simply tongue-in-cheek. As far as Sirk was concerned, the title of this autumnal romance is ironic ('heaven is stingy'). The question is whether the powers that be will allow middle-aged widow Cary (Jane Wyman) a chance for happiness with a handsome, woodsy younger man, Ron (Rock Hudson, in an array of lumberjack shirts).

Sirk understood the allure of surfaces, and small-town New England is gorgeously rendered, all ideal homes and spotless eiderdowns of snow. It's so disturbingly picture-perfect you may want to tear it up. Did Sirk sometimes wish that he could? The movie certainly rustles with discontent. Ron and Cary's love affair, fracturing social convention, takes place under the disapproving eyes of Cary's children and her tittle-tattling neighbours. It's a film full of rhyming contrasts: the big, open windows of Ron's home versus the curtain-twitching of the country-club set; the way Ron uncorks a wine bottle with his teeth, while another of Cary's suitors cautiously sips a single cocktail. And at its heart lies a terrifying image of immurement, as Cary's face is reflected in the screen of the TV set her priggish son has given her.

Wyman gives a sober, almost expressionless performance, and Sirk makes the actress's blankness work for her. Hudson provides a good-looking set of muscles as the Thoreau-like hero; the sight of him crooning 'I make the flirty eye at you' is one of the film's chief pleasures. Heaven may be stingy, but Sirk's swooping crane shots and swelling score put it in its place.

THE DISC

Sirk's delirious, acid-drop colours look freshly sprayed on this DVD. With their overtones of psychic violence, they can leave the viewer dizzy. Strong reds and yellows are favoured throughout the movie, and Agnes Moorehead's orange lipstick practically corrodes the screen.

The extras include fascinating snippets, no more, from the 1979 BBC documentary 'Behind the Mirror: A Profile of Douglas Sirk'. The director discusses his pre-Hollywood career in Germany, and his ambivalence towards melodrama: 'I was trying to give that cheap stuff meaning.' The DVD also features an illustrated essay by Fassbinder, as well as the fabulously OTT trailer: 'Love was not gentle with these two.' (MAXIE SZALWINSKA)

Amadeus

(USA, 1984) Director's Cut
2-disc Special Edition

Director: Milos Forman
Label: Warners (all territories)
Region: Any
Discs: 2

THE FILM

A conventional biographical treatment of Wolfgang Amadeus Mozart could have been a plodding, enervating affair that failed to shed much light on the nature of creative genius. The brilliance of Peter Shaffer's 1979 play *Amadeus* was to analyse instead the *effects* of genius by dramatising the rivalry that developed between the established Viennese court composer Antonio Salieri and the young upstart from Salzburg. Salieri becomes embittered that God selected a clownish, boorish womaniser as a vessel for bequeathing his heavenly music to humanity, while sensing − rightly − that his own work will be consigned by history to the dustbin of mediocrity. By trying to sabotage Mozart's career and drive him into an early grave, Salieri knows he is warring against the arbitrariness of Divine Destiny itself, giving his confessions − delivered in old age following a suicide attempt − the ring of true pathos.

Fortunately, Forman's lavish, award-strewn adaptation retains the play's virtues while successfully opening out the material to provide a satisfying sense of how Mozart's classic operas would have first been performed and received. Forman shot entirely on location in communist Prague, reaping the benefits of the original 18th-century architecture while keeping the acting centre stage. F Murray Abraham delivers a richly nuanced performance as Salieri − his cynical, supercilious façade melting as he succumbs to the raptures of his adversary's music − while Tom Hulce's prosaic boyishness (complete with falsetto giggle) is wholly appropriate. The entire enterprise, of course, remains rooted in its glorious music − Sir Neville Mariner's orchestrations and Twyla Tharp's choreography are class acts − while it remains one of the few films to make the process of musical composition exciting (particularly the climactic scene in which the dying Mozart dictates his *Requiem* to Salieri). Admittedly, the American accents take a little adjusting to, but they're part and parcel of Forman's aim to blow the cobwebs off the era and contemporise the milieu. As Europuddings go, this one still tastes delicious.

THE DISCS

An excellent package, featuring a superb transfer of the 20-minute-longer Director's Cut in both Dolby Digital 5.1 and Dolby Surround 2.0. There's a revealing commentary from Forman and Shaffer (who've clearly not resolved *all* of their creative differences), and a decent hour-long making-of with plenty of engaging anecdotes − including Abraham's gruelling sessions at the hands of makeup maestro Dick Smith, change of leading lady after Meg Tilly tore a ligament, and the production's attempts to uncover the spies and bugs of Prague's secret police. (ANDY RICHARDS)

Amores Perros

(Mexico, 2000)

Director: Alejandro Gonzáles Iñárritu
Label: Optimum (UK)
Region: 2 (PAL)
Discs: 1

THE FILM

Inviting superficial comparisons with *Pulp Fiction* thanks to its tripartite structure, jarring violence and jumbled chronology, Alejandro Gonzáles Iñárritu's brilliant debut is far more than a Tarantino knock-off, and along with Alfonso Cuarón's *Y Tu Mamá También* (also starring the superb Gael García Bernal) put millennial Mexican cinema squarely on the map. Post-modern playfulness is low on Iñárritu's agenda, and instead he uses his three stories – all linked through a dramatic car crash and the pivotal use of dogs – to offer a panoramic social commentary on the interlocking social strata of Mexico City, alongside an urgent moral exhortation that – in a dog-eat-dog world – compassion is our best strategy for survival.

Scripted by novelist Guillermo Arriaga, the story strands all inhabit separate genres, although each deftly overlaps the others. The first is a seedy slice of social realism, with Octavio (Bernal) falling hard for his brother's wife and entering his Rottweiler in fights to try and scrape together enough cash for them to make a fresh start. The second is a cruel, Buñuelian fable of a vain supermodel (Goya Toledo) crippled in the car crash, who loses her pampered pooch beneath the floorboards of the apartment she's just moved into with her magazine-publisher lover; as her life disintegrates, she listens to her dog starving and being gnawed by rats. The third is a psychological character study of a hitman and former Communist revolutionary (Emilio Echevarría) who, having been consumed with bitter self-loathing, decides to reform his life and attempt a reconciliation with his estranged daughter.

Putting his background in directing adverts to good use, Iñárritu's dazzling visuals – all edgy handheld camerawork, aggressive jump-cuts and an otherworldly colour palette – give his film a gripping immediacy. This is particularly true of the first story, with its claustrophobic family tensions and astonishingly visceral dogfights, although the film saves its biggest emotional punches for its final section. *21 Grams* would later prove that, despite their obsession with the way chance events can turn our lives upside down, the first collaboration of this dynamic director-writer team was no fluke.

THE DISC

The Optimum release offers an excellent anamorphic transfer that does justice to Rodrigo Prieto's stunning cinematography (the use of non-colour-corrected sodium lighting to give scenes a sickly cast is particularly effective). There are also several additional scenes with director's and writer's commentary, a trailer, poster gallery, production featurette and a brace of Iñárritu's music videos.
(ANDY RICHARDS)

Andrei Rublev

(Russia, 1966)

Director: Andrei Tarkovsky
Label: Artificial Eye (UK)
Region: 0 (PAL)
Discs: 2

THE FILM

Intended as a patriotic epic to mark the 50th anniversary of the October Revolution, Tarkovsky's *Andrei Rublev* straddles the crucial fault-line in Russian culture between Orthodox Christianity and Soviet Communism. In eight spectacular episodes, the film chronicles the life of the titular 15th-century monk and icon-painter. Driven to silence and inactivity by the horrors of the Tartar invasions (rendered in astonishing action sequences), Rublev is reinvigorated by a glimpse of the power of faith in the world. His paintings, held from view until the predominantly monochrome film's colourful coda, are works of devotion, and Tarkovsky gambles that they speak down the ages; likewise, the event that restores Rublev's faith, the casting of a giant bell, is meant to have a comparable effect on the audience.

If in these respects *Andrei Rublev* appeared, to the consternation of the Soviet bureaucracy, to follow Orthodox belief, in which religious iconography, belonging to a transcendental realm, is deemed actually to embody what it represents, Tarkovsky's style plays on the meaning of the 'materialist' philosophy imposed by the authorities, suggesting the lingering traces of religious faith within it. Sometime film theorist Slavoj Zizek has said that 'in Tarkovsky's universe, we enter the spiritual dimension only via intense direct physical contact with the humid heaviness of earth', and it's this politically ambiguous sense of the material, earthy nature of artistic production that prevails here, with a long sequence built around Rublev rooting around in the muck for dyes. Demanding patience and engagement, Tarkovsky makes duration an active element in his film, not simply a factor of its running time.

THE DISCS

There are multiple edits of *Andrei Rublev* on DVD (Criterion call theirs, running some 25 minutes longer, the 'definitive director's cut', something Tarkovsky might have disputed). RusCiCo's version, released by Artificial Eye, has the advantage through its selection of supporting material. Culled from the Russian state film archives, the extras on *Andrei Rublev*, each intended to help situate the film for Western viewers unfamiliar with its background and the historical era it recreates, are thrillingly miscellaneous in origin and style. Ranging from a dance sequence clipped from Eisenstein's *Ivan the Terrible* (by way of contrast with Tarkovsky's slower, less preordained style) to documentaries on bell-ringing, pagan ceremonies, and the church murals of Theophanes the Greek, they simultaneously provide context and demand it themselves, figuring as artworks in their own right. One newsreel from the Union of Militant Atheists, on the joys of anti-religious iconoclasm and church demolition, documents the conversion of a church into a workers' cinema to an unholy union of choral music and pop-metal.

(HENRY K MILLER)

Angels in America

(USA, 2003)

Director: Mike Nichols
Label: HBO (USA) / Warners (other territories)
Region: 1 (NTSC) / 2 (PAL)
Discs: 2

THE FILM

This rendering of Tony Kushner's monumental eight-hour play cycle lives up to the name of the channel that produced it: Home Box Office (HBO), a byword in quality television such as *The Sopranos*. The channel pushed itself yet further with this magnificently cinematic adaptation, budgeted at $60 million for six hours of profound entertainment. Few US movies offer such value for money, and this two-disc set is endlessly rewatchable.

The many wonderful characters carry the viewer through this grand rewriting of the Bible and the American dream. There are dozens of them, in interlocking relationships in parallel real and fantasy worlds (think Oz), played by top-notch actors – many taking two or more roles. Meryl Streep is the heart of the soap opera within the epic drama as Mother Pitt, a Mormon matriarch whose life is altered when her closeted son Joe (Patrick Wilson), a Republican politico, calls her to announce that he's gay, and promptly disappears. He's off having an affair with nerdy liberal Louis (Ben Shenkman), who has just left his HIV-positive boyfriend Prior (Justin Kirk) to his Cocteau-addled dreams.

For all the homoerotic comings and goings, it is the journeys and performances of the women that centre the story. Mother takes her doped-up daughter-in-law Harper (Mary-Louise Parker, brilliantly dilating not only her pupils but her entire persona) under her wing after Joe's flight, and these two abandoned women help Prior. Caring for him in hospital, Mother has a magnificent erotic encounter with the titular Angel (Emma Thompson of the magnificent vowels), who has descended on flaming wings to inform Prior that he has to save the world by stopping change.

Naturally, he then visits Heaven, where the Angels of the Continents have been abandoned by God in an *Orphée*-like wasteland, while Louis is given a chance to redeem himself by stealing Roy Cohn's AZT – terrifying, given that Cohn is played by a scenery-spitting Al Pacino. He's given this mission by Prior's ex-ex Belize (a barnstorming Jeffrey Wright), charge nurse and drag queen, whose powerfully eloquent vision of a heaven much like San Francisco will give you shivers every time.

THE DISCS

No extras are included, and none are required. It's impossible to resist watching all six hours of this extravaganza in one sitting, to get the full emotional force of the grand finale. With a beautiful widescreen transfer showing exactly why this miniseries won five Golden Globes, the main event is all you need. (SOPHIE MAYER)

The Films of Kenneth Anger Volume One

(USA, 1947-54)

Director: Kenneth Anger
Label: Fantoma (USA)
Region: 1 (NTSC)
Discs: 1

THE FILMS

Spanning the first half of Anger's career, these films are the wellspring of American underground filmmaking, still genuinely startling in their audacious combinations of personal history and esoteric, often occult symbolism. Their narratives adhere only to the dictates of dream logic. The 16mm short *Fireworks* (1947) – made when the fledgling auteur was just 17 – was a direct rendering of a nightmare (influenced by Los Angeles' wartime Zoot Suit Riots) in which he was beaten and raped by a gang of sailors. Its theme of the transformative powers of sexual desire and ritualistic violence would remain central to Anger's work, while the precise choreography of his players establishes his perennial fascination with the stylisations of ballet and mime.

Puce Moment (1949), a tantalising fragment of a larger, aborted project called *Puce Women*, is Anger's nostalgic homage to silent movie stars; it opens with a fetishistic procession of dresses given to him by his grandmother, a former Hollywood dresser to the likes of Clara Bow. *Rabbit's Moon* (1950), shot in Paris, combines Japanese fairytales with characters from the Commedia dell'Arte to rapturous effect, functioning both as a universal tale of unrequited love and an autobiographical portrait of a striving artist's soul. Its witty use of '50s doo-wop songs showed how perfectly Anger could marry music to his images. In *Eaux d'Artifice* (1953) he cuts his images of a 'Water Witch' roaming a nocturnal water garden to Vivaldi's 'Winter', the close-ups of gushing water blending with the strings as they build to an ecstatic climax.

At 38 minutes, *Inauguration of the Pleasure Dome* (1954) is the most substantial work here, and unleashes the full range of Anger's intellectual erudition – in particular, his growing fascination with the *Magick* of Aleister Crowley. A taste of its phantasmagoric flavours: Anaïs Nin appears as the Moon Goddess Astate, her head encased in a birdcage; avant-garde filmmaker Curtis Harrington is Caligari's somnambulist Cesare; and Anger himself plays Hecate in a monochrome silent movie tribute. Throw in a slew of cabbalistic symbols and a goblet of hallucinogenic ambrosia and you have perhaps the cinema's most truly decadent masterwork.

THE DISC

Fantoma has done an excellent job with this disc, collecting together transfers of recent painstaking digital high-definition restorations by the UCLA Film Archive (and a 1993 restoration of *Inauguration*). The disc comes with a lavish booklet (featuring storyboards for the unrealised *Puce Women*), and Anger himself contributes a fascinating commentary to each film, which certainly helps decipher some of the esoterica. This release whets the appetite for Volume 2 and the presentation of the epochal *Scorpio Rising*. (ANDY RICHARDS)

Apocalypse Now: The Complete Dossier

(USA, 1979/2001)

Director: Francis Ford Coppola
Label: Paramount (USA)
Region: 1 (NTSC)
Discs: 2

THE FILM

Orson Welles abandoned plans to film Joseph Conrad's novel *Heart of Darkness* and made *Citizen Kane* instead. Thirty years later Coppola returned to the idea, this time with George Lucas slated to direct, guerrilla documentary style, on location in the middle of the Vietnam conflict. (Imagine how different the history of movies might have been!)

In 1976 Coppola took over the reins himself, for what would prove to be a tumultuous 18-month shoot in the Philippines, and the project mushroomed into a spectacular, hallucinatory phantasmagoria of war, arguably the high point – or at any rate the climax – in Hollywood's artistic renaissance of the 1970s.

Martin Sheen is Willard, dispatched up-river to terminate bonkers green beret Colonel Walter Kurtz (Marlon Brando). Kurtz has 'gone native' and become a political liability. It is implicit that, while his methods may be extreme, Kurtz's madness only reflects the imperatives of US foreign policy.

This is an extraordinarily powerful film – for once, the epithet 'sensational' is appropriate – but it's also flawed and frustrating, as Coppola's rejigged 'Redux' cut from 2001 acknowledges. With yet more additional scenes, this DVD propagates the notion that *Apocalypse Now* remains an organic work-in-progress.

THE DISCS

Pedants – and indeed completists – will complain that 'The Complete Dossier' is a misnomer. A few extras from earlier editions are missing, including trailers and footage of the destruction of the Kurtz compound. (They were present on a third disc issued exclusively to Circuit City stores in the US . . .)

Also AWOL, and more damagingly: the documentary *Hearts of Darkness*, based on Eleanor Coppola's warts-and-all chronicle of the shoot (apparently withheld from DVD for contractual reasons). This elision skews the *Dossier* to emphasise post-production work, with only the commentary track as partial counterweight.

On the other hand, this very reasonably priced package gets you the 1979 original and the controversial extended Redux editions of this landmark film, with introductions and an expansive, insightful commentary by Coppola; a 17-minute audio recording of Brando reading TS Eliot's *The Waste Land*; a dozen never-before-seen 'additional scenes'; documentaries on the film's groundbreaking editing and sound design, and even a couple of Easter eggs (in one, screenwriter John Milius discusses the genesis of the title). Aspect ratio is 2.00:1 and the soundtrack is Dolby Digital 5.1. Both films are divided into two parts over two discs. You will want to devote time to this one. (TOM CHARITY)

The Apu Trilogy

(India, 1955/1957/1959)

Director: Satyajit Ray
Label: Artificial Eye (UK)
Region: 2 (PAL)
Discs: 3

FILM TITLES: *Pather Panchali* ('Song of the Little Road'), *Aparajito* ('The Unvanquished'), *Apur Sansar* ('The World of Apu')

THE FILMS

Akira Kurosawa once commented that 'Not to have seen the cinema of Satyajit Ray means existing in the world without seeing the sun or the moon'; indeed, Ray's majestic trilogy opened the eyes of the West to Indian cinema in the same way that the Japanese master's *Rashomon* did. Based on a 1939 novel by BB Bandyopadhyay, Ray's debut *Pather Panchali* depicts the life of an impoverished Brahmin family in a Bengali village, particularly the experiences of five-year-old Apu (Subir Bannerjee). Influenced by the social realism of De Sica and the unjudgmental humanism of Renoir, Ray's episodic narrative unfurls with a spellbinding naturalism, following the rituals and rhythms of work and play, life and death. While Apu's priest father dreams of writing plays and poems, his mother frets about the practicalities of food and clothing, and an old woman known as 'Auntie' (a show-stealing performance from Chunibala Devi) tells fairytales to Apu and his older sister. The film lyrically evokes the pleasures of childhood through encounters with sweet sellers, travelling theatre troupes and steam trains, while an incident with a stolen necklace becomes an important staging-post in Apu's moral education. The arrival of the monsoon, though, ushers in a family tragedy, culminating in the trilogy's first – but far from last – scene of wrenching heartbreak.

The first sequel *Aparajito* focuses on the rift that opens between a teenage Apu (Smaran Ghosal) and his mother (Karuna Bannerjee) when his academic success at school wins him a scholarship to study in Calcutta. Few films have so precisely captured the complex ebb and flow of affection and resentment that children feel towards their parents, and reflected the difficulty of reconciling personal ambition with community loyalty. Public interest in the fate of his hero pushed Ray into making a third film, *Apur Sansar*, in which, after subjecting Apu to dramatic extremes of happiness and grief, Ray finally bequeaths him one of the most resolutely affirmative endings the cinema has offered.

THE DISCS

Artificial Eye's transfers reproduce Subrata Mitra's luminous photography to fair effect, complemented by Ravi Shankar's enthralling music. The discs also offer excellent notes by Ray biographer Andrew Robinson, excepts from a BBC Omnibus special (including an interview with Ray), stills, and a rather turgid 'Movie Masterclass' segment in which a class from the National Film and Television School pick through clips from *Apur Sansar*. (ANDY RICHARDS)

Atanarjuat: The Fast Runner
(Canada, 2000)

Director: Zacharias Kunuk
Label: Columbia TriStar (USA) /
Alliance Atlantis (Canada)
Region: 1 (NTSC)
Discs: 1 / 2

THE FILM

Canadian films always feature 'weird sex and snowshoes', as author Katherine Monk titles her book. With *Atanarjuat*, the viewer is clear from the first, mysterious moments that, while we're not in Cronenberg country any more, the film explores the same complex ties of sexual desire and jealousy that characterise Atom Egoyan's *The Sweet Hereafter*.

There's also snow, if not snowshoes. Filmed north of the Arctic Circle, on the lands where its characters lived, and its largely non-professional cast still live to tell their ancestors' tales, *Atanarjuat* is alive to and through the way its epic narrative is embedded in the landscape. Astonishing light and utter dark reflect the moral core of the story, in which two brothers, Amaqjuaq (Pakkak Inukkshuk) and Atanarjuat (Natar Ungalaaq) challenge the rule of an evil shaman (Paul Qulitalik).

The shaman's curse led to the installation of a brutal usurper, Sauri (Eugene Ipkarnak), whose son Oki (Peter-Henry Arnatsiaq) lords it over Atanarjuat and Amaqjuaq, the sons of the usurped and murdered chief, Kumaglak (Apayata Kotierk). Atanarjuat wins Oki's promised bride Atuat (Sylvia Ivalu), causing thoughts of vengeance to occur not only to Oki, but to Oki's sister Puja (Lucy Tulugarjuk), who desires Atanarjuat. Some sexual misdemeanours, an ambush, a murder, and Atanarjuat finds himself fleeing for his life, naked, across the spring sea ice.

This sequence is all the more stunning because it's beset by danger: to Atanarjuat, to the crew shooting it on a dog sled skimming over the fragile ice (shown in the end credits), to the social order in the myth and to indigenous ways of life in the present. *Atanarjuat*'s unlikely and wonderful success at Cannes (winning the 2001 Caméra d'Or) – and Atanarjuat's in learning how to heal his community – offer hope as wild and beautiful as the film.

THE DISCS

There's a choice here that shouldn't have to be made, between image quality and extras. Columbia USA's disc has zero extras, but the picture is a straight port of the original video master (*Atanarjuat* was shot on Digi Beta, then transferred to film for its theatrical release). Alliance Atlantis's is taken from a telecine back to video from that film interpositive – four generations removed from the original, in other words, and all the blurrier for it. But it does give you a whole second disc of extras. There's an innovative fact track that accompanies the movie, offering insights into Inuit culture and myth; a production diary; a featurette on the film's art direction, and another on the story's legend; as well as extensive introductions to the cast, crew and Isuma Igloolik, the world's first indigenous production company.

Having taken it all on board, it's worth watching the film again – without English subtitles, for the sound of the Inuktitut language and gestural storytelling. (SOPHIE MAYER)

Au Hasard Balthazar

(France, 1966)

Director: Robert Bresson
Label: Criterion Collection (USA)
Region: 1 (NTSC)
Discs: 1

THE FILM

Alas, poor Balthazar. The sweet, unassuming donkey in what is one of Robert Bresson's most celebrated films is beaten, kicked, terrorised with fire crackers, made to perform at a circus, flayed, whacked, and eventually left bleeding to death on top of a hillside. Close-ups on his face, of which there are many, portray a near-anthropomorphic suffering and martyrdom that has only ever been rivalled by Maria Falconetti in Dreyer's *The Passion of Joan of Arc*. Jean-Luc Godard has described the film as 'the world in an hour and a half'.

Pure and almost beautiful in its austerity, *Au Hasard Balthazar* follows the donkey from its bucolic childhood, through to its later shackling and ill treatment, and its clip-clopping but ultimately ill-fated bids for freedom. To him are attracted both kind and deeply unkind individuals. Among the former is Marie (Anne Wiazemsky), an innocent girl who is drawn to local roughneck Gerard (François Lafarge) who abuses her and eventually leaves her stripped naked, locked and gang-beaten in a room. Everything about him – his leather garb, motorbike, the manic pop songs that soundtrack his prowlings – suggest that his wickedness, so morbidly alluring to Marie, represents the way that modernity invades rural life – or brings into relief its dark heart.

Au Hasard Balthazar is a harrowing passion play whose precise meaning, artfully left porous by Bresson, has been endlessly disputed since its release in 1966. Its themes of suffering and redemption, as well as its use of actors whose stilted motions make them almost indistinguishable from models, are characteristic of the director's work; not so its telling use of music (Schubert's *Piano Sonata No. 20*) which amplifies a sound design full of lonesome breezes and clanking chains. A final scene in which Balthazar lies dying surrounded by sheep is one of the most unforgettable in 20th-century cinema.

THE DISC

A characteristically elegant Criterion package includes a thoughtful essay by James Quandt arguing against a transcendental reading of *Balthazar*, and a video interview with Donald Richie in which he rhapsodises with great feeling about its fundamental mystery. Best of all is *Un Metteur en Ordre*, a 1966 French television special in which the likes of Godard, Louis Malle and Marguerite Duras shower Bresson with praise. JLG describes him as 'a Grand Inquisitor' and likens the film to Pascal's *Discourse on the Passion of Love*. Also interviewed are Wiazemsky and Lafarge who contribute quietly thoughtful interpretations of the film's fathomless depths. (SUKHDEV SANDHU)

Avant-Garde: Experimental Cinema of the 1920s and '30s
(USA/France/Germany/Netherlands, 1921–47)

Directors: Various
Label: Kino Video (USA)
Region: 1 (NTSC)
Discs: 2

THE FILMS

For a moment in the 1920s an art cinema emerged in the European capitals, independent of the major studios, and with a sizeable audience not merely among intellectuals but – in France at least – in popular ciné-clubs across the country. Bringing together dabbling artists, Russian émigrés and rebellious industry professionals, the avant-garde was a hot-bed of competing groups and theories, fired by diverse modernisms – especially Dada and surrealism. Partisans of these latter groups, among them Antonin Artaud, Marcel Duchamp and Man Ray (all of whose film work is represented here), perceived in the movie camera – commonly seen as a mechanical recording instrument – the potential both to make strange the visible world of objects and to give objective, physical presence to images of the mind.

For all the controversies it initiated (art versus commerce, form versus content, realism versus abstraction etc.), the avant-garde was united in its opposition to the conventional story-film, demanding total freedom of both subject matter and treatment in their mission to make cinema an autonomous medium, independent of the theatre and capable of showing things inaccessible to the established arts. Many of the results of this grand experiment are included here: Hans Richter and Viking Eggeling's work with abstract forms; Jean Epstein's fragmented narrative; Eisenstein's early attempt at non-naturalistic sound, made for walking-around money during his 1929–32 world tour. Naturally there were as many misses as hits, but in the process the avant-garde established a moving-image repertoire that has nourished mainstream and the less-exposed cinema alike ever since, as well as providing an apprenticeship for directors like Jean Renoir and Luis Buñuel.

THE DISCS

The avant-garde film's wide influence has long been out of proportion to its limited accessibility, having more in common with the traditional art-object – 'auratic', existing in only a few prints, often confined to galleries – than the mechanically reproduced commercial film. 'The few films which might justify the category of "art",' wrote the novelist Henry Miller in 1939, 'died almost at their inception.'

Often without star performers – sometimes without actors – and seldom of regular 'feature' length, in many ways the avant-garde film ill-fitted the cinema and videotape eras. The DVD format, well-matched to short work, has the potential to rescue it from the shadowy half-life it has led since its '20s golden age ended. Kino's package, which features extensive notes by the film historian Elliott Stein, redresses a historical imbalance. (HENRY K MILLER)

L'Avventura

(Italy, 1960)

Director: Michelangelo Antonioni
Label: Criterion Collection (USA)
Region: 1 (NTSC)
Discs: 2

THE FILM

Michelangelo Antonioni's *L'Avventura* is a high-modernist masterpiece that revolutionised film grammar and established the northern Italian intellectual as the master formalist of European art cinema. Like that other great formalist, Hitchcock, Antonioni conveys meaning through rigorous technical and compositional methods. Unlike Hitchcock, his strategies are austere, open-ended and decidedly anti-dramatic. Landscape and architecture become objective correlatives for characters' inner realities (in a break from neorealism), and his compositions often evoke an underlying absence. The viewer is given space to project his or her own meaning onto the frame.

L'Avventura was the first in a series of stylistically and thematically related films (followed by *La Notte*, *L'Eclisse* and *Il Deserto Rosso*) which followed an alienated female protagonist's quest for self identity and spiritual truth within a morally ambiguous world. They offer studies of the impossibility of communication and the complexities of modern erotic relationships, or what Antonioni called 'sick Eros'. Although he denied being a moralist, all the director's films are biting social critiques.

The plot of *L'Avventura* is simple: a girl disappears during a yacht trip in the Mediterranean. Her friend (Monica Vitti) and fiancé (Gabriele Ferzetti) search for her and in the process begin an affair. The missing girl is soon forgotten and the love story takes centre stage. This 'disappearance of the disappearance', to quote Pascal Bonitzer, alarmed many when the film first came out. But even more perplexing for audiences was Antonioni's formal style. At the film's Cannes premiere, audiences yelled 'cut, cut!' as rigidly composed shots lingered long after characters left the frame. The critics, however, awarded the film a special jury prize 'for a new movie language and the beauty of its images'. Antonioni films are often interpreted as pessimistic. Yet ultimately his cinema has a clear positive function: to express a new way of seeing.

THE DISCS

Dependable Criterion does it again with this superb set, now relatively hard to come by. Disc 1 contains an intelligent audio commentary by film historian Gene Youngblood. On the second, Jack Nicholson (Antonioni's star in *The Passenger*) reads a couple of the director's essays and talks briefly about his personal experiences with *il maestro*. But the highlight is Gianfranco Mingozzi's 58-minute 'Antonioni: Documents and Testimonials' from 1966. While offering a record of Antonioni at work, it's perhaps more interestingly a portal into the Italian intellectual culture of the '60s, a time when painters, critics and filmmakers argued passionately and idealistically about truth in art. (JONATHAN RAFMAN)

Back to the Future Trilogy

(USA, 1985/1989/1990)

Director: Robert Zemeckis
Label: Universal (UK)
Region: 2 (PAL)
Discs: 4

THE FILMS

During the 1980s, Steven Spielberg was more concerned with bringing to life the Boys' Own adventure comic serials of his childhood than reliving the tragedy of the Shoah. As well as directing the joyfully cornball WWII flick *Raiders of the Lost Ark*, he produced the shlocky *Gremlins* and *The Goonies*, and oversaw the first instalment of the *Back to the Future* trilogy, a rollicking tale of time travel, skateboarding and rock 'n' roll with Oedipal undertones. Michael J Fox played Marty McFly, a family-troubled teenager who seeks refuge in the friendship of the local eccentric inventor (Christopher Lloyd). For want of gainful labour, Doc Brown turns his DeLorean sports car into a time machine; McFly straps himself inside, presses all the right buttons and finds himself stuck in 1956, where his teenage mother promptly falls in love with him.

Tightly plotted and generously directed, the film and its '50s nostalgia went down a storm with Baby Boomer audiences and their kids, so Zemeckis filmed a pair of sequels back-to-back, extending their backdrops to two more periods beloved by Hollywood and its attendees: the Wild West and the not-too-distant future. Despite an increasingly brow-furrowing plot of competing timezones and alternate universes, Zemeckis and writer Bob Gale kept a tight grip throughout, never allowing sentimentality to get the upper hand and maintaining the overriding spirit of a straightforward Saturday afternoon sci-fi serial.

THE DISCS

Universal seems to be churning out unstoppable multiples of this box set, whose mass of extras has now overflown onto four discs in the UK and Australia. Forensic inquiry suggests there may be one commentary track (with Gale and producer Neil Canton) less per film than on the three-disc US set, but you can still hear Gale and Zemeckis on all three features. Spread amongst those are copious interviews with cast and crew, pop-up trivia, various making-of docs (one made especially for the DVD), deleted scenes, out-takes, short films about set and prop design and Industrial Light and Magic's special effects, FAQs about the intricate plotting, and pop videos with Billy Ocean, Huey Lewis and ZZ Top. The bonus fourth disc adds more Q&As and deleted scenes (and siphons off some of the extras previously crammed onto the three discs). The films have also been slightly reframed for the widescreen release, but you'd have to be disturbingly nerdy to notice. The Dolby Digital 5.1 sound is superb.

(PETER WATTS)

The Battle of Algiers

(Algeria/Italy, 1966)

Director: Gillo Pontecorvo
Label: Criterion Collection (USA)
Region: 0 (NTSC)
Discs: 3

THE FILM

Pauline Kael called Pontecorvo 'the most dangerous kind of Marxist, a Marxist poet'. *The Battle of Algiers*, Pontecorvo's fiercely intelligent film about the Algerian war of independence, is anything but prosaic. The movie begins with French troops storming the casbah, before revealing in flashback how they crushed the insurgency and flushed out its leadership. It shows the cat-and-mouse aspect to the conflict, and the ruthless use of terror and violence by both sides pursuing their determined ends.

Starkly shot in newsreel-style black and white, the film recreates the insurrection without a single inch of documentary footage. Pontecorvo wanted audiences to think they were seeing recorded events, so he damaged the reels to make them look like archival footage, and used handheld cameras and amateur actors. Former Algerian revolutionary Yacef Saadi plays himself. Jean Martin, the only professional actor in the film, is terrific (and terrifying) as Colonel Mathieu, the leader of the occupying forces.

Current events have brought the movie sharply into focus again. In 2003 the Pentagon arranged a screening to see what counter-insurgency lessons might be learnt from it. Four decades on, *The Battle of Algiers* has lost none of its power, relevance or lucidity.

THE DISCS

The Battle of Algiers remains a template for political cinema, so it's hardly surprising that one of the chief attractions of Criterion's exemplary three-disc edition is a series of interviews with directors inspired by the film, including Spike Lee, Oliver Stone and Steven Soderbergh. The late Palestinian cultural critic Edward Said also presents a diverting documentary about Pontecorvo.

These two features are the highlights of the second disc; the third considers its legacy. A short documentary called 'Remembering History' deals with the Algerian struggle for independence and includes exclusive interviews with leading historians and revolutionaries such as Saadi. Former US National Security and counterterrorism adviser Richard Clarke explores the film's current relevance, while, in an excerpt from Patrick Rotman's documentary *L'ennemi Intime*, French officers discuss using torture to combat terrorism in Algeria.

Rounding off the set are a short film documenting Pontecorvo's return to Algeria 30 years after it won independence, a 56-page book featuring extracts from the original screenplay, and an essay by scholar Peter Matthews. (JAMES CLASPER)

The Beast

(France, 1975)

Director: Walerian Borowczyk
Label: Cult Epics (USA)
Region: 0 (NTSC)
Discs: 3

THE FILM

A young, wealthy American arrives at the crumbling château of her fiancé, a faintly inhuman French nobleman peculiarly absorbed in the breeding of horses, whose family home is dank with decadent secrets and deviant lusts. Local tales of a monster, half-bear, half-wolf and entirely priapic, infect the sleep of the bride-to-be, and Lucy dreams of a ravishment in the woods in which, Angela Carter-style, the woman's desire for the beast far outstrips its bad-boy intentions. The rampant accompaniment of frantic harpsichord and shaggy gorillagram costuming are very funny, and surprisingly sexually intense.

Polish director, animator and poster designer Borowczyk was, by his own intent, a legend whose work gleefully danced on the boundaries between art and pornography, exploitation and the erotic. As an accredited member of the '70s Euro art-cinema scene, he was widely fêted on the festival circuit – he won a Berlin Silver Bear for a 1966 short and competed for the Palme d'Or with *A Story of Sin* in 1975. Critical doubt started to set in with his presentation of *Immoral Tales* as a work-in-progress at the 1974 London Film Festival, however, and hardened into certainty that he'd gone off the rails when he took one of the shorts that made up this portmanteau work and created *The Beast*.

Though it's a stunningly detailed period piece with an exquisite focus on textures, surfaces and objects, notwithstanding a Henry James homily on old world versus new, and despite its surrealist solemnity about its self-consciously Freudian symbolism, it earned Borowczyk a reputation as a purveyor of soft porn (something he did nothing to discourage), and he was felt to have irreparably damaged his reputation. Audiences, however, took their pleasure where they found it and enjoyed the adult acknowledgment of lust, the black comedy of manners and the richness of style. The film played in Paris for over a year, and has maintained a cult status ever since.

THE DISCS

Borowczyk's short film, 'Une Collection Particulière', extols the virtue of sublimating the erotic urge into the art of collection, and ideally the same approach would apply to a DVD of *The Beast*, as no single set truly suffices. For sheer weight and an excellent transfer, Cult Epics' three-disc set wins out, though the exhumed 16mm behind-the-scenes footage is silent and unedited (feature-length!) at Borowczyk's behest, and the alternative 'Director's Cut' version of the film is for completism's sake only. (REBEKAH POLDING)

Beau Travail

(France, 1999)

Director: Claire Denis
Label: Artificial Eye (UK)
Region: 2 (PAL)
Discs: 1

THE FILM

LP Hartley's oft-quoted assertion that 'the past is another country' takes new and powerful meaning in Claire Denis' ninth feature film, *Beau Travail*. Through extended, temporally indeterminate flashbacks, the memories of Galoup (Denis Lavant), a former sergeant of the French Foreign Legion, evoke the vast, dry horizons of Djibouti, on the Horn of Africa. There, neatly contained within white stone walls, lies the Legion's jarringly obsolete world, with its ordered rituals and hierarchies, its training exercises honed to pointless purity. A colonial past lives on anachronistically in a country indifferent to it, while Galoup's present, discharged existence in exile in Marseille is rendered meaningless by the loss of that structured life.

The narrative that emerges is based on Herman Melville's posthumously published novella *Billy Budd*, and Benjamin Britten's opera adaptation haunts the film's soundtrack. Denis takes the skeleton of this tale of a jealousy-fraught triangular relationship and remoulds it into a multi-layered exploration of power and desire – the driving forces of much of her filmmaking. Galoup is the definitive legionnaire: perfectly conformist and, as sergeant, the enforcer of conformity in the ranks, holding the Legion and his commanding officer, Forestier (Michel Subor), in the highest esteem. The balance is threatened with the arrival of the beautiful Sentain (Gregoire Colin). He quickly wins Forestier's affection, revealing Galoup's 'admiration' to be something more akin to passionate love. As a bitter, disruptive violence seeps into their unit's ordered existence, the viewer remains aware of the distance separating their world from the Djiboutians, who look on with a kind of bemused tolerance, surveying a former power turned in upon itself.

What makes the film particularly compelling is its attention to the sensual forms and forces of the masculine body. Agnès Godard's luminous cinematography closes in on skin and sinew, beautifully conveying the patterns of contact and separation that structure affective and social relations. The imposing landscape and unwavering heat are rendered stunningly visceral, drawing the viewer into another world – one whose beauty and violence demand repeated exploration.

THE DISC

Artificial Eye can usually be relied upon for a high-quality transfer and their edition comes up sharper than New Yorker Video's Region 1 version. Extras are low-key, featuring only the theatrical trailer and several filmographies. Francophones may wish to sample the France Télévisions edition. The aspect ratio has been altered in the pan-and-scan transfer and there are no subtitles, but it does have an audio commentary by the director. (ISABELLE McNEILL)

Before Sunrise & Before Sunset

(USA, 1995/2004)

Director: Richard Linklater
Label: Warners (all territories)
Region: Any
Discs: 2

THE FILMS

It's easy to forget just how unfashionable Richard Linklater's *Before Sunrise* first looked back in 1995, when, if American movies engaged with dialogue at all, it was with the postmodern hipster flippancy of *Pulp Fiction*, and a storyline about two protagonists meeting cute (on a train en route to Vienna, with just the night to spend together) seemed certifiably sentimental pap. Credibility and conviction were just off the radar.

In fact, if *Before Sunrise* owed anything to anyone, it was to the moral amblings of Eric Rohmer (with a titular nod to Murnau's *Sunrise*) – but one of its many wonders is its unassailable naturalism; its resonance emerges from the lifelikeness and liveliness of its two characters, doing their best to make good the magic of this moment in time. *Carpe noctem*! Ethan Hawke's love-spurned American tourist Jesse and Julie Delpy's bashful Sorbonne student Celine, earnest and idealistic the both, are the film's key plot points, and as they comb Vienna by night, confiding their hopes, hang-ups, passions and impressions, they incarnate their notion that what meaning life provides must be in the connections made between people.

Less easy to forget, perhaps, was the magic of catching up with Jesse and Celine again, after a nine-year lacuna for all concerned. The first film left them agreeing to rendezvous six months later; *Before Sunset* begins with the harsh reality of their failure and separation, and only because Jesse has turned their first encounter into fiction do they find each other again, at his reading in a bookshop in Paris. With but half an afternoon to share, they talk about all the water passed under the bridge – his passionless marriage, her rage at life's disappointments – and their unquenchable longing for that lost night of promise. A rare sequel in real follow-on time, *Before Sunset* is simultaneously even more naturalistic than its predecessor, and even more resonantly layered: entwining fiction and fate, idealism and make-believe, and folding the actual life changes of its actors and its viewers into its mix, it achieves a profound intimacy between its characters and ourselves.

THE DISCS

It would be nice to think these beautiful films might one day get the fulsome DVD treatment afforded other Linklater movies (there's a bountiful Region 1 disc of his lucid-dream trip *Waking Life*, and bumper Criterion Collection editions of both *Slacker* and *Dazed and Confused*). The current editions play fine, but carry no extras worth writing home about, unless you count a Quebecois-French dub track for *Before Sunset*. Try watching the two discs nine years apart.

(NICK BRADSHAW)

La Belle et la Bête

(1946, France)

Director: Jean Cocteau
Label: Criterion Collection (UK)
Region: 1 (NTSC)
Discs: 1

ENGLISH TITLE: *Beauty and the Beast*

THE FILM

Once upon a time there was a poet, a painter, a sculptor, a writer and a maker of avant-garde films called Jean Cocteau who decided to make a movie, a fairy-tale film for the mainstream. The hopes of a nation's film industry were riding on him, as France emerged from Nazi occupation and struggled to rebuild. As Cocteau records in his production diaries, the filmmaking was certainly not easy: cameras jammed, stock ran short, aeroplanes ruined take after take and beautiful Jean Marais, Cocteau's lover and star, was plagued with boils. Yet out of this darkness came a film of light wit and charm, influencing many, from Peter Greenaway to the Disney studio.

Much of the film's grace stems from the beauty of Josette Day, a statuesque blonde with a round face straight out of Vermeer and a uniquely delicious smile. Like Disney's later Belle, Beauty is an animated young woman whose inner and outer goodness do not preclude a lively flirtatiousness, nor a near-animal appreciation of her luck when, at the close, she realises she's getting her beau and her beast in one. With a strong flavour of Rousseau, the Beast is in fact portrayed from the outset as a worthy suitor: though he may lack civil table manners, his is a noble if savage nature in sharp contrast to the petty bourgeois materialism of Beauty's grasping sisters, profligate brother and foolish father whose plucking of a rose from a mysterious castle sets the story in train. This strong sense of worldliness and sharp social comedy ground the film's enduring enchantment. Amidst much magic one moment, conjured by Cocteau with tricks of the surrealist cinema trade, transcends: using real actors, curtains and reversed footage the bodiless, gliding arms bearing lit candelabra create an image of awesome beauty unreachable by CGI.

THE DISC

Even by Criterion's high standards this disc is outstanding, as delightful as a rose in a magic castle. A picture sharp as the sisters' tongues and as soft as Beauty's tender heart allows you to see the film as Cocteau wished, while the lavish extras allow you to see pretty much everything else: trailers, stills, warm-hearted cast and crew interviews in two intelligent documentaries, not one but two commentary tracks, a charming booklet of notes and the original fairytale. Best of all, Philip Glass's seductive opera score can be played as an alternative soundtrack, an unexpected and absorbing pleasure. (REBEKAH POLDING)

Bicycle Thieves

(Italy, 1948)

Director: Vittorio De Sica
Label: Arrow (UK)
Region: 0 (PAL)
Discs: 1

ORIGINAL TITLE: *Ladri di Biciclette*

THE FILM

Few premises are as startlingly simple as that of De Sica's classic: Antonio Ricci needs a job so that his family can eat; he's offered one bill-posting, which requires a bicycle; he pawns all the household linen to get one; the bicycle gets stolen. This high point of Italian neorealism has continued to inspire other socially conscious directors down the years, not least the young Ken Loach, who made a similarly questing work in *Cathy Come Home*.

The cast is filled with amateur actors, as De Sica strives for as much *verismo* as he can cram into 84 minutes. Lamberto Maggiorani makes his Ricci a granite-faced working-class hero driven to desperate measures, while Enzo Staiola as young son Bruno winningly strives to belie his tender years and grasp the gravity of his father's economic situation.

Perhaps, though, there is one world-renowned star: the city of Rome itself, free at last from the wartime troubles of *Rome, Open City*. Cinematographer Carlo Montuori reminds us that we're watching a country in the grip of socio-political change, with sweeping shots (copied in a later Italian classic, Pasolini's *Mamma Roma*) of scrubland punctuated by new apartment blocks. As ever in transitional times, it's those at the powerless end of the food/hunger chain who suffer, and De Sica leaves us in no doubt that life, in the 1940s at least, wasn't sweet on the peninsula.

THE DISC

On the evidence of 'Timeless Cinema: A Documentary on Vittorio De Sica', a career overview made by the Italian state broadcaster RAI, it was a wonder that De Sica got any films made at all. Whenever he was on set or location, up popped a pesky RAI reporter to call him by his surname and ask a series of dopey questions.

De Sica's early career as an actor in and director of light commercial films is judiciously given little airtime. Italians obviously like to think their national treasure emerged fully formed at the age of 44 with *Shoeshine* (1946). Yet for a man who took it upon himself to portray his country's post-war travails to the world, De Sica comes across as remarkably jolly. He tells of his ruse to avoid directing German propaganda – get a commission from the Vatican and take two years to complete it – and also how he gambled away one film's financing in casinos along the French Riviera. Sophia Loren stands by his side at premieres, smoking away and looking elegantly bored as Signor RAI continues to witter away. Retro Euro-programming at its best. (FIONA MOUNTFORD)

The Big Lebowski

(USA, 1998) Special/Collector's Edition

Director: Joel Coen
Label: Universal (UK/USA)
Region: 2 (PAL) / 1 (NTSC)
Discs: 1

THE FILM

'What makes a man, Mr Lebowski?' According to arguably the Coen bros' most accomplished amalgam of matters high- and low-brow to date, the answer seems to be located somewhere between moral deportment and groin: like an extended pun on the term 'private dick', this post-Chandler investigative comedy follows Bridges' unlikely hero, a shamblingly lazy hippie drop-out, through an uproariously motley LA in search of virtue (and his carpet), and in defence of his 'johnson'. The plot – thick as Kahlua – accommodates nihilist former krautrockers, fluxus artists, Malibu porn moguls, tearaway Minnesotan farm-girls, paraplegic fake millionaires, TV-Western writers in iron lungs, neo-Jewish Vietnam vets, paedophile bowlers and Saddam Hussein. Somewhere in this babel, there's also a wander-in cowboy narrator, emblem of the old straight-backed 'man's gotta do . . .' ethos, of which the film semi-seriously posits the Dude as a modern repository.

It takes a few viewings to relish just how richly this ostensibly tubby comedy actually works – and scores don't quite clarify how the Coens made it do so. Key ingredients include the endlessly quotable dialogue, an inspired cast of actors clearly relishing those lines, and T Bone Burnett's jukebox soundtrack, with its exhumations of Dylan's 'The Man in Me' and Kenny Rogers and the First Edition's 'Just Dropped In'. After an unspectacular cinema release, the film has become such guaranteed entertainment (this writer rates it as the best colour comedy bar none) that a 'Lebowski Fest' now tours the US, making a minor celebrity of film producer's rep Jeff Dowd, the real-life model for the Dude. The Coens are sometimes taxed with being so arch as to be aloof from their characters, but the sheer inclusiveness of characterisation here testifies to *Lebowski*'s genial spirit: in its cockeyed celebration of manly humility and the benign side of the Californian bacchanal, it proves the Coens as the true inheritors of the spirit of Preston Sturges.

THE DISC

Though the title's a cheek, this 'Collector's Edition' (also available in the rather random Coen Brothers Collection box set) marks a modest improvement on the film's first release on disc. Newly added are a mock introduction by one Mortimer Young, film historian, and another in the Coens' fictive gallery of industry oddballs, plus a gallery of Jeff Bridges' set photography and production notes; still in place are a teaser trailer and a making-of featurette in which the Coens speak, albeit giving little away. The reframed, remastered transfer is perhaps fractionally sharper than was – but after ten years of cult groundswell, a better-referenced edition is surely due. Lebowskiheads can hunt down 2005's limited edition Region 1 Achiever's Edition, boxed with photo cards, character coasters and a bowling towel. (NICK BRADSHAW)

The Big Red One –
The Reconstruction

(USA, 1980/2004) 2-disc Special Edition

Director: Sam Fuller
Label: Warners (UK/US)
Region: 1 (PAL) / 1,2,3,4 (NTSC)
Discs: 2

THE FILM

The first version of Sam Fuller's peerless war movie turned up in dog's dinner form in 1980. Fuller's epic account of the First Infantry ('The Big Red One') ricocheting from battlefront to battlefront during WWII had been turned into a shoot 'em up, *Dirty Dozen*-style exploitation pic. Twenty-four years later, to mark the 60th anniversary of D-Day, it was restored to something closer to what its late director had intended, recovering more than 40 minutes of footage.

While the restored version makes more sense of some aspects of the story, it doesn't have a comfortable narrative trajectory. It's still a messy affair, but that was the point. War – at least as experienced by Fuller when he was serving with the US infantry in Sicily or on Omaha Beach or in liberated Germany – was an inchoate affair. He shows, arguably more honestly than any other film-maker, the squalor and the boredom of the soldier's life alongside the terrifying adrenaline rush of battle.

Just occasionally, the film lapses into Boy's Own machismo, but at least it does so with style and humour. Take, for example, the scene in which Lee Marvin (in one of his greatest performances as the battle-hardened sergeant) throttles a German officer who accosts him in a hospital ward. 'I can understand you being horny, Fritz, but you've got bad breath,' he sneers as he squeezes the life out of the man.

What really makes *The Big Red One* special, though, is its lyricism and affinity for the helpless victims of war, most notably the children. More recent directors like Steven Spielberg and Terrence Malick have made bigger-budgeted WWII movies with much more elaborate set-pieces, but neither had Fuller's genius for capturing seemingly throwaway moments that show the pity and horror of war in microcosm. The boy trying to bury his decomposing mother or the doomed Sicilian girl weaving flowers round Marvin's helmet . . . moments like these have an impact and authenticity that no blockbuster can match.

THE DISCS

As if to make up for the cavalier way the movie was treated first time round, Warners have produced a lavish two-disc set, showcasing the work of both Fuller and the film's restorers. There's a commentary from critic Richard Schickel, who oversaw the recreation, two 'anatomies of a scene' and a hefty inside look at the repair job; there's also an hour-long TCM portrait of Fuller as a soldier and war-movie director, and a 1946 US government propaganda film about life in the infantry, 'The Fighting Fist'. (GEOFFREY MACNAB)

The Big Sleep

(USA, 1946)

Director: Howard Hawks
Label: Warners (USA)
Region: 1 (NTSC)
Discs: 1 (double-sided)

THE FILM

Evoking profound nostalgia for Hollywood even among those born after its demise, *The Big Sleep* is a mess of contradictions. Nominally a detective thriller, its plot – not exactly lucid in Raymond Chandler's source novel – is famously incomprehensible, and the film's popularity demonstrates how far cinema is enjoyed, if not conceived, as a non-narrative form. However fantastic the film is in most respects, for admirers it's an intimate documentary by director Howard Hawks on its stars; the most memorable scenes consist of Humphrey Bogart and Lauren Bacall trading dirty jokes.

Though the film was no B-movie, it was a decade and more before it won any critical reputation, and as a cult it stands less for the classical Hollywood of the '30s and '40s than the cinephilia that rode the French New Wave in the early '60s. The *Cahiers du Cinéma* critics were struck above all by Hawks' consistency – the mark of a true 'auteur'. Arguing that *The Big Sleep* transcended the *policier* genre, Claude Chabrol found in 1955 that 'deep roots and firm connections link it to the body of Hawks' work'. Hawks, it was said, worked across most genres, but always ended up making a Hawks picture, defined by stylistic economy, cynicism and – perhaps most importantly – women who talked back.

THE DISC

The notion of the director's cut, privileged object of the special-edition DVD fan's connoisseurship, is just one example of auteurism's manifold influence on film culture. *The Big Sleep* package (R1 only) offers both Hawks' cut and the 'original' – but in doing so it reveals the unbearable anti-auteurist truth. The version that underpinned Hawks' elevation as an auteur was imposed by the studio. Unfavourable responses from test audiences kept Hawks' initial version on the shelf for a year before Bacall's high-powered agent leant on studio boss Jack Warner to re-shoot, losing the tiresome scenes explaining the plot and instead playing up the Bogart–Bacall chemistry.

It was only at Bogart and Bacall's insistence that Hawks was employed on these re-shoots, and it was through this convoluted and collaborative process that the scenes so beloved by its later partisans were dropped in. David Thomson, the film's most eloquent champion, has said of these added scenes that 'without their pleasure, their fun, we might be made more aware that we don't know what the hell the film is about'. If Thomson is right, it's at the expense of *The Big Sleep*'s reputation as an auteur film; but not of its manifest pleasures. (HENRY K MILLER)

The Blair Witch Project
(USA, 1999)

Directors: Daniel Myrick and Eduardo Sanchez
Label: Pathé (UK)
Region: 2 (PAL)
Discs: 1

THE FILM

Myrick and Sanchez's no-budget 1999 frightener is arguably even more effective on the small screen, partly for the added jitters of watching purported 'home movie' footage on a TV set, partly because it's easier to be scared on your own. Heather Donahue, Mike Williams and Joshua Leonard (playing under their own names) are the student documentary-makers who go down to the woods to investigate long-standing rumours of supernatural goings-on and get a big surprise: having lost their bearings, they witness mysterious and increasingly threatening events that escalate from uncanny bundles of twigs to ultimate destruction.

Dispatching their three actors into the Maryland undergrowth with cameras and backpacks, Myrick and Sanchez subjected them to (almost) the same ordeal as their self-named characters, eliciting plausibly panicked performances and allowing for the *vérité*-style use of the footage the actors recorded themselves. Making a virtue of its miniscule budget, the film derives its considerable impact from tapping into fundamental fears: being lost and being in the dark, both literally and metaphorically. Central to its credibility is the timely notion that its leads – especially Donahue – are chronically reluctant to put down their cameras and engage in their predicament without the protection of the lens.

THE DISC

Despite being shot on 16mm film and Hi8 video tape, *The Blair Witch Project* stands as a key text of the digital era, if only for the enormous role played by the internet in generating anticipation (and eventually extraordinary profit) for the picture through the cultivation of a stand-alone mythology to which the film itself was ostensibly a mere documentary footnote – an approach which proved influential on projects such as *A.I. Artificial Intelligence* and the TV series *Lost*. The DVD is of a piece with this approach: bonus material includes a historical Blair Witch timeline and the full-length faux-documentary 'Curse of the Blair Witch', which set out the back-story from 1785 to the eerie 'discovery' of the feature footage itself. Director interviews and the commentary (from Myrick, Sanchez and producers Robin Cowie, Gregg Hale and Michael Monello) drop the act, offering insights into the development of the mythology and the impact of the film's success on the local area, including a plea to fans that the characters would have done well to heed: 'Stay away from Burkittsville. Please!' (BEN WALTERS)

Blood Simple

(USA, 1984) Director's Cut

Directors: Joel and Ethan Coen
Label: Universal (USA)
Region: 1 (NTSC)
Discs: 1

THE FILM

The writing, producing and directing debut of Joel and Ethan Coen, *Blood Simple* remains a landmark of US independent cinema. Exploring a backwoods America largely untouched by Hollywood since the noir heyday of the '40s, the Coens breathed new life – drawn in part from exploitation cinema – into the genre. The four saps at the centre of this stupefyingly *un*simple triple-cross plot have all the freedom of movement of chess pieces, acting almost exclusively out of ignorance, jealousy or greed; and yet the film is anything but predictable, operating according to some hard-boiled variant of Heisenberg's uncertainty principle.

Leavening the film's movie-brat mixture of mannerist dialogue and baroque *mise en scène* with a dose of gothic-horror-movie humour, the Coens leave you forever unsure if they're taking the piss. Sometimes taken for heartlessness, the brothers' authorial poker face is an essential element in all their films, the opacity of their intentions being part of the post-modern fun.

THE DISC

Taken at face value, the claim of 'Director's Edition' made for this DVD would be outrageous – you'd have to watch the two versions simultaneously to spot the difference. Venturing into the extras, however, it becomes clear that the Coens have taken the opportunity to send up the very notion of the director's cut. The 'new' edition is introduced by one Mortimer Young of Forever Young Film Restoration, who claims that the film was shot at a time when 'filmographic techniques were in their infancy', and boasts that 'the boring parts have been taken out and other things . . . added'.

There's no extra-textual evidence that the DVD is a ruse, but it would be hard to imagine anyone being taken in by the commentary (or 'exegetical notes') performed by Forever Young's Artistic Director, Kenneth Loring. For the most part this is a concoction of outright lies and absurd score-settling, but things get really interesting when Loring, in an epic flight of fancy, sketches out the 'real' director's cut – rejected after the film's failure with preview audiences. This imaginary *Blood Simple*, which appends a subplot involving an Eastern European dictator played by Gene Kelly, and without which, Loring claims, the characters' motivations are all but inscrutable, is a conceit out of Nabokov, throwing yet another spanner in the interpretative works. However facetious, the director's edition of *Blood Simple* adds more of value to the original than any more sincere re-edit could have managed. (HENRY K MILLER)

The Blue Angel

(Germany, 1930)

Director: Josef von Sternberg
Label: Eureka (UK)
Region: 2 (PAL)
Discs: 2

THE FILM

Dietrich's first major role, as the *outré* nightclub singer Lola Lola in Germany's earliest sound film, made her a star and inaugurated her remarkable collaboration with Josef von Sternberg. Emil Jannings played Professor Rath, an upstanding teacher who, introduced to Lola's world by his pupils, is seduced and – after losing his job and self-respect – returns to his classroom to die.

Sternberg's mastery of composition and lighting imprints the film with his strong, Expressionist visual style, and his narrative methods are often subtle and ironic, as when the chimes on a clock sound Papageno's aria from *The Magic Flute*, expressing his desire for a wife. He also makes use of parallels: the joyful moment at their wedding when bride and groom crow after the magician produces eggs contrasts with Rath's terrifying noises on stage when working as the conjuror's stooge. The film is built on a series of contrasts: between the classroom (space of responsibility and respectability) and the nightclub (representing desire, excitement and transgression); between Lola Lola and the Professor (paradoxically, he is shown to be the unrealistic and irrational one); and between Rath and the strongman Mazeppa, who is poised to become Lola Lola's new lover. Dietrich's incarnation of the seductress is extraordinary, and established her enduring screen persona: she and Sternberg present Lola Lola as a complex character – by turns friendly, contemptuous, loving and scornful – whose motivation is ultimately unfathomable.

THE DISCS

For commercial reasons, the film was shot in both English and German versions (Dietrich was markedly more comfortable with the English language than the rest of the cast), and Eureka devotes a disc to each. The German version includes parallel versions of a classroom scene which bring out the differences in compositions, Jannings' performance and reaction shots of the boys. In a 1971 interview filmed in Stockholm, Dietrich recalls hearing about the success of *The Blue Angel* – but Ufa, the studio which made the film, did not pick up her option, so she followed Sternberg to Paramount. Also included is her October 1929 screen test, in which she sings 'You're the Cream in My Coffee'. Performing it again 34 years later back in Stockholm, she dryly remarks that it was not because of her singing that she was offered the part. (ADAM STREVENS)

Blue Velvet

(USA, 1986) Special Edition

Director: David Lynch
Label: MGM (USA)
Region: 1 (NTSC)
Discs: 2

THE FILM

Conceived at the height of the Reagan family-values era, at a time when most movie teenagers were fretting about what to wear to the prom, David Lynch's murder-mystery *Blue Velvet* remains genuinely disturbing: a rare English-language riff on the violence of sex, and what happens when bodies come together after dark.

Charting young Jeffrey (Kyle MacLachlan)'s investigations into the severed ear he finds in a field – an amateur-detective adventure that leads through the bedroom wardrobe of Isabella Rossellini's nightclub chanteuse Dorothy Vallens into the sordid underworld of Dennis Hopper's depraved gangster Frank Booth – it's amongst a select band of multi-layered American films that strike you in different ways with every new viewing, each time resisting definitive interpretation. Is *Blue Velvet*, as some have claimed, a key entry in the cinema of misogyny? If so, why is Rossellini's Vallens one of the most complex female characterisations of the '80s?

Technically and formally, the film is every bit as intricate. Lynch's sound design should give home cinema systems everywhere a workout, and the film is full of easily missed verbal and visual puns which tend to the disconcerting rather than funny. Look at how the tangled hosepipe in the opening scene mocks the valves of Jeffrey's stroke victim father, and listen for the chainsaw in the local radio jingle, with its sinister suggestions of further carnage. Laura Dern's girl-next-door Sandy puts it best: 'It's a strange world, isn't it?'

THE DISCS

Sanctuary's two-disc UK edition is a marked improvement on the ruinous original Castle release, not least for being presented in the full anamorphic 2.35:1 aspect ratio, with an image contrast that brings out Lynch's masterful use of light and shade. Extras include a decent 30-minute documentary, 'Strange Desires', in which various Lynch collaborators deconstruct the film's all-American surrealism, and an extract from BBC2's late, lamented film show *Moving Pictures*, in which JG Ballard puts the movie forward as the best film of the '80s.

Devotees, however, plump for MGM's R1 Special Edition, which maintains the excellent image and sound quality while offering up a superior selection of extras. There's an alternative 70-minute doc, 'Mysteries of Love', featuring new interviews with most of the key players (and archive talk-time with Lynch), a montage of deleted-scenes stills, a photo gallery, and the 1986 *Siskel and Ebert* review, again illustrating the diverse reactions the film continues to provoke. Further Easter-egg vox pops consider robins, misogyny, McDonalds and coffee shops. (MIKE McCAHILL)

Borat: Cultural Learnings of America for Make Benefit Glorious Nation of Kazakhstan

(USA, 2006)

Director: Larry Charles
Label: 20th Century Fox (UK)
Region: 2 (PAL)
Discs: 1

THE FILM

American comedy has been testing taboos around bad taste with some vigour over the last decade or so, but Kazakhstan's second most famous TV personality takes bad manners to the level of an art form. Borat is a disingenuous Groucho Marx, an outsider eager to assimilate despite his ingrained sexism, homophobia and anti-Semitism. The great 'cultural learning' underlying his odyssey across the United States is how much common ground he finds along the way.

If Sacha Baron Cohen's Ali G suckers the egos and condescension of the elite, Borat is a more insidious satirist, playing on the courtesy of ordinary folk to expose their latent prejudice. A dinner scene with a party of hospitable southern Christians on Secession Drive is a tour de force of social discomfort, as the guest 'innocuously' makes ever-greater demands on their forbearance. The scene is fascinating, worthy of Buñuel for the way it probes the limits of bourgeois etiquette. As is often the case in this movie, race is the great divider: when he invites a black hooker into the house his hosts finally throw them out. A later scene with a group of Frat boys ends with them lamenting the demise of slavery.

But it's at the Tennessee rodeo that Baron Cohen really shows his balls. First he elicits xenophobic and homophobic comments from the rodeo manager (not hard to do). Then he stands up in front of the entire crowd and delivers a rousing speech pledging support of George Bush's 'War of Terror'. The crowd keeps right on whooping as Borat describes the slaughter in bloodthirsty detail. Their cheers change to jeers when he sets about massacring the Stars and Stripes by substituting the lyrics of the Kazak national anthem.

THE DISC

Baron Cohen and three co-writers earned an Oscar nomination for the screen-play . . . it would be interesting to know just how much of this moc-doc was scripted. This relatively parsimonious disc doesn't supply answers, only a straight face. The first and most original gag comes with the disc itself, manu-factured to look like a bootleg. The menus extend the joke, offering options like 'Make Scene Choosing' and 'Censored Footages', the latter adding up to another 16 minutes of deleted scenes, some of it as funny as the film itself. Under 'Propaganda' you'll find Borat attacking Conan O'Brien's pubis, defending Kazakhstan from Uzbek slurs outside the White House and making sexy time with Martha Stewart and Jason Leno. Select Hebrew in the Language options to activate an alert signal. (The Region 1 disc features the same supple-ments in a different order; it just lacks a DTS soundtrack.) (TOM CHARITY)

Born in Flames

(USA, 1983)

Director: Lizzie Borden
Label: First Run Features (USA)
Region: 1 (NTSC)
Discs: 1

THE FILM

Not so much *Medium Cool* as totally hot, Borden's feminist classic mixes up documentary footage and low-budget science fiction to imagine a revolution wearing its dancing shoes. A major influence on riot grrl culture, *Born in Flames* tells its story of the Women's Liberation Army through news bulletin-like chunks of narrative broken up by beautifully choreographed montages of women working, and scored by the punky sounds of the underground. The events of the film are narrated by three competing voices: the women's underground radio stations Phoenix and Ragazza; male surveillance voice-overs; and the reporters at the Socialist Youth Newspaper, who follow the government party line. There's been a bloodless socialist revolution, bringing a government focused on labour rights to power. But that doesn't extend to gender rights, and many women are being laid off, sent back to the home and attacked on the streets. A women's army has formed in reaction, led by a militant named Adelaide Norris.

Adelaide hooks up with a feminist liberation army in the Western Sahara, and on her return from freedom fighting, she is thrown into jail and tortured by the secret police. Pictures of her supposed suicide make the news and galvanise the army, with the support of the radio stations and, eventually, the socialist women reporters, whose coming to consciousness guides the viewer. What a summary can't convey is the outrageous energy and daring of the film. It's not only riot grrls that studied it, but the creators of many films that advocate media anarchy, revolution in the head and quasi-documentary speculative fiction, from *The Blair Witch Project* to *V for Vendetta*. And yet the film is smarter than any of them, politically and aesthetically, sharing more in common with New York experimental cinema and early rap than with commercial spectaculars.

It's the final sequence that proves jaw-dropping science fiction doesn't need tons of money thrown at it to be eerily relevant years later, as the women's army prepares for its final, audacious act: bringing down US telecommunications systems by planting a bomb under the World Trade Center. This is cinema at its most dangerous and oneiric: miss it at your peril.

THE DISC

It's a miracle that this film even exists, and a double miracle that it finally exists on DVD after two decades of festivals-only availability. The DVD is taken from a print with sharp colour and good sound. There's also a trailer and an interview with the director. But little can beat the thrill of owning a piece of history that still suggests a potent future. (SOPHIE MAYER)

The Bourne Supremacy

(USA, 2004)

Director: Paul Greengrass
Label: Universal (all territories)
Region: Any
Discs: 1

THE FILM

Doug Liman's 2002 *The Bourne Identity* was a solidly appointed retro spy-flick, showcasing a unexpectedly good Matt Damon as little-assassin-lost Jason Bourne, even if it tended to hop about its Old Europe locations with more brisk efficiency than genuine urgency. *The Bourne Supremacy* is the same movie happening now, in worse weather, and at twice the speed; its sheer pace is a startling virtue, whipping up Robert Ludlum's standard Cold War espionage games into the kind of geopolitical cyclone that could almost give you frostbite.

Universal's craftiest move was handing the reins over to British docudrama specialist Paul Greengrass, whose *Bloody Sunday* was a masterclass in fly-on-the-trigger-finger realism, and who penetrates Bourne's dawning moral consciousness — you try unkilling — with much the same acuity. It's all played strictly for real, in other words, and Bourne's existential crisis, however much it seems a pulp abstraction or pretext for staggeringly cool car chases across central Moscow, does play out in a creepily recognisable white-collar climate of abrupt lay-offs and covert clean-ups and frantic rear-covering, in which only total retrograde amnesia might manage to clear out one's ethical hard drive. Among Bourne's agency pursuers, the infighting between a brusquely unflappable Joan Allen and a superbly fatigued Brian Cox charges up its political dimension with bitchy animus, and they're both helped by screenwriter Tony Gilroy's expressive way with monosyllables. ('Does this scan?' fires off Cox. 'I mean, at all?') *Interpreters* and *Constant Gardeners* be damned: if Greengrass edited *War and Peace* you could read it in an hour and not miss much and, if it's post-millennial thrills with a conscience you're after, *The Bourne Supremacy* beats any and all comers into a cocked hat.

THE DISC

This single-disc edition crams more in than most double discs, albeit in bite-sized chunks even a Guy Pearce in *Memento* could manage. Greengrass extols the franchise's USP as 'action that exhibits intelligence', whether Bourne's using the Berlin train timetables to plan a down-to-the-second getaway or finding multiple deadly uses for a rolled-up magazine. Crucial, too, is that his world look 'unconsidered', which is to say that the movie's unfussy framing and handheld immediacy puts you right there, running on instinct, having to think 24 life-or-death thoughts a second. Lean and to the point, these extras scan perfectly. (TIM ROBEY)

Bowfinger

(USA, 1999)

Director: Frank Oz
Label: Universal (USA)
Region: 1 (NTSC) / 2 (PAL)
Discs: 1

THE FILM

The last hurrah of Steve Martin as a force for high-comic good, *Bowfinger* shows off its screenwriter and star's mix of cynicism and sentiment to beguilingly stupid effect. It is, like his earlier self-scripted *L.A. Story*, a wonky love letter to Tinseltown. But it's sharper, more fanciful and freakier than anything Martin did since the silly films he made with Carl Reiner at the start of his film career. The premise is preposterous, even if it echoes the real story of Russian film-maker Sergei Komarov, who shot Mary Pickford and Douglas Fairbanks goofing around for the camera while on holiday in the Ukraine, and then stuck the footage into his film *Potseluy Meri Pikford* (1927) as if it were part of the story. Here, bargain basement auteur-in-waiting Bobby Bowfinger (Martin) tries to hook action star Kit Ramsey (Eddie Murphy) for Chubby Rain, a shlocky new alien-invasion thriller funded to the tune of $2,100. The paranoid, testy Ramsey is having none of it, but our ruthless yet hopeless, Ed Wood-ish hero ropes him in anyway, getting his unwitting cast to accost Ramsey in the street in full alien garb while the cameras are rolling.

The mix of snappy storytelling and unforced ensemble fun adds up to a wondrous rarity: a big-screen comedy that's subtle and broad, wide-eyed and cynical (see also: *Galaxy Quest*). Oz and Martin can't always sustain that playful tone, but the comically adept cast play the high-concept set-up for real, not least in a pair of performances from Murphy that remind you why he's great. His total commitment to the material raises the stakes whenever he's on, whether as fractured Ramsey or his hopeless brother Jiff. If there's a funnier scene than that of Ramsey being pursued in an underground car park by a dog in high heels, then it must be the scene in which Bowfinger films petrified Jiff crossing from one side of a busy freeway to the other. Shame that neither Martin nor Murphy have come anywhere close to equalling this since.

THE DISC

Region 1 has DTS 5.1 sound, but otherwise there's nothing to choose between the UK and US discs. If you can bear the repetition, director Oz's commentary track shows that, while he's no great stylist, he's thought hard about how to sustain a feature-length comedy. Main points has he three: 1) Keep it snappy; 2) Keep it fluid ('I always let the actors mess around and improvise on the last take. Eddie/Steve/Robert Downey Jr came up with that line on the spot.'); and 3) Keep it real ('We used a lot of natural light in this scene. I didn't want it to look like a movie set.'). There's also a smattering of out-takes and deleted scenes. (DOMINIC MAXWELL)

Brief Encounter

(UK, 1945)

Director: David Lean
Label: Granada (UK)
Region: 2 (PAL)
Discs: 1

THE FILM

It's so easy to mock *Brief Encounter*. There's the Received Pronunciation for a start, the endless cups of tea and the chirpy lower classes who pop up occasionally to offer a bit of light relief from all the soul-searching. But name another celluloid moment as visceral and wrenching as that when Celia Johnson and Trevor Howard decide to do the noble thing. Upper lips may be stiff, but the hearts under the ration-book clothing are pounding.

Both David Lean's direction and Noel Coward's screenplay ooze a decorous restraint that seems alien in today's follow-your-heart-and-damn-the-consequences world, coming as they do from a 1945 Britain schooled in self-sacrifice over self-serving. It never looked good for housewife Laura and doctor Alec, but then they weren't looking for it. Contentedly if uninspiringly married to other people, they are simply going about their unassuming middle-class business when specks in eyes and busy restaurants complete with lunchtime orchestras conspire to throw them together. Thereafter, they are consigned to a furtive romance agonisingly measured out in the teaspoons of the refreshment room at Milford Junction.

It feels almost voyeuristic to intrude on this intensely personal passion, played out to the plaintive strains of Rachmaninoff's *Piano Concerto No. 2*. Johnson achingly suggests the burden of her increasingly tangled web of domestic deceits and Howard shines with the ardour of a good man who can't believe that the love he feels can be so wrong. Your dad was right: they don't make films like this any more, and the loss is all ours.

THE DISC

If you like to nurture thoughts of Trevor Howard curing small children of polio in his free time, don't read the cast biographies; it seems he was an off-screen roaring boy, not unaccustomed to nights spent at His Majesty's pleasure when the bar bills got the better of him. The theatrical trailer shows that marketing sorts were just as keen on giving away all the plot twists 60 years ago as they are today. What we lack now, though, are the accompanying captions redolent of wartime public information broadcasts. 'All will follow their problem with emotion and understanding', instructs one.

Brief Encounter's two producers reminisce in suitably misty-eyed fashion in the 25-minute documentary featurette, whose makers were somewhat hamstrung by a lack of living cast members. All is not lost, however: they did manage to track down Beryl the station tearoom girl. (FIONA MOUNTFORD)

Bringing Up Baby

(USA, 1938)

Director: Howard Hawks
Label: Warners (USA)
Region: 1 (NTSC)
Discs: 2

THE FILM

The screwball romance formula isn't all that complex: fling together a chalk-and-cheese couple, establish an antagonistic flirtation, scatter the path to sexual consummation with highly improbable impediments, and let the hysteria build. This definitive take on the genre succeeds by taking every element to a crazed extreme. The resulting pell-mell dash mirrors its own central romance by uniting utter freeform anarchy with pernickety precision.

Cary Grant plays stuffy, sexually repressed palaeontologist David Huxley, who's about to be swallowed whole – matrimonially speaking – by the strait-laced Alice Swallow (Virginia Walker) when the pursuit of a million-dollar museum grant leads him into altogether more effervescent waters. A golf-course encounter with elegant but exasperating heiress Susan Vance (Katharine Hepburn) throws both bursary and engagement off-course, as Susan proves herself to be peculiarly inextricable from David's professional and romantic fortunes. Then there's the runaway leopard, the mad aunt, the drunk Major, and the misplaced dinosaur bone . . .

Hawks's film is so overflowing with charm and invention that it's hard to believe it initially flopped at the box office. It showcases its two stars at their finely tuned finest – while their clashing characters provide a charming retort to that old question about what happens when an irresistible force meets an immovable object. Hepburn is a madcap, maddening delight; Grant proves wholly disarming in an uncharacteristically donnish and emasculated role. Combined with such gracefully authoritative direction from Hawks, and one of the most relentlessly funny scripts ever written, *Bringing Up Baby* ultimately transcends the conspicuous absurdity of its plot to establish itself as an oddly touching metaphor for the power of love to overwhelm good sense and logic. Every boy-meets-girl comedy undertaken since has striven for the same frenetic energy and starry romantic chemistry; most, including the 1987 Madonna/Griffin Dunne remake *Who's That Girl*, have fallen short.

THE DISCS

This double-disc set includes a playful but insightful commentary by Peter Bogdanovich, who knew Hawks, and drew inspiration for his 1972 comedy *What's Up, Doc?* from *Bringing Up Baby*. Disc 2 carries two documentary features. 'Cary Grant: A Man Apart' gives a complete portrait of the much-loved actor (and doesn't shy away from addressing his drug use or his sexuality), with input from his co-stars, directors, friends and fans. 'The Men Who Made the Movies: Howard Hawks' is an informative portrait featuring copious archive interview footage with Hawks himself. Also included is a Hawks trailer reel, and two comic shorts from the year of the film's release, 'Campus Cinderella' and the cartoon 'A Star is Hatched'. (HANNAH McGILL)

Bring Me the Head of Alfredo Garcia

(USA, 1974)

Director: Sam Peckinpah
Label: MGM (USA)
Region: 1 (NTSC)
Discs: 1

THE FILM

A savagely downbeat, grim journey through Mexico's criminal borderlands, *Alfredo Garcia* is Peckinpah's most personal film, and a favourite amongst his admirers. The endlessly watchable Warren Oates is a natural for Bennie, a saloon-bar piano player who was down on his luck and then discovered that life has a basement. It's a startlingly bleak, yet captivatingly human performance, allegedly based on Peckinpah himself; Oates apparently even borrowed Sam's shades for the role. With the beautiful Elita (Isela Vega), and eventually the rotting head of the title in tow, Bennie sets out to claim a bounty from a mysterious group of criminal bureaucrats. As things go from bad to vicious, Bennie's grip begins to slip and he descends into a hell of booze, bullets and *bandidos*.

Peckinpah's twisted, embittered take on the American dream is populated by a succession of sleazy, corrupt lowlifes, all dragging themselves through the dusty hell of 1970s Mexico, forever under the shadow of Nixon's America. It's a vile, grubby existence: sweat-slicked, bloodstained and permanently sticky with alcohol, where nobody gives a shit and violent death is as much an option as pouring another drink.

On its release *Alfredo Garcia* was hated by critics, who found its unabashed misanthropy difficult to stomach, but it has since carved a niche as a superior piece of filmmaking that transcends any attempts at pigeonholing. Peckinpah himself often claimed that it was the only one of his films that was truly *his*. Driven by Oates' delirious performance and Peckinpah's raw, masterful direction, *Garcia* represents a very personal odyssey by a very angry man. Like its director, it's something of a drunken, incoherent, nihilistic bastard, but you'll never regret inviting it into your living-room. Look out for a mean-assed cameo from Kris Kristofferson.

THE DISC

In the UK we get nothing but a deep down and dirty 1.85:1 print of the film in roaring mono. Americans get a trailer and a great three-way discussion between Peckinpah experts Paul Seydor, Garner Simmons and David Weddle. The trio, who refer to it as 'the hangover film of the '60s', are clearly in love with it (one even appears as an extra in the opening sequence), and take great pleasure in conducting this live autopsy, providing plenty of insight into Peckinpah the man, and the special hatred he reserved for then recently ex-President Nixon, to whom this film might be considered a middle-finger tribute.

(MARK PILKINGTON)

Bus 174

(Brazil, 2002)

Director: José Padilha
Label: Metrodome (UK)
Region: 2 (PAL)
Discs: 1

THE FILM

Often compared with the fictionalised hold-up thriller *Dog Day Afternoon*, *Bus 174* is a more telling indictment of the society in which its story takes place. On 12 June, 2000 Sandro di Nascimento boarded a bus on route 174 in the centre of Rio de Janeiro, taking its occupants hostage. Over the next five hours, more than 30 million Brazilians watched events unfold on television. Happening as it did outside one of the local network's studios, Sandro's every move was captured on film, including his own death at the hands of the police.

José Padilha's riveting documentary investigates what drove Sandro to his crime. His story is that of many of the homeless children who roam the streets of Rio. Unlike the residents of the surrounding *favelas*, the street urchins are not recognised as citizens and as such fall prey to unscrupulous and sadistic members of the police force. The turning point in Sandro's life was the massacre at Candelaria Church in 1993, when police opened fire on 70 sleeping children, killing seven. Sandro was one of the survivors, but a number of his friends were murdered. According to people who knew him at the time, he became withdrawn after the ambush, losing contact with the few family members he had.

Bus 174 is damning in its criticism of the Brazilian state and nation, and its lack of interest in the street children (as *Jornal do Brasil* wrote upon the film's release, 'All of us are on Bus 174'). Padilha's film also argues that the tragic outcome to the siege was as much the fault of a disorganised police force, and, though never excusing Sandro's crime, attempts to explore the reasons for his actions. Through archive footage and scrupulous research, including interviews with members of the police force, street gangs, Sandro's family and his social worker, *Bus 174* is a compelling portrait of social injustice, and an exemplar of the new Latin American film wave.

THE DISC

None of the film's quality is lost in transfer, evident in the stunning opening aerial shot over Rio. The extra interviews, though occasionally insightful, could have done with tighter editing as they repeat many of the comments made in the film. The most impressive extra is the gallery of photographs of Rio street children and gangsters taken by Alexandre Lima, *Bus 174*'s assistant director, which were exhibited in London when the film was originally released. (IAN HAYDN SMITH)

By Brakhage: An Anthology
(USA, 1954–2001)

Director: Stan Brakhage
Label: Criterion Collection (USA)
Region: 0 (NTSC)
Discs: 2

THE FILMS

'Imagine an eye unruled by man-made laws of perspective, an eye unpreju-
diced by compositional logic, an eye which does not respond to the name of
everything but which must know each object encountered in life through an
adventure of perception. How many colours are there in a field of grass to
the crawling baby unaware of "green"?'

The visionary words, the manifesto calling, are of Stan Brakhage, magus
and maker of a moving image utterly removed from the story-lined, characterised imperatives of feature-form cinema. Brakhage, who died aged 70 in
2003, from a cancer likely caused by the coal-tar dyes he used in his nearly
400 8mm and 16mm films, was a poet in light, a painter in motion of the
phenomenal world whose avowed intention was to give his viewers God. This
would transpire via a filmmaking that prioritised the metaphorical, abstract
and subjective voices in a ceaseless dialogue between consciousness and the
world, and has resulted in some of the 20th century's most remarkable works,
in any medium.

Working with celluloid every which way, from handpainting frame-by-frame
to scratching the emulsion with his fingernails, from nine-second ultra-fragments
to four-hour epics of imaginative intensity, Brakhage created a body of work
that both fuelled and shaped the American filmic avant-garde and remains its
most complete achievement. Whether in *Mothlight*, where he pasted moth
wings directly onto the film strip, or *Window Water Baby Moving*, where he
filmed the birth of his child in a cubist, mystical union with the luminous day,
he constantly pushed formal and thematic boundaries. His films, he said, were
'essentially preoccupied by, and deal imagistically with, birth, sex, death and
the search for God'. So, *The Act of Seeing with One's Own Eyes* is an unflinching
look at autopsy bodies and his seminal *Dog Star Man* deploys wildly distorting
lenses, solar flares and paint to depict the creation of the universe.

THE DISCS

For an artist who often made only a second of work a day, and whose sense of
texture, rhythm and detail was without match, any translation into another
medium will raise questions. But it is hard to imagine a more empathetic and
accomplished assembly than Criterion's exemplary double-disc anthology. A
model of curation and presentation, it offers over two dozen of Brakhage's
most important works, in digital transfers and from new master prints. There's
also a contextualising interview with the master, and an essay by Brakhage
authority Fred Camper (whose website, fredcamper.com, offers extremely
detailed comparisons of the work on film and DVD). (GARETH EVANS)

Cannibal Holocaust

(Colombia/Italy, 1979)
25th Anniversary Collector's Edition

Director: Ruggero Deodato
Label: Grindhouse Releasing (USA)
Region: 0 (NTSC)
Discs: 2

THE FILM

Dogged by controversy from the moment of its release, Ruggero Deodato's *Cannibal Holocaust* remains a rare instance of a film that really is as grisly as it's cracked up to be. The opening title sequence, flying over an Amazon bend accompanied by Riz Ortolani's lush, delicate score, signals from the get-go that this is going to be something more than your regular no-brainer gorefeast. The choice of Ortolani for the score was entirely deliberate. It was his music for Cavara and Jacopetti's blockbusting 1962 *Mondo Cane* that helped set the tone for the exploitation documentary format that Deodato emulates here.

The film's first section follows an expedition to locate a lost crew of documentary filmmakers (themselves convincingly portrayed by Deodato's crew). Overcoming the usual jungle perils, the team eventually find their way to a tribal village where, amongst the human remains, they locate the crew's personal belongings and film canisters. Back in the US, TV producers sift through the footage, revealing the brutal truth of the team's exploitative ways, and their eventual demise at the hands of a cannibal tribe. As we view (on grainy 16mm) the parade of atrocities staged by the documentary team to look like acts of tribal fury, the lines between reality and fantasy, human and animal, right and wrong, become increasingly blurred. The scenes of human cruelty are genuinely brutal and shocking, but it's the scenes of cruelty to animals that will have people reaching for the off switch, and which ultimately saw the film banned all over the world.

Whether consciously or not, the film is highly reminiscent of the dubious late-1960s anthropological films that purported to depict the brutal rites of the Amazonian Yanomami tribe. If the wider narrative framing device sounds familiar, talk to the makers of *The Blair Witch Project*.

THE DISCS

The two-disc Grindhouse edition is a lovingly assembled, fan-led affair. A striking anamorphic transfer of the full 96-minute film (and alternative 'animal cruelty-free' version) is complemented by audio and picture-in-picture commentaries from Deodato and actor Robert Kerman. On the second disc, an hour-long Italian documentary, 'In the Jungle', covers the controversy surrounding the film, with making-of footage and some candid memories from cast and crew. There are also interviews, photos and Easter eggs. Limited to 11,111 copies, the set now sells at a premium; Siren Visual Entertainment's Australian Collector's Edition is identical, and Grindhouse's single-disc Deluxe Edition reproduces the same cut and many of the extras. If you're setting out to watch hardcore atrocity cinema, there's no point cutting corners . . . (MARK PILKINGTON)

Capturing the Friedmans
(USA, 2003)

Director: Andrew Jarecki
Label: Tartan Video (US)
Region: 2 (PAL)
Discs: 2

THE FILM

'My eyes were in the right direction but my brain saw nothing,' says Elaine Friedman, desperately trying to describe how she felt when she first saw the illegal pornography owned by her husband Arnold. Her story is one of many covered in director Andrew Jarecki's unsettling documentary *Capturing the Friedmans*, which won the Grand Jury Prize at Sundance.

Jarecki's film explores the child-abuse scandal that engulfed a Long Island middle-class Jewish family in the late '80s. When the post office caught retired schoolteacher Arnold mail-ordering child pornography, police raided his house and discovered a stash of illegal magazines. Worse still, Arnold and his teenage son Jesse were later accused of molesting dozens of children in after-school computer classes.

Capturing the Friedmans explores several fascinating aspects of the case, from the elusiveness of truth and fickleness of perception (different testimonies and revelations are disclosed in carefully see-sawing fashion), to the Friedman children's seemingly compulsive need to videotape their experiences, like outrunners of our modern confessional media culture. Jarecki struck gold with these hours of home video, including heartbreaking images of the family's final Passover together and footage of Jesse's last night with his two brothers. A compelling study of sorrow, shame and denial, Jarecki's film is an object lesson in the fallibility of memory and the fragility of family.

THE DISCS

Quite apart from the appalling crimes Arnold and Jesse are alleged to have committed, what makes *Capturing the Friedmans* such disquieting viewing is the murky legal swamp surrounding the case. Tartan wades deeper with this two-disc Special Edition.

Disc 1 has an interview with Jarecki and an astute audio commentary with him and editor Richard Hankin. Together, they discuss technical aspects of the film, address frequently asked questions, and show particular sensitivity towards the Friedmans. There's also a half-hour interview with Jarecki conducted by critic Tom Dawson (the only addition to HBO's otherwise identical R1 edition).

A repository for material that didn't make the final cut, Disc 2 includes a disturbing interview with the prosecution's star witness and an introduction to several alleged accomplices not mentioned in the film. There's footage from its Long Island premiere, which saw the judge speak out, and from a Tribeca Film Festival screening which triggered an altercation between several audience members. And we get the original 20-minute doc Jarecki had been making – about eldest brother David's career as a children's entertainer – when he stumbled on the skeletons in the Friedman family closet. (JAMES CLASPER)

Carnival of Souls

(USA, 1962)

Director: Harold A Harvey
Label: Criterion Collection (USA)
Region: 1 (NTSC)
Discs: 2

THE FILM

The very definition of a midnight movie, Harold A 'Herk' Harvey's micro-budget *danse macabre* was shot for $17,000 on location around Salt Lake City and Lawrence, Kansas, carelessly released by a virtually bankrupt distributor, and all but vanished. Harvey went back to making educational and industrial films for the Lawrence-based Centron Corporation, and his sole feature would be lost to us if it weren't for some enterprising programmer on one of the cultier American TV networks. Repeat play on the late-night schedules gradually gained it a following and, 27 years on, Harvey gave his blessing to a 1989 theatrical re-release which enshrined it as a bona-fide favourite both on the horror festival circuit and, belatedly, on DVD.

Even more fundamentally than Romero's *Night of the Living Dead* (see **Trilogy of the Dead**), Harvey's film depends on its minimal resources – stark monochrome photography, crudely recorded organ score – for eerie, hallucinatory suggestibility. Plundering its structure from the Ambrose Bierce story 'An Occurrence at Owl Creek Bridge', it follows car-crash survivor Mary (Candace Hilligoss) as she recup-erates from near-drowning and takes a job as a church organist in Salt Lake City, visited all the while by a silent, staring ghoul played by Harvey himself. The director wanted his film to have 'the look of a Bergman and the feel of a Cocteau', and he triumphed on both counts, particularly during the splendid climax at the abandoned Saltair Pavilion amusement park, a Mormon mecca sitting on the shores of the Great Salt Lake, and one of the most deliciously uncanny locations in horror history. Mary's molestation by a lecherous boarding-house neighbour (Sidney Berger) and the imagery of groping hands also fascin-atingly prefigure Polanski's *Repulsion*.

THE DISCS

Criterion have lavished an almost obscene amount of love on this cherished cult item, putting presentations of many more canonical classics to shame. There's no trade-off between the superior picture quality of the original, 78-minute cut (pristinely remastered from a duplicate negative) and the slightly less spruce 83-minute director's cut, since we get both, the latter graced by intermittent audio commentary from Harvey and his screenwriter, John Clifford. Essays on the history of the Centron Corporation and Saltair – the former accompanied by over an hour's worth of vintage excerpts from their films, and the latter graced by an array of extraordinary, Kubla Khan-like period photos – provide all the context you could possibly want. (TIM ROBEY)

Carrie

(USA, 1976) Special Edition

Director: Brian DePalma
Label: MGM (all territories)
Region: 1 (NTSC) / 2 (PAL)
Discs: 1

THE FILM

Carrie feels like a classic now, but it came from almost nowhere. An unproven director, whose main claim to fame was an early thumbs-up from Pauline Kael; a first novel by a Maine English teacher, Stephen King, which even he later dismissed as sub-par; and a cast full of virtually unknown twenty-somethings playing stroppy, horny teens, topped, in the role of a tormented wallflower who can move things with her mind, by the weird star of that Terrence Malick film, and, playing her religious nutjob mom, a semi-retired former ingenue in her first screen role for 14 years.

Measures of the movie's astonishing success – as pop entertainment, as a capsule of its moment, and as a long-lived cult favourite – are to be found not only in Sissy Spacek and Piper Laurie's shock Oscar nominations, but in the careers it launched: De Palma's, King's, John Travolta's. And the film did for senior proms in cinema what *Jaws*, the year before, did for the becalmed waters around a beach resort.

The true horror apex, in terms of good old emotional investment, pity and awe, was never Carrie's telekinetic payback, oddly anticlimactic any way you splitscreen it. It was the pig's blood. Always the pig's blood. You want to race up, slice through the rope, and give Nancy Allen a bitch-slap every time you watch it. The astounding Spacek makes Carrie's ritual humiliation almost too much to bear, from her wrenchingly vulnerable shower scene onwards. And De Palma and Laurie brilliantly pillage the domestic mother-daughter duets for jet-black satire, making the whole movie click, hilariously, and heartbreakingly, as a fire-and-brimstone Gothic riff on the exaggerated pain of every adolescence.

THE DISC

Almost all the film's available talent has been rounded up for a clutch of special-edition featurettes here, with the notable exception of Travolta (who still receives cheeky second billing for his walk-on part). The supporting cast allow themselves wry if clearly aggrieved smiles about De Palma's manipulative rehearsal techniques, and there's a wickedly abrupt cut from PJ Soles talking about a high-pressure hose bursting her eardrum to De Palma stonily saying 'Everyone who dies is involved in this Greek tragedy . . .' Screenwriter Lawrence D Cohen is particularly good company, discussing alternative drafts of the script, and the legendarily short-lived Broadway musical in which Betty Buckley (terrific as gym teacher Miss Collins) took on the Laurie part. It sounds like a scream. (TIM ROBEY)

Casablanca

(USA, 1942) 2-disc Special Edition

Director: Michael Curtiz
Label: Warners (worldwide)
Region: Any
Discs: 2

THE FILM

When all the timeless lines and yearning glances have gone by once again, the impression left is one of flawless balance: cynicism with starry-eyed sweetness, romance with action, sleek choreography with a certain thrilling and surprising looseness. The look of Michael Curtiz's much-loved and endlessly quoted wartime romance is all-pleasing contrasts, too – silvery lights against inky darks, and crumpled Humphrey Bogart next to luminous Ingrid Bergman. He's ex-pat bar owner Rick, who keeps his vulnerability, his patriotism and his heart of gold firmly under wraps; she's the woman from his past who passes through and brings them all seething back to the surface. The sideline characters are no less memorable: Claude Rains as the 'just like any other man, only more so' Captain Renault; Dooley Wilson as Rick's piano man and confidant Sam; Peter Lorre as Ugarte, dealer in black-market exit visas; and Paul Henreid as Victor Laszlo, the romantic rival with unimpeachable virtue on his side. The original play had never even been performed when Jack Warner optioned it, and the film was regarded by all involved as a rather modest undertaking – yet *Casablanca* has made an indelible cultural mark, and aged just beautifully.

THE DISCS

A gorgeous transfer is accompanied by four hours' worth of artefacts and anecdotes, offering plenty for devotees and neophytes alike. Background is filled out by two commentaries – a manic and irreverent one by US critic Roger Ebert, and a more sober one by film historian Rudy Behlmer – and three documentaries. 'Bacall on Bogart', presented by the star's widow, features his earliest screen appearances as well as interviews from friends like John Huston and Katharine Hepburn. 'As Time Goes By: A Tribute to Casablanca', also voiced by Bacall, is a dense elaboration of the film's origins that includes priceless interviews with key behind-the-scenes players. Only 'The Children Remember', an interview with Bogart's son Stephen Bogart and Bergman's daughter Pia Lindstrom, is on the vapid side.

Smaller scraps include a set of brief but subtly revealing out-takes and two additional scenes (all sadly without sound); the scoring-stage sessions (which include an alternate take of 'As Time Goes By'); and mesmerising production ephemera ranging from trailers and publicity shots to script notes and tense office memos. There are even three alternative takes on the whole story: a 1943 radio version, a 1955 TV adaptation, and a cartoon spoof featuring the entire Looney Tunes stable. (HANNAH McGILL)

John Cassavetes: Five Films

(USA, 1959–1977)

Director: John Cassavetes
Label: Criterion Collection (USA)
Region: 1 (NTSC)
Discs: 8

FILM TITLES: Shadows, Faces, A Woman Under the Influence, The Killing of a Chinese Bookie, Opening Night

THE FILMS

With the completion of his debut *Shadows* in 1959, John Cassavetes defined what it means to be an independent filmmaker. As with most of his subsequent films, he financed and distributed it on his own, using money raised from his acting gigs. This unrelenting determination to remain faithful to his personal vision underpinned a level of emotional truth near unrivalled in film history, as these five of his best manifest.

Populated with jazz musicians, hipsters and awkward young lovers, and infused with raw spontaneity, *Shadows* is an authentic document of life in Manhattan in the late '50s, and a portrayal of timeless human dramas. Although the final version was almost entirely scripted, the film developed out of two years of improvisation. In *Faces*, Cassavetes depicts a failing middle-class marriage with uncanny detail. A scathing attack on bourgeois values, the film nonetheless transcends reductive moralistic statements. *A Woman Under the Influence*, arguably Cassavetes' greatest film, portrays the psychological breakdown of Rowlands' suburban housewife Mabel. Both Rowlands and Peter Falk, as her befuddled husband, offer remarkable performances. *Opening Night* is the story of an aging Broadway actress (Rowlands) who witnesses the death of a young girl outside the theatre one night, triggering her own downward spiral into depression and alcoholism; it's a meta-cinematic study of the struggle to communicate life through art. *The Killing of a Chinese Bookie* has a charismatic strip-club owner (Ben Gazzara) pressured into committing a hit for the mob in order to pay off his gambling debts. Like much of Cassavetes' cinema, the film examines a failed yet heroic struggle to realise the American dream.

Cassavetes stops us totally sympathising with any of his characters, yet his love for them shines through no matter their flaws. Perhaps only Jean Renoir's films present humanity so compassionately while remaining so devastatingly honest.

THE DISCS

Optimum offer a very decent package of these films in the UK, but Criterion's box set is a whopper. Included is 'A Constant Forge' by Charles Kiselyak, a respectable 200-minute documentary on Cassavetes' life and art, over two hours of video interviews with his stock company of actors, an excellent short film by cinematographer Al Ruban, 'Lighting and Shooting the Film', which details how *Faces* was shot, and a 68-page booklet of essays and interviews. As usual Criterion's transfer quality is superb. The two best essays are by critic Kent Jones and novelist Jonathan Lethem, but no words do justice to the distinct experience of watching a Cassavetes film. (JONATHAN RAFMAN)

Céline et Julie vont en Bateau

(France, 1974)

Director: Jacques Rivette
Label: BFI (UK)
Region: 2 (PAL)
Discs: 2

ENGLISH TITLE: Céline and Julie Go Boating

THE FILM

Rivette may be the most elusive of all the French New Wave directors. At once baffling and utterly absorbing, his sprawling feature films are epic in both complexity and duration, with stories that resist genre classification. A primary concern has been the role of the viewer, and Rivette's use of narrative to explore our relationship with both cinema and the world we inhabit is nothing short of visionary. His films are long with purpose, expressive of his belief that movies should activate us, rather than pacify us, challenging us to think for ourselves.

Céline and Julie is his most joyful work. A collaboration with screenwriter Eduardo de Gregorio and its stars Juliet Berto and Dominique Fournier, it follows the adventures of two best friends who meet after a playful chase on foot through the streets of Paris. They come upon a mansion where an ominous melodrama is perpetually unfolding: two well-manicured women (Bulle Ogier and Marie-France Pisier) vie for the affections of a wealthy creep (Barbet Schroeder, the film's producer) and his daughter, who, it becomes clear, is in imminent danger. The story-within-a-story is conveyed in fragments, as Céline and Julie travel between its world and theirs through the power of magical candies.

The film's use of theatre and performance is signature Rivette; critic David Thomson remarked that, in its dissolution of the boundary between reality and imagination, Céline and Julie is 'the most innovative film since *Citizen Kane*'. The charming pairing of Julie, a mischievous librarian fixated on witchcraft, with the impetuous Céline, a magician and compulsive storyteller, echoes *Gentlemen Prefer Blondes*' Monroe and Russell (Rivette was an early Hawks champion), but their unapologetic autonomy firmly situates the film in the heyday of feminism. Céline and Julie is a pleasure to watch, both a playful narrative escapade and an exhortation to an enlightened kind of spectatorship.

THE DISCS

Benefiting from the film's 2006 restoration, the BFI's transfer is very clean and true to the low-contrast colours of the original. Extras on the second disc include Jonathan Romney's 18-minute introduction to Rivette's cinema and informative discussion of C&J. A two-minute short, RW Paul's silent *The Haunted Curiosity Shop* (1901), echoes the spirit of the film, and a special bonus is Alain Resnais's rare, masterful short *Toute la memoire du monde* (1956), a documentary essay on the old National Library of France. The booklet includes colour photos and interviews with Labourier, Berto and Rivette, as well as words by the late Tom Milne and Susan Seidelman, who cites Rivette's influence on *Desperately Seeking Susan*. (VERA BRUNNER-SUNG)

The Cell

(USA, 2000)

Director: Tarsem Singh
Label: New Line Platinum Series (USA)
Region: 1 (NTSC)
Discs: 1

THE FILM

Tarsem's *The Cell* notches another entry in the perversely inexhaustible genre of serial-killer procedurals, but its spectacular visions and troubling ironies deserve and reward repeated viewings. From its first stylised sequence of rippling dunes, couture gowns and sallow demon-children in the Namibian desert, *The Cell* strongly implies that its fundamental plot formula is only a bare hook on which to hang some opulent fantasias: a Khan-like emperor with purple satin capes that whip around the entire perimeter of his ten-storey throne room; a horse that is vivisected by huge panes of glass, through which its still-beating heart can be glimpsed; a ceiling-sized chandelier built of lambent coins and seashells; still shots that embroider themselves around the edges with gold filigree and breathing flowers; a desolate panorama of arid, gray furrows, where parched, open-mouthed women sit in stony expectation of some unseen immi-nence in the dark sky.

Sometimes these images tip too far into excess or rely on broad psychological clichés, and yet the devilish, despairing wit of *The Cell* lies in how it ascribes those very clichés and dangerous dualisms not to the killer (Vincent D'Onofrio), though he is clearly enslaved to his own cruel iconographies, but to the professional empath (Jennifer Lopez) and the crusading cop (Vince Vaughn). If the breathtaking visuals and roiling imagination of *The Cell* aren't enough to recommend it, consider it as a provocative antonym to *The Silence of the Lambs*. The evil avatar is not an impermeable object like Hannibal Lecter but an endless series of inroads, recesses and internal projections; the ostensible heroine does not prove her mettle so much as she betrays her prejudices and principles, ending the movie, despite her best intentions and final close-ups, in much worse shape than when she started – and with terrible blood on her hands.

THE DISC

For a company that quickly started selling its DVDs at cut-rate prices, New Line sure packs in a lot of sumptuous extras. Indeed, the disc of *The Cell* shares the film's own willingness to toss a lot of material at the audience and see what sticks, from two excitable commentaries to an isolated track of Howard Shore's cacophonous score to an 'empathy test' that boots you out once your 'emotional IQ' dips too low. An inter-active diagram of the human brain explains the difference, to all ye who enter here, between the somatosensory cortex and the parietal lobe. Best of all are the affable and well-illustrated dissections of the film's most elaborate set-pieces and technical processes by visual effects supervisor Kevin Tod Haug, who previously teased out the manias and emblems of a troubled mind for David Fincher's *Fight Club*. (Note that other, 'international' editions include a scene featuring D'Onofrio's killer masturbating over a corpse in the main cut of the film, rather than a deleted-scene extra, as here; the trade-off is this disc's second commentary with the production team.) (NICK DAVIS)

Le Cercle Rouge
(France, 1970)

Director: Jean-Pierre Melville
Label: Criterion Collection (USA)
Region: 1 (NTSC)
Discs: 2

ENGLISH TITLE: *The Red Circle*

THE FILM

Director Jean-Pierre Melville claims 'I try to be as conventional as possible.' *Le Cercle Rouge* shows why this can be a valuable aim. While the story – the heist of a Parisian jeweller by a trio of outsiders – may be conventional, its execution is original and entrancing.

The opening, for instance, is standard for a *policier* – an escape by captured killer Vogel (Gian Maria Volonté) from police captain Mattei (André Bourvil) on the Marseilles–Paris train. But Melville's genius lies in the escape's pacing. A slow, wordless build-up, intercut with the jail release of gangster Corey (Alain Delon), concentrates on the minutiae: Vogel feigning sleep while crafting a lock-pick, Mattei wearily preparing for bed. Then, a brief explosion of energy as Vogel kicks through a window and jumps off the train. This pattern recurs throughout the film: Corey's lengthy and lovingly photographed game of billiards in Marseilles is interrupted by gangsters, the death of one of whom is recorded in a single one-second shot. What could be merely perverse in the hands of a lesser director is instead inspired; the details are never redundant, and the moments of action are made more intense by brevity.

Reflecting Melville's love of American cinema, *Le Cercle Rouge* is a hybrid of Western and film noir; cowboys and sheriffs clad in trenchcoats and fedoras and transplanted into cold, gloomy Paris. These are tough, unemotional men (there are no female speaking parts), whose dialogue is sparse. We can empathise with Mattei's wry comment on seeing a video of the robbery: 'They're not much for talk.' Delon, in particular, is magnificent, a taciturn enigma resignedly aware that he cannot escape the red circle (a recurring visual image) that has trapped him with his fellow conspirators.

THE DISCS

An entertaining 2003 interview with assistant director Bernard Stora is the highlight of Criterion's extras disc. He recalls Volonté's one-man, two-day strike, perhaps because he found Melville's politics insufficiently radical, and describes Melville's method of transforming Bourvil from music-hall comic to hard-boiled detective (essentially, buy him a good suit and hat). The contemporary interviews on the disc are less revealing, including one especially vacuous chat show appearance by Melville and Delon (sample question: 'Is there a potential loner in you?'). Perhaps it would have been more valuable to have the whole of the 1971 *Cinéastes de notre temps* episode on Melville instead, rather than just some idiosyncratic but fascinating excerpts. The picture is sharper and ruddier than on the also worthy R2 BFI disc, which includes a scholarly commentary and alternative features. (JOE PERKINS)

La Cérémonie

(France, 1995)

Director: Claude Chabrol
Label: Metrodome (UK) / Homevision (USA)
Region: 0 (PAL) / 1 (NTSC)
Discs: 1

THE FILM

Wryly dubbed 'the last Marxist film' by its director Claude Chabrol, this adaptation of Ruth Rendell's novel *A Judgement in Stone* – relocated to Brittany from rural Suffolk – continues the explorations of power, guilt, class consciousness and transgressive violence that have preoccupied the veteran French director since he kick-started the Nouvelle Vague with *Le Beau Serge* back in 1958. Sophie (Sandrine Bonnaire) is hired as a live-in maid for a well-heeled family living in a secluded mansion near St Malo. Shy and intensely private, she endures their well-meaning condescension while desperately trying to conceal her illiteracy, as well as disturbing events from her past. When she forms a friendship with the volatile postmistress Jeanne (Isabelle Huppert), who is nursing emotional wounds of her own, the stage is set for a fatal clash between bourgeois complacency and the resentful sociopathy of their putative social inferiors.

Chabrol, like Brian DePalma, has often been derided for his cribbings from Hitchcock, but here he's distinctly uninterested in the mechanics of suspense and plot and acutely aware of psychology's shortcomings in accounting for criminal deviancy; thanks to the nuanced playing of his cast, judgments remain provisional and shifting rather than cast in stone. Once again, Chabrol's creative partnership with Huppert (begun with *Violette Nozière* in 1978 and still going strong with *L'Ivresse du Pouvoir* in 2006) proves as fruitful as his earlier collaborations with Stéphane Audran, and the actress delivers another of her compelling portrayals of a woman on the verge; Bonnaire, meanwhile, in the less showy role, invests Sophie with an unnerving inscrutability while never entirely forsaking the audience's sympathy. Chabrol also provides Jacqueline Bisset with a minor 'comeback' role as Sophie's employer, while fledgling star Virginie Ledoyen makes a strong impression as her wilful stepdaughter.

THE DISC

Second Sight (on a disc now reissued by Metrodome) have made a good fist of the transfer and subtitling of this edition, although biographical and filmographic details of the prolific Chabrol, his strong cast and Rendell herself (whose writings would later inspire Almodóvar's *Live Flesh* and Claude Miller's *Betty Fisher and Other Stories*) would have been appreciated. However, there is a decent making-of that clarifies the film's deviations from its literary source and the director's openness to input from his actors. (ANDY RICHARDS)

Un Chien Andalou & L'Age d'Or
(France, 1929/1930)

Directors: Luis Buñuel & Salvador Dalí / Luis Buñuel
Label: BFI (UK)
Region: 2 (PAL)
Discs: 2

THE FILMS

'Once upon a time . . .' reads the opening caption to *Un Chien Andalou*, in what remains the most provocatively misleading opening line ever. We're promised a conventional fairytale, but what we get is a motiveless, utterly unwatchable slicing of a damsel's eyeball, followed by a voyage into the unconscious as exhilaratingly ungraspable today as it must have been in 1929. Of the two cinematic collaborations between Luis Buñuel and Salvador Dalí – brought together in this rigorous BFI package – the 17-minute *Chien* is certainly the more fun. It was fuelled by a passionate complicity between the two Spaniards, and, for all its oddness, it's a playful and impeccably even-toned piece of work.

Where it impishly teases the viewer with its sexually charged dream-logic juxtapositions of ponies and pianos, breasts and buttocks, ants and armpits, *L'Age d'Or*, made the following year, is essentially a manifesto for the revolutionary side of Surrealism. By this point, the two Spaniards were at loggerheads, and the film was chiefly the work of the more politically radical Buñuel, who, perturbed at the earlier film's success, was determined to make something that would really bother the bourgeoisie. The result was a 64-minute barrage of anti-clericalism that launches with footage of belligerent scorpions and lurches, via cod-historical reconstructions and heaven knows what else, to a scene that depicts Christ emerging from an orgy. A 'golden age' indeed! But then, of course, its predecessor features not so much as one hair of an Andalusian dog. Three-quarters of a century on, cinema has yet to offer a diptych either sillier, or more serious.

THE DISCS

As academic Robert Short points out, so original and influential were these films that you could legitimately approach them from their place in either Dalí or Buñuel's oeuvre, in subversive art, in erotica, or in Surrealism. For his introduction and his thoroughly erudite commentaries, he picks the last of these, counter-intuitively suggesting that both films should in fact be read as a reaction against the abstract cinema of their time. Man Ray and others had tried to fuse Surrealism and celluloid and had fallen flat on their faces: what these two inveterate mischief-makers did, by brilliant contrast, was to form an 'unholy pact with Hollywood', lulling the spectator with conventional cinematic cues and then repeatedly slamming him with outlandish content. Short is equally elucidating on both films (his dissection of their openings alone could fuel an entire essay), and his pithy booklet rounds off a package that anyone who has ever thrilled to any work by Dalí, Buñuel or even David Lynch is strongly advised to acquire. (MARK MONAHAN)

Children of Men

(USA, 2006) 2-Disc Special Edition

Director: Alfonso Cuarón
Label: Universal (all territories)
Region: Any
Discs: 2

THE FILM

At some point in the near future, women become infertile and humanity faces extinction. But, as our rumpled hero Theo (Clive Owen) observes, even before then 'the world went to shit'. Britain is apparently the one survivor of the Long War, and its population and totalitarian government are preoccupied with fighting terrorism and keeping out immigrants, unto the rapidly approaching species death. When a resistance group led by Theo's ex – the slippery 'Fishes' – discover Kee (Claire-Hope Ashitey), the first pregnant woman in 18 years, among the 'fugees', he's enlisted to get her to the equally shadowy Human Project. All does not to go to plan, and Theo and Kee are thrown into a breathless chase across Kent and Sussex into the hell that is Bexhill, now a West Bank-style prison town.

The suspense narrative is in some ways a pretext for the exploration of team Cuarón's vividly imagined dystopia. Drawing on the visual Esperanto of the past decade – from Diana to 7/7 via Guantanamo – the Britain of 2027 is all too plausible, partly owing to cinematographer Emmanuel Lubezki's *caméra-stylo* approach. Built out of extraordinary, digitally assisted but unostentatious long takes, *Children of Men* offers an immersive experience conceived for the DVD format, with much of the story's filigree – its pitting of Theo's hard-won optimism of the will against religious millenarianism – hidden away in the margins of the constantly moving frame.

THE DISCS

A radio DJ in the film ironically refers to our present as 'that beautiful time when people refused to accept the future that was just around the corner', and *Children of Men* is clearly meant as a commentary on contemporary politics. As a result the standard 'views expressed in interviews or commentary are those of the individuals speaking . . .' rider probably applies more than usually to Universal's seminar of activists and academics. The keynote comments come courtesy of Slavoj Zizek, a huge fan of the film invited by Cuarón to hit the unsuspecting consumer with his coveted brand of Hegelian-Lacanian knowledge. Mostly comprising non-dramatic shots abstracted from the film, the image track for Zizek's discussion of the 'paradox of anamorphosis' backs up his argument that 'the true focus of the film is there in the background'. The technique is taken further in a longer symposium titled 'The Possibility of Hope', which explores the real-world concerns of the film – global warming, the post-modern condition, the necessity of political idealism – using a seamless mixture of found footage and B-roll from the *CoM* shoot. (HENRY K MILLER)

Chinatown

(USA, 1974)

Director: Roman Polanski
Label: Paramount (all territories)
Region: Any
Discs: 1

THE FILM

Film noir bursts its banks in Polanski's extraordinary, seething LA opus, as the tawdry professional concerns of the cynical private dick expand to mythic proportions. JJ Gittes (Jack Nicholson) takes on a standard-issue marital infidelity case, but nothing, from the wife to the other woman to the nature of the offence, is what it seems. Soon he's up to his nose in a high-level conspiracy to manipulate land prices through the illegal diversion of water. Water department chief Hollis Mulwray can't offer much insight, since he's face-down in the reservoir, and his icily glamorous widow Evelyn (Faye Dunaway) has secrets of her own to keep.

Chinatown smooths the way to its lividly melodramatic climax with lush colours, painterly compositions and delicately witty dialogue, creating a deceptive atmosphere of arch, classy restraint before letting rip with the fire and brimstone. This trajectory is mirrored in Dunaway's performance: pristine '30s fashion plate at the start, howling wraith out of Greek tragedy by the end. A lesser film might have been unbalanced by the sheer weight of ideas shouldered here, but Robert Towne's deftly crafted script and Polanski's muscular direction ensure that *Chinatown* maintains absolute poise. Nicholson has simply never been better, while the presence of legendary director John Huston as corrupt patriarch Noah Cross offers a final back-handed nod to old Hollywood.

THE DISC

Modern-day movie icons don't come much more colourful than Roman Polanski, Robert Towne and *Chinatown*'s producer Robert Evans, so the three-headed retrospective interview that accompanies this DVD is lively and illuminating. Plenty good enough, in fact, to stimulate the desire for a full commentary, which is sadly lacking here. A film of *Chinatown*'s stature, with a legendarily eventful production history to boot, arguably merits a meatier package; a contribution from Jack Nicholson, for instance, would have been an invaluable addition, given that this film – as Evans observes – provides perhaps the single finest showcase for his versatile gifts.

Still, there are plenty of good anecdotes to be going on with. Evans remembers drawing together the film's key players, and observing its rocky progress to classic status; Towne recalls the vice cop whose observations about his beat inadvertently provided the film with its title ('The best thing to do when you're in *Chinatown* is as little as possible'); while Polanski comments upon Dunaway's annoying makeup habits, his own unforgettable cameo as a nose-slashing hood, and his squabbles with Towne over the film's ending. Subtitles, language options, scene selection and the theatrical trailer are also included.
(HANNAH McGILL)

Cinema 16: British Short Films

(UK, 1958–2001)

Directors: Various
Label: Warp Films (UK)
Region: 2 (PAL)
Discs: 1

THE DISC

Given the impediments to short-film programming at the cinema, and the random-access capabilities of the DVD, you'd think the new medium should be a cinch for showcasing shorts. Certainly there are some excellent director-led collections out there (see the Jonze, Cunningham, Svankmajer and Brakhage sets reviewed in this book), and of course many instances of shorts accompanying features as extras. As a magazine format, though, the DVD never quite fulfilled its promise; perhaps, between the difficulties of rights clearance and the limits to audience eclecticism, it's still not so easy. Still, there have been compilations from curators such as Resfest and onedotzero, and festivals such as Slamdance and Clermont-Ferrand – and then there's British producer Luke Morris' Cinema 16 series, the most prestigious of the lot.

Morris' format is simple: 16 short films, each with by a commentary by its maker, collated by geographic region (Britain/Europe/North America) but otherwise a determined grab-bag of styles and genres. The British and European Short Films discs are Region 2 PAL, and good quality transfers; the American is Region 0 NTSC, and serviceable (interlaced rather than progressive), with only nine of the films accompanied by a commentary. (NICK BRADSHAW)

THE FILMS

It would take an insanely eclectic film fan to enjoy everything on this set, but the European shorts are probably the most consistent, with excellent contributions spanning early Godard and Svankmajer to Jan Kounen and Chris Morris, and two bona fide classics from Nanni Moretti (humble arthouse homage *The Day of the Premiere of Close-Up*) and Patrice Leconte (*Le Batteur du Bolero*, or 'The *Bolero* Drummer', a wonderfully dry send-up of Ravel's tortuous rondelay). The Americans range from Andy Warhol to George Lucas via the early shorts of Tim Burton, Alexander Payne, Gus van Sant and Todd Solondz; best are the experimental works: Maya Deren's classic *Meshes of the Afternoon*, DA Pennebaker's city symphony *Daybreak Express* and Standish Lawder's reverse-escalator snapshot *Necrology*.

The British disc brilliantly encompasses early Ridley Scott and Peter Greenaway, and calling cards as diverse as Lynne Ramsay's lovely *Gasman* and Jim *I Know What You Did Last Summer* Gillespie's nasty *Joyride*, but it's our headline choice for one reason, John Smith's *The Girl Chewing Gum*. A brilliantly simple formalist joke in which Smith's voice-over 'directs' the contents of an single-shot documentary street scene, it's an abundantly resonant riff on art's interplay of description and prescription, documentary observation and creative imagination; it's also an all-too-rare introduction (on DVD) to one of Britain's finest filmmakers.

Citizen Kane

(USA, 1941) Special Edition

Director: Orson Welles
Label: Universal (UK)
Region: 0 (PAL)
Discs: 2

THE FILM

In 1939, when 24-year-old Orson Welles, sensational star of the stage and air, finally submitted to the siren call of Hollywood, RKO made him the beneficiary of the most outrageously generous contract a novice actor-director had ever received. By the time that contract bore fruit almost two years later, Welles' genius had been triumphantly confirmed, and the studio almost destroyed. Used to having his own way with source material and material resources, Welles gave scant thought to the fact that his film – a portrait of a media baron whose career was unmistakably modelled on William Randolph Hearst's, even if his charismatic narcissism owed more to Welles himself – might arouse the wrath of its model, who indeed marshalled the full force of his empire against the picture. In the end, *Citizen Kane* did see its way to release and immediately established its critical status as a masterpiece: as well as ensuring terrific performances from a cast new to the screen, Welles had succeeded in galvanising the talents of collaborators whose superlative abilities the studio system rarely exploited to the full, yielding baroque photography and superb sound design. Yet, perhaps understandably, *Citizen Kane* failed to find an audience: beginning in conspicuously disorienting fashion, it has neither heroes nor villains and its mystery yields neither solution nor redemption, just a sense of loss and another thing to be burned. For all its aesthetic delights, it offers cold, un-American truths about the unknowability of people and the futility of acquisition. It remains one of Hollywood's most brilliant and anomalous achievements.

THE DISCS

As well as an informative (if sometimes banal) commentary from Ken Barnes and an extended making-of featurette presented by Barry Norman, the two-disc Special Edition includes evocative production sketches and revealing photos of Welles on set with his little-seen brother Richard and studio sponsor George Schaefer. There's also a fully itemised budget for *Kane* ($379.50 on livestock rental, $1,600.61 on wig purchase, $1,476.58 on stenographic labour). Most fascinating is the original trailer for the film: Welles was always more comfortable as a vocal than a physical presence, and as a ringmaster rather than losing himself in a role; accordingly, he appears in the trailer only as a voice, summoning light like the God of Genesis and marshalling his actors for display. Having introduced them he has them talk about Kane on the telephone – a suitable foreshadowing of the maelstrom of gossip in which the film was engulfed. Many alternative extras, and a slightly overzealous digital restoration on Warners' R1 SE. (BEN WALTERS)

City Lights

(USA, 1931)

Director: Charlie Chaplin
Label: Warners (UK)
Region: 2 (PAL)
Discs: 2

THE FILM

Chaplin mistrusted sound − not merely because it would rob him of pantomime's universality, but because of its technical limitations. In *City Lights*, he made an ingenious concession, by featuring music and sound effects, but not dialogue. The tramp meets a blind flower girl (Virginia Cherrill), and by taking on jobs variously unpleasant (shovelling manure) and dangerous (boxing − a brilliant sequence), and enlisting the help of a changeable millionaire, he restores her health and sight. At the close of the film, he meets her again after being mistakenly jailed, tries to flee but is identified when she touches his hand.

The plot is simple and effective (the reversal of fortunes, whereby the broken tramp is offered money by the now seeing and prosperous girl, is especially poignant), while the episodes of slapstick and pathos finely complement each other. The blindness theme is an inspiration, not merely because of its emotional impact in a visual medium, but because of its dramatic possibilities: the flower girl mistakes the unseen tramp for a millionaire, only to discover his wretched state as a result of his own kindness. The recognition scene, filmed with restraint and ineffably moving, may be Chaplin's finest achievement. James Agee famously remarked: 'It is enough to shrivel the heart to see, and it is the greatest piece of acting and the highest moment in movies.' This is the film that Chaplin cited as his favourite: 'Well, I think I liked *City Lights*. I think it's solid, well done. *City Lights* is a real comedy.'

THE DISCS

Film historian David Robinson points out that Chaplin worked longer and harder on the film than on any other − yet, when completed, it flowed effortlessly. The final scene still amazed and gratified him in his old age. Peter Lord, of Aardman, praises Chaplin's use of movement, which has been an inspiration to animators. For Lord, Chaplin's greatness lies in his range: he did many things so well. The tramp was once the world's best-known figure, and Chaplin's fame comes across in extraordinary footage of him being mobbed in Vienna. Also included is Georgia Hale's screen test, which suggests that, although more experienced, she would not have been as effective as Cherrill in playing the flower girl. (Chaplin considered replacing Cherrill with Hale, but was unable to do so as the production was too far advanced.) The only vice with Warners' set is some marked image cropping; a R1 version from Image Entertainment is better, and slightly brighter, but carries fewer extras. (ADAM STREVENS)

Clerks

(USA, 1994) 10th Anniversary Edition

Director: Kevin Smith
Label: Miramax (UK/USA)
Region: 2 (PAL) / 1 (NTSC)
Discs: 3

THE FILM

Along with Robert Rodriguez's *El Mariachi*, Kevin Smith's convenience-store comedy was the film that forged the do-it-yourself creation myth of 1990s American independent cinema, and became a key text for an entire generation of short-termers. Shot for $25,575 over long nights and the counter where Smith himself worked, it's the tale of Dante (Brian O'Halloran), called into work on his day off to preside over random egg inspection, impromptu rooftop hockey and accidental necrophilia – not to mention a best friend, Randal (Jeff Anderson), who arrives from the video shop next door, determined to annoy as many customers as possible.

Back in the day, the Sundance festival was small enough for filmmakers to form their own incestuous mesh of influences: *Clerks* shares both Richard Linklater's ear for slacker discourse and a Tarantino-like fondness for choice foulmouthery and leftfield pop-cultural reference points. The monochrome ennui can seem like a studied lift from Jim Jarmusch, and smart-arse chapter headings were specifically designed to attract the attentions of students, but Smith is a populist at heart, making you share Dante's distress ('I'm not even supposed to *be* here today!') while writing ferociously funny punchlines ('In a row?', 'Ooh, *Navy SEALS*!') and diatribes that continue to resonate with anyone who's ever had to bow and scrape for minimum wage.

THE DISCS

Handing a scratchy tape into Sundance in 1993, Smith would scarcely have imagined his film would later be repackaged as a deluxe three-disc box set. Two commentaries illustrate more or less perfectly the time-honoured contrast between youthful exuberance and hard-won life experience. The original laserdisc commentary, recorded on the set of *Mallrats*, finds supporting player Jason Mewes apparently drunk under a table and everybody else cock-a-hoop over Anderson's engagement to co-star Lisa Spoonauer. A second track, recorded in 2005 over the rough cut (included here, downer ending intact), has Smith musing over the performance of *Jersey Girl*, Mewes drying out and Anderson shrugging his shoulders over the break-up of his marriage. Otherwise, this is the definitive record of an of-its-moment cult movie, complete with *Clerks*-related animation, shorts, a Soul Asylum video, audition tapes, a retrospective documentary, DVD-ROM features and a punchy Q&A session. Most features come with rambling, discursive, off-the-cuff introductions by Smith and producer Scott Mosier; their extended riff on Jeff Healey, the blind pianist in the Patrick Swayze vehicle *Road House*, is almost worth the RRP in itself. (MIKE McCAHILL)

The Cloud-Capped Star

(India, 1960)

Director: Ritwik Ghatak
Label: BFI (UK)
Region: 0 (PAL)
Discs: 1

THE FILM

Where the Indian director Satyajit Ray fashioned a long and renowned career making poised, finely etched miniatures, his more restless compatriot Ritwik Ghatak managed a bare handful of movies, voluptuous in their ambition and outrage, yet mostly overlooked in their day and now forgotten. A communist, alcoholic, and unfailing critic of human exploitation, he mixed in his films rapturous portraits of his native Bengal with forceful tragedies of (usually female) peasant suffering; the scars left by the division of his homeland in 1947 were expressed in the rent bodies of his protagonists, and in turn in the fissuring language of his films themselves.

The first part of a trilogy about the refugees of Partition, *The Cloud-Capped Star* is one of his best films, and one of his few popular successes – a furiously told story of the betrayal of an educated country girl, Neeta, at the hands of her usurious family, an inconstant suitor and her own self-sacrificial nature. Shouldering the role of breadwinner after her father suffers a workplace accident, she defers her studies and marriage to the intellectual Sanat, only to find her family conniving in her exploitation: while her feckless elder brother idles his days away dreaming of musical stardom, her mother encourages Sanat's transfer of affections to the younger daughter, Geeta. By the time Neeta recognises the truth of her plight, she has contracted tuberculosis, her body revolting against her self-neglect. (Ghatak would later suffer with TB himself, until his early death.)

Ghatak's signature blend of picaresque realism and aesthetic transgression is most starkly evident in his soundtrack, which juggles songs by Bengal's folk hero and Nobel laureate Rabindranath Tagore with non-diegetic inserts (the superimposed sounds of whip lashes, or hot frying oil) that offer a sometimes hysterically suggestive commentary on the drama. Using melodrama, like Douglas Sirk, as a framework for political critique, Ghatak pulls out all the cinematic stops; his style at times bears comparison to the early Soviet montage artists, at other times to neorealism. All in all, though, there's nothing quite like it.

THE DISC

Kudos to the BFI for this release (Ghatak's later Advaita Malla Barman adaptation *A River Called Titas* is also available, although his *Subarnarekha* would also be nice), and for forgoing region-coding for the benefit of international buyers. The transfer quality is good, though there is occasional speckling on the source print. Besides a Ghatak biography, there's one extra, a genial hearthfire-style commentary at home with Derek Malcolm, ranging over Ghatak's ouvre in general and *The Cloud-Capped Star* in particular. (NICK BRADSHAW)

Un Coeur en Hiver

(France, 1992)

Director: Claude Sautet
Label: Koch Lorber (USA)
Region: 1 (NTSC)
Discs: 1

ENGLISH TITLE: *A Heart in Winter*

THE FILM

'It's the story of a man who refuses love', notes Sautet in an interview on this DVD. 'And when the love offered is Emmanuelle Béart's, you have to be crazy to refuse it.'

Un Coeur en Hiver is a modernist love triangle that combines the acidity of film noir with the enigmatic poignancy of Ravel, whose *Violin Sonata* and *Piano Trio* provide both the film's musical accompaniment and its emotional framework. The violin lead is played (literally) by Béart's Camille, a professional musician as self-contained as she is stunning. Accompanying her are the two partners in a violin-making firm, André Dussollier's suave front officer, Maxime and Daniel Auteil's backroom craftsman, Stéphane. Both play their roles impeccably: that is, while the married Maxime charms up business and romance, Stéphane is the steady hand and the glue, furnishing the polished sounding-boards for his clients' art, and the dispassionate alibis for his partner's indiscretions. Camille is the deal breaker. Maxime soon moves in with her, but Stéphane too hints at interest, thereby catching hers. What lies behind his modesty? He retreats, she steps into the breach. Proud, smitten, ruffled, she throws herself at his barricades – what does he feel for her? – but he denies them both: she speaks of feelings, he insists, to which he has 'no access'.

Is he cautious, complacent, deferential, fearful, self-abnegating, heartless, cruel? Sautet keeps us guessing; perhaps Stéphane himself doesn't know. But there are riptides of emotion beneath these characters' (and the film's) Parisian refinement: it's in the nuances of their looks and pauses, and perfectly resonates in the performances of the Ravel. Auteil has never essayed such merciless ambivalence; Béart never such a searing blend of hauteur and hurt. Rarely have the heart's perversities been charted with such subtle and sublime realism. This is a masterpiece of mature French cinema.

THE DISC

It's a sign of the film's ambiguity that its director suggests three different formulations at various points amongst the interview extras. In a scrappy 'Excerpt from Claude Sautet Documentary', he cites the inspiration of Lermontov's story of two officers who compete to seduce a princess, in *A Hero of Our Time*; later he describes the film as '*Othello* from the point of view of Iago'. In a promotional TV interview (there's also one with Dussollier) he talks of Stéphane's impotence before 'the violence' of Camille's emotions, 'the way men are destabilised by this realistic approach, this urge women have to experience feelings and the couple'. The 'Rare Interview' with him mostly discusses his 1988 film *A Few Days with Me*. The progressive, anamorphic, HD transfer is colder than Second Sight's unadorned UK disc, but apparently supervised by DoP Yves Angelo. Audio is 5.1, and sweet. (NICK BRADSHAW)

Come and See

(Belarus, 1985)

Director: Elem Klimov
Label: Nouveaux Pictures (UK)
Region: 2 (PAL)
Discs: 2

THE FILM

There are war films, then there are films about war. *Come and See* falls into the latter category, and could rank amongst the most intense films you'll ever come face to face with.

It follows the trials of Florya, a young teen who joins the Russian partisans heading off the murderous German advance of 1942, during which, according to this film, 628 Belarusian villages were razed to the ground, along with their inhabitants. Initially a fresh-faced innocent, Florya is furious to be rejected from the advance party by his squadron's leader. By the film's end, we and Florya know why. Never has war on screen seemed so brutal, harrowing and real.

Filming *Come and See* must have been something like hell. The production designers famously used live military explosives and ammunition in the battle sequences to ensure an authentic feel. Indeed the film sometimes feels more like a documentary shot on location in 1942 than a piece of fiction. Things got so distressing for first-timer Alexei Kravchenko, who plays Florya, that he was given hypnotherapy treatment for some of his more traumatic memories from the shoot. (Thankfully, interviewed recently for this DVD, he seems to have come out of it remarkably cheerfully.)

It's not all grim realism, though. Despite the blood and fire, Klimov includes several sequences of sustained hallucinatory intensity and visionary, transcendent beauty, aided in no small way by Oleg Yanchenko's powerful electronic score and stunning Steadicam work from Alexei Rodionov. It took Klimov eight years to get the go-ahead to make his masterpiece and, though it was globally praised, and he was barely in his 50s, he never made another film.

THE DISCS

Disc 1 features a beautiful print in dubbed or subtitled versions. Disc 2 contains interviews with Klimov, Kravchenko and production designer Victor Petrov. All vividly convey the intensity of the shoot, which translates so visibly to the finished film. A photo album consists of stills and some interesting behind-the-scenes shots, but the real bonus is a pair of WWII Soviet propaganda newsreels, which provide fascinating and gruesome historical context, and evidence of the level of truth that *Come and See* attains. (Other regions split the film across two discs.) (MARK PILKINGTON)

The Company

(USA, 2003)

Director: Robert Altman
Label: Columbia Tristar (USA)
Region: 1 (NTSC)
Discs: 1

THE FILM

When the Joffrey Ballet of Chicago opened their doors to Altman, a self-confessed novice in their medium, for what turned out to be his penultimate film, it's hard to know what they thought they were letting themselves in for. More baffled than reverential, this is hardly a genuflection to the art form: why should it be? Instead, we get a lot of luvvie posturing courtesy of artistic director Alberto (a fun Malcolm MacDowell) . . . but it isn't going for the sour satire of *Prêt à Porter* either. Frankly, it's hard to say *what* exactly *The Company*'s doing, unless we put it this way: it's about ballet, and it also is one.

Any mastery of dance depends on an illusion of effortlessness, and that's precisely the trick Altman pulls off here. The movie has almost no plot and almost no point: the same could be said of *Les Sylphides*. What makes both worth watching is the fluidity of movement, the expert control of space, the simulation of a world in gestures. Altman-as-choreographer has often led us a merry dance, if you think of that famous opening shot in *The Player*, or his juggling of massive ensembles in the likes of *Nashville* and *Short Cuts*. Here, whether it's Neve Campbell preparing for her big audition or James Franco's apprentice chef whisking her up scrambled eggs, the filmmaking has the same supple attentiveness to the quality of the moment, the exact feel of it. Ballet becomes an excuse for Altman to make a supremely graceful film about almost nothing.

The curious magic of the experience is that in coming to this artistic realm with so few preconceptions, Altman made a movie that honours the evanescence of dance, its fleeting rapture, and found a perfect way to marry it up with his own medium. Scene for scene, *The Company* is at once the most featherlight of all this director's movies, the least essential in a lot of ways, and the closest to unimprovable.

THE DISC

Sony's disc feels like a multimedia press release for the awestruck film Altman didn't actually make — it even contains a featurette called 'The Passion of Dance'. Still, the great man has an easy, compliment-packed rapport with Campbell on their commentary, which reveals the full extent of the Joffrey's collaboration, and how Barbara Turner incorporated a lot of their anecdotal experiences into her screenplay. Andrew Dunn's cinematography glints superbly in anamorphic widescreen, and the 5.1 sound captures all the buzz and bustle in every frame. For ballet purists who aren't necessarily Altman purists too, there's an option to watch the dance sequences in isolation from the film. (TIM ROBEY)

The Company of Wolves

(UK, 1984)

Director: Neil Jordan
Label: Granada (UK)
Region: 2 (PAL)
Discs: 1

THE FILM

Neil Jordan's bizarre portmanteau fantasy is a lush, dangerous set of stories about awakening desire, revolving around a Brothers Grimm-like village and the tales told by a wise old granny (Angela Lansbury, caricatured but convincing) to her granddaughter (Sarah Patterson). As befits a film book-ended by a teenager's dream, the effects are lurid and macabre. The cast do well to flesh out their fairytale characters, Stephen Rea particularly impressive as a sinister 'travelling man'. All Granny's stories involve the overlap of wolves and men, and both eventually come calling for the two females.

Based on a set of Angela Carter stories, the film has no central plot; it's complex viewing, and subtext is as important as looks, notwithstanding Anton (*Batman*) Furst's genuinely beautiful sets. There's a kind of grisly magnificence to the most important scenes: in particular, a wedding banquet that degenerates into chaos as the guests sprout fur and burst their clothes, and a scene in which a groom rips off his face to reveal a wolf's head forming from the meat beneath.

Roses drip blood, milk turns red, and the devil causes a boy to race through puberty, turning into a man, then a wolf. The imagery becomes increasingly ferocious and sexualised, following our heroine from the comfort of childhood into the alluring, dangerous world of adults. This is neither *The Crow* nor cutesy Tim Burton fare: *The Company of Wolves* is ultimately a disturbing, hallucinatory journey into the Freudian underworld of the story of Red Riding Hood.

THE DISC

This edition comes with a very literate booklet ('The Scenes Dossier') explaining the background, symbolism and literary origins of the story: slightly apologetic, perhaps, but useful in making sense of what is a fractured and allegorical film. Otherwise, the extras are a little disappointing. The menu screen suggests the compilers understood the nature of the film: sinister, childish figures flutter against a puppet-show backdrop. The trailer is dated but cerebral and gory, and there are some production stills. Everything is well and good, but the film is so rich, and peculiar that you want more.

The saving grace is Neil Jordan's commentary. In a discussion with Robert Ross, he explains the way the film was inspired and made, with close reference to Carter's stories. Informative rather than fun, it's a good opportunity to hear how a highly original feature was created on a limited budget. (TOBY FROST)

Con Air

(USA, 1997)

Director: Simon West
Label: Buena Vista (UK)
Region: 2 (PAL)
Discs: 1

THE FILM

Made at the height of the post-modern action era, Jerry Bruckheimer's first solo project without his OTT production partner Don Simpson (departed to the big John Belushi bathroom in the sky) is hardly a huge leap away from their blockbusting collaborations *Beverly Hills Cop*, *Top Gun* and *Days of Thunder*. It neatly encapsulates all that's best (and brilliantly bad) about his overblown, testosterone-fuelled oeuvre; indeed, it's basically *The Rock* on a plane.

As there, Nicolas Cage plays our shamelessly clichéd hero. An impossibly noble former US ranger with a life-is-like-ah-box-ah-chocolates drawl, his Cameron Poe ends up imprisoned for manslaughter after defending his impossibly blonde and devoted wife's honour. He's just about to make parole on his young daughter's birthday – aww! – when his flight home gets sky-jacked by a dream crew of notorious crims led by one Cyrus 'the Virus' Grissom (branded by John Cusack's Dostoevsky-quoting Federal Marshal Vince Larkin as 'a poster child for the criminally insane'. You may recognise the features of John Malkovich).

'We are in the transportation business. We transport audiences from one place to another,' Bruckheimer once proclaimed. Yet though *Con Air* starts as confidently too-quick-for-thought (credit to Scott Rosenberg's unusually sharp script), it's increasingly overloaded by ever more grandiose set-pieces, not to mention its magnificent support cast of movie-stealers. The heavy freight includes Ving Rhames, Colm Meaney and Steve Buscemi, whose unforgettably clammy psycho paedophile, all dolls, tea parties and Hannibal Lecter insinuation, even out-creeps Malkovich. Come the 75-minute mark, the film's only remaining recourse is to start blowing itself up, which it does in true Bruckheimer style, the Las Vegas-strip finale being a monster crash-landing in more ways than one.

THE DISC

Anamorphic widescreen and Dolby 5.1 provide the bare minimum bangs for your buck; elsewhere, the movie's high production values don't extend to the disc. The Region 1-only 'Unrated Extended Edition' (with an extra seven minutes of gristle!) released in May 2006 has even fewer extras than the paltry selection here: the trailer; a perfunctory four-minute on-set featurette with Nic Cage et al offering insights along the lines of 'it's an interesting concept'; and 'The Destruction of Las Vegas', a bolted-on three-minute logistics shoot. There's no director's commentary – surely Brit-for-hire Simon West could have found a moment after his subsequent career high of *Lara Croft: Tomb Raider* to knock one out? (LARUSHKA IVAN-ZADEH)

The Conformist

(Italy, 1970)

Director: Bernardo Bertolucci
Label: Paramount (USA)
Region: 1 (NTSC)
Discs: 1

THE FILM

Bertolucci's masterpiece is exile cinema many times over: in the matter of its plot, and in the lineage of both its dazzling visual style and thematic concerns. Titular anti-hero Marcello (Jean-Louis Trintignant) is a Fascist agent sent from Rome to assassinate his former professor, now an anti-Fascist dissident in Paris. As he hunts down his target, Marcello reflects on his self-willed conformity, shaken by the attentions of the professor's seductive wife Anna (Dominique Sanda). The flashbacks which make up the body of the film are idealised to the point of distortion – a stratagem which occasions any amount of cinephiliac invention from Bertolucci and his cinematographer Vittorio Storaro – as Marcello attempts to construct for himself (and us) a plausible explanation for his decisions, which the film's coda, set during Fascism's death throes in 1943, pulls apart.

Paris in 1938, the year of Anglo-French collusion in the fall of Spain and Czechoslovakia and the collapse of the Popular Front, is a chilly, desolate place, and Marcello's prey is already neutered. The conformist speaks on behalf of his ghostly peers, outcast intellectuals of the '30s like Herbert Marcuse (*One-Dimensional Man*) and Wilhelm Reich (*The Mass Psychology of Fascism*) whose attempts to meld Marx and Freud, continued in their American exile, lie behind Bertolucci's own thinking; correspondingly, the film's Oedipal scenario is articulated in the manner of directors who were likewise forced to abandon Europe by the rise of Fascism – temporary Parisians Max Ophüls and Fritz Lang most noticeably. After Bertolucci's break with the '60s New Wave and its enthusiasm for post-war Hollywood, *The Conformist* marked a 'return of the repressed', a reckoning with recent history and the course of European cinema that set the tone for its next decade.

THE DISC

As befits a benchmark in cinematography, *The Conformist* has been given a faultless transfer. The extras comprise about 40 minutes of interviews with Bertolucci and Storaro. The former is, as ever, an engaging performer, claiming to have pitched the project on the basis of his girlfriend's description of Alberto Moravia's source novel, without having read it himself. His recollection of the initial response to *The Conformist* testifies obliquely to its standing as a visual primer to the '70s. Bertolucci says that, even after its acclamation at the New York Film Festival, it took a letter signed by Francis Ford Coppola – who would later employ Storaro on *Apocalypse Now* – and other New Hollywood luminaries to clinch the film's US distribution. (HENRY K MILLER)

The Conversation

(USA, 1974)

Director: Francis Ford Coppola
Label: Paramount (USA) / Buena Vista (UK)
Region: Any
Discs: 1

THE FILM

It hinges on an inflection – something surveillance whiz Harry Caul's recording equipment can't quite register – as he pieces together the hushed dialogue between two people he doesn't know but might, just might, be helping to have killed. Such is the outline of probably the great paranoid thriller of the 1970s (a decade hardly low on them) and the Hollywood film most routinely cited as Watergate-flavoured. What's easy to forget is that Coppola had written the script in the late 1960s, and wrapped production days before the break-in at Democratic HQ, qualifying the movie as the most eerily prescient of its political age. But with Paramount bugging him to finish the script for *The Godfather*, *Part II*, Coppola handed *The Conversation* over to supervising editor Walter Murch, who tinkered away for a full year in the cutting room before either was happy with it.

Indebted to its director's pet European auteurs, above all Antonioni (and not just *Blow Up*, from which it borrows its pieced-together conspiracy idea), the movie's creepy detachment of style stands in marked contrast to the operatic gestures of *The Godfather* diptych on either side. The loneliness of its obsessions and the fascination with technology always marked it out as Coppola's most personal film, the one with a driven, insecure central character closest to his own heart. David Shire's wandering piano motifs lend a sad irony to Harry's quest, and Gene Hackman gives the performance of a lifetime.

THE DISC

Coppola's own commentary, as on *The Godfather* trilogy, is a disappointingly pedantic affair you'll struggle to sit through. Better to flip over to the separate audio track by Murch, which is spottier but fascinating. It's hard not to feel for him: in his first fully paid-up gig as a professional editor, his first task was poring over every inch of footage for 'the conversation' itself, surreptitiously captured in multiple six-minute takes using six cameras overlooking San Francisco's Union Square. You do the maths. Murch makes clear how many of *The Conversation*'s felicities and ambiguities emerged through trial and error in the cutting room – if ever a film was pretty much written in post-production, this one was. The real shocker is that the re-reading of Frederic Forrest's key line ('He'd kill us if he got the chance') was a last-minute brainwave on the editor's part to solve confusion at test screenings, proof that necessity really can be the midwife to genius. Plus: an on-set doc catches Coppola trying to sing. (TIM ROBEY)

The Corporation

(Canada, 2003)

Directors: Listed below
Label: Metrodome (UK) / Zeitgeist Films (USA)
Region: 2 (PAL) / 1 (NTSC)
Discs: 2

DIRECTORS: Mark Achbar, Jennifer Abbott and Joel Bakan

THE FILM

A stand-out title in the recent new wave of documentary filmmaking, this collaboration between director Mark Achbar, writer Joel Bakan and editor Jennifer Abbott forms a meticulously researched, shrewdly balanced and yet starkly slanted history of corporate activity over the last century.

Certainly, the anti-globalisation lobby will find much here to support their arguments, though the filmmakers grant equal time to former Shell chairman Sir Mark Moody-Stuart as they do Michael Moore. *The Corporation*'s strength is that it understands both points of view, recognising that a bank account and a conscience need not be mutually exclusive. Still, the film argues, corporate reach is now such that few areas of life remain untouched by its constituent institutions' own-brand psychopathy.

There are no easy solutions, and yet the lasting impression is of a film less apocalyptic than optimistic: it plants a thousand seeds in your mind. Naomi Klein is one interviewee, and the film adopts much the same proactive tone as her *No Logo*, which shocked the reader with the gravity of the situation before working towards a renewal of hope. *The Corporation* is similarly studded with signs of independent life, tiny glimmers of light amid the darkness. 'Fissures', Klein calls them. Beats gaps, I guess.

THE DISCS

There's enough material here to keep anyone out of the office for days. Disc 1 offers twin commentaries, Q&A footage, a handful of deleted scenes, and a 40-minute filmed radio interview marking Bakan's appearance on Janeane Garofalo's *Majority Report* show. A short feature on the film's marketing campaign is complemented by a pair of trailers: one for *The Corporation*'s North American release, the other for Achbar's 1992 film *Manufacturing Consent*, a profile of radical thinker Noam Chomsky.

The real meat is to be found on Disc 2, in the form of additional interview footage there simply wasn't room for even in a 2½-hour film. Viewable by both interviewee and by topic, with appropriate weblinks, this talking-heads gallery finds Chomsky speaking about the responsibilities of activists, Moore on using humour as a weapon, Klein on the limitations of modern party politics. And Milton Friedman declares 'I don't believe in democracy.' With its variety of opinions, this is about as democratic as the DVD experience gets; few packages leave the viewer feeling so well informed, or so inspired to learn (and maybe *do*) more. (MIKE McCAHILL)

Coup de Torchon

(France, 1981)

Director: Bertrand Tavernier
Label: Criterion Collection (USA)
Region: 0 (NTSC)
Discs: 1

THE FILM

The early '80s ushered in a spate of style-fixated neo-noirs, with *Blade Runner* and *Body Heat* jostling against remakes like *Against All Odds* and *The Postman Always Rings Twice*. Tavernier's *Coup de Torchon* shares these films' interest in moral quandaries and criminal contagion, and was adapted from a bona fide hardboiled source (Jim Thompson's 1964 novel *Pop. 1280*), but there all similarities end. Tavernier's film, in fact, stands as a genuine cinematic oddity – a kind of *anti*-noir that challenges audience responses with its enigmatic plotting and ambiguous characterisations while revelling in its rare ability to be both profoundly serious and hilariously irreverent.

Tavernier and his co-screenwriter Jean Aurenche relocate the action from Thompson's Deep South to colonial French West Africa in 1938. Philippe Noiret plays Lucien Cordier, the police chief of a small village whose masculine dignity is constantly affronted by his superiors, various local pimps and bullies, and his wife (Stéphane Audran) – who seems to be having an affair with a character who may (or may not) be her brother. At the end of his tether, Lucien embarks on a string of cold-blooded murders – although whether each is motivated by a moral impulse or calculating self-interest remains teasingly murky. By giving Noiret's genial persona some violent shadings, Tavernier denies viewers an easy source of identification, keeping them constantly off-balance. Likewise, Cordier's mistress Rose (Isabelle Huppert) is less a traditional femme fatale (in Thompson's novel she was nakedly venal) than a puckish free spirit, affectionate rather than manipulative. As elsewhere in his films (particularly *The Judge and the Assassin* and *The Bait*), Tavernier enjoys confounding our expectations of human behaviour, militating against snap judgements and reassuring resolutions.

The film's fluid sense of character is reinforced by its lengthy, sinuous Steadicam shots, which glide restlessly through the village, unable to pin down any of the action for long. Shooting entirely on location in Senegal, Tavernier successfully evokes the sweat and clutter of a trading outpost, far removed from the picturesque exoticism of other evocations of the colonies. By highlighting the milieu's endemic racism (a perfect analogue to Thompson's Deep South), he also further muddies the film's moral waters: what role should conscience play in a world which holds some forms of human life cheaper than others?

THE DISC

Criterion have again done us proud with a crisp transfer that conveys the rich variety of the African light. As well as the trailer and a rather bizarre alternative ending, the disc also contains a meaty interview with Tavernier, in which his evident fondness for the film and frequent collaborator Noiret shines through.
(ANDY RICHARDS)

Crash
(Canada/UK, 1996)

Director: David Cronenberg
Label: New Line (USA)
Region: 1 (NTSC)
Discs: 1

THE FILM

Pity the wayward soul who intends to rent Paul Haggis' angsty sketchbook of America's racial subconscious and instead settles in with Cronenberg's homonymous opus of automotive erotica. And yet, praise the good fortune of this same soul, since Haggis may have copped the Oscar, but it's Cronenberg who earns the seal of art.

By any reasonable standard, *Crash* does remarkable justice to the narrative and thematic content of JG Ballard's flagrantly transgressive novel, and yet its most scandalous gesture is its refusal of subversive energy; Cronenberg flouts every existing code for representing sex in popular film without turning his film into a sideshow attraction or a rebel yell against prudery or convention. *Crash* is about cool stylistic confidence, sleek concision, crouching silences and prowling camera movements. The movie has the colour and the feel of chrome plating and the purring calm of an Aston Martin engine. There's plenty more under this hood: a brilliant mood piece on urban alienation, a deadpan comedy about two lovers whose every detour leads them back to each other, and important omens of the surgical economy that Cronenberg would later bring to the schizophrenic dioramas of *Spider* and the seriocomic gangster drama *A History of Violence*. Aspiring editors and adventurous composers would do well to look and listen.

Most of all, though, *Crash* suggests that sexual subcultures and social iconoclasts don't always crave attention, that their pleasures are not symbols or metaphors, and that they don't give a hoot about shocking, changing or in any way engaging the mainstream. The small cabal of characters in *Crash* live and die for each other, yet they don't seem to care if anyone else is watching. The film, ingeniously rendered and powerfully provocative, nonetheless exists to please itself. *Crash* neither placates its detractors nor plays to their salacious indignation, and that's probably the biggest and best fuck-you of all.

THE DISC

Like the film, the DVD of *Crash* cuts right to the quick with a bare-bones presentation. Aside from the most perfunctory add-ons (cast bios, subtitles), the only distinguishing feature is an on-screen menu where the viewer opts between censored and uncensored versions of the film, and even of individual scenes as selected from the chapter menu. So, the DVD asks, are you in, or are you out? (NICK DAVIS)

Cries and Whispers

(Sweden, 1972)

Director: Ingmar Bergman
Label: Tartan Video (UK)
Region: 0 (PAL)
Discs: 1

THE FILM

Question: What's black and white and red all over? Answers: a tabloid news-paper, a nun in a blender, and Ingmar Bergman's *Cries and Whispers*, which uses these colours exclusively to paint a remarkable, unsettling portrait of one household steeped in unhappiness. Of the three sisters at its centre, Agnes (Harriet Andersson), dying of an unspecified cancer, seems best off: no matter how much pain she's in now, at least she knows relief is imminent, in the form of death.

There's no such respite for the other two. Maria (Liv Ullmann) saw her husband commit suicide in front of her; and the repressed Karin (Ingrid Thulin) has started to hear and see things which just aren't there. Or are they? Bergman here takes what he was theorising about in his earlier *Persona* and *The Silence* – the distance between people – and applies it practically to a dramatic situation, with characters who have been isolated from society (because of their wealth? their sex? their sisterhood?) and left to rot.

Intensity is built from the simplest of elements. On DVD especially, this seems a key text for budding cinematographers. Sven Nykvist's cold scarlets – at once unworldly and unyielding, a backdrop of permanence against which human decay can be measured – are a marked contrast with, say, Godard's Maoist reds, the coats of life and death that graced *Schindler's List* and *Don't Look Now*, or the russet of Liv Ullmann's hair. In a similar vein, Bergman's frequent fades – like blood coursing across the screen – express a potent bodily horror. And everywhere, there are ticking clocks: a painful reminder that, in this instance, time is not the great healer, but only making matters worse.

THE DISC

Two text-based features help analyse this most complex of works. From within, Bergman's own writings define 'the motionless camera' used in the film, permitted only to take one step forward or back. Perhaps only the director of *The Seventh Seal* could arrive at the camera-as-chess-piece, but the idea of 'move-ments' – not just spatial, but musical – appears to have preoccupied Bergman during *Cries and Whispers*: the title, we learn, is taken from one critic's review of a Mozart quartet. From without, Philip Strick eloquently sets the film in context, identifying how it was made during an especially bleak period in Bergman's life. There's also some discussion of the film's symbolism and themes, and details of Roger Corman's incongruously cheery involvement with its distri-bution. (Criterion offer a comparably fine edition featuring a Swedish television interview with Bergman and actor-writer Erland Josephson, and notes by histor-ian Peter Cowie.) (MIKE McCAHILL)

Crouching Tiger, Hidden Dragon
(USA/China, 2000)

Director: Ang Lee
Label: Sony (all territories)
Region: Any
Discs: 1

THE FILM

Ang Lee described his sensuous foray into Chinese *wuxia pian* movies as 'Bruce Lee meets Jane Austen', and it's a pretty neat summary. Certainly *Crouching Tiger*'s far from a regular example of the ancient genre of martial arts chivalry, which dates back to the Tang Dynasty (618–907 AD). Though exciting and kinetic, the film's famous weightless fight scenes, in which Chow Yun Fat, Michelle Yeoh and company spring up walls, across rooftops and among lush green trees, emphasise grace over clashing and crunching.

The script, co-written by perennial Lee collaborator James Schamus, has a distinct feminist edge and languid pace (there's 15 minutes' exposition before any action). Despite revolving around possession of Chow's mythical Green Destiny sword, it's mostly concerned with character and parallel tales of frustrated love. One story pairs expert sword-wielders Fat and Yeoh, who repress their feelings for each other out of respect for Yeoh's long-dead fiancé; the other unites young, headstrong aristo (and secret martial arts master) Zhang Ziyi and lowly Mongolian horseman Lo (Chang Chen).

The lack of action climaxes irked Chinese audiences, as did Hong-Kong-born Fat and Malaysian Yeoh's mangling of Mandarin. But *Crouching Tiger*'s contemplative pace offers singular pleasures, its exquisite cinematography, choreography (by *The Matrix*'s Yuen Wo Ping) and Tan Dun's score layering it with subtlety and beauty. Indeed most Western *wuxia pian* first-timers were entranced and the film scooped four Oscars, including best foreign-language film.

THE DISC

A feature-length commentary by Lee and Schamus, with Schamus serving as de facto interviewer. Together they offer useful nuggets about the cross-cultural script – explaining Mandarin jokes and the film's martial art of *wudan* (an inner-directed counterpoint to the more flamboyant *shaolin*) – as well as a story about Alan Rickman and farting horses.

There's also an interview with Yeoh, who appears to have mothered the shoot along (venturing out on location in the Gobi desert, though not needed for any scenes), plus a making-of featurette, 'Unleashing Dragons', which includes more of Lee, Schamus and Yeoh, as well as Chow Yun Fat, Tan Dun and cellist Yo-Yo Ma (who apparently played the score on a $3 million cello). Two trailers, a photo gallery and filmographies round off the package. (Sony's alternative Superbit Edition drops the extras, devoting the disc space to a distinctly minor improvement in video quality; it's swell enough here already.)
(NICK FUNNELL)

The Work of Director Chris Cunningham

(UK, 1995–2002)

Director: Chris Cunningham
Label: Mute Films (UK) / Palm Pictures (USA)
Region: 2 (PAL) / 1 (NTSC)
Discs: 1

THE FILMS

Chris Cunningham has led the pop video deeper into the realms of art than anyone else. A self-confessed *Blade Runner* addict, he was raised in the Suffolk fenlands, next to an airforce base, and this curious backdrop of dreamily melancholic East Anglian countryside and the constant high-tech droning of F1-11 fighters was to lodge itself deep in his psyche, and later in his work. This DVD (the jewel of Palm's excellent, currently six-strong 'Director's Series') brings together the pick of his music promos and various other tidbits in a dazzling, disturbing collection that survives endless revisiting.

Cunningham's notorious pieces for unforgiving electro pioneer Aphex Twin, aka Richard James, are the two that remain most likely to have you (depending on constitution) either goggle-eyed with wonder or cowering behind the sofa. The earlier of the two, 'Come to Daddy', matches the music's furious energy with a kinetic and frankly terrifying vignette of an old woman being accosted first by a marauding horde of warped mini-twins, and then by a wizened demon who emerges, screaming, from a television set; the later, orgasmically inventive 'Windowlicker' is stranger still. Leftfield's 'Afrika Shox' is an urban black-magic nightmare shot with a cool beauty worthy of Michael Mann, Squarepusher's 'Come on My Selector' is an apoplectic and blackly funny slice of high-tech nonsense – but there are passages of relative serenity, too, in the charged cyber-sex of Björk's 'All Is Full of Love' and the deliquescent moonscapes of Madonna's 'Frozen'. Whatever their content, what these little celluloid grenades all leave the viewer with is the nanosecond-precision of Cunningham's fusing of sound and light, and his endless, explosive creativity. That, and a compulsion to hit 'play' just one more time.

THE DISC

Although this sort of inevitably bitty collection doesn't lend itself to stark separation of 'main feature' and 'extras', it makes sense to consider the pop videos as the meat, and everything else (docs, commercials, excerpts from video installations) as accompaniments. Admittedly, the latter are not the fattest pickings, but it's interesting to see that weird Sony PlayStation 'mental wealth' plug (the one with an alien-headed girl talking in a sexy Scottish accent) in the context of Cunningham's wider canon, and his admission elsewhere that he's always been 'obsessed with engineering and industrial robotics' explains a lot. As for Björk's reference to 'Come to Daddy' – 'This Aphex Twin video happened, and everybody knew: here comes a genius' – one can only nod one's head in awed agreement. (MARK MONAHAN)

Dancer in the Dark

(Denmark, 2000)

Director: Lars von Trier
Label: New Line (USA)
Region: 1 (NTSC)
Discs: 1

THE FILM

'I used to be a communist, so you know, I believe in all of that, dancing around the machines.' So testifies writer-director von Trier amid the commentary track on *Dancer in the Dark*, a sublimely invigorating and deeply dismaying film that constantly asks what we dare to believe, and ruefully mourns what we used to believe.

Björk, everyone's favorite Icelandic imp, stars as Selma Jezkova, a Czech factory worker in the abstracted Pacific northwest, dreaming of tap-dancers while she operates a machine press, losing her eyesight while saving money to guard her son from the same destiny. With von Trier at the helm, it's no surprise that Selma's pristine intentions will be pulverised by a cruel world; any glimmers of transcendence within her suffering are much more muted than they were in *Breaking the Waves*. And yet, the film braids an earnest, eccentric and weirdly uplifting mélange of tones and motifs into its narrative of catastrophe. We relish the crude exuberance of Selma's musical fantasies, the saturated greens of the forest, the doting loyalty of Selma's best friend Kathy (a superb Catherine Deneuve), the pinwheeling shapes and vital sounds of stage and screen musicals.

Somehow Selma's own naïveté and her pugnacious attachment to skewed ideals become a strange source of joy; the weary singing of workers on a flatbed train, the ballets of rural poverty, even the resurrected, crooning body of a murdered villain are sites of uplift as well as regret. *Dancer in the Dark*, even more than von Trier's earlier *Medea*, is a Greek tragedy for modern times, where unlikely characters cut strange, poetic swathes through their predetermined fates. The infinite points of view – some sequences engaged as many as 100 cameras – transform the screen into a theatre in the round, eliciting emotion and prompting reflection from every conceivable angle.

THE DISC

The making-of documentary is a model of its kind, enriching our sense of the enormous technical challenges and philosophical quandaries involved in making this film. Alternate scenes and a montage of the film's musical numbers will intrigue the movie's fans, but the real treasure is the candid and intensive commentary track, where von Trier and his producer recall the Passion of the Björk, who clashed notoriously with her director. By turns impassive, sympathetic and severe, von Trier admits the inordinate demands he places on his actors, even as the movie builds a strong aesthetic case for the extremity of his methods. (NICK DAVIS)

Dances with Wolves

(USA, 1990) Special Edition

Director: Kevin Costner
Label: Pathé (UK)
Region: 2 (PAL)
Discs: 3

THE FILM

Has there ever been an Oscar-winning movie that cineastes liked to hate more than *Dances with Wolves*? In 1991, Kevin Costner's directorial debut mugged Martin Scorsese's mob movie *Goodfellas* and walked away with seven Oscars, including Best Picture and Best Director. It looked like a three-hour vanity project, with a pompous score and a pious voice-over, by a first-time director who thought he was John Ford. And yet, with this three-disc Special Edition, Pathé presents the argument for the defence.

An epic western about a disillusioned soldier who joins a Sioux tribe, *Dances with Wolves* is sombre, violent and deeply moving. Costner plays Lt John Dunbar, a Civil War veteran who asks to be posted to the frontier 'before it's gone'. He soon befriends the magnificently attired native Americans and falls in love with Stands with a Fist, a Sioux widow, played with panache by Mary McDonnell.

The original version of the movie ran just over three hours. The Special Edition adds about an hour of footage, fleshing out the love story, highlighting Dunbar's estrangement from his own culture, and emphasising the senseless destruction of the great plains. Elegantly photographed by Dean Semler and majestically scored by John Barry, *Dances with Wolves* is spellbinding stuff – a violent western, a touching romance, and a requiem for the fabled horse culture of the West.

THE DISCS

Film students take note: Kevin Costner's audio commentary is a masterclass in film production. His marathon discussion with producer Jim Wilson unpicks just about every aspect of the movie, from working with animals, scouting for locations, and financing, to Elsa Zemparelli's Native American costume design, the difficulties of working as an actor-director, and the film's commercial and critical reception. A case in point is their discussion of the Sioux buffalo hunt. The crew ended up using some 2,000 buffalo, at the time the largest herd in North America, and had seven cameras running simultaneously.

All of which puts the Special Edition's numerous other extras in the shade. The chief attraction is a 90-minute making-of doc called 'The Creation of an Epic: A Retrospective', which features interviews with almost everyone involved. Not to be outdone, Semler and editor Neil Travis provide an alternative audio commentary. Travis explains how he battled to produce a three-hour cut of the movie, while Semler discusses filming during the magic hour and taking his wife shopping in Beverly Hills on Oscar night. There are also four shorter featurettes, 'Native American' subtitles, animatronic buffalo and a DTS sound-track option. (JAMES CLASPER)

Daughters of the Dust
(USA, 1991)

Director: Julie Dash
Label: Kino Video (USA)
Region: 1 (NTSC)
Discs: 1

THE FILM

In 1992, almost a century into the cinema's life as a public art form, Dash's *Daughters of the Dust* became the first movie directed by an African-American woman to receive commercial release in the United States. Happily, *Daughters* is a landmark for artistic as well as historical reasons – an ode to, and not just an occasion for, complicated nostalgia and celebration tinged with melancholy. Central to every scene is the lustrous beauty of the Sea Islands off the Georgia coast and the detailed, idiosyncratic culture of their inhabitants at the turn of the twentieth century. These Gullah or Geechee populations, of African descent, had worked as slaves in past generations without ever migrating to the mainland, and without assimilating their language, customs and spiritual beliefs with those of the American South.

Within this general context, we weave back and forth among several characters and plot strands: a young woman carrying a child born of rape; her inconsolable husband; her formidable great-grandmother, wedded to the land but worried for her fraying family; a gorgeous prodigal daughter who returns home with a female companion after years of ill repute; a young black woman in love, controversially, with a Native American man; a Christian missionary and a dapper photographer who come to escort the family as they prepare to leave the island; and the sprightly figure of an unborn child, assuaging pain, revelling in play and awaiting her first breath of life. Writer-director Dash weds an anthropologist's eye to a historian's brain and, at times, a sentimentalist's heart. The film is often romantic, often exquisitely so, but never naïve. In drawing on American, Caribbean and African film styles and motifs, Dash uniformly embraces the vitality of her characters without losing sight of their bruises or their differences.

THE DISC

Kino, the same company that sponsored *Daughters'* theatrical release, provides an immaculate and expansive showcase on DVD, catering especially to the teachers, historians and enthusiasts of black culture that have sustained the film as a modern classic. On her commentary track, Dash is mellow and eloquent in describing her influences, some of which, including clips of Spencer Williams' ethnographic films of the 1940s, are furnished on the disc. The silent reel of emblematic images that Dash used as a fundraising tool are remarkably revealing of the practical contexts of independent filmmaking, training unfamiliar viewers – as the full feature would later do – to peek into an unrepresented world and to disrupt almost every prevailing stereotype of black culture and typography in American film. (NICK DAVIS)

David Holzman's Diary

(USA, 1967)

Director: Jim McBride
Label: Second Run (UK)
Region: 0 (PAL)
Discs: 1

THE FILM

It's July 1967 on the Upper West Side. The Vietnam war and the Newark riots blast out of every radio set, but, although recently unemployed and classified A1 – 'perfectly American' – by the draft board, David Holzman (LM Kit Carson) has weightier things on his mind. Accompanied by his loyal friends Eclair and Nagra, Nouvelle Vague fanboy David sets out to record his somewhat aimless life – and, less consensually, that of his girlfriend Penny – on 16mm film in order to tease out some kind of existential truth. This *Diary* is the purported result.

As David's friend Pepe points out, 'as soon as you start something, whatever happens in front of the camera is not reality any more; it becomes part of something else. It becomes a movie, and you've stopped living somehow.' In an uncanny prophecy of the age of social networking websites and reality television, he learns that obsessive self-documentation is not a reliable route to self-knowledge, still less happiness. Jim McBride's ingenious debut is at once an insider satire of the New York underground – at the height of its 15 minutes' worth of fame when the film was shot – a no-budget *Rear Window*, and a painfully honest relationship comedy.

THE DISC

As *cinema scope* magazine's resident DVD evangelist Jonathan Rosenbaum points out in his excellent sleevenotes, although *Holzman* has had very limited theatrical exposure over the decades, with films of its kind 'we're speaking more about the quality of the response than about the quantity of respondents'. Second Run lives up to its name in finally giving this well-remembered but little-seen film the quality presentation it deserves. Rosenbaum, a member of the McBride circle in '60s New York, records that Carson and McBride had been working on a book about *cinema vérité* for MoMA before making the film, and naturally compares their shift from criticism to critical filmmaking with that of their Parisian idols, Godard in particular. McBride also gives a colourful account of the production in a filmed interview.

The icing on the cake is his follow-up feature, *My Girlfriend's Wedding* (1969), a portrait of a magnificently haughty Englishwoman who has come to New York 'because of the revolution'. For the most part an interview film typical of the Warholian underground, this breaks out at the end in a stop-motion flight across the big country when director and lover/subject/star set out for San Francisco. It's McBride's *vivre sa vie*. (HENRY K MILLER)

The Deer Hunter

(USA, 1978) Special Edition

Director: Michael Cimino
Label: Warners (UK)
Region: 2 (PAL)
Discs: 2

THE FILM

1978 was the year Hollywood faced up to Vietnam. Coppola finally wrapped on *Apocalypse Now*, while Hal Ashby's *Coming Home* and Cimino's *The Deer Hunter* duked it out at one of the most politicised Oscar ceremonies ever. One of Ashby's stars, Jane Fonda, denounced Cimino's film as racist and re-actionary without even seeing it, but it won anyway, and proved such a runaway box office success that United Artists, hoping lightning might strike twice, threw their money into the era-changing debacle of *Heaven's Gate*. Cimino's reputation stands or falls on these two movies, which is to say it stands, thanks: *The Deer Hunter* still reverberates down the years as both a primal scream of a war film and a penetrating diorama of the American consciousness.

Not without its narrative problems — the first third never quite achieves the Altmanesque observational looseness it's after — the movie comes into spear-sharp focus during the 'Nam section, where the rightly celebrated Russian roulette scenes stand in metaphorically for the torturous randomness of war and being at war. One close-up on Christopher Walken's squirming hell tells us more about the Vietnam experience than two whole hours of pitched battle in 2003's *We Were Soldiers*, and if the escape downriver has all the raging suspense of *Deliverance*, the homecoming's straight out of Homer. However tentatively hopeful the sentiment, 'God bless America' has never sounded so small-voiced, so thoroughly *defeated*, as it does in the final scene of Cimino's blue-collar odyssey, which is still exactly the scarring ordeal it should be, an unruly behemoth howling out scarcely articulable feeling.

THE DISCS

Cimino discusses in a second-disc interview how he structured the film around the internment sequence, his tussles with Universal over the running time, and the test screening he claims to have sabotaged to keep it at the length he wanted. (The director's battered myth needs all the puffing up it can get, evidently.) There's also input from a barking mad John Savage, whose substantial performance as Steven is an important complement to De Niro and Walken; his macho-sentimental reminiscences are embarrassingly heartfelt. And cinematographer Vilmos Zsigmond (whose work here, slightly iffy transfer notwithstanding, is exemplary) gets a well-deserved segment too. Cimino's drily defensive audio commentary (with US critic FX Feeney) is less worthwhile. (Optimum's new 2-disc special edition has all the same extras and a new Dolby 5.1 soundtrack; there's little to choose between them.) (TIM ROBEY)

demonlover

(France, 2002) Unrated Director's Cut

Director: Olivier Assayas
Label: Palm Pictures (USA)
Region: 1 (NTSC)
Discs: 2

THE FILM

Moments into Assayas' pervy and paranoid cyber-thriller, we drop into a tense sequence of high-stakes corporate sabotage, the kind that often requires an hour of exposition. Connie Nielsen, coldly lethal, a Valkyrie of white-collar malfeasance, poisons her boss's in-flight bottle of Evian. Literally from the moment *demonlover* hits the ground, the world crawls with kidnappers and counterspies, cranks and throbs with the sounds of machinery and machination, gleams and twitters to the pervasive pulse of hypermedia. Across narrative compartments, among varying film stocks, extending and revoking chances for audience identification, the plot gets thicker and grimier: French and American companies vie for licensing rights to a Japanese franchise of pornographic anime, leading to more conspiracies and assassinations, and then to horrific intimations of a clandestine racket in live-streaming torture.

A *Videodrome* for the internet generation, a *Mulholland Drive* for the post-cinema age, *demonlover* confounds the logic of narrative as it burrows further into psychic and social anxieties about violence, sexuality, capitalism and media. Even its wildest, boldest conceits pose direct, visceral questions about the future of voyeurism, the perversity of money and power, the brutalities of men toward women and of women towards women. Perhaps too obviously, *demonlover*'s contrasts between sleek and frizzy images, between ethereal music and echoing screams, between detached observation and direct gazes at the audience, demand that we scrutinise our own orientations, our own appetites, our own complicity in a world of seduction, comeuppance and increasing irreality. This Cannes pariah looks more and more like a keyhole into its epoch.

THE DISCS

Shop carefully: the Lions Gate pressing of *demonlover* is visually dull and poorly subtitled, and many DVD packages in America and Europe have blurred or excised the most daring sexual imagery. In line with the film's own themes, the most complete and entrancing of the available DVDs is also the most sinister: amped sounds, unflinching images, even a hidden Easter egg in the second-disc menu that conveys you into the torture website only partially glimpsed in the uncensored film. This DVD also comes equipped with candid, articulate interviews with Assayas (one of them a long Q&A session on a college campus), two featurettes that showcase how the images and the Sonic Youth soundtrack came into being, and self-consciously hip but nonetheless interesting reflections by the lead actors. (NICK DAVIS)

Maya Deren: Experimental Films

(USA, 1943–59)

Director: Maya Deren (with Alexander Hammid)
Label: Mystic Fire (USA)
Region: 1 (NTSC)
Discs: 1

THE FILMS

With Veve A Clark's monumental three-volume biography *The Legend of Maya Deren* slowly moving to completion, following on from Martina Kudlácek's documentary *In the Mirror of Maya Deren*, Deren's reputation as visionary avant-garde filmmaker is further cemented by this DVD. Although much talked about, Deren's films are rarely seen, and this disc includes not only the better-known 1943 surrealist short *Meshes of the Afternoon* (rescored in 1959), but all of Deren's finished cinematic work.

Her many early influences – Gestalt psychology from her father, Imagist poetry, anthropologist and choreographer Katherine Dunham, with whom Deren worked – are subtly visible in her extraordinary burst of work in the mid-1940s. *Meshes*, co-directed with her then husband Alexander Hammid, is an eerie film about a woman (Deren) encountering multiple versions of herself in a dream that portends violence to, or by, her partner (Hammid).

The innovative use of editing dominates her next film, *At Land* (1944), which includes an appearance by John Cage. Like Cage's work, *At Land* has a complex mathematical algorithm, hinted at by a chess game on the beach, behind its sequence of impossible spaces connected by Deren's graceful movements. Two dance films, *A Study in Choreography for the Camera* (1945) and *Meditation on Violence* (1948), continue the director's exploration of editing, with dancers appearing to leap across the cut. *Ritual in Transfigured Time* (1945–46) is full of dancing bodies, but is also an unsettling poetic account of a young woman's coming of age that draws on Deren's anthropological studies of dance's ritual functions.

Between 1950 and 1959, Deren worked tirelessly to promote avant-garde film, and focused her creative energy on an unfinished research project on Haitian Vodoun, excerpted here. Her final completed film, *The Very Eye of Night* (1952–59), is startlingly contemporary and mesmerising, with its abstract starburst patterns of white silhouettes of dancers moving across the sky. Deren's cinematic revolution was one you can dance to.

THE DISC

As well as an excerpt of *Divine Horsemen: The Living Gods of Haiti*, which was edited after Deren's death by her second husband Teiji Ito, there is *The Private Life of a Cat*, a winning study of feline domesticity in Deren and Hammid's New York apartment. There is also a useful selection of Deren's quotes, hopefully inspiring the viewer to acquire Documentext's excellent collection of essays, *Essential Deren*. (SOPHIE MAYER)

Les Diaboliques

(France, 1954)

Director: Henri-Georges Clouzot
Label: C'est la Vie (UK)
Region: 2 (PAL)
Discs: 1

THE FILM

So noir was Henri-Georges Clouzot's clammy chiller – part fright flick, part detective thriller, part marital tragedy – that a good deal of its inky blackness rubbed off onto Hitchcock as he prepared *Psycho*. Hitchcock even riffed on Clouzot's end-credits plea not to give the dénouement away, using his poster to threaten late arrivals with locked doors at the picture house. But it's in their uneasy atmospheres that the kinship is most obvious, even if the Frenchman's film has none of the Englishman's sardonic touch. Set largely at a tatty boarding school in the Paris suburbs, *Les Diaboliques* is driven by the sadistic headmaster (the ever-excellent Paul Meurisse) and two teachers, his hard-bitten mistress (Simone Signoret) and fragile wife (Véra Clouzot, wife of the director). Spouse and mistress team up to kill the tyrant, in a grim scene that involves poison and a full bathtub, but his body vanishes, and accounts of sightings – a vengeful ghost? – start coming in . . .

Queasiness is kept at a lively simmer by suggestively gloomy lighting, the characters' steady mistrust and enmity, the brilliant choice of a school for a setting (the nastiness feels nastier for occurring in such proximity to innocent tykes) – and, unlike *Psycho*, without any help from music: there's none outside the first and last credits. Clouzot was famous for his misanthropy – seen at its most pungent in his handling of two minor characters, a quiz-mad misery-guts and his shrewish wife – and the shoot was an ordeal: Signoret and Mme Clouzot loathed each other, and the martinet director browbeat his wife, was barely on speaking terms with the other two leads, and forced Meurisse to spend a whole day up to his neck in water. But the on-set bitterness sharpened the tale's sour stew of fear and deceit, and *Les Diaboliques* was the most successful film of Clouzot's career. Jeremiah Chechik directed an indifferent Hollywood remake, starring Sharon Stone, Isabelle Adjani and Chazz Palminteri, in 1996.

THE DISC

Les Diaboliques has been less fortunate in its DVD treatment than Clouzot's other better known films, notably *Le Corbeau*, *Quai des Orfèvres* and *Le Salaire de la Peur* (*The Wages of Fear*), all of which exist in bonus-rich editions. C'est la Vie's release of *Les Diaboliques* is the most amply furnished, and even then only dishes up the trailer and still-screen filmographies for Clouzot and the main actors. The transfer is acceptable, if occasionally on the grainy side.
(SIMON CROPPER)

Die Hard

(USA, 1988) Special Edition

Director: John McTiernan
Label: 20th Century Fox (UK)
Region: 2 (PAL)
Discs: 2

THE FILM

A film that gets better and better with each viewing, *Die Hard* is a two-hour serotonin shot that's still able to make grown men want to get sockless and prise open lift doors.

Back in 1988, it ramped up the visceral thrills of the big dumb action movie with a solid dose of domestic drama. New York cop John McClane (Bruce Willis) lands in Los Angeles on Christmas Eve to visit the family he hasn't seen since his wife (Bonnie Bedelia) upped sticks after a big promotion the previous July. He's feeling pretty redundant as a dad and husband, until a gang of terrorist-thieves, headed by sharp-suited German Hans Gruber (Alan Rickman), invades her sparkly new high-rise office block and takes everyone hostage.

Meticulously assembled, *Die Hard* succeeds through close attention to onscreen space, logical plotting, well-timed wit and lively casting – Rickman, Reginald VelJohnson as McClane's ground-bound cop ally, De'Voreaux White as ebullient limo-driver Argyle, not to mention Willis, who proves a far more sympathetic hero than a Sly or an Arnie. It leaves you thoroughly engrossed in McClane's one-man crusade round Nakatomi Plaza as he picks off the gang and tries to save his wife, updating the traditional American tough guy for the corporate age. The iconography of skyscrapers, terrorists and explosions, meanwhile, offers unforeseen resonance post 9/11.

THE DISCS

Disc 1 features an admirably detailed feature-length commentary by McTiernan and production designer Jackson DeGovia, both getting deep into the nitty-gritty of the script, sets and editing. Be warned though: McTiernan's remark about the film's basis in *A Midsummer Night's Dream* may induce splutters of disbelief. Another track finds visual effects producer Richard Edlund nattering over a few chapters, while a cast and crew text commentary delivered in subtitles proves much more edifying. There's also a version of the film with one re-inserted deleted scene.

Disc 2 is a more rag-bag affair, including a reel of deleted, alternate and blooped scenes, the film's newscast footage, magazine articles and some gimmicky scene- and sound-editing workshops. Also in the mix is an interactive slide-show, the script, a glossary of technical terms, trailers and featurettes. Unlike the first disc's goodies, little of it adds much to your appreciation of the film, but die-hard fans should enjoy. Not the crispest of transfers, but there's a DTS soundtrack. (NICK FUNNELL)

Directors Commentary

(TV) (UK, 2004)

Director: (TV Director)
Label: Granada (UK)
Region: 2 (PAL)
Discs: 2

THE FILM

First shown on British television in 2004, Rob Brydon's *Directors Commentary* only emphasises its conceptual strangeness with this appearance on DVD. Assuming the role of toff-accented helmer Peter De Lane, Brydon rambles over a range of justly forgotten ITV shows – the costume drama *Flambards*, sitcoms *Only When I Laugh* and *The Bounder* – each 'ep' bracketed with what the marketing people call an 'interactive menu'. Taking the opportunity to shower insincere compliments on colleagues, condescend to the audience, and badmouth rivals and exes, De Lane gradually exposes himself as an ingratiating shit. As in his breakthrough series *Marion and Geoff*, Brydon is a master of character revelation through partial disclosure.

Much of the series' comedy emerges from the juxtaposition of De Lane's hopeful pretensions ('In the script it simply said "japes", and I think I achieved that') with the utter banality of the image track. The most unremarkable composition is transformed by his commentary into a 'trademark De Lane three', and in this way the programme becomes an implicit 'commentary' on the idea of directorial authorship that is the rationale for the form itself. After all, are these flatly lit and poorly scripted TV shows significantly less formally adventurous than the bulk of film and television production? Or, conversely, is anything of value added to these audio-visual entertainments – never intended to be preserved in digital code – by this kind of supplementary material?

THE DISCS

'Meta' is the only word for the extras on *Directors Commentary*, which include, somehow, deleted scenes and – of course – a commentary from a putatively out-of-character Rob Brydon on two episodes. Claiming that part of the inspiration for the series stemmed from disappointment with his own lacklustre performance as commentator on the *Marion and Geoff* DVD, Brydon proceeds somewhat inevitably to run out of things to say, proving a 'worse' commentator than his alter ego De Lane – though he does reveal that the shows were re-edited for the commentaries and explain the title's lack of an apostrophe along the way. 'Behind the Scenes' is simply Brydon and his collaborators crammed into a tiny recording studio, spending half an hour agonising over five minutes of the finished programme, all in real time. On paper very boring, this proves a surprisingly insightful glimpse into the creative process – a rarity among making-ofs – detailing the combination of pedantry, brainstorming, and inspired ad-libbery that goes into making De Lane sound like a man who has half his mind on the parking meter. (HENRY K MILLER)

DodgeBall: A True Underdog Story

(USA, 2004) Extreme/Unrated Edition

Director: Rawson Marshall Thurber
Label: 20th Century Fox (all territories)
Region: Any
Discs: 1

THE FILM

Some time between *Zoolander* and *Starsky & Hutch*, the gaggle of comic actors now known as the 'Frat Pack' became an irresistible box office force, reviving the *National Lampoon–Saturday Night Live* strain of pre-PC humour with a saving dash of we-know-this-is-dumb-(honest) irony. Benefiting from neophyte Thurber's zippy direction (not usually a Pack strongpoint), the subtitle of *DodgeBall: A True Underdog Story* tells you pretty much all you need to know about its plot, which takes the shape – if not the tenor – of an über-generic sports movie.

Pitching body fascist White Goodman (Frat MVP Ben Stiller) against slacker Peter La Fleur (indie refugee Vince Vaughn) in the inevitable tournament, *DodgeBall* wins partly by making it very nearly possible to take the 'underdog' theme seriously. Apart from a career-best performance from Stiller (showing off a lurid painting of him grabbing a bull by the horns: 'It's a metaphor . . . but that actually happened'), it's also a film of fine supporting characters, memorably Rip Torn as Patches O'Houlihan, a foul-mouthed, monstrous extrapolation from the stock 'firm but fair' coach figure. Meanwhile, sportscasters Gary Cole and Jason Bateman's absurdist stream-of-consciousness commentary on the contest itself is an easily missed comedy goldmine.

THE DISC

DodgeBall's extras and (equally abundant) Easter eggs are the occasion for some unheralded *Curb Your Enthusiasm*-style self-reflexivity, playing on Thurber's inexperience. Edgiest of all is the main commentary, with Vaughn cast as his obnoxious *Swingers* alter ego, belittling the director ('Pretty much just set up a camera and let me go, huh?'), and Stiller, turning up late for the recording, playing up the petty-tyrant persona also on show in *Curb* and Ricky Gervais's *Extras*, more than a little preoccupied and claiming he only did the film as a 'solid' to his co-star. One way or another the commentators exit halfway through, leaving the studio staff to play the commentary for *There's Something About Mary* for the remainder of the run-time. The 'real' director-and-star commentaries – fun but inessential – are hidden away as Easter eggs.

As so often with Frat Pack comedies, typically heavily improvised and lightly plotted, the notion of 'deleted scenes' is an archaism: much of the footage cut from the theatrical version is as good as what was left in. On DVD the theatrical *DodgeBall* is one attraction among many, and most of the extras are devised in the same spirit of entertainment as the main event. (HENRY K MILLER)

La Dolce Vita

(Italy, 1960) 2-disc Collector's Edition

Director: Federico Fellini
Label: Koch Lorber (USA)
Region: 0 (NTSC)
Discs: 2

THE FILM

Fellini's epic portrait of a man whose nobler impulses are smothered by the decadence of the society around him seems more relevant than ever in our contemporary culture of vapid 'celebrities', media feeding-frenzies and bright young things. Marcello (Marcello Mastroianni) was once a serious writer, but is now a gossip columnist and a fixture of Rome's modish party scene. While his suicidal fiancée (Yvonne Furneaux) languishes at home, he spends his nights chasing tittle-tattle — and flirting with promiscuous socialites and vainly pursuing a buxom starlet (Anita Ekberg). He admires his friend Steiner, a philosopher with a loving family whose life is seemingly untainted by the temptations of the 'dolce vita' (sweet life); but in a world where older values are being replaced by shallow hedonism (the film's famous opening sequence shows a statue of Christ being carried away by a helicopter), Marcello may have left it too late to recover any meaning in his life.

Made after the successes of his neorealist period and before his slide into lazy self-indulgence, this film stands as one of Fellini's richest. Ekberg cavorting in the Trevi fountain is only one of many memorable scenes — including the hoax sightings of the Virgin Mary by a group of children, Marcello's cruel feathering of a female partygoer, and the dawn encounter between some jaded revellers and a washed-up sea creature that reflects their own dead-eyed monstrousness back at them. If Fellini may sometimes seem half in love with the circle of hell he's depicting, moments like these remind us that the wildest satires are often the most fiercely moral at heart.

THE DISCS

Koch Lorber supplements its excellent remastered anamorphic transfer and soundtrack in two alternative sets. The cheaper 2-disc Collector's Edition features film historian Richard Schickel's solid (and slightly stolid) commentary and an affectionate introduction from director Alexander Payne, as well as a jumble of archive television and film clips with Mastroianni and Ekberg, video footage of Fellini touring the Cinecitta studios and Rome, and some wacky shorts, called 'Fellini TV', left over from *Fred and Ginger*. There's also a photo gallery and demonstration of the restoration job on the film.

The aptly titled and distinctly pricey Deluxe Set replicates the second disc, and adds a third that includes an excellent hour-long documentary about composer Nino Rota and a later and more substantial interview with Ekberg, along with further vox pops with Fellini and actors, writers and pals. It's boxed in a faux-leather case with photos, an Ekberg poster and a 40-page booklet, containing behind-the-scenes pics and a decent essay. One for die-hard fans and scholars. (ANDY RICHARDS)

Don't Look Back

(USA, 1967) 65 Tour Deluxe Edition

Director: DA Pennebaker
Label: Sony (UK) / New Video (USA)
Region: 2 (PAL) / 1 (NTSC)
Discs: 2

THE FILM

We can only wonder whether Pennebaker truly realised what a gift he'd been handed when Albert Grossman – Bob Dylan's manager at the time – approached him to make a documentary of the artist's 1965 solo tour of England. It was a point at which Dylan's music – hitherto mainly the provenance of folkies and the liberal intelligentsia – was finding a mass youth audience, and the star was now inspiring the same frenzied fascination as the era's pop bands. This document remains unique as a portrait of an artist completely rewiring the circuit boards governing popular music, politics and poetic expression – armed only with a guitar, a harmonica and an attitude. And, naturally, it's the latter that gives the film its meat, with Dylan slyly baiting the uncomprehending journalists sent to see what all the fuss is about while parrying their questions about categories and content ('My real message? Keep a good head and always carry a light bulb'). Decked out in shades, leather jacket and rockabilly quiff, he's truly a spaced oddity in drab Wilson-era Britain. It's hardly surprising that the Joneses weren't hip to this particular hep-cat though; by the time Pennebaker's film was released, Dylan had plugged in with the Hawks, swept round the world and blown *everyone's* mind.

Despite having editorial veto, Dylan creditably allowed Pennebaker to keep scenes that are hardly flattering to his star subject (in particular, an ugly drunken argument over a broken glass). Of course, it's a given that Dylan is 'performing' for much of the film, especially as he's never seen alone. His orbiting entourage provide plenty of incidental intrigues: Joan Baez is cruelly sidelined, while a running riff on Dylan's rivalry with rising folk artist Donovan culminates in the American topping one of the Scotsman's fey songs with a pointed rendition of 'It's All Over Now, Baby Blue'. The film's longevity is ultimately guaranteed by Pennebaker's primitive but spellbinding 16mm concert footage – capturing that precious, fleeting sense that art might just change a world.

THE DISCS

As well as a fine transfer, Disc 1 of Docurama's set includes useful biogs of the film's *dramatis personae*, an alternative version of the proto-music video for 'Subterranean Homesick Blues', and five complete audio tracks of Dylan performances from the tour. A commentary from Pennebaker and tour manager Bob Neuwirth highlights the various serendipities that allowed this *cinéma vérité* touchstone to form. A second disc features a new Pennebaker film '65 Revisited assembled from outtakes from the original shoot, while the set also includes a reproduction 1968 tie-in book and a flipbook of the cue-card sequences. (ANDY RICHARDS)

Don't Look Now

(UK, 1973) Special Edition

Director: Nicolas Roeg
Label: Optimum Releasing (UK)
Region: 2 (PAL)
Discs: 2

THE FILM

Would you dream, after the drowning of a loved one, of trying to recover in a city of canals? That's the first mistake made by John (Donald Sutherland) and Laura (Julie Christie) in Roeg's elliptically terrifying adaptation of Daphne Du Maurier's short story. Unlike its source, Roeg's film opens with the scene of their daughter's death in her little red mac, prefigured by a crimson stain spilling across the photograph of a Venetian church. The editing – this has got to be one of the most suggestively and brilliantly cut films of all time – is already establishing the central idea of inevitability, involving a Resnais-like slippage across past, present and future in which every detail steathily accrues.

Nothing that happens in the movie, however shockingly random-seeming, is anything other than the only outcome Roeg's jigsaw of portents will permit. And yet it's the joy of this rich, compassionate and marvellously unsettling film that it houses such life: rumpled, unconstricted, vitally acted life. Sutherland and Christie create a deeply tender and convincing portrait of a couple outwardly doing fine, but hiding their own grief from each other even in their most private moments. The movie may be about getting lost in a labyrinth, misreading the signs, or sorrows coming to us in battalions, but its most celebrated sequence, an exquisitely filmed sex scene between husband and wife, lets them find each other, perfectly, first.

THE DISCS

This new Optimum edition has the distinct edge in picture quality over earlier transfers, adding a ruminative Roeg commentary, a solid introduction by Alan Jones, and an interview with Pino Donaggio, who debuted as a film composer with this famously lush, operatic score. Ported over from the Warner Bros disc is 'Looking Back', a 20-minute featurette dominated by charmingly conversational input from Roeg, who talks up coincidence and déjà vu as universal motifs, and the suitability of Venice's sound maze for his MC Escher-like vision. Editor Graeme Clifford, later a director of sorts (*Frances*, *Gleaming the Cube*) takes perhaps excessively modest credit for his own contributions, subserviently placed to Roeg's overall 'exercise in film grammar', while prolific DP Anthony B Richmond (*Candyman*, *Legally Blonde*) somewhat overstates the ruthless demarcation of the colour red in the frame – check out Julie Christie's boots! It's amazing to learn that one of the most memorable sex scenes in cinema was shot handheld in just an hour and a half. For Roeg, interestingly, Christie's enigmatic smile on the funeral barge is to be interpreted as a kind of victory. Her darlings are safe now. (TIM ROBEY)

Donnie Darko

(USA, 2001)

Director: Federico Fellini
Label: Koch Lorber (USA)
Region: 0 (NTSC)
Discs: 2

THE FILM

In one episode of *The Simpsons*, Homer staggers through a portal linking Groening-land and the cine-world of our own. Tyro Richard Kelly's justly feted debut offers a smart riff on what would happen if all of Springfield were to pass through the wormhole. Puffed-up clouds over Middlesex, Virginia, and credits scroll as turbulent youngster Donnie (Jake Gyllenhaal) scoots through the town which for the next two hours will comprise our universe. That evening: dinner with his family – super-smart liberal sister, precocious younger tot, tetchy dad who's happiest watching football on TV and sad-eyed mother (Mary McDonnell, quite wonderful) trying to maintain some standards – and a domestic quarrel which refreshingly *doesn't* point to creepy suburban dysfunction. We feel at home here, because thanks to Kelly's adroit borrowings of type and generous handling of his characters it's like we've known these people for years. Ditto those other characters whose path Donnie will repeatedly cross: an unruffled school principal, a brainwashed gym mistress, and celebrity motivational guru Jim Cunningham (Patrick Swayze), who with his washed-up marketing shtick should clearly go into business with Krusty the Clown.

But Kelly's masterstroke, and what makes his film so affecting, is his observation – in the middle of a sci-fi mash! – that people's actions in Middlesex are necessarily bound by the sort of natural causes and consequences never glimpsed in day-glo Springfield. When Donnie floods the school and defaces its statue it's not youthful high spirits driving him but a profound mental disorder; bullied at the bus-stop for her weight, a plump girl hides under her ear-muffs, scarred, for the rest of the movie. And when, in the most *Simpsons*-like incident of all, an aeroplane engine randomly falls on the Darkos' house, a draped body is stretchered out through the hallway and we realise, shocked, that Donnie's predicted end of the world has indeed come to pass: and that life will go on without Bart.

THE DISCS

The original R1 Fox disc has galleries, music spots, and a cluster of deleted expositional scenes which Kelly would unwisely restore for his clunky 2004 Director's Cut, available in a two-disc R2 set from Metrodome. Much more fun is to be had with the commentaries, where we learn that Kelly would have cast Maggie Gyllenhaal as Donnie's elder sister even if she weren't (pause) a good actress, and that Drew Barrymore's duties as executive producer extended to 4 a.m. conference calls to the Netherlands to secure permission for Donnie in one scene to discuss the Smurfs' genitalia. If it's been troubling you, the official Dutch line is that the Smurfs are indeed hermaphroditic. (PETER VÁSÁRY)

Dr. Strangelove or: How I Learned to Stop Worrying and Love the Bomb

(UK, 1964)
40th Anniversary/2-disc Special Edition

Director: Stanley Kubrick
Label: Columbia TriStar
Region: 2 (PAL) / 1 (NTSC)
Discs: 2

THE FILM

It takes balls to play the end of the world for laughs. At the height of the Cold War, it would have been safer, surely, to indulge in liberal hand-wringing by casting Gregory Peck in *On the Beach* or Henry Fonda in *Fail-Safe*. Off the back of *Lolita*, however, Kubrick re-enlisted Peter Sellers, called up counter-cultural scribe Terry Southern, and turned the prospect of nuclear obliteration into a very '60s sex comedy, a film premised on one last big bang for mankind.

Dr. Strangelove was engaged in its own form of brinksmanship: envisaging a credible worst case scenario – rogue US general orders his bombers to nuke Moscow – and discussions likely to have been heard at the highest levels of government, then seeing how far events might be pushed towards absurdity. A credit sequence of quasi-pornographic plane-refuelling establishes the tone, but among those hot-to-trot characters frustrated in the voluptuous darknesses of Ken Adam's sets, there's a President Kissoff and a Staines, even before Nazi loon Strangelove wheels himself on.

Sellers is simply very funny in three very different roles, never more so than as RAF Group Captain Lionel Mandrake, grudgingly prepared to forgive his Japanese torturers for making 'such bloody good cameras'. Those who label Kubrick humourless often overlook this, perhaps the most potent and ironic of all screen comedies, and amongst the most perverse: a laugh riot with gunshots and whiteouts for punchlines.

THE DISCS

To quote Slim Pickens' Major Kong: 'A fellow could have a pretty good weekend in Vegas with all this stuff.' No prophylactics or chewing gum, alas, but Columbia's Special Edition can be found packaged with postcards, Peter Bryant's altogether terse source novel *Two Hours to Doom*, and liner notes by Roger Ebert, who overrates George C Scott's performance, but otherwise nails the film's innate seriousness as its source of humour and makes intelligent points about the ending.

The discs assemble several documentaries blessed with terrific archive footage. Alexander Walker, Spike Lee and Robert McNamara – together at last! – discuss the political backdrop, writers and performers pay tribute to Sellers, a making-of dissects the film's unshot prologue and unusable custard-pie epilogue, and there's a feature on Kubrick's early career. Alongside publicity material, filmographies and trailers, there's also an extended interview with McNamara, who scarcely throws off his reputation as a stickler for efficiency by keeping a close eye on his watch throughout. (Sony's limited R2 Reel Edition collector's box includes all this with glossy stills and a tin can.) (MIKE McCAHILL)

The Draughtsman's Contract
(UK, 1982)

Director: Peter Greenaway
Label: BFI (UK)
Region: 2 (PAL)
Discs: 1

THE FILM

What a seductive little Rubik's Cube of a movie *The Draughtsman's Contract* is. Peter Greenaway's first and (by a mile) best full-length feature, it certainly hints at the misanthropy that would sink its talons into his subsequent canon, but devotees of Agatha Christie novels, wantonly ripped bodices and late 17th-century history and horticulture are unlikely to care a jot. Anthony Higgins is the flouncing, pencil-waving stud hired by Mrs Herbert (Janet Suzman) to deliver 12 drawings of her husband's estate – Groombridge in Kent was used – in return for 12 intimate encounters with her. For a while, he appears to be cock of the roost, until Mr Herbert's horse is found ominously riderless, and the draughtsman begins to twig that he has been framed every bit as immaculately as his studies.

Greenaway's teasing intelligence is everywhere – in the hypnotic, baroque script, the rigorous visual formalism, the immaculate narrative clockwork – and the result is a feast for the eyes, the ears (thanks to Michael Nyman's dynamic score), and that part of the intellect that likes to gorge on crosswords and sudokus. It's also, in its bizarre way, a hoot from first to last frame, and must be the only picture ever to conclude with a statue trying, and failing, to eat a pineapple.

THE DISC

Even Greenaway's harshest detractors would have to concede that this is a mightily alluring DVD. One neat then-vs-now extra reveals just what a glorious job has been done with the remastering, and the film itself only grows with each viewing as you scour it for clues that went unnoticed the last time. There's a decent introduction from Greenaway, too, yet it's his commentary that makes the disc a must-own. It speaks volumes about his attitude to actors that 47 minutes pass without his mentioning a single one by name, but then, ideas are his concern. He reveals that the entire plot is rooted in the otherwise forgotten, almost insanely arcane Married Woman's Property Act of 1694, and he talks with such fluency on everything from landscape gardening to the classical significance of the pomegranate that the film often becomes merely a gorgeous visual backdrop to his words. Juicy nuggets abound, too. It turns out that the immaculate if chilly pictures that feature in the movie were by his own hand, and that the Meissen tea-set used towards the end was insured for ten times *Draughtsman*'s entire budget – a testament to Greenaway's commendable fiscal discipline, not to mention his impeccable taste in porcelain. (MARK MONAHAN)

The Earrings of Madame De . . .

(France, 1953)

Director: Max Ophüls
Label: Second Sight (UK)
Region: 2 (PAL)
Discs: 1

THE FILM

'Viennoiserie', a term bandied around in the extras here, is a useful gloss on Ophüls's creamy, delectable surface style, not to mention his trademark penchant for the waltz. But if it suggests some kind of calorific flippancy, it's going to need modifying. Equally, hailing the formal precision of his oeuvre – if nothing else, this could be the most unerringly *precise* film you'll ever see – might easily give an impression of coldly impersonal, film-as-panopticon technique. And that's an even worse misperception, since to experience Ophüls's films is not just to be dazzled, but ravished, ruined and left inconsolable.

If Ophüls is famed for one thing only, it's for the empyreal effortlessness of his gliding sequence shots, here taking in not just a night at the dances for flirtatious society beauty Louise (Danielle Darrieux) and her cautious suitor Baron Donati (Vittorio De Sica), but a whole week of waltzes, each pivoting on the lightest of turns into the next. The camera doesn't just observe the couple, embarking on a scandalous affair before our eyes, but belongs to them: it is caught within their emotional forcefield, magnetised.

Louise's diamond-heart earrings, a wedding gift from her patient but controlling husband General André (Charles Boyer), have by this point been surreptitiously sold, declared stolen, secretly returned, discreetly given away, cashed in for gambling chips, bought in Constantinople and recklessly presented back to her by the unwitting Baron. Captured in close-up by the film's first and last shots, they tell her tale, meaning only as much to her as their last bestower; not unlike that pesky hankie in *Othello*, they also lure in the green-eyed monster, representing a token here of actual, not imagined, infidelity. Louise's final act is to leave them at the altar with a prayer – one that doesn't procure her and her Baron's safety, but, in one of cinema's most serenely ironic endings, allows them union and peace.

THE DISC

By releasing this along with *Le Plaisir* (1952), *Letter From An Unknown Woman* (1948) and *The Reckless Moment* (1949) to comprise their four-film, separately priced 'Max Ophüls Collection', Second Sight leave only *La Ronde* (1950) and *Caught* (1949) as no-shows on DVD among his major late works. (*Lola Montès* (1955) can be sourced from Fox Lorber.) The transfer's fine, though far from spotless.

There are two extras, both splendid: a filmed interview with Ophüls' friend and colleague Alain Jessua, who isn't too vain to remember his main task as third AD, namely scooping up horse poo; and a tremendous video essay by Tag Gallagher, whose sparkling aesthetic insights make you wish he'd provided a full commentary. Get this description of Ophüls's dancing lovers: 'They get dizzy, they fall down, sometimes they die.' (TIM ROBEY)

Edward II
(UK, 1991)

Director: Derek Jarman
Label: Image Entertainment (USA)
Region: 1 (NTSC)
Discs: 1

THE FILM

There are some things you can't do with a stage production. Have the characters genuinely whisper to one another and still be heard by the audience. Show a face-off between hundreds of Act Up! demonstrators and hundreds of riot police. Watch the production 15 years later.

Derek Jarman's background in theatre is evident in the poised performances in his adaptation of Christopher Marlowe's *Edward II*, and the brilliant use of a haunting set (the film was shot in the basement of the Hammer studios in weeks). But there's nothing stagey about the drama. At a swift 90 minutes, Jarman discovers the glorious soap opera at the heart of Marlowe's play, and plays it for all its contemporary relevance. Council members with Thatcher hair tut-tut about the king's love affair with Gaveston, played by Andrew Tiernan as a semi-feral rent boy locked in deadly competition with a magnificent Tilda Swinton, as Edward's wife Isabella, for the role of queen of England.

Steven Waddington's Edward, dancing with Gaveston through a series of set pieces that have the hallucinatory brilliance of the best of 1980s music videos, brings both sweetness and sympathy to his role as the king who would be a boy, and he and Swinton are well-matched performatively and physically. The contrast between their pale skin and their red hair sets up the film's palette – and, in a way, Jarman's definition of love – of white sets slashed with the red of costume and emotion.

Swinton called Jarman 'the best bloody user of cardinal red in British cinema', and one could watch this film as an essay on the colour red: Annie Lennox's lipstick cutting her monochrome countenance and the dresses of the Elektra Quartet seem frighteningly bold in the murky political world through which strides the queen's lover and Gaveston's persecutor Mortimer (Nigel Terry), dressed in military camouflage.

The film glows with immediacy – not just political (although the questions it raises about identity, leadership and prejudice have become no smaller), but visual. Jarman may not have written the book on British cinema but, with his unique and much-missed combination of joie de vivre, autodidactics, cheek, gorgeousness and outrage, he adapted it definitively.

THE DISC

In 2002, *Vertigo* magazine launched the Derek Jarman Memorial Lecture at the Edinburgh International Film Festival and invited Tilda Swinton to be the inaugural speaker. Her fierce, unabashed address (shown here in full) restores Jarman to his position among the brightest and best of British film. (SOPHIE MAYER)

Sergei Eisenstein: The Sound Years
(Soviet Union, 1938/1945/1958)

Director: Sergei Eisenstein
Label: Criterion Collection (USA)
Region: 1 (NTSC)
Discs: 3

FILM TITLES: *Alexander Nevsky*, *Ivan the Terrible (Ivan Grozny)*, *Parts I and II*

THE FILMS

Sergei Eisenstein's pioneering, visually striking films extended the lexicon of modern cinema. Yet, though many continue to identify the granddaddy of Soviet celluloid solely with the densely edited 'montage' techniques of his 1920s pro-revolutionary silents, *Strike*, *Battleship Potemkin* and *October*, his work took a no-less influential turn towards high spectacle in the sound era.

Returning to the Soviet Union after a thwarted spell in Hollywood, where the studios deemed his style too idiosyncratic, Eisenstein found himself smeared as an anti-populist 'Formalist' by the Communist authorities. *Alexander Nevksy*, a rousing propaganda piece based on the patriotic 13th-century folk legend of Prince Alexander's heroic vanquishing of the dastardly Teutonic knights, was his first attempt to win back favour; the topical anti-German theme drew such approval from Stalin that no cultural commissar subsequently dared alter it. Using traditionally trained actors, rather than 'types', the film drew on Eisenstein's early training as a theatre designer, but it also continued his experiments with form, synchronising his imagistic rhythms with those of Prokofiev's original score. Grandiose sequences like the momentous battle on a frozen lake (pilfered lock and stock by Olivier's *Henry V*) still pack an impact to rival anything in **Lord of the Rings**. Less triumphant was the unfinished *Ivan the Terrible* trilogy, a mesmeric, highly charged portrait of the Russian founder's accumulation of power and increasingly paranoid brutality. Distilling Russia's experience of both World War II and Stalin's Terror, the films mix the stylistic expressionism of Japanese kabuki theatre, El Greco and Disney (and include Eisenstein's first, tantalising use of Technicolor) – but it was *Part 2*'s implicit political critique that Stalin belatedly descried and suppressed. Ill health prevented Eisenstein seeing through any revisions (or finishing the third part), and this broken masterpiece was first shown ten years after Eisenstein's death, in 1958.

THE DISCS

You could pick holes with the image quality – visible scratches and dirt remain, especially on *Nevsky*, and though High Definition, the transfers aren't progressive – but these discs showcase an awesome restoration job. Audio is less good; again, Criterion can point to an uphill battle against the wretchedness of sound facilities in Stalinist Russia, but *Nevsky* would seem to come with a non-original soundtrack.

Word counts can't do justice to the extras, which include a *Nevsky* commentary and copiously illustrated essay on the score, an all-too-fleeting sketched reconstruction of Eisenstein's destroyed *Bezhin Meadow*, and his (and others') essays about the same. (A new three-disc Tartan collection containing *Potemkin*, *Strike* and *October* is now available on R2.) (LARUSHKA IVAN-ZADEH)

Election

(USA, 1999)

Director: Alexander Payne
Label: Paramount (all territories)
Region: Any
Discs: 1

THE FILM

Released midway between Monicagate and the Stolen Election of 2000, Alexander Payne's second film sketches a political system defined by media-led prurience and barely concealed fraud. Pitching naked self-interest, in the form of frontrunner Tracy Flick (Reese Witherspoon), against the purported civic duty of sad-sack civics teacher Jim McAllister (Matthew Broderick, all signs of Ferris Bueller's cockiness abraded), in a flyover state high-school election that interests no-one but its participants, Payne's choice of genre and setting is bitterly apposite for his satirical purposes.

When Mr McAllister makes overprivileged jock Paul Metzler (Chris Klein) his anti-Flick candidate, the business of fostering democracy – conceived as the choice between Coke and Pepsi – gets hopelessly entangled in class resentment, sexual jealousy, and sibling rivalry. 'The weak,' says Tracy's pushy mom, 'are always trying to undermine the strong', and in its treatment of McAllister's attempts to induce Tracy's comeuppance, Payne's allegory approximates the jaded moral vision of Graham Greene's *The Quiet American*, enlivened by a measure of teen-movie sass.

Unlike the election itself, the drama is never rigged: McAllister has broken all the rules; but is he morally justified? As third-party anti-candidate Tammy Metzler has it, the go-getters take part 'just to put it on their transcripts so they can get into college', so isn't Tracy's only real crime precocity in the face of the schoolyard's all-pervasive egotism, demagoguery, and apathy? Even in the chilling epilogue, which confirms all of McAllister's – and the audience's – fears about the destination of school-age overachievers, his motivation remains terminally compromised, and his means confound his ends.

THE DISC

With *Election*, Payne became an exponent of 'Indiewood', the mini-golden age of the late '90s and early 2000s when subversive elements like David O Russell (*I ♥ Huckabees*), Andersons PT (*Magnolia*) and Wes (*The Royal Tenenbaums*), and Payne himself were able to infuse a string of studio-backed pictures with an 'indie' sensibility. Although his film was produced by MTV and features big-name stars, Payne's commentary plays up its small-scale, local qualities. Unusually for a teen movie, *Election* was shot in a functioning school during term-time, and all the extras and many of the cast (including Chris Klein) were recruited on location in Omaha, Nebraska. Payne's cinematic frame of reference runs to Milos Forman and Akira Kurosawa rather than John Hughes, and perhaps most tellingly he claims that he'd not seen *Ferris Bueller's Day Off* before casting former teen icon Broderick. (HENRY K MILLER)

Elf

(USA, 2003)

Director: Jon Favreau
Label: Entertainment in Video (UK)
Region: 2 (PAL)
Discs: 2

THE FILM

It may be that history will best recall Will Ferrell as the comic whose likeably moronic impersonations made George W Bush appear electable. But if you're looking to get to the heart of Ferrell's appeal, *Elf* is the place to start. True, Frank the Tank from *Old School* has bare buttocks, *Anchorman*'s Ron Burgundy has a massive erection, and *Talladega Nights*' Ricky Bobby likes to imagine the tiny baby Jesus in golden fleece diapers – but it's Buddy the Elf who best personifies the mix of innocence and inappropriateness that makes Ferrell so funny, and so touching.

Like most of Ferrell's characters, Buddy is basically a child in a man's body. He's not a biological elf, but a human who was raised by elves at the North Pole, and is now looking for his real father (James Caan) on the mean streets of New York City. His upbringing has left him disarmingly open and guileless, so he does things most people would censor: loudly and proudly proclaiming his love for his dad, his love for a shy shopgirl (Zooey Deschanel) and, above all, his insatiable love for sugar, in all its varieties.

Hyperactive, high on Christmas cheer, striding around in his tight green stockings, Buddy is a misfit with no understanding of the rules of human behaviour – and he's proud of it. Ferrell plays all of this dead straight, without any winking to the audience. However flawed Buddy's belief system might be, he buys into it completely. This makes him vulnerable, so over the course of the film, he becomes loveable as well as ludicrous: we want him to live happily ever after.

It's this kind of unironic sincerity that makes the story work so well; screenwriter David Berenbaum and director Favreau deserve enormous credit for it. For even if you're not a Ferrell fan, *Elf* is that rarest of treats: a truly heart-warming family film. It genuinely seems to believe in Christmas spirit – not the grossly inflated extravaganza of commercialism that we've come to know, but the simple making of space in our lives for the possibility of magic, wonder and good cheer.

THE DISCS

The two-disc package comes with many extras, but none of them feel invaluable. The deleted scenes offer only minor variations on the material in the movie. There's also a behind-the-scenes featurette, with a film-school class for children, but the only real reason to buy this DVD is the film itself. (SF SAID)

The Empire Strikes Back

(USA, 1980)

Director: Irving Kirshner
Label: Fox (all territories)
Region: Any
Discs: 2

THE FILM

George Lucas's follow-up to his all-conquering *Star Wars* was the film that set the standard for blockbuster sequels, as well as establishing the tradition for trilogies to have a dark core. There's a serious, mythical, evergreen grandeur to the events that unfold in *The Empire Strikes Back* (in which everything goes very wrong for our band of rebel heroes), from its satisfying, dovetailing twin plots and stirringly choreographed combat scenes to the shrewdly inconclusive ending, and one is also reminded just how much *The Phantom Menace* et al later suffered from Harrison Ford's absence. But there are still grins to be had, too, at Jedi master Yoda's oddly Germanic habit of verbs at the end of sentences putting, at Darth Vader's Tourettes-ish inability to stop yabbering mid-duel and at the sight of Vader throttling *Grange Hill*'s very own Mr Bronson.

THE DISCS

'I don't know where you get your delusions, laser-brain.' So says uppity Princess Leia to cocksure admirer and buckaneer Han Solo, not far into *The Empire Strikes Back* — yet Lucas might legitimately have aimed this less-than-Wildean barb at himself. The particular 'delusion' of the billionaire 'laser-brain' in the mid-'90s was that it would be desirable not just to re-master the three original movies, but also to add tricksy little bits of computer-generated imagery to existing scenes, as well as inserting entirely new ones. (See also: *E.T.*) Lucas's argument? That he had merely waited for the technology to catch up with his imagination.

All very well, except that *The Empire Strikes Back* needs no further gilding: it was already a stupendous piece of entertainment, with special effects supremely and sublimely of its time. In this sense, it remains Hollywood's last great stop-motion movie, and, watching the original now, thankfully supplied entirely untouched on a second disc, it's possible to be entirely blown away by the intricate magnificence of the set-pieces while also happily wondering, 'I know this was done with models — but *how*?' The shortcut of CGI dents this pleasure, and such awful add-ons as the whizz through the newly wrought Cloud City in the last act add nothing in dramatic terms and shriek 'fake'. And Lucas's new addiction to having digital space-traffic endlessly wooshing past in the background is as bizarre as it is irritating — you long for a mid-air pile-up.

All that said, the obsessive, tinkering child in Lucas that made him mess around with the original is the very same that made his universe so compelling in the first place, and the remastering on the 'updated' version (Disc 1) is of course visually and sonically superb. Lucas should have saved himself a lot of bother and left it there. (MARK MONAHAN)

Les Enfants du Paradis

(France, 1945)

Director: Marcel Carné
Label: Criterion Collection (USA)
Region: 0 (NTSC)
Discs: 2

ENGLISH TITLE: *Children of Paradise*

THE FILM

Made in France during the Occupation, *Les Enfants du Paradis* mixes fact and fiction. The real-life characters of the famous mime Baptiste Debureau, who performed at the Funambules in mid 19th-century Paris, the actor Frédéric Lemaître (Pierre Brasseur) and the murderous criminal Lacenaire (Marcel Herrand) are all in love with an invented figure, the minor actress Garance (Arletty, in an imperishably luminous performance), whose independence and love of life captivate them. The true match is between Debureau and Garance, but it is frustrated by events, and when the lovers are reunited at the close of the film Garance leaves out of deference to Debureau's wife and child.

Les Enfants du Paradis was the zenith of the collaboration between screenwriter Jacques Prévert and director Marcel Carné, and an unusually ambitious project: not only did it take three years to complete and require a huge budget (25,000 extras were hired for the carnival scene), but in wartime France materials were extremely scarce. Fortunately, Alexandre Trauner's magnificent sets, stretching a quarter of a mile, were somehow constructed (though both he and composer Joseph Kosma had to work clandestinely, because of their Jewish origins).

Paradoxically, this most celebrated work of the Golden Age of French cinema (billed by its distributor as 'The French *Gone with the Wind*') is above all a tribute to the theatre: the curtain rises and falls on both parts; all of the major characters are, in some sense, performers; and the relationship between life and art, dream and reality, is a recurring refrain (thus, for instance, does Lemaître use his jealousy of Debureau when playing Othello). The epic sweep of *Les Enfants du Paradis*, its splendid gallery of characters, its compelling romantic fatalism, its legendary cast and its symbolism as an example of French resilience have made it a classic of world cinema.

THE DISCS

Criterion's loving trove splits the film over two discs, the better to maintain video quality with a high bit-rate, and handily replicating the intermission of the theatrical original. You also get two different Carné scholars' commentary for your money. Brian Stonehill handles Part 1 (his 1990 interview with Carné also adorns the 28-page booklet, along with an essay by historian Peter Cowie), and provides a dense account of the film's background and production history. Over on Part 2, Charles Affron pushes the thematic interpretation further, exploring the film's multiple ironies and frames-within-frames. This disc also includes production stills and design illustrations, and Jacques Prévert's original treatment, while back on the first disc, Terry Gilliam introduces the film, hymning an era 'when poetry and big budgets went hand in hand . . .' (ADAM STREVENS)

Eternal Sunshine of the Spotless Mind

(USA, 2004) Special Edition

Director: Michel Gondry
Label: Momentum (UK)
Region: 2 (PAL)
Discs: 2

THE FILM

The inimitable collision of screenwriter Charlie Kaufman and Michel Gondry, *Eternal Sunshine of the Spotless Mind* tells the heartbreaking story of a failed relationship — twice. In a movie bubbling over with ideas, Jim Carrey inverts his screen image as Joel Barish, a painfully shy New Yorker devastated by his ex-girlfriend Clementine's decision to have him professionally wiped from her mind. Choosing to return the disfavour — courtesy of memory-erasure specialists Lacuna, Inc — Joel begins to recall his fondest memories of their relationship and desperately tries to hide them inside his head — setting up some of the most imaginative and touching moments in recent cinema.

Watching Joel's memories disintegrate is like flicking through a collection of love letters, only to see them scattered forever by a sudden breeze. By exploring the aching melancholy of a love affair slipping away, *Eternal Sunshine* becomes a kind of rococo Rorschach test for our own broken relationships. And yet, for all its wistfulness, Michel Gondry's second feature is immensely clever and wildly entertaining. Ellen Kuras's cinematography is dreamlike and disorienting, while Kate Winslet has never been kookier. And, under Gondry's impish eye, *Eternal Sunshine* uses high-tech visual invention to trawl depths of emotion and intellect rarely glimpsed in fare from Hollywood today.

THE DISCS

Eternal Sunshine's intimate charm is perfectly matched to the small screen, and this two-disc special spills over with endlessly entertaining extras. As well as several deleted scenes, a Polyphonic Spree music video, and an infomercial for Lacuna, there's a bafflingly awkward mutual interview between Gondry and Winslet, other conversations with the cast and crew, and a fascinating 20-minute doc, 'Inside the Mind of Michel Gondry', that explores the visual wizard's flights of fancy.

Further treats are scattered throughout the commentary that Gondry and Kaufman share. Predictably droll — à la Nicolas Cage in *Adaptation* — Kaufman strikes a tone somewhere between insouciance and apathy, allowing Gondry to be the chattier of the two. Listen out for his analysis of the infamous scene at the heart of the movie, in which Joel realises he's losing his most cherished memories. But the real highlight of Gondry's commentary is the tenderness with which he equates the movie's exploration of memory with a conversation he had with his father shortly before he died. Momentum package their version of this Special Edition with a copy of Kaufman's screenplay. (JAMES CLASPER)

E.T.: The Extra-Terrestrial

(USA, 1982) Collector's Edition

Director: Steven Spielberg
Label: Universal (UK)
Region: 2 (PAL)
Discs: 3

THE FILM

The little bald chap? The Oscar that controversially went to the other little bald chap, Gandhi? The sobbing in your local cinema? The memories of Spielberg's enduring family favourite are legion. Me, I tend to think of that pre-pubescent drug addict waiting to happen, Drew Barrymore, all lisping, pigtailed sweetness opposite Henry Thomas as brooding, intense young Elliott.

To commemorate his 20th anniversary, the oddly dimensioned scaly fellow with the extensible neck and light-up index finger was given a whole set of enhanced visual effects. The CGI certainly makes him look spiffy, if somewhat cutesy and soft-edged. (Guns were also digitally replaced with walkie-talkies, and the word 'terrorist' redubbed as 'hippie'.)

Yet Spielberg, following up his *Close Encounters* theme of otherworldly connection, is too canny a filmmaker simply to give us lonely moppets and lovable aliens. A tense family situation — the three kids are left in the care of stressed single mom Dee Wallace after a particularly nasty divorce — is reinforced by stark cinematography. It shows their house, in the very Spielbergian setting of suburban San Fernando Valley, looking eerily like a spaceship come to rest on a barren plain. No wonder E.T. eventually decides to try out his newly developed telecommunications skills.

John Williams's soaring score, an instant classic, is the perfect accompaniment for Elliott's airborne bicycle ride across the face of the moon. This intuitive little boy alone saw that difference did not spell danger, that all you needed was love rather than massed armed response. And there's a thought that echoes down the decades.

THE DISCS

Spielberg's computer-generated nip-and-tuck job on his prodigal alien was not universally celebrated, so best track down this Collector's Edition, which includes the original theatrical cut as well as the 20th-anniversary version, both anamorphically enhanced with optional DTS soundtracks. (The American equivalent is now out of print, and made a hash of the information on its packaging.)

Most of the extras are sandwiched on Disc 2 between the two versions of the movie, and divide fairly evenly between retrospective docs about E.T.'s 'evolution and creation', designs, photographs and marketing, and the 20th-anniversary reunion of cast and crew in 2002. Henry Thomas (subsequent credits: *Frog Dreaming* and *Psycho IV*) looks agitated, even as he comments on the enchanting audition tape in which he cries on tap. Barrymore gushes winsomely and Spielberg talks engagingly about his 'most personal film', inspired by his parents' divorce. (FIONA MOUNTFORD)

The Exorcist

(USA, 1973) Director's Cut,
aka The Version You've Never Seen

Director: William Friedkin
Label: Warners (all territories)
Region: Any
Discs: 1

THE FILM

This one-time box office smash and runaway cultural phenomenon has lost little of its original power, thanks largely to the unwavering seriousness with which director Friedkin and screenwriter William Blatty (adapting his own novel) treat their potentially preposterous subject matter. The Catholic Church raised objections to the film at the time, but they could hardly have secured a better advertisement for their services than this tale of the demonic possession of 12-year-old Regan (Linda Blair) and the heroic intervention of two priests, veteran exorcist Father Merrin (Max Von Sydow) and Father Karras (Jason Miller) – a Doubting Thomas who in facing down evil manages to overcome his own spiritual qualms.

Along with other iconic horror films from the era (from *Night of the Living Dead*, see **Trilogy of the Dead**) and *Rosemary's Baby* through to *The Omen* and *It's Alive*), this film situates its crisis right at the heart of the family unit. The spectacle of a pre-pubescent girl projectile vomiting, issuing a stream of profanities, masturbating with a crucifix and driving her mother (Ellen Burstyn) to her wit's end acts as a neat metaphor for the era's intense inter-generational conflicts, while raising the bar for screen shocks to a level that arguably no film has seen fit to top since. Friedkin had demonstrated with *The French Connection* how documentary-style realism could grip a mass audience, and here he takes the same approach to supernatural events – as if to prove that the devil really *is* in the detail. The film goes for a slow-burn build up – including an atmospheric prologue in Iraq, and the futile interventions of an impotent medical establishment (from Ritalin prescriptions to a bloody arteriogram) – before unleashing its barrage of innovative Dick Smith-supervised special effects. Until the arrival of Jason Vorhees and Michael Myers, this film created a fleeting sense that horror films didn't have to be solely the provenance of teenage boys, and – whatever the merits of its metaphysics – the bravura conviction of its storytelling still grips like a vice.

THE DISC

Not a true 'Director's Cut', this new version of the film is ten minutes longer than the original release, and has reinstated scenes that were probably closer to Blatty's heart than to Friedkin's (including Merrin's speculations about the demon's motives in choosing a little girl as his victim), as well as the infamous 'spider walk' sequence; there are also several optical demon effects added to existing shots. This release also includes a new commentary by Friedkin that clarifies the narrative, but fans will also want to seek out the standard DVD release, which includes Mark Kermode's excellent 'The Fear of God' documentary as well as separate commentaries by Friedkin and Blatty. (ANDY RICHARDS)

Eyes Without a Face

(France/Italy, 1959)

Director: George Franju
Label: Criterion Collection (USA)
Region: 1 (NTSC)
Discs: 1

ORIGINAL TITLE: Les Yeux sans Visage

THE FILM

With most modern-day horror films aspiring merely to subject viewers to a nerve-rending endurance test, Franju's cult classic is a reminder that the genre is also the repository of some of cinema's most potent poetry. Adapted by Pierre Boileau and Thomas Narcejac (the team behind the source stories of *Les Diaboliques* and *Vertigo*) from a novel by Jean Redon, the film sets out to compete with the likes of Hammer Horror in the *Grand Guignol* stakes, while at the same time incorporating elements of tender, ethereal beauty that echo the Surrealist fantasies of Jean Cocteau.

The plot is pulp perfection: brilliant Parisian surgeon Dr Génessier (Pierre Brasseur) is responsible for a car crash that seriously damaged the face of his daughter Christiane (Edith Scob). With the help of his assistant Louise (Alida Valli), he abducts girls and attempts to perform experimental skin grafts to restore his daughter's ravaged features. Génessier's actions are appalling – his victims are sacrificed on the operating table, and then disposed of by Louise – but they are motivated by his guilt over the accident and a love for his daughter. If he is hardly a conventional 'mad scientist', then Christiane is far from a traditional movie monster; with her flayed face hidden by a delicate porcelain mask, she is a prisoner in her father's mansion, haunting its corridors and stairways like a restless wraith. As Génessier perseveres in his obsessive, murderous quest, his daughter is finally driven to a terrible act of rebellion against his patriarchal tyranny.

Almost a half-century on, in an era when televised surgery is a daily entertainment, Franju's medical procedure scenes still pack a punch. But it is other macabre moments that give the film enduring resonance: the opening sequence with Louise driving her 2CV through the night, glancing nervously at the corpse sat in the back seat, its hat pulled low to conceal its lack of a face; or the haunting final shot where Christiane walks slowly away into the darkness, newly liberated doves fluttering around her, to an ambiguous apotheosis.

THE DISC

The Criterion edition is of a typically high standard, and as well as a remastered transfer contains *Le Sang des Bêtes*, Franju's fascinating 1949 documentary about Parisian abattoirs that – like the main feature – follows the Surrealist strategy of juxtaposing images of violence and tenderness. There are also archival interviews with Franju, Boileau and Narcejac, and trailers that reveal how the film was dubbed and repackaged for the US market as *The Horror Chamber of Dr Faustus* and served up on an exploitation double bill with *The Manster* ('Half man! Half monster!'). (ANDY RICHARDS)

F For Fake

(France, 1974)

Director: Orson Welles
Label: Criterion Collection (USA)
Region: 0 (NTSC)
Discs: 2

THE FILM

Welles' last completed feature (unless you count the filmed lecture *Filming Othello*), this is also a rare Welles film that wasn't compromised in post-production battles, though ironically enough it emerged from someone else's abandoned documentary.

According to Welles' partner, Oja Kodar, he was only supposed to narrate François Reichenbach's portrait of art forger Elmyr de Hory. Then de Hory's biographer, Clifford Irving, hit the headlines when his Howard Hughes autobiography was exposed as a fraud – at which point Welles convinced Reichenbach to let him loose with his footage, incorporating his own inimical musings on the art of lies, trickery and the fallibility of 'experts' (Pauline Kael was querying Welles' contribution to the script of *Citizen Kane* at the time).

Running through the rushes at his Moviola like a magician shuffling a deck of marked cards, Welles makes great show of celebrating the art of the lie, but only to conjure the shadow of 'the fake fake'. 'I'm a charlatan,' he claims, but only a fool would believe that. When the fun and games are over, we're left with Welles' touching reverie over Chartres, and his equally emotional, though unarticulated, effusion for the warmth and beauty of Oja. That and a spry, witty escapade of a movie which actually calls itself *?: About Fakes*. Shhh! Don't tell anyone! It's a secret.

THE DISCS

Eureka's Masters of Cinema Region 2 release has much to recommend it – indeed a Welles completist may feel compelled to check out Jonathan Rosenbaum's 28-minute video piece, an audio commentary by cameraman Gary Graver with critic Bill Krohn, and especially the booklet of essays by Fred Camper, Joseph McBride, Peter Tonguette *et al.*

Nevertheless, the Criterion double-disc is the essential edition here. Again, Graver contributes an audio commentary, this time with Welles' companion Oja Kodar, and this time Rosenbaum supplies liner notes. There's a video intro by Peter Bogdanovich, a workmanlike 1992 documentary on de Hory, plus then-and-now *60 Minutes* interviews with Clifford Irving. Better yet, there's a nine-minute (!) trailer Welles made for his film, and still we're not done: what makes it a must-have is the feature-length documentary *Orson Welles: One Man Band*. Hardly the last word, Vassili Silovic's collaboration with Kodar is nevertheless a fascinating scrapbook of late Wellesian odds and ends, including tantalising clips from *The Other Side of the Wind*, *The Dreamers*, *Magic Show* and much more besides. It's material you won't find elsewhere. (TOM CHARITY)

Fanny and Alexander

(Sweden, 1982)

Director: Ingmar Bergman
Label: Criterion Collection (USA)
Region: 1 (NTSC)
Discs: 5

THE FILM

'Ej blot till lyst', or 'Not merely for pleasure', proclaims the slogan painted at the top of 11-year-old Alexander's puppet theater, filmed in rich colour and deceptive scale in the opening shots of *Fanny and Alexander*. True, this warm, expansive, unimprovable film does not exist 'merely for pleasure', and as Alexander and his younger sister Fanny navigate their childhood, they will lose their father, shudder at their mother's grief, cling to each other amidst the iron rule of a devout, despotic stepfather and escape their grim(m) fate through a magical transport to a shadowy, whispery world of illusions that they don't quite understand.

But they will also romp with their governess, soak in the holidays, give and receive love, marvel at stories and images, dart like minnows within and around their sprawling family. The film, as ample and detailed as a Victorian novel, is spry with humour, succulent in sensory delights, sly with its unexpected leaps and its dollops of magical realism. Clearly, it's the creation of a master filmmaker, a devotee of the theatre, a connoisseur of opera and music, a great eater, a great worrier, a childlike dreamer, a melancholy senior, an ardent lover and an estimable ringleader with a lifetime's share of genius actors and craftsmen at his side.

THE DISCS

Criterion has avoided the key mistakes of the Artificial Eye DVD, which cropped the images, brightened the colours and lightened the contrasts of the master print, subtly but surely distorting the textures and meanings of the film. By contrast, Criterion's deluxe presentation exceeds even their own high standards, obeying the low light and gaslight hues of key scenes but capturing all of the sprightly colour and dazzling nuance in the rest of the movie. Even better, this set encompasses the three-hour film beloved by the world, the five-hour cut heretofore confined to Swedish television and the two-hour documentary about the making of the film that played in cinemas as a stand-alone feature.

Best of all – yes, even better than that! – the whole set is replete with sublime add-ons, covering Bergman's memories of a full dozen of his films, a fond and sweeping commentary track by Peter Cowie, models of sets and costumes, illustrated reminiscences by most of the crucial behind-the-scenes talent and much, much more. Like the film it so gorgeously showcases, the DVD set is sublimely generous and sprawling with characters, each speaking in his or her own memorable voice. (NICK DAVIS)

Fantômas

(France, 1913)

Director: Louis Feuillade
Label: Artificial Eye (UK)
Region: 2 (PAL)
Discs: 2

THE FILM

The movies lost their innocence just about here, with Gaumont's five-part adaptation of Pierre Souvestre and Marcel Allain's hot pop-literary property *Fantômas*, an infernal crime saga untethered from any moral overload. It relates the battle of wits between Parisian criminal mastermind Fantômas, an endlessly resourceful 'master of disguise', and the indefatigable Inspector Juve, who like his nemesis seems to have at least nine lives, but never quite gets to light that cigar.

If it's striking seeing the edifices of modern TV serials finding their shape here – the pre-titles plot recaps, the character-gallery credits, the musical motifs, not to mention the vertiginous cliff-hangers at the end of each episode – it's even more remarkable how casually amoral the drama is. Fantômas is as indelibly evil as he is indecipherable, dispatching minions, lovers, passing and distant strangers with nothing but alacrity, but the film plays his duel with Juve as an entertainment; there's no back story, no motivation, no bourgeois sermonising. Fantômas is also diabolically ingenious, a creation midway between Moriarty and the modern serial killer. Episode 3, 'The Corpse That Kills', sees him availing himself of a borrowed hand in ways that must have inspired Hannibal Lecter. Perhaps the movies also lost their shackles here?

Feuillade was an interesting directorial case, from a time (pre-Griffith!) when film directing was not conceived of as an ego-channelling role. Reputedly conservative by instinct, like the stories' writers, he cranked out these pulp dramas, staging jewel heists, prison breaks, car chases, train crashes and house demolitions for popular edification. It may not be too much to find in this an unconscious foreshadowing of the easy annihilation of WWI. As Kim Newman discusses in his extra on the disc, Feuillade's quick-fire filmmaking must have involved a degree of automatism that may have appealed to many of the movies' fans, not least the Surrealists. There's a democratic/demotic modernism here: the film is conceived in the same spirit of high-tech mass communication as the new cars and trains seen in Feuillade's location scenes. Taking the trick film out of the studio, *Fantômas* and its follow-ups, *Les Vampires* and *Judex*, began to remake the real world.

THE DISCS

Kim Newman's loquacious 20-minute discourse on the *Fantômas* phenomenon is the only extra on Artificial Eye's disc (Francophones will find far more on Gaumont's untranslated French set). The transfer quality is quite ravishing – there's just one lost scene, replaced with a flagged-up surrogate. Information about the soundtrack would have been welcome, but it's certainly crisp and resonant, sonically and dramatically. (NICK BRADSHAW)

Far from Heaven

(USA, 2002)

Director: Todd Haynes
Label: Entertainment in Video (UK) /
Universal (USA)
Region: 2 (PAL) / 1 (NTSC)
Discs: 1

THE FILM

A sure sign you're watching a class-act '50s melodrama is that you come to overlook all which might now seem dated or artificial and start forming real emotional attachments to the characters. Todd Haynes's meticulous 21st-century attempt to recreate this most unfashionable of genres initially appears to be making problems for itself by aiming for a style now half a world and half a century away. By its end, though, *Far from Heaven* has forced jaded viewers' eyes so wide open that we too begin flinching whenever it looks as though one of the principals is going to get hurt.

The Whittakers – mom Cathy (Julianne Moore), pop Frank (Dennis Quaid) and their two young children – appear to be the model American family, the epitome of everything Frank's employers, the Magnatech corporation, stand for. Problems arise, however, when Frank starts coming home late from the office, and Cathy seeks the companionship of her black gardener (Dennis Haysbert) to compensate for the increasing emptiness she finds in a once-happy household.

Consider it the Technicolor fantasy of another CW: Carol White, the etiolated heroine of Haynes's previous *Safe*. In a film in all senses queer enough to make even straight men appreciate the virtue of good interior design, Moore and Quaid are shot, lit and dressed to look like movie stars at the height of Hollywood glamour, their finely tuned performances at the heart of the director's obsessively magnificent tragedy: that of a woman holding on to the illusion of the perfect family and the ideal home right through to the bitter end.

THE DISC

The prevailing richness of colour in the feature makes *Far from Heaven* an ideal demonstration of the DVD image anyway, but on the extras front there's a classy trailer, and several short featurettes. A ten-minute making-of finds Haynes talking about the Sirk influence and his clearly felicitous collaboration with composer Elmer Bernstein, while 'The Filmmaker's Experience' is an all-too-brief filmed Q&A with Haynes and Moore.

Slightly more enlightening is another in the Sundance Channel's 'Anatomy of a Scene' series, in which Haynes, Moore, costume designer Sandy Powell and editor James Lyons amongst others dissect the film's eventful house-party sequence. And Haynes himself provides a genial, literate commentary: he's clearly smuggled key texts by Sirk, Brecht and Fassbinder into the booth with him. (MIKE McCAHILL)

Ferris Bueller's Day Off

(USA, 1986) Bueller . . . Bueller . . . Edition

Director: John Hughes
Label: Paramount (USA)
Region: 1 (NTSC)
Discs: 1

THE FILM

A small but much-cherished time capsule from a moment when the line 'How could I possibly be expected to handle school on a day like this?' set to Sigue Sigue Sputnik could sound like the most exhilarating call to arms. These days, kids bunk off with no effort whatsoever, but in John Hughes's enduring comedy, Matthew Broderick's Ferris did it in style.

Few teen movies speak this directly to their audience, addressing that adolescent sense of a life stretching out endlessly, with only odd authority figures standing in the way. Other Hughes scripts used high school as a stage on which to play out teenage hopes and fears. Here, by ridiculing Jeffrey Jones's pricelessly uptight principal Rooney and Ben Stein's dullard economics teacher, Hughes is dismissive of the institution, championing instead the self-taught and instinctive: baseball games as substitutes for gym class, followed by a whirlwind tour of the Chicago Museum of Art.

Entirely absent are the interchangeable hunks and babes of most modern teen-pics; in their place, indelible characterisation: we cheer not the hero's rebellion so much as his resourcefulness and loyalty, his desire to do right by his girl and his best friend. Accepted wisdom is that the older you get, the less persuasive you find Broderick's boyish charm in the lead role, and the greater the desire to box Ferris Bueller's ears; so see it while you're still young, or at least young at heart.

THE DISC

The 20th-anniversary 'Bueller . . . Bueller . . . Edition' offers several lovingly compiled featurettes. 'Getting the Class Together' details how the film was cast, tracking down most of the key players – and Kristy Swanson, a fleeting *Ferris* cameo – as they are now. Amongst the revelations: Jennifer Grey looks better today than she ever did in her twenties, and Ferris's parents – actors Cindy Pickett and Lyman Ward – were actually dating during the production. (Their reappearance here is guaranteed to make devotees feel *really* ancient.)

A particular treat is 'The World According to Ben Stein', a latter-day collection of *Bueller*-related anecdotes in which one of the smartest figures in American comedy explains what Kurt Cobain and George W Bush have in common, and outlines his vision of human beings as 'ungrateful and self-pitying bipeds'. Director Hughes's commentary track on the previous Standard Edition (still available in the UK) has been removed from the update, alas, and he's now represented only in the form of interview footage from 1986, looking for all the world like the runner-up in a Mike Read lookalike contest. (MIKE McCAHILL)

WC Fields
Comedy Collection
(USA, 1933–40)

Directors: Edward Sutherland, Norman Z MacLeod, George Marshall, Edward F Cline
Label: Universal (USA)
Region: 1 (NTSC)
Discs: 5

FILM TITLES: *International House, It's a Gift, You Can't Cheat an Honest Man, My Little Chickadee, The Bank Dick*

THE FILMS

Bitterness and booze: William Claude Dukenfield, aka Charles Bogle, aka Otis Criblecoblis, aka Mahatma Kane Jeeves, aka Uncle Claudie, aka Bill, aka WC Fields, was a man of few guises. In his youth, a phase it's hard to imagine him submitting to, he was a mute vaudeville juggler, an art learned on sufferance while peddling vegetables with his abusive Cockney-emigrant father. In his more fully rounded latter years, he added byzantine wordplay and aphoristic self-asides to his shtick, and thus was born the great un-juvenile ('I never smoked a cigarette until I was nine'), antidote to all that is cute, coy, sanctimonious and cornball in Hollywood.

His films couch a deliciously acerbic worldview, with their hectoring harridans, monstrous children, officious jobsworths, and salvation in both the bottle and the unsteady hand of fate, but the best of them (those he wrote himself) also testify to his love of a tall tale and the ad-libbed life, teetering from one ramshackle scenario to another. If his poison-pen portraits of small-town America make David Lynch look sweet-toothed, his narratives anticipate the softer idiosyncrasies of *The Simpsons*. Universal's collection is, at least, fittingly random. *International House* (1933) saw Paramount almost literally parachuting their new comedy property, beer bottle in hand, into a skittish all-star portmanteau plot about a business expo in China, intended as a '*Grand Hotel* of comedy'. *You Can't Cheat an Honest Man* (1939) is a circus mishmash with too much of Edgar Bergen's creepy ventriloquist, although Fields makes an admirably roguish ringmaster. And the comedy western *My Little Chickadee* (1940) is a misbegotten attempt to yoke Fields's dissident talent to Mae West's: the two stars could barely share a set, let alone a scene.

Still, here be two certified classics: *It's a Gift* (1934) and *The Bank Dick* (1940), both key distillations of the Fields purview. The former sees his storekeeper Herbert Bisonette prevailing over blind customers and fruitless mail-order California orange groves; the latter finds his barfly Egbert Sousé turning his hand to film directing and bank warding, corrupting his daughter's fiancé and poisoning a dutiful accountant. It's topped by the fastest, funniest car chase in the movies, back projection and all. (A companion Volume Two set now offers further essentials: *The Old Fashioned Way, Man on the Flying Trapeze, Never Give a Sucker an Even Break . . .*)

THE DISCS

Beautiful transfers in a hardback box set. The lesser films come with trailers, and there's a substantial if rudimentary life-of doc, in which friends and family testify to Fields's equally over-large off-screen legend. (NICK BRADSHAW)

Fight Club

(USA, 1999)

Director: David Fincher
Label: 20th Century Fox (USA)
Region: 1 (NTSC)
Discs: 2

THE FILM

Taking you inside the mind of an anonymous, jaded yuppie (Edward Norton) whose response to his well-cushioned malaise is to troll support groups for any kind of human contact, *Fight Club*'s all-embracing satire starts dark and gets darker. After our man falls in with sometime cinema projectionist Tyler Durden (Brad Pitt), whose seductive and subversive personal philosophy splices Nietzsche, Herbert Marcuse and Zen Buddhism, he discovers a route to self-knowledge via consensual pummelling that's as ominous as it is ridiculous. Though he's initially in awe of Tyler's way with a slogan ('It's only after we've lost everything that we're free to do anything'), when the titular organisation takes off their strange partnership becomes a case, as Tyler's on-off girlfriend Marla (Helena Bonham Carter) has it, of Dr Jekyll and Mr Jackass.

Fincher, the MTV auteur behind *Se7en*, and his collaborators, working from a droll adaptation of Chuck Palahniuk's novel, crafted one of the most technically innovative films of the CGI era, its unobtrusive tricknology employed not, crucially, as spectacle but as thought made visible. From dazzling 'where's your head at?' start to definitive 'where do we go from here?' finish, *Fight Club* will leave you reeling.

THE DISCS

Radically different on second viewing, *Fight Club* is a DVD classic, lovingly produced right down to its phoney anti-piracy warning. With extras enlarging on every stage of the production in cult-pleasing detail, you decide your own level of involvement. The pre-production stage alone is covered as storyboard panels, as a number of layers of computer effects, as a costume designer's sketch, and as a location scout's video – some of these with multiple commentaries. Something of an eve-of-the-millennium time capsule, the film's distinctive publicity campaign is, perhaps surprisingly, one of the DVD's highlights – notably a spoof consumer catalogue ('Is your feng-shui properly aligned? If so, take a hard look at your life') that connects the film to the moment of the Seattle riots and Naomi Klein's *No Logo*. Capping all this are four commentary tracks in which Fincher talks about his work in advertising (a means 'to just, you know, play with the tools'), Edward Norton defends the film, 'so obviously about what goes wrong when a bunch of fratboys start taking themselves too seriously', against charges of fascism, and Brad Pitt relates his love for Radiohead, the soundtrack candidates whose *The Bends* and *OK Computer* albums are this film's morose pop equivalent.

(Extras on the R2 PAL disc are subtly different, though there are three fewer commentaries, and the image is marginally less sharp. Four seconds of BBFC-imposed cuts to the fist-fights were waived for the 2006 Special Edition.) (HENRY K MILLER)

The Film Noir Classic Collection, Vol. 1

(USA, 1944–50)

Directors: Listed below
Label: Warners (USA)
Region: 1 (NTSC)
Discs: 5

FILM TITLES: *Out of the Past, Murder, My Sweet, Gun Crazy, The Asphalt Jungle, The Set-Up*
DIRECTORS: Jacques Tourneur, Edward Dmytryk, Joseph H Lewis, John Huston, Robert Wise

THE FILMS

'Film noir' was a term first coined by French critics to describe the glut of stylish Hollywood thrillers made available to them after the end of WWII, alluding to the films' low-key, shadowy lighting style and brooding pessimism, as well as linking them to *série* noir paperbacks. This indispensable collection unites two archetypal private eye classics with three equally seminal films reflecting the influence of the noir style on other developing genres. Tourneur's *Out of the Past* (1947) is perhaps the best of all noirs. Based on Daniel Mainwaring's novel *Build My Gallows High*, it features many characteristic elements: a tough-talking, wisecracking hero (Robert Mitchum) ensnared in a tortuous plot; a beautiful, duplicitous femme fatale (Jane Greer); a suave, debonair villain (Kirk Douglas in an early role); flashbacks with a fatalistic voice-over narration ('And then I saw her coming out of the sun. And I knew why Witt didn't care about that forty grand') and lashings of moody chiaroscuro. Dmytryk's 1944 *Murder, My Sweet* (based on Raymond Chandler's *Farewell, My Lovely*, the film's British title) had set the template for many of these elements, and remains immensely enjoyable thanks to a winning against-type performance from crooner Dick Powell (as Chandler's 'white knight' investigator Philip Marlowe), memorable character turns (notably Mike Mazurki as Moose Malloy), entertainingly vivid voice-over ('I was a toad on a wet rock. A snake was looking at the back of my neck'), and experimental hallucinatory sequences.

Later in the decade, Lewis's cult B-movie *Gun Crazy* (1949) featured Peggy Cummins as a memorable femme fatale, a circus sharp-shooter who seduces the equally gun-obsessed John Dall and leads him on an increasingly murderous robbery spree. In its explicit linking of eroticism and violent transgression, this tale of *amour fou* was a clear forerunner of Arthur Penn's *Bonnie and Clyde*. Huston's *The Asphalt Jungle* (1950), an influential 'caper' film, follows a gang who perform a daring jewel heist only to be undone by bad luck and weaknesses of character; its depiction of crime as 'a left-handed form of human endeavour' gave its motley crew – particularly Sterling Hayden's hoodlum Dix – a certain tragic nobility. Wise's *The Set-Up* (1948), finally, remains one of the great boxing films, telling a taut real-time tale of a washed-up fighter (Robert Ryan) falling foul of a mobster even as he regains his dignity in the ring; its tawdry poetry chimes perfectly with noir's shadow world.

THE DISCS

The Set-Up features a commentary by Wise and Martin Scorsese, who discusses the film's influence on his own *Raging Bull*. The other titles each feature an informed commentary by a noir specialist, setting the achievements of each film within their studio production context. The transfer quality is well nigh unimpeachable, and the price is a snap. (Two further volumes are nearly as strong.) (ANDY RICHARDS)

Final Destination 2
(USA, 2003)

Director: David Ellis
Label: Entertainment in Video (UK)
Region: 2 (PAL)
Discs: 1

THE FILM

At time of writing, this warped little series stands at three in number, but it's the second instalment that remains Grand Vizier. A 24-carat guilty pleasure, it treads a line of sublime deftness between white-knuckle tension and gross-out flair of the 'I really don't believe that just happened' kind. As always in the triptych, Death is cheated, this time when Kimberly (AJ Cook), off for a weekend with her chums, predicts a horrific car crash moments before it happens, thereby saving her own – and six others' – lives. But Death is also miffed, and subsequently employs everything from pigeons and plate-glass to an airbag and an airborne fence to claim the survivors.

While not quite Tarkovsky, then, it's acted and constructed with a necessarily straight-faced conviction, and amounts to one of the most immaculate interweavings of CGI and stunts that Hollywood has yet delivered. The opening pile-up, in particular, is choreographed with a murderous, balletic brilliance, and the rest of the film bolts along like a modern-day *The Omen*, but with the humour, imagination and yuk dials cranked up to a glorious 11 – as you might hope from a flick with such an inspired, idiotic oxymoron for a title.

THE DISC

If ever a commentary echoed the mood of its movie, this disc's 85 minutes of often hilarious, epically un-PC nonsense is it. Director Ellis, producer Craig Perry and the two screenwriters all contribute, but barely seconds have elapsed before you completely forget who's talking. Of course, they're all extremely professional filmmakers (which is why *FD2* works so well), but their impression of a quartet of baggy-trousered, sex-obsessed teenage doofuses is uncanny. One of them starts talking promisingly about the 'trap' of making a horror-movie sequel – but then a breast-bearing scene looms and he's interrupted with, 'Hey now! Hey now!' and then, upon production of a nipple, 'Now THAT! Look at THAT!' 'I forgot everything,' laments the original speaker.

In fact, all this ribaldry is punctuated with plenty of respectable insights, and there's also a very enjoyable 30-minute documentary that sets the film in a surprisingly solid historical context. (NB there's mounds of tripe on the DVD, too.) But the commentary is the thing, and as the foursome proceed to rip their film to shreds, sparing not even a hapless, flapping goldfish, it's best simply to order a pizza, switch off your IQ and go along for the ridiculous ride. (MARK MONAHAN)

The 400 Blows

(France, 1959)

Director: François Truffaut
Label: Tartan (UK)
Region: 2 (PAL)
Discs: 1

ORIGINAL TITLE: *Les Quatre Cents Coups*

THE FILM

Oft-imitated, never surpassed, François Truffaut's legendary first feature is dedicated to his *Cahiers du Cinéma* mentor André Bazin, whose famous predilection for the long take found its most luminously simple expression here. Louis Malle and Claude Chabrol had already pitched in with their debuts *Lift to the Scaffold* and *Le Beau Serge*, but it was *The 400 Blows* which, premiering at Cannes in 1959, seemed the definitive manifesto for the French New Wave's freewheeling aesthetic and stood out from the pack as a captivatingly personal work.

For the autobiographical role of 12-year-old rebel schoolboy Antoine Doinel, Truffaut found the remarkably talented Jean-Pierre Léaud, who would continue to play the character in four further films charting his quizzical progress into adulthood. What the ongoing Doinel saga could never recapture was this film's air of complex realist nostalgia for Truffaut's adolescence, which seeps into it from the first frame as Jean Constantin's unforgettable music, a light and sad melody plucked from the air, accompanies besotted travelling shots of the Parisian rooftops. (Cinematographer Henry Decaë, having worked several times with Jean-Pierre Melville already, was top of the payroll.)

Antoine's bits of mischief in the classroom – he's unlucky enough to get caught repeatedly – set him on the road to delinquency, but the film's subjects are as much his solitary ecstasy on a fairground whirligig and the businesslike way he lays the family dinner-table. His eventual escape from a boys' reformatory – shades here and throughout of Vigo's *Zéro de Conduite* – precipitates a headlong flight to the sea, where Antoine ends the movie both liberated and trapped, caught on the threshold of an ambiguous future, and gazing back, as Truffaut's shot freeze-frames, to ask himself and us, 'What next?'

THE DISC

Elevating this Tartan disc to consideration alongside the pricier Criterion import is its inclusion of Truffaut's superb 1957 short 'Les Mistons', of major interest as his first directorial credit. Focusing on a gaggle of boys and their obsession with the pert, cycling Bernadette (Bernadette Lafont, from Eustache's *La Maman et la Putain*), it's a coarse but energetic sketch for the masterwork to follow, establishing a formative debt to Italian neorealism. *The 400 Blows'* original trailer, splicing in raves from Henri-Georges Clouzot and Jean Cocteau, is an added boon. (TIM ROBEY)

Four Weddings and a Funeral

(UK, 1994) Special Edition

Director: Mike Newell
Label: MGM (UK)
Region: 2 (PAL)
Discs: 1

THE FILM

Forget Mr Bean. Forget *Love, Actually*. Try extra hard to forget *Bridget Jones: the Edge of Reason*. And wipe from your memory the ghastly spectre of both Wet Wet Wet and also Andie MacDowell's line about not noticing the rain. Done it? Excellent. Because – those hiccups aside – *Four Weddings and a Funeral* is not just the most successful British comedy of all time, it is also one of the best, a fact obscured by the wet drizzle of romcoms that followed in its wake and its writer's (and star's) subsequent formulaic track record. *Four Weddings* may have spawned an entire genre, but the film itself is the kind of emotionally satisfying, character-based, *cynical* comedy which Ealing Studios once specialised in – with the very '90s addition of sex, pop music and much more swearing. That Curtis could include nine 'fucks', one 'fuckity fuck' and one 'bugger' within minutes of the opening titles and still not spook a family audience testifies to his comedic charm, and that of director Mike Newell (*Donnie Brasco, Harry Potter and the Goblet of Fire*) and star Hugh Grant.

Crucially, the pace and the performances in *Four Weddings*, particularly those of Grant, Simon Callow and the late Charlotte Coleman, still feel fresh and spontaneous – this gang of friends, unlike the ones in *Notting Hill* et al, actually seem to like one another. And Grant has never bettered the defining role of his career, the aggressively diffident Charles, whose every 'um', 'er', and 'fuck-a-doodle-do' was painstakingly mapped out by the actor in rehearsal; in fact, the whole film is a masterclass in comic judgement. Except the line about the rain. Oh, and that bit on the South Bank . . .

THE DISC

A tenth-anniversary Special Edition of *Four Weddings* was released in 2004. Like previous DVDs, the film is presented in its original theatrical aspect ratio of 1.85:1, but this is the first time an anamorphic transfer has appeared. There are three featurettes (all adequate), trailers, a picture gallery and promotional spots – so far, so standard. But both the deleted scenes and commentary are more interesting. None of the deleted scenes are remarkable in themselves, but they emphasise how well Newell and Curtis appraised their material; if it was cut, it was cut for a good reason. As for the commentary, the writer, director and producers cover a wide range of topics in an affectionate, bantering, amusing manner – one of those entertaining commentaries that make the viewer feel good about an already feel-good film. (ANDY MILLER)

Frankenstein & Bride of Frankenstein

(USA, 1931/1935)

Director: James Whale
Label: Universal (UK)
Region: 2/4 (PAL)
Discs: 2

THE FILMS

Generally considered the jagged, cloud-swept pinnacle of the Universal horror series, and certainly the two that have most successfully weathered the passage of time, James Whale's *Frankenstein* films still make for engrossing, rewarding and disturbing viewing.

The original *Frankenstein* may no longer be frightening, but thanks to the combination of Boris Karloff's moving performance as the monster, the tragic alcoholic Colin Clive's Henry Frankenstein, Whale's sensitive direction, Ed Keye's striking, Expressionist production design and Jack Pierce's and Ken Strickfaden's electrifying laboratory equipment, it's far more satisfying than all of its tombmates. Except one ...

Freed from the restraints of Mary Shelley's original, Whale's *Bride of Frankenstein* is unique: strange, complex, funny and camp in the extreme, largely due to the wonderful Ernest Thesiger as Dr Pretorius, the ultimate mad scientist. Viewers are spoiled for choice: as well as Thesiger we get Karloff again, this time with some unforgettable spoken scenes, Elsa Lanchester as both the Bride and, in a meta-historical prologue, as Mary Shelley and then, to cap it all, a family of doll-sized homunculi. Fresher, funnier and more imaginative than anything else in the Universal monster series – indeed, than any number of horror films that have followed – *Bride of Frankenstein* remains a benchmark for fantastic cinema.

THE DISCS

A new seventy-fifth anniversary Universal edition of *Frankenstein* boasts a better transfer and improved extras, but this UK double-disc still shines for having both films, plus two documentaries. The first, presented by the dean of Universal Monster Studies, David J Skal, puts the first film into the context of horror history, from Shelley's novel through various stage adaptations to the present day. The second, hosted by a breathless Joe Dante (*Gremlins*), focuses on the making of *Bride*, with some interesting discussions about its censorship battles. Both contain incisive commentaries from film historians, trailers and various other extra nuts and bolts. Hardcore Frankenstein fans might want to seek out the Region 1 Legacy Collection edition, which also crams *Son of*, *Ghost of* and *House of Frankenstein* onto two very affordable discs, along with an alternative commentary by historian Rudy Behlmer – or even the massive Monster Legacy Collection which includes the contemporaneous *Dracula* and *The Wolf Man* series. For sheer quantity, they're certainly better value, although there are reports of problems with the compression in some players – and with the films following *Bride*, it's a serious case of diminishing returns, the monster having strayed into serious end-of-the-line B-movie territory. (MARK PILKINGTON)

Gallivant

(UK, 1996)

Director: Andrew Kötting
Label: BFI (UK)
Region: 2 (PAL)
Discs: 2

THE FILM

Andrew Kötting is one of Britain's most intriguing artists, and perhaps the only filmmaker currently practising who could be said to have taken to heart the spirit of visionary curiosity and hybrid creativity exemplified by the late Derek Jarman. Formally exploratory and aesthetically innovative, like Jarman he is also a great collaborator, building around his various projects a community of shared interest, while anchoring his prolific production in an ongoing report on the lives of those closest to him.

His 25-year progress to date has moved from early live-art inflected, often absurdist pieces, ripe with their own internal logics and skewed mythologies, through darkly comic shorts – teasing out the melancholy surrealism at the heart of contemporary Englishness – to two resolutely independent features that take landscape and journeys as the springboards for visually striking and structurally inventive enquiries into identity, belonging, history and notions of community.

In all Kötting's work, there is a more or less active reclamation of deep strains of popular experience and folk memory for the digital age. At the same time, his oeuvre is underpinned by a psycho-geographical approach to place, meaning the layered reading of territories, urban and other, via signs of all kinds and without prejudice as to the source or status of the prompt.

The above has come together most winningly in his award-winning debut feature, the accessibly experimental *Gallivant*. An unscripted camper-van journey around the entire British coastline in the company of his grandmother and his daughter Eden (then eight years old and suffering from the rare Joubert's Syndrome) allows Kötting to excavate all his interests at length. Multiple filmstocks, found footage, non-synchronous sound, home-movie reveries and encounters with a host of distinctive personalities all make for richly textured, humorous and fascinating viewing. At its heart, though, are the affecting relationships, across three generations, of family members learning about both the country they inhabit and themselves. It's a genuine one-of-a-kind road movie, and a unique British film.

THE DISCS

Beautifully packaged, with two fully illustrated booklets boasting insightful notes by Kötting, an extended treatment for *Gallivant* and a very fine essay by Iain Sinclair, this double-disc set boasts nearly three hours of extra material. Eleven shorts, drawn from across Kötting's oeuvre, are included. They range from the Keatonesque japes of his debut 'Klipperty Klöpp', through the cross-Channel comedy of 'Là Bas' and the suburban holiday mayhem of 'Smart Alek', to 'Jaunt', with its parodic travelogue, and the dark introspection of 'Me'. A two-screen work, 'Visionary Landscapes', made from Super-8 *Gallivant* out-takes in collaboration with musician and Pogues co-founder Jem Finer, is also included.

(GARETH EVANS)

Gandhi

(UK/India, 1982)

25th Anniversary Edition

Director: Richard Attenborough
Label: Sony (all territories)
Region: any
Discs: 2

THE FILM

Not one for the movies at the best of times, Gandhi would surely have hated the film of his life – epic, star-studded, multi-Oscar-winning, historically flaky and, worst of all, directed by an Englishman. But despite its Western peccadillos, Richard Attenborough's *Gandhi* is a sterling triumph – its story of how this London-trained Indian lawyer went from battling injustice in South Africa to non-violently liberating his nation proves as irrepressible as the man himself.

The film's main problem, one an opening disclaimer shows it's only too aware of, is the age-old biopic stumbling-block of compression. Events that would have played out over weeks or months – Gandhi's wife's initial refusal to clean the Ashram latrine, for instance, or his fellow independence leaders' conversion to the path of non-violence – suddenly rear up, are instantly resolved, then forgotten, and the effect is to turn Gandhi too much into some invulnerable, loin-clothed superhero.

But when it's firing on all cylinders the film delivers some rousing moments – Gandhi's first explanation of non-cooperation to a crowd of South African Indians ('through our pain, will we make them see their injustice'), the clear-eyed logic of his anti-British campaign ('in the end you *will* walk out because 100,000 Englishmen simply cannot control 350 million Indians if those Indians refuse to cooperate'). Half-Indian Ben Kingsley radiates dignity, determination and mischievousness in his monumental lead performance, while it's great fun ticking off the Raj of old-guard luvvies as they appear: John Mills, John Gielgud, Trevor Howard, Nigel Hawthorne, Michael Hordern, Edward Fox (not to mention a young Daniel Day-Lewis).

All told, it's a film that works despite itself. Whether advertently or not, scenes of carnage raise stimulating doubts about Gandhi's philosophy, while its glossed-over complexities – um, why *exactly* was he assassinated? – simply spur you to further investigation. An alluring and entertaining primer.

THE DISCS

Disc 1 features a good transfer, which retains the original intermission, and a predictably gushing commentary by Attenborough. Disc 2's goodies comprise no less than nine making-ofs, including one on the famous funeral scene and its staggering 400,000 real, completely non-digitised extras. It also features interviews with Attenborough about casting and music, and another with Kingsley from back in 2000, in which he can't resist regaling us with anecdotes about the uncanny accuracy of his performance. The highlights, though, are four vintage newsreels of the real Gandhi, including a rare interview – in which he doesn't seem much like Kingsley at all. (NICK FUNNELL)

Ghost in the Shell Movie Double Bill

(Japan, 1995/2004)

Director: Mamoru Oshii
Label: Manga (UK)
Region: 2 (PAL)
Discs: 3

THE FILM

What is I? How am I alive? What is the proof of my identity? Delicately, power-fully, poignantly, the two *Ghost in the Shell* films capture the eerie loneliness of existential imaginings, the painful struggle with self-awareness that is the burden of human consciousness. As in *Akira*, *Blade Runner*, *Robocop*, *The Terminator* and the *Matrix* series – all part of these films' networks – these questions are explored on the borderlines of humanity, through hybrid inhabitants of the age now dawning in which the boundaries between computers and their makers have become profoundly blurred. It is a key theme of much Japanese animation, apt for a medium concerned with manufacturing life – a mission accomplished with breathtaking beauty in these two films. While *Ghost 1* deliberately strove to bring anime to the international mainstream with unparalleled visual density, *2* moved the format beyond belief with a richness of 2D, 3D and computer graphics that render each frame vitally aglow.

The story is lit from within by the deep and unspoken love between the lead characters, elite cyborgs Batou, a wry Special Forces-type with a charac-teristically noir cynicism and sensitivity, and the exquisite and extraordinary Major Motoko Kusanagi, leader of the Section 9 squad dedicated to combating high-level cyber crime. Their quest to bring down a super-hacker code-named 'The Puppetmaster' coincides with the Major's search for self-certainty, and in *1*'s finale her consciousness (or 'ghost') disappears into the vastness of the net. Batou's investigations continue into murderous dolls and the meaning of 'life' in the more meditative second film, the balance shifting from action adventure to retro-styled reverie overseen by an intangible Guardian Angel . . . Electro-chorale soundtracks, scenes of gunfighting acrobatics and fading geisha robots blend into the decadent cityscapes of future Hong Kong. The disorientation of the plunge into a world full of alien technologies melts into utter enrapturement.

THE DISCS

To have both halves of this continuous narrative in one box set is worth the slight loss of unremarkable extras (chiefly other anime trailers) entailed in choosing this over the special edition of *1*. Making-of featurettes for both films give professional insights into animation techniques (including gunfire testing in Guam) while the rambling commentary by Oshii and his chief animator on *2* amusingly reveals how different two memories of one film production can be. The English dubs are disappointingly unnuanced, but high-quality sub-titling allows you to appreciate the excellent Japanese vocal performances.

(REBEKAH POLDING)

The Gleaners and I

(France, 1999)

Director: Agnès Varda
Label: Zeitgeist (USA)
Region: 1 (NTSC)
Discs: 1

ORIGINAL TITLE: *Les Glaneurs et la Glaneuse*

THE FILM

This extraordinary cine-essay by Agnès Varda, a director too often neglected in histories of the Nouvelle Vague, was one of the first to profit from the flexibility and cheapness of handheld digital cameras. The film is a fierce and loving salvage operation that rescues from present-day French condescension the lives of those men and women who bend down for a living: those who pick up what fruit and vegetables are left after harvest; those who hang around urban market stalls at closing time to gather food that's been abandoned; those who wander suburban streets at night collecting the goods that affluent house-owners have prematurely junked.

Varda was born in 1928, and made *The Gleaners and I* at an age when most directors' best work is long behind them. She exploits the new camera, which she calls 'stroboscopic, narcissistic, hyper-realistic', in the service of a resistance cinema, one that marries the personal to the political in a style that is never affected or self-aggrandising. She includes mistakes – such as the time she's so busy swaying in time to the melodies sung by a family of squatter-farmers that she forgets to switch the 'off' button and ends up recording her feet. The silliness – and charm – of these moments is off-set by a deep sadness too: she films her withered skin, mulls on the ageing process, and never tries to mask the loneliness of many of her subjects.

Varda is both ruminative and motorik. She tramps through fields, ploughs down motorways, busies towards the objects of her fascinations. She seems to possess a divining rod – at once artistic and ethical – for locating the power and poetry that resides in the most neglected corners of the world around her. It's an enabling curiosity, one that can't help but make us want to go out and look at, through and to the edges of the world we find outside the cinema.

THE DISC

The DVD is decked out with a sequel, *The Gleaners and I: Two Years Later*, in which Varda revisits a number of the itinerants and eccentrics from the original documentary. Some have died, others have given up alcohol or been treated for psychiatric problems. Varda also visits some of the many hundreds of people who wrote to her to recount their own gleaning anecdotes or to send her heart-shaped potatoes; 'the film', observe one artistic couple, 'put us back in touch with ourselves – and life'. Varda's *Gleaners* production notes are also included, along with liner notes by *New York Times* critic AO Scott. (SUKHDEV SANDHU)

The Go-Between
(UK, 1970)

Director: Joseph Losey
Label: Optimum (UK)
Region: 2 (PAL)
Discs: 1

THE FILM

In 1953, Joseph Losey fled America for the UK to avoid being blacklisted. He cut his British teeth on the obligatory motley assortment of *Robin Hood* TV episodes and Hammer Horror thrillers, including, thanks to his script interventions, one of their finest, darkest moments, a bleak, chilling Oliver Reed vehicle about radioactive children called *The Damned* (1962). Yet it was his fascinated outsider's view of English society, in particular its decaying class system, that caused him to be fleetingly adopted as a national treasure.

The Go-Between, based on L.P. Hartley's 1953 literary classic, is in many ways a companion piece to Losey's most popular and critically acclaimed film, *The Servant* (1963), both pitch-perfectly penned by Jewish, working-class outsider Harold Pinter. Based on Robin Maugham's 1949 novella, *The Servant* peeked askance at Britain's smothering hierarchical social system through the homosexually-charged master–servant relationship between Tony (James Fox) and Barrett (Dirk Bogarde). *The Go-Between*, set in 1900, similarly counterpoints upper/working-class central protagonists, both tragically locked in their roles. In this case hairy tenant farmer Ted (Alan Bates) fancies the delicate bloomers off Miss Marian (Julie Christie), the young lady up at The Hall, intended to be married to an eligible but oblivious Viscount (sidelined Edward Fox). The twist on this slightly embarrassing Mills & Boon scenario is the boy who becomes their 'go-between'. Non-U, middle-class Leo (a wonderfully natural and naïve Dominic Guard) is a guest of the house. At 12 years old, his long golden summer of childhood is on the delicate cusp of adolescence – hastened by his role as pandering postman for the couple's illicit and torrid messages.

As with *The Servant*, Losey's classically composed frames corset the characters the more entirely within their formal, gilded cages. Despite the dreamy Merchant-Ivory setting, this is no nostalgic love letter to an England past. Hartley's 'The past is a foreign country: they do things differently there' is one of literature's most famous opening lines, though it proved an elegy to Losey's own career – he barely did much of note after.

THE DISC

The lack of special features is perhaps to be expected, given that Pinter doesn't participate on DVD extras and Losey and Bates both have the excuse of being deceased. However, an increasingly crackly print distractingly spatters over Pinter's final, lingering pauses. The mono sound flattens the melodrama of Michel Legrand's magnificently doom-laden piano chords. Fingers crossed that a superior anniversary re-release is in the offing. (LARUSHKA IVAN-ZADEH)

The Godfather
DVD Collection
(USA, 1972/1974/1990)

Director: Francis Ford Coppola
Label: Paramount (UK)
Region: 2 (PAL)
Discs: 5

FILM TITLES: *The Godfather, Part I*; *The Godfather, Part II*; *The Godfather, Part III*

THE FILMS

The first two *Godfather* films tower over the blessed but unlikely circumstances of their creation – a studio which didn't know what they had, a director who wasn't sure what he'd got himself into, and a lead actor, Al Pacino, who spent the first few weeks of the shoot wondering when he was going to get fired. This, like Don Vito Corleone's own story, is the myth of humble beginnings and the forging of an empire; but like his son Michael's it is also the story – more compelling, we suggest – of not knowing where to stop. Without *Part III*, the *Godfather* saga would be nothing more nor less than the quintessential achievement of 1970s American cinema, but with it there's a tragic dimension to that achievement, which now looks – in part thanks to Coppola's own failure to get more than halfway back up it – like an unscalable plateau from a different era of Hollywood economics.

Look at the endings: *Parts I* and *II* have among the most remarkable final shots in American movies, because they're stamped less with hard narrative closure (*cf.* the fat lady singing in clunky *Part III*) than a sure, fatalistic, and peerlessly economical sense of what's in store – Diane Keaton's Kay shut out, and then Michael, alone in the garden and keeping counsel only with ghosts. Where was there left to go? *Part II* travelled both forwards and backwards to show how Don Vito's rise to power (De Niro, understudying Brando) mirrors Michael's doomed interpretation of his keep-it-in-the-family legacy. But *Part III* had no ideas left. Coppola thinks it's his *King Lear*, but it's more like his cut-rent *Oedipus at Colonus*, all about men blindly flailing with their daughters in the wilderness – and allowing themselves to be pulled back into what was already, monumentally, a done deal.

THE DISCS

You need this set, but it would be nice if the extra materials dug a little deeper and weren't content just to bask in the films' sepia glow of popularity and acclaim. The trifling three-and-a-bit-minute segment on Gordon Willis' cinematography is embarrassing enough without getting everyone's Oscar acceptance speeches thrown in into the bargain, though it's fun spotting meddlesome Paramount honcho Robert Evans look stony-faced as *Part II* beats his beloved *Chinatown* to Best Picture. Coppola couldn't be called the most perceptive of self-critics on his rambling, often garbled commentaries, though there's the odd bit of buried gold and some choice anecdotes about Brando; the feature-length 'A Look Inside', made during production on *Part III*, is a good one-stop source for background. *Part II* is split frustratingly across two discs, but otherwise it's a technically immaculate package. (TIM ROBEY)

Gone with the Wind

(USA, 1939) 4-disc Collector's Edition

Director: Victor Fleming
Label: Warners (all territories)
Region: Any
Discs: 4

THE FILM

More people have seen *Gone with the Wind* than any other film. It was made only through the obsessive persistence of producer David O Selznick, who required the services of four directors, several cinematographers and over 12 uncredited screenwriters. Setting the personal against the social, the conflicts of Rhett Butler and Scarlett O'Hara against the battles of the Civil War, the film compellingly sustains its more than three-hour narrative (Margaret Mitchell, the novel's author, declined to write the screenplay, which was undertaken by Sidney Howard).

The casting is crucial: it's impossible to imagine anyone but Clark Gable as the swaggering but ultimately vulnerable Rhett, or another actress than Vivien Leigh as the selfish, indomitable Scarlett, who embodies the resilience of the Old South. Hattie McDaniel, incomparable as Mammy, became the first African American to win an Academy Award. Replete with unforgettable images – the burning of Atlanta, the flight to Tara, the street of dead and dying Confederate soldiers – and graced with William Cameron Menzies' superb designs and Max Steiner's magnificent score, *Gone with the Wind* holds its place as a classic and a legend.

THE DISCS

Warners' edition is appropriately lavish, spreading the glowingly restored film over two discs and devoting a further two to extras. 'The Making of a Legend' documents Selznick's long search for his Scarlett (which began before he had either script or money for the film), as well as his drive and compulsive desire for control. Olivia de Havilland (Melanie) recalls how distressed she and Leigh were when George Cukor, who was always sympathetic to actresses, was replaced as director by the macho Victor Fleming – but Fleming succeeded in revitalising the production.

The shoot was troubled and often chaotic, with crises over the script, the directors and money (as well as objections from the censors to Rhett's use of the word 'damn'), but eventually half a million feet of footage were cut to 20,000, and the Atlanta premiere was a triumph. The film became the highest-grossing of all time. The DVD also offers documentaries about the leading man and lady: Gable was initially reluctant to play Rhett, fearing that he would not match readers' preconceptions of the character, whereas Leigh understandably coveted what is arguably Hollywood cinema's most prestigious female role, and campaigned adroitly to gain it. (ADAM STREVENS)

Goodbye, Dragon Inn

(Taiwan, 2003)

Director: Tsai Ming-Liang
Label: Wellspring (USA)
Region: 0 (NTSC)
Discs: 1

THE FILM

A young man takes shelter inside a crumbling Taiwanese movie palace showing King Hu's 1966 martial arts classic *Dragon Inn*. The lonely ticket-taker makes herself dinner and wanders up to the projectionist's booth to share it with him. So begins director Tsai Ming-Liang's stunningly sad celebration of movies and movie-going.

As Hu's ground-breaking film plays to a sparse audience, various stories unfold in the auditorium. The ticket-taker checks in on the projectionist; the young man cruises for an anonymous encounter in the hallways; and an older man holds back tears as he watches the images on screen.

Goodbye, Dragon Inn reduces Tsai's famously low-key aesthetic to its core. Meticulously composed, exquisitely framed, and stripped almost entirely of dialogue, it resonates with hypnotic beauty. And yet, for all its minimalism, critic Jonathan Rosenbaum has noted, 'it manages to be many things at once: a failed heterosexual love story, a gay cruising saga, a melancholy tone poem, a mordant comedy, a creepy ghost tale'. Above all, it's a portrait of loneliness and a hymn to the shared experience of cinema.

THE DISC

Tsai Ming-Liang carved out a niche for himself as Taiwan's master of melancholy with previous films such as *The River* and *What Time Is It There?*, a deliciously droll meditation on anomie and angst. Wellspring includes the original trailers for both movies, along with the one for *Goodbye, Dragon Inn*. They supply the garnish for the main course here: a short called *The Skywalk is Gone*. Conceived as an epilogue to *What Time Is It There?*, it picks up the story some time later. The young Taiwanese girl who moved to Paris with a watch bought from a boy on a pedestrian overpass returns home. Caught jaywalking on the same stretch of road, she pleads her innocence to a cop, convinced that there used to be an overpass there.

Precious little happens in the film. The devil is in the detail and Tsai excels at letting haunting moments unfold on camera. Casting his spell, he refuses to spare us from the aching sadness we feel as the girl wanders the streets looking for the boy. And the film's tantalising conclusion – a devastating indictment of urban anomie or perhaps a wry comment on dwindling employment opportunities – lingers long in the mind. (JAMES CLASPER)

The Gospel According to St Matthew
(Italy, 1964)

Director: Pier Paolo Pasolini
Label: Tartan (UK)
Region: 2 (PAL)
Discs: 1

THE FILM

It's one of the sweet ironies of world cinema history that, *pace* Mel, a gay Marxist poet managed to get in the last word on Jesus Christ. Pasolini wasn't just any old non-believer, but an artist of fearsomely *outré* politics and sensibility; that said, for all the controversy it aroused on both left and right, you couldn't call his treatment of Matthew's gospel shockingly subversive so much as radically fly-on-the-wall. It's as if Jesus (played as a righteous proto-communist bad-ass by Catalan economics student Enrique Irazoqui) had had a documentary crew following him about from birth, recording the walking on water and the feeding of the five thousand with matter-of-fact diligence, while egging him on to furious tirades about the plight of the Galilee dispossessed.

But Pasolini doesn't just hijack the greatest story ever told and turn it into a prosaic social manifesto; following the text with reverent care, his film climbs mountains, grapples with the sacred, and achieves a lush, transfixing grace. Don't fiddle with the Dolby – that really is a blues spiritual (Odetta's astonishing 'Sometimes I Feel Like a Motherless Child') playing when we first meet John the Baptist, the most goose-pimply step in a constantly surprising cross-cultural musical odyssey that takes us from Bach to Billie Holiday and back again. The entirely non-professional peasant cast and dusty Calabrian locations (re-used by Gibson) make this a neorealist gospel at heart, but its unadorned simplicity reaches for transcendence, not least when Pasolini uses his medium literally to work miracles – a deformed leper approaches Christ, asks to be made whole again, and all it takes is a cut.

THE DISC

There's a daunting choice of five editions out there, three of them boasting (annoyingly non-removable) English subtitles. We've plumped for Tartan's for its clean and pleasingly soft image quality, and because at least the font's quite nice. Purists with good Italian might prefer Gaumont's similar-looking French disc or Kinowelt's significantly brighter German one, both of which give you the option to watch them subtitle-free. Tartan's has bare-minimum extras (filmographies, and good notes by British critic David Parkinson), but the trade-off with a poor, murky transfer and nasty burnt-in subtitles is too great to make the Region 0 (NTSC) Water Bearer edition, despite a purportedly decent Pasolini doc in the extras, your stand-alone recommendation. Certainly don't bother with Image Entertainment's effort, the runt of the litter for being dark, scratched, extra-free, badly subtitled *and* unforgivably squished. All discs are in Dolby Digital 2.0 mono except Gaumont's, which is 1.0. (TIM ROBEY)

The Graduate

(USA, 1967)

Director: Mike Nichols
Label: Momentum (UK)
Region: 2 (PAL)
Discs: 1

THE FILM

Few films can be distilled into a single word. For the generation that Godard dubbed 'the children of Marx and Coca-Cola', though, the word 'plastics' triggers a wave of nostalgia for Benjamin Braddock, Mrs Robinson and the timeless sound of Simon & Garfunkel. Released at the tail end of the '60s, *The Graduate* went on to receive eight Oscar nominations and launched Dustin Hoffman's career. He plays Braddock, a listless college graduate who returns home to southern California disillusioned with the career path his parents expect him to take. Desperate to break out of their goldfish-bowl existence (they even buy him a diving suit for his 21st birthday – and make him model it), he begins a seedy affair with one of their friends, the irrepressible Mrs Robinson, then dates her naïve daughter Elaine. The film finds the absurdism in baby-boomer disaffection; it still looks like a comedy classic.

Based on an obscure novel by Charles Webb, *The Graduate* was directed by Mike Nichols, whose visual flair – droll symbolism, stylish symmetry and slick jump cuts – has been much imitated and rarely bettered. Yet the film's enduring popularity derives from several superb performances. Hoffman has never been goofier, nor Katherine Ross more beguiling than as Elaine. Four decades on, however, it's Anne Bancroft as Mrs Robinson – a fiery furnace of sexual longing, drunken abandon and failed dreams – whom we remember best of all.

THE DISC

The Graduate was almost a very different movie. The producers originally wanted the lead roles to be filled by Ronald Reagan, Candice Bergen, Robert Redford, and Doris Day. According to screenwriter Buck Henry in 'The Graduate at 25' – a retrospective documentary made in the mid '90s, included here – they opted for Dustin Hoffman after he did a screen test.

But Henry might have told them what to expect. He saw Hoffman on stage in New York playing a handicapped German transvestite and says Hoffman was so impressive that it was 'impossible to believe he wasn't at least one of those three'. Henry's cheerful reflection is one of several that comprise Momentum's charming package. Along with producer Lawrence Turman, Henry discusses the movie's legacy and adapting Webb's novel for the screen. Other highlights include the original trailer, which almost reveals the entire plot; a 64-page book about Nichols' career; and an interview with Hoffman, in which he admits to getting into trouble for once patting Ross's buttocks. You get much more of this last on the R1 MGM disc – 22 minutes as opposed to four here – but Momentum's anamorphic 2.35:1 transfer is much cleaner and truer. (JAMES CLASPER)

La Grande Illusion

(France, 1937)

Director: Jean Renoir
Label: Criterion Collection (USA)
Region: 1 (NTSC)
Discs: 1

THE FILM

Of the great classics, Jean Renoir's *La Grande Illusion* is probably the most misrepresented. There are film taxonomists who'd have you believe it's a 'warm tribute to man's essential humanity', a 'plea for understanding between nations', 'an anti-war film'. Far from idealistic, however, or even hopeful, it's a tale in which barriers stand taller than brotherhood (no accident that most of it plays out in prison) – barriers of class, language and expectation, shatterproof and at best semi-porous.

In his portrayal of French POWs circa 1917, based on his own wartime memories and those of a French fighter pilot, Renoir certainly nails much of what's absurd in military endeavour: the propaganda, bureaucracy and petty tyranny. But social absurdity exercises him more, and the diagnosis isn't rosy or simple. Even the much commented-upon rapport between aristocrats de Boieldieu (Pierre Fresnay) and his Junker gaoler von Rauffenstein (Erich von Stroheim), frequenters of the same derbies and, it's hinted, the same woman, is full of cracks: their talk flickers between French and English, their different social tolerances are illustrated at least three times, and in the end one shoots the other.

Renoir lets hardly a scene go by without presenting a difference of outlook, from the low-key joshing an ex-teacher gets for his love of Pindar to the bitter exchange of insults by salt-of-the-earth Lieutenant Maréchal (Jean Gabin) and generous Jew Rosenthal (Marcel Dalio) – perhaps the film's most memorable scene. But Renoir's social tableau is so rich, and his *mise en scène* so light and fluid, it's easy to miss what's under your nose; blatant didacticism – as when a token black soldier is ignored by cellmates as he tries to show them a painting he's finished, 'Justice Pursuing Crime' – is rare. *La Grande Illusion* is the work of a realist, not an idealist, and its 'great illusion' is life itself.

THE DISC

Criterion's DVD presents the film in a restored digital transfer, created from the recently rediscovered camera negative. Extras include an audio essay by film historian Peter Cowie; Renoir's 1956-filmed foreword in which he discusses the film and his own war experiences; a radio excerpt in which Renoir and von Stroheim accept *La Grande Illusion*'s Best Foreign Film prize at the 1938 New York Film Critics Awards; a restoration demonstration; and a well-equipped booklet, with Renoir's 'letter to the projectionist', an essay on Renoir by von Stroheim, and another about the film's title. (SIMON CROPPER)

Grave of the Fireflies

(Japan, 1988)
Special Edition / Collector's Edition

Director: Isao Takahata
Label: Optimum Asia (UK) /
Central Park Media (USA)
Region: 2 (PAL) / 1 (NTSC)
Discs: 2

THE FILM

Anime has a strong sub-genre of worthy educational movies about World War
II, many made for television or as part of local-history exhibits, ranging from
the twee and dreary to the superlative. But *Grave of the Fireflies* is in a class
all of its own, outshining even the Hiroshima anime *Barefoot Gen* by cutting
between two children's harrowing last days in post-surrender, famine-struck
Japan, and their haunting of the modern world, in which their ghosts stare
entreatingly at oblivious commuters.

Brother and sister Seita and Setsuko are left orphaned and homeless by the
firebombing of Kobe. Traumatised by the sudden end of their childhood, they
struggle and fail to survive, waiting for adult intervention that never comes.
Studio Ghibli co-founder Takahata's adaptation of Akiyuki Nosaka's semi-
autobiographical novel chronicles their slow decline in an uncaring and
preoccupied world, in one of Japanese animation's few unquestionable masterpieces.

Takahata's movie is a terrifying, quiet apocalypse, the mirror image of the
fun-loving pastorals of Hayao Miyazaki's *My Neighbour Totoro*, with which it
shared a double bill on its original release. Children's games in the countryside are constantly shadowed by the spectres of starvation and disease – a fate
the audience has already seen, since the entire story is told in flashback from
the moment that the lone, emaciated Seita starves to death in a railway station,
breathing his last while preoccupied travellers step around him.

THE DISCS

Optimum's two-disc UK release is a straight port of the 2002 Central Park
Media R1 Collector's Edition, painstakingly remastered, with a digital noise
clean-up and decent extras. Ghibli discs currently lack commentary tracks –
the main contributors have better things to do, and the studio is reluctant to
give rhetorical weight to third-party punditry by allowing it to accompany a
film in real time. Instead, as with other recent DVDs of Ghibli releases, the
spare space on the main disc is occupied by shot-by-shot storyboards, running
alongside the film, viewable with the Angle Change button. A bonus disc
contains author and director interviews, an introduction from Roger Ebert,
real-world locations and a Historical Perspective featurette that deftly places
events in context. Online bargain hunters should beware the 1998 bare-bones
R1 release, also from Central Park Media, many copies of which have entered
the second-hand market as Ghibli fans upgrade to the two-disc set. (JONATHAN
CLEMENTS)

Grease

(USA, 1978) Collector's Edition

Director: Randal Kleiser
Label: Paramount (all territories)
Region: Any
Discs: 1 (USA) / 2 (elsewhere)

THE FILM

1950s High School America has been made over many times for the big screen. As a subject, it's a sure-fire attractor of baby-boomer bucks, but there's often a genuine appeal to go alongside the nakedly nostalgic commercial grab. Of this mini-genre, taking in flicks as diverse as *The Last Picture Show*, *Back to the Future* and *Diner*, 1978's *Grease* is perhaps the most straightforward celebration of America's last era of innocence.

Adapted from a slightly earthier stageplay, *Grease*'s showcase of the world's oldest teenagers singing the decade's catchiest showtunes (by Jim Jacobs and Warren Casey) continues to hold uncanny appeal for successive generations who wouldn't know Cold War paranoia if you dropped the big one on them. In a plot kept simple to hang the dance routines and black leather jackets on, John Travolta and Olivia Newton John's on–off relationship plays out against a box-ticking backdrop of James Dean stereotypes – the stageplay even featured a reference to Sal Mineo, excised when he was killed while the film was in production – but spun with sufficient wit, good intentions and self-awareness to make the corn part of the charm. We can even overlook the chauvinist fantasy ending, or choose to see it as an early example of female empowerment, should you buy the whole Girl Power thing.

THE DISC(S)

After a derisory twenty-fifth anniversary release in 2002, Paramount have gone to town with the 2006 two-disc Collector's Edition, otherwise known (in the USA) as the bumper single-disc Rockin' Rydell Edition – early pressings of which packed a mini T-bird leather jacket so you can dress the gerbil like Danny Zucco. Leathered or not, the discs themselves include a stack of featurettes including a making-of and a pointless but entertaining doc about '50s car and soda shops, deleted scenes (in black and white), photo galleries, and interviews from the release party of the original DVD, which includes the cast reuniting for a quick burst of 'Summer Nights' and 'You're The One That I Want'. There's also a commentary track by director Kleiser, in which we learn about product displacement in the soda fountain (Coca-Cola ads had to be obscured because of a deal with Pepsi) and Travolta's good side (his left), while the high point for many will be the karaoke-style subtitles so you can sing along, girl v boy, to your heart's content. The picture has also received a much-needed touch-up, and the remixed Dolby 5.1 sound is just what your Kenickie-obsessed doctor ordered. (PETER WATTS)

The Green Ray

(France, 1986)

Director: Eric Rohmer
Label: Arrow (UK)
Region: 2 (PAL)
Discs: 1

ORIGINAL TITLE: *Le Rayon Vert*

THE FILM

Now well into its fifth decade, Eric Rohmer's richly consistent body of work stands as a testament to the complexity of human desires and the eternal tug-of-war between the head and the heart. This mid-period masterpiece, part of the 'Comedies and Proverbs' cycle, is entirely representative of his strengths – the beguiling simplicity of its tale belying the subtle sophistication of its methods.

Parisian secretary Delphine (Marie Rivière), single since breaking up with her fiancé two years ago, finds herself at a sudden loose end when a friend cancels their summer vacation. Desperate to escape the capital over the summer, she has several abortive attempts at holidaying – firstly with friends in Cherbourg, and then alone in the Alps and at Biarritz – hoping to find true love, but suspicious of men and fiercely self-critical of her own ability to form relationships. With her fragile, quivering soul hiding behind a brittle carapace, Delphine is a quintessential Rohmer heroine – her attempts to open herself to experience repeatedly undermined by an earnest over-intellectualising of her predicament.

Rohmer's unapologetically intimate canvas, the naturalistic performances of his actors and his precise attention to details of time and place make this drama of the heart as engaging as any other in his oeuvre. His long takes compel an audience to 'read' his characters not only through their lengthy conversations but also through the often more telling nuances of glance and gesture. The film's beating pulse can be felt most deeply in three wordless sequences in which Delphine finds herself profoundly alone in an apparently indifferent natural landscape, culminating in her visiting Biarritz's 'Cavern of Love' only to find it flooded by the sea. As ever, though, Rohmer proves generous to his characters, and a series of green leitmotifs arrayed through the film, culminating in an anxious wait for a glimpse of the titular 'green ray' itself – at once a natural sunset phenomenon, and a literary conceit from Jules Verne signifying the revelation of self-knowledge – hints at a gentle breeze of supernatural providence steering his lovelorn heroine towards a safe harbour.

THE DISC

The picture quality on the Arrow disc is adequate if not outstanding, though that's primarily due to the limitations of the original 16mm shooting stock. Along with a trailer, the disc also includes a short radio interview from the reclusive Rohmer in which he discusses his approach to music and colour in the film. The DVD is also available in Arrow's eight-film 'Eric Rohmer Collection'. Avoid the poor R1 Fox Lorber version, retitled 'Summer'. (ANDY RICHARDS)

Gremlins & Gremlins 2: The New Batch

(USA, 1984) Special Edition/(USA, 1990)

Director: Joe Dante
Label: Warners (USA)
Region: 1 (NTSC)
Discs: 2

THE FILMS

Treading a fine line between comedy and horror, *Gremlins* was a product of some of Hollywood's most fertile minds. Chief among them was gleefully subversive director Joe Dante, who, aided by canny screenwriter Chris Columbus, uses the film's opening act to introduce us to one of those small-town idylls beloved by executive producer Steven Spielberg, before spending the rest of the movie resolutely trashing the whole enterprise via some of the '80s' most malevolent rubber monsters. The catalyst is Gizmo, a cute and cuddly creature called a mogwai, given to young dreamer Billy (Zach Galligan) as a Christmas present. Gizmo comes with a set of rules, the satisfyingly methodical breaking of which has unseasonably hellish consequences as Gizmo spawns siblings that aren't so much cute and cuddly as downright evil.

Thanks to Spielberg's gift for storytelling and Dante's for anarchy, the film zips along, mixing black comedy and classic horror with broad social satire, cinematic references and masochistic slapstick. It was such a success Warners asked for more, but 1990's *Gremlins 2: The New Batch* may not have been what they had in mind. On the DVD's excellent accompanying commentary, Dante explains that the studio were so desperate for a hit they gave him carte blanche: the stupendously silly result announces its intent from the off, with a truncated pre-credits Daffy Duck/Bugs Bunny routine, written and directed by Chuck Jones. This is *Gremlins* by way of Loony Tunes.

The action is moved to a high-tech tower block in New York, where the plot of the first film merrily repeats itself, only with less of the story and more of the anarchy. This could feature cinema's only Brechtian gag involving Hulk Hogan (an Easter egg on the DVD allows you to see an alternate version of this scene featuring John Wayne); it's certainly the first to reference both *Rambo III* and Susan Sontag and to end with a roomful of mutated monsters singing Sinatra and paying homage to Busby Berkeley.

THE DISCS

The US double-set offers the Special Edition of *Gremlins* where the UK *Gremlins Collection* bundles the plain old extras-free version. Though not the last word in SEs, the sound and image are remastered to some effect, and Dante provides two ticklish commentary tracks with his actors, producer and gremlin designer. Even more so on his *G2* commentary, Dante is in his element, highlighting many of the blink-or-you'll-miss-'em visual gags and offering information, wisecracks, technical knowledge and self-deprecation throughout. The second disc also features a short 'on location' documentary (predictably 'hijacked' by gremlins) and a solid 20 minutes of deleted footage, mostly jokes, that includes the entire Chuck Jones pre-credits cartoon sequence shortened for release after it confused audiences at test screenings. (PETER WATTS)

Groundhog Day

(USA, 1993)
Collector's Edition/Special Edition

Director: Harold Ramis
Label: Sony (all territories)
Region: Any
Discs: 1

THE FILM

Probably the only romantic comedy to embrace Buddhist philosophy (and to make a film's repetitiveness into its main selling point), *Groundhog Day* makes full use of a simple conceit to offer humour and morality in equal measure. Bill Murray stars as Phil, a heroically misanthropic weatherman forced to the dismal one-horse town of Punxsutawney, Philadelphia on a freezing February morning, to see whether the local groundhog (a chipmunk) will emerge from his annual hibernation. If he does, and sees his shadow, local tradition proclaims that winter will carry on for another six weeks. Murray, accompanied by producer Rita (Andie McDowell) and cameraman Larry (Chris Elliott), has a hatred of Punxsutawney that borders on the pathological, so imagine his horror when he awakes the next morning to find the previous day repeating itself in its entirety — the same song on the alarm clock, the same conversation with the same person in the same street, the same groundhog, the same day. He's caught in a temporal loop, doomed to follow the same experience day after day, his actions having no consequence or repercussion.

At first he reacts with despair, embracing self-destruction, gorging on food, drink, violence and sex. Next he turns to self-improvement, then charity and generosity, and finally self-sacrifice, but all to no avail: whatever he does, whoever he helps (or doesn't), he wakes up on 2 February. When salvation eventually arrives, its shape won't surprise anybody familiar with romantic fiction, but the message is as appealing as the medium is clever.

THE DISC

The main draw is director Ramis' witty and informative, if somewhat sparse, commentary. Back-up comes in the form of a rudimentary 30-minute doc called 'The Weight of Time', which attempts to balance a thought-provoking examination of time and existence with trivia about the making of the film. There are also cast and crew filmographies. While the visual transfer isn't perfect — there are a few blemishes — sound quality is excellent, with the film making surprisingly good use of the Dolby Digital 5.1 track. A satisfyingly straightforward package (despite the 'special' tag). The R1 version also offers DTS sound. (PETER WATTS)

La Haine

(France, 1995)

Director: Mathieu Kassovitz
Label: Criterion Collection (USA)
Region: 1 (NTSC)
Discs: 2

THE FILM

Some liken Mathieu Kassovitz's volatile urban drama to *Do the Right Thing*, but Spike Lee's film had an even-handedness to it; *La Haine* is an anti-police tract, a clenched fist. The title means 'hatred' or, in the tough urban vernacular, anguished rage – always in the air in the multi-ethnic ghetto where the action unfolds. The three main characters – gunned-up Jewish skinhead Vinz, black boxer Hubert and North African wisecracker Saïd – lead dead-end lives: no jobs, no girls, few family ties. Vinz has found a revolver and wants to avenge the shooting of a friend by police, and as the hours tick by the tension mounts . . .

Fuelled by Kassovitz's own anger after the killing of a North African teenager in police custody, and as powerful in its picture of inarticulate aggression as Scorsese, clearly a reference (Vinz does *Taxi Driver* to the bathroom mirror), *La Haine* won the Director's Prize at Cannes in 1995. Kassovitz was 26, it was only his second feature and the timing was perfect: it was a media sensation, and little wonder. Though *La Haine*'s message is unsophisticated and pessimistic, it crackles with energy and panache, and as a wake-up blast for France's complacent middle class, its aim could not have been better.

THE DISCS

You can barely drive a knife between this Criterion edition and Optimum's three-disc R2 Ultimate Edition, both prepared in the wake of the pan-France riots of November 2005, which spotlit how little had changed in the decade since the film's release. Both have new Kassovitz commentary tracks (testaments to the director's continued combination of razor-sharp instinct, swagger and simplistic thinking). Both include the 90-minute Canal Plus documentary '*La Haine* – Ten Years On', made from interviews with everyone from the actors and director to the press attaché, and afix a selection of on-set and audition footage, and colour-timed rough cuts, before the film's conversion to black and white. Both carry new English subtitles that don't translate 'Asterix' as 'Snoopy'(!). Optimum's offers liner notes by Keith Reader (reprinted from *Sight & Sound*), Criterion's by Ginette Vincendeau; both carry the text of Kassovitz's 2005 war of letters with then minister of the interior, now French president, Nicolas Sarkozy.

Criterion's visuals are marginally sharper, however, and the set also carries a sharp 15-minute introduction by Jodie Foster, as well as a compelling round-table featurette with sociologists Sophie Body-Gendrot, Jeffrey Fagan and William Kornblum, comparing *banlieu* resentments in France and the USA. Optimum's third disc, a CD, instead offers you the film's soundtrack. (SIMON CROPPER)

Hairspray

(USA, 1988)

Director: John Waters
Label: New Line Home Video (USA)
Region: 1 (NTSC)
Discs: 1

THE FILM

As if we ever needed more proof of what a paradoxical, messed-up country America is, consider the career of John Waters. His first two decades as a film-maker produced some of the sickest, most obscenely funny exercises in bad taste ever to grace a cinema screen, earning him the well-deserved title the Pope of Trash. With his regular Baltimore-based ensemble fronted by the late, great, inimitable drag queen Divine, Waters catalogued just about every conceivable affront to good taste. From interspecies coprophagy (Divine eating poodle shit in *Pink Flamingos*) to self-rape (Divine again, in *Female Trouble*, playing both male and female roles), Waters and friends did, and filmed, it all.

Long-term filthophiles were stunned when the relatively family-friendly *Hairspray* popped out in 1988, but it doesn't take long to realise that it's bona fide Waters, and a classic. Regular cast members Divine, Mink Stole and Mary Vivian Pearce are all here, aided and abetted by Ricki Lake, Sonny Bono and Debbie Harry, amongst others. Also maintained is the no-holds-barred social satire – this time turning on some of those favourite American preoccupations, weight, race, fame and rock 'n' roll. We're also treated to several moments of classic gonzo Waters, though now the taste is probably poor-to-questionable, rather than simply bad.

Stretch marks and all, *Hairspray* is a near-faultless piece of all-singing, all-dancing, good-time rock 'n' roll entertainment, currently conquering the world as a sanitised stage musical. Who would have believed it!?

THE DISC

The songs sound great in either Dolby 5.1 or 2.0 Surround, while the campy colours look mighty fine in 1.85:1 widescreen. New Line's Region 1 disc has a commentary by John Waters and Ricki Lake lacking on the UK disc, so seek that one out if you can. There's a lot of history here, not least the tragic death of Divine shortly before the film's release, and Ricki Lake's subsequent rise to superstardom as an American TV talk-show host (though only after losing some weight). (MARK PILKINGTON)

Hannah and Her Sisters

(USA, 1986)

Director: Woody Allen
Label: MGM (USA/UK)
Region: Any
Discs: 1

THE FILM

More than being Woody Allen's best movie, *Hannah and Her Sisters* ranks as the eminent Chekhovian comedy-drama of the American cinema, and makes a serious run at being the best American film of its decade. It's also funnier than all get-out, full of jokes that are rooted in particular voices and situations, rather than one-liners from Allen's notepad of good ideas. As if this all weren't enough, the movie is admirably wise, willing to follow its characters through successes as well as mistakes without hustling to flag which is which.

Working within an autumnal palette and abetted by modest but incisive camerawork – nowhere better than in the muted emotional climax of a lunch shared by Hannah and her sisters – Allen finds the kind of emotional centre that eluded him in most of his subsequent films, but which, to be fair, eludes many filmmakers through their entire careers. Family and marital relationships are placed under pressure but also valued for their resilience, and the typical obsession with mortality actually serves as a credible context for the follies, gambles, longings and comforts that define the middle of life. Diane Wiest and Barbara Hershey are miraculous, but the entire cast shares credit for this pinnacle.

THE DISC

As always with Allen films, and as usual for MGM releases, the movie stands virtually alone on DVD. Granted, the trailer reminds us how comfortable studios felt in 1986 to offer the public a simple taste of a movie's cast and tone, without trotting out the full buffet of plot points. Perhaps the chance to watch the film dubbed in French will gratify Woody's own Europhilia, though it's doubtful whether 'On a besoin de sperme' really works as a punch-line.

Otherwise, *Hannah* refuses any supplementary features, but Allen fans should probably resist our urge to grouse about this, and to think long and hard about how pleasurable or sincere an Allen commentary track would likely manage to be. Instead, sate yourself with insider challenges like spotting the Richard Jenkins and Julia Louis-Dreyfus cameos, and savour the memory of when Allen's films were sufficiently strong, confident, and layered as not to require any outside supports. (NICK DAVIS)

Happiness of the Katakuris

(Japan, 2001)

Director: Takashi Miike
Label: Tartan Video (UK) / Chimera (USA)
Region: 0 (PAL) / 1 (NTSC)
Discs: 1

THE FILM

Since bursting his way into Western consciousness with the shocking *Audition*, Takashi Miike has proven himself one of the world's most versatile and controversial filmmakers. From low-key character pieces like *Rainy Dog* to the outrageous violence of *Ichii the Killer*, Miike's range as a director would seem to know no boundaries. He also habitually makes around four films a year, not all of which make it to the West, so it's difficult to keep up with his oeuvre, let alone know where to start watching.

No one film is truly representative of Miike, but *Katakuris* is perhaps his most immediately accessible and consistently entertaining. A musical comedy about a family who set up a motel in the remote Japanese countryside, ultimately resorting to murder to find the peace and happiness that they crave, it presents Miike at his warmest, and most frenetic. From its surreal claymation opening sequence, through a number of wild J-pop song-and-dance numbers (including a *Thriller*-style zombie boogie), the film is by turns sharp, goofy, funny and elaborately outrageous.

While much of the humour refers to Japanese pop culture – for example, the casting of well-loved film, TV and music stars in self-parodying roles – there's a persistent air of joyous delirium, with the cast breaking out into elaborate song and dance routines at the drop of a hat. You'd have to be dead not to enjoy it.

THE DISC

Presented in anamorphic 1.77:1 and Dolby 5.1, the DVD looks and sounds as crazy as a family of singing murderers trapped inside a shiny plastic disc. Miike provides an audio commentary and an interview, which serve as a good introduction to the director and his work. First-timers will no doubt be startled by the speed with which Miike works (hence his prodigious output), and his benign but overwhelmingly enigmatic presence. The 30-minute making-of doc may be a little strenuous, but it gives us Westerners an insight into some of the more culture-bound gags in the film, as well as the sense of a cast and crew having a *really* good time. (MARK PILKINGTON)

Happy Together

(Hong Kong, 1997)

Director: Wong Kar-Wai
Label: Kino Video (USA)
Region: 0 (NTSC)
Discs: 1

THE FILM

Happy Together was the first Wong Kar-Wai film to deal with the reality of a relationship rather than the yearning romantic agony of unrequited love – though that reality turns out here to be another kind of cyclical self-torment. Make-up-break-up lovers Lai Yui-Fai (Tony Leung) and Ho Po-Wing (Leslie Cheung) arrive on the other side of the world – Buenos Aires – in the hope of starting over, but their co-dependence proves as mutually corrosive as ever: holed up in a shabby bedsit, Po-Wing takes a kind of delight in flaunting his extramural activities while Yui-Fai struggles to break his compulsion through the hard labour of low-paid work and a friendship with a young traveller (Chen Chang).

Aesthetically, the film is of a piece with Wong's earlier work, taking a fractured chronological approach that more strongly echoes the operation of memory itself than that of conventional narrative; the use of pop and tango music is extraordinary, both ironic and intensely moving, while the visuals – again created with cinematographer Christopher Doyle – offer a similarly remarkable conflation of the grubby and sublime. An uncomfortably intimate portrait of individual identity in crisis, *Happy Together* can also be read as a sly political allegory: made as Hong Kong was returned to China, its unhappy bedfellows offer an abject lesson in the painful consequences of enforced togetherness.

THE DISC

Although the disc of *Happy Together* offers only one substantial bonus feature, it's one of the best making-of films around. Made around the film's locations a year or so after the initial shoot, Kwan Pun-Leung and Amos Lee's *Buenos Aires Zero Degree* offers intriguing insights not only into Wong's working methods but into notions of exile and otherness common to both the subjects of his film and the circumstances of its production. Thanks to Wong's notoriously open-ended, improvisatory technique, his cast and crew found themselves marooned, like Lai and Ho, on the other side of the world, increasingly alienated from home. Perhaps, Leung hints, this was the director's plan all along . . . Combined with the benefits of access to the film's considerable left-over footage – the casualties of a Wong final cut are not just deleted scenes but deleted characters, plotlines, even fundamental narrative premises – this constitutes an exceptional document of how what is there can be defined by what is missing.

The film is less well served by its presentation on current DVDs. Of the two editions that include the extra doc, Kino's has consistently stronger colour than Artifical Eye's R2, except in a 14-second sequence after the opening credits, which it mistakenly renders as black and white. (AE's sound is also poorer.) (BEN WALTERS)

Harlan County, U.S.A.

(USA, 1976)

Director: Barbara Kopple
Label: Criterion Collection (USA)
Region: 1 (NTSC)
Discs: 1

THE FILM

'Fire in the hole!' a coal miner cries out in the musty, subterranean darkness of the opening image. In his thick Appalachian accent, only moments before he detonates a whole sheet of rock, a metaphor rings clearly: this movie is prepared to chip away at rough, thick walls of ideology and injustice, moving on dangerous ground toward its own explosive revelations of exploitation, intimidation and violence.

The candour and force of the film's representation of a miner's strike in eastern Kentucky remain constant through *Harlan County, U.S.A.*, and yet, only seconds later, the movie discloses its deeper and subtler strategies, the core of its character. Beneath a jaunty banjo and the high, twangy tenor of David Morris (singing a worker's hymn by Merle Travis), the spry, colourful men of Harlan County lie tummy-down on the conveyor belt that ferries them below ground. The camera and the microphone follow along, just as they follow into picket lines, courtrooms, doctor's offices, press conferences and the extraordinary organising meetings of the miners' indomitable wives.

The genius and the soulfulness of *Harlan County, U.S.A.* lie in how the film maintains and elucidates its grasp on moral principles and political axioms in moments of exuberance, comedy, fellowship, fatigue, tenderness and musical performance. These impressions, borne of the filmmakers' long and fully immersed observations, reveal the heart, the stakes and the fire of the protest, no less than when a squadron of strike-breakers pummel the camera and shoot at the film crew, no less than when a wet fragment of a worker's brain is found on the ground where he stood for his cause. A transcript, a manifesto, a songbook and occasionally an absurdist delight — witness the conversation between the policeman and the miner shooting the breeze on a Wall Street sidewalk — *Harlan County, U.S.A.* ranks not only as one of America's landmark documentaries but as of one of its essential films, of any stripe.

THE DISC

After years of unavailability on DVD, the film enjoys a resplendent and informative treatment from Criterion. Testimonies and commentaries by director Kopple, editor Nancy Baker, featured singer Hazel Dickens, filmmaker John Sayles and early champion Roger Ebert enrich our sense of this brave, difficult production. Kopple tells the story of her three-person crew, including herself, driving off the side of a mountain on their second day in Kentucky, crawling out of their totalled vehicle and walking for miles with their equipment to the first picket line. Thus did a trio of 'hippie New Yorkers' win the full trust of the initially sceptical miners, and thus did they set the tone for a film that pulls no punches and admits no obstacles in telling important truths. (NICK DAVIS)

Heat

(USA, 1995) 2-disc Special Edition

Director: Michael Mann
Label: Warners (all territories)
Region: Any
Discs: 2

THE FILM

Even in a world that includes *Sunset Boulevard* and *Chinatown*, writer-director Michael Mann's 1995 thriller *Heat* might justifiably be considered the most magnificent of all LA movies, a cinematic banquet with so many delicious courses that it's hard to know where to start. An indispensable addition to the heist genre, it's also an extraordinarily deft interweaving of doomed love stories, with violent, beautiful, unforgiving Los Angeles shining every bit as much as Al Pacino (as cop Vincent Hanna) and Robert De Niro (as his bankrobber quarry Neil McCauley).

Mann's glossy remake of his own 1989 TV-movie *LA Takedown* remains the richest expression of his fascination with police and criminal methods, and, even by his own intimidating standards, the attention to detail he invests in both Hanna's and McCauley's actions is astounding. He paints his characters' private lives and implied back-stories – the 'emotional fall-out' – with similar love, and the result is a film at least as rewarding the twentieth time around as the first. It's also ravishingly shot and heroically well-acted and, as an exercise in supercharged tension and thunderous release, the central heist and subsequent gun battle are pretty much unrivalled on film.

THE DISC

If *Heat* is, as first assistant director Michael Waxman adroitly puts it, 'like watching the six o'clock news, only amped up 100 per cent', much of its plot might, in fact, have cropped up on such a bulletin at one time or another. A tireless researcher, Mann based Neil McCauley on a real-life, high-flying criminal of the same name, who – as in the film's famous meeting between Pacino and De Niro – genuinely did share a latte with his ultimate nemesis, policeman Chuck Adamson, in an Illinois coffee-shop. The pivotal, ill-fated robbery was suggested by a dreadfully botched supermarket heist of 1964 and, for Waingrow, the psychopath whose loose tongue ruins McCauley's plans, Mann found inspiration in a criminal who ratted out a 'crew' in Chicago and was later found nailed to a shack on a north Mexican ranch.

Essentially a top-to-bottom case study of every last aspect of the film, this set includes a five-star commentary from Mann, an exhaustive, three-part making-of doc (including interviews with everyone important) and a full 11 deleted scenes. The award for Most Arresting Character Insight goes to Pacino, for suggesting that Hanna's loopy highs might be cocaine-induced. But it's Amy Brenneman, so serene as McCauley's girlfriend, who most deftly sums up *Heat*. The film concludes with Hanna and McCauley alone at last, one of them fatally wounded. And, as Brenneman says, '*That's* the love story.' (MARK MONAHAN)

Hedwig and the Angry Inch
(USA, 2001)

Director: John Cameron Mitchell
Label: New Line (USA)
Region: 1
Discs: 1

THE FILM

There are four words that should never be used when writing about the extraordinary *Hedwig and the Angry Inch*: 'rocky', 'horror', 'picture' and 'show'. Richard O'Brien's cavalcade of camp cast a long shadow on John Cameron Mitchell's film, or at least on its marketing campaign. It's a rock musical, about a drag act, with a tradition of audience participation, right? Right? The public duly stayed away.

Hedwig and the Angry Inch is its own special creation. A comparison with *Rocky Horror* would suggest tacky, kitschy, (im)pure fun. While *Hedwig* certainly has its moments of trashy euphoria – for instance, the exhilarating climax of 'Wig in a Box', when a Winnebago wall falls away to reveal Hedwig and the Angry Inch (the band) rocking the entire trailer park – it is also a film suffused with a quality entirely lacking in the earlier movie: pain. Not simply the physical pain of Hedwig's botched sex-change operation, but Hedwig's pain at being alive and jilted; jilted by her husband Luther and subsequently by the public, and jilted by Tommy Gnosis (Michael Pitt), who leaves her and becomes a huge star playing Hedwig's songs. The film's ambiguous ending hints that only one outcome can deliver Hedwig from her pain, but that redemption will mean setting aside the wigs and the make-up that have always been her salvation.

Two further qualities mark *Hedwig* out. Stephen Trask's indie-rock score is superb, and has spawned an album of cover versions featuring many of the artists who inspired the songs in the first place: Sleater-Kinney, The Breeders, Rufus Wainwright, Fred Schneider of the B-52s. And, quite apart from writing the script and directing the film, John Cameron Mitchell's performance as Hedwig is astonishing – funny, bewitching and heartbreaking. What this all adds up to is a musical which feels triumphantly modern, both in its setting and in its liberated attitude to gender and sexuality – in other words, no 'Time Warp' required.

THE DISC

Long story short, long story short . . . *Hedwig and the Angry Inch* is a musical that grows in stature with every viewing; the anamorphic widescreen transfer and options of 5.1 or stereo sound only enhance a movie which is perfect for DVD. The commentary by Mitchell and director of photography Frank DeMarco is thoroughly excellent – Mitchell sounds as energised as ever by a project on which he has worked for years. There is a decent batch of deleted scenes and an option to allow the devotee to access their favourite songs. Best of all, the accompanying documentary is substantial and enlightening, covering both the original stage production and the shooting of the film. Fabulous stuff, in all senses. (ANDY MILLER)

Hellraiser Puzzle Box

(UK, 1987/1988; USA, 1992)

Directors: Listed below
Label: Anchor Bay (UK)
Region: 2 (PAL)
Discs: 4

DIRECTORS: Clive Barker, Tony Randel, Anthony Hickox

THE FILMS

Hellraiser is an old-fashioned, deadly serious horror film, a retelling of *Faust* that replaces knowledge with 'pleasure', as dished out by the artistically mutilated Pinhead (Doug Bradley), a mixture of ghost, devil and grim reaper. When the decadent Frank (Sean Chapman) summons the demonic Cenobites, he is dragged into a cruel hell, which he can only escape if his old lover Julia (Clare Higgins) can collect enough blood to bring him back. It's a ghoulishly accomplished film about desperation and desire, disturbing and extremely grisly, that combines the traditions of horror and ghost stories with a subtext of its own.

Clive Barker makes a strong directorial debut, adapting his own novella. He plays with ideas of indulgence and sado-masochism, but the film is really a brilliant exercise in dread. The sense of claustrophobic fear mounts as Barker skilfully threatens to reintroduce his depraved Cenobites, while Higgins and Andrew Robinson, as Julia's oblivious husband Larry, help make an excellently disturbed *ménage à trois*.

The trilogy moves from horror to gory fantasy in *Hellraiser II: Hellbound*, a brave, flawed attempt to bring some originality to the task of a sequel that remains repellently inventive until its rather formulaic ending. Higgins is refined and sinister, and Kenneth Cranham makes a splendidly deranged psychiatrist, at once coldly murderous and oddly sympathetic in his need to know more.

Despite a promising beginning and decent characters, *Hellraiser III: Hell on Earth* plays to a teenage market and lacks depth. There are some moments of quality, but the film ends firmly in slasher territory.

THE DISCS

The three films come boxed in their own replica of the Configuration that opens the path to Hell. Impressive? Tacky? An eccentric English affability pervades the behind-the-scenes extras for *Hellraiser*: less so for *Hellraiser II*, whose commentary reveals how the original's success was beginning to be exploited. In the *Hell on Earth* extras, one gets the impression that the cast and crew all struggle not to use the phrase 'sold out'. An extra disc contains two short films by Barker, both arty and unrewarding.

It's intriguing to compare Barker and Bradley in these extras. Although they were once part of the same avant-garde troupe, Barker has clearly come to resent this concentration on his early work, while Bradley remains philosophical about the grotesque role that pays his wages. All Barker's commentaries are witty and shrewd, though, and it's intriguing to watch him chart the progress not just of his characters, but of the money-making archetype that Pinhead has become. (TOBY FROST)

Herzog Kinski (aka Werner Herzog Box Set 1)

(West Germany/Germany, 1972–99)

Directors: Werner Herzog
Label: Anchor Bay (all territories)
Region: 2 (PAL) / 1 (NTSC)
Discs: 6

THE FILMS

The New German Cinema dominated the art-house cinema of the '70s much as the French New Wave had done in the '60s, and Werner Herzog was at once its figurehead and its odd man out. Before starring in Herzog's conquistador adventure *Aguirre, the Wrath of God* (1972), Klaus Kinski was the wild-eyed villain of a hundred spaghetti westerns. *Aguirre* and their four subsequent collaborations would put them in the Godard–Karina league, the psychological fall-out from this most volatile of director–actor relationships being picked over in Herzog's documentary *My Best Fiend* (1999), made some years after Kinski's early death.

Each of their films takes place, figuratively and often literally, somewhere in the contested interzone between sanity and madness, culture and barbarism. Kinski, as the jungle colonist in *Aguirre* and *Fitzcarraldo*, acts out his devotion to the European ideal with a fervour that threatens to corrupt its very foundations – or reveal their original corruption. By contrast with his subjects' passionate involvement, Herzog's camera affects a pitiless impartiality towards these human-sized conflicts, the director's vision characterised by the artist-critic Manny Farber as 'a droll, macabre, romantic, zestful wrathfulness at God's work'. Shooting guerrilla-style on hostile terrain, Herzog achieved a precarious grandeur, his no-tech visual effects – rats overrunning a misty market town in *Nosferatu* (1979), a riverboat being dragged over a Peruvian mountain ridge in *Fitzcarraldo* (1982) – appearing paradoxically *un*real.

THE DISCS

The Herzog legend, in which shooting conditions on his films paralleled the fictions being enacted, is duly printed, his commentaries demonstrating little genuine desire to play down the impression of a three-way mind-meld of the 'visionary' Herzog, the 'madman' Kinski, and their films' similarly overreaching protagonists. For all he claims that 'the only thing that counted was what you would see on the screen', there's no doubt that this long-cultivated legend dies hard. The *Fitzcarraldo* shoot, already the subject of Les Blank's documentary *Burden of Dreams* (1982), is just as interesting as the film itself (if not more so), and Herzog's commentary takes in malaria, self-administered amputation, and war – such stories are, after all, an integral part of Herzog's auteur status. An occasional actor himself, it's hard not to hear Herzog's commentaries as well-prepared performances, and in substance and commitment they're a world away from the contract-fillers found on the vast majority of films. The box set as a whole is a welcome novelty among the minimal packages typical of foreign-language DVDs. (HENRY K MILLER)

High Art
(USA, 1998)

Director: Lisa Cholodenko
Label: Universal (USA)
Region: 1 (NTSC)
Discs: 1

THE FILM

The art and life of cult photographer Nan Goldin haunt Cholodenko's alluring debut film. Like Goldin's portraits of friends and lovers in her cluttered, seedily glam Bowery pad, the film glows with chemical-bright colours. And like Goldin's most famous work, it's a ballad of sexual dependency.

High Art focuses on Syd (Radha Mitchell), a bright-but-naïve assistant editor on a trendy photo mag. Her head is turned by reclusive snapper Lucy Berliner (a fierce, knotty turn by former bratpacker Ally Sheedy), who lives in the boho loft upstairs.

The women's mutual professional and personal seduction is complicated by Lucy's addiction to heroin and to her lover Greta (Patricia Clarkson), a washed-up Fassbinder actress who spends her days lounging about in her undies and catnapping in restaurants.

Cholodenko builds her story from careful looks, glances, glassy stares and tantalising glimpses. The film has been dismissed by some as Cassavetes-lite and too chic for its own good, but the emotional crosscurrents between Lucy and her lovers make it more than an artful snapshot of the beautiful and the fated.

Clarkson's Greta, wriggling her snaky body on a rumpled bed, is a magnificently out-to-lunch creation, and yet her final plea for Lucy to stay is so excruciatingly intimate it seems almost wrong to be listening in. Mitchell and Sheedy, meanwhile, generate a nervy chemistry. We feel the insistent tug of attraction between them within the movie's wider tangle of infatuation, ambition and art snobbery. When Syd, in bed with Lucy, says: 'You look so serious', the latter's deadpan reply is: 'I'm kinda hot. That's kinda serious.' Sheedy, and the tinglingly sexy camerawork and lighting, make us believe it. The ending, with its nod to *All About Eve*, is peremptory, and there's a misjudged cameo by Tammy Grimes, but *High Art*'s hothouse languor is hard to resist.

THE DISCS

This transfer has an eyedrop clarity. The disc comes with a dumbed-down trailer that whitewashes *High Art*'s lesbian theme, but the writer-director's commentary on her low-budget movie is a must for indie film buffs.

Cholodenko cast actors and non-actors (Anh Duong, a painter and ex-model with a Modigliani face, plays Syd's snot of a boss), and a few of the scenes were improvised. The oppressive temperature of the shoot (in a Brooklyn loft during a heatwave) helps explain Syd's sweaty upper lip and the film's woozy, drenched mood. All the pictures on Lucy's walls were donated by photographers, including one from Goldin. Cholodenko also tells how Sheedy chased after the part of Lucy, a role she identified with strongly, and the one she should be remembered for. (MAXIE SZALWINSKA)

The Hired Hand

(USA, 1971) Collector's Edition

Director: Peter Fonda
Label: Tartan Video (PAL)
Region: 2
Discs: 2

THE FILM

'Peter Fonda is riding again, moving fast, living hard' runs the publicity material for *The Hired Hand*, hoping to exploit the incredible success of *Easy Rider*. It must be one of the more misleading advertising campaigns, since this slow-paced, intelligent western is at its best in the intimate domestic scenes between Harry (Fonda) and Hannah (Verna Bloom), the wife he abandoned for a life on the trail seven years earlier.

The emotional core of the film, she is no Penelope. When Harry decides that 'it's just a waste living this way', and returns home with long-time partner Arch (Warren Oates), Hannah takes them on as hired hands and tells them to sleep in the barn. We later learn that several previous hired hands have been invited into her bed, before being dismissed when they thought this meant they could dominate her life. Hannah's unflinching, unapologetic explanation of this choice is superbly portrayed by Bloom, as is her later vulnerability when Harry leaves her for the final time.

This is a film by debutants, including Fonda, directing for the first time, composer Bruce Langhorne and set designer Lawrence G Paull (*Blade Runner*). Sometimes the result is clumsy, as in the overuse of dissolves and still frames. But this is compensated for by innovative and beautiful cinematography, well exhibited in this luxuriously restored version. Consider the opening shot – a tilt down from the sun to a sparkling Rio Grande. Or the closing one – an extravagant 150-second shot of Arch's return alone, panning from the overwhelmed Hannah to Arch as he opens the barn door, taking up his place as the latest hired hand.

THE DISCS

A new documentary, 'The Return of the Hired Hand', is the principal attraction of the extras disc. Bloom emphasises the richness of her role compared to other female characters, while many cast and crew members remember the happiness of the shoot (aided by the availability of marijuana). But perhaps of most interest is the obvious importance of Fonda's relationship with his father in his filmmaking career. The main references he cites are two of Henry's classic westerns, *My Darling Clementine* and *The Ox-Bow Incident*, and he claims that he wanted to replicate the look of the former in colour. Otherwise, there are the usual trailers and (rightly) deleted scenes, plus a rambling audio commentary by Fonda. The transfer is anamorphic and there are alternative DTS, Dolby 5.1 and 2.0 Stereo soundtracks. (JOE PERKINS)

Hiroshima Mon Amour

(France/Japan, 1959)

Director: Alain Resnais
Label: Criterion Collection (USA)
Region: 1 (NTSC)
Discs: 1

THE FILM

Radiating with astonishing intensity, *Hiroshima Mon Amour* is a swooningly romantic meditation on memory and the fear of forgetting the past. At first glance, it's the story of a love affair several years after the atomic bomb brought WWII to its conclusion. Emmanuelle Riva, in her film debut, is utterly arresting as a French actress who recalls a doomed relationship she had many years earlier and realises she can't live without a mysterious Japanese architect she meets.

Shot with elegant precision by Takahashi Michio and Sacha Vierny, and based on a screenplay by Marguerite Duras, Resnais' film is also an exquisite essay about the passage of time and the decomposition of memory. It saw Resnais pioneer the use of flash cuts and voice-over narration not only to drive the narrative but also to act as an emotional counterweight – a technique adopted by many later directors, among them Terrence Malick.

Watch the film soon after any Malick movie, American critic Matt Zoller Seitz has written, and 'you'll sense a direct evolution from there to here, a line that brings us through the French New Wave and into 1960s European art cinema and their English and American equivalents'. Indeed, *Hiroshima Mon Amour* is a modernist masterpiece, its contribution to world cinema immeasurable.

THE DISC

Film historian Peter Cowie offers a restlessly informative, occasionally scene-specific commentary. A third soundtrack option removes the players' voice-overs and allows you to focus on Georges Delerue and Giovanni Fusco's modernist score.

There are two interviews with Resnais: a sphinx-like 1961 TV encounter discussing his early career, and an audio-only interview from 1980 about *Hiroshima Mon Amour*'s making. There are two with Emmanuelle Riva, too; the 2003 sit-down, recorded for this disc, is a useful reminiscence, but most disarming is the beautiful alfresco profile she offers from the film's premiere at Cannes. You also get eight minutes' worth of Marguerite Duras' 'screenplay annotations', read over the relevant film scenes, and a hefty booklet with a Kent Jones introduction, the text of a 1959 *Cahiers du Cinéma* critics' confab on the film involving the likes of Rohmer, Rivette and Godard, and Duras' pen portraits of the film's two protagonists. There's a visible scratch down the film's luscious opening sequence of dissolving bodies; otherwise, this looks like another definitive edition from Criterion. (JAMES CLASPER)

Histoire(s) du Cinéma

(France, 1989–1998)

Director: Jean-Luc Godard
Label: Gaumont (France)
Region: 0 (PAL)
Discs: 4

THE FILMS

Histoire(s) du Cinéma is an extraordinary series of eight video films that explore Godard's personal approach to the history of cinema. Through a collage of clips, paintings, photographs, music and interviews, the filmmaker ponders cinema's present, past and missed opportunities. Weaving fleeting fragments into a dense tapestry of cultural references, the works are composed around the flow and rhythm of music rather than a conventional narrative of a history. Like dreams, however, the strange logic of their form is thronging with compelling visual and conceptual possibilities. Produced in a video-editing suite with experimental playfulness, the montage flickers, dissolves and superimposes images, often marking them with titles or slogans.

It may sound esoteric, but in fact the series deserves a wider audience, as an audio-visual re-imagining of the contemporary aesthetic of the 'sample', beloved of popular electronic music. The cited films may not all be familiar to younger viewers, but their range is surprisingly wide, including silent movies, cartoons, westerns and even porn alongside revered Italian neorealism and Godard's own oeuvre. For this is, above all, a personal work of memory, a life imagined through celluloid, in the way we all might do with our own patchwork of filmic experience. Discovering the diversity of cinema, and its intermingling with other arts through the prism of Godard's creative and iconoclastic mind, is a delight, a provocation and challenge. The sheer wealth of material and juxtaposition makes DVD the ideal viewing method, enabling the viewer to roam through the films freely and pause vividly on striking or mysterious images.

THE DISCS

Until recently the only commercially available edition of *Histoire(s)* was a five-disc Japanese box set from Imagica (2001): beautiful but expensive, and subtitled only in Japanese. In April 2007, Gaumont finally released this long-awaited version. The style-conscious Japanese set the bar high in the design stakes, so it's a pleasant surprise to discover an equally covetable box set from Gaumont: such an aesthetically exploratory and satisfying work deserves beautiful presentation. The question on everyone's lips on its release, however, was whether or not it would have English subtitles. The layering of texts makes subtitling challenging, so Gaumont have opted for a minimal, but crucial, translation of Godard's voice-over. This is perfectly adequate, though some inscriptions and film clips will be in French. More's the pity that the fascinating extras – two Cannes press conferences and Godard's *2 X 50 Ans de Cinéma Français* – do lack subtitles and are therefore mostly inaccessible to English-speaking audiences. Still, this is more than made up for by the stunning impact of the *Histoire(s)* films themselves. (ISABELLE McNEILL)

The Hitcher

(USA, 1986) Special Edition

Director: Robert Harmon
Label: Momentum (UK)
Region: 2 (PAL)
Discs: 2

THE FILM

'My mother told me never to do this', jokes Jim Halsey (C Thomas Howell), offering a lift to John Ryder (Rutger Hauer) one stormy night on a lonely desert highway. Five minutes later – with the stranger holding a knife to his eyeball and describing what it's like to slide the blade in – he's starting to realise that mother knows best. The pair are soon embroiled in a complex game of cat-and-mouse, with the stakes building as fast as the body count. Inspired by the Doors' 'Riders on the Storm', this road/action/horror hybrid is pulp poetry of the first order – a gruelling but purifying rite-of-passage with the steely intensity of sacred ritual.

One of the keys to the film's uniquely unsettling atmosphere is the way it plays the wide open spaces of the American south-west off against the claustrophobia of its core psychodrama. In this, it is something of a companion piece to screenwriter Eric Red's other mid-'80s cult classic *Near Dark* (directed by Kathryn Bigelow), another film that plays fast-and-loose with genres and takes its hero for a feverish walk on the wild side. But if Red wins *auteurist* kudos, then first-time feature director Harmon deserves credit for keeping proceedings razor-taut, orchestrating the low-budget, high-octane mayhem with the same aplomb as a James Cameron or George Miller, and putting his cinematographic background to good use to give a seductive sheen to his stark visuals (perfectly complemented by Mark Isham's brooding electro-score).

Sensibly, the film never entirely rationalises its central relationship, leaving teasing suggestions that Ryder is a spectral presence or even Halsey's alter ego. As he did so memorably in *Blade Runner*, Hauer finds in his homicidal loner a disarming pathos. There are flickers of tender respect in the symbiotic bond that develops between the two men; one is forced to reach deep into himself to recover a primal resourcefulness, while the other – like Brando's Kurtz – craves release from the prison of his own monstrousness.

THE DISCS

The Momentum package is first-rate, boasting an excellent anamorphic transfer that shows off the widescreen visuals to full advantage. In addition to the trailers, filmographies and cast and crew commentaries, there's a solid making-of (clarifying, among other things, Hauer's many creative contributions to his character), screenplay samples, and two revealing shorts – Harmon's self-funded calling-card *China Lake* and Hauer's arty directorial debut *The Room*. (ANDY RICHARDS)

Hoop Dreams

(USA, 1994)

Director: Steve James
Label: Criterion Collection (USA)
Region: 1 (NTSC)
Discs: 1

THE FILM

James' landmark documentary charts the rise and fall and rise again of two contrasting black teenagers in contemporary America, united by their love of basketball. Arthur Agee Jr is a terrifically confident youngster from a troubled background. Faced with a 90-minute commute to school everyday, and a father who shows up at an inner city basketball court to score crack from his dealers while his son looks on, it's no surprise his big-match temperament should be so shaky. Agee's contemporary William Gates has the support of a loving, stable family, scholarships, and the president of Encyclopaedia Britannica herself, but he's prone to recurring injuries and a deep personal insecurity.

Made originally for public television, *Hoop Dreams'* great virtue is a patience that allows James the time to choose from over five years of material, in ways that a work originated for the cinema probably wouldn't. Playing the long game, in this instance, pays off. At any point in the film, one of the boys is on the way up, one on their way down, an often painful dichotomy that makes one marvel at the filmmakers' luckiest of breaks.

A fascinating piece of evidence in the nature-versus-nurture debate, *Hoop Dreams* also offers a document of the changing face of ghetto fashion from the mid-'80s onwards; a bizarre cameo from Spike Lee, who turns up at summer camp insisting these rookies are mere cogs in a machine; and several moments of true grace. It's there when the camera finds Gates's wife fast asleep, babe in arms, during one of the biggest matches of the season; when Agee loafs about, shooting imaginary hoops, as his mother does her hair in preparation for her community college graduation; and especially when Gates returns, alone, to his old school gym – away from all the hoopla, just a boy, a ball and a basket.

THE DISC

The difference between the UK and US DVD releases illustrates contrasting attitudes towards what is perhaps still considered, on this side of the Atlantic, merely a film about basketball. Where the Region 2 edition disappoints with only production notes and a trailer, the Region 1 disc – a product of the excellent Criterion Collection – offers two commentaries (one with the filmmakers, the other with Gates and Agee) and clips from the *Siskel & Ebert* shows that proved so instrumental in bringing *Hoop Dreams* to international prominence. (MIKE McCAHILL)

Hou Hsiao-Hsien Classic Movie Collection 1983–86

(Taiwan, 1983–86)

Director: Hou-Hsaio Hsien
Label: Sino Movie (USA)
Region: 0 (NTSC)
Discs: 4

FILM TITLES: *The Boys from Fengkuei, A Summer at Grandpa's, The Time to Live and the Time to Die, Dust in the Wind*

THE FILMS

What to do about Hou? Revered by many cineastes as one of the finest working filmmakers, he's a victim of his own exceptional aesthetic, too refined and demanding for the market. He shoots in long, composed, fluid takes, but it's his elliptical angle on story and emotion that's most unusual for audiences weaned on Western drama. Understated, episodic and immersive, it's a method whereby 'the part shows the whole'; let it embrace you and it's not difficult so much as disconcertingly easy. Hou is in fact a neorealist in the mould of Ozu and Satyajit Ray, his subject time and the ineluctibility of change, his films, meditative, spacious, richly textured expressions of memory and loss.

Perhaps we're lucky that he's represented on DVD at all, but it's best to avoid Fox Lorber's shoddy Region 1 transfers of his delicate Chinese-brothel saga *Flowers of Shanghai*, and *The Puppetmaster* and *Good Men, Good Women*, the more challenging parts of his supremely ambitious trilogy on Taiwan's 20th-century history. The modern-day *Millennium Mambo* and *Café Lumière*, as released respectively by TF1 Vidéo in France and Wellspring in the US, are better transferred, but maybe not the best introductions to the Hou project. For that, we're recommending this supposedly limited-edition (but at the time of writing quite easily obtainable) box set of his four early personal works – including *The Boys from Fengkuei* (1983), *A Summer at Grandpa's* (1984) and *Dust in the Wind* (1986) – rural reminiscences that contrast innocence and experience, the shrinking countryside and growing city, and the widening gulf between mainland China and breakaway Taiwan.

Amongst them, *The Time to Live and the Time to Die* (1985) is his near-masterpiece, a semi-autobiographical portrait of a family displaced from the mainland that's steeped in quiet humour, nostalgia and remorse. Straddling two time-frames – Ah-Hsiao as a wayward boy and a petty-delinquent youth – it's punctuated by the deaths of his unsettled parents and senile grandmother, but never turns to melodrama. As Hou charts these lives touched by the tragedy of exile, the sense of generational attrition and waste becomes all the more heartbreaking for his clear-eyed acuity.

THE DISCS

Plushly boxed with a 56-page hardcover colour booklet, sadly only in Mandarin, the discs carry no extras, but sport fairly clean, faithful transfers of all four films. Onscreen menus are also Mandarin-only (except for the subtitle selection), and there are minor hiccups in the subtitled English, but these are mere niggles. (NICK BRADSHAW)

The House of Mirth

(UK, 2000)

Director: Terence Davies
Label: Cinema Club (UK)
Region: 2 (PAL)
Discs: 1

THE FILM

Davies' adaptation of Edith Wharton's acerbic portrait of New York high society in the early 20th century is a stunning testament to just how powerful period costume drama can be in the hands of a master filmmaker and an impeccable cast. As Wharton's heroine Lily Bart, Gillian Anderson may have distanced herself from *The X-Files'* world of alien abductions and paranormal plots, but here she finds herself the victim of an intricate conspiracy no less deadly for being concealed behind a veneer of civilised decorum.

As the film opens in 1905, Lily is contemplating her options in the marriage market for which her entire upbringing has been preparing her: she is disdainful of several circling suitors, while the man she really loves, lawyer Lawrence Selden (Eric Stoltz), isn't wealthy enough to bankroll her extravagant lifestyle. This rift between her romantic aspirations and her ingrained pragmatism leaves her vulnerable to the vicious opportunism of some of her social set – particularly sleazy Gus Trenor (Dan Aykroyd, his familiar avuncularity hiding unexpected menace) and serial adulteress Bertha Dorset (a brilliantly reptilian Laura Linney). After making some crucial errors of judgement, Lily finds herself exiled to the lonely fringes of high society, where she will have to sacrifice her own moral integrity if she hopes to be rehabilitated.

As a study in the way genteel social rituals can be a front for almost inhuman cruelty, Davies' film is as icily effective as *Dangerous Liaisons*: 'My dear, the world is vile' observes one of Lily's few allies, and this society of vain nouveaux riches is certainly that. But this film never succumbs to flamboyant histrionics, and the formal restraint of its characters gives the nuances of their speech and the subtleties of their gestures tremendous significance. In his emphasis on Lily's stoic dignity in the face of impending tragedy, Davies takes his cues from the masterworks of Mizoguchi and Ophüls (particularly *Letter from an Unknown Woman*), coaxing a revelatory performance from Anderson that helps make this tragedy of wasted opportunities and misplaced trust a shattering experience.

THE DISC

This fine release features an excellent 2.35:1 transfer that does credit to the film's exquisite, painterly tableaux (derived partly from John Singer Sargent portraits). There are various production featurettes, deleted scenes, and a commentary from Davies elucidating the departures his script made from the novel and the challenges of using Scottish (predominantly Glaswegian) locations to substitute for America's East Coast. (ANDY RICHARDS)

Howards End

(UK, 1992) The Merchant Ivory Collection

Director: James Ivory
Label: Merchant Ivory/Home Vision Entertainment (USA)
Region: 1 (NTSC)
Discs: 2

THE FILM

Emotionally repressed toffs drooping around pretty places in bonnets and corsets: received wisdom about the Merchant Ivory oeuvre is well entrenched. But if anything is going to make the naysayers reconsider, it has to be this finest work from the team's most fruitful period. Merchant had a winning habit of tweaking budgets so that the limited money available ended up onscreen, which means Edwardian England looks lavish in both town and country. But it would just be toffs in pretty places were it not for the skill of screenwriter Ruth Prawer Jhabvala. Forster's 1910 novel is scalpel-sharp underneath its surface gentility, and Jhabvala ensures that this richness of both character and theme – class conflict, the possibility of absolute honesty between two people – makes it through unmolested.

Topping everything, though, is Emma Thompson's Oscar-winning turn as Margaret Schlegel, the role that this oft-underrated performer was surely born to play. Sister to Helena Bonham Carter's idealistic Helen, Thompson's Margaret is refreshingly practical in her compassion. As *A Room with a View* also showed, one of Merchant Ivory's many talents was assembling the perfect cast. Each of Forster's three conflicting worlds – bohemian Schlegels, business-minded Wilcoxes, poor but aspiring Basts – is brought to compelling life by British Equity's finest. Vanessa Redgrave reins in her customary whimsy as ailing Mrs Wilcox, while Prunella Scales, as the Schlegels' jolly Aunt Juley, makes us marvel all over again at her ability to speak without pausing for breath. Even the famously grumpy Forster would have to admit that the prose and the passion connected splendidly.

THE DISCS

Legend tells that the late Ismail Merchant could win anyone around after one of his legendary homemade curries, and there's testimony to this and other aspects of the Merchant Ivory 'family' in the new 42-minute featurette 'Building Howards End', made for this disc. Merchant (excitable, Indian) and Ivory (laconic, American) come across like a comedy double act. Bonham Carter is, as ever, outshone by her hair. Costumier Jenny Beavan and production designer Luciana Arrighi also talk shop, both here and in a separate short doc about the film's design.

Hopkins and Thompson turn up briefly on the pocket-sized original 1992 making-of, and there's also the odd but not unwelcome inclusion of a documentary from 1984, 'The Wandering Company', which spans M-I's first 20 years before their first Forster adaptation, *A Room with a View*, flung them into the limelight. Robert Emmet Long's sleeve notes are most handy, and apart from all this, the film's sound and image (a new transfer from the original interpositive) are quite radiant. (FIONA MOUNTFORD)

I ♥ Huckabees
(USA, 2004)

Director: David O Russell
Label: 20th Century Fox (UK)
Region: 2 (PAL)
Discs: 1

THE FILM

In an age of easy consensus, it's a joy to stumble on an honest-to-God, love-it-or-loathe-it movie like *I ♥ Huckabees*, a madcap satire on corporate and anti-corporate creeds which tends to have half its audience hissing with annoyance while the other's in hysterics. Jason Schwartzman stars as Albert Markovski, a manic environmental activist seeking counsel from a pair of 'existential detectives' (Dustin Hoffman and Lily Tomlin) who preach the interconnectedness of things and mean to get to the bottom of his screwy neuroses. Trying to placate Albert's fury with Huckabees, a Wal-Mart-esque retail chain that has humoured and then thwarted his attempts to fight urban sprawl, they rope in his slick nemesis Brad Stand (a fantastic Jude Law), Huckabees poster-girl Dawn (Naomi Watts), and their existing client Tommy (Mark Wahlberg), a nihilistic, anti-petroleum-campaigning fireman – just don't call him 'hero'.

Anarchic to its core, the movie plays ping-pong with its characters' life philosophies, bringing in Isabelle Huppert to extol futility by getting Albert and Tommy to bash themselves in the face with a rubber ball ('Don't call it "the ball thing" – call it pure being!' she insists). By allowing the ideas to take on a barely containable life of their own, Russell goes one up on both his Gulf War comedy *Three Kings* and his undervalued screwball farce *Flirting with Disaster*. He gets a amazingly funny performance out of Walhberg, whose knuckleheaded idealism explodes in a dinner-table spat with a family of card-carrying libertarians, and there's an inspired run of scenes in which Brad's whole personality crumples after hearing his oft-told, grotesquely self-serving anecdote about Shania Twain played back to him on tape. You'd be mad to try and swallow *Huckabees* wholesale, but it can be relished again and again for Russell's scattershot comic coups, and though there are quite a few missed targets in the mix, the bullseyes win out.

THE DISC

Stick the Fox DVD in and the first thing you get is, dismayingly, a trailer for the Queen Latifah/Jimmy Fallon vehicle *Taxi*. It's uphill from there: Russell waxes philosophical in a solo commentary and has a bit more fun duetting with Schwartzman. Out-takes allow those so inclined to watch Jude Law being knocked down again and again, Dustin Hoffman farting, and Huppert being incomprehensible; the japes continue in a montage called 'Miscellaneous Things People Did', which features Russell bounding in and delightedly announcing 'I've broken into my own scene!' If the meta-fun gets too much and you'd rather your corporation-chastising comedy played by the rules, there's an inside look at Fox's *Robots*. (These extras and more are available on the pricey R1 two-disc Special Edition; Fox's R1 single disc only carries the commentaries.) (TIM ROBEY)

Ikiru

(Japan, 1952)

Director: Akira Kurosawa
Label: Criterion Collection (USA)
Region: 1 (NTSC)
Discs: 2

THE FILM

Ikiru, which means 'to live', is that rare thing, an unmorbid film about dying. Intimations of mortality were its germ – 'Sometimes I think of my death, I think of ceasing to be,' wrote Kurosawa, 'and it's from these thoughts that *Ikiru* came' – and fill its first frame, an X-ray of the hero's stomach darkened by the cancer that will kill him. Watanabe, played to perfection by Kurosawa-veteran Takashi Shimura, is a pen-pushing bureaucrat jarred from somnambulism by the news that he has just months to live. In the scramble to give his life meaning, he grabs a chance to turn an inner-city wasteland into a playground, thus remaking the world and himself at the same time; and then, in a bold directorial stroke, he dies with the final third of the film still to play, leaving his family and associates to chew over (and largely misinterpret) the message of his last actions.

Ikiru is occasionally disparaged for its moments of piety and sentimentality, but it's nevertheless, in the main, a no-nonsense, even harrowing film – and a fairly cynical one, at that. In the words of Donald Richie, in *Ikiru* 'Kurosawa managed an (uneasy) truce between the part of him ... that says social endeavour is the answer and the part ... which knows perfectly well it is not.' Its artistry is breathtaking – so much so it has become a textbook for directors and editors – and it's also funny (gallows humour) and very moving: if your eyes stay dry, have a chest X-ray taken. Your heart's probably missing.

THE DISCS

Criterion's characteristic care and attention have gone into this double-disc *Ikiru*: restored sound and image (the picture is still sometimes scratchy, though not distractingly so), and decent extras. The film comes with commentary by Stephen Prince, author of an excellent study of Kurosawa's cinema, *The Warrior's Camera*. Disc 2 passes on *A Message from Akira Kurosawa: For Beautiful Movies*, a 81-minute documentary made by Kurosawa Production in 2000, built around interviews with Kurosawa on the sets of his late-period films. More relevant and less hagiographic is the 41-minute documentary about *Ikiru* from the Japanese TV series *Akira Kurosawa: It is Wonderful to Create*, the interviews here all conducted long after the film was made and more honest about the demands of working for the exacting director. We hear from actors and actresses (including Shimura), co-writer Hideo Oguni and members of the crew. (SIMON CROPPER)

Imitation of Life

(USA, 1959)

Director: Douglas Sirk
Label: Universal (USA)
Region: 1 (NTSC)
Discs: 1

THE FILM

Sirk's final film, a calculated spin on John M Stahl's Oscar-nominated 1934 weepie of the same name, is the definitive achievement of a career spent smuggling meaning into melodrama. In earlier movies such as *All That Heaven Allows* and *Written on the Wind*, Sirk had set himself the task of using all the available resources of high-gloss 1950s' studio filmmaking – contract stars, sumptuous cinematography, gaudy sets and swooning romantic scores – to erect an almost oppressive edifice of all-American artificiality, only to fill it with his spitefully recurring demons of unhappiness and personal failure. *Imitation of Life* is quintessential Sirk from the title on down – as a remake, it even gets to be an imitation of an imitation – and starts off by stuffing its opening credits with a glittering, treacherous cascade of what can only be paste jewels. The equally ersatz Lana Turner, in the lead role of hopeful actress and single mother Lora Meredith, occupies her essentially functional part with what looks like one eye on the profits – she got half – and becomes increasingly subordinate to the movie's beaten, despairing tone, deliberately splintered storyline, and terrible gulfs of unrequited feeling. As Lora's daughter Susie, apple-pie ingénue Sandra Dee slots into the *mise-en-scène* wearing a camouflage of indistinct pastel frocks, so sexless and placid a part of the furniture that it's a shock when she develops a crush of her own on square-jawed photographer Steve (John Gavin, himself an archetypal slice of '50s Hollywood beefcake).

All this is but preamble to the real point of the picture, which is the struggle of Lora's black housekeeper Annie (the marvellously affecting Juanita Moore) to cling on to some maternal claim over the light-skinned Sarah Jane, played as a nasty, petulant eight-year-old by Karin Dicker, and as a flagrant wildcat of an eighteen-year-old, cavorting incognito in luridly styled Manhattan nightclubs, by the unforgettably assured Susan Kohner. Sarah Jane's determination to pass holds up a mirror to the baseless prejudice of the whole era – Kohner, tellingly, is white – and Sirk uses reflections, again and again, to confront his characters with the consoling illusions they're both peddling and entrapped by.

THE DISC

Universal's anamorphic transfer is passable, even if problems with the Eastmancolor stock mean that the colours are sometimes a little hazy. The movie's available as a twofer with Stahl's original, but neither disc has significant extras beyond the plummy trailer here. Criterion or someone should get on the case, and they can amend another frankly disturbing oversight: neither Moore nor Kohner feature on the front cover. (TIM ROBEY)

Innocence

(France, 2004)

Director: Lucile Hadzihalilovic
Label: Artificial Eye (UK)
Region: 2 (PAL)
Discs: 1

THE FILM

In the forest, there is a school.

In a coffin, there is a girl.

Thus are new pupils delivered – dazed, but breathing – to a sealed, self-governing, man-free world where the uniform is tennis togs teamed with big functional boots, and each year-group is denoted by colourful hair ties. Why is it like this? Because. The days pass much as the average boarding schoolgirl's, with the same mix of ribbon-twirling, bullying and lessons, though there are just two teachers, imparting an unusual curriculum of ballet and off-kilter natural history, and hardly a book in sight. There's also a large wall surrounding the premises. Is this prison or paradise? Scenes of girls in white dresses idyllically gambolling through sunny days suggest bliss, yet cinematic convention and accumulating details of tweenage discontent combine to convince us there's some big bad going on in these woods, and a mystery develops around where the older girls go at night.

Hadzihalilovic was previously known for her work with Gaspar Noé, editing and producing his *Seul Contre Tous*, which delivers with shocking force the punchline that *Innocence* teasingly withholds. Is this a brilliantly realist portrait of girlhood or a metaphor for the dark path to civilisation? Are these girls, so sweet and so savage, innocence incarnate or proof that no such state exists – and, if it did, would we dirtied old cynics be able to see it? The film very deliberately offers us multiple symbols to read it by – the cycles of rain and rivers, butterflies flying and pinned, ticking clocks, coffins, caverns – but you're still never quite sure if there's sexual depravity at work or if it's all in your mind . . . And perhaps that's what makes this film great. Almost entirely visual (the dialogue is both spruce and sparse), it's a pure picture paradox, the sort of highly sexed philosophical conundrum one might expect from a French film based on a piece by Frank Wedekind, writer of the *Lulu* plays (see ***Pandora's Box***). But don't let that put you off: it's a ravishing piece of cinema and an exhilarating watch.

THE DISC

Anything less than this excellent transfer would fail this film, which builds its conviction on the cinematographer's dense, pre-Raphaelite palette. The menu is gorgeous, glowing and fading like memories of childhood, though the extras it offers are basic. Still, the trailer is as brilliant and intriguing as a Fabergé egg and the straight-to-camera interview with Hadzihalilovic is a thoughtful statement from a thoughtful director, proposing some unexpected influences (horror maestro Dario Argento chief amongst them), interesting points about gendered reactions to the film, and useful tips on the filmmaker's craft. If only the disc, like the pupils, came in a coffin. (REBEKAH POLDING)

Invasion of the Body Snatchers

(USA, 1978)

Director: Philip Kaufman
Label: MGM
Region: Any
Discs: 1

THE FILM

Jack Finney's 1955 novel about the takeover of a small Californian town by pod people has proved a virulent enough seed in itself: as well as Don Siegel's 1956 Cold War classic, we've had Abel Ferrara's 1993 stab set in the environs of a US military base, and goodness knows how many barely-disguised imitations. Kaufman's San Francisco-bound remake trumps even Siegel's version, quite simply because the focus of its sociopolitical paranoia is the *least* specific, resisting tidy allegory and sending out tendrils of uncontrolled anxiety every which way – towards commercial institutions, at America's growing therapy culture, into the home. Leonard Nimoy's shrink, for one, reckons there's 'some kind of hallucinatory flu going around', making the likes of Elizabeth (the delightful and underrated Brooke Adams) suspect their loved ones have been replaced by doppelgänger aliens. But his soothing psychobabble rings hollow indeed when he turns out to be one of them. Terser and more intuitive are the brilliantly chosen words of a Chinese launderette owner, buttonholing Donald Sutherland's public health official for advice about his wife: 'She *wrong* . . .'

The first half is all mounting panic on the streets, conjured through skewed tableaux of everyday urban routine. Audible even when it's not visible is a ubiquitous fleet of rubbish trucks secretly towing away binfuls of human ash, and that's Kevin 'No relation' McCarthy, sole survivor of Siegel's version, still running about and bellowing his hysterical warning to anyone who'll listen. Sutherland's 'fro is the single dated special effect as this mutates into cinema's finest-ever chase movie for hypochondriacs, fielding a sterling squad of freak-out players from Jeff Goldblum's constantly disgruntled intellectual to the inspired Veronica Cartwright, clapping her hands over her ears in a terrifying knockout of a last scene. The only way these characters still know they're human is by toppling right over the edge of a nervous breakdown.

THE DISC

Michael Chapman's beady cinematography is slightly at the mercy of a rudimentary non-anamorphic transfer, but MGM's Dolby 2.0 does a pretty good job with the unsettling sound design and Denny Zeitlin's wacko, bells-and-whistles score, which sounds like it was genuinely composed on another planet. The only extra to speak of is a feature-length commentary from Kaufman, but it's a good one: dry and modest, appreciative of his cast's endeavours, revealing on the nitty-gritty. The movie, a contemporary classic that remains vaguely underappreciated, could do with a lick of polish as it nears its thirtieth birthday, but then couldn't we all. (TIM ROBEY)

The Iron Giant

(USA, 1999) Special Edition

Director: Brad Bird
Label: Warners (all territories)
Region: Any
Discs: 1

THE FILM

Ted Hughes and Andrew Davidson's 1968 children's book *The Iron Man* is a dark, though ultimately redemptive tale of war and peace. This adaptation manages to maintain the original's edge, and also its heart.

Set in a brilliantly depicted 1950s America, the familiar tale of one boy and his giant alien robot is played out against a background of paranoia about pretty much everything: Communists, atomic devastation and, of course, the ever-present alien menace. When young Hogarth Hughes finds the metal-eating monster (voiced by Vin Diesel) dazed in the forest, he must protect it from the suspicious townsfolk of Rockwell, Maine, and the prying eyes of a paranoiac government agent. Hogarth and the man-machine take refuge with a local Java-guzzling Beatnik, but are unable to avoid a confrontation with the self-destructive forces of Americana.

Emotionally honest without resorting to mawkishness, the sharp script contains enough self-referential satire and visual humour to keep both adults and kids beaming throughout. The animation combines pen-and-ink illustration with subtle CGI, resulting in a refreshingly stylish look that manages to feel entirely modern while still harking back to simpler times. Overlooked by filmgoers on its initial release, despite a warm reception from critics, *The Iron Giant* has since been recognised as a classic of modern animation. That director Brad Bird's next feature was the Pixar smash *The Incredibles* has done nothing to dent its predecessor's reputation.

THE DISC

The Special Edition disc, presented in a dazzling new 2.35:1 widescreen transfer, has had numerous extras bolted on, key amongst them an in-depth 13-part making-of featurette that shows the painstaking process of making a cel-animated feature. There are also eight deleted scenes, including an alternate opening; a commentary from Bird and his animation team; two in-depth sequence analyses; and an interview with Vin Diesel about being the man behind the mask. (MARK PILKINGTON)

ivansxtc.

(UK/USA, 2000)

Director: Bernard Rose
Label: Tartan (UK)
Region: 2 (PAL)
Discs: 2

THE FILM

To experience ecstasy means, literally, to stand outside one's self, something well-heeled Hollywood agent Ivan Beckman (Danny Huston) has made a career of doing. His sharkish grin and suave flattery have got him in many a door, and so long as he never lets that mask slip, he'll continue to be the industry's darling. But at what price? And what happens to the rest of him when the collector comes knocking?

Both Tinseltown cautionary fable and bleak requiem for a lost soul, Rose's film operates in a mode of harsh, daylit realism that pulls very few punches. It's better for eschewing the safe darkness of Altman's *The Player*, which trekked off into an artificial thriller-land archly removed from the real world; the tone here, matched by stark digital photography, is closer to the excruciating awkwardness of good Dogme. When Ivan's death from a lung tumour is announced in his office boardroom, there's not much shock, just smirking incredulity, the world's briefest moment of silence, and a rush towards 'damage control'. We then backtrack to his final days, a blur of coke-snorting, deal-making and smothered anxiety as a man not allowed to be ill starts coughing up blood.

The movie's two sources – Tolstoy's *The Death of Ivan Ilyich* and the shock suicide of Rose's own one-time agent Jay Moloney – are unlikely bedfellows, but their pairing gives it a brazen quality, not so much for the usual acerbic film-biz muckraking as for its unapologetic solemnity and almost savage lack of irony. There's a highly entertaining turn from Peter Weller as Ivan's star client Don West, an over-the-hill action hero who parties hard and keeps his wife firmly out of sight, but even he seems faintly disgusted by the machinations of Ivan's colleagues mere hours after his death. Really, the film belongs to Huston, in a role you can imagine Jack Nicholson nailing 20 years ago: he movingly captures the bubbling horror beneath this huckster's gregarious charm offensive. Rose, who got his ticket in with the oneiric fantasy *Paperhouse* (1988) and the terrific Clive Barker adaptation *Candyman* (1992), fell out with the system soon after – *Immortal Beloved* (1994) and *Anna Karenina* (1997) bear the scars. But, save perhaps for an OTT funeral scene, this doesn't come across as the intemperate sideswipe of a former whizz-kid nursing his sour grapes. It is a plea, in the end, for a little bit of humanity.

THE DISCS

While the grandiosity of Rose's opening – shots of LA's empty boulevards scored to Wagner's *Tristan & Isolde* – sits somewhat oddly on DVD, the movie is mostly well-suited to this medium, its digital visuals crisp and involving. Extras are on the minimal side, with Chris Roberts' film notes providing the only real background, while a few party scene out-takes give you some extra hellraising for your buck. (TIM ROBEY)

Jaws

(USA, 1975) 2-disc Special Edition

Director: Steven Spielberg
Label: Universal (all territories)
Region: Any
Discs: 2

THE FILM

The film that demonised the great white shark, and was in turn vilified for heralding the new wham-bam age of effects-loaded blockbusters, Spielberg's breakthrough is a masterclass of simplicity, storytelling and suspense. Its plot centres around a Long Island coastal village whose tourist population suddenly becomes the target of a series of savage shark attacks. Chief Brody (Roy Scheider), the town's gnarled, principled sheriff, finds himself engaged in some ferocious battles, first with the town mayor, reluctant to close the beaches for fear of losing valuable revenue, and then with the shark itself. Famously, because Spielberg's rubber shark kept malfunctioning, the young director was forced to improvise, and when the shark makes its first much-delayed appearance, it's all the more terrifying for the built-up anticipation.

Spielberg was ultimately making a scary monster B-movie – as epitomised by the oft-cited but actually rather hammy three-men-in-a-boat 'narrative context' scene with Scheider, Richard Dreyfuss and Robert Shaw – but his intuitive ability to judge what will simultaneously scare and captivate an audience, allied to his consummate gift for storytelling, makes this a superior example of the genre. Viewed today, *Jaws* has the easy familiarity of films like *Casablanca*, *Psycho* and *The Godfather*, with iconic scene following iconic scene (and a score by John Williams to match); try to watch it with a *Jaws* virgin to remind yourself of its visceral evocation of cinema at its most base level of sheer, straightforward excitement.

THE DISCS

Seeing as it's one of Hollywood's most popular and highest grossing films, it's no surprise that there have already been a number of versions of *Jaws* released on DVD. This two-disc set came out in 2005 for the film's 30th anniversary. The first disc features the film (with exquisite sound and vision), deleted scenes, shark facts and an on-set featurette which includes rare behind-the-scenes footage of Spielberg in action. The second disc is largely given over to an excellent two-hour documentary, 'The Making of Jaws', which appeared in truncated form on the 25th anniversary DVD (and was originally shot for the 20th anniversary Laserdisc version), but is well worth seeing in full. The other big draw is the 60-page booklet that comes with the package – an excellent photographic accompaniment to a cinematic treat. (PETER WATTS)

The Humphrey Jennings Collection

(UK, 1942–46)

Director: Humphrey Jennings
Label: Film First (UK)
Region: 0 (PAL)
Discs: 1

THE FILMS

Who was Humphrey Jennings? A painter, photographer and poet who helped launch Surrealism in Britain. A literary historian with a peculiar sense of the poet's relationship to his public, whose life's work was an anthology tracing the effects of industrialism in the British mass mind. And a founder of Mass Observation, an eccentric group of amateur sociologists and cultural theorists. But it was with his wartime film work, revered within British film culture for over 50 years, that Jennings came closest to fulfilling the polymathic potential that was dashed by his accidental death aged 43 in 1950.

Commissioned, like most of his films, as Ministry of Information propaganda, the almost wordless *Listen to Britain* (1942) is a 20-minute tour of the home front covering a single day. Within his compositions and later in the cutting room, Jennings and editor Stewart McAllister fashioned an associative montage of images, of sounds – and of images with sounds – to capture what he considered the war-forged beginning of a new classless society. Breaking with the didacticism of the Soviet school of editing, and featuring neither story nor characters, nor even a commentary – the 'voice-of-God' being a cornerstone of the classic British documentary – the film is itself quietly revolutionary.

A Diary for Timothy (1946), only twice as long, is nonetheless an exponential expansion in technique and scope. The subject is again the home front, during the too gradual transition to peace in 1944–45, but settling on four characters as counterpoint to the first six months of baby Tim's life. The film's 'voice' belongs not to God but to the novelist EM Forster, his commentary a doubting, sometimes agonised discourse on the prospects facing Tim's generation in the post-war world. The almost-feature-length *I Was a Fireman* (aka *Fires Were Started*, 1943) is what Jennings called a 'mixture of slapstick and macabre blitz reconstruction', featuring East End volunteer firemen practically 'as themselves'. Commenting on Jennings's decision to encourage the maximum of participation from his performers, Lindsay Anderson, in his 1954 essay 'Only Connect', made the eloquent judgement that 'Jennings's people are ends in themselves'.

THE DISC

Film First's package trumps the competition with landmark tributes from filmmakers of two generations: the disc has the excellent profile 'Humphrey Jennings: The Man Who Listened to Britain' (2000), directed by Kevin *Touching the Void* MacDonald, while the booklet reproduces Anderson's 'Only Connect'. The three films are taken from the best prints available. (HENRY K MILLER)

The Jerk

(USA, 1979) 26th Anniversary Edition

Director: Carl Reiner
Label: Universal
Region: 1 (NTSC)
Discs: 1

THE FILM

Steve Martin's iconic, career-launching turn as Navin R Johnson is the kind of role the words 'wacky' and 'zany' were invented for. Navin is a happy dunderhead, astonished to discover he's adopted – despite being the only white guy in an all-black Mississippi family. On his 18th birthday this pre-Gump innocent leaves home 'to find his special purpose', and after surviving room and board in a petrol-station gents' cubicle, a crush on a circus stuntwoman and regular run-ins with a deranged assassin, he makes rich with the invention of the 'Opti-Grab' glasses attachment, only to find that money doesn't buy ya happiness.

Martin's put-upon madcap schtick – as perfectly timed and nuanced as that of Chuck Jones's Wile E Coyote – is what carries this oddball show. Unlike later, more consistent efforts like *Dead Men Don't Wear Plaid* and *The Man With Two Brains*, both similarly penned by Martin and directed by Carl Reiner, *The Jerk* is far more a film of scattered, brilliant, quotable moments than a satisfactory whole – i.e. frankly better in the memory. Particularly draggy is the cutesy-pie love story with Bernadette Peters – a dire warning of Martin's many schmaltzy horrors to come. Still, for sheer wild and crazy physical comedy, he's arguably never topped *The Jerk*. It's a reminder that he truly could once make you laugh so hard you'd snort popcorn out your nose.

THE DISC

Martin's early, funny movies have been woefully served by DVD – most originally turning up, and some still only available, in murky panned-and-scanned editions. Now presented in a decent, if slightly softened, anamorphic transfer, the film looks better than it sounds: the new Dolby 5.1 mix barely dresses up the original stereo soundtrack, and there's a slight hiss running under it throughout.

The new extras aim for quirky, but mostly fall flat. 'Ukelele Gal' Janet Klein helps us 'Learn How to Play "Tonight You Belong to Me"' – so you can twang alonga Martin as he woos his lady. 'The Lost Filmstrips of Father Carlos Las Vegas de Cordova' feature further multifarious pet abuse by a modern-day impersonator of the film's cat-juggling priest. There are also those old standby fillers, a theatrical trailer and production notes – but no commentaries. Universal still need to take a leaf out of their own superior release of Martin's 1999 return to form *Bowfinger*. (HD version now available.) (LARUSHKA IVAN-ZADEH)

La Jetée & Sans Soleil

(France, 1962/1983)

Director: Chris Marker
Label: Nouveaux Pictures (UK)
Region: 2 (PAL)
Discs: 1

THE FILMS

Few filmgoers have seen a Chris Marker film. Fewer still know what he looks or sounds like. But this wilfully recessive French director, born in 1921, has for well over 40 years been a revered figure for those who dream of an expanded cinema that can utilise the technical and aesthetic possibilities opened up by the emergence of multimedia visual culture, and at the same time create art-works that do not fall prey to the amnesiac, surface-over-depth tendencies that are a feature of this image-overloaded era.

La Jetée is Marker's best-known work, if only because it was remade as *Twelve Monkeys* by Terry Gilliam in 1995. The black-and-white original, a mere 28 minutes in length, consists entirely of still photographs (apart from one shot of a woman's eyelids opening and closing), over which a narrator delivers a precise yet resonant story about a young boy who sees a woman at a Parisian airport and then a man shot dead. An apocalypse befalls the earth, but the boy survives and grows up to become a man who is tested on by government scientists keen to use his abiding memories of the beautiful woman in order to travel back in time and restore the world to its former condition.

Sans Soleil, like *La Jetée*, is a strange, hybrid work that fuses speculative fiction, travelogue and philosophic reverie to create a memorable example of the cine-essay form. Floating, both in terms of geography and mood, between Guinea, Iceland and Japan, it consists of a series of letters predicated on the notion that the great question of the 20th century was 'the co-existence of different notions of time', and exploring the relationship between war, memory and history. Its invocation of the 'melancholy comfort of the tiniest of things', and especially the post-modernist Orientalism of its claim that contemporary Tokyo was 'a comic strip. It's Planet Manga', would later be re-echoed by Sofia Coppola's *Lost in Translation*.

THE DISC

A 16-page booklet contains the script of *La Jetée* and an autobiographical essay by Marker about the first film he made while at school. It featured images of the director's signature motif – cats. His collaborator remarked grumpily, 'Nobody can do a movie with still images.' The nine-minute 'Chris on Chris' is an intriguing essay-doc by noted film writer Chris Darke that includes all-too-short interviews with Marker associate Michael Shamberg and Terry Gilliam, the latter particularly eloquent about the excellent editing on *La Jetée*. (A Criterion Collection edition was in the works at the time of going to press.)

(SUKHDEV SANDHU)

Johnny Guitar

(USA, 1954)

Director: Nicholas Ray
Label: Universal (UK)
Region: 2 (PAL)
Discs: 1

THE FILM

'Never seen a woman who was more like a man – she looks like one, acts like one, and sometimes makes me feel like I'm not.' Thus saloon boy Sam on his butch boss Vienna (Joan Crawford) in Nicholas Ray's delirious gender-bending western, unimprovably summed up by François Truffaut when he said Ray's cowboys 'circle and die like ballerinas'. Crawford, for her part, keeps changing back into trousers, in part to complicate the manly status of her troubled, gun-spurning paramour Johnny (Sterling Hayden), who rides into town as a railroad pass is being blasted through the mountainside, only to find Vienna at all kinds of loggerheads with the locals.

Everything in this lurid Trucolor panto is camply a-twirl, from Vienna's never-used but ever-revolving roulette wheel ('I like to hear it spin!') to the howling sandstorm outside and the whiplash volte-faces of key players at bits of bad news. When Vienna semi-helps the Dancin' Kid (Scott Brady) and his bandit crew hide out, the movie serves up a McCarthy-esque witch-hunt to rival *The Crucible*, as a torch-wielding lynch mob descend on the saloon, compel Kid associate Turkey (Ben Cooper) to turn informant, and ready the noose. Chief Inquisitors certainly don't come much more blood-crazed or self-deluding than squeaky spinster Emma Small (Mercedes McCambridge), who scurries through proceedings like a vicious elf, denying her hots for the Kid by hanging him, and setting Vienna's joint ablaze with a horny glee McCambridge wouldn't top until *The Exorcist*. Ray would carry on reinventing the form and psychology of movie melodramas throughout the '50s – suicidal teen angst in *Rebel Without a Cause*, suburban-issue-movie-gone-wild in *Bigger Than Life* – but this remains his finest and most operatic spin on genre, at once doolally and spellbinding, as well as a persuasively grim treatment of persecution and the power of the posse. It's a western so unstable you can't even run for the hills, because the hills are exploding.

THE DISC

No one loves *Johnny Guitar* more than Martin Scorsese, whose brief introduction is all we get here by way of extras. He's certainly got the measure of the movie: its influence is right there in *Alice Doesn't Live Here Anymore*, with its clay-red skies, abused but tough heroine, and strumming man-friend coming a-knocking. Ray's output is shamefully under-served on DVD generally, but at least Universal's smart transfer, right from the first succulent yellow-on-blue credit, does this one justice. (TIM ROBEY)

The Work of Director Spike Jonze

(USA, 1994–2003)

Director: Spike Jonze
Label: Mute Films (UK) / Palm Pictures (USA)
Region: 2 (PAL) / 1 (NTSC)
Discs: 1

THE FILMS

A hipster household pseudonym well before hitting the big-screen big time with *Being John Malkovich* and *Adaptation*, Jonze was world famous for 15 or so minutes' worth of joyous promotional videos. By casting the Beastie Boys in an unremembered '70s cop show (*Sabotage*), projecting Weezer into 'Happy Days' ('Buddy Holly'), and orchestrating the 'Umbrellas of San Fernando Valley' clip for Björk ('It's Oh So Quiet'), Jonze defined the retro aesthetic of the mid '90s. If '80s post-modernism, all surface sheen and hard edges, had stressed ironic distance, the Jonze school called on a hazy celebratory nostalgia – in the case of 'Buddy Holly' for an earlier moment of pop revivalism – and appeared to relinquish any aspiration to cool. It was the in-joke that everyone got.

Before routine set in, former skateboarder Jonze made a 180, turning from conventional performer-led pieces to work with European dance acts Daft Punk ('Da Funk') and The Chemical Brothers ('Elektrobank'). Rather than give these largely instrumental tracks a spurious 'face' for MTV, he shot two short-story films with little or no obvious connection to the music: a moving tale of big-city alienation for Daft Punk, and a miniature teen movie (starring his then girlfriend Sofia Coppola) for The Chemical Brothers. 'Praise You' for Fatboy Slim rolled out the eccentrist Jonze brand just ahead of his move to Hollywood (as director of *Malkovich* and actor in *Three Kings*), with the director himself leading an amateur dance troupe in a merry sidewalk dance.

THE DISC

The random-access capacity of the DVD has made it an ideal platform for the music video – somewhat neglected, despite its acknowledged role as Hollywood's avant-garde, in the years before the format took off. 'The Work of Director Spike Jonze', which brings together the bulk of his short work, belongs to Palm's lovingly curated series of auteur anthologies, which includes entries from Jonze associates Michel Gondry and Mark Romanek. The director himself is mostly absent from the disc, breaking cover only in an accompanying inter-view book, and leaving the commentaries to his musical collaborators. Although Jonze, under the alias Richard Koufey, features prominently in a documentary on the convoluted 'Praise You' story, he plays his role, as in the video itself, entirely straight.

No mere collection of odds and ends, and more than a warm-up for the features that followed, this DVD packs more ideas than most directors manage in their whole careers. (HENRY K MILLER)

Journey to Italy

(Italy, 1953)

Director: Roberto Rossellini
Label: BFI (UK)
Region: 2 (PAL)
Discs: 1

ORIGINAL TITLE: *Viaggio in Italia*

THE FILM

The intertwining of documentary and fiction in film (think of Kiarostami's *Close Up*, or Michael Winterbottom's *In This World*) is sometimes conceived of as a purely recent phenomenon. In fact it's been a strategy for as long as movie cameras have been mobile enough to take out into the world, and certainly describes the aspirations of the neorealist movement that flowered so remarkably in post-war Italy, with the films of Vittorio de Sica, Roberto Rossellini, Lucino Visconti and Federico Fellini. Rossellini's war trilogy – *Rome, Open City*, *Paisa* and *Germany, Year Zero* – remain keystones of that movement, but he held true to its tenets even when moving focus from social privations to the more private travails of the heart.

A portrait of a marriage on the rocks, starring his then-wife Ingrid Bergman, *Journey to Italy* openly courts viewing as an record of reality: we watch Bergman and George Sanders, discomforted by Rossellini's emphasis on unprepared interacting, playing an English couple, Alex and Katharine Joyce, journeying through Naples to sell a house Alex has inherited. It starts on the open strada, and ends in an impasse of market traffic, capitulation and an embrace. In between, as the two begin to wend their separate ways, he tying up business and flirting, she visiting the local sights, Rossellini steers their slight story down the scenic route, taking time to contemplate life's evanescence in the shadow of Vesuvius and its smouldering substructure. The landscape photography is beautiful, and crucial: less a road movie or *Sunrise*-style romance than a ghost story, the film is steeped in the spectres of lost lovers and civilisations, war, poverty and more. Hollywood narrative certainties are laid to rest; the promise of cultural exchange (between English and Italians, or perhaps Swedes and Italians) is queried; and – viewed today – two dead film stars can still be seen acting out this misleadingly modest passion play.

THE DISC

High on quality if not quantity, the BFI's disc features a sterling transfer, and one substantial extra, a lucid and illuminating commentary track by British critic Laura Mulvey. Digging through the film's layers of meaning, she calls the film 'a milestone of modern cinema', and traces its influence from Godard (notably *Le Mépris*) and Antonioni (*L'Avventura*) to Wong Kar-Wai (*Happy Together*). It makes you want to go straight back to the film . . . (NICK BRADSHAW)

Junebug

(USA, 2005)

Director: Phil Morrison
Label: Eureka (UK)
Region: 2 (PAL)
Discs: 2

THE FILM

Amid the bonanza of so-called 'Indiewood' productions that graced filmdom's awards season in 2005–06 – a pack led by *Brokeback Mountain, Good Night and Good Luck, Capote* and *Crash* – there wasn't much room for the year's real find. A movie of genuinely independent spirit and ethos, *Junebug* lacked both the star power to get itself noticed and the issue hook to make it newsworthy: it was merely wonderful, a bittersweet comedy of manners to make Ozu proud.

Amazing that the film's barely-known creators and pitch-perfect ensemble cast achieve this from a set-up that could be glibly glossed as *Meet the Parents* for the Sundance crowd, but there you go. Chicago art dealer Madeleine (Embeth Davidtz) is killing two birds with one stone in a quiet corner of North Carolina: trying to sign a borderline-insane outsider artist (Frank Hoyt Taylor); and meeting her in-laws. Rake-thin, tightly-wound and somewhat older than her new husband George (Alessandro Nivola), Madeleine instantly clashes with his possessive bruiser of a mother (Celia Weston) and struggles to get a word out of his kindly but withdrawn dad (Scott Wilson) or constantly pissed-off younger brother (Ben McKenzie). The only Johnsten family member she scores a hit with is the latter's heavily pregnant wife Ashley, a daft chatterbox played with utterly winning, unpatronising candour by Oscar-robbed Amy Adams.

This is a movie about a home and a family who tacitly understand each other in ways their visitor can't hope to decode yet, for all the sincere efforts she's making. Morrison and screenwriter Angus Maclachlan stage a remarkable Sunday church gathering, where Nivola does angelic hymn duties and Davidtz looks on in wonder at this man she doesn't have the measure of yet: there's not a trace of that kneejerk secular panic usually prompted by indie sojourns to the Bible belt. Next to the rancid red-state/blue-state satire of something like Todd Solondz's *Palindromes*, *Junebug*'s non-judgemental embrace of every character, its dry intelligence and essential kindness, make it worth its own song of praise.

THE DISCS

This two-disc UK edition ports over all the features from Sony's R1 disc, but you get the better PAL picture. Chief among the extras is a chatty love-in with Davidtz and Adams, the former embarrassingly forgetting the names of key cast members ('Frank . . . er . . .') and revealing her surprise that a lot of audiences didn't like Madeleine much. Morrison, it's clear, knew exactly what he was doing with her, and with Adams, whose performance seems all the more special when you take a look at her indecisive audition clips. There are also ten deleted scenes, any one of which would have ended up as the weakest in the movie: all hail the instincts of Morrison and his editor Joe Klotz. A Q&A with Adams in London, some cursory behind-the-scenes snippets and a gallery of Ann Wood's specially-commissioned artworks round out the package. (TIM ROBEY)

Kabhi Kushi Kabhie Gham

(India, 2004) Collector's Edition

Director: Karan Johar
Label: Yash Raj Films (USA)
Region: 1 (NTSC)
Discs: 2

ENGLISH TITLE: *Sometimes Happy, Sometimes Sad*, aka *Happiness and Tears*

THE FILM

Backdrop to a million weddings and fan re-enactments across the globe, the gorgeous, opulent and genuinely heartwarming *Kabhi Kushi Kabhie Gham* (or *K3G*) was the most expensive and highest-grossing Indian film of all time until 2005's *The Rising*. Interestingly, it toppled director Karan Johar's previous, debut feature *Kuch Kuch Hota Hai* from this illustrious perch. While *Kuch Kuch* revivified an ailing industry by pioneering contemporary urban-set plots, a more MTV-music style and integrated musical numbers, *K3G* represents a return to the classics, a lavish homage to the traditional Bollywood masala of love, tears and laughter without losing Johar's top stylistic touch.

That the film stars Amitabh Bachchan, the reigning monarch of Bollywood cinema for over 30 years (and BBC's Superstar of the Millennium) adds an amusing frisson to this story of cross-generational conflict. With his real-life partner, the adored actress Jaya Bachchan, he plays the rich industrialist parent to *Kuch Kuch*'s star Shah Rukh Khan, whose mega-wattage dominates the younger Bollywood scene. As their adopted son, Rahul, Shah Rukh defiantly strikes out on his own by marrying not their choice of bride, but a girl from the wrong side of the tracks. It takes the interventions of a younger brother and many trips to London (including Bluewater Shopping Centre) for the family to heal their rift and come together for the traditional wedding finale. A jumbo pack of tissues may be required by the tender-hearted, such is the dramatic force of this celebration of family values as young and old come together in the final dance number. With songs that include a title track sung by playback legend Lata Mangeshkar (plus hilarious usage of 'It's Raining Men'), tremendous choreography by Farah Khan and a veritable legion of superb star performers, this offers a near-embarrassment of contemporary Bollywood cinema riches.

THE DISCS

Be sure to track down this deluxe Collector's Edition of *K3G*, available for the same price as the single disc version, and offered as standard by plenty of UK-based Bollywood DVD specialists. The transfer quality is as good as the single disc, the packaging considerably classier and there are 80 minutes of glossy extras, including a good making-of documentary. In a nice touch, the deleted scenes (including a cameo by Amitabh's son Abishek Bachchan and a further British shopping centre scene, this one filmed at Bicester Village) are presented by the director. (REBEKAH POLDING)

The Buster Keaton Collection

(USA, 1923–27)

Directors: Listed below
Label: mk2 (France)
Region: 2 (PAL)
Discs: 10

DIRECTORS: Buster Keaton, Roscoe 'Fatty' Arbuckle, John G Blystone, Edward F Cline, Donald Crisp, Clyde Bruckman, James W Horne, Charles Reisner

THE FILMS

For rhythm, flow, poetry, wit and sheer cask-strength excitement, the silent comic auteur Buster Keaton trumps them all. His greatness is not just in the inventiveness of his gags, the precision and elegance of his camerawork, the touching fortitude of his screen persona – nor merely the one-off amalgam of comic talents in the one performer, unequalled for breakneck physical prowess and just as sweet in small-scale business. Watch his forward flips down a 45-degree slope in *Seven Chances* (1925) and gasp, then the lovely underwater repair in *The Navigator* (1924).

No, Buster endures because he made real films of real human understanding – his railroad masterpiece *The General* (1926), for example, was described by Orson Welles as '*the* Civil War film' – that were neither gag conveyor belts nor sentimental stick-up. Delightful touches abound: the pre-Harryhausen claymation dinosaur of *Three Ages* (1923), the rickety train and flexible track of *Our Hospitality* (1923), the absurd luxury of the campsite in *Battling Butler* (1926). Granted, his movies are very much of their pre-Depression time, the plots – usually love stories – vaudevillian and schematic, but they also bear comparison to Pirandello and Beckett, which is more than one can say for Chaplin's work. In short: some of the funniest, most intelligent, most exhilarating cinema ever made.

THE DISCS

One box, ten discs, all ten six-reeler films Buster made as an independent, from *Three Ages* to *Steamboat Bill, Jr* (1927). The set isn't cheap, but the quality of its presentation, from the sleek black tin – aptly resilient – to the restoration of the films, is unmatched by Keaton packages elsewhere. The films not already mentioned are *Sherlock Junior* (1924), *Go West* (1925) and *College* (1927), but star of the set is a spotless *The General*, purged of every fleck of dirt and watery flutter of light. British critic David Robinson supplies three pithy introductions and three 'Frame by Frame' audits of dangerous stunts. A muffed rooftop-to-rooftop leap in *Three Ages*, where Buster falls short and plummets out of frame, is eye-popping enough – and then he turns the out-take into a gag with canvas awnings and a drainpipe (that's what Beckett meant by 'fail better'). Other extras include a handful of Buster's two-reeler shorts, archive footage of the Mississippi floods, cartoons, a Kodak ad he made in the '60s and a 1949 episode of 'The Buster Keaton Show'. mk2 is a French label, but the films all have their original US intertitles and the French subtitles can be turned off. (SIMON CROPPER)

Kill Bill: Vols 1 & 2

(USA, 2003/2004)

Director: Quentin Tarantino
Label: Buena Vista (UK) / Universal (Japan)
Region: 2 (PAL (UK) / NTSC (Japan))
Discs: 2

THE FILMS

Pure cinematic coup de grâce, or junked-up jerk-off? An extension of Tarantino's talent, or a betrayal of it? You can cut *Kill Bill* any which way: that's surely the name of QT's post-modern mix-and-match game. But to state the obvious, your taste for ultra-violent, hyper-stylish cartoon revenge operas may come into play. This is one such, in spades.

Tarantino riffles through blaxploitation, samurai, ninja, yakuza, kung fu, anime, noir, spaghetti western and Tex-Mex tropes, layering homage upon riff upon rip-off upon the disinterred plots of *The Bride Wore Black*, *Lady Snowblood* and *I Spit on Your Grave*. As he'll tell you, Tarantino also digs the idea of playing Svengali to a hot Hollywood muse and, as von Sternberg was to Dietrich, so 'Q to U' (-ma Thurman) in the age of recycled '70s jogging suits and Eastern action pin-ups. *Kill Bill* is, *inter alia*, a fanboy fantasy tribute to womanhood, from its refinement of the kicking-chicks flick to Thurman's Bride's killer maternal instinct, and shy of the moral import of, say, Elmore Leonard, it's no more frivolous than any of Tarantino's films. What it offers, more than ever, is sheer cocksure braggadocio: testosterone to match the oestrogen, blood, spunk and swagger.

THE DISCS

Re the *V1* v *V2* chop. With their split cinema release, the belated characterisation, motivation, reflection and closure provided in *V2* showed its predecessor to be one long, loud, lurid teaser. At home, the two films' ten chapters can be more readily re-sampled, highlighting the Saturday-morning serial structure of the enterprise. Tarantino has long spoken of a prospective bumper edition of the films combined. That might be good reason to hold off from first dipping into these artificially separated discs, functional but surely far from the final word. Each comes with a glossy 20-minute promo skim-sample and a couple of live song performances, respectively by the 5,6,7,8s and Robert Rodriguez's Chingon; *V1* also includes three trailers, and *V2* a single uncontextualised deleted scene. Sound is good, with DTS options on both; image is better on *V2* than the cartoonishly edge-enhanced *V1*.

Japanese versions are longer: *V2* lingers an extra 45 seconds at the Mexican brothel, but Tarantino's 'full-strength' version of *V1* ships several buckets more blood in its myriad extra shots (see the IMDb's 'alternate versions' section for chapter and verse), and restores colour to the House of Blue Leaves sequence made black and white to placate the blood-shy MPAA. You'll have to fiddle with the subtitle toggling, though, and some of the interview extras are unsubtitled. (NICK BRADSHAW)

The Killers

(USA, 1946/1964)

Directors: Robert Siodmak, Don Siegel
Label: Criterion Collection (USA)
Region: 1 (NTSC)
Discs: 2

THE FILM

The world could have been a very different place had American voters thought more carefully about Ronald Reagan's final screen role. In Don Siegel's cold and lurid adaptation of Ernest Hemingway's short story *The Killers*, the Gipper plays a crime lord – and a pretty loathsome one too.

Siegel's movie was the second attempt to bring *The Killers* to the screen. But where Robert Siodmak's 1946 film noir version remained faithful to the original story, Siegel's concentrates on two assassins trying to discover why one of their victims, a former racing driver working at a school for the blind, stood still as they gunned him down.

Originally made for television, *The Killers* was deemed too violent by Universal, who released it theatrically. Meticulously plotted and tightly assembled, it gets its snap from a stellar cast. Lee Marvin is coiled, fierce and merciless. Angie Dickinson is bewitching as Sheila Farr, the femme fatale who double-crosses her boss, and John Cassavetes is typically solid as Johnny North, the killers' passive victim. And Ronald Reagan? He was so revolted by the nastiness of his character that he went into politics. Go figure.

THE DISCS

'A very tragic story, filled with deeper truth', said the young Andrei Tarkovsky about Hemingway's short story. Tarkovsky, a student at the All-Russian State Institute of Cinematography, then turned it into a 20-minute short film – one of five versions of the story on Criterion's double-disc edition. As well as Tarkovsky's stylish number, there's a 1949 radio adaptation starring Burt Lancaster and Shelley Winters, a reading of the original story by actor Stacy Keach, and the two movie adaptations – Robert Siodmak's 1946 film noir classic and Don Siegel's 1964 remake.

By way of supplements to all that, there are three elegant essays – among them an article by author Jonathan Lethem and Paul Schrader's seminal 'Notes on Film Noir'; an interview with Clu Gulager, who appeared in the 1964 version; excerpts from Don Siegel's autobiography, read with deadpan drawl by actor Wolf Wolverton (according to Siegel, buying Ronald Reagan a Cobb salad convinced the future president to accept a role in his movie); and an interview with screenwriter Stuart Kaminsky. He says that different eras produced different versions of the same story – prompting his tantalising question, 'If someone were to do *The Killers* again, what would they do?' (JAMES CLASPER)

Kind Hearts and Coronets

(UK, 1949)

Director: Robert Hamer
Label: Criterion Collection (USA)
Region: 1 (NTSC)
Discs: 2

THE FILM

KH & C is one of the greatest British films, and one of the most unclassifiable – as if Oscar Wilde had come back from the dead as scriptwriter and Luis Buñuel were the director attached. Such a project is a long way from the cosy moralistic fare of much of Ealing, and indeed *KH*, as scripted and directed by Robert Hamer, the alcoholic *'poète maudit'* of British cinema, is provocative, amoral stuff – if only for the glee with which its protagonist Louis Mazzini (Dennis Price) takes his class revenge.

His draped Edwardian dandy is on a mission to kill every upper-class twit who stands between him and the D'Ascoyne family fortune (all played by Alec Guinness, in a cross-dressing kaleidoscope of cameos). Louis' mama (née D'Ascoyne) had committed the class sin of marrying beneath her – and an Italian! – so she and son were dispossessed. *KH* brings sly savagery to its satire of that great British taboo of class; its anti-hero's wardrobe and urbane version of 'up yours' helped inspire the emerging figure of the Teddy Boy to shape a working-class parody of the Edwardian toff about town.

The film treads on other taboos, not least sex. Most British cinema either sniggers about sexuality or portrays it in serious tones, more out of dutifulness than any desire to explore its complexities. Joan Greenwood, however, as Sibella, the married object of Louis' lusts, does more with her voice than most British actresses have managed since with trunkfuls of lingerie and parades of nudity. She makes her every syllable a come-on, every word bear the promise of naked flesh.

The voice-over makes it a wordy film in other ways, too. The language is lapidary yet rhythmic, in constant shifting relationship to the images and action. No wonder such counterpoint inspired Scorsese into *Goodfellas*, another work of gleeful amorality. And no wonder *KH* became a favourite of Buñuel, who was enchanted by its incendiary take on the world. There's more political tendency in Hamer's cinematic wit than in the whole dun-dreary corpus of British social realism.

THE DISCS

Criterion's well-heeled edition, now available in limited numbers, is not for paupers, who should content themselves with the Anchor Bay offering (also R1) and its droll family-tree menus, available stand-alone or boxed with its Ealing brethren in 'The Alec Guinness Collection'. Those of means can avail themselves of another plum from the CC stable, with its cut-glass transfer, 75-minute BBC documentary on Ealing, photo archive and learned Philip Kemp liner essay, not to mention a 1975 *Parkinson* episode in which Guinness discusses his role in a forthcoming sci-fi curio called *Star Wars*. (PAUL TICKELL)

King Kong

(USA, 1933) Special Edition

Director: Merian C Cooper and Ernest B Schoedsack
Label: Warners (USA)
Region: 1 (NTSC)
Discs: 2

THE FILM

It may have grossed billions, but the global box office success of Peter Jackson's 2005 *King Kong* is just same old same old for this monster classic. Since its release in 1933, the movie has enjoyed numerous triumphal returns to the screen, inclusion in innumerable all-time-greats lists, and the dubious honour of being known as Hitler's favourite film. Its story of a girl, a guy and a really big monkey speaks of the destruction of man's inner urges, the raging beast, by the forces of civilisation ranged against him: capitalist greed, urban living, military planes and Women. Much discussion takes place as to the deleterious effect of the fairer sex on a man's strength of character, and the famous eulogy – 'it was beauty killed the beast' – is rather a reminder that messing with girls always leads to no good than recognition of the soul and profounder feeling seen in Jackson's re-ape. This original Kong really is a brute, utterly terrifying in his rampages through jungle and city, his movement authentically animal thanks to the pioneering stop-motion genius of Willis O'Brien. No less powerful a performance is given by Kong's co-star, Fay Wray, whose famously forceful lungs (she is often described as the very first 'scream queen') have sometimes overshadowed the plucky naturalism she brings to her part.

When Wray died in 2004, the Empire State Building was darkened for 15 minutes in tribute.

THE DISCS

Though the ape-proof tin-boxed Collector's Edition with programme and post-cards was sadly limited, you can still experience an awesome adventure through fantastic film history via the two-disc collection. Produced by pre-eminent film historians Kevin Brownlow and Patrick Stanbury, the documentary *I Am King Kong!*, the boy's-own life story of Merian C Cooper, is a riot: the man got kicked out of the military, shot down in a plane, captured by Bolsheviks, adopted by Persian tribesman and made movies about it all as he went. Snatches of his words (and Wray's) can be heard on the commentary track, which honours the tired old voice of masterly animator Ray Harryhausen, but to truly understand the technical achievement of the film it's the king-size seven-part documentary that you need. Starting with test footage of *Kong*'s predecessor, *Creation* (also included as a separate feature), this follows the development of the special effects through the impassioned eyes of present-day animators who reverence the film so fervently they devote several months to re-creating the lost 'spider-pit sequence'. And yes, they are led by one Peter Jackson . . . (REBEKAH POLDING)

The King of Comedy
(USA, 1983)

Director: Martin Scorsese
Label: 20th Century Fox (USA)
Region: 1 (NTSC)
Discs: 1

THE FILM

In terms of box-office receipts, *The King of Comedy* is reputedly Martin Scorsese's least successful film. On its release in 1983, three years after the triumph of *Raging Bull*, critics were either baffled or inflamed by Pupkin's progress, Pauline Kael going so far as to assess it as 'grossly insensitive, coldhearted . . . a bad movie'. But while it's true that only a copywriter or a sociopath would describe this as a hilarious, feel-good comedy – one of the original, woeful marketing tacks – it is far from being a bad movie; in fact, it stands as one of the most perceptive and prophetic films of the modern media age.

Robert De Niro plays the unctuous Rupert Pupkin who, abetted by a certifiably obsessive Sandra Bernhard, plots to kidnap talk-show host Jerry Langford, an authentically jaded performance by comedian Jerry Lewis. In a series of toe-curling set-pieces and an epilogue which appears deliberately to echo and parody his own *Taxi Driver*, Scorsese (with writer Paul D Zimmerman) dissects the contract of love and loathing between performer and fan, hovering somewhere between black comedy and despair. But that was then. In the celebrity-obsessed 21st century, the infamous final line of Pupkin's stand-up routine – 'Better to be king for a night than schmuck for a lifetime!' – seems to have been adopted by media and public alike as a piece of advice rather than a warning, the motto of a thousand reality shows. Twenty-five years ago, Rupert Pupkin wanted to be Jerry Langford; these days, it appears a disturbing number of people want to be Rupert Pupkin . . .

THE DISC

With an anamorphic transfer and its original 1.85:1 aspect ratio, this is as good and as grubby as you would hope – Times Square has never looked dingier. There are only a couple of deleted scenes, both featuring Lewis rather then De Niro, frustrating when one considers how much extra, improvised material was shot (rumours of De Niro persistently needling Lewis, in character, are rife). In addition to the trailer, a TV spot and a stills gallery, there is also a basic 20-minute documentary featuring Scorsese and Bernhard but, again, no De Niro. Admirers of this unique movie can only hope that, like *Mean Streets*, *New York, New York* and *Raging Bull*, there will be a Special Edition along soon.

Note: the Region 1 and 2 editions of *The King of Comedy* are more or less identical; Region 1 just shades it if you are after more audio options. (ANDY MILLER)

The Kingdom I & II

(Denmark, 1994/1997)

Director: Lars von Trier
Label: Zentropa Entertainment (Denmark)
Region: 2 (PAL)
Discs: 4

ORIGINAL TITLE: *Riget I* and *II*

THE FILMS

The appearance of an arcane ambulance outside Kingdom Hospital sets off a series of events linking a psychic patient, the ghost of a young girl, the victim of clinical malpractice, an arrogant neurosurgeon and a medical staff presided over by department heads who belong to a Masonic-like lodge. To make matters worse, the hospital itself, built on top of an age-old swamp, is slowly sinking into the ground.

The Lars von Trier film that even his detractors could like, *The Kingdom* finds the *enfant terrible* of European cinema at his most playful, creating a hybrid of ghost story, soap opera, black comedy and thriller. Originally commissioned for television and shot either side of *Breaking the Waves*, these two five-hour series are entirely original takes on the hospital dramas that dominate the small screen, using hand-held cameras, grainy film stock and murky lighting to disorientate and disturb.

Opening with a mood-setting prologue in the swamp that existed hundreds of years before the hospital was built, *Kingdom I* sees the ghosts of the past appear on the wards and relations between hospital staff break down. Following the bizarre birth of an adult baby at the end of the first instalment, *Kingdom II* substitutes ghosts for the grotesque, featuring an outlandish turn – even by his standards – from Udo Kier, as the oversized infant. Trier's concern with the hubris of modern medical practice belies many of the film's narrative strands. Where Lindsay Anderson's similarly anarchic *Britannia Hospital*, or the Stephen King-penned US remake of von Trier's series failed, *The Kingdom* succeeds in its sideswipes against doctors playing God, de-personalisation of the patients and hospital administrations out of control.

THE DISCS

Try to source this (now rare) Danish set, rather than any of the inferior or incomplete other editions out there. As it was originally made for TV, the transfers are good, even if the films look like they were shot through dirty bathwater. The limited commentary is amusing, with von Trier on fine, if infantile form, informing us that his amusing summations at the end of each series were performed minus his trousers. There are few extras, which include a bizarre pop video for the theme song, as well as adverts directed by von Trier for a Danish newspaper, ranging from a bizarre sketch in a sauna to a series of monologues featuring actor Ernst-Hugo Järegård in various guises.
(IAN HAYDN SMITH)

Kiss Me Deadly

(USA, 1955)

Director: Robert Aldrich
Label: MGM (USA)
Region: 1 (NTSC)
Discs: 1

THE FILM

Mickey Spillane loathed the changes that director Robert Aldrich made to his 1953 novel (drug traffickers became dealers in something far more precious and powerful, while granite-jawed hero Mike Hammer was presented as unambiguously sadistic and dislikable); yet the film's critical reputation has come to far outshine Spillane's own. One of cinema's most striking pre-title sequences sets the edgy tone. A thin, short-haired woman (Cloris Leachman, in her first film role) runs half-dressed down a road, her jagged breathing weirdly amplified on the soundtrack. Hammer (Ralph Meeker) stops for her – and the trouble he picks up has as little in common with his usual 'bedroom dick' work as this film does with the smoother, glossier end of film noir. The harsh angles and high-contrast black and white cinematography reference German Expressionism; the violence is brutal; and there's nothing sexy or playful about Hammer's interaction with the raw, nervy women he encounters. Hammer might be the closest thing we have to a good guy here, but Meeker's extended snarl of a performance renders him scarier than some of the villains. This is a film that plays out on the verge of hysteria. After such a build-up, only a truly explosive ending would suffice – and Aldrich doesn't diasappoint.

The film's direct stylistic influence upon the more scholarly breed of contemporary directors is a further source of fascination. David Lynch nabbed the strobe-lit corridors and burning beach house for *Lost Highway*, while the mysterious glowing box foreshadows both Alex Cox's *Repo Man* and Quentin Tarantino's *Pulp Fiction* (though the latter denies the connection).

THE DISC

Along with subtitles and scene selection, the disc offers the original theatrical trailer, which represents a fascinating example of the bombastic mis-selling of an awkward movie (the voice-over promises 'Girls Fleeing in Terror from Things Beyond Description!', while the clips emphasise kisses and exposed thighs, leaving the impression of a sexed-up stalk-and-slash thriller). There's also a chance to compare two different endings, both of which have been accepted as 'definitive' in their time. The original US cinema cut concludes the film in abrupt, truncated style, which contradicted the screenplay and studio synopsis; some speculate that the mangling was a studio editor's slip, although there is evidence of impositions by local state censors. Aldrich's intended ending, included here, was shown abroad (although in Britain the BBFC imposed heavy cuts elsewhere in the film), and restored to the film from his personal print in 1997. The back of the UK DVD box also promises both endings, but you only get the longer. (HANNAH McGILL)

Kung Fu Hustle

(Hong Kong/China, 2004)

Director: Stephen Chow
Label: Columbia TriStar
(UK/Europe/Hong Kong/Korea)
Region: 2 (PAL) / 3 (NTSC)
Discs: 1 / 2

THE FILM

Director-producer-writer-actor Chow, veteran of around 60 films in his native Hong Kong, crashbanged into Western consciousness with the deliriously deranged *Shaolin Soccer*, a musical that mixed cartoon kung fu with magic-realist football and filled a gap you didn't know existed. As warm-hearted and relentlessly violent a comedy as you're ever likely to see, it was shoddily released in the cinema, hacked and dubbed, and still hasn't received the DVD treatment it deserves (although even the knocked-up version is worth a scope). Fortunately, there were no such problems with Chow's follow-up, the excellent *Kung Fu Hustle*, which was garlanded on cinematic release and comes here beautifully presented in a giftbox special edition DVD.

A Mel-Brooks-meets-Quentin-Tarantino-style homage to myriad martial arts films, only with jokes, dancing and the odd nod to Looney Tunes, the film stars Chow as a cheap hood who wants to join the fearsome local axe gang, and subsequently gets caught in the middle of their row with the unexpectedly feisty residents of rundown Pigsty Alley. Chow borrows far and wide – from westerns, Buster Keaton, James Cagney and Busby Berkeley musicals, as well as the Chinese kung fu serials of his youth – but never stoops to dread irony, Zhang Yimou-style pomposity or Jackie Chan's gurning slapstick. His innovations are delightful – a *Road Runner*-style chase scene; a human kung fu bullfrog – and the result is a film that's original, brilliant and very funny.

THE DISC(S)

Avoid the Region 1 edition, which has taken a couple of cuts and had some of the bloodshed toned down. The UK giftbox edition comes with some essential collectables – playing cards, keyring, inflatable axe and sweatband (how have you managed to live without them?) – but all Region 2 releases have the same extras: out-takes, a couple of deleted scenes, poster art, commentary (not as revealing as you'd hope), a good 20-minute interview with Chow and a decent making-of doc. You can watch *KFH* dubbed or subtitled, and the anamorphic widescreen is as good as befits a high-budget film. If that's not enough for you, hunt out one of the Region 3 Korean special editions – one comes in a leather case with a hardback picture book; the other features a fine Samuel L Jackson-narrated documentary, 'The Art of Action', which looks at the history of the martial arts genre. (PETER WATTS)

L.A. Confidential

(USA, 1997)

Director: Curtis Hanson
Label: Warners (all territories)
Region: Any
Discs: 1

THE FILM

'Unfilmable' is one of those labels that film directors see as more of a challenge than a warning, and so it was with *L.A. Confidential*, a powerful, dense noir based on James Ellroy's idiosyncratic, superior pulp thriller. Director Curtis Hanson and writer Brian Helgeland took necessary liberties with Ellroy's Byzantine plot and placed his focus on the detailed evocation of lowlife and illusion in 1950s Los Angeles. The action centres around three policemen (Kevin Spacey, Russell Crowe and Guy Pearce) asked to find a balance between principle and ambition when they get drawn into a complex case of high-level greed and corruption after a massacre at a late-night diner.

Spacey is excellent, oozing sleazy charm as a cop more in love with the image than the reality, but the latter two are breathtaking: Crowe's Bud White is a demented, pugilistic, righteous angel; Pearce's Ed Exley a man of introspective, cold cunning. Solid back-up includes Danny De Vito as a muckraking hack and Oscar-winning Kim Basinger as a Veronica Lake lookalike and the film's pivotal squeeze. Following a direct line from Bogart, Cagney and Nicholson, this is self-hating Hollywood filmmaking at its finest, both homage and accusation: a cinematic and spiritual *mea culpa*.

THE DISC

No director's commentary on this decent disc, but it's otherwise loaded with useful extras. Los Angeles-philes should first turn to the nifty interactive map that allows the viewer to take a virtual tour of the key locations used by an LA-saturated film, with comments from Hanson. Making-of doc 'Off the Record' details the history of the film, concentrating mainly on the difficulty of adapting Ellroy's novel. Extremely informative, it includes interviews with all major cast and crew members (including Ellroy and Hanson), plus screen tests.

Finally, there's a fascinating short in which Hanson explains his original pitch: he used various images of Los Angeles, both iconic and forgotten, to show prospective producers how he intended this most visual of films to look. The three shorts make for a satisfying complement to one of Hollywood's more intelligent offerings of the 1990s. (Rumours of a new special edition were unconfirmed at the time of going to press.) (PETER WATTS)

Labyrinth

(UK/USA, 1986) Collector's Edition

Director: Jim Henson
Label: Sony (USA)
Region: 1 (NTSC)
Discs: 1

THE FILM

Labyrinth is legendary, not only to a generation of women who grew up idolising teenage heroine Sarah (Jennifer Connolly), but to producers and execs, who discovered the amazing possibility that video could create (remunerative) cult hits out of films with poor box-office takings.

One of the pleasures of growing up with the film, from cinema through video to DVD, is how it changes with you. On DVD, you can move forward frame-by-frame to identify startling Henson signatures. The length of *Labyrinth*'s trivia page on IMDb is testament to the loving care of team Henson, whose muppety creatures populate the labyrinth, ruled over by the Goblin King, Jareth (David Bowie). Sarah accidentally brings his world into hers when she wishes that the Goblin King would take her annoying infant step-brother. When Sarah recants, Jareth challenges her to solve his labyrinth, populated by Sarah's childhood toys brought to life, and possessed of all the dreamy illogic one would expect from a film scripted by ex-Python Terry Jones.

Bowie, who supplied five original, haunting songs for the soundtrack, reprises his persona from *The Man Who Fell to Earth* and *The Hunger* as a preternatural inhuman beauty, and his scenes with 16-year-old Connolly have a disturbing, fairytale sexuality. Sarah's fascination with the elaborately-coiffed Jareth and his tight jodhpurs is both the absorbing heart of the movie, and instructive, in that Sarah learns how to see through and resist his cruel attractions. There are no other performances *per se*, just the act of wild imagination – the way all children build fantastic tales out of family lives and toys' adventures – brought spectacularly and satisfyingly to life in a surprisingly radical reminder that nothing is as it seems, and authorities have no power over us but what we give them.

THE DISC

No explanation of Bowie's hairstyle is offered, but the UK and American Collector's Edition sets provide plenty of other creature features, from master goblineer Brian Froud's original character sketches to a sweet making-of featurette. Most of the extras are static galleries (photos, storyboards, filmographies), though for the full '80s spirit there's an original trailer alongside the vintage-posters gallery. The main event is beautifully remastered, with sound so clear that you can hear every rude word mumbled by the wee creatures that turn the stones around. The US Collector's Edition trumps the UK version with the inclusion of collector's postcards and a collector's booklet, although at the time of writing those collectors had pushed the price into the premium bracket. (SOPHIE MAYER)

The Lady Eve

(USA, 1941)

Director: Preston Sturges
Label: Criterion Collection (USA)
Region: 1 (NTSC)
Discs: 1

THE FILM

In a few frenzied years in the early 1940s, Preston Sturges set a filmmaking pace few have come close to touching. One of the very first major Hollywood writer-directors, he turned out a breathless run of supersonic screwball comedies – *The Great McGinty*, *Christmas in July*, *Sullivan's Travels*, *The Palm Beach Story*, *The Miracle of Morgan's Creek*, *Hail the Conquering Hero* – that took the genre to unprecedented heights of sophistication and farce. And within the films, the pace was just as extraordinary: if their rococo chitchaw evinces his background as a screen scribe, his sleek visual sense and ringmastery of an inimical company of players provided for some equally uproarious screen antics. A frequent punctuating Sturges refrain is a furiously speeding train, evidently the sensation he wished to impress upon his audience.

Surely his most perfect concoction, *The Lady Eve* exemplifies his exceptional ability to have his satiric cake and eat it. Fondly skewering both the airs of the mating game and the (dis)graces of the rich and mighty, it plays out the fall – biblical and literal – of Henry Fonda's virginal ale heir Charles Pike, a teetotal sort first met collecting snakes up the Amazon. On a cruise ship back to civilisation he takes a tumble for Barbara Stanwyck's card sharp, a to-the-manor-born hustler who equally falls for him. Resolving to match his ingenuousness with her sincerity (if he's on the level then she can be too), she runs into his priggishness at the first hurdle. And so, smarting for retribution – or perhaps to deliver a crash course in the many faces of girls 'good' and 'bad', and the right and proper foolishness of love – she transforms into the Lady Eve Sidwich, an avenging angel in English aristo's clothing . . .

THE DISC

Criterion's edition is a typical bang-up job. Film scholar Marian Keane offers a richly interpretive commentary, musing on the film's dynamics of innocence and knowledge, truth and performance, difference and sameness, and the gullibility integral to both film viewing and falling in love. There's the complete recording of a 1942 Lux Radio Theater adaptation of the film with Stanwyck and Ray Milland in lieu of Fonda; a gallery of the film's costume designs by the great Edith Head (to whom *The Incredibles* paid homage); a brief appreciation by Peter Bogdanovich; and a fulsome photo scrapbook, alongside the film's original trailer. The video transfer (from a 35mm duplicate negative and 'sweetened' magnetic track) is duly dazzling.

You'll also want Sturges' other films, greater and lesser, and can get *The Lady Eve* and most of them on the seven-disc 'Written and Directed by Preston Sturges' (R2), aka 'Preston Sturges – The Filmmaker Collection' (R1). The price is good, the transfers mixed, the extras paltry (trailers, a booklet of bios, and Terry Jones' underwhelming R2-only *Lady Eve* commentary). It's also badly lacking *The Miracle of Morgan's Creek* – but a decent Paramount R1 disc is available for a song. (NICK BRADSHAW)

The Last Picture Show

(USA, 1971)

Director: Peter Bogdanovich
Label: Columbia TriStar (UK/USA)
Region: 2&4 (PAL) / 1 (NTSC)
Discs: 1

THE FILM

Peter Bogdanovich's second film – the work that would make his name, and overshadow the rest of his career – takes place in the early 1950s, in a small, dusty Texas town where there appears nothing for the resident teenagers to do except catch a movie and wait to die. In the early '70s, young moviegoers couldn't help but empathise: these kids are peaceniks who would rather make out with one another than fight their elders' battles; one early gag has the older townsfolk repeatedly bemoan the school football team's tackling ability.

'You're rich and miserable,' local sweetheart Jacy (Cybill Shepherd) tells her faded mother (Ellen Burstyn), 'I don't want to be like you.' In the final scene, some kind of reconciliation is offered, but this intergenerational *détente* is liable to count for nothing as the lasting legacy of the '50s – teenage rebellion and American involvement in South East Asia – blows in.

The Last Picture Show remains one of the quieter, more ruminative films made by the '70s movie brats, with ballads on the jukebox and Bogdanovich's broad-canvas style tempered by writer Larry McMurtry's precision eye for small-town poetry. The cast forms a melancholy parade: former stars (Ben Johnson), stars-to-be (Shepherd, Jeff Bridges, Randy Quaid), actors who never quite made it (the Bottoms boys, Timothy and Sam) and actresses who should have been bigger (Burstyn, Cloris Leachman). Outside on Main Street, winds rustle the leaves, buses head off into the unknown, and we're left to witness a moment passing, gone forever.

THE DISC

The 'director's cut' tag seems an unnecessary fuss over the inclusion of one one-minute scene restored shortly after the film's Oscar success and, given Bogdanovich's erudite commentaries elsewhere (*Targets, Paper Moon*), it's a pity there's no talk track here. The highlight is '*The Last Picture Show*: A Look Back', which continues the retro theme through interviews with most of the film's key players. As directed by Laurent Bouzereau, presently the go-to guy for DVD extras, this delves a little deeper than usual: we learn how the townsfolk were unhappy with the film's portrayal of teenage sex, and Shepherd is as forthright as ever discussing Bogdanovich's tyrannical qualities and her battles with *Playboy* over stills from the skinny-dipping scene. Also included: filmographies, the original trailer and a featurette with a youthful, somewhat haughty Bogdanovich repeating many of the anecdotes heard elsewhere. The film looks as luminous as it ever did. (MIKE McCAHILL)

Late Spring, Early Summer & Tokyo Story

(Japan, 1949/1951/1953)

Director: Yasujiro Ozu
Labels: Tartan Video (UK); also Criterion Collection (USA)
Region: 2 (PAL) – Tartan; 1 (NTSC) – Criterion
Discs: 3 (Tartan)

ORIGINAL TITLES: *Banshun, Bakushû, Tokyo Monogatari*

THE FILMS

Yasujiro Ozu made 53 films. One of them (*Tokyo Story*) regularly makes the all-time top-ten lists. The other 52 are seldom discussed, perhaps because it's been so hard to see them in the West, until now. But this box set places *Tokyo Story* in its proper context, as part of a wider project.

Ozu worked with a loyal company of collaborators, most notably actors Setsuko Hara and Chishu Ryu. In all three of these films, Hara plays a woman called Noriko. They're not strictly a trilogy, as each Noriko is subtly different; but there are so many connections between the films that they're best seen as a triptych.

They all deal with a common question: what happens to human values in the face of modernity? In *Tokyo Story*, an ageing couple visit their grown-up children, and realise that they have no place in their world. *Early Summer* deals with the difficulties of being a modern woman in a traditional setting.

A sense of disappointment and regret runs through the films, transformed by acceptance into grace. The feeling is most powerfully evoked in *Late Spring*, in which a widowed father realises that it's best for his daughter to marry, though this will leave him alone in the world. She doesn't want to abandon him, but he persuades her through an elaborate charade in which he hides his true feelings. Only when she's gone, and he is sitting on his own at home, peeling an apple, does he finally drop his head – and it is one of the most heartbreaking moments in all of cinema.

In all these films, Ozu's style is remarkably controlled and precise. He favoured one static shooting position, and used the simplest domestic objects – doors, stairs, tables and chairs – to create precise geometries that visually manifest his characters' inner spaces, and the social ties and obligations that bind them together. The result is exquisitely understated – but, at its best, intensely moving.

THE DISCS

The Tartan box is a good place to start if you're new to Ozu. It features all-new subtitles, acclaimed as the most accurate yet, but the NTSC transfers are not attractive, and the extras are disappointing: no commentaries or background material, just trailers and photo galleries. For confirmed fans seeking something richer, the Criterion single discs for *Late Spring* and *Tokyo Story* are highly recommended. (SF SAID)

Laura

(USA, 1944)

Director: Otto Preminger
Label: 20th Century Fox (USA)
Region: 1 (NTSC), 2 (PAL)
Discs: 1

THE FILM

Preminger's *Laura* is a murder mystery about a woman who isn't dead, told by a supercilious narrator who is, and solved by a necrophiliac. At least, that's one interpretation. It's also about a painting. Watch the moment carefully when Dana Andrews' detective, McPherson, is transfixed by the portrait of the dead Laura (Gene Tierney) above the fireplace in her apartment. Whisky in hand, he dozes off. And he's suddenly awakened by the real, live Laura entering her living room like Lazarus. 'You're alive,' says McPherson, rubbing his eyes. Or is he still dreaming?

Preminger took over the film from Rouben Mamoulian. It was his first major success, got five Oscar nominations, and proved that his dry, ironic, distanced style could work at the box office. But it's the film's deft psychological layering that makes it a masterpiece. David Raksin's score ushers us into a *Vertigo*-like spiral of romantic obsession – the music seems to be Tierney's birthright, and we instantly understand why everyone's in love with Laura and needs to possess her.

Sitting spiderishly astride the movie is Clifton Webb's dapper and poisonous Waldo Lydecker, a role supposedly based on *New Yorker* theatre critic Alexander Woolcott. Lydecker's gay, you've got to assume, but his hold over Laura is nonetheless the movie's most intoxicating. 'I hope you'll never regret what promises to be a disgustingly earthy relationship,' goes his sign-off to the happy couple, the highlight of a screenplay as bright and bevelled as a sapphire.

THE DISC

Laura's genesis always has been the stuff of film-historical legend. In her terrifically perceptive commentary, scholar Jeanine Basinger describes it as an 'accidental classic' in the *Casablanca* mould – a movie Fox initially accorded B status, only for the script, direction and performances to come together more perfectly than anyone could have predicted. Basinger, interrupted every now and then by genial bits of anecdote from composer David Raksin, is superb on the subtle glories of the film's lighting and production design, too. Historian Rudy Behlmer, on a separate track, offers a well-researched account of the movie's journey from page to screen, quoting extensively from Darryl F Zanuck's memos to Preminger on matters of casting and characterisation. We learn that a different ending was shot, tested and then (rightly) discarded; and that a key montage during Lydecker's flashback was trimmed back, supposedly to avoid upsetting homesick GIs with too much glitz. Those trimmings are here, and also A&E biographies of Tierney and Vincent Price. (TIM ROBEY)

The Leopard

(Italy/France, 1963)

Director: Luchino Visconti
Label: Criterion Collection (USA)
Region: 1 (NTSC)
Discs: 2

THE FILM

Just like John Webster, Luchino Visconti had the gift of seeing the skull beneath the skin. Rather than death's austerity, what fascinates Visconti is the lush sweetness of decay. *The Leopard* is coloured by the riches of rot: autumnal shades indoors and a white-hot light outdoors strip away the last of Sicily's distinct society in the face of Italian unification. Watching the film is like being absorbed utterly into an oil painting; in some ways, only its length and social complexity betrays its adaptation from a literary source: Giuseppe di Lampedusa's masterpiece.

The central plot of the film, the romance between dashing young aristocratic Tancredi (Alain Delon), who joins Garibaldi's red shirts, and fiery Angelina (Claudia Cardinale), a merchant's daughter, acts as historical foreshadowing as rural traditions fall sway to the rise of the bourgeoisie and the hushed sounds of Italian nationalism can be heard. But only the driest political economist would halt at that level: the film (and its beautiful leads) is as richly textured and gorgeously complex as the tapestried palatial abode of Prince Salina (Burt Lancaster), Tancredi's uncle and the film's moral centre.

As in a fairytale, the film proceeds through the resplendent logic of dinners, hunts and balls without ever losing its burning melancholy. The three central characters seem on the verge of the Brechtian revelation that they are just actors in a larger historical drama, especially Angelica, whom Cardinale embodies with a blazing erotic intelligence that raises her above the traditional fairytale princess. She appears to emit the warm colours captured by Giuseppe Rotunno's cinematography, making the closing scene at the ball — and her dance with Prince Salina — in every way the film's beating heart. Even dubbed into Italian, Lancaster radiates both gravitas and fragility, expressing an entire way of life coming to a dignified end.

This is a film of endings, and it manages it superbly: the audience is given a release that can only be described as spiritual, like entering a darkened cathedral from the blinding heat of the midday sun.

THE DISCS

This long-awaited DVD release is taken from a digitally restored print that, for the first time for English audiences, presents the full-length film with subtitles. For Burt Lancaster fans, or those who remember fondly seeing the film at the cinema in its attenuated English dub, a remastered version of the English release appears on a second disc. (SOPHIE MAYER)

The Life and Death of Colonel Blimp

(UK, 1943)

Directors: Michael Powell and Emeric Pressburger
Label: Criterion Collection (USA)
Region: 0 (NTSC)
Discs: 1

THE FILM

Extrapolated from David Low's comic-strip creation, Powell and Pressburger's 1943 epic is as bold and colourful as any animated film. It's propaganda, but propaganda for the kind of country that could handle a satire of its officer class (and what Low called the 'feudal-aristocratic tradition') at the height of war. Given the name of Clive Candy, Blimp (Roger Livesey) begins the film an Edwardian relic whose Queensberry rules approach to war has been rendered obsolete by the Blitzkrieg and by the army of bolshy young men conscripted to fight it. In a typically iconoclastic Powell and Pressburger move, the critic Raymond Durgnat noted, 'Blimp's fumbling is contrasted not, as one might expect, with an ordinary Briton, but with the direct, efficacious, and manlier gallantry of his Prussian counterpart,' Theo Kretschmar-Schuldorff (Anton Walbrook).

Taking Clive and Theo's ambivalent friendship, viewed in flashback, as an allegory for 40 years of Anglo–German rivalry, the film construes Britain's imperial adventures as at once a symptom of emotional dishonesty and a diversion from having to face up to its lonely consequences. Made at the height of the British studio system the film was, as such, extensively the product of European émigrés – not only the Hungarian Emeric Pressburger, but also French cinematographer Georges Périnal and German designer Alfred Junge. Famously, Churchill wanted to ban it; if *Blimp* never quite suffered this dramatic fate, the critical establishment, largely committed to drab realism, managed to neglect the film for 20 years to much the same effect.

THE DISC

Martin Scorsese fell in love with a butchered print of *Blimp*, seen in black-and-white on New York television, during his movie-mad childhood, and was instrumental in promoting the British Film Institute's full-length Technicolor restoration seen here. Scorsese – whose devotion to the Powell-Pressburger team is as well-documented as it is, he says, 'unaccountable' – introduces the commentary, recorded for a laserdisc release in 1988, but the main attraction is the late director Michael Powell, his impressive drawl counterpointing his acolyte's trademark rat-a-tat delivery. Perhaps alone among his generation of filmmakers in providing a DVD commentary, Powell (b. 1905) is a natural. By turns whimsical, paying special attention to his ex-fiancé Deborah Kerr's various hats, and analytical ('Max Ophüls could have done better'), Powell's commentary is a singularly personal treat. In a typically thoughtful edition, the Criterion disc provides background both on the Powell-Pressburger team and on David Low, many of whose fearlessly anti-appeasement cartoons are reproduced here.
(HENRY K MILLER)

Lilo and Stitch

(USA, 2002)

Directors: Dean DeBlois & Chris Sanders
Label: Disney (Australia)
Region: 4 (PAL)
Discs: 2

THE FILM

'*Ohana* means family, and family means nobody gets left behind – or forgotten.'
So Lilo tells her pet dog Stitch in this unusual Disney film. It's a shame that
Disney doesn't seem capable of taking her advice: many of its classics get left
behind when it comes to DVD availability and extras. Luckily, *Lilo and Stitch*
isn't one of them.

Lilo's family is not of the Disney (evil step)mom and pop variety. Similarly,
Lilo is not a sylphlike paleskinned brunette, but a healthy indigenous Hawaiian
kid. Her sister Nani (voiced by Tia Carrere) is no princess: she's a luau waitress, and her would-be boyfriend David is a fire-breathing slacker. Lilo feeds
sandwiches to fish, and bites a white girl who insults her. That combination
of lovable whimsy and amoral violence means a teenage Lilo would fit perfectly
into *Buffy the Vampire Slayer*'s Sunnydale but, as a six-year-old, she's 'troubled'
– and hardcore social worker Cobra Bubbles (voiced by, and modelled on, Ving
Rhames) is on her and Nani's case.

They have three days to shape up, but the classical Hollywood shtick ends
there. The puppy that Lilo adopts turns out to be as whimsical and amoral as
she is. After all, he's a blue, six-armed, indestructible alien experiment
programmed to be evil, and therefore exiled from his home planet. Cue mayhem:
a space chase, alien mad scientists in drag, Elvis medleys, Roswell jokes,
surfing, the spectacular demolition of Lilo's house (Stitch, in the kitchen, with
a chainsaw) and a subtle critique of colonialism. Seriously. The glorious anarchy
is untempered by sentiment, and yet the film is full of simple, moving moments
in which the tight-knit misfit family is threatened by forces, both galactic and
bureaucratic, beyond their control. If you've ever wondered why Disney films
couldn't be as subversive as Warner Bros cartoons, and why Warner Bros characters lacked the affable charm of Disney protagonists, then this genius alien
experiment is for you.

THE DISCS

If you want the warm fuzzies to last, skip the dire sequel, and check out the
two-hour making-of documentary, with its innovative 'footnote' system that
takes you to the deleted scenes being discussed, including the original ending,
in which a plane flies through canyons of tower blocks, which was deleted
during the final stages of production in September 2001. There are also music
videos, games designed to stimulate children's memories and imaginations, and
a surprisingly educational (and inoffensive) series of 'postcards' about Hawaii.
The UK edition replaces a scene from the film featuring the use of a washing
machine as a hiding place, lest we get ideas. (SOPHIE MAYER)

Lisa and the Devil

(Italy/West Germany/Spain, 1973)

Director: Mario Bava
Label: Raro Video (Italy)
Region: 0 (PAL)
Discs: 2

THE FILM

Tourist Lisa (Elke Sommer) winds up stranded at a remote villa outside Toledo, Spain, home to a bizarre aristocratic family apparently in thrall to their charming butler, played by Telly Savalas.

Starting out as a respected cinematographer, Mario Bava soon made a name for himself as a director of striking low-budget films like *Black Sunday*, *Planet of the Vampires*, and *Danger Diabolik*. After some financial success, he was given free reign by producer Alfredo Leone to make the film that he wanted, and *Lisa and the Devil* was the result. A film of rich and unparalleled beauty, its loose, dream-world narrative is peppered with high Gothic symbolism and long, lingering glances, all suggestive of thoughts and deeds on the cusp of the unreal. Possessed by a history of lust, murder and the love of the damned, the family seem permanently doomed to re-enact their sinister past, trapped in a Byzantine hall of mirrors, and watched over by the bemused, lollipop-slurping Savalas. (Telly would carry his trademark lolly into his next role – Kojak.)

Some may be frustrated by Bava's baroque approach to story, but they're missing the point, as did producer Alfredo Leone. Haunting and beautiful as the original is, Leone had *Lisa* brutally re-edited, with new 'possession' footage, starring a no-doubt puzzled Robert Alda (father of Alan!), inserted to make the film more commercial in the wake of *The Exorcist*. Renamed *House of Exorcism*, it became a film to be generally avoided, though a comparison of the two makes for an interesting exercise. The real tragedy, though, is that many have confused it with Bava's original.

THE DISCS

The Raro edition (see *www.rarovideo.com*) includes both films, in far better condition than Image Entertainment's Region 1 disc. *Lisa* is presented in a richly coloured 1.85.1 widescreen print, with options of the Italian or English soundtracks – though there are a couple of weird lip-synching errors that are presumably present in the original. An interesting one-hour documentary, 'Exorcising Lisa', details the film's troubled history, and includes interviews with Bava's son and assistant Lamberto, now a filmmaker in his own right. A Mario Bava filmography and biography round out the package nicely. (MARK PILKINGTON)

The Little Foxes

(USA, 1941)

Director: William Wyler
Label: MGM (USA)
Region: 1 (NTSC)
Discs: 1

THE FILM

A dab hand at the confined literary adaptation, Wyler might have needed two goes at Lillian Hellman's lesbian-themed classic *The Children's Hour*, but he instantly nailed *The Little Foxes*, her despairing 1939 melodrama about money-making and marital skulduggery in America's turn-of-the-century Deep South. A Broadway smash with Tallulah Bankhead, the play was snapped up by Samuel Goldwyn, but Wyler insisted that the part of scheming matriarch Regina Giddens ought to go to the far more popular Bette Davis. Goldwyn agreed, and Bankhead — also ousted by Davis for the screen version of *Dark Victory* (1939) — went ballistic.

More friction was to follow. This was Wyler and Davis's third collaboration after the Oscar-strewn *Jezebel* (1938) and *The Letter* (1940), but they never worked together again because of a sharp creative difference on how Regina should be played. Wyler wanted to soften the character and give her moments of wit and sympathy, but Davis stuck to a resolutely diamond-hard interpretation, much as Bankhead had, arguing there was simply no other way the role could work.

It's hard not to take the ladies' side. Regina drags home her terminally ill husband Horace (Herbert Marshall) to get his sign-off on a sweatshop business deal she's been brokering with brothers Ben (Charles Dingle) and Oscar (Carl Benton Reid) — but getting his assent proves harder than she'd imagined. Davis, plastered in ageing makeup and constantly rearranging her hideous thatch of curls, plays Regina not just as a calculating gorgon but as the ultimate domestic stage manager: she's forever shifting furniture about to suit her purposes, hovering with intent at the top of the stairs, even turning up the lamplights to defuse an intimate moment between her daughter (cowed Teresa Wright) and the suitor (Richard Carlson) she doesn't favour.

This was Gregg Toland's other assignment the year he shot *Citizen Kane*. His main coup is heightening Davis's bloodcurdling dominion with low angles whenever possible, but the bravura deep focus also allows a key supporting character, Oscar's neglected wife Birdie (Patricia Collinge), to be poignantly marginalised in the blocking. Davis, Wright and Collinge got Oscar nominations. Hellman's anti-capitalist theme, cued up by a Song of Solomon epigraph — 'Take us the foxes, the little foxes, that spoil the vines, for our vines have tender grapes' (2:15) — could hardly ring out more potently: the film's near-perfect.

THE DISC

DVD hasn't been a particularly kind medium to Wyler, beyond the obligatory four-disc special edition of *Ben-Hur* (1959). While most of his essential films — *Dodsworth* (1936), *The Best Years of Our Lives* (1946), *The Heiress* (1949) — are available in some form, these MGM discs do them the bare minimum of courtesy: all you tend to get are the theatrical trailers. Picture quality is at least reasonable. (TIM ROBEY)

London & Robinson in Space
(UK, 1994 & 1997)

Director: Patrick Keiller
Label: BFI (UK)
Region: 2 (PAL)
Discs: 2

THE FILMS

Patrick Keiller's signature works, which these two films are generally recognised as being, are pleasingly hard to describe. To call them documentaries, albeit ones that start from fictional conceits, seems wholly inadequate. They occupy a critical and creative space somewhere between cine-essay, haunted travelogue and psychogeography. Prefiguring the writings of WG Sebald, they may also be seen as audio-visual palimpsests that allow us to glean three centuries of European thought on topics such as public space, the residual power of Modernism, and both urban and rural ambulation.

The nominal subject of *London* is 'the problem of London' itself. Set against the backdrop of the fourth successive Tory General Election victory in 1992, it features a series of carefully framed static shots of its shopping malls, eerie suburbs and post-IRA-bomb topographies. This is the capital before its much-vaunted 'swinging' incarnation in the late 1990s. A place that is at once outmoded and troublingly new: the anachronistic rituals of the monarchy are played out on the streets alongside the increasingly grabby privatisation of the public realm by the City. The narration, voiced by Paul Scofield in the kind of plummy tone used by James Mason in Norman Cohen's *The London That Nobody Knows* (1967), has the droll melancholia associated with elderly Oxbridge dons.

In *Robinson in Space*, based on Daniel Defoe's *A Tour Through the Whole Island of Great Britain* (1724–1727), the unnamed narrator has been commissioned by an international advertising agency to examine the 'problem of England', in which capacity he and his gay friend Robinson make several journeys across the country to places as diverse as the West Midlands, Sellafield and Blackpool, the final town being posited, with what degree of irony is unclear, as a kind of utopia-in-Albion. Along the way, apparently history-less green spaces are revealed as the sites of power plants, intelligence bases and post-modern manufacturing zones. They are eerily soundless.

THE DISCS

These films, particularly *London*, have had considerable impact on left-field British image-producers such as Paul Kelly (who, with the band Saint Etienne, made the London-themed *Finisterre*) and Nick Relph and Oliver Payne. The BFI's well-packaged double-DVD set includes a 32-page booklet that contains two appreciative essays: 'The Secret City' by *Get Carter* director Mike Hodges and 'London: Necropolis of Fretful Ghosts' by noted psychogeographic writer Iain Sinclair. The booklet also contains an interview between Keiller and historian Patrick Wright. (SUKHDEV SANDHU)

The Loneliness of the Long Distance Runner
(UK, 1962)

Directors: Tony Richardson
Label: BFI (UK)
Region: 2 (PAL)
Discs: 1

THE FILM

There are a few great movies about sport: *Raging Bull*; *The Hustler*; *This Sporting Life*. [And *Kingpin* – Eds.] But there is only one about the heroism of not playing up and playing the game – British director Tony Richardson's last 'kitchen-sink' drama, *The Loneliness of the Long Distance Runner*. Richardson had previously directed screen adaptations of John Osbourne's *Look Back in Anger* and *The Entertainer*, and Shelagh Delaney's *A Taste of Honey*; here he teamed with Alan Sillitoe, who adapted his own short story for the screen, just as he had adapted his novel *Saturday Night and Sunday Morning* for Karel Reisz (a hit in 1960).

Using natural light, extensive location shooting and youthful extras plucked from real borstals, Richardson's film is unusually ambitious in tone by the standards of kitchen sink. It is also graced with the debut screen appearance of Tom Courtenay, who turns in a magically insolent performance as Colin Smith, the anti-social tearaway given the chance to 'redeem himself' in a sports-day run against the local public school. Although the symbolism of Church, state and army at the film's climax may seem heavy-handed – the crowd is dotted with priests, colonels etc. – it remains a uniquely exhilarating moment in cinema. This is a movie about rebellion, as youthful and impassioned as it must have seemed 40 years ago (it was released in the USA with the hilarious title *Rebel with a Cause*). And it continues to exert its influence on disaffected young men to this day. Reputedly, Tom Courtenay's character gave his name to the greatest musical refuseniks of the 1980s – The Smiths.

THE DISC

This BFI DVD edition upholds the high standards set by previous company releases, including a small stills gallery and text biographies of Tony Richardson, Alan Sillitoe and the Free Cinema movement. On the commentary film historian Robert Murphy talks about both the film and the genre of kitchen sink itself; he reveals that the BBFC was so outraged by what it saw as Smith's conniving disregard for authority that they described the film as communist propaganda. The commentary also includes interspersed reminiscences from both Courtenay and Sillitoe. In addition, there is a video essay by the film's cinematographer Walter Lassally which sheds (natural) light on the location shooting for the film. The DVD has been mastered from a recent print (2002) and looks as good as you would expect. If you see it, grab it; there are indications this edition is already deleted. (ANDY MILLER)

The Lord of the Rings: The Fellowship of the Ring

(NZ/USA, 2002)

Special Extended DVD Edition

Director: Peter Jackson
Label: New Line (USA) / LNK (Portugal) / Village Roadshow (Australia)
Region: 1 (NTSC) / 2 (PAL) / 4 (PAL)
Discs: 4/5

THE FILM

The Passion of the Hobbit. That was my pre-viewing take: a slavish adaptation aimed at brainwashed devotees of a badly-written fantasy. As a confirmed Tolkien atheist, I looked forward to mocking wide-eyed earnestness while suffering outrage at the misogyny, racism and poor narrative technique.

Popcorn in hand. Lights down. Mockery on standby. And then: Cate Blanchett's cut-glass voice like a light in places where no light shines, condemning men who 'above all, desire . . . power'. Feminist Tolkien? I was in.

I still deny that Tolkien is a fantasy god, but I effusively embrace Peter Jackson as the Messiah. Jackson's gift is to summon not just a story but a world, light-drenched and dark-shadowed. For me, it's Viggo Mortensen's does-all-his-own-stunts performance as dirty-fingernailed swordsman Aragorn that embodies the three-hour convince-athon thrust on an unsuspecting public by a merry band of woodworkers, armourers, digitisers, and Hobbit stand-ins. Aware as I was of all the craft and trickery that had gone into realising every last hairy foot, the film came across like Mortensen's ranger: sweaty, passionate, hard-riding and utterly convincing. Only Jackson could take a fantasy epic and make it grip by the force of its wholehearted realism.

THE DISCS

The Fellowship blew my mind on the big screen, but it was on DVD, where the homely elements that make up Hobbiton could be savoured in detail, that the film truly came alive. Of the DVD's 46 chapters, 24 consist of either new or extended scenes. Even those who saw the cinema release five or six times would find it difficult to spot the additions. Who would want to? Their seamless integration means that they offer fantasy's deep pleasure of extended world-building – more Hobbity warmth, more elven floatiness, more Morian gloom.

Like the films themselves, the DVD extras – a combination of stills and extensive video diaries – work hard to satisfy Tolkien nuts with proof of Jackson's loving dedication, and offer film buffs 11 documentaries, forming what amounts to film school taught by the fellowship behind *The Fellowship*. Warning: watching all the extras is a lifetime commitment, with hidden Easter eggs, DVD-ROM content and – oh yes – two more box sets to buy . . .

(It's worth checking *dvdcompare.net* to navigate the sprawl of alternative editions. The Special Extended Editions contain the longer versions of the movies; some versions also offer the theatrical cuts for comparison. The Collector's Gift Sets big up to five discs, with a National Geographic 'Beyond the Movie' special, and toys. For purposes of PG certification, the UK editions truncate the 'Day in the Life of a Hobbit' featurette and cut entirely an MTV Movie Awards Easter egg clip, featuring Jack Black, Sarah Michelle Gellar and genital piercing.) (SOPHIE MAYER)

The Lost Honor of Katharina Blum

(West Germany, 1975)

Directors: Volker Schlöndorff & Margarethe von Trotta
Label: Criterion Collection (USA)
Region: 0 (NTSC)
Discs: 1

THE FILM

Schlöndorff and his then-wife von Trotta were branded 'terrorist sympathisers' for this fierce attack on what they saw as the forces undermining Germany's fledgling democracy from within. Post 9/11, their film's depiction of a society living in fear of homegrown terrorists and the attendant trampling of civil liberties by a reactionary state apparatus manages to perfectly skewer the contemporary zeitgeist all over again. Katharina Blum (Angela Winkler), a divorced domestic cleaner, is arrested after a one-night stand with a suspected anarchist terrorist (Jürgen Prochnow). She stubbornly refuses to betray his trust and disclose his whereabouts, even as the police and tabloid hacks contrive to break her resolve and smear her reputation. Aided by the precise, steely blue cinematography of Jost Vacano (a frequent Paul Verhoeven collaborator), the film renders Katharina's harrowing experiences with almost documentary clarity, while Winkler's beautifully controlled performance gives the measure of her mounting indignation at her life being manipulated to fit a dubious political agenda: the moment at which she trashes her flat in frustration is truly painful to behold.

If the film damns the police for their crass insensitivity and bureaucratic inflexibility, it reserves its bitterest ire for the yellow press. The film's source novel – by Nobel prize-winner Heinrich Böll – had been written as a direct response to his own demonisation at the hands of the daily tabloid *Bild-Zeitung* (which he criticised for its alarmist coverage of the Baader-Meinhof gang). Katharina's personal nemesis is not the ruthlessly careerist police chief, but rather the unscrupulous hack who weasels his way into an intensive care ward to question her dying mother, and it is his betrayals that eventually spur this political 'innocent' into murderous retaliation. It is precisely Katharina's political naivety that finally makes her ordeal so moving; in her stoical resistance to the oppressions of patriarchal paranoia, she becomes transfigured into a kind of saintly Everywoman.

THE DISC

Once again Criterion come up trumps, delivering a spanking new digital transfer supervised by Vacano along with textbook 24-bit audio remastering. Excerpts from a 1977 documentary on Böll, as well as new interviews with the directors and Vacano, help contextualise the film's production in the turbulent social realities of mid-'70s Germany, confirming its status as a brave document of a dangerous time as well as the first commercial feather in the New German Cinema's cap. (ANDY RICHARDS)

Magnolia
(USA, 1999)

Director: Paul Thomas Anderson
Label: Entertainment (UK)
Region: 2 (PAL)
Discs: 2

THE FILM

Paul Thomas Anderson's exhilarating three-hour treatise on Those Elements We Cannot Control, set over one eventful day in the San Fernando Valley, forms arguably the most ambitious undertaking in late 20th-/early 21st-century American cinema. Essentially, *Magnolia* is constructed as a sprawling obstacle course, testing the faith and endurance of both viewers and characters at every turn. Take Julianne Moore's extraordinary pharmaceutical freak-out in your stride, and you might stumble at the cast bursting into song; and that's even before beasts (*pace* Exodus 8:3) start falling from the sky.

Keep up, however, and you'll discover a true epic of intimacies, a master-piece of trivia that fuses together the cursory and the critical with audacious sleight of hand. Anderson's authorial credit reads 'PT Anderson', and the spirit of Barnum pervades much of a film that vacillates throughout between show-manship and spontaneity. Amongst the happy-sad human clowns, a who's-who of modern American acting (Moore, Philip Seymour Hoffman, William H Macy, Felicity Huffman, Philip Baker Hall) is complemented by the odd surprise: at the very least, *Magnolia* begs to be seen as one of the few films that dares to cast Tom Cruise — sharkish grin, incipient couch-vaulting madness and all — as a seemingly incorrigible power-freak.

THE DISCS

A suitably idiosyncratic selection. A smattering of out-takes prove certain elements (giggling, hand-eye co-ordination, Luis Guzman) really can't be controlled, while budding misogynists get more of Cruise's Frank Mackey. The tantalising trailers and TV spots do a very decent job narrowing down and clarifying the themes of what must be amongst the broadest of film canvases, and hardest to encapsulate; slightly less forthcoming is the Anderson-directed video for Aimee Mann's 'Save Me', in which the main cast do their level best to appear entirely miserable. (Did they not get overtime?)

Pride of place, though, goes to a 75-minute video diary, an entertainingly anecdotal account of a shoot that almost inevitably dragged on beyond schedule. As a record of Anderson's varying working methods, it's pretty good: we see him in precise, intense collaboration with Moore, mucking around with Hoffman, and letting Macy take the rise out of him. In a peculiar coda, Anderson gets girlfriend Fiona Apple to act out the role of 'Magnolia', an unruly infant who embarrasses and repels everyone with her shrieking-dancing routine. And you thought the frogs were weird . . . (MIKE McCAHILL)

Louis Malle Volume One

(France, 1957-63)

Director: Louis Malle
Label: Optimum World (UK)
Region: 2 (PAL)
Discs: 4

THE FILMS

This collection of Malle's first four features gives a sense of the impressive eclecticism that would characterise his career — a mark of versatility, doubtless, but also perhaps the reason why he was never fêted as much as European contemporaries with more unified styles and themes. *Lift to the Scaffold* (1957), while being a far more conventionally suspenseful noir than *Breathless*, still radiates *nouvelle vague* chic — from its moodily iconic breakthrough performances from Jeanne Moreau and Maurice Ronet as the ill-fated adulterers, to the mesmerising Miles Davis improvisations on the soundtrack. Moreau was equally memorable in Malle's second feature *Les Amants* (1958) as a bored provincial *bourgeoise* who finds unexpected liberation in a tryst with a young archaeologist she's only just met; kissing her child goodbye, she leaves the cloying comforts of husband and hearth and strikes out into the unknown. At the time of initial release, it was this generous non-judgementalism (perhaps the closest thing to Malle's defining quality) towards adultery, as much as the film's sexual frankness, that stirred controversy and made the film a taboo-busting *cause célèbre*.

For his next feature, Malle struck out on an altogether different tack by tackling an 'unadaptable' novel by Raymond Queneau. The result, *Zazie dans le Métro* (1960), hasn't dated as gracefully as much of Malle's other work — its frequent homages to silent-film slapstick (intended as cinematic analogues to Queneau's verbal pyrotechnics and pastiches) are now likely to evoke the spectre of Benny Hill. Still, they certainly provided a few pointers for Richard Lester's '60s work, and the film also introduced us to the multifarious talents of Philippe Noiret. *Le Feu Follet* (1963) was another dramatic shift, a sombre depiction of an alcoholic ex-soldier (Ronet) contemplating suicide but hoping to find some semblance of value that will stay his hand. This was perhaps the closest Malle came to a truly 'personal' film (a good friend had killed himself), and its compassion, lack of contrivance and measured approach to its sensational subject matter are the hallmarks of this undervalued director's greatest works.

THE DISCS

All of the Optimum discs have been transferred with good contrast and detailing, and each disc contains an interview with Vincent Malle, the director's brother, who helps contextualise these early works. Also included is Malle's 18-minute 1962 Tour de France documentary *Vive le Tour!* (also on the highly recommended five-disc Criterion Eclipse collection 'The Documentaries of Louis Malle'). Optimum's five-disc Volume Two collection is also worthwhile, although its three best films — *Murmur of the Heart*, *Lacombe Lucien* and *Au Revoir Les Enfants* — are available in a superior Criterion box set. Completists will want to note that Criterion's single-disc *Lift to the Scaffold* has a slightly superior transfer to Optimum's. (ANDY RICHARDS)

Man with a Movie Camera
(USSR, 1929)

Director: Dziga Vertov
Label: BFI (UK)
Region: 2 (PAL)
Discs: 1

THE FILM

Dziga Vertov's last silent movie has proved to be a film for all seasons. Adopted as a mascot in the 1960s both by revolutionaries keen to show they knew more than merely Eisenstein and by the new documentarists who'd taken on Vertov's slogan 'cinema truth', it's since become probably the best-known of all silents because of its knowing self-reference and the way it synthesises a whole lost world of '20s innocence. It's also one of the movies contemporary musicians most enjoy playing to.

Showing that 'life caught unawares' could be as fascinating as fiction was at least what Vertov wanted to prove with this manifesto film. After supervising newsreels and making promotional films for the Soviet state for a decade, this was his bid to make an artistic experiment in the spirit of Constructivism – a movie about what cinema could and should be. Following the life of the city (actually several collaged together) from dawn to evening, he shows a cinema audience mesmerised by seeing how what they're watching was made. Who needs fictional trash, he asks, when they can see the cameraman (his brother Mikhail) perilously gathering images from a speeding car and motorbike, from beneath a train and on top of a factory chimney?

Only on film can they experience the dizzying life of the modern city, with image piled on image. And also grasp how that film is made, when Vertov's editor, and wife, Svilova is shown stopping it, joining it to other shots, then magically setting it back in motion. Vertov claimed he was demystifying in the name of 'communist decoding', but was condemned for 'formalism' when Stalin wanted films with a simple upbeat message of loyalty to the Party. Ironically, this very formalism has ensured its survival when all the propaganda is forgotten or tainted.

THE DISC

The BFI's disc of Vertov's masterpiece offers an extraordinary range of choice, making it one of the most versatile of historical DVDs. Since there was no original score, musicians are free to improvise and silent-movie specialists, the percussive Alloy Orchestra follow Vertov's cues in their powerful rhythmic accompaniment, which lends real excitement to many passages. But if you prefer modern electronics, there's also an alternative score from In the Nursery. The best guide to the film's many subtleties is Latvian-born film historian Yuri Tsivian, who contributes a commentary and has ensured that the opening titles are fully translated, which throw down Vertov's challenge before the rest of the movie neatly demonstrates that no further explanation is needed. (IAN CHRISTIE)

The Manchurian Candidate

(USA, 1962) Special Edition

Director: John Frankenheimer
Label: MGM (USA)
Region: 1 (NTSC)
Discs: 1

THE FILM

One of the most potent films of the Cold War, Frankenheimer's delirious combination of dark political comedy and psychological thriller even-handedly satirises the Right, the Left and conspiracy theories through a plot of Byzantine complexity. It follows Bennett Marco (Frank Sinatra), as he discovers that an entire American patrol was captured during the Korean War and brainwashed by Communists. Marco's former comrade, Congressional Medal of Honour winner Raymond Shaw (Laurence Harvey) has been programmed to assassinate a presidential nominee at a Madison Square Gardens rally.

Shaw's mother (the superb Angela Lansbury) plots with the Russians and Chinese to install her simpleton husband, Senator John Iselin (James Gregory) in the White House, so she can gain control from behind the scenes – but she then plans to use this power against her former accomplices when she learns that the automaton killer they have produced for her is her own son. Both he and her husband are her stooges – ironically, the former is a Communist tool, while the latter is constantly warning of the Red menace. Frankenheimer draws attention to the artifice of the media by placing TV monitors within the frame, and indeed his film erases trust in the representation of politics: nothing is what it seems, and any manipulation of the public is possible.

THE DISC

In his commentary track, Frankenheimer recalls how *The Manchurian Candidate* was at first turned down by all the studios. He is proud of overcoming rejection and making a film which took on Senator McCarthy, on whom the rabidly anti-Communist Senator Iselin is clearly based. The film version of Richard Condon's novel became viable because Sinatra immediately agreed to appear. The project was favoured by Kennedy despite concern in some quarters about the treatment of the Russians. Frankenheimer rehearsed for two weeks before shooting, and in filming used techniques he had employed in television, working with wide-angle lenses in real locations. The structuring of the extraordinary nightmare sequences, with their 360-degree pans, was boldly entrusted to writer George Axelrod, despite his utter lack of editing experience. The results were a triumph. The entire crew was excited to be working on the film, and writer, director and star recall it with great satisfaction – for Sinatra, it was the high point of his acting career. (ADAM STREVENS)

Manhunter

(USA, 1986) Special Edition

Director: Michael Mann
Label: Momentum (UK)
Region: 2 (PAL)
Discs: 2

THE FILM

In 1991, Jonathan Demme's adaptation of *The Silence of the Lambs* – the second novel in Thomas Harris' Hannibal Lecter trilogy – became only the third picture ever to bag all five big Oscars. However, a fairly small, very smug group of filmgoers knew that Harris' evil genius had already had a far more satisfying cinematic outing, just five years earlier. With *Manhunter*, writer-director Mann – then best-known for his glossy cop series *Miami Vice* – looked to the first in Harris's trilogy, *Red Dragon*. In his first of several collaborations with the prodigiously gifted cinematographer Dante Spinotti, he delivered an unsettling, unforgettable, highly influential thriller, favouring visual and psychological detail over guts and grand guignol.

William Petersen (more recently of the thematically similar television series *CSI*) plays Will Graham, the FBI profiler who formerly caught Lecter – then spelt Lecktor – by learning to think like him, but gave himself a crushing breakdown in the process. Now, he finds himself called out of traumatised retirement to catch a particularly vicious new serial killer, one Francis Dolarhyde, aka the 'Tooth Fairy'.

The film is bursting with terrific performances – Graham's troubled, brilliant agent; Joan Allen's blind victim-to-be – but, inevitably, it's the psychos who steal the show. Tom Noonan is a six-foot-six-inch monolith of raging, at times pitiful psychosis as Dolarhyde, and Brian Cox's Lecktor makes Anthony Hopkins's later turn look downright meretricious. Above all, the film is high on the dangerous thrill of Graham's chase, and one can only gawp, riveted, as he edges ever closer towards his deranged quarry.

THE DISCS

Manhunter's career on DVD is itself a tortuous tale of 'true theatrical cuts', 'theatrical/hybrid prints' and 'restored director's cuts' partly or entirely grubbed from analogue videotape. Momentum's remastered, anamorphic special edition includes the latter two remixes. The 'director's cut', or what Mann call his 'preferred version', works out three minutes longer, and it's only the justifiably extended and reinstated scenes that bear the blight of poor source tapes.

There are also substantial extras: featurettes on the film's making and its look, a booklet with Will Graham's 'case notes' – and a terrific director's commentary. As Mann points out, police 'profiling' didn't even exist as a term in 1986, and this was the first film ever to give the phenomenon serious attention. He's particularly good on Lecktor – 'such a charismatic character that I wanted the audience almost not to get enough of him' – and boldly describes him as 'a wish-fulfilment character' for his constant ability 'to work his will'. As with the film proper, Mann's intellectual rigour and fascination with forensics blaze throughout. (MARK MONAHAN)

Marathon Man

(USA, 1976)

Director: John Schlesinger
Label: Paramount (all territories)
Region: Any
Discs: 1

THE FILM

'Is it safe?' inquires escaped Nazi dentist Christian Szell (Laurence Olivier) of unsuspecting Columbia grad student Tom Levy (Dustin Hoffman), referring – though Tom, strapped in terror to the chair, has no idea – to the contents of a safe-deposit box Szell has skulked out of hiding in Uruguay to claim. The plot of John Schlesinger's movie is wildly confusing beyond this – try working out exactly what Levy's brother (Roy Scheider) is up to in the first third before Szell knifes him in the stomach, embroiling Tom in the whole business – but it stands up as a singular example of the 1970s Hollywood thriller as an arena where anything goes, jazzed up by Schlesinger's beady, adrenalised direction in ways that make it sweat-inducing to this day. It's not just the root-canal torture that's memorable: the movie has a technically brilliant set-piece in every reel, from the opening car-rage spat between two elderly Manhattan motorists to an excruciatingly realistic *mano à mano* in a Paris hotel suite.

What we get is less the usual connective tissue of plot than, if you like, violence itself as an organising principle – Schlesinger, on his first genre assignment, seems to jump to whichever story strand he can milk for maximum shock and awe at any one time. Olivier's visit to Manhattan's diamond district, say – where he's recognised and catcalled by a hysterical victim – is horribly tense and resonant despite the script's absurd manoeuvres required to get him there, and Hoffman's bafflingly tenuous involvement in his own storyline actually helps the paranoia click. Almost unimprovably directed and acted given its outright mess of a screenplay (from William Goldman's hardly more coherent novel), *Marathon Man* is a reminder of how little the screen's best thrillers, from *The Big Sleep* to Michael Haneke's *Caché*, actually need to make overarching sense when what's going on in sequence after sequence is reward enough.

THE DISC

Hoffman relates the famous 'Dear boy, why don't you just try acting?' anecdote with eyes decidedly downcast: he was the one who first quoted it, but no-one ever printed Olivier's follow-up remark about how, given all of his own stage acrobatics, he was hardly one to talk. That's in a featurette called 'Remembering *Marathon Man*'; we also get an original promo film called, very naffly, 'The Magic of Hollywood', in which producer Robert Evans, still basking in the glory of *Chinatown*, perches on his desk at Paramount and gives us the hard sell as only he knows how. There's a slightly fawning send-off for Olivier on his last day's shooting, and miscellaneous rehearsal footage too. (TIM ROBEY)

Maria Full of Grace

(USA/Colombia, 2004)

Director: Joshua Marston
Label: Icon Home Entertainment (UK) / HBO (USA)
Region: 2 (PAL) / 1 (NTSC)
Discs: 1

THE FILM

While Steven Soderbergh's *Traffic* covered many aspects of Latin American drug trafficking – the US war against drugs, law enforcement on either side of the Mexican/US border, drug-addicted Americans – it missed one crucial perspective: that of the drug mules. With his memorable debut, writer/director Joshua Marston fills the gap.

Marston dares to give a human (and Spanish-speaking) face to the stereotype, seeking to understand what drives a mule to take such risks – the least of which is getting caught. A clean three-act structure involves a depiction of his heroine's life in rural Colombia, a clinical, frightening explication of the drug-muling process, and a final section in New York, where the consequences must be faced. As a whole, it is a brilliant synthesis of politically engaged, non-judgemental social realism in the Ken Loach tradition, and nerve-shredding thriller.

Catalina Sandino Moreno plays the eponymous 17-year-old, suffocating in a routine whose parameters are poverty and conformity. Tired of her arduous job in a rose plantation, an ungrateful family eating up her pay cheques and a dullard boyfriend who barely flickers when she announces she is pregnant, the spirited Maria is searching for an escape route when a mule scout smells her desperation.

The stand-out scenes are those in which Maria has to swallow several dozen drug pellets (the actress's discomfort inseparable from the character's) and the nail-biting flight to New York: how will Maria and her fellow mules hold their nerve through customs, when we get twitchy with an extra bottle of duty free? Throughout, Marston eschews the drab aesthetic that usually accompanies such material, for crisp, colourful, thoughtful compositions, to which the DVD does justice. And despite the handheld camera, his is an unobtrusive gaze, fixed firmly on the remarkable Moreno. In her first film, this brave actress never searches for our sympathy, but earns it in an incredibly emotional final reel.

THE DISC

Marston's superior commentary adds a new dimension to the experience of the film. This includes a history of Colombia's 40-year civil war (the dangers of which forced the production to shoot in Ecuador) and some very icky details of the customs shake-down in the US; a host of interesting casting choices, among them the retired drug-pellet packer who brought along his own equipment, and the film's producer playing a drug lord; a lexicon of drug-running practices ('triple-packing', 'shotgunning') and the truth of Moreno's pellet scene. Did she, or did she not, swallow? (DEMETRIOS MATHEOU)

The Marx Brothers
Silver Screen Collection
(USA, 1929–33)

Directors: Listed below
Label: Universal (USA)
Region: 1 (NTSC)
Discs: 6

FILM TITLES: *The Cocoanuts, Animal Crackers, Monkey Business, Horse Feathers, Duck Soup*

DIRECTORS: Robert Florey and Joseph Stanley / Norman Z MacLeod / Victor Heerman / Leo McCarey

THE FILMS

Pomp and pride may never have faced fiercer foes than Minnie Marx's irrepressible offspring, Jewish vaudevillians who took to the new talkies like chimps seizing the zoo intercom. Between Groucho's unchecked verbal barbs, Chico's delinquencies of language and logic, and Harpo's persuasive approximation of an overgrown four-year-old, the Marxist modus operandi constituted an anarchic assault on the full gamut of human institutions, from authority, civility, work and romance to rationality itself.

This collection of their five Paramount comedies – made before MGM softened them up – wends from the beach and jungle to the corridors of state. *The Cocoanuts* (1929) serves as an appetiser – creaky in execution as well as narrative, with Groucho as a proto-Basil Fawlty hotelier vying to rip off the wealthy denizens of a Florida beach resort. *Animal Crackers* (1930) is similar but better, with his Captain Spaulding returning to high society from a safari expedition, and Chico and Harpo bringing the wilderness behind.

Right in their stride now, *Monkey Business* (1931) has the quartet (if we are to include Zeppo, comical only inadvertently) as singing stowaways on a steamliner to America, making like mob goons and Maurice Chevalier. *Horse Feathers* (1932) finds Groucho running Huxley College as a less-than-successful den of iniquity, and ends with Harpo overhauling the rules of football. All of which builds to *Duck Soup* (1933), the *ne plus ultra* of political satire, in which derelict political patronage consigns the banana republic of Freedonia to the leadership of Groucho's Rufus T Firefly. The Marxes' aggressive-absurdist humour is given untrammelled rein – no love songs! no harp solos! – in what's also their most cinematically witty and savvy offering, down to the split-second-perfect mirror sequence.

THE DISCS

These DVDs preserve all the pops and scratches of extant prints of the Marxes' work (*Horse Feathers* is the scrappiest) and, while the movies were clearly somewhat crudely crafted, the world is still waiting for Universal to grant its comedy legacy the same TLC it has bestowed on, say, the Hitchcock canon. Warner's feature-packed box of the Marxes' lesser later MGM comedies surely shows the way.

Still, it's good to be able to replay the films without adding to the wear and tear (and to skip faster through Harpo's po-faced harp interludes). This Region 1 set comes with a nice if hardly exhaustive booklet of film images and Groucho quotes plus a dispensible sixth disc of the brothers' '70s *Today Show* appearances. The R2 equivalent offers instead a surfeit of the Marxes' worst: *A Girl in Every Port*, *Love Happy* and *Room Service*, all for completists only. (NICK BRADSHAW)

Master and Commander: The Far Side of the World

(USA, 2003) Special/Collector's Edition

Director: Peter Weir
Label: 20th Century Fox (all territories)
Region: Any
Discs: 2

THE FILM

Peter Weir's worlds have always been intriguingly self-contained – think of *The Truman Show*'s hermetic biosphere, the Amish idyll in *Witness*, or Harrison Ford's rainforest-living experiment in *The Mosquito Coast*. This made Weir absolutely the perfect director to adapt Patrick O'Brian, whose books go about creating a dauntingly detailed miniature society on board ship. 'This little wooden world' is how Russell Crowe's gruff captain, Jack Aubrey, describes his vessel, speaking with the wistful devotion of a man who knows no other home. By the end of this grand and beguiling movie you understand precisely why.

The great, joyful perversity of *Master and Commander* is how brusquely it gets the rip-roaring adventure stuff out of the way. The grand historical narrative cruises past an ocean away, and it's not even a moment of truth, particularly, for the HMS *Surprise* and her crew, patrolling the South American coastline in the year 1805. As far as fraught seamanship during the Napoleonic Wars can be, it's business as usual.

But *what* business. Weir's way with images – 'HOLD FAST' printed on the knuckles of an old sea dog, silhouetted clamberings in the rigging, Crowe's eyes intent as the compass spins – turns this into an experience that's all the more evocative for being so unusually abstract. And yet the bond between Aubrey and ship's doctor Maturin (a wonderfully sarcastic Paul Bettany) still rests at the very heart of the movie, a sublime ode to courage, duty and companionship in the eye of the storm.

THE DISCS

A clue to the purity of Weir's intentions here was his determination 'to hardly touch land', outside the beautiful scenes on the Galapagos Islands, where the second disc's ample array of featurettes also frequently weigh anchor. Preparing for an arduous sea shoot, Weir swotted up with the usual sources – accounts of Spielberg's travails on *Jaws* and Huston's on *Moby Dick*. But production on *M&C* seems to have gone remarkably smoothly, so much so that it's nigh-impossible to tell which scenes involve the real, specially reconstucted period frigate, which the replica mounted on gimbals in a studio tank, which the scale models and which the CG ones. More troublous, we hear, were the stars' efforts to get their violin and cello technique down: 'I sound like I'm trying to climb into a squirrel,' ventures Bettany, with a grimace. A charming and considered package. (TIM ROBEY)

The Matrix

(USA, 1999) Collector's Edition
2-Disc Set

Directors: Larry and Andy Wachowski
Label: Warners (all territories)
Region: Any
Discs: 2

THE FILM

Holy Baudrillard, an ideas movie from Hollywood! Part one of the Wachowski brothers' *Matrix* trilogy is an industry landmark, giant cash cow, teenage daydream, film factory product at its slickest; all of the above, and a goad to mental exertion. How else to account for its buffet spread of ideas from the Bible, Eastern philosophy, simulacra theory, Lewis Carroll, mangas, superhero narratives and any number of movies (Hong Kong ones especially)? Plot in brief: hacker Neo (Keanu Reeves), yanked from the titular illusory world contrived by a race of malevolent machines, joins the rebellion and has kung fu installed in his skull like so much software.

Cue robots, evil goons in black suits and shades, much slo-mo kicking, shooting and acrobatics – mental acrobatics, that is. 'Welcome to the desert of the real', intones guru Morpheus (Laurence Fishburne) without cracking a smile. Is he talking about Hollywood? Is technology good or bad, or both? Why are the trilogy's second and third parts not a patch on the simultaneously innovative *and* derivative, wry, savvy and consistently thrilling first? The Columbine gunmen were *Matrix* fans – is that significant? What does the *Matrix* video game do to the primacy of the film text? Why, it's a film-studies dream ticket – or, as Neo would say: 'Whoah.'

THE DISCS

DVD seems made for *The Matrix* – or at least, the freeze-frame button does: without it you're unlikely to notice that Morpheus's retro TV set is a 'Deep Image' model (and that's an allusion to gnosticism and Philip K Dick). Disc 1 carries the feature and two good commentaries: the first by film critics who didn't like the film, *Variety*'s Todd McCarthy, *Vogue*'s John Powers and *Biographical Dictionary of Film* author David Thomson, all strong on the cinematic allusions; the second by philosophers who did like the film, Dr Cornel West and Ken Wilber, both free with exclamations of amazement and references to Descartes, Schopenhauer and 'synechdochic character'.

Disc 2 has three hours of music and documentary 'pods' aplenty: all the dope on the part-fetish, part-sacerdotal outfits, the CGI, the sound design and the martial arts choreography. Some pods are more po-faced than others (the visual effects supervisor's explanation of 'bullet time' will do nothing for recruitment) and the two-hour feature doc *The Matrix Revisited* is a hotch-potch of talking heads: the Wachowskis in teenager garb and postures, Keanu in professor mode and Carrie-Anne Moss sounding slightly peevish. But all in all, an essential package: find its Easter eggs with the Internet. (Both discs are also available as part of the mind-boggling ten-disc Ultimate Matrix box set, along with the dismal sequels, the *Animatrix* toons and much, much more . . .) (SIMON CROPPER)

Norman McLaren: Master's Edition

(UK/US/Canada, 1933–83)

Directors: Listed below
Label: Soda (UK) / Home Vision (USA)
Region: 2 (PAL) / 1 (NTSC)
Discs: 7

DIRECTORS: Norman McLaren; **Co-directors:** Evelyn Lambart, Claude Jutra

THE FILMS

No-one made movies – as in moving images – purer than Norman McLaren, a pioneer of the art of animation for half a century. McLaren proclaimed that 'animation is not the art of drawings that move, but of movements that are drawn', and brought the nostrum to life in more than 70 relentlessly inventive, imaginative shorts, displaying a synaesthetic mastery of the musical possibilities of visual rhythm, shape and colour. His was an experimental cinema of the most direct and engaging kind: 1949's *Begone Dull Care*, for instance, a perfection of the technique of painting and scratching directly on celluloid, is an unassuming masterpiece, splashing out prolific licks of frolicking shapes, colours and patterns to an Oscar Petersen Trio original.

McLaren brought his love of dance to bear on the documentary form as a Glasgow student in the early '30s; made several anti-war films at the GPO Film Unit, where he also began to experiment with synthetic sound; and worked independently in the US for two years before John Grierson hired him to found the National Film Board of Canada's animation department. His technical virtuosity spanned 2-D cut-out animation (the visual numbers game *Rhythmetic*, *Le Merle*), multi-plane 3-D (*A Phantasy*), chalk drawings (*Là-haut sur ces montagnes*), systematic cross-fading (*C'est L'Aviron*), and stop-motion live action, or 'pixillation' (the Oscar-winning war allegory *Neighbours*).

There's a surrealistic playfulness to even his most abstract films, such as *Lines Vertical* and *Mosaic*, explorations of the geometry of harmony and balance. It's that choreographic expressionism that underpins all his work, from fluid musical works such as *Begone Dull Care* to representational films such as his dance trilogy, *Pas de Deux*, *Ballet Adagio* and *Narcissus*. *Pas de Deux* in particular is an ethereally beautiful reverie, superimposing the silhouettes of two dancers in the optical printer and thus tracing the trails they leave in their wake.

THE DISCS

The National Film Board of Canada calls their 65th-anniversary release of this gargantuan box set 'a jewel in the crown of film history', without hyperbole. The seven discs include 58 of McLaren's remastered films, 38 digitally restored; tests and unfinished films; 14 short thematic documentaries and Donald McWilliams's excellent feature-length portrait *Creative Process*; technical notes, filmed interviews and audio clips with McLaren, and excerpts from his writings – in all, some 130 video and audio documents. For a more digestible introduction to McLaren's art, Milestone's deleted two-disc 'Norman McLaren – Collector's Edition' set may still be obtainable; but once you've seen a promise of this treasure, you'll likely want it all. (NICK BRADSHAW)

Memento

(USA, 2000) Special Edition

Director: Chris Nolan
Label: Pathé (UK)
Region: 2 (PAL)
Discs: 3

THE FILM

'What's the last thing you remember?'

'My wife.'

'That's sweet . . . '

'Dying. I remember my wife dying.'

This exchange, between former insurance investigator Leonard (Guy Pearce) and barmaid Natalie (Carrie-Anne Moss), elegantly distils writer-director Christopher Nolan's poetically edgy thriller *Memento*, and Leonard's sorry life: he exists only to find and kill the man who both murdered his wife and caused his 'condition', a crippling inability to make new memories. The catch, for us, is that the main narrative is presented in reverse-chronological order, with the 'last' scene coming first. Yet what could have been an annoying gimmick proves an inspired way of putting us inside Leonard's head: we have some idea of the immediate future, but we're forced to cobble together the past from the Polaroids, notes and body-tattoos that are his pitiful substitute for a short-term memory.

Like an epically unreliable narrator, Pearce carries the film magnificently, rage, confusion, sadness, frustration and grim determination playing on his flawed features, and Nolan also coaxes first-rate support from Moss and the wonderfully weasely Joe Pantoliano. As a step up from Nolan's accomplished 1998 debut *Following*, as a blacky comic film noir, a disquisition on the failings of memory, and circuit-training for the mind, *Memento* is pretty much perfect. Indeed, unforgettable.

THE DISCS

Even before *Memento* left cinemas in 2000, many filmgoers were breathlessly speculating: would the DVD release allow it to be watched chronologically? The answer is 'yes', although even here you're made to work a little: the main menu of Disc 2 lists only four options, but hitting the '5' button on the remote will unearth a hidden fifth. Predictably, the film in this order is no substitute for the final cut, but it is tremendous fun as an elaborate, explanatory footnote, as well as a different picture in its own right.

As for the rest of this stuffed-to-the-gunwales release, several of the extras are unlikely to be of interest outside film-studies classes, but there are decent interviews with Nolan and Pearce, and the former's main-feature commentary is further proof of the intelligence that has made this Londoner one of modern Hollywood's most compelling craftsmen. As he memorably suggests, what *Memento* does best is to draw out for its entire 108 minutes 'that moment when you know that something's wrong, but for a minute you forget what it is that's hanging over you'. And, in marked contrast to so many mindlessly gushing DVD commentaries, his extensive praise for Pearce's performance is merely clear-sighted gratitude for the sensational piece of cinema that the actor helped him deliver. (MARK MONAHAN)

Le Mépris

(France/Italy, 1963)

Director: Jean-Luc Godard
Label: Criterion Collection (USA)
Region: 0 (NTSC)
Discs: 2

ENGLISH TITLE: Contempt

THE FILM

When Jean-Luc Godard made his debut with *Á Bout de Souffle*, the Hollywood cinema he had championed as critic and now paid homage to as director was out of creative breath. *Le Mépris*, his first and only big-budget, all-star movie, allegorises this falling-off as the corruption of weak-willed French writer Paul (Michel Piccoli), hired by the philistine American producer Prokosch (Jack Palance) to adapt Homer's *Odyssey* for the veteran German director Fritz Lang (played by the veteran director Fritz Lang). Bound up in their struggle for the soul of European culture is Paul's disintegrating relationship with his wife Camille (Brigitte Bardot). Not for the last time, Godard declares the 'fin du cinéma'.

Paul's tragedy, Godard once said, is that he's a character from European art movies who wants to be a hero in a western; against Lang's classicism, he conceives of Ulysses as a 'modern-day neurotic', projecting his marital strife onto Homer's epic. As the critic Jonathan Rosenbaum noted, the film is built from 'frequent slippages between stars and characters, characters and caricatures, films and ideas about films', and in this case director and character. Substituting widescreen lateral tracks and long takes for New Wave jump-cuts and hand-held camerawork, Godard crafted a surpassing instance of 'Antoniennui', devoting a third of the running time to an agonizingly authentic argument between the two lovers, all conducted in a single location.

THE DISCS

The presence of 'BB', then at the peak of her fame, ensured that the production of *Le Mépris*, already a film about filmmaking, was a hall of mirrors affair, exhaustively covered by the international paparazzi (a relatively fresh word at the time). The Criterion edition includes two documentaries, 'Contempt: Bardot et Godard' and 'Paparazzi', the latter an intriguing artefact addressed directly to Bardot. An analysis of her stardom in the manner of Roland Barthes or Edgar Morin's *The Stars*, it anticipates Godard and Jean-Pierre Gorin's less flattering *Letter to Jane* (1972).

The English-dubbed version of the film, included as an extra, is fascinatingly awful – Godard included a translator as a major character in the narrative, mediating relations between the principals as well as making dubbing unnecessary, so the film's US distributors had to invent redundant dialogue for her. Elsewhere an hour-long conversation between Godard and Lang transmitted in 1967 contains what must be one of history's more unusual blooper reels, showing Lang performing numerous takes of his apparently spontaneous answers. (HENRY K MILLER)

Metallica: Some Kind of Monster

(USA, 2004)

Directors: Joe Berlinger & Bruce Sinofsky
Label: Paramount (US & UK)
Region: 2 (PAL) / 1 (NTSC)
Discs: 2

THE FILM

Rising from San Francisco in 1983, Metallica revitalised heavy metal music by pioneering a harder, faster, lyrically ominous sub-genre known as thrash. Albums like *Ride the Lightning* and *Master of Puppets* provided a dynamic alternative to the lightweight fluff peddled by Mötley Crüe, Bon Jovi et al. However, the quartet's success dovetailed with tragedy. In 1986, their tourbus crashed in Sweden, killing talismanic bass player Cliff Burton. His replacement was Jason Newsted: a talented, dependable dude who was never fully accepted by founding members James Hetfield (vocals, guitar) and Lars Ulrich (drums, ego). As the group passed their commercial peak, Hetfield descended into alcoholism. Meanwhile, notorious motormouth Ulrich initiated legal action against internet file-sharing site Napster, ruining Metallica's reputation as a band of the people.

Some Kind of Monster was commissioned by Ulrich and conceived as a fly-on-the-studio-wall piece about the group's tenth LP, *St Anger*. As the film's title suggests, it's actually a document of dysfunction. Remarkably, the millionaire musicians gave Berlinger and Sinofsky intimate access to two years of turmoil, from Newsted's departure in January 2001 to the record's release in June 2003. We see alpha male Hetfield submit to rehab, only to find his drink problem replaced by a communication breakdown with the tactless Ulrich – an erstwhile tennis prodigy whose fearsome Danish father makes a tellingly brusque appearance. 'Performance enhancement coach' Phil Towle is hired to ease the creative process; at $40,000 a month, his self-regarding psychobabble merely heightens the tension. Sating the voyeurism of a public used to reality TV, *Some Kind of Monster* was a cinematic hit and has been credited – alongside Ondi Timoner's *Dig!* – as spearheading a new wave of music films with non-specialist appeal. Hilarious and excruciating, it also echoes Rob Reiner's classic rockumentary *This Is Spinal Tap*. Unfortunately for Metallica, that one was fiction.

THE DISCS

The seven hours of extras include 40 additional scenes (short, pointless), soporific commentaries (by the directors and band alike), plus a promotional video. The 'Premieres' section is much livelier, featuring candid (and often quite funny) press conferences at Sundance and the San Francisco Film Festivals. One caveat: despite its warts-and-all status, this is still an authorised documentary. If you don't follow metal, it's easy to get the impression that *St Anger* was a triumph against the odds. In fact, the album so underwhelmed both fans and critics that Metallica no longer play any of it in concert. (MANISH AGARWAL)

Metropolis

(Germany, 1926/2002)

Director: Fritz Lang
Label: Eureka (UK)
Region: 2 (PAL)
Discs: 2

THE FILM

Fritz Lang was one of two central pillars of the *Cahiers du Cinéma* critics' temple of 'pure cinema' (the other was Hitchcock), and none of his films better embodied their ideal than his ill-fated, monumental folly *Metropolis*. Conceived to out-Griffith Hollywood, it employed – so legend has it – 30,000 extras, lost its producer his job and flopped on release; it was one of the Nazis' favourite films; in later life, even Lang disparaged it.

As storytelling it's a woefully sappy piece of work (co-written with Lang's then wife, Thea von Harbou) – a paranoid, Freudian-cum-humanist sci-fi epic wherein the son of the city's overlord gets a social conscience, a mad inventor designs a female robot to goad the masses to revolt, the walls fall down – and all is forgiven in a heavily symbolic handshake. As cinema, however, it's a paragon, a delirious dream of almost unequalled symbolic and visual power. Its radical montage, transformations (a monstrous machine into the idol Moloch, a robot's mask into a human face) and cityscapes influenced dozens of sci-fi films, from *Things to Come* to *THX 1138*, *Star Wars*, *Blade Runner* and *Dark City*. This is cinema as conjuring trick, and it still works wonders.

THE DISCS

This typically fine set from Eureka's Masters of Cinema collection presents the film in as near authentic a version as is ever likely to exist, swelled by snippets from the bowdlerised versions pooled by archives in Germany and around the world. Even so, a quarter of the footage is missing, presumed lost (gaps are bridged by painstakingly detailed intertitles, and the score, Gottfried Huppertz's original, has been newly arranged to adapt to the truncations), and the reinstatement of the extra footage was a matter of educated guess-work. At least the picture quality is unambiguous, thanks to a careful and comprehensive digital restoration.

Extras include meticulous commentary by film historian Enno Patalas; a 44-minute doc, 'The Metropolis Case', that unpacks the film's visual trickery (lots of mirrors, miniatures and multiple exposures); a nine-minute piece on the restoration process, backed up by notes on the same in the 28-page booklet; and a wealth of production snaps, stills from the missing segments and sketches. The booklet also squeezes in contemporary testimony from cast and crew, and an essay by critic Jonathan Rosenbaum. The Masters of Cinema collection also includes Lang's *Dr Mabuse, the Gambler* and *Spione*. (SIMON CROPPER)

Metropolis

(Japan, 2001)

Director: Rintaro
Label: Columbia Tristar (UK)
Region: 2 (PAL)
Discs: 2

ORIGINAL TITLE: *Metoroporisu*

THE FILM

This twenty-first-century Japanese anime isn't merely a cartoon version of Fritz Lang's 1927 classic. With an original screenplay by the venerable Katsuhiro Otomo (*Akira*, *Roujin Z*), *Metropolis* is actually adapted from the 1949 work of ground-breaking illustrator Osamu Tezuka, who, inspired by Lang's iconic robot, created his own manga comic homage.

In Tezuka's dystopian *Metropolis*, technology is fetishised and reviled in turn; rich leaders wage war while the disenchanted proletariat revolt against machines who plaintively ask: 'Why do humans use violence to resolve their problems?'. Japanese detective Shunsaku Ban arrives in the sprawling city with his young nephew Kenichi, intending to arrest corrupt scientist Dr Laughton. What their mission uncovers, however, is Laughton's ultimate brainchild: ethereal beauty Tima, a surrogate daughter for the megalomaniac Duke Red, constructed to control the Ziggurat ('the culmination of mankind's long history of scientific achievement'); essentially, Tima's a tool of world domination with a pretty face.

Audiences familiar with the kitsch cartoon hero *Astro Boy* will recognise Tezuka's cutesy style and, initially, the 2D protagonists appear oddly simplistic against the burnished CG art deco backdrops. But Otomo's typically sophisticated script drives this slickly paced adventure, combining bittersweet humour and resonant horror, particularly in the climactic scenes.

As retro-futurism forms the pulsing undercurrent of *Metropolis*, an honourable mention goes to its vintage jazz and blues soundtrack, featuring director Rintaro on bass clarinet. In arguably the most striking scene, an apocalypse unfolds to the romantic croon of Ray Charles's 'I Can't Stop Loving You'. Tentatively distributed in Western cinemas, *Metropolis* is crucial entertainment for anime fans, but this deeply emotive, accessible take on a timely fantasy should sway broader audiences on DVD – it charges the imagination and tugs at the heartstrings.

THE DISCS

The power of *Metropolis* translates impressively to DVD – the rich colour palettes and vast, detailed settings remain thrilling to behold in anamorphic widescreen, with crisp sound in Dolby 5.1. The English dubbed dialogue has more of a kids' cartoon quality than the original Japanese, but subtitles do come in English, Hindi or Dutch. The bonus disc still looks sharp, but the extras are a tepid side-order to the striking main feature; besides a photo gallery, Rintaro and Otomo filmographies, comparisons between different stages of animation, and a basic 'History of *Metropolis*' storyboard, there are two rather dry interview-based docs. In the 'Animax Special: the making of *Metropolis*', Rintaro reveals that the late Tezuka never wanted to have his early comic adapted into animation, while Otomo simply explains: 'I tried to create a science fiction adventure that is full of dreams.' Intriguingly, Fritz Lang doesn't seem to get a mention at all. (ARWA HAIDER)

Monty Python and the Holy Grail

(UK, 1975) Collector's Edition Boxed Set

Directors: Terry Gilliam & Terry Jones
Label: Sony (USA/UK)
Region: 2 (PAL) / 1 (NTSC)
Discs: 2

THE FILM

The Pythons' daffy combination of high and low cultural influences found its first cinematic fruition in *Holy Grail*, a cracking Arthurian comedy that embraces the Celtic mythology of Ancient Britain as much as the medieval genre's cinematic clichés. This was the first time the Pythons were able to break out of the ghetto of Oxbridge-influenced, sketch-based TV comedy to produce a full-length narrative and, although the result is inescapably episodic in tone, there's sufficient lunacy and intelligence on display to keep things moving along.

The tone is set early on: two peasants harvesting mud debate the merits of anarcho-syndicalism, while Arthur, Lancelot and the other Knights of the Round Table sent to find the Holy Grail explain that because they can't afford real horses, they'll have to bang coconut shells throughout the picture. Deft, daft and sly, the film is eminently quotable and, while the Christian-baiting follow-up *The Life of Brian* might be more coherent, it can't match the wit and invention of *Grail* scene for scene. There's also more of the Pythons' trademark visual deconstruction, which reaches its logical conclusion at an anticlimax that's both bold and silly.

THE DISCS

Attention to detail has always been a Python trademark through numerous spin-offs, and fans will revel in the ephemera here, including Terry Gilliam's sketches of ideas that were never filmed, behind-the-scenes photos and advertising posters. Palin fronts an educational film called 'How To Use Your Coconuts', and there are karaoke versions of the film's songs, an 'on location' doc from the BBC vaults, an informative new 45-minute documentary in which Jones and Palin revisit locations, scenes translated from Japanese and another immaculately rendered in Lego. The film is also presented in a 'killer rabbit' version, offering pop-up stats (often emphasising the film's low budget), two good commentary tracks from the surviving Pythons (Chapman died some years ago), a full 24 seconds of additional footage, and subtitles filched from *Henry IV, Part II*, for people who don't like the film.

All extras are accessed from gorgeous Gilliam-designed menus, which make better use of the Dolby Digital 5.1 sound than the film itself. This edition comes with a paperback of the screenplay, but you can also get a Special Edition that omits the hard copy. Given the general quality of the package, one has to assume that the video's few nicks and blemishes are due to faults on the original film stock rather than the result of a poor transfer. (PETER WATTS)

Moolaadé

(Senegal/France/Burkina Faso, 2004)

Director: Ousmane Sembene
Label: Artificial Eye (UK)
Region: 2 (PAL)
Discs: 1

THE FILM

With a career spanning four decades, Ousmane Sembene is regarded as the founder of post-colonial African cinema. Already established as a leading novelist, he travelled to Gorki Studios in Moscow in 1962 to study filmmaking. Back home from 1968, Sembene pioneered the use of African languages in cinema and became both internationally celebrated and a local hero in West Africa. When *Moolaadé* won the Un Certain Regard Award at Cannes in 2004, it was in many ways a lifetime achievement award, and a recognition of the existence of a vibrant, essential African cinema.

The film also won on its own considerable merits. Like many of Sembene's films, it puts its politics in people – here in Collé, a Bambara village woman in Burkina Faso. Collé almost died from the traditional circumcision ceremony performed by the village's Salidana (female elders), and later helped her daughter escape excision. When four young girls flee the ritual and seek sanctuary ('*moolaadé*'), Collé – with the support of her neighbours and her reputation as a witch – faces down the elders and places a boundary of sanctuary around her home.

Collé's daughter Amasatou, taunted as a '*bilakoro*' (dirty woman) by the Salidana, is planning to marry Ibrahima, the son of the village chief, whose return from Paris brings the confrontation between Collé and the Salidana to a head. Collé has to stand up to the chief, her abusive husband, and her own fears (vividly realised in two dream sequences) to protect the young women. The confrontation between power and the powerless has predictable consequences. The chief seeks to cut the women off from the outside world by driving out the itinerant salesman Mercenaire, and taking away the radios whose sounds are a constant, brilliantly effective presence throughout the film.

The final sequence, of the women gathering together to defy the tribal council as their radios burn, is a vividly stirring call to action, and utterly convincing given the courageous performances (many from first-time actors), especially Fatoumata Coulibaly as Collé and the luminous Salimata Traoré as Amasatou. This fantastic introduction to the riches of African cinema combines the measured grace of a lifetime's filmmaking with the vital energy of a political activist.

THE DISC

The interview with 81-year-old Sembene encompasses the political motivation behind the making of *Moolaadé* and the breadth of his distinguished career. The behind-the-scenes featurette gives some insight into filmmaking conditions and the experiences of the film's cast, and there's a promo video by the Foundation for Women's Health Research and Development, detailing the reality of '*moolaadé*'.
(SOPHIE MAYER)

The Errol Morris Collection

(USA, 1980–88)

Director: Errol Morris
Label: Optimum (UK) / MGM (US)
Region: 2 (PAL) / 1 (NTSC)
Discs: 3

FILM TITLES: Gates of Heaven, Vernon, Florida, The Thin Blue Line

THE FILMS

Errol Morris's first three documentaries provide an excellent introduction to one of the most accomplished non-fiction filmmakers at work today. They also highlight the strengths of his best work, balancing detailed character study with an acute sense of narrative control.

Gates of Heaven remains an oddity, even for Morris. It is an account of two pet cemeteries, one beset by the avarice and financial mismanagement of one of its owners, with the other succeeding as an ongoing concern for a family who take pride in cherishing the resting place of, for some owners, their best friend. Its pace is relaxed, allowing characters' stories to unfold naturally. An adept interviewer, Morris takes great care to steer clear of ridicule. His interest lies in allowing his subjects to express their feelings for their pets and if their behaviour appears odd Morris ensures that the eccentricity is presented affectionately rather than as freakish.

If Norman Rockwell's dream of perfect America were to become nightmare, it would surely fall somewhere between Grant Woods's *American Gothic* and Morris' *Vernon, Florida*. Featuring a cast of characters that must have made the director's college lecturer, Werner Herzog, jealous, the film offers a wry take on small-town American life. Almost bereft of female subjects, it is a strange and mesmerising film that once again avoids ridicule through the director's sensitive handling of each character, from the turkey-obsessed hunter to a late convert to the idea of tarring and feathering wrongdoers.

The Thin Blue Line was Morris' breakthrough. A landmark in factional film, where documentary and dramatic reconstruction are seamlessly blended, it achieved notoriety by questioning the dubious investigation that followed the shooting of a law enforcement officer in Dallas County, Texas. As a result, the case was reopened and the conviction of Randall Adams, then residing on death row, was overturned. Once again, Morris' approach is subtle, slowly peeling away the layers of untruths surrounding the case. However, rather than content himself with revealing a gross miscarriage of justice, Morris explores a system under pressure to find a culprit at any cost and presents the central figure of Adams as a complex and not entirely sympathetic character rather than a victim. Accompanied by Philip Glass's mesmeric score, it's a powerful and compelling film.

THE DISCS

All films are transferred well, paying attention to Morris's subtle use of natural light in the framing of his subjects. Extras are paltry: on the Optimum set, Nick Broomfield's brief, entertaining, but hardly informative introductions to each film; on the R1 MGM, a single episode ('Mr Personality') of Morris's *First Person* TV series. (IAN HAYDN SMITH)

MouseHunt

(USA, 1998)

Director: Gore Verbinski
Label: DreamWorks (all territories)
Region: Any
Discs: 1

THE FILM

One of the most anarchically good-natured studio pictures of the last decade, *MouseHunt* is what the Coen brothers might produce if they attempted a mash-up of Fincher's *Panic Room*, Eisenstein's *October* and Hanna-Barbera's *Stop the Pigeon*, and were feeling in a good mood. When string visionary and cigar aficionado Mr Smuntz dies, he leaves his sons Lars (Lee Evans) and Ernie (Nathan Lane) a factory, some spoons and a huge great rambling mansion, boasting a rich architectural pedigree and an uninvited lodger. In the ensuing run of events, the brothers hit one another with blunt objects, blow up the house with a bug bomb and set fire to Ingrid and Hilde, two distinctly un-Belgian hair models from Belgium.

With the movie's title usefully getting the plot out of the way, Verbinski and his team are free to allow themselves some fun, as we cut to an unbroken gallop of fake sheikhs, Dadaist non-sequiturs and a priceless performance from Maury Chaykin as a wealthy connoisseur with a taste for two-tone shoes and maraschino cherries. Kids can keep *Shrek* or even – dare we court outrage? – *Toy Story 2*: *MouseHunt* is true family entertainment for grown-ups, with cheery nods to Michael Mann and Scorsese, shades of Upton Sinclair as factory employees go on strike in the snow, and a comic sensibility straight from *New Yorker*-era Thurber, with added Gouda. Studio-lot palm trees 'accidentally' glimpsed swaying in the background give this multi-million-dollar creature an artfully ramshackle feeling: but artful is very different from arch, and being clever very different from brittle superiority. There's a deathbed scene here offering a truer, more sympathetic account of giving up the ghost than anything outside *The Death of Mr Lazarescu*, and the opening title card offers an apophthegm – 'A world without string is chaos' – which could sustain half a dozen Sunday sermons. A genuinely nice film, plus Lee Evans offers a pretty convincing impression of what it might feel like to have a mouse in your underpants.

THE DISC

Unfortunately no commentary, but there's partial compensation with two ace trailers and lots of footage which didn't make it into the final cut. Most of the excised material is significantly cruder than the finished movie, but Christopher Walken fans will regret the omission of three scenes featuring his deranged pest exterminator. 'A baker discovered droppings in the cup cakes', he says, doing his best Captain Ahab impression. 'Can you imagine? Children's. Cup. Cakes.' (A R1 DTS version is also available without the extras.) (PETER VÁSÁRY)

Mrs Harris
(USA, 2005)

Director: Phyllis Nagy
Label: HBO (USA)
Region: 1 (NTSC)
Discs: 1

THE FILM

Annette Bening must be the unluckiest actress in the history of the Oscars: imagine being beaten twice by Hilary Swank. She blooms in Nagy's *cause célèbre* mystery, giving a brilliantly haggard performance as Jean Harris, the former school headmistress who killed her lover, the Scarsdale diet doctor Herman 'Hy' Tarnower (Ben Kingsley).

Things begin on 10 March, 1980, the night Jean squeezed the trigger after driving for hours in the bucketing rain to Hy's suburban New York pad. The shooting is shown the way Harris described it, as a botched suicide attempt and a messy struggle over a gun. Later, it's played out from the prosecuting attorney's point of view: Jean kills with intent.

In between, the narrative hopscotches between trial scenes, flashbacks of the couple's 14-year affair and grainy mock-doc segments in which Jean and Hy's friends and enemies speak to camera. We're treated to a smorgasbord of tasty cameos from Mary McDonnell, Ellen Burstyn, Philip Baker Hall and Cloris Leachman, among others.

Kaleidoscopic in tone, *Mrs Harris* doesn't offer a tidy moral package. It is a compelling and moving examination of romantic folly and its rancid aftermath, obliteration, and the vexatious distance between men and women. Nagy's script is clear-eyed without being malicious or, at any rate, more malicious than necessary.

Despite their capacity for self-mockery and tart badinage ('You're a real bastard, aren't you?' 'Sure. I'm your bastard . . . '), both Jean and Hy are self-deceivers, and Nagy brings a precise intelligence to the tragi-comic manslaughter and murder scenes, in which spilled bullets bounce all over the bathroom floor like pills. Bening's Jean, zonked out on uppers and downers, has an extraordinary *Uncle Vanya* moment: after she tries to shoot herself with a malfunctioning handgun, she gives an exhausted laugh that makes you gasp. And she has someone to play off in Kingsley's Hy, a heartlessly affable, geekily charismatic womaniser.

Take your pick of the death scenarios: either way, *Mrs Harris*'s cumulative understanding of a crime of passion is unnerving in how close it comes to forgiveness.

THE DISC

From the summery richness of the scenes before Hy's death to the asphalt feel of the courtroom episodes, this picture looks good. Supplementary features include an all-too-short selection of first-hand accounts of the case. There's a commentary by the two leads, and a measured, eloquent one from first-time writer/director Nagy. The movie's painstaking period detail extends to a sound-track of '60s and '70s pop songs about obsessional love, all heightening the sense of devotion as a kind of trap. (MAXIE SZALWINSKA)

Mulholland Drive

(France/USA, 2001)

Director: David Lynch
Label: Vision Video (UK)
Region: 2 (PAL)
Discs: 1

THE FILM

It's hard to believe that *Mulholland Drive* was a salvage job. That ABC saw the 88-minute pilot for the TV series they'd commissioned and, in a decision right out of the creepily Byzantine studio wranglings the film itself depicts, didn't want it. Certain off-shoots in the movie – a lot of the material involving Justin Theroux's bamboozled hot-shot director, and a hysterically funny set-piece with a hit man (Joe Pellegrino) – do feel like little buds of subplot that would have been nurtured to fullness in subsequent episodes. But the damnedest achievement of David Lynch's film – it's perhaps his most drop-dead alluring, and emotionally overwhelming – is making even the apparently tangential stuff work within the reconstituted fever-dream it gives us.

We start, after a wacky jitterbug dance number, with amnesiac 'Rita' (Laura Elena Harring) stepping from a car crash, and wandering the hill-tops above the winking lights of LA. Betty (Naomi Watts, wondrous) is drawn to Tinseltown for her own reasons: she's a talent-show winner, fresh off the boat and hoping to ace her big audition. The pair are thrown together in the flat owned by Betty's Aunt Ruth, and busy themselves with puzzling out the iden-tity of Rita – or maybe it's Diane? – which has something to do with the deal Adam (Theroux) is trying to put together, and something else to do with a festering corpse in a *Day of the Locust*-style stucco apartment complex.

It's two-thirds of the way in that Lynch pulls off one of the most startling structural coups in modern film, sucking his heroines into a little blue box and flipping Betty's dreams of stardom over to reveal their fetid, desperate flipside. Now *she*'s Diane, the offers have dried up, and the gurgling underbelly of the Hollywood chimera is exposed. *Mulholland Drive* presents a poster image and its yellowed reverse, a fantasy and its malicious disappointment: it finds a shuddering, keening poetry in the abyss between them.

THE DISC

The film is indispensable, but here's hoping this bare-bones disc gets an update soon – all we get is a trailer, cast and crew biogs and a clutch of bland, nuggety interviews from Cannes 2001. Lynch is his usual thoroughly weird and cryptic self, letting drop only that all his characters are dealing with 'questions of identity', which is a bit like saying Norman Bates has mummy issues. (Optimum's cheeky 2007 'Special Edition' contains all the same extras on a second disk, at double the price.) (TIM ROBEY)

My Little Eye

(UK, 2002)

Director: Marc Evans
Label: Momentum (UK)
Region: 2 (PAL)
Discs: 2

THE FILM

By some distance the most accomplished film in the recent cycle of reality-TV-inspired horror movies, Brit director Evans' chiller zooms in on five young wannabes hand-picked by a get-rich-quick website to live for six months in a remote cabin under round-the-clock surveillance. The arrival of a programmer who's never heard of the contestants at first seems like a joke about the nano-celebrity that such reality entertainments engender, but slowly doubts are raised about the purpose and existence of the whole operation.

Evans pulls off a distinctive look, obsessively and meticulously collecting his data from the mikes and cameras of the webcast (in pens, torches and shower nozzles, all the better to see our victims with), and creating a familiar *Big Brother* world with its own sealed-in tensions. The slow but effective build-up puts unusual meat on the bones of its characters, as they bicker and are sometimes amazingly callous towards one another, but somehow win the audience's sympathy as all hell breaks loose.

Just when you think it might cheat the rules of its own game by reverting to a psycho-in-the-house pic, *My Little Eye* makes the far more disturbing suggestion that the real monsters – perhaps a shady operative referred to as 'The Company' – are still out there. It's a rare modern horror movie brave enough to have its young leads return the gaze of their contemporaries in the audience, and where filmmakers and characters alike seem to be asking the same question: who are the sickos still watching this shit?

THE DISCS

An excellent, innovative package, most notable for an interactive mode which allows viewers to 'log on' to the fictional website and watch the film on web browsers with updating odds, access to auditions and deleted scenes (also available to view separately), alternative camera angles and a day counter. For extra sadism, listen to The Company – revealed as a couple of leery technoheads – plotting the contestants' downfall.

Elsewhere, fans of regional accents should find much to cherish as Welshman Evans and Geordie producer Jon Finn banter their way through an entertaining, honest commentary and reveal which of *The Breakfast Club* refused to allow their image to be used within the film. (Clue: it wasn't Anthony Michael Hall.) There's an instructive making-of and a panoply of promo spots, while a gallery shows off the Nova Scotia location in all its snow-covered glory. (MIKE McCAHILL)

My Own Private Idaho
(USA, 1991)

Director: Gus Van Sant
Label: Criterion (USA)
Region: 1 (NTSC)
Discs: 2

THE FILM

Idaho is the most beautiful and lasting trace of the heady days of the early 1990s: grunge was in and the Pacific Northwest was its spiritual home, bisexuality was edgy verging on hip and Riot Grrl band The Voodoo Queens hymned Keanu Reeves in their song 'Kenuwee Head'. They sang: 'He's the most bodacious boy you ever saw / When will he be more than just a picture on my fridge door?' In *My Own Private Idaho*, that's when. In a totemic scene, Reeves and fellow teen dream River Phoenix are magazine cover boys, lined up on racks. Except the magazines are more *Barely Legal* than *Just Seventeen*. In this dream(y) sequence, Scott Fortune (Reeves) reveals that he's a rich boy slumming as a hustler, Narcissus to Mike Waters' (Phoenix) adoring Echo. Just as Scott is eventually defined by his fortune, so narcoleptic Mike is like water: a drifting soul with liquid eyes.

While the film received bitter fame after Phoenix's overdose death, with fans and commentators reading his portrayal here for signs of pathology, Reeves' consummate performance marks *his* wasted potential. As he would with Nicole Kidman in *To Die For*, Van Sant's camera seduces Reeves into revealing his magnetic nastiness, as well as his clumsy tenderness towards the disintegrating Mike as they traverse the USA. The 'fucked-up face' of middle America is as much a character, and as simultaneously compelling and tragic, as the leads.

In the course of their picaresque journey from Portland to Boise looking for Mike's mom, they encounter a Rabelaisian range of characters, especially the magnificent Bob Pigeon (William Richert), a prince of thieves borrowed from Shakespeare's Falstaff. Like Mike, Bob nurtures a crush on Scott, who is equal parts Prince Hal and Patrick Bateman, and will betray them both.

Van Sant's hallmark is his visualisation of interiority: from the crashing houses that bring on Mike's narcolepsy to the tableaux of sculpted bodies enjoying polymorphous perversity. Conjuring a symbolism that fuses Andrew Wyeth and Kenneth Anger, Van Sant enters the American psyche, bringing the perfect house of the American dream crashing down in order to build his own.

THE DISCS

Criterion excel themselves, creating not so much a box set as a fetish object. *Idaho* benefits from a sexed-up digital transfer that allows you to appreciate every drug-opened pore on the leads' faces. Disc 2 (and accompanying essay collection) provides everything you could ever need to understand/drool over *Idaho*, even if you came from Mars. Todd Haynes, Jonathan Caouette and JT LeRoy offer a snapshot of *Idaho*'s impact on queer culture. (SOPHIE MAYER)

Naruse: Volume One

(Japan, 1951, 1954, 1955)

Director: Mikio Naruse
Label: Masters of Cinema (UK)
Region: 2 (NTSC)
Discs: 3

FILM TITLES: *Repast, Sound of the Mountain, Flowing*

THE FILMS

How do you film the endless anti-drama of everyday life – the petty exchanges and compromises, the struggle to raise your prospects, the quiet attrition of your dreams – without alienating your audience? Do you simply aim for relevance (and coherence)? Naruse was an arch exponent of the 'women's movie', meaning that predominantly female filmgoers either side of the war turned out for what critics, Westerners and latter-day audiences have struggled to appreciate. (The Japanese call the genre *shomin-geki*: slice-of-life.) Studio heads took issue, too. 'Naruse, we don't need two Ozus,' his boss at Shochiku groused, kicking him over to Toho. His scenes have 'no ups or downs; the tone is too flat'. Kurosawa, though, saw beneath the surface calm to the 'fast-raging current underneath'.

Indeed, his admirers hold him as the third great master of the first generation of Japanese cinema, alongside Ozu and Mizoguchi. But his heroines don't suffer in such style as Mizoguchi's: never martyrs, they are practical, flawed people fighting an uphill battle for self-determination. ('If they move even a little,' he noted of his characters, 'they quickly hit the wall.') And where Ozu's intimate tableaux etch life's major domestic transitions – marriage, death – and his images respire and transcend, Naruse's are resolutely concrete and caught in that flow of time. People don't die in Naruse, they go on. Every shot pushes forward these affirmations of financial constriction, emotional isolation and residual stoicism.

Watch these debut Naruse DVDs chronologically, and then Criterion's *When a Woman Ascends the Stairs* (1960), and you can see Naruse work through the meagre career alternatives available to Japanese women as modernity rushes on. *Repast* and *Sound of the Mountain* both star the angel-faced Setsuko Hara as lonely suburban housewives, no longer cherished by their working husbands, sizing up the dubious fruits of freedom in one and sheltering in an impossible intimacy with her father-in-law in the other. *Flowing* is an ensemble piece set in the latter days of a geisha house, whose old economy of beauty and refinement is on the retreat, and where female solidarity and foresight are almost as scarce resources as money. Not that the brasher new world of entrepreneurialism is any easier, as the desperately seeking bar hostess of *When a Woman* . . . knows. Love, emancipation: these are but trace scents on the wind.

THE DISCS

Both this hefty box set and Criterion's disc come with different mash-ups of writings by Naruseans Audie Bock, Philip Lopate and Catherine Russell; MoC's with relaxed commentaries by Lopate and Kent Jones (two brief, *Sound of the Mountain*'s full-length), Criterion's by Japanese-film vet Donald Richie. The only gripe with the image quality is that *SotM*'s blacks dim whenever the subtitles appear. Otherwise, gems. (NICK BRADSHAW)

Nashville

(USA, 1975)

Director: Robert Altman
Label: Paramount (USA)
Region: 1 (NTSC)
Discs: 1

THE FILM

Robert Altman's kaleidoscopic masterpiece is a contradictory beast: a film whose main theme is the failure of Watergate-era America to cohere effectively as a community, but that is – in itself – a triumph of collaborative creativity. Its epic sweep takes in no less than 24 main characters during the countdown to a presidential primary in Nashville, and remains the best example of the innovative Altman style – creating extemporised 'events' within a loose narrative framework, encouraging improvisation, and then covering the whole chaotic mix with multiple cameras and microphones.

Altman takes a satirical skewer to the heart – or rather, the place where the heart should be – of the town's music machine, just as he later would to Hollywood in *The Player* and High Fashion in *Prêt-à-Porter*. In this world, smarmy country stars like Haven Hamilton (Henry Gibson) get rich peddling glib patriotic anthems, while desperate wannabes at the bottom of the ladder are exploited, mocked or ignored. Meanwhile, a cynical advance man (Michael Murphy) is trying to get the music establishment to support his third-party candidate at a rally. Other characters are defined by their vacuousness (Shelley Duvall's 'LA Joan'), their insensitive womanising (Keith Carradine's narcissistic folk star Tom), and their astonishing pretensions (Geraldine Chaplin's inspired comic creation 'Opal from the BBC'). Even the most likeable folk, like Lily Tomlin's gospel singer Linnea, patiently signing with her deaf children while their father (Ned Beatty) looks on in exasperation, are lonely and troubled. In Altman's state-of-the-nation address, all of the idealism and engagement of the previous decade has vanished in a haze of self-interest and insincerity.

But despite its pessimism, this remains a wildly entertaining film, a free-wheeling musical extravaganza incorporating plenty of memorable comic vignettes. Many of the songs were written by cast members themselves and, while they're not always great, they're perfect expressions of character and theme: the film's best scene features Carradine performing his own Oscar-winning 'I'm Easy' to a crowded bar, watched by four women he's involved with who each think he's singing just to them. They're deluding themselves, of course; but in this film – which climaxes with a communal rendition of 'It Don't Worry Me' following an pointless assassination – who isn't?

THE DISC

This edition features an excellent widescreen transfer and a Dolby Digital 5.1 soundtrack. There's also an interview and commentary by Altman, shedding light on his approach to filming, the response of the Nashville community to the film, and the film's prescient foreshadowing of John Lennon's murder. (ANDY RICHARDS)

New York, New York

(USA, 1977)

Director: Martin Scorsese
Label: MGM (UK)
Region: 2 (PAL)
Discs: 2

THE FILM

If, in 1976, you were making a straight-faced pastiche of the 1930s MGM musical and looking for a female lead, you couldn't have a more obvious choice than Liza Minnelli, a performer culturally and genetically steeped in the heightened expressiveness of the form. And if you were looking for a male lead, who better than . . . Robert De Niro?

New York, New York is a film distinguished by incongruity, not just in its casting but in its characters and, crucially, its very conception. De Niro's Jimmy Doyle is one for instant gratification, whether pranking, punching or playing his sax; Minnelli's Francine Evans is one who lives in hope, only falteringly admitting of her voice, but then letting it out loud. They meet after the war, when he barges his way into her heart, and see their careers grow together and in opposition to each other during back-projected cab rides and across a variety of heightened sound-stage settings. Indeed, another of the film's great incongruities, and perhaps the one that most alienated its earliest audiences and critics, is the way Scorsese worshipfully recreates a bygone cinematic mode of flagrant artificiality – the studio musical, for crying out loud! – yet endows its characters with a distinctly contemporary emotional rawness. A pastiche, yes, but utterly sincere, *New York, New York* takes the power of the movies to move us every bit as seriously as it dissects the loving battle of its leads. File it somewhere between *Singin' in the Rain* and *Far from Heaven*.

THE DISCS

The 163-minute film presented here is the 1981 version, which restored (*inter alia*) the 'Happy Endings' closing sequence, a bravura production number without which the picture is now unimaginable. Watching the film leaves no doubt about Martin Scorsese's adoration of the cinema of his youth, but his commentary (which is somewhat sporadic and interlaced with less interesting comments from critic Carrie Rickey) and interviews on this double-disc set lay out the contrast he noted even then between the city he grew up in and the city he saw on screen – the two New Yorks of the title? (Kerb height is the clinching distinction, apparently.)

Minnelli also offers insights into the experience of shooting on stages used by and with colleagues of her parents, though there's no contribution from De Niro. The original ending is also included – a sweeter scene, more downbeat in its implications. MGM's R1 disc fits the same extras on a single disc.
(BEN WALTERS)

Night Moves

(USA, 1975)

Director: Arthur Penn
Label: Warners (USA)
Region: 1 (NTSC)
Discs: 1

THE FILM

The title of Penn's neglected '70s classic refers in part to a winning chess gambit ('three little knight moves') that a player – to his eternal regret – failed to spot. Los Angeles-based private investigator Harry Moseby (Gene Hackman) has had an obsession with piecing together clues ever since tracking down the parents who abandoned him. He accepts an assignment from a faded Hollywood starlet to find her runaway jailbait daughter (Melanie Griffith's first significant role), but the initially straightforward case soon develops into a labyrinthine intrigue involving murder, treachery and sunken treasure; like other jaded shamuses in Watergate-era America (*Chinatown*'s Jake Gittes and *The Conversation*'s Harry Caul included), Moseby finds that figuring out all the angles is a tougher game than it used to be, and that in a world of endemic corruption a stalemate is the best you can hope to play for.

Reuniting with Penn after *Bonnie and Clyde*, Hackman delivers a brilliantly shaded performance as Moseby – a man whose fundamental decency has become compromised by the tawdriness of his profession; in one of many fine moments in Alan Sharp's screenplay (conceived in the tradition of Ross Macdonald's PI novels), Moseby compares his youthful idealism as a professional ball player at the time of JFK's assassination to the seedy adultery cases he found himself working at the time of Bobby Kennedy's death less than five years later. With his own marriage collapsing around him, Moseby's whole sense of self is pinned on the need to understand the plot he's caught up in. Penn's film makes an interesting companion piece to Robert Altman's 1973 *The Long Goodbye*, with which it shares some Malibu settings and a sardonic sense of humour, as well as a 'white knight' protagonist whose moral impulses seem sadly anachronistic. Ultimately though, Moseby is denied even the moment of climactic self-definition afforded to Elliot Gould's Marlowe, and *Night Moves* concludes with an image of futility and frustration that echoes – and rivals – that of Herzog's *Aguirre, Wrath of God*.

THE DISC

A decent transfer of an essential film, with a brief making-of featurette showing Penn in action on location. A commentary from Hackman or a Penn specialist would have been a real treat, although at least the film's beguiling, enigmatic charms remain intact. (ANDY RICHARDS)

Night of the Demon

(UK, 1957)

Director: Jacques Tourneur
Label: Sony (USA)
Region: 1 (NTSC)
Discs: 1

THE FILM

Japan's *Ring* cycle of horror flicks, with their hot-to-trot premise of a cursed snuff video, never acknowledged their debt to the master practitioner of the good-old English ghost story. MR James's *Casting the Runes*, filmed by Jacques Tourneur as *Night of the Demon*, pivots on a deadly piece of parchment which dooms the bearer to being stalked by a 'frightful friend' (a quotation from Coleridge's *Rime of the Ancient Mariner*) unless he can slip it into the possession of someone else in the allotted time. In the film, Dana Andrews' sceptical psychologist locks horns with an urbane devil worshipper (the marvellous Niall McGinnis) who whips up a storm in one skilfully achieved sequence – a favourite of Tourneur – to impress his still stubbornly non-believing opponent.

Most famous for not showing us the cat people in *Cat People*, Tourneur was here compelled to shoot a puppet of the monster, which – despite long-circulated rumours that the studio brought it in against his will – is really quite imaginatively deployed except in extreme close-up. Ted Scaife's black-and-white cinematography works spooky wonders with the opening, as a terrified professor (Maurice Denham) pays a last-ditch visit to Karswell's estate to try and overturn the curse, before being followed home through narrow country lanes by the very embodiment of a gnarled, fire-breathing medieval woodcut. We also get the best use of the British Museum's reading room since Hitchcock's *Blackmail*, and what's hugely impressive about *Night of the Demon* in general is how, with a French director and American money, it manages to remain palpably true to the tradition of James in conjuring such a thoroughly British atmosphere of occult dread.

THE DISC

The cover promises a 'double feature' with *Curse of the Demon*, which is quite a cheek: it's the truncated American release of the same movie, about 13 minutes shorter with key chunks of exposition missing. The cuts were so clumsily done that many of them happen in mid-dissolve, and Columbia executives also saw fit to fiddle with the credits, relegating Andrews' co-star Peggy Cummins to below-the-title status and McGinnis still further. By sheer accident the 1987 US laserdisc of the film was struck from a British print – they just swopped the title card – which perhaps explains why the longer version looks the cleaner here; with both cuts side-by-side for the first time, hardcore devotees will be able to compare and contrast until the cows come home. (TIM ROBEY)

The Night of the Hunter

(USA, 1955)

Director: Charles Laughton
Label: MGM (USA)
Region: 1 (NTSC)
Discs: 1

THE FILM

What were you scared of when you were small? Was it dropping your teddy, the bad man in the shadows or losing your dad? For the two doughty Depression-era tots whose troubles Laughton depicts in his one work as director, these fears are what waking dreams are made of. As their father is hanged by the neck for robbery, an itinerant preacher arrives in town, seduces the townsfolk with hellfire harangues and inveigles himself into their home by marrying their mother, the dappy, doe-eyed Shelley Winters.

That the preacher is played by the laconically menacing Robert Mitchum should have given them warning, as should the blood-freezing way he says 'Children . . .' Although famously disinterested in vetting his film roles, Mitchum was an acquaintance of Laughton, shared his anti-religious zeal and rebellious streak and took on this quirkily expressionist project at the peak of his fame. It was a shrewd move: his performance has from the outset been revered as a high point in lowlifes, his huge frame seldom shot better than in the looming silhouettes created by extraordinary cinematographer Stanley Cortez (who also shot the dreamy black and whites of Welles' similarly un-classifiable *The Magnificent Ambersons* (1942)).

For Laughton, however, the project was less than successful, with the film poorly received on release; it was enshrined in the National Film Registry of the Library of Congress as 'culturally significant' only after his death. Too late, too, comes the handsome homage paid by recent American cinema: the sensual aliveness of landscape of Terrence Malick, the lyrical American Gothic of David Lynch, the mawkish yet steadfast moralism running through the works of the Coens. It is they, cineaste jesters, who offer to the film perhaps its finest tribute: the gentle horror of Winters drowned, her streaming hair swaying in the current becomes goggle-eyed Jon Polito with a floating toupee in the suitably monochrome *The Man Who Wasn't There*.

THE DISC

The film's theme of innocence versus evil is best served by the richer blacks and brighter whites of the R1 disc, which also boasts double the number of chapter divisions. The advertised 'Collector's Booklet' is nothing more than a sleeve note and chapter list, but for more enlightening reading material, seek out Davis Grubb's original novel. The 1953 bestseller was translated straight to the screen with scarcely a flutter of lost pages, and everything from the hallucinatory feel of the voyage downstream and the child's-eye view to the rabbits that crouch by the bank is there in the prose. It's an extraordinary insight into the precision of Laughton's achievement and a rich re-immersion in the world of the film. (REBEKAH POLDING)

A Nightmare on Elm Street

(USA, 1984) Infinifilm Edition

Director: Wes Craven
Label: New Line Infinifilm (USA)
Region: 1 (NTSC)
Discs: 2

THE FILM

Listen to a bunch of ten-year-olds talking horror movies at the back of the bus and you can tell who's seen the first *Nightmare* film. S/he's the one who knows it's not a comedy. Sod the sequels' dream warriors and psychokinetics: what's scary in *Nightmare* is that Freddy Krueger could be coming for *you*. Most other trademarked maniacs from the early '80s are vigilantes for a warped puritanical justice, dispatching post-coital couples and incipient yuppies as though taking orders from a Jerry Falwell/Pol Pot action committee. Craven's canny move is to ditch the prurience and opt instead for the pitiless dream logic of the fairytale and the bogeyman.

Nightmare is a beautifully unjudgemental film, with Freddy's hapless targets a bunch of regular teenagers suffering bad dreams. After chirpy cheerleader Tina is cut to pieces during a sleepover, there's a terrific scene where apple-pie heroine Nancy (Heather Langenkamp) visits Tina's bad-boy lover (Nick Corri), under arrest for the murder, in a police cell. Corri protests his innocence, of course, but in his biker jacket he also confesses to Nancy that he is *frightened*: and in this tussle of vanity and fear there's a lovely sense of being human in a bad place.

There are some wasted opportunities here: we could have done with a bit more unease about the role of the grown-ups, and there are some gestures towards a paranoid thriller which subsequently go nowhere. But Craven keeps things creepy throughout, packing the movie with images to haunt the middle of your night: Freddy's extendable arms, a body-bag full of eels and a corridor monitor hiding behind the corner. Best of all, a colour scheme that has percolated its way right into the popular consciousness: red and *black* stripes is Dennis the Menace, but red and *green* is something nastier altogether.

THE DISCS

A good remastered special edition from New Line, with featurettes, alternative endings and two busy commentaries. With John Saxon (Nancy's dad) Zen-like and silent throughout, and Langenkamp primarily concerned to point out that she's since had surgery to remove the cyst on her forehead, it's a good thing that Craven manages to keep things bubbling along by himself. He points out Daryl Hannah's brother making a doomed bid for the big time as 'Surfer no. 1', tells some good stories involving *that* prosthetic tongue, and offers an account of how Johnny Depp came to be cast in his break-out role: nothing to do with Craven, apparently, and all to do with Craven's teenage daughters. (PETER VÁSÁRY)

La Niña Santa
(Argentina, 2004)

Director: Lucrecia Martel
Label: Artificial Eye (UK)
Region: 2 (PAL)
Discs: 1

ENGLISH TITLE: *The Holy Girl*

THE FILM

With *La Ciénaga* ('The Swamp') (2001) and *La Niña Santa*, Lucrecia Martel has established herself as the most distinctive director of the 'New Argentine Cinema' of the late '90s and early 2000s. Martel is deliciously unique, in fact: in her perspective, her *mise en scène* and the richly textured, almost tangible atmospheres that she drapes around her stories.

La Niña Santa is a sly, sensual and very mischievous account of a 16-year-old girl stumbling between the indoctrinations of her Catholic education and her burgeoning sexuality. Amalia (the intriguingly sullen-faced María Alche) lives with her mother Helena (Mercedes Morán) in a sprawling hotel, currently enlivened by a medical convention. While the girl is listening to a theremin player in the street, a man moves close behind and touches her. This is Dr Jano (Carlos Belloso), one of the doctor-delegates staying at the hotel. And Amalia decides to 'save' his soul.

It's unclear to what extent her pursuit of the middle-aged man is shaped by spiritual vocation, or teenage crush – the likelihood being that the girl doesn't know herself. Meanwhile, having sparked Amalia to life, the married medic is now flirting outrageously with her mother – the hotel and its popular thermal pool becoming the setting in which these ambiguous emotions heat up.

Martel's characters are variously lonely, disaffected and randy; the air around them is moist with family dysfunction (a recurring theme for her) and emotional lethargy. The film's jaundice, though, is counterbalanced by mischief and invention. As a writer, Martel sprinkles her scenario with symbolism and wonderfully pithy dialogue. As a director, she combines close-ups, editing and sound (the mix resonates with lapping water, catechism and the bizarre tunes played on the theremin) to create a mood of mystery and amusement.

THE DISC

This is a typical Artificial Eye package: the film quality well reproduced, the features unflashy but rewarding. A cute making-of totally captures the film's strange, languid atmosphere, the theremin humming behind the reflections of Martel, her producer Lita Stantic (a canny champion of New Argentine Cinema), the cast and crew. We learn of Pedro Almodóvar's support of the project, and how Martel (who cuts a very elegant figure on the set) used to visit the hotel as a child – just one aspect of her own experience that informs the film. The long interview further reveals a very smart and engagingly uncommon individual. (*La Ciénaga* is available on R1 from Homevision.)

(DEMETRIOS MATHEOU)

The Complete Works of Yuri Norstein

(USSR, 1968–79)

Director: Yuri Norstein
Label: Films by Jove (USA)
Region: 0 (NTSC)
Discs: 1

THE FILM

To know Yuri Norstein is to sing his praises. His animation – a magical blend of hand-textured drawings, enigmatic, idyllic storytelling, pastoralism and motifs from Russian legend, art and music – may be hard to explicate, but not to appreciate; it's a shame to keep it to the connoisseurs. The films belong on film, but they also have a poetry and an intimacy that you want to hold close and return to again and again.

This gem of a DVD, home-printed cover and all, collects all of his authored works to date, including two early co-directed pieces. *25th – The First Day* (1968) is a paean to the artistic aspirations unleashed by Russia's October Revolution, mixing the 'formalist' artistry of Malevich, Shostakovich, Eisenstein and others with the broken political promises of Lenin. *The Battle of Kerjenets* (1971) is a more straightforward parade of Russian victories over foreign invaders, borrowing from medieval frescoes and icon paintings.

His signature films are fables that finesse the animation of cut-outs on multiplane glass to an extraordinary level of depth and gestural detail (although Norstein's mastery is equally in his versatility: he'll mix in flat pencil drawings, real water drop, even live-action fireworks). *The Fox and the Rabbit* (1973) is a daffy parable of pertinacity, in which a dispossessed bunny finds help not from blowhard bears and bulls, but a pipe-smoking, cutlass-wielding, have-a-go cockerel. *The Heron and the Crane* (1974) tells of the four seasons of mutual courtship and denial, with a wry simplicity further honed in *The Hedgehog in the Fog* (1975), whose protagonist loses himself in the wonders and terrors of the temporal world, before finding his place to gaze at the stars.

Norstein's masterpiece, the autobiographical *Tale of Tales* (1979), is a hymn-like collage of childhood memories, a scrapbook reverie, an interrupted lullaby. A boy shares his apple with the crows and drifts into daydream . . . a little wolf carries a baby through the woods; men are whisked away from their women, to return from war as alcoholics; and the wind blows . . . Norstein calls it 'about eternity'. Festival polls of animators voted it the best animation of all time in 1984 and again in 2002.

THE DISC

These films are also available on Jove Films' Masters of Russian Animation DVD series, cut with those of Fyodor Khitruk and lesser works. Transfer quality is very decent. There's one extra: a 15-minute extract from *Magia Russica*, a doc on Russian animation, featuring Norstein and his tools on screen, plus a sizeable clip from *The Overcoat*, the unfinished Gogol adaptation that has occupied him for the past quarter of a century. These days he's known as 'The Golden Snail'. (NICK BRADSHAW)

Oldboy

(South Korea, 2003) Special Edition

Director: Park Chan-wook
Label: Tartan Video (UK)
Region: 2 (PAL)
Discs: 2

THE FILM

A hyper-kinetic, Grand Guignol rethink of *The Count of Monte Cristo*'s protracted revenge narrative, and a defining text in the artistic and commercial explosion of South Korean cinema, *Oldboy* is pulp horror on an operatic scale. Dae-Su Oh (Choi Min-sik) is an average middle-aged failure, fond of the bottle and neglectful of his small daughter. One drunken night, he's waylaid by an umbrella-wielding figure, and spirited away to spend 15 years in solitary imprisonment. No explanation is offered; nor can our increasingly unhinged hero come up with any clues from his own past to explain the scenario. When he's just as abruptly released, he embarks upon his own investigation, with the help of a delicate sushi waitress (Kang Hye-Jong) to whom his shaggy appearance and deranged manner are apparently irresistible.

Park Chan-wook marshals the cartoonish excesses of the story (based upon a manga by Tsuchiya Garon) with a pitch-perfect blend of solemnity and rakish humour, a tonal balancing act that's reflected in visuals that are as considered in their shady elegance as in their near-surreal luridness.

THE DISCS

This is an exemplary DVD package, aimed at devoted fans. Indeed, its comprehensive range of behind-the-scenes extras presents the making of *Oldboy* as such a warm and positive collaborative experience, you could almost forget that the film's narrative takes in incest, torture, mass murder and the consumption of living sea creatures.

Park provides three frank and illuminating commentaries – one solo, one in the company of cinematographer Jeong Jeong-hun, and one with actors Choi, Yu Ji-tae and Kang – while a second disc of extras dissects the film in documentary form. In a geeky but endearing touch, the actors are questioned not by an interviewer, but by the director himself and an assembled gang of fans. Kang, we discover, spent half of her wages buying treats for the crew; Yu, despite his gloomy demeanour, is a keen karaoke singer; and Choi has a pleasing deadpan wit. ('I felt sorry for the octopus,' he notes of the infamous scene in which his character consumes live seafood. 'I bit it hard.') The entire behind-the-scenes crew also get their chance to comment ('I like the crew better than the film,' one states). The film's comic-book origins, elaborate production design, CGI effects and music are all explored in full, as is the experience of taking it to Cannes in 2004 and winning the Grand Prix du Jury. (HANNAH McGILL)

On Her Majesty's Secret Service

(UK, 1969) Ultimate Edition

Director: Peter Hunt
Label: Sony/MGM (UK/USA)
Region: 2 (PAL) / 1 (NTSC)
Discs: 2

THE FILM

Not just the best Bond film ever but one of the best movies of the 1960s, *OHMSS* is a marvellously clear-eyed work about the lure of status, institutions and blood. Most Bonds feature a cursory three-minute pit-stop in Whitehall before getting down to business on a beach; *OHMSS*, by contrast, never really leaves Whitehall's rarefied world of Dorset limestone and the hush of privileged access. This is Fleming's world, not Connery's, where good money is old money, where Bond is as attracted to his prospective father-in-law's gravitas as he is to fiancée Tracy (Diana Rigg) herself, and where the prospect of a place in *Burke's Peerage* offers Blofeld the sort of thrill he'll never get from simply impregnating chalet girls with Dutch elm disease.

It's also an immensely lonely world, where anyone not born to privilege is an outsider looking in. Bond knows what to say *chez* M, Draco or Blofeld, but there's little prospect of him playing host himself. Throughout the film there's a numbing sense of melancholy, culminating in the immaculately-staged chase scene after Bond has escaped the mountain lair as he tries to elude Irma Bunt's heavies among the crowds at a winter festival: Christmas, we realise, is something which happens to other people.

Early longueurs yes, hypnosis idiocy yes, George Lazenby yes yes yes, but there's still lots of stuff here which would stand up well even to *The Bourne Supremacy*. Brilliant aerial footage in the second ski sequence as assorted goons pursue Bond and Tracy into an avalanche, some terrific cutting as Tracy seduces Blofeld while Draco's helicopters approach the mountain top and a stupendous John Barry score which I remember desperately humming at the age of 12 while having to run cross country at school.

THE DISCS

Good picture quality and brassy sound on the Ultimate Edition double disc, along with plenty of nice extras and lots of fan-boy junk. A bewilderingly dreadful trailer introducing 'Rigg, Diana Rigg . . . this one's got style and class', and a documentary narrated by Patrick McNee including such insights as the fact that director Hunt 'knew the importance of communicating with his actors'. In place of a commentary there's a loose assemblage of nostalgic vox pops. George Baker is stoical about the fact that Fleming really wanted him to play Bond, lots of production assistants talk about Hunt's dapper appearance – 'You know, there really was a bit of Bond to him' is the general consensus – and we learn that former chalet girl Catherine von Schell now runs a B&B, 'in France'. (PETER VÁSÁRY)

On the Waterfront

(USA, 1954)

Director: Elia Kazan
Label: Columbia Tristar (all territories)
Region: Any
Discs: 1

THE FILM

In *On the Waterfront*, Marlon Brando gives one of his most famous performances, as Terry Molloy, a longshoreman and ex-boxer who battles a corrupt
union. The power of Kazan's film comes partly from its realism: the narrative
was based on a real-life story; the film was shot mainly on location, using
natural light; and real dockers appeared in it. Kazan, however, added a symbolic
dimension, in which the suffering Terry is presented as a Christ-like figure;
his justification of his collaboration with the Crime Commission has been read
as Kazan's coded apologia for co-operating with Senator Joe McCarthy's House
for Un-American Activities Committee and its anti-Communist witch-hunt.

On the Waterfront is particularly celebrated for the taxi scene, in which Terry
accuses his brother Charley (Rod Steiger) of ruining his life by making him
throw a vital fight: 'You don't understand. I could have had class. I could have
been a contender.' It is a remarkable moment in many ways: Terry gently
pushes aside the gun Charley is pointing at him, and says what he must say,
not with anger and bitterness, but in a tender, grieving tone. Charley tries to
put the blame on Terry's manager, but finally accepts his guilt and, in effect,
signs his own death warrant – he is killed for failing to deliver Terry to corrupt
union boss Johnny Friendly (Lee J Cobb). In a scene lasting four minutes, an
entire existence is summed up and changed. These unforgettably intense –
even transcendent – performances may be Brando's and Steiger's greatest
screen achievements.

THE DISC

A featurette called 'Mastering the Method' is devoted to the 'contender' scene,
which Steiger sees as a heartbreaking moment of lost love, where Terry realises
that he was betrayed by the brother he so much admired. It was not easy to
film, because Brando would sometimes improvise, departing from the script
in order to explore the characters' backgrounds – and he even departed from
the set to see an analyst, leaving Steiger to work alone. Kazan disclaims credit
for the scene, saying that he left it to the actors, who knew what they were
doing. He points out that it is the ambivalence of Brando – at once tough and
sensitive – which makes his impact so great. Of all his films, Kazan says, it is
On the Waterfront which most exactly realises his intentions. (ADAM STREVENS)

Once Upon a Time in the West

Director: Sergio Leone
Label: Paramount (all territories)
Region: Any
Discs: 2

(Italy/USA, 1968) Special Collector's Edition

THE FILM

Comprising a string of references to classic westerns, and set in an imaginary west itself defined by the movies, Leone's epic flirts with redundancy, but from the opening sequence onward it's clear that this is no ordinary homage. Replaying and up-ending *High Noon* at Warholian duration, to a pop-minimalist 'score' made up of treated found sounds, the scene announces both Leone's departure from the 'spaghetti western' cycle that had made his name and the arrival of a new style in action cinema, corresponding to Jean-Pierre Melville's reinvention of the gangster movie with *Le Samouraï*. When Henry Fonda, icon in John Ford's films of everything right and true and decent in the national character, appears as the mercenary killer Frank, hired by rail baron Morton to eliminate all opposition to the tracks' progress across the continent, all bets are off.

Part-scripted by the young leftist Bernardo Bertolucci, *Once Upon a Time in the West* proposes an analogy between the westward drive of big capitalism dramatised in the film and the flooding of European screens with American movies. Rewriting Nicholas Ray's canonical *Johnny Guitar*, another lament for the passing of the old west, as a radical text, Bertolucci was among the New Wave cinephiles who sought to express their revulsion at US imperialism in Vietnam in a newly critical attitude to Hollywood cinema. (A flop in the States and Britain, *Once Upon a Time . . .* played for years in Paris.)

The finished film is a Mexican stand-off of style, genre and history, combining Bertolucci's ambivalent take on the post-war western, Leone's near-nihilistic black humour, familiar from his *Dollars* trilogy with Clint Eastwood, and a signature widescreen *mise en scène* pitched midway between the contemporary American avant-garde and the European art movie. These elements play off each other in unexpected ways, making the film's relationship both to the historical west and to the western genre a complex affair, somehow nostalgic and analytic, allusive and iconoclastic, coarse and lush – all at once.

THE DISCS

Generally poorly received on release, and shown in a number of versions in different countries, *Once Upon a Time in the West* has nonetheless won a cult following, well represented in the DVD's extras. Anchored by Professor Christopher Frayling – as much an enthusiast as an academic – and featuring a number of celebrity admirers, the commentary and supporting documentaries help contextualise the film's intricate weave of historical and cinematic references. Sharp images on both NTSC and PAL versions. (Hardened fans who speak Italian can shop for the Italian Cine Video Corp edition that preserves an old extended cut of the film, running five minutes longer.) (HENRY K MILLER)

Onde Jaz O Teu Sorriso?

(France/Portugal, 2001)

Director: Pedro Costa
Label: Assírio & Alvim (Portugal)
Region: 2 (PAL)
Discs: 1

ENGLISH TITLE: *Where Does Your Hidden Smile Lie?*

THE FILM

Movies about making movies tend to focus on the bustling bits: the dealing (*The Player*), the shooting (*Day for Night, Hearts of Darkness*), even the media junket (*America's Sweethearts*). If there's anything that they like to elide, it's the editing process, wherein those raw transcripts of sound and image are coaxed, cajoled or simply allowed to slip into their final form. What are the aesthetic, even ethical choices being made in that dark room?

There's elision in Portuguese filmmaker Costa's precious record of Danièle Huillet and Jean-Marie Straub editing their 1999 film *Sicilia!*, but it's designed to engage the viewer's imagination, rather than duck the challenge of filming inaction. At least Costa's subjects are a pair, with fulsome opinions. (Indeed, they're one of cinema's great couples, working together for 43 years until Huillet's death in 2006. Costa made this documentary for the venerable French series of filmmaker portraits *Cinéastes de Notre Temps*.) Straub is the cock of the roost, smoking, pacing, firing off movie quotations and perorating on the means and ends of an artist. He talks about form and content, realism and fantasy, close-ups and match shots, Chaplin's attention to movement and the privilege of their uncompromising filmmaking method. Huillet works at the flatbed and interjects corrections. 'It's hard not to talk bullshit,' Straub opines in mid-argument. 'No it's not, you just shut up,' Huillet snaps back.

The film is an object lesson in more ways than one. 'Genius is nothing more than a great deal of patience,' Straub approvingly quotes from 'someone'. The Straubs work 10–5 and make five cuts a day. Costa hewed his documentary from 150 hours of mini DV footage. He could never have made it on celluloid, and nor does he offer their style of multi-angle coverage (rather, the same striking angles, brooding colours and long static takes deployed in his own docudramas *In Vanda's Room* and *Colossal Youth*), but the credo is the same: look closely, diligently; don't cut corners. Huillet's real voice is palpable as we comb her footage with her, back and forth, looking for the crucial flicker of a smile in an actor's eye, the one right frame to cut on. The film's a beautiful testament, to both her and her hubbie.

THE DISC

. . . is also lovely. Both versions of Costa's movie are here – the 104-minute theatrical and 72-minute TV cuts – along with six 'Bagatelles', or out-takes. Ported directly from 'film-look' progressive video, they look gorgeous, but so too do the two extra Straub shorts, 'The Wayfarer' and 'The Knife Grinder', made alongside *Sicilia!*. The accompanying book is sadly Portuguese-only, but the disc is assiduously multilingual (Portuguese/English/Italian). It's not widely available, but I had no problems ordering it from *cdgo.com*. (NICK BRADSHAW)

Orlando
(UK, 1992)

Director: Sally Potter
Label: Artificial Eye (UK)
Region: 2 (PAL)
Discs: 2

THE FILM

There can be no doubt about the enduring and wide-ranging appeal of this film, starring Tilda Swinton as the title character who lives 400 years of British history and (gender) politics. Adapted from the beloved novel by Virginia Woolf, Sally Potter's award-laden film set a new standard for costume drama with its sexy, witty script and performances.

Orlando, a bored young nobleman (and later, noblewoman) who aspires to be the soul of his era, finds the staples of historical drama rather empty: neither love and war (when he is a man) nor marriage and fabulous frocks (when she is a woman) hold any appeal or bring greatness. S/he'd rather be an artist, an observer and chronicler – and so the film becomes Orlando's cinematic autobiography.

The film's daring sweep allows it to incorporate unforgettably magnificent sights that are visually ravishing and politically resonant: Queen Elizabeth arriving in a night procession (serenaded by Jimmy Somerville); *Othello* performed by an all-male company on the frozen Thames; the palace of the Khan of Khiva (Lothaire Bluteau) as England tries to take control of Central Asia; and the cold glass-and-steel glamour of London in 'the present'.

Connecting all these disparate places and times is Orlando, whom Swinton gives a charm and insouciance best expressed through her witty, complicitous address to camera. Whether evaluating her newly female body, swooning with passion in the arms of Russian princess Sasha (Charlotte Valandrey) or Byronic hero Shelmerdine (Billy Zane), Swinton imparts to Orlando a self-awareness and sense of irony that retains its wonder at the world s/he admits us to.

The Orlando that we find seated beneath the great oak at the end of the film is – and is not – the same as the Orlando who sat beneath it at the start, 400 years, one sex change, and the birth of a daughter ago. As Orlando says, with cool irony, after her sex change, 'No difference at all.' But this film made all the difference: launching the careers of its director and star, and injecting British cinema with daring, originality, passion and a queer sensibility as knowing and warm as Orlando's to-camera gaze.

THE DISCS

An entire bonus disc of extras puts Sony Classics' Region 1 release to shame. Behind-the-scenes docs follow the film from shooting (in Saint Petersburg and Uzbekistan) to its reception, specifically a press conference at its Venice Film Festival bow. Potter also provides an interview and commentary over select scenes, and there's a photo gallery. (SOPHIE MAYER)

The Others

(Spain/France/USA, 2001)

Director: Alejandro Amenabar
Label: Buena Vista
Region: 2
Discs: 2

THE FILM

When art-house darlings with self-penned scripts start to play around with studio money, something usually gets lost in translation. Yet after Spanish successes with *Tesis* and *Open Your Eyes*, Chilean-born writer-director Alejandro Amenabar here scored a major success with a work boasting not only a big budget and an A-list star, but also, thankfully, considerable thematic coherence. *The Others* is defined (as was *Open Your Eyes* before it) by its acute understanding of limbo: a filmmaker with one foot in Europe and one in America tells a story, set during the final days of WWII, in which all Nicole Kidman's good housekeeping can't prevent her photosensitive charges coming under threat from the other side.

We're left somewhere between war and peace, good and evil, the living and the dead. Shying away from the chilly narrative chicanery of *The Sixth Sense*, Amenabar transports us from one state to the next with great ease, and invests the last-reel revelations and explanations with a trademark tenderness that insists love – even a love in limbo, between ghosts – is the most powerful force of all. European sensibility coupled to American showmanship, resulting in the best of both worlds: Gothic horror that's both scared of the dark *and* afraid of the light.

THE DISCS

Solid supplementary material. 'A Look Inside *The Others*' is a better-than-average making-of, folding in critical input and some cursory assessment of the film's unexpectedly strong box-office performance; meanwhile, Amenabar reveals he cast Kidman for her 'underused' eyes. Along with an affable commentary track (absent from Dimension's R1 equivalent), it proves more revealing than anything in 'An Intimate Look at Director Alejandro Amenabar', several minutes of negligible on-set footage.

The other substantial extra, leftfield documentary 'Xeroderma Pigmentosum: What Is It?', offers more proof that Amenabar might have become a doctor if he hadn't ended up behind a camera. This short film reveals the photosensitivity disease affecting the two young children in the feature isn't just a screenwriter's gimmick, but a recognised medical phenomenon. DVD extras, by their very nature, tend to be analytical rather than emotional, and few make one inclined to shed a tear; yet the sight of young Katie Mahar at her first birthday party, blowing out the solitary candle with a face full of blisters, is genuinely heartbreaking. A good example of what can be done with special features given a little extra care and research. (MIKE McCAHILL)

Pandora's Box

(Germany, 1929)

Director: GW Pabst
Label: Criterion Collection (USA)
Region: 1 (NTSC)
Discs: 2

THE FILM

A silent film that post-dates the advent of the talkies, adapted from two turn-of-the-century plays by the Wilhelmine playwright Frank Wedekind, *Pandora's Box* remains one of the most startlingly modern of movies. Its greatness is inextricably bound up with its iconic leading turn by the famously bob-haired Louise Brooks, a Hollywood fugitive whose commingling of artless naturalism and fearless carnality, both here and in Pabst's follow-up *Diary of a Lost Girl*, could not unreasonably be called revolutionary.

Made at the apex of Weimar German cinema, *Pandora's Box* encapsulates that era's combustive mix of modernism and pessimism, as the Jazz Age roar of liberation, innovation and globalisation readied to break. The Depression and rise of Nazism famously fed into film noir, with its femme fatales and brooding sublimation of Expressionism, but *Pandora's Box* was already ahead of the game. Flame to the story's many moths, Brooks's sexually uninhibited Lulu is as much victim as villain, chaperoned by the twins Eros and Thanatos as she tumbles happy-go-unluckily from Berlin's revue stages and drawing-rooms to the brutal backstreets of foggy London.

Liberated and child-like, wide-eyed and cunning, Lulu may be a mass of contradictions, but as played by Brooks, she's also a reactive figure, chimeric and unknowable, a *tabula rasa* for her audiences' projections – in short, a modern movie actress. Like the same year's *Un Chien Andalou* and *The Passion of Joan of Arc*, *Pandora's Box* implicates the spectator in male assaults on a woman, elaborating the camera's newfound capacity for voyeurism, sadism and sexual alienation. Pandora's mythic 'box' becomes a metaphor not just for Lulu's contested body, but for the cinematic apparatus itself.

THE DISCS

Perhaps inevitably, *Pandora's Box* did not make its way into the world unscathed. The French reworked its lesbianism and concocted a gay love triangle. The Americans saved Lulu by recruiting her for the Salvation Army. Criterion's edition boasts the longest extant version, restored in 1997 and now remastered for Brooks' centenary. You also get a choice of four (!) different scores, and a very erudite commentary by scholars Thomas Elsaesser and Mary Ann Doane. A second disc hosts two documentaries: 'Looking for Lulu', an hour-long portrait of Brooks' remarkable career, and Richard Leacock and Susan Steinberg Woll's 'Lulu in Berlin', an audience with the venerable flapper herself. Leacock and Pabst's son Michael record shorter reminiscences for the DVD, and there's a gallery of 50 stills. The booklet – no, book – offers a J Hoberman introduction, Kenneth's Tynan's epic 1979 *New Yorker* Brooks profile-cum-pilgrimage, and the lady's own sharp 1965 dissertation 'Pabst and Lulu' for *Sight & Sound*, all illustrated in gorgeous silver tint. Is this not to die for? (NICK BRADSHAW)

Paris, Texas

(France/West
Germany, 1984)

Director: Wim Wenders
Label: Fox Home Entertainment (USA) / Anchor Bay (UK)
Region: 1 (NTSC) / 2 (PAL)
Discs: 1

THE FILM

A man, in a suit and a red baseball cap, emerges from the desert on the Mexican border, virtually catatonic and gripped by a self-protective amnesia. He's Travis (Harry Dean Stanton), or used to be: his eyes gaze mournfully out of a forgotten face, and he patrols the dry Texan flatlands like a shellshocked ghost. His brother Walt (Dean Stockwell) brings him home, but can't fill the ragged hole Travis's wife Jane (Nastassja Kinski) opened up when she left him, dumping their son Hunter (Hunter Carson) on Walt's doorstep.

Father and son hit the road, and the movie – which won the Palme d'Or for Wim Wenders in 1984 – becomes a quest for wholeness and healing, one essayed against a backdrop of urban scenery that isn't quite finished, all cranes and half-constructed billboards. Like other macho missions such as the rescue of Princess Leia in *Star Wars* and George C Scott's hunt for his daughter in Paul Schrader's *Hardcore*, Travis and Hunter's journey harks back to John Ford's seminal gone-native western *The Searchers*, particularly in the dawning implication that they might not like what they find, and that Jane may not *want* to be found. (She's working at a peep-show parlor in Houston.) The screenplay, by Sam Shepard and LM Kit Carson (Hunter's dad) gives both Stanton and Kinski long, reflective last-act monologues in which they make a monumental effort to reconnect through mirrored glass, but seem individually sealed off in their own sad stories. Working with the great Dutch cinematographer Robby Müller (*Ghost Dog*, *Breaking the Waves*), Wenders tramps across America's wastelands to often extraordinary effect, mapping out an epic of personal loss and alienation as boundless as the scrub.

THE DISC

Chief extra here is a ruminative Wenders commentary, particularly attentive to visual minutiae and a must-listen for any budding cinematographers out there. These days, Wenders points out, skies and clouds would be prettified to order in post-production – as throughout Peter Jackson's *King Kong*, say – but back then he and Müller only got them the way they wanted using Polaroid filters. They also ignored the usual lab advice to 'correct' green neons in the frame because they wanted roadside America to be bathed in its true, livid light. The movie was shot in sequence and with only half a script at first; Shepard, off filming *Country* in Iowa, faxed in the peep-show scenes which were carefully rehearsed, performed in uninterrupted takes and shot through a one-way mirror, just as they appear. (TIM ROBEY)

Partie de Campagne

(France, 1936)

Director: Jean Renoir
Label: BFI (UK)
Region: 2 (PAL)
Discs: 1

ENGLISH TITLE: *A Day in the Country*

THE FILM

Never did such a wisp of a film resonate so richly. Seemingly a mere snapshot of a riverside picnic and a brief ensuing dalliance, Renoir's 40-minute tone poem finds grace and heartbreak to colour a lifetime in the blush of cherry trees, the song of nightingales, the flowing of the river and the clouding of the sky.

The film is set, like the Guy de Maupassant short story from which it is taken, on a summer's Sunday in 1860, on the banks of the Seine; Renoir recreated that no-longer-rural-idyll in Montigny-sur-Loing, where his father Auguste had painted. A Parisian ironmonger, Monsieur Dufour, brings his family to a country inn; while he and his doltish shop assistant Anatole, betrothed to Dufour's hapless daughter Henriette, engage in Laurel-and-Hardy-esque burlesque, Henriette and her mother Juliette catch the eyes of a couple of local rakes, Henri and Rodolphe. Fishing rods are produced to divert the menfolk, boats furnished for the women, and a light afternoon's elopement ensues, Rodolphe and Juliette fooling boisterously while the more fastidious Henriette and Henri finally surrender to their passions in the shade of a tree.

The sucker punch – the rallying of 'real' time – comes with the transition to the film's coda. As forecast several times during the action, the weather turns; a squall whips up, rain-clouds lash the water as the camera pulls rapidly away, and only with the advent of a screen caption do we realise the succinctness of the metaphor: 'Years passed with Sundays as bleak as Mondays. Anatole married Henriette, and one Sunday . . . '

Renoir had written his screenplay for clement weather, true to Maupassant's story; the rained-out location shoot left its own mark on the film, just as the immediacy of nature touches Henriette and Henri. Production was finally abandoned, and the film was only fully edited ten years later, by Renoir's editor and former partner Marguerite Renoir. It's often called unfinished, but like the lovers' lingering memory of the stolen kiss at the film's core, it's testament to how the most fleeting experience and tenuous events leave their mark on the human heart. An impressionist masterpiece, suffused with light and liquid feeling, it stands with Vigo's *Zéro de Conduite* as the cinema's greatest featurette.

THE DISC

In a well-tempered commentary, Philip Kemp talks us through the vicissitudes of the film's production (Renoir liked to describe his cast and crew as his 'family', but on this shoot he became an increasingly absent patriarch), and offers some incisive analysis of the film's interplay of nature, time and social class. The mood and craft of the production can also be glimpsed through some 40 minutes' worth of raw out-takes and screen tests from the Cinémathèque Française's archives. The transfer is lovely; the disc is a keeper. (NICK BRADSHAW)

Partner

(Italy, 1968)

Director: Bernardo Bertolucci
Label: NoShame (USA)
Region: 1 (NTSC)
Discs: 2

THE FILM

European cinema was thoroughly entwined with the student uprisings of the late '60s, anticipating, documenting and reflecting on the Paris 'événements' and sparking debates on aesthetics and politics that still smoulder today. Godard was the central figure in the shift among young filmmakers toward political commitment, applying the theories of Bertolt Brecht to the screen in an attempt to undermine the cinema's impression of reality and do away with narrative conventions. A director of uncommon lyrical gifts, Bertolucci was in many ways an unlikely disciple of the most famous Swiss Maoist, and *Partner* is an acute expression of his need 'to be doing battle with those you love the most'.

Relaying a situation more than a plot, *Partner* concerns Giacobbe (Pierre Clémenti), a theatre teacher who lives among towering book-sculptures, and his revolutionary double. A follower of Antonin Artaud, Giacobbe's double believes in the need to 'abolish the difference between the stage and stalls'. In his view revolution is a play carried out on the streets, equating the film audience with the real-world 'spectators' whom this performance is meant to awaken. Perversely, street theatre becomes a way of 'throwing the mask away' and revealing one's true desires, conceived as a revolutionary force. Just as Giacobbe oscillates between rhetoric and romance, so Bertolucci alternates gorgeous cinematography with Artaudian direct-to-camera address.

THE DISCS

NoShame's inspirational package contains then-and-now interviews with Bertolucci, whose *The Dreamers* revisited the revolutionary cinephilia of his youth. 'I didn't want to call a film "political" if the only political thing in it was the plot', he explains. Revealing that Situationist slogans freshly minted on the Left Bank barricades were incorporated into the film by the Frenchman Clémenti, who flew to Paris each weekend during the film's production in May 1968, Bertolucci conjures up a fizzily synchronistic age.

The DVD, now in limited supply, also includes an extraordinary full-length 1969 feature, *His Day of Glory*, directed by the Italian film critic Edoardo Bruno, and incorporating some unused footage from *Partner*. Mostly comprising lengthy discussions on political aesthetics and revolutionary strategy, it's probably most viewers' idea of hell; but it comes closer to the authentic tenor of argument in the wake of May than any film I've seen, and as a psychodrama of post-revolutionary pessimism it parallels early Fassbinder. Its credo on cinema applies to both films here: 'the spectator must actively participate in the show with his vigilant attention and critical spirit'. (HENRY K MILLER)

The Passenger

(France/Italy/USA/Spain, 1975)

Director: Michelangelo Antonioni
Label: Sony (all territories)
Region: Any
Discs: 1

THE FILM

We're first introduced to David Locke (Jack Nicholson) in the middle of the North African desert. A burned-out television journalist, he's searching for guerrilla forces to cover in some post-colonial civil war. Before we learn any more, he has swapped identities with a dead businessman back at their hotel. As his jilted wife and producer try to figure out what's happened, Locke – criss-crossing Europe as a gunrunner for the rebels – gets embroiled in the very war he was trying to report on.

You don't so much watch *The Passenger* as tangle with it. 'Every audience is tied to certain habits in the way that they look at film,' said director Michelangelo Antonioni. 'If they don't have the same articulation of scene, they get lost.' What you think are flashbacks are really films seen by other characters; conversations turn out to be tape recordings; people disappear, one character says, 'every time they leave the room'.

Though it has all the elements of a Z-style political thriller, *The Passenger* teeters on the brink of abstraction, threatening to and finally succeeding in abandoning altogether the story's main action, just as its anti-hero yearns to leave his life for another. But if Locke has to improvise a new life for himself, so the viewer has to learn again how to watch movies.

THE DISC

Not a commercial success, *The Passenger* was bought outright by Nicholson in the early '80s. Why he kept the movie, which he calls 'probably the biggest adventure in filming that I ever had', out of circulation for so long remains obscure, but despite this lacuna his commentary remains one of the more entertaining – and weirdly moving – star tracks. Never particularly illuminating, there's nonetheless something in Nicholson's whiskey-and-cigars drawl that pulls you in. It's clearly a film he loves inside and out.

Co-writer Mark Peploe's commentary couldn't be more different – for him the film is still a site of conflict, its discourse on the ethics of documentary, which one gathers formed the core of the original script, far from resolved. A clip we see from Locke's film, meant to explain his sense of impotence in the face of horrific violence, is in fact 'found' footage of a man being executed. If within the film this fragment crystallises the reporter's professional crisis, so the scene proved a major point of contention in the film's making, and Peploe is still audibly upset at its inclusion. (HENRY K MILLER)

The Passion of Joan of Arc

(France, 1928)

Director: Carl Theodor Dreyer
Label: Criterion Collection (USA)
Region: 1 (NTSC)
Discs: 1

THE FILM

The Maid of Orléans was canonised in 1920, nearly 500 years after the English burnt her at the stake. By that measure, the half-century that Carl Theodor Dreyer's awesomely fervent passion play suffered censure by censor, producers' scissors and studio fire (twice!) seems a trial period any saint could endure. By the time Dreyer died in 1968 the film was only circulating in grubby and bowdlerised prints; but in 1981 a copy of his original cut was found in the closet of a Norwegian mental institution and, after a major Franco-Danish restoration project, the film could again be recognised as one of the supreme achievements of European silent cinema.

Working from the historical records of Joan's trial, Dreyer collapsed the action into a single day. Arraigned before an inquisitorial court determined to discredit her claims of being sent by God, she is mocked, manipulated and threatened with torture; finally, deliriously weak, she signs a recantation, only to retract it again from her cell – raising the stakes, as it were, with her increasingly dismayed persecutors.

Dreyer orchestrates these scenes as a pounding procession of gothic imagery, a visual conflagration echoing that between the forces of temporal tyranny and spiritual piety. The extreme camera angles and off-kilter sets recall not only contemporary German Expressionism, but the pre-perspective painting of the pre-Renaissance; the editing momentum equals *Battleship Potemkin*'s for impact. Aiming to film the soul and religious intensity of a 15th-century peasant girl, Dreyer deployed his vast sets, almost never seen in their entirety, not so much for their impact on the viewer directly as on his actors, whom he frames in a litany of stringent, sculpted close-ups. He believed in the face as the window to the soul, and Renée Falconetti's tremulous focal turn as Joan opens up one of the most transcendentally moving vistas in all cinema.

THE DISC

Dreyer intended the film to screen without music, but Criterion's excellent edition offers, as well as that option, Richard Einhorn's inspired 1995 composition *Voices of Light*, an unsurpassable accompaniment. The film's digital restoration is superlative (there are illustrated discussions about both the film's blighted release history and its reconstruction, along with similar notes about its production design). Dreyer scholar Casper Tybjerg's 'audio essay' is a lucid and comprehensive commentary track. There are also excerpts of an audio interview about Falconetti with her daughter Hélène, an essay by Einhorn about his music, a promo film about its recording, a booklet with his libretto and medieval source texts, and a short Dreyer treatise on 'realised mysticism' in the sleeve notes. (NICK BRADSHAW)

Sam Peckinpah's The Legendary Westerns Collection

(USA, 1961-73)

Director: Sam Peckinpah
Label: Warners (USA)
Region: 1 (NTSC)
Discs: 6

THE FILMS

As Paul Schrader once remarked, Peckinpah 'chiselled the gravestone' for the western just as Orson Welles did for film noir. These four films – the solid core of his filmmaking achievements – perfectly convey his romantic yearning for the Old West with its imagined codes of honour and male camaraderie, coupled with a resigned, fatalistic understanding of how fragile those values can prove as the modern world encroaches. Just as he saw himself as a man out of time – an outlaw maverick obsessively pursuing his art while locking horns with philistine studio suits – so he was fascinated by men (and almost exclusively men) who couldn't adapt to a changing world. *Ride the High Country* (1961) was the film which first won him his spurs: it used 'classic' western elements to spin an elegiac tale of betrayal and redemption in which nobility triumphs over avarice and self-interest. But it was with 1969's *The Wild Bunch* that Peckinpah really staked his claim, bringing a down-and-dirty realism to the genre (including unprecedented displays of mass carnage) while sending his anachronistic outlaw gang out in an ecstatic blaze of heroic glory; in their death throes these stone killers prove scorpions among mere ants.

Bloody Sam's masterpiece struck a chord with Vietnam-era audiences, but he chose to follow it up with *The Ballad of Cable Hogue* (1970), a gentle tragi-comedy in which Jason Robards' eponymous prospector briefly realises the American Dream – turning a desert waterhole into a profitable enterprise while winning the heart of Stella Stevens' feisty prostitute – before the modern world comes crashing in. It was Peckinpah's personal favourite of his works, but he replaced its playful lyricism with a mournful despair in his last period western – *Pat Garrett and Billy the Kid* (1973) – which treats the grizzled lawman's killing of his former friend as the ultimate defeat: a betrayal of both the Spirit of the West and the best part of himself.

THE DISCS

As with some anamorphic transfers, these discs suffer from a slight softness of image, but are the best currently available. All four films feature illuminating commentaries from a group of Peckinpah scholars, which are particularly good at elucidating the differences in the two versions of *Pat Garrett* included here – the long 1988 Turner Preview version and a 2005 Special Edition (combining the best of the Turner version with the original theatrical cut). The set's various documentaries interview key Peckinpah collaborators to build up a picture of a driven, difficult man, who – hounded by the demons of drink, drugs and despair – rode roughshod over his personal relationships in pursuit of his epic visions. (The UK R2 versions of *PG&BTK* have cuts to scenes of cock-fighting and a horse fall.) (ANDY RICHARDS)

Peeping Tom
(UK, 1960)

Director: Michael Powell
Label: Criterion Collection (USA)
Region: 1 (NTSC)
Discs: 1

THE FILM

Michael Powell once described *Peeping Tom* as a movie about a film fan, a cruel joke that fails to make his classic thriller any less uncomfortable to watch. On the surface, it betrays a fondness for deviant sexual behaviour, amateur psychology and cold-blooded murder. At its core, though, it's a lurid meditation on the voyeurism inherent in any audience.

German actor Karl-Heinz Böhm is genuinely creepy as Mark Lewis, the son of an eminent psychologist who deliberately filmed and tormented him for research purposes. Now a focus puller in a London film studio, Mark is obsessed with filming the deaths of young women, turning the camera on his victims at the point of death. Released the same year as *Psycho*, *Peeping Tom* shares with Hitchcock's film a fixation with violence and transgressive sexual behaviour.

The British press took a much dimmer view. Dismissing the movie as 'sick', they effectively destroyed Powell's career overnight. Perhaps he cut too close to the bone. Making us watch one girl's death through Mark's camera, Powell not only reminds us of our own involvement in her death, but reveals quite how seedy the movie-going experience can be too.

THE DISC

'Look out! Look out! Look out!' screamed *Peeping Tom*'s original theatrical trailer. 'Take care, for you are now alone with a killer!' The producers needn't have bothered with the warning – audiences stayed away in droves after the movie was panned by critics. 'The only really satisfactory way to dispose of *Peeping Tom* would be to shovel it up and flush it swiftly down the nearest sewer,' ran one of the kinder reviews. 'Even then the stench would remain.'

And yet, as Criterion's superlative special edition reminds us, *Peeping Tom*'s stench has merely sweetened over time. Film theorist Laura Mulvey's thoughtful audio commentary typifies the movie's enduring academic appeal, while the documentary 'A Very British Psycho', made for Channel 4, examines *Peeping Tom*'s reception and subsequent reappraisal, featuring interviews with Alexander Walker, Powell, Böhm and Anna Massey.

But the indisputable highlight is the documentary's introduction to *Peeping Tom*'s screenwriter Leo Marks, who worked as a codebreaker during the war and was fascinated by psychoanalysis. 'The greatest code of all was the unconscious and Freud appeared to have deciphered it,' Marks says. 'Perhaps not accurately or altogether, but what an attempt he made.' You could say the same for *Peeping Tom* too. (JAMES CLASPER)

Pee Wee's Big Adventure

(USA, 1985)

Director: Tim Burton
Label: Warners (USA)
Region: 1 (NTSC)
Discs: 1

THE FILM

From his beginnings as an adult stage comedian, through glory days as a movie star and hit kids' TV show host to, finally, his humiliation and ignominy in a Florida porno-cinema, the rise and fall of Pee Wee Herman (or was it his alter-ego Paul Reubens?) would make for a fascinating biopic. In fact it's something Reubens has long talked about, but until then there's always this, his first dazzling entry into our world. The story goes that Reubens selected Tim Burton to direct what would be both their first features on the strength of Burton's short *Frankenweenie*. The result would launch both their careers, Reubens going on to warp young minds on Saturday mornings for years to come, Burton becoming a famously hit-and-miss A-list director.

Pee Wee presents them both at the top of their form. As he sets out into the big, wide world in search of his beloved bicycle, Pee Wee is a deranged, hyperkinetic man-child, reminiscent at times of Jerry Lewis, but with a healthy dose of cinematic PCP keeping things wild and strange. Seen through the eyes of Burton, Reubens and his late co-writer Phil Hartman (the voice of *The Simpsons*' Troy McClure), Pee Wee's world is still our world, but one magically transformed into a giant toyshop of the mind, populated with larger-than-life characters and garish colour schemes.

Brimming over with imagination, invention and more than slightly twisted humour, *Pee Wee's Big Adventure* is a film that will either speak directly to the dreamy kid inside you, or simply confuse the hell out of it.

THE DISC

Considering its large and loyal fan base, the film justifies a double-disc edition, though there's plenty here to keep us entertained. The quality of the film is top notch, as is the Dolby 5.1 soundtrack, while Danny Elfman's score is given the five-star treatment with its own commentary by the composer. The main commentary comprises banter between Reubens and Burton, which though enjoyable, doesn't shed a huge amount of light on the film itself. A good selection of deleted scenes, in which we meet more bizarre characters from Pee Wee's world, including the Amazing Larry and his amazing flying wig, more than compensate. (MARK PILKINGTON)

Performance

(UK, 1970)

Directors: Donald Cammell & Nicholas Roeg
Label: Warners (UK/USA)
Region: 2 (PAL) / 1 (NTSC)
Discs: 1

THE FILM

Forever teetering on the brink of incoherence, pretension and self-indulgence, but never quite tumbling into the abyss, Cammell and Roeg's high-wire experiment finally succeeds through its potent distillation of the social, sexual and cultural energies swirling around 1968's 'swinging' London. The symbiotic relationship between its two principal 'performers' – reclusive rock star Turner (Mick Jagger) and Chas (James Fox), the brutal underworld enforcer holing up in his Notting Hill mansion – enacts the era's fascination with the worlds of violent crime and the new breed of celebrity popstars; these spheres intersected in the bohemian, aristocratic Chelsea set which Cammell inhabited and from which the film was born. Warners were banking on a Jagger vehicle that they could market to the counterculture, but they balked at the heady, alienating blend of Borges, Burroughs, Anger and Artaud concocted by the filmmakers – as well as the almost unprecedented intensity of the onscreen sex and violence. In Britain though, *Performance* has always had its cult among those who appreciate its status as a key homegrown gangster film and as a unique collaboration between some of the country's most gifted visionaries.

The rumours surrounding the production (including Fox's immersion in East End crime and his post-film breakdown, as well as assorted sexual and pharmacological shenanigans) may have helped preserve the film's notoriety over the subsequent decades, but it's less the whiff of authentic decadence than the film's utopian idealism that is most striking today. Turner and his lovers Thurber (Anita Pallenberg) and Lucy (Michèle Breton) set about dismantling Chas's macho, repressed psyche to release his feminine energies, while for Turner Chas is a conduit for recovering the creative demon that has forsaken him. In a film obsessed with mirrorings and 'mergers', their final fusion is an extreme form of liberation, where even death is reconfigured as a transcendental headtrip. The film's formal experimentation (kaleidoscopic, asso-ciative editing) has come to be associated with Roeg's future oeuvre, but Cammell's stock has risen significantly since his suicide in 1996, and the project's intellectual ambitions and rich tapestry of cultural allusions are now more properly attributed to his erudite sensibilities and fruitful associations within the Chelsea set.

THE DISC

Warners' crisp new transfer brings out the intensity of the film's saturated colours, while the Jack Nitzsche-curated soundtrack has been given a sonic spruce-up (one glitch aside, when Turner raises his glass to Old England, but the sound of his toast disappears). A decent new featurette, 'Influence and Controversy', includes interviews with Pallenberg, producer Sandy Lieberson and critic Colin McCabe, and provides some fascinating background (Cammell originally wrote the script for Marlon Brando rather than Fox), as well as unpicking some of the film's esoteric symbolism. (ANDY RICHARDS)

Persona

(Sweden, 1966) Special Edition

Director: Ingmar Bergman
Label: MGM (USA)
Region: 1 (NTSC)
Discs: 1

THE FILM

Persona is a film of constant astonishments, but perhaps its biggest surprise is that Bergman's masterpiece, for all its earned comparisons to *The Waste Land* and *Ulysses*, remains so potently accessible. Despite withholding its monumental secrets from scholars and first-timers alike, the movie's confessional atmosphere, erotic gravity and emotional warfare prove seductive and scalding to all who enter here. After the opening montage of slinking spiders, nailed hands and corpse-like faces, the central storyline between Liv Ullmann's suddenly mute actress and Bibi Andersson's star-struck and garrulous nurse arrives, perversely, as a sort of relief.

Bergman's formal ruptures – the soundtrack of dripping water, the sutured faces of the actresses, the crisis when the film literally cracks and burns – retain every ounce of their strangely frightening power. *Persona* has thus invited no shortage of sweeping assessments: as the final word against myths of identity, a schizoid mirror held up to history's traumas, the last nail in the coffin of 'interpretation'. But are we wrong to hear a contagious note of fright in these rationalised responses? Has any film ever offered a stronger, purer taste of unreturned infatuation, of killing resentment and desperate pleading, of the prodigious sexuality in certain kinds of silence? *Persona*, immaculate, radiates Big Ideas and basic human feelings at the same time, surpassing all comers in its ability to stitch them all together in a sort of sinister catharsis.

THE DISC

Available on its own or as part of MGM's five-disc set with *Hour of the Wolf*, *The Passion of Anna*, *The Serpent's Egg*, and the extraordinary *Shame*, *Persona* has been scrupulously rendered through a new digital transfer. The infinite shades of white and grey, the eerie seaside mists and the black, rugged beach: all of it looks exquisite and pops right off the screen. The 'Poem in Images' featurette sports interesting testimonies from Bergman, Ullmann and Andersson; disciples will shudder to learn that the film almost wasn't made. Shorter, isolated interviews with both actresses are squarely directed at the lore of Bergman's on-set liaison with Ullmann – debatable in their relevance, but weirdly compatible with the film's own obsession with erotic secrets.

Really, the only supplement that fizzles is the commentary track from Marc Gervais, a Bergman biographer and Jesuit priest whose bizarrely chirpy rhetoric, calling his listeners 'boys and girls' and coining words like 'complexificated', fails to illuminate much, especially in a film so deeply attuned to the limits of language. (Tartan's R2 edition is notably brighter than the MGM, with fewer extras, but does suggest some image cropping on the latter.) (NICK DAVIS)

A Personal Journey with Martin Scorsese through American Movies

(UK/USA, 1995)

Director: Martin Scorsese
Label: BFI (UK)
Region: 2 (PAL)
Discs: 1

THE FILM

Scorsese's 225-minute history of US cinema is an enthusiastic canter through some 50 years of the medium, told in dozens of film clips and archive interviews with the likes of Welles, Wilder, Ray, Capra, Cassavetes and Ford. Personal it is: these are the films that inspire Scorsese, the contents of his 'imaginary museum', and he cheerfully admits the selection won't be objective or academic. So there's a perceptible emphasis on movies of the 1940s and 1950s – the formative films Scorsese watched as a kid – and he brings down the curtain at the end of the 1960s, declining to comment on his peers. Though the museum has room for high and low, much of the curator's affection goes to marginal, undervalued filmmakers – Delmer Daves, Phil Karlson, Joseph H Lewis, King Vidor, Jacques Tourneur – and he omits some major figures almost entirely: Hitchcock, for instance, barely gets a mention.

Scorsese is an engaging guide, trenchant and epigrammatic – 'Movies are a medium based on consensus', 'More than a plot, Murnau offered visions, a landscape of the mind' – and his decision to swap slavish chronology for a set of loosely connected themes is a fine touch. 'The Director's Dilemma' weighs the compromises a film artist may have to make to keep working inside the Hollywood system ('Do you make one for yourself, one for them?'); 'The Director as Smuggler' examines film subtexts; and under the heading 'The Director as Storyteller' Scorsese considers native American genres the western, the gangster film and the musical.

Between the clips he talks straight to camera, weaving industry lore with his own memories: guiltily snipping, as a child, illustrations out of a book on movies borrowed from the New York Public Library, or being taken to see *Duel in the Sun* by his mother. Finally, he has a word of advice for would-be filmmakers: 'Do it like painters used to do, study the old masters, enrich your palette. There's always so much more to learn.' Earlier on, though, he confesses that the work ethic, at least in his case, is only half the story: 'As with heroin, the antidote to film is more film.'

THE DISC

Personal Journey was a BFI/Channel 4/Miramax co-production for TV. The disc has no extras other than on-screen biographies and filmographies of the filmmakers under discussion. Incidentally, Scorsese has also made a history of Italian cinema along similar lines: *My Voyage to Italy* (1999), available from the US on the Miramax label. (SIMON CROPPER)

Petulia

(USA, 1968)

Director: Richard Lester
Label: Warners (USA)
Region: 1 (NTSC)
Discs: 1

THE FILM

With *Shampoo* (1975), Hal Ashby delivered a rueful retrospective satire on the moral confusion sweeping America in 1968, but it was an earlier Julie Christie film – Dick Lester's brilliant but undervalued tragi-comedy *Petulia* – that showed the inside track on a nation spinning crazily off its moral axis. With Vietnam playing out on America's TV sets, Lester dissects the 'casual violence' of people's relationships, and the inability of individuals to overcome insecurities and form meaningful ties with those they purport to love. Archie (George C Scott) is a successful surgeon whose gnawing boredom with life's lot has just driven him to walk out on his wife and kids; he's given a second roll of the dice when he meets wilfully eccentric socialite Petulia (Christie, at her most beguiling), and they embark on a peculiarly extended courtship that promises to bring out the best in each of them. Gradually, though, Archie comes to realise that Petulia's breezy front hides fearful disappointment with her abusive marriage to her naval architect husband (a suavely chilling Richard Chamberlain), and her guilt over a young Mexican boy whose life has become a casualty of their marital mind-games.

Frequently very funny, the film leaves a bittersweet aftertaste, withholding any easy redemptive epiphanies from its characters; if they remain mired in the pains of their pasts, it's ultimately because their better intentions aren't sufficient to help them locate their moral bearings in a society that has foundered on the rocks of self-interest and political apathy. Lester has a lot of fun whisking us around a series of San Francisco locations that highlight the shallow gimmickry and vapid consumerism of over-automated late-'60s America – from roller-derbies and trained penguin displays to mechanised motels and hospital rooms with false-fronted TV sets (designed to encourage patients to rent the real thing). The overwhelming sense of dislocation extends to the film's fractured chronology and elliptical edits, which rather than feeling like voguish affectations are a perfectly apt way of depicting a world where everything is in flux; they also – fascinatingly – anticipate the future *modus operandi* of director Nic Roeg, here impressively rounding off his last main stint as cinematographer for hire.

THE DISC

The fine, detailed transfer does justice to the film's riot of day-glo psychedelia, and helps show off Christie's Arlette Nastat outfits to the max. A new making-of gives a useful perspective on the Haight-Ashbury scene and the Summer of Love that gifted the movie its evocative backdrop, as well as teasing out the film's relationship to its John Haase source novel *Me and the Arch Kook Petulia*. (ANDY RICHARDS)

The Piano

(Australia/New Zealand, 1993)

Director: Jane Campion
Label: Optimum (UK)
Region: 2 (PAL)
Discs: 2

THE FILM

Ada McGrath (Holly Hunter) is a 19th-century Scotswoman who has refused to speak since she was six years old. She arrives in New Zealand as the purchased bride of a taciturn colonist, but neither she nor her fatherless daughter (Anna Paquin) make any easy concessions to domestic custom. Ada's proud resolve is shared by the film, which forges ahead into tense, exotic circumstances and allows us, indeed forces us, to fend for ourselves within its fertile landscape of desire, violence, envy and enigma. The piano in Jane Campion's magisterial film is an instrument, a voicebox, a prize, a symbol, a concept, a thing-in-itself, a means of communication and a bulky rampart against it. Campion's ingenuity is to read all the same paradoxes into human personality and sexuality. Her film looks askance at daily life, brimming with unexpected angles and an almost subconscious language of images and tones, and yet it stares forthrightly into extraordinary conflicts: the worst of what people do to each other, and the remarkable, ambiguous ways in which we save each other. None of this, of course, would be possible without the flawless cast, the superb locations, the eccentrically beautiful score and the utterly persuasive production design.

THE DISCS

Heretofore available only in an undistinguished and feature-free version, *The Piano* finally attains a proper showcase, with an impressive gallery of key creative personnel gathered for the occasion. Campion and producer Jan Chapman provide a chummy but detailed commentary track, but even more illuminating are the generous interviews with both women as well as composer Michael Nyman, all furnished on the second disc. Campion speaks for a full, congenial hour about her creative process (including glimpses at her sketch-books), her casting decisions and varying methods with different actors, her close collaboration with her cinematographer, and her charmingly ambivalent response to the film's Oscar successes. Chapman elucidates with passion the role of an independent film producer, specifically when securing international funds for a risky screenplay, and Nyman, without winning any trophies for modesty, sheds valuable light on how and why the film was tailored to the score, rather than the more customary reverse. A shorter making-of featurette from the time of the film's production expands to include the lead actors' perspectives. Best of all, the print transfer exquisitely captures the rolling waves, the plashy mud, the burnished glow of the interiors, and the eerie, aqueous light of the New Zealand bush. (NICK DAVIS)

Pickpocket

(France, 1959)

Director: Robert Bresson
Label: Criterion Collection (USA)
Region: 1 (NTSC)
Discs: 1

THE FILM

Pickpocket bowed in the same year as *Breathless* and **The 400 Blows**. Though critical response was lukewarm at first, the film has by now installed itself just as highly in the canon of world film and influenced subsequent generations just as profoundly. In fact, this 75-minute masterpiece is often touted as Bresson's most accessible film, partly due to its surprising sensuality, but the arresting simplicity of the film's surface and plot give way on further inspection to dazzling complexities and crucial enigmas. Does Michel (Martin LaSalle), the titular thief, act out of naturalistically evoked poverty and desperation, or is he a figure of existential alienation? What exactly is the scale of his prior transgressions? Why does the film mention but elide a two-year interval of hedonistic debauchery in London? On what is his bond with the catlike but nurturing Jeanne (Marika Green) finally based? These and other riddles eddy and shimmer beneath the film's famous visual regime, composed equally of Bresson's caressing close-ups of thieving hands and his carefully cultivated visual and moral distance.

THE DISC

In her interview for the illuminating 'Models of *Pickpocket*' featurette, Marika Green attests that actors from different Bresson films are often stand-offish toward each other, defensive about their private confidences and working methods with their mercurial director: 'Each of us, her own experience, her own Bresson.' The *Pickpocket* DVD, replete with enticing extras, bespeaks its own interesting version of internal rivalry. Gary Indiana contributes an observant but roundly contrarian liner-notes essay, emphasising the film's subversive erotics and alleging 'the uselessness of Christian faith' as a governing theme. James Quandt, author of a book on Bresson, declines to extemporise and instead recites a scripted commentary track, blending more conventional takes on Bresson's spiritual and visual hallmarks with backstage anecdotes about, for example, the cinematographer's dislike of the film.

Paul Schrader's introductory segment pitches Bresson as a patron saint of the 1970s generation of American filmmakers, and, in a 1960 French television segment, two hilariously austere interviews quiz the great man himself, asking, 'Do you think people understand you?' and 'Your film is unlike most others. Are you aware of that?' Each featurette, its own experience, its own Bresson — their claims no less emphatic for being so divergent, and all of them highly provocative for thinking about the director and his film. (The slightly blurrier transfers from MK2 and Artificial Eye share most of the same DVD supplements but not the Quandt commentary, the Schrader introduction, or the controversial Indiana essay.) (NICK DAVIS)

Planet of the Apes

(USA, 1968) 35th Anniversary Edition

Director: Franklin J Schaffner
Label: 20th Century Fox (all territories)
Region: Any
Discs: 2

THE FILM

The year 1968 was a tricky moment for Hollywood to fund a despairing political allegory about the misuse of civilisation, but then 20th Century Fox just
thought they were making a monkey movie. It was producer Arthur Jacobs
who bought up the rights to Pierre Boulle's novel, touted it around the studios,
and only after make-up tests managed to persuade Fox head Richard D Zanuck
that the idea of established actors going ape could be anything other than
laughable. The starring clout of Charlton Heston gave them not only the green
light but an unexpected source of resonance: his stranded astronaut chomps
cigars and has a Nietzschean moan about the contemptibility of his fellow
man, only to be thrust to the bottom of an even baser planetary hierarchy
when he's captured and enslaved by lower primates.

Director Schaffner, rising to the occasion as rarely before or later, gives us
a tense and spacious arrival in a barren land, while Jerry Goldsmith's startlingly experimental score deploys ram's horns, Brazilian cuikas and goodness
knows what else to bring an ethnic disorientation to the thrill of the chase.
From there, the investigation of ape society – a three-tier caste system with
orang-utans as the judiciary, chimps as the intellectuals, and gorillas as the
muscle – culminates in an almost McCarthy-esque courtroom smackdown that
was largely the work of once-blacklisted screenwriter Michael Wilson. But it
was Rod *Twilight Zone* Serling who came up with that matchless zinger of an
ending, one of the classic doomsday tableaux of 1960s iconography. It socks a
fiercely disgruntled vision right home.

THE DISCS

The two-hour-plus, Roddy-McDowall-hosted documentary 'Behind the Planet
of the Apes' is the real meat on the second disc, and offers a handy trawl
through the sequels as well as an extremely detailed account of the first
film's production history. We get the original make-up test in which Edward
G Robinson, earmarked for the part of orang-utan theologian Dr Zaius, helped
sell the studio on the premise (he eventually ducked out because the latex
took so long to apply). Zanuck's professed unawareness about even the most
basic level of social commentary in the movie beggars belief, but plenty of
lip-service is given to it elsewhere. Available either in a six-disc box set or
in a subsequently repackaged stand-alone edition, the material here predates
Tim Burton's 2001 rehash and makes it all the easier to ignore. (TIM ROBEY)

Point Blank

(USA, 1967)

Director: John Boorman
Label: Warners (USA)
Region: 1 (NTSC)
Discs: 1

THE FILM

Overlooked at the time of its release, *Point Blank* is now recognised as one of the definitive films of its era: avant-garde filmmaking backed by a gripping narrative and powerful performances.

After a stunning, hallucinogenic opening sequence, this New Wave noir weaves an intricate, multi-layered web of dreams, lies and memories before gathering for a brutal final act. Lee Marvin has rarely been better than as Walker, the stoic, silent, hard-bitten gunman betrayed and left for dead by a faceless, bureaucratic enemy called The Organisation. Fed clues by a mysterious man in black, Marvin slowly pieces together the tattered fragments of his life, the trail leading him to the recently decommissioned island prison Alcatraz, where it all began. The young Boorman keeps a firm grasp on the action, though there's a thrilling sense that both we and Walker could be engulfed at any minute by the writhing, labyrinthine plot. With innovative camerawork, stunning sound design and a consummate sense of style, revenge has never tasted so bitter or looked so good.

Point Blank has since become a genre touchstone, influencing everything from Mike Hodges' *Get Carter* to *The Limey* and beyond. For some reason, Donald Westlake's original novel, *The Hunter*, was remade in 1999 as *Payback*, starring Mel Gibson – but he ain't no Lee Marvin and it ain't no *Point Blank*.

THE DISC

A dazzling 2.35:1 print is complemented by a fascinating discussion between Boorman and fellow director and fan Steven Soderbergh, whose own *The Limey* owes more than just a tip-of-the-hat to the film at hand. While Boorman remains rightly evasive about the meaning of some of the film's more oblique moments, he does reveal some startling behind-the-scenes insights. Particularly intense was the tension between stars Angie Dickinson and Lee Marvin (safe to say, some of the slaps she gives him in one of the film's most memorable scenes were probably meant to hurt). A separate two-part featurette details the trials and tribulations of being the first crew to shoot on Alcatraz since its decommissioning in 1963. (MARK PILKINGTON)

The Roman Polanski Collection

(Poland/UK, 1957-66)

Director: Roman Polanski
Label: Anchor Bay (UK)
Region: 2 (PAL)
Discs: 4

FILM TITLES: *Knife in the Water, Repulsion, Cul-de-Sac,* plus early shorts

THE FILMS

Rounding up the vast majority of Polanski's work made prior to *Dance of the Vampires* (1967), this Anchor Bay box set encapsulates the most assured, original and brilliantly sustained segment of the director's quixotic career. His Polish debut feature *Knife in the Water* (1962) – a taut psychological thriller set almost entirely on a small yacht – is a supremely economical piece, using subtle shifts in the relationships between its three characters (a bickering couple and a young hitchhiker they've picked up) to explore themes of power, humiliation and betrayal that would recur throughout Polanski's career. The film's success gave a fillip to Polish cinema, helping it shrug off the strictures of social realism, while giving its brightest new star a ticket to a career on the other side of the Iron Curtain.

His next project arose through lucky opportunism: he hooked up with London-based Compton Films, a seedy distribution outfit keen to diversify into more prestigious ventures, and proposed a *Psycho*-style horror thriller. The resulting film – *Repulsion* (1965) – became one of the landmarks of the genre: a scary, psychologically acute portrait of a young Belgian manicurist (Catherine Deneuve) undergoing a mental breakdown when left alone by her sister in their Kensington flat. The film's repertoire of expressionist effects (including hands grasping from walls, wide-angle visual distortions and expanding sets) perfectly conveyed the heroine's incipient madness, rooted in her crippling shyness and fear of sexual contact.

Basking in more critical and commercial acclaim, the director was now able to return to a pet project – *Cul-de-Sac* (1966) – which Compton had been earlier unwilling to finance. Reconfiguring the triangular psychodrama of *Knife* into a tale of a brutish gangster (Lionel Stander) invading the lives of a mismatched couple (Donald Pleasance and Françoise Dorléac) living in a remote castle on Northumberland's Holy Island, Polanski once again delights in exploring the cruel games people play to shore up their fragile psyches. Mixing Pinter and Beckett to absurd, disturbing effect, the film unnerves with its sly shifts in tone from tragedy to black comedy and back again, often within the same scene: if it evokes Tarantino or the Coens, that's because – like these other Polanski classics – it casts an impressively long shadow.

THE DISCS

Anchor Bay's transfers are reasonably sharp, although completists will want to track down Criterion's edition of *Knife in the Water*, which has the edge in picture quality. Each film boasts trailers, bios and a decent new featurette revealing plenty about the challenges of these difficult low-budget shoots, while *Repulsion* has a commentary from Polanski and Deneuve. The fourth disc includes eight of Polanski's early shorts (mostly produced at the Lódz film school), which illustrate his nascent talent while fascinatingly prefiguring his later work. (ANDY RICHARDS)

Porco Rosso

(Japan, 1992)

Director: Hayao Miyazaki
Label: Buena Vista (USA)
Region: 1 (NTSC)
Discs: 2

THE FILM

If animation is a kind of sorcery, Hayao Miyazaki ranks as one of its very grandest wizards, his films achieving, through a celebration of the human capacities of artisanship, imagination, self-knowledge and worldly engagement, a transcendent state of grace and affirmation. Flight is his favourite metaphor, and from *Nausicaa Valley of the Wind* to *Spirited Away* and *Howl's Moving Castle* he has sent feisty princesses, teenage witches, forest sprites and the hearts of his audience alike leaping and soaring through the air.

Arguably his most personal and touching film as well as his most eccentric, *Porco Rosso* contrives to make pigs fly, its hero a porcine fighter pilot plying his trade as a mercenary in the skies of the Adriatic between the wars. Marco once flew in squadron as an ordinary man, but now lives piggishly alone on an island hideaway with his beautiful but ageing Savoia seaplane (a Miyazaki original). The world, however, is not for leaving him in peace and, beset by buffoonish brigands, a grandstanding yankee rival and Mussolini's fascist police, not to mention his pining childhood friend Gina, Marco is grudgingly drawn back into the fray.

A scenario that would seem to be the stuff of farce (think Bottom in *A Midsummer Night's Dream*) is played out with tremendous dignity: steeped in Miyazaki's Europhilia, the film revives the gallant spirit of such classics as *Only Angels Have Wings*, *A Matter of Life and Death* and Roald Dahl's flying stories, while, as a comment on lost idealism and political engagement, it's at least the equal of *Casablanca* or *To Have and Have Not*. There's action in the aerial sequences, and comedy in the fights, but what lingers longest is the fragile romanticism of the milieu and old-fashioned cel drawings. Like Marco, perhaps, Miyazaki is the last of a rare breed.

THE DISCS

Disney's Region 1 double-disc set gets the nod here. It shares with the Optimum UK version a fleeting interview with Studio Ghibli MD Toshio Suzuki, full storyboards, and trailers both Japanese and Disneyed.

One addition is what you might call a dubbing-of doc, 'Behind the Microphone', a slightly gushing profile of the American voice cast at work. But if you're collecting, better pick the version that has not just Japanese and American language tracks (the latter, with a gruff Michael Keaton as Marco, just slightly over-simplified), but also the Jean Reno-led French version, which Miyazaki professed to prefer to the original. (NICK BRADSHAW)

Predator

(USA, 1987)
Special Edition / Collector's Edition

Director: John McTiernan
Label: 20th Century Fox (all territories)
Region: 2 (PAL) / 1 (NTSC)
Discs: 2

THE FILM

When Arnold Schwarzenegger and Carl Weathers clasp hands in greeting-as-confrontation at the outset of *Predator*, their eyes locked and biceps bulging, the tone is set. Schwarzenegger plays Major Alan 'Dutch' Schaefer, who heads up a US Army Special Forces team consisting of some of the 1980s' most eminent muscle men, soon to be stalked in the South American jungle by an extra-terrestrial hunter with a penchant for hot weather and making trophies of America's finest.

As with many action films of the era, the Cold War and the ghosts of Vietnam hang heavy over proceedings. But more importantly *Predator* harks back to the seminal monster movies of the 1950s (and some have even claimed its heritage in the Old English poem *Beowulf*). Like contemporary remake *The Thing* and the soldiers-versus-space-beings *Aliens*, it brings a visceral dynamism to the genre with its deftly executed violence and gore. Never letting the pace drag, and eschewing the trivialities of character development, McTiernan pits ego and machismo against a refreshingly sophisticated adversary, and gleefully watches the body count rise. Alan Silvestri's pounding score jacks up the tension, as does the infrared 'Predator vision', McTiernan holding off until the climactic showdown before the manhunter finally shows its face.

The film owes a great deal of its success to Stan Winston's instantly iconic creature (an in-flight conversation with James Cameron apparently inspired those trademark mandibles). Beyond that is the sheer red-blooded entertainment on show: the destruction of a large portion of rainforest as the soldiers open fire indiscriminately at their unseen assailant, the raft of quotable action hero lines, and one of Arnie's best performances as an all-American soldier with a thick Austrian accent.

THE DISCS

The Special Edition features a host of extras (some as Easter eggs), but the real enjoyment lies in the seven featurettes that take you 'Inside the Predator', – particularly the documentary 'If It Bleeds, We Can Kill It'. The latter is a treasure trove of revelations about the testosterone-fuelled atmosphere of the shoot: the cast would get up before dawn to train and secretly pump weights to look the most buff for filming; the imposing Sonny Landham was so unstable that he needed a bodyguard to protect the cast and crew from him; and the diminutive Jean-Claude Van Damme, wouldn't you know it, was lined up to play the Predator, but dropped out when he wasn't offered a name credit. (DAN FRANKLIN)

Psycho

(USA, 1960) Special Edition

Director: Alfred Hitchcock
Label: Universal (France)
Region: 1 (PAL)
Discs: 2

THE FILM

There's a crude but reliable litmus test for movie notoriety, and that's when one scene or snatch of dialogue becomes shorthand for a whole film. *Citizen Kane* has 'Rosebud!', *Basic Instinct* the uncrossing of Sharon Stone's legs; and in *Psycho* there's 'the shower scene', pretty much the most picked-over three minutes in movie history. With it, Hitchcock bumped off his heroine (Janet Leigh) a third of the way into the story – all part of his plan to 'direct the audience' (for which read 'wrong-foot') – and made three days' work last forever. Everyone's seen it; many have stolen from it; some – like Mel Brooks in *High Anxiety* – have made fun of it: rare honours for a low-budget film shot in black and white.

Film-goers liked it, too. *Psycho* was Hitchcock's biggest commercial success ($819,000 to make, $40 million at the box office) and the most reluctant to lie down: Anthony Perkins reprised his role as wacko motel keeper Norman Bates in two film sequels and one TV movie, then Gus Van Sant did a shot-for-shot remake in 1998. And still the original stands up to viewing and re-viewing, devilishly droll and slippery, craftily scripted and cast, masterfully shot. Just don't take it too seriously: it's a game, one of the darkest and best ever played.

THE DISCS

The latest, 45th anniversary UK set looks outwardly splendid in its glossy, blood-red slipcase; shame about the rather meagre serving of lo-fi extras. First, a 12-minute excerpt from the American Film Institute's Lifetime Achievement ceremony (1979) – eminently Hitchcockian insofar as parts of it make the flesh crawl. James Stewart makes a speech and a regal Ingrid Bergman gushes 'Alfred Hitchcock is an adorable genius' – which prompts a cutaway to a motionless Hitch, looking as though the neighbour's dog has soiled his back lawn. Once the applause has died down, however, he comes to life and makes a graceful, gently mocking speech of his own. Second, a half-hour colour interview for the Masters of Cinema TV series, in which the director talks about his early career, tells a handful of funny stories and twice ducks a question about the importance of sexuality in his work.

Absent is a sturdy 94-minute making-of doc, familiar from many previous versions of the disc. Find it on Universal's French special edition along with the above docs, newsreel footage, photos, drawings and a shower-scene comparison with and without music. The best set of extras, perhaps inevitably, comes with the R1 15-disc 'Alfred Hitchcock: The Masterpiece Collection' box set. (SIMON CROPPER)

The Pusher Trilogy

(Denmark, 1996, 2004, 2005)

Director: Nicolas Winding Refn
Label: Momentum (UK)
Region: 2
Discs: 2

FILM TITLES: *Pusher, Pusher II: With Blood on my Hands, Pusher III: I'm the Angel of Death*

THE FILMS

Clearly made on a shoestring, *Pusher*, set on the mean streets of Copenhagen, positively pulses. The frenetic, docu-real direction thrives off the magnetism of Kim Bodnia as small-time dealer Frank, whose over-ambitious money-borrowing and deal-breaking makes him the lowest morsel on a cut-throat food chain, at the mercy of middle-aged Serbian drug-lord-cum-amateur-chef Milo (the oleaginous Zlatko Buric) and his strangely endearing heavy, Radovan (Slavko Labovic). Alongside the hyperactive Tonny (the superb Mads Mikkelson), Frank's hangdog demeanour casts them as a sort of comedy duo, akin to a couple of teenagers pushing the limits with their incessant and salacious back-and-forth. His relationship with his prostitute girlfriend (and his inability/refusal to have sex with her 'paid-for pussy') imparts an air of loveless melancholy. And when, at the film's climax, she runs away with the little cash he has scraped together, the shot of Bodnia's expression conveys hopelessness, bewilderment and resignation all at once. In a way, it's a feelgood movie in negative, leaving you counting your lucky stars that you are not, like Frank, totally, utterly and irredeemably fucked.

Coming eight years after the first film, the two sequels pick up with Tonny and Milo for some affectionate, though no less abrasive portrayals of family life. In Tonny's case he must come to terms with a newborn baby and the criminal family of his father, 'The Duke', all of which verges on high melodrama. Though the third film is the weakest of the three, it's still highly entertaining: having to prepare for your demanding daughter's twenty-fifth birthday party is no mean feat for Milo while simultaneously fending off small-time crooks, harbouring human traffickers and disposing of corpses. From teenager to young father to ageing custodian, the trilogy could itself be seen as an examination of the male condition; that and the perils of trying to shift too much dope.

THE DISCS

Nothing too special here, but the first film gets its own disc and a making-of documentary that shows Refn's bum fluff in all its glory (and the interesting genesis of the film from a late-night director's spot on Danish TV). The film itself is presented anamorphically, with 5.1 audio. The two sequels lack gripping extras but do have a director's commentary, cast and crew profiles, photo galleries and trailers. (DAN FRANKLIN)

Q: The Winged Serpent
(USA, 1982)

Director: Larry Cohen
Label: Anchor Bay (UK)
Region: 2 (PAL) / 0 (NTSC)
Discs: 1

THE FILM

'This building deserves to have its own movie,' thought Larry Cohen while looking up at New York's feathered, pyramid-capped Chrysler building. One week's pre-production (including script-writing), a few favours called in from friends like David Carradine and Richard Roundtree, 18 days' shooting and $1.1 million later, *Q* was born.

The film shows what happens when a small-time crook (the inimitable Michael Moriarty, who later made a career as a cabaret singer) meets a hungry Mesoamerican dragon god. From the opening shot of a skyscraper-window cleaner getting his head torn off, through the assorted sunbathers, construction workers and criminals who also become bird food, it's clear that this is something special. Shot on the hoof, with Cohen rewriting the script on a scene-by-scene basis and the actors constantly improvising new dialogue, *Q* has a freshness that you'll only realise is lacking from regular Hollywood fare – and most other indie flicks – when you see this one.

Awash with witty sight gags, razor-sharp performances, tear-jerkingly nostalgic stop-motion creature animation from Dave Allen and Peter Kuran (who would later work on *Men in Black* and other major FX fare) and some of the best pre-9/11 views of the city you'll ever see, *Q* is quite probably one of the best creature features of all time.

THE DISC

The film looks great and is presented in both 1.78:1 and 1.85:1 formats, while the squawks and screams will reverberate through the canyon city of your living room in both 6.1 DTS and 5.1 Dolby Surround. A nice bonus is a PDF file containing an original press pack, newspaper and media cuttings and a fake NY newspaper heralding *Q*'s arrival. Meanwhile, in a wonderful commentary, Cohen outlines his filmmaking philosophy – 'make sure you're the only person who knows what's going on', 'they're all excursions into lunacy' – and provides a glimpse of what might have been: *Q* starring Bruce Willis and Eddie Murphy. Now that's scary. (MARK PILKINGTON)

Brothers Quay – The Short Films 1979–2003
(UK, 1979–2003)

Directors: Steven and Timothy Quay
Label: BFI (UK) / Zeitgeist (USA)
Region: 2 (PAL) / 1 (NTSC)
Discs: 2

THE FILMS

London residents since studying at the Royal College of Art in the late 1960s, identical American twin brothers Stephen and Timothy Quay are among the most original filmmakers in the world. It seems no accident that one sounding of their name suggests a point of departure, a threshold and leaping off into the unknown, where what the horizon promises is as forbidding as it is enthralling because, for over 30 years, they have created a body of work visionary in intensity and operating with the sensuous logic of a fever dream.

Renowned for their extraordinary puppet animations, inspired by the pioneering oeuvre of Czech Surrealist **Jan Svankmajer** and drawing on the heightened, phantasmagoric literature of eastern and central Europe (Kakfa, Robert Walser, Bruno Schulz *et al*), they create densely-loaded fables, where power struggles unfold in labyrinthine spaces beyond linear time-frames, where all things are charged, 'animated'. Operating on the borderland between material reality and metaphysical unease, the Quays deploy objects, inhabited by experience of a viscerally textural kind, as totems of richly imaginative transformation. Their frame becomes a repository of arcane, sometimes hermetic wisdoms, informed by a host of visual, literary, musical and philosophical elements that alchemically inspire the dazzling cinematography and *mise en scène* at work. Crafting a cinema of child-like unsettlement and wonder that works deep into the unconscious, the Quays, both of them, are truly singular and vital talents in a world of ever-reducing horizons.

THE DISCS

Continuing the remarkable renaissance of BFI DVD production, this immaculate publication was conceived and extensively supervised by the Quays themselves, in collaboration with the Institute's Michael Brooke. (The R1 Zeitgeist set is a straight port of the BFI set with different artwork, plus an essay by critic Michael Atkinson.) The care and concern in presentation extends throughout, from the stills on discs and casing, through Brooke's insightful A–Z essay on the Quays' universe, the original text treatment for *Street of Crocodiles* (perhaps their most famous film) and, of course, the shorts themselves.

Split energetically across the two discs ('films' and 'footnotes'), 13 titles are included. They range from the eponymous tribute to their mentor Svankmajer (1984) and a take on the Gilgamesh myth, *The Unnameable Little Broom* (1985), through the idiosyncratic music videos *Stille Nacht I-IV* (1988–93) and the archive exposure of *The Phantom Museum* (2003), to what might be their masterpiece, *In Absentia* (2000), a lacerating, Stockhausen-scored study of madness.

All are restored and remastered, alongside 180 minutes of extras, including alternative versions, interviews, pilot projects and idents. Selected commentaries and a video introduction by the brothers give fascinating context. An artwork in its own right. (GARETH EVANS)

Raging Bull

(USA, 1980) Ultimate Edition

Director: Martin Scorsese
Label: MGM (UK)
Region: 2 (PAL)
Discs: 2

THE FILM

Raging Bull was to be – he insisted at the time – Scorsese's last film. He was disillusioned with filmmaking, and this, the third part of a loose New York trilogy, was to be his final statement about male identity, violence and redemption – themes he'd already mapped out in *Mean Streets* and *Taxi Driver*. Based on the autobiography of 1949 world middleweight champion Jake La Motta, the 'Bronx Bull' who'd known delinquency, rigged fights, boxing triumph, divorce, prison and an unlikely reinvention as a music-hall comedian, the project was unusual in being driven by an actor: Robert De Niro talked up the idea of a film adaptation for five years before Scorsese, no boxing fan, agreed.

De Niro trained with the real La Motta for the fight sequences, ate his way to a 60-pound weight gain to play the character in his music-hall years, and won an Oscar (in sympathy?) for his pains. Shot almost entirely in black and white, its fights superbly filmed and its dialogue honed to taut perfection, *Raging Bull* has not an ounce of fat on it. It's considered by many to be Scorsese's masterpiece: a hell of a comeback.

THE DISCS

There are three instructive commentaries: one by Scorsese and his long-serving editor Thelma Schoonmaker, another by members of the crew and cast (without De Niro or Pesci, though both contribute to other extras), and a third by a wheezy La Motta.

Disc 2 has five docs weighing in at around 20 minutes apiece, each covering a different aspect of the film: one examines its development, another gets in the ring to monitor the painstakingly mapped-out fight sequences (and the screams of elephants, horses and other animals used by sound effects specialist Frank Warner). Schoonmaker tells a lovely story about visiting the projection booth in one New York cinema and finding the projectionist about to snip out La Motta's home-movie footage, the only segment of the film in colour: he'd thought it came from a different film, spliced in at the lab by mistake. In a stand-alone item La Motta tells some of his old music-hall jokes, and elsewhere remembers going to see the finished film with his ex-wife Vickie. 'Was I that bad?' he'd asked. 'No – you were worse!' (This set should not be confused with the inferior UK Special Edition, also on two discs and released in 2000, though MGM haven't helped by also terming this edition a special edition in its Region 1 incarnation.) (SIMON CROPPER)

Raise the Red Lantern

(China/Hong Kong, 1991)

Digitally Remastered Edition

Director: Zhang Yimou
Label: Era (Hong Kong)
Region: 0 (NTSC)
Discs: 1

THE FILM

Movie viewers born to the digital era may associate Zhang Yimou only with such virtual razzle-dazzle as *Hero* and *House of Flying Daggers*, with their sweeping landscapes-as-colour-schemes, or *The Curse of the Golden Flower*, with Gong Li's embonpoint-as-landscape. But there was a time when his films, along with those of his Fifth Generation compatriots Chen Kaige and Tian Zhuangzhuang, emerged like messages of dissent in a bottle, rare and daring revelations from behind the great wall of Chinese repression. Zhang's early works may have cloaked themselves in period garb and lavish style (he trained as a cinematographer), but they were ripe with frustrations, defiance and disorder that seemed bigger than the world of their dramas. Their rebellious protagonists were invariably women, Zhang's muse Gong Li headlining a series of feminised riffs on genre movies: *Red Sorghum* (1987) was a women's folk bacchanal, *Ju Dou* (1990) a twist on the James M Cainian adultery melodrama.

Raise the Red Lantern is a women's prison movie, though it doesn't exactly flaunt the kick-ass catharsis of a Roger Corman B-flick. Based on Su Tong's novella in his collection, *Wives and Concubines*, it casts a traditional Chinese patriarch's mansion as Bluebeard's Castle, where tradition justifies petty rites and power hierarchies, and polygamy is a metaphor for the art of divide and rule. 'Kowtow to our ancestors', Gong's headstrong inductee Songlian is told on her first day as the master's Fourth Mistress. Privileges accrue to the master's nightly choice of bedmate: 'If you can manage to have a foot massage every day,' advises a wise maid, 'you'll soon be running this household.' But these are favours, not rights, to be curried through obeisance and ingratiation. Each night's patronage ceremonies (the raising of red lanterns outside the anointed bedroom; the jingle of those foot-massage hammers) echo around the palace, sounding impotence in three spurned bedrooms and hearts.

Each mistress resorts to a different self-protection strategy – weaselling, foolery and in Songlian's case a catalogue of stubbornness, deceit and good old cat-fighting. Zhang finds sly humour in their petty plays, and isn't blind to the old finery of their palatial trappings – but it's a corrupt beauty, closed to the outside and governed by the dead. More modern than, say, Mizoguchi's heroines, the women go down fighting, but the tragedy is that they fight alone.

THE DISC

Avoid Era's first shot at this transfer; their second (progressive, anamorphic) master is far improved – a little soft, but rich and warm. Subtitles are legible and optional, with just the occasional minor typo. Extras remain minimal: a picture gallery and spoiler-heavy trailer. You can get it from *yesasia.com* (listed as 'Hong Kong version'). A R1 MGM disc was in the works at the time of writing. (NICK BRADSHAW)

Ratcatcher

(UK/France, 1999)

Director: Lynne Ramsay
Label: Criterion Collection (USA)
Region: 1 (NTSC)
Discs: 1

THE FILM

Working-class life in Scotland has traditionally been figured in a dour social realism that owes more to sociological inquiry than it does to art. Lynne Ramsay's debut full-length feature is steeped in that aesthetic, yet transcends it with such canny verve and self-confidence that upon its release in 1999 the film was immediately heralded as a major contribution to the slim canon of British art-house cinema.

A supremely stylised and oblique period drama, one that works hard to avoid the inane chirpiness of 'I Love the 1970s'-style TV programmes, it's set during the dustbin collectors' strike of 1973 in which piles of rubbish lay out in the streets of tenemented Glasgow. A young boy called James (William Eadie), the son of a borderline alcoholic, roams the council stairwells, rat-infested back alleys and canal paths. He's on the cusp of adulthood, hastened there perhaps by the accidental drowning of one of his friends, alive to the quotidian cruelties of local boys but unable to do anything about them. The film takes place as much in the drifting, porous spaces of his own psyche as it does in tough-man Glasgow.

The tastefully muted cinematography of Alwin Küchler and Ramsay's own almost fetishistic obsession for small details – the bloody scab on a girl's knee, the dirty socks on another character's feet – evoke not so much the blighted underclass landscapes associated during the 1990s with Richard Billingham's 'Ray's A Laugh' photographic series, but the choreographed griminess of fashion snappers such as Corinne Day. Ramsay, unlike Bill Douglas, whose 'My Childhood' trilogy she has cited as an influence on her work, is drawn to the visual challenges of her material more than its moral or political dimensions. Naturalistic elements are married to off-kilter sound design and moments of surreal whimsy such as a scene in which a mouse called Kenny ascends to the moon hanging from a red balloon.

THE DISC

The road to *Ratcatcher* can be followed on the three short films that Criterion have bundled together: 'Kill The Day', 'Gasman' and 'Small Deaths', the latter winning the Jury Prize at Cannes in 1995. An elegant essay by critic Lizzie Francke is supplemented by a characteristically pugnacious filmed interview with Ramsay during the course of which she knocks the National Film School she attended, champions poetic modes of cinematic naturalism, and elaborates on the importance she attaches to music and sound design. (SUKHDEV SANDHU)

The Red and the White

(Hungary/USSR, 1967)

Director: Miklós Jancsó
Label: Second Run (UK)
Region: 0 (PAL)
Discs: 1

THE FILM

In Ukraine circa 1919, borders shift as suddenly and arbitrarily as loyalties, and victory turns to rout in a second as the revanchist Tsarists fight to the last ditch against the Bolsheviks to secure the territory for greater Russia. *The Red and the White* is concerned with those caught between two crumbling empires – Hungarian prisoners of war who have taken up the revolutionary flag to ensure their release from captivity. Mocking the Manichaeanism of its own title, the film was not well received by its Soviet sponsors, who wanted a clear-cut celebration for the October Revolution's golden jubilee.

Ranging over a contested patch of ground near the Volga river, Jancsó's film – in a sense identical with Jancsó's landscape – is populated by desperate men and terrorised women, his focus switching between either side without ceremony, following the bitter reversals of fate that befall both sides with apparent equanimity. Claiming that 'even the best film is primitive', Jancsó declined to pry into his characters' motivations – declined, finally, to offer up characters at all. 'People are constantly running about, riding horses, shooting, rushing back and forth, and that's it. That is the maximum we can achieve.'

With its bare minimum of exposition and characterisation, *The Red and the White* is a near-anthropomorphic vision of undirected and unpredictable historical change, realised in what the critic Raymond Durgnat dubbed 'photo-topography'. Advancing what would become his trademark style, Jancsó's famous sequence shots match complex choreography of action with elaborate camera movements and widescreen compositions in long takes.

THE DISC

The first in Second Run's projected series of Jancsó discs is meant to introduce the festival circuit and art-house hero of the late '60s and early '70s as a director whose somewhat abstract films are both deeply rooted in Hungarian culture and shaped by its recent history. The accompanying booklet contains a wide-ranging interview with the octogenarian auteur, covering his apprenticeship in the late '40s under the pioneer theorist Béla Balázs (who persuaded him to abandon theatre for film), life under Russian occupation, and his strong sympathies with central European Jewish culture. This is the subject of the disc's other main attraction, the opening film in Jancsó's documentary series *Message of Stones* (*Kovek uzenete*). With little other than its lack of dialogue in common with the rest of the Jancsó canon – at least as it's known in the West – this is a fly-on-the-synagogue-wall account of a tiny but resilient tradition.
(HENRY K MILLER)

The Red Shoes

(UK, 1948)

Directors: Michael Powell and Emeric Pressburger
Label: Criterion Collection (USA)
Region: 1 (NTSC)
Discs: 1

THE FILM

It's difficult to describe the innovation and importance of this film, which seems to spring straight from the collective unconscious. Like Jean Cocteau making *La Belle et la Bête* in 1945 France, the Archers (directors Michael Powell and Emeric Pressburger) turned to fairytales to capture the imagination of post-war Britain. Their belle is aspiring ballet dancer Victoria Page (Royal Ballet principal Moira Shearer) and their beast Boris Lermontov (Anton Walbrook), Diaghilev-esque director of the Ballet Lermontov, whose unrelenting aesthetic ambitions lead him to ask Vicki to dance the lead in a new ballet, *The Red Shoes*, scored by brilliant young composer Julian Craster (Marius Goring). Vicki's fate is tied to the girl's: once she has put on the red shoes, she is inexorably drawn into the tragic spiral of the narrative.

Hans Christian Andersen's source tale of the girl who is so enamoured of her shoes that she is condemned to dance in them to her death is given a sophisticated meta-theatrical setting as the Archers create a fantastic Europe of emigrée ballerinas, first nights at Covent Garden and horse carriage rides along the cliffs of Monaco. Glamorous, vivid and urbane, this richly appointed film seems a world away from a Britain struggling with the wrecked aftermath of WWII. But as well as a fantasia of how the other half live, the film offers an intensely realised sequence of psychological trauma that recalls the Archers' earlier war films and looks ahead to *Peeping Tom*.

This sequence is at the heart of the film, within the first performance of *The Red Shoes* ballet. Vicki becomes lost in a Surrealist netherworld that lifts off from the stage and becomes cinema, as she falls through clouds, dances with a newspaper, is possessed by demons and sees Julian mounting the stage to dance with her. This stunning entry into Vicki's psyche, mixing painted sets, live action and early special effects, has earned the film a permanent place in cinema history – and it will move any viewer who has ever been caught up in art or love.

THE DISC

There are some charming inclusions: a gallery of memorabilia belonging to Martin Scorsese, who is famously obsessed with the film, even wearing Lermontov's shirt while directing; a reading from the witty novelisation written by the directors; and, most magically, the storyboards for *The Red Shoes*'s ballet sequence, which can be viewed alongside the filmed ballet. (SOPHIE MAYER)

Requiem for a Dream

(USA, 2000)

Director: Darren Aronofsky
Label: Momentum (UK)
Region: 2 (PAL)
Discs: 1

THE FILM

A slick adaptation of Hubert Selby Jr's gritty novel, *Requiem for a Dream* is one of the most stylish movies ever made about addiction. Proving that π was no fluke, Darren Aronofsky's second feature is an unflinchingly forensic examination of four souls trapped in a downward spiral of degradation and despair.

Much of the movie's success is due to Ellen Burstyn's startling performance as Sara Goldfarb, a Brooklyn housewife measuring out her life with diet pills and daytime television. As Sara's amphetamine addiction worsens and psychosis looms, Burstyn appears to wither before our eyes.

Displaying a deft touch behind the camera, Aronofsky and cinematographer Matthew Libatique capture the horror of dependency and the mundane routine of addiction. Sharp sound effects and whiplash editing fuse to illustrate the rituals of drug consumption: pupils dilate, dollar bills are rolled, heroin cooks in a spoon. Propelled by Clint Mansell's sinister score, *Requiem for a Dream* surges like an ocean and rises towards an appalling climax of mental instability and physical degradation. Yet the film is achingly tender, too: exquisite moments between Harry and Sara hint at what might have been.

THE DISC

Hubert Selby Jr would read aloud from his novel to prepare Ellen Burstyn for her portrayal of Sara Goldfarb's descent into electroshock-therapy hell. Jaw-dropping footage of Selby's performance and Burstyn's response is one of the more astonishing special features on Momentum's single-disc release. Other highlights include Burstyn talking to Selby about spirituality and death, an analysis of the scene in which Sara 'speed cleans' her apartment; and Darren Aronofsky's fascinating audio commentary.

Aronofsky unpicks his movie with enthusiasm and poise, balancing rewarding technical insight with affectionate anecdotes about his cast and crew. Moving fast to keep up with the movie, he discusses everything from Selby's novel and working with Burstyn to shooting in Coney Island and creating 'hip hop montage'. It's insightful stuff, a case in point being Aronofsky's discussion of the scene in which Sara finally loses her mind. Its fusion of sound, photography, special effects, and production design was 'like conducting an orchestra', he says. And Aronofsky isn't afraid to broach the movie's difficult subject matter either, arguing that almost anything can be used to fill the void in our lives. (JAMES CLASPER)

The Roaring Twenties

(USA, 1939)

Director: Raoul Walsh
Label: Warners (USA)
Region: 1 (NTSC)
Discs: 1

THE FILM

The acme of Warner Bros' '30s style and maybe the quintessential Prohibition movie to boot, this was the first film Jimmy Cagney made with the brilliant Raoul Walsh. An indispensable studio workhorse, Walsh built up a celebrated flair for tough-guy pictures – typically westerns, Errol Flynn swashbucklers and a handful of classic gangster melodramas – throughout his 52-year career. He might have starred in them, too, if a jackrabbit hadn't pounced through the windscreen of his jeep, taking his right eye out just before *In Old Arizona* (1928). They don't make movie directors like Walsh any more.

As for Cagney, Eddie Bartlett isn't one of the pug-faced star's legendarily vicious hoods – try Tom Powers in William Wellman's *The Public Enemy* (1931) or Arthur 'Cody' Barrett in Walsh's later *White Heat* (1949) – but a figure of some pathos. At heart, he's a solid citizen, a plucky WWI doughboy who comes home to New York, can't get his old job back, and enlists a few war buddies to start a taxi firm. When the liquor ban kicks in, they turn to bootlegging, and we're treated to one of Walsh's fantastic newsreel-style montages, all tumbling rows of bottles and hip flasks being swigged on back seats. There's the obligatory shot of a fender being wrapped around a tree, just so we know nationwide alcoholism wasn't all high jinks. And then comes 1929, banknotes fluttering uselessly from the sky on Wall Street, and one hell of a hangover.

The script, based on the rags-to-riches-to-rags story of real-life racketeer Lawrence Fay, is a bumper compendium of Jazz Age clichés, but Walsh's propulsive direction and savvy casting knock it out of the park, principally by shaping the characters into such sturdy archetypes. Humphrey Bogart, just on the cusp of leading-man stardom, signs off with one of his sneering heavies as Eddie's casually murderous colleague/nemesis George, trampling over everyone and everything to make it big. Priscilla Lane's love interest, a demure nightclub chanteuse, is absurdly wholesome for the speakeasy. But you can't beat Gladys George as hardbitten hostess Panama Smith, charging her customers extra for enjoying themselves, and toting her own sad torch for Eddie. Cagney wouldn't return to the gangster genre for a good decade – this said it all.

THE DISC

Ever loving with their archives, Warner Bros went to town with this wonderful disc, which contains a bounteous array of newsreels, trailers and other nostalgic odds and ends, a full feature commentary by UC Davis film professor Lincoln Hurst, and a cracking 17-minute appreciative featurette with contributions from Scorsese and Andrew Sarris. Hurst unimprovably nails Walsh's directorial style with the expression 'windmilling energy' – why didn't I think of that? And the glories of Ernest Haller's cinematography are hard to miss on this high-contrast transfer. (TIM ROBEY)

Roger & Me

(USA, 1989)

Director: Michael Moore
Label: Warners (all territories)
Region: Any
Discs: 1

THE FILM

Anyone criticising *Fahrenheit 9/11* for its loose adherence to journalistic principles should go back to the first five minutes of this, Michael Moore's debut
documentary, which detail how the filmmaker was fired from a San Francisco
tabloid after disagreeing with his editor once too often. In the Moore legend,
this is a crucial moment: the point this filmmaker leaves the fourth column
behind to pursue his own agenda.

Rather than latent egotism, the 'me' of the title here suggests how personal
Roger & Me – a hometown story told by a local boy made good – really is.
Recounting General Motors' betrayal of Flint, Michigan in painfully funny
(and sometimes just painful) fashion, this is Moore's least problematic film to
date: driven by justifiable outrage, with the director's trademark use of humour,
telling juxtaposition and pop music already well in place. (Few films have
better understood the bittersweet sting of the Beach Boys 'Wouldn't It Be
Nice?') As entertaining as it is illuminating, and as much about individuals as
it is about politics, this is the *ur*-text of the recent documentary renaissance.
Stay tuned through the end credits for the grimly ironic final gag.

THE DISC

The trailer – featuring Moore reading from his own glowing reviews – is
perhaps a sign of things to come. Yet the director's commentary track – recorded
in the summer of 2003, after his Oscar success with *Bowling for Columbine* –
allows for a better glimpse of the humanity behind the much-reported ego.
While his first words concern the 'AOL Time Warner' footnote currently
adorning the Warner Bros logo, Moore is thoroughly gracious towards the
studio throughout, not just for their extensive promotional activities, but for
the aid they provided for many of those featured in the film.

Fifteen years on from the film's production, he's able to express nostalgia
for the days when his interviewees would open up willingly, suspecting their
contributions would only turn up 'on cable access at four in the morning'.
There's also an update on how Flint's doing today: not good, and Moore
confesses to finding the film hard to watch because he attained personal success
but couldn't save the town. Hardened Moore-ophobes may carp that the
commentary brings up one of the film's greyer areas ('there are no dates in
the film') without elaboration, but otherwise this package is a much-needed
reminder of a major modern filmmaker's considerable virtues. (MIKE McCAHILL)

Eric Rohmer's Six Moral Tales

(France, 1963–72)

Director: Eric Rohmer
Label: Criterion Collection (USA)
Region: 1 (NTSC)
Discs: 6

FILM TITLES: *The Bakery Girl of Monceau, Suzanne's Career, My Night with Maud, La Collectioneuse, Claire's Knee, Love in the Afternoon*

THE FILMS

It starts with desire, in its byzantine windings. Rohmer encapsulated the stories in his first film series this way: 'While the narrator is looking for a woman, he meets another one, who occupies his affection until he finds the first woman again.' Then come words: flirtation, evasion, investigation, contemplation, rationalisation and outright fabulation; in the words of Molly Haskell, 'an endless round of glittering verbal manoeuvres that constitute the late twentieth century's most literate tales of love'. Rohmer's protagonists are men and women of the tongue, but their talk says more than they would say. As their author wrote in a 1948 manifesto, 'There are not enough lies in the cinema.'

Rohmer spins his characters' lies with exquisite precision. They gleam with hidden insights, but they are also resolutely credible: there is nothing fake or fantastical about his cinema, which is designedly a window onto real, quotidian bourgeois life. 'Start with what you know,' runs the adage, and while Rohmer's films observe some of the truest female characters in cinema, his Moral Tales focus on men, and specifically the ways they court and relinquish girls and women. Thus we have a Parisian student toying with a shop girl in lieu of the more uptown object of his affections; two students finding tenuous common cause in the exploitation of another working girl; an affianced provincial Catholic intellectual holding off the temptations of a beautiful divorcee over a night in her bedroom; two St Tropez vacationers determined to set an attractive and sexually active young girl on the straight and narrow; a holidaying diplomat entertaining an obsession with a teenage girl's knee; and finally a married office worker, deliberating on a potential affair in his lunch break.

Rohmer's films satirise male sanctimony, and shrewdly document the shifting sands of the sexual revolution. Their timeless moral generosity, though, lies in their recognition of the vexations of free will: in the agonies of choosing between fidelity and promiscuity, faith and spontaneity, predetermination and chance; in the moral rudiments and spiritual ramifications of choice itself. Deep in the navel of the French bourgeoisie, Rohmer films something resembling the soul.

THE DISCS

The above quotes are all from Criterion's valuable book of essays accompanying the six films (the bigger book is of Rohmer's original stories, written before the film). Each film is individually slip-cased, the transfers supervised by Rohmer and quite astounding. The extras include five of his shorts, from 1951's 'Presentation, or Charlotte and Her Steak' to 1999's 'The Curve', a new, rare and lovely interview conversation with the master conducted by his old producer Barbet Schroeder, interviews with actors and others via archive TV programmes – and since God moves in inscrutable ways, a video afterwards by Neil LaBute. (NICK BRADSHAW)

A Room for Romeo Brass
(1999, UK)

Director: Shane Meadows
Label: Momentum (UK)
Region: 2 (PAL)
Discs: 1

THE FILM

The sort of modest, one-for-me marvel that a filmmaker sometimes slips out when bigger projects are failing to fly, *A Room for Romeo Brass* is an unassuming tale of two happy-go-lucky schoolboy pals that, without ever undercutting its naturalism, suddenly wallops you in the face with a darkly dramatic reminder of the fearful mess festering under many a stone. Romeo and Knocks (Andrew Shim and Ben Marshall) are neighbours whose friendship is shaken up by the intrusion of a sad-sack older lad, Morell, making a deluded attempt to get into the pants of Romeo's big sister Ladine. Shane Meadows recruited his old school mucker Paddy Considine to incarnate Morell's latent menace, and you can see why this debut performance shot him off on an acting career; the delinquency, volatility and pathos he brings to the screen are extraordinary.

Unlike his follow-up features *Once Upon a Time in the Midlands* and *Dead Man's Shoes*, Meadows doesn't hide behind genre jokiness here; working from a script by his own childhood buddy Paul Fraser, he roots the film in people and experience, and his characterisation is unerring. The two kids are portrayed in all their semi-innocent mischief, mulishness and irresponsibility (chip-guzzling Romeo is presumably the Meadows surrogate), and their neighbouring families are a source of both vulnerability and strength. Particularly key are their fathers, neither the last word in maturity; while Knocks's boyish dad (James Higgins) is a fount of embarrassment and enforced humility, Romeo's estranged old man (Frank Harper) is both the cause of Romeo's ill-judgement and, after a fashion, his salvation.

A mis-marketed flop on its UK theatrical release, *Romeo Brass* still has the deliciousness of a well-kept secret. Devotees speak of the film with a gleam in their eyes. Come join their ranks.

THE DISC

Like the film, the DVD isn't the showiest package (the sound is plain Dolby Stereo, and you shouldn't expect a multi-disc reference-standard Ultimate Collector's Edition any time soon), but it's quite ripe. Extras include Meadows' 'video diary' – a silent three-minute collage of behind-the-scenes footage – and a trailer, but the real gem is the larky commentary between him and Considine, a rich mix of useful insights and laddish irreverence (the pair cut out for a burger halfway through). Hang on through the closing credits, too, over which Considine reveals his uncanny gift for mimicry. (NICK BRADSHAW)

Rosetta & La Promesse

(Belgium, 1996/1999)

Directors: Luc and Jean-Pierre Dardenne
Label: Artificial Eye (UK)
Region: 2 (PAL)
Discs: 2

THE FILMS

The adjective 'Bressonian' only gets you so far with Belgium's celebrated Dardenne brothers, whose films can sound like dour, schematic slogs until you've been initiated. They've been honing their unmistakable brand of over-the-shoulder social realism since a series of TV documentaries in the late 1970s, but it was the 1999 Palme d'Or winner *Rosetta* which first brought them major international attention and acclaim. Never letting its teenage trailer-park heroine (the lumpily convincing Emilie Dequenne) out of our sight, the Dardennes document Rosetta's grim-faced struggle to find and hold down a job, ultimately wresting control of a waffle stall away from the well-meaning Riquet (Fabrizio Rongione), who's the closest thing she's got to an ally. Lying in bed on her own, Rosetta chants 'I have a normal life' like some kind of self-help mantra, but the movie makes clear that she deprives herself of just that through the all-but-superhuman exertion required to attain it. The bristling determination of her daily rituals, as she peddles secondhand clothes and sets prohibited fish-traps in the murky river surrounding the park, speaks only of a circuitous hopelessness; when she tumbles into the water (an over-emphatic nod to Bresson's *Mouchette*), the fight to escape the sucking mud is virtually the highlight of her day.

The Dardennes have made subtler films than *Rosetta*, and one of them is the 1996 *La Promesse*, a blazingly compassionate moral drama with key roles for their regular actors Olivier Gourmet (*Le Fils*) and the then 15-year-old Jérémie Renier (*L'Enfant*). As in *Rosetta* and both those later films, the context here is the never-ending cycle of transactions and betrayals – petty or large – which define life on or below the breadline. Its pivotal moment arrives when Igor (Renier) makes a promise to a dying Burkinabe immigrant, Amidou, whom his father Roger (Gourmet), a slum landlord, has been illegally housing and employing. Amidou falls from some scaffolding and asks Igor to look after his wife and baby, which he surreptitiously attempts to do while the hard-hearted Roger does everything possible to get rid of them. Igor's dawning Samaritanism typifies the Christian dimensions of the Dardennes' work – their obsession with carpentry is a giveaway – but the move towards redemptive allegory doesn't soften the grimy and fearful reality of these milieux so much as switch on a hopeful shaft of light.

THE DISCS

A good value twofer from Artificial Eye with a reasonable smattering of extras, including pub-table interviews with the brothers pre and post their Cannes success, galleries, trailers and filmographies. Transfer quality is even a bit clearer and sharper than TF1's French *Rosetta*. (TIM ROBEY)

The Royal Tenenbaums
(USA, 2001)

Director: Wes Anderson
Label: Criterion Collection (USA)
Region: 1 (NTSC)
Discs: 2

THE FILM

The Royal Tenenbaums is a thing of rare beauty – a comedy that breaks your heart as often as it makes you laugh. Wes Anderson's wildly imaginative third feature tells the story of the dysfunctional Tenenbaum family, brought together after years of estrangement.

Cantankerous to the core, Gene Hackman triumphs as Royal Tenenbaum, the elderly patriarch who decides to make amends with his long-neglected wife and children. Claiming he has only weeks to live, Royal returns to the family home, joined by his three grown-up kids, Chas, Richie, and Margot.

All of them were childhood prodigies who came off the rails following the collapse of their parents' marriage. As the movie's narrator Alec Baldwin deadpans, 'all memory of the brilliance of the young Tenenbaums had been erased by two decades of betrayal, failure, and disaster'.

Hackman's crabbiness threatens to steal the show, but the entire cast sparkles. Gwyneth Paltrow, Ben Stiller, and Luke Wilson are heartbreaking as Royal's emotionally stunted children; Anjelica Huston is regal as his wife Etheline; and Danny Glover, Bill Murray, and Owen Wilson all chip in wittily.

The Royal Tenenbaums makes great eye-candy, too. Robert Yeoman's cinematography is meticulously composed, and David Wasco's production design, full of marvel. But the movie never chokes on its charm. Despite its quiet despair and aching sadness, *The Royal Tenenbaums* remains a riotously amusing expiation of one family's guilt.

THE DISCS

The *Tenenbaums* two-disc edition is a treasure trove of extra features, and Anjelica Huston lends it two of the best moments, albeit unintentionally. First she boasts about introducing Wes Anderson to eggs Benedict, apparently quite serious about the matter, and then she sets fire to her hair while holding a birthday cake. The producers preserve her dignity by concealing the incident as an Easter egg.

There are fascinating extras elsewhere on the disc, including several deleted scenes, the original trailer, on-set photography, Wes Anderson's storyboard, his brother Eric's paintings of Margot's plays and Richie's murals, and a radio segment explaining how a painting by Mexican artist Miguel Calderon made it into the movie. There are also interviews with the main actors: Bill Murray is typically dry, Gene Hackman somewhat supercilious, and Ben Stiller surprisingly serious.

But the best extra is Albert Maysles' 'With the Filmmaker' portrait of Anderson. It illustrates the director's obsession with getting every detail right, from the carpet in the Tenenbaum house to the colour of Chas's hair in the murals. Anderson's commentary track (unique to Criterion's R1 version of this otherwise broadly available set) also bears out that perfectionist passion. (JAMES CLASPER)

The Saddest Music in the World

(Canada, 2003)

Director: Guy Maddin
Label: Soda Pictures (UK)
Region: 2 (PAL)
Discs: 1

THE FILM

The Saddest Music in the World, adapted from a short story by Kazuo Ishiguro, is Guy Maddin's closest foray into mainstream cinema, though still steeped in the charm and absurdist humour of much of the director's work.

It is 1933 and the town of Winnipeg has again been voted 'the world capital of sorrow' by *The London Times*. Legless local beer baroness Lady Port-Huntly (Isabella Rossellini) announces a competition to discover the saddest music in the world. Among the arrivals is swaggering Chester Kent (Mark McKinney), returning home in the colours of the US, and his brother Roderick and father Fyodor, representing Serbia and Canada. As each country vies for the $25,000 prize, renewed grievances amongst the Kents threaten to upend the competition.

Often compared to silent cinema, Maddin's films feel more like pioneering works from a parallel world. The camera techniques (colour filters, iris shots etc.) and declamatory performances bear the hallmark aesthetics of that bygone era, but the narratives conjure up a much stranger environment, ruled by primal instincts and desires.

Saddest Music has the offbeat lunacy of *Hellzapoppin* as shot by *The Cabinet of Dr Caligari*'s Robert Wiene. Playing an amputee whose glass prosthetic legs are full of beer, Rossellini is both glamorous and grotesque. Maddin makes the most of the first real star to appear in his films, resulting in one of her most memorable roles since her work with David Lynch. Nostalgic, but never sentimental, for an imaginary past, Maddin conjures up one of his most fully realised worlds, the film's satirical elements ensuring light relief while never eclipsing the drama of the characters' lives.

THE DISC

Soda's edition trumps both MGM's Region 1 disc, which omits several key extras, and TVA Films' Canadian release, which gets the reproduction of the main feature all wrong. Soda's excellent transfer retains the print's texture, down to the subtle light and colour changes. Maddin is thorough in discussing his approach to filmmaking in his entertaining and informative commentary, most of it in conversation with McKinney. They also discuss the real Winnipeg (where, we are informed, it is illegal to drink alcohol whilst stood at a bar), an inspiration behind much of Maddin's work. The accompanying hour-long featurette *Cowards Bend the Knee* is a more extreme example of Maddin's work, though no less rewarding for it. The three shorts play out like minor sketches, although 'Sissy Boy Slap Party' — imagine Jean Genet directing the Marx Brothers — has to be seen to be believed. (IAN HAYDN SMITH)

Safe

(UK/USA 1995)

Director: Todd Haynes
Label: Tartan Video (UK)
Region: 2 (PAL)
Discs: 1

THE FILM

'Where am I? Right now?' whimpers palely afflicted trophy wife Carol White (Julianne Moore): and when in one sequence director Todd Haynes glides her home from a doctor's surgery through the dip-lit night-time Hollywood hills we could be seeing a redhead Camilla Rhodes from *Mulholland Drive*. *Pace* Lynch, however, you don't need doppelgangers for existential horror: one person wheezing in an empty room will do just fine. Moore's airtight blankness and Carol's obsessive devotion to a patch of yellow roses doesn't mean that ten-year-old Rory's stepmother is an alien, but like E.T. she's sickening and like E.T. it's the world that's doing it. This sly and scary take on the issue-of-the-week movie has been championed as a take on 1980s consumerism, but that's doing Haynes a wretched disservice: *Safe* would be a pallid thing indeed if the director really confined his sights to those shiny yuppie pathogens – teal-coloured settee sets, Kenny Loggins aerobics sessions – which inhabit the movie's opening hour.

The magnificent second part is bolder altogether. Picking up clues as to her condition from the white noise of late-night radio static and dead-eyed hospital informercials, a newly introspective Carol discovers the pleasures of self-hood; through the lithium haze of composer Ed Tomney's score she heads to Wrenwood, a new-age retreat in the desert outside Albuquerque, in the hope of replacing toxic anomie with a new life of beansprout regimens and baggy-sweatered holisticism. A problem solved, *Koyaanisqatsi* sages will nod, but the rest of us are soon feeling pretty queasy. Does telling yourself that you've taken charge of your life actually mean that you have? Either which way, self-diagnosis is clearly quite as addictive as self-medication, and we know what happens to Mrs Goldfarb in *Requiem for a Dream*. You feed a cold and you starve the flu: but what do you do if you're suffering from the greatest AIDS metaphor that cinema has yet come up with? Not what Carol does, anyway.

THE DISC

Some nice bits on the pleasingly incongruous audio commentary with Haynes, Moore and producer Christine Vachon, particularly when the three of them assess the odds as to whether the child actor playing Rory has got married yet. Moore's pretence not to remember meeting Haynes at a Seattle film festival – she was in town shooting *Assassins*, it emerges – usefully prickles up the mutual admiration, while Haynes keeps a running tally of scenes shot round at his grandparents' place. They tidied it up a bit, apparently, to get the Kubrickian feel. (PETER VÁSÁRY)

Salesman

(USA, 1969)

Directors: Albert and David Maysles
Label: Criterion Collection (USA)
Region: 0 (NTSC)
Discs: 1

THE FILM

The Maysles brothers were pioneers of American 'direct cinema', making documentaries that eschewed voice-over and talking heads to create intimate, candid portraits of people and their livelihoods, typically constructed from hundreds of hours of observational footage. Many of their films, such as the Rolling Stones concert film *Gimme Shelter* and *Grey Gardens*, on the eccentric Jackie O relatives Edith and Edie Beale, have become cult classics. But the brothers' first feature was on a decidedly less glamorous topic: travelling Bible salesmen. Co-credited to their frequent editor Charlotte Zwerin, it is a landmark documentary: an aesthetic masterpiece, extraordinary for both its compassionate handling of its subjects and its profound socio-cultural insight.

Salesman follows four men working for the Mid-American Bible Company as they travel the country peddling their wares to poor and working-class Catholic families. Venturing into private homes, we watch their sales pitches with horror or humour, but also suspense. We join them in dismal motel rooms and cafeterias, and at sales meetings where their superiors hail selling as the ultimate form of self-actualisation – and by extension, failure to sell as personal deficiency. Each man tackles this challenge differently, and the film comes to focus on Paul Brennan, whose poor sales correlate with his increasingly bitter cynicism. What emerges is not only an inescapably affecting portrait of a man in a particular time and profession, but also powerful perspective into the inner workings of American consumer capitalism, religion, and the human condition.

As David says in an old interview on the DVD, *Salesman* should make us 'depressed as hell'. But the filmmakers are also encouraging us to examine our own lives and livelihoods, and this is what allows the film to transcend its historical context. In this golden age of media exploitation, we would all do well to experience *Salesman* – a sensitively crafted, intimate human drama of epic proportions.

THE DISC

There's little to choose in terms of transfer and sound quality (excellent all round) between this disc and the new UK edition from Masters of Cinema, which has a different set of interview-led extras and a 36-page booklet containing rare vintage photography. What the R2 edition lacks is Criterion's wonderfully insightful commentary by Albert Maysles and Zwerin, recorded in 2001 (David passed away in 1987). There's also an oddly shot but informative 1969 television interview with the brothers by *Newsweek* critic Jack Kroll, and a National Public Radio interview with James Baker, the last surviving salesman, from 2000. Both editions deliver the goods – go with whichever you can get your hands on. (VERA BRUNNER-SUNG)

Salvador
(USA, 1986)

Director: Oliver Stone
Label: MGM (all territories)
Region: Any
Discs: 1

THE FILM

Less an essay in forensic dialectics *à la* his beloved Eisenstein or Pontecorvo than a try-out for the save-one-life template fine-tuned in 1997's *Welcome to Sarajevo* and other exercises in narrativising carnage, Oliver Stone's not-quite directorial debut looks a lot more conventional in form now than it must have done in 1986. Nevertheless, this is still fearsome, angry stuff, which Washington State Department analysts grappling with a newly alienated Latin America would do well to re-watch. One hopes that it's Stone's commitment to a Kierkegaardian larger truth rather than his background in working with Alan Parker which makes him so little concerned with human realism – check out that early scene where as-yet-unredeemed scuzzball hack Peter Boyle (James Woods) and ersatz Samoan attorney Dr Rock (Jim Belushi) cross the El Salvadorean border, and ask yourself what's really going on – but there's no-one else to touch him for the pit of the stomach and the end of the gun: as a colonel in sunglasses Juan Fernandez is as frightening now as he was 20 years ago, and you see why Paul Hogan wanted him for *Crocodile Dundee II*. The kitsch factor mounts toward the end, as rebels skelter on horseback down cobbled streets and Woods takes to lamenting that both sides are as bad as each other, but the death of John Savage's Capra-esque reporter is duly affecting, and there's a good handful of spineless and complicit US officials upon whom you end up sincerely wishing violence.

Question: what is it about 1986 American movies and people talking top secret with parrots in the background? A scarlet macaw trying to look unobtrusive here as right-wing goons plan to murder Archbishop Romero, and another gracing Kelly McGillis's pad when Tom Cruise is 'debriefed' in *Top Gun*: thank God Russo-American relations warmed at Reykjavik, because the reds were clearly deep undercover.

THE DISC

When real-life Boyle tells how he originally decided to cover the El Salvador conflict 'not as a surfer, but as a journalist', everything else on the DVD is going to suffer by comparison. Stone's audio commentary keeps the *Apocalypse Now* thematic going with regular accounts of the 'madness' on set, and we catch a whiff of his John Milius-like self-regard when he suggests that he should have been called Oliver South. (Not that it was this film *alone* which changed the White House's late Cold War policy, he admits: such epiphenomena as economic cycles were also apparently quite important.) On the puff-piece documentary, meanwhile, Woods tells how he decided to quit the movie one day after almost being killed on the Mexican set, and Stone recounts how he telephoned ahead and asked that road blocks be set up to stop him. Road blocks? You heard. (PETER VÁSÁRY)

Salvatore Giuliano

(Italy, 1961)

Director: Francesco Rosi
Label: Criterion Collection (USA)
Region: 1 (NTSC)
Discs: 2

THE FILM

Francesco Rosi's first signature film crosses noir with neorealism to delve into recent Sicilian history. By turns a bandit, political terrorist and mafia captain, the film's title character, whose still-unsolved 1950 murder provides the central mystery, is made the prism through which Rosi views the mechanisms of state, judicial and mafia power, as Sicily casts off Fascist rule and then fights by the same covert means for independence from Rome. Though the film is not without characters, Rosi, while retaining his mentor Visconti's feeling for the Sicilian landscape and the non-pro actors who inhabit it, takes the total political situation as his subject, rather than the plight of individuals within it.

While based so far as possible on documentary evidence, the film does not claim omniscience, and the reasons behind the final downfall of Giuliano and his outfit, in which mafia politics and turf wars within the civil and military authorities converge, are presented in part as conjecture. Within this meticulously devised frame, the first half of *Salvatore Giuliano* is a superb guerrilla-war film, the second a near-satirical courtroom drama in which only the judge is really interested in unravelling the truth. Rosi's film advances on neorealism by interrogating, rather than seeking to reflect, that diaphanous thing 'reality'.

THE DISCS

Politically engaged before it was fashionable, Rosi has remained, at least within Anglo-Saxon film culture, something of a poor relation to the heirs of neorealism who lit up Italian cinema in the early '60s. As the inventor of the intelligent political thriller, paving the way for Gillo Pontecorvo and Costa Gavras, his reputation is higher in Europe, and in a booklet essay here *Positif* magazine eminence Michel Ciment hails him as the Eisenstein of the postwar era. Criterion's outstanding double-disc – the first in a series of Rosi releases from the label – is designed as an introduction to a neglected master.

Peter Cowie's expertly timed and valuable commentary moves from close-up sequence analysis to wide-angle consideration of the historical context – both of the film and of the Salvatore story – without once losing focus. Two documentaries provide further insights into Rosi's life and work, one of them made for Italian television and hosted by the man himself in his apartment. Taking us through photo albums and visiting the graves of old collaborators, it's an informal, unpretentious self-portrait, though one with room for a video tribute from celebrity fan Martin Scorsese. (HENRY K MILLER)

Santa Sangre

(Mexico/Italy, 1989)

Director: Alejandro Jodorowsky
Label: Anchor Bay (UK)
Region: 2 (PAL)
Discs: 2

THE FILM

Chilean émigré Jodorowsky's reputation as a crazed cinematic genius rests on just three films, but is justly deserved. If *El Topo* was his western and *The Holy Mountain* his religious epic, then *Santa Sangre* is his horror film. It's also probably the most accessible and (relatively) coherent of the three.

Felix, the young son of a circus ringmaster and a crazed religious cult leader, leads a troubled, blood-drenched upbringing surrounded by freaks, clowns and madmen. After witnessing his parents horribly mutilate each other, he is driven over the edge and incarcerated in an asylum, where he remains until adulthood. Rescued by his mother, now an armless cabaret performer, Felix becomes a tool of her terrible revenge on past tormentors – and on anyone who would threaten the bond between mother and child.

Starring Jodorowsky's own two sons, a permanently drunk Guy Stockwell and countless non-professionals – including a blind guitar troupe, transgender wrestlers, coked-up Down's Syndrome kids, slum dwellers and hundreds of chickens – and shot entirely in Mexico City, *Santa Sangre* is a lavish wonder to behold. It's also a wonder to hear, with a wild soundtrack of Perez Prado mambo tunes and Mexican brass bands.

THE DISCS

Presented in a beautiful, near-pristine print, the film looks great. 'I don't like normality!' confesses Jodorowsky during an enlightening and entertaining audio commentary with Alan Jones. He expounds on the joys of the irrational, the difficulties of filming in Mexico City and the pleasures and pain of using street people instead of actors. The second disc includes Louis Mouchet's excellent documentary *La Constellation Jodorowsky*, in which the great man talks about his life in theatre, film, tarot and comics; plus a lengthy deleted sequence and a short film, *Echek*, by Alexandro's son Adan. The soundtrack is offered in Dolby 2.0, Dolby 5.1 and DTS Surround. (MARK PILKINGTON)

Sátántangó
(Hungary, 1994)

Director: Béla Tarr
Label: Artificial Eye (UK)
Region: 2 (PAL)
Discs: 3

THE FILM

Equally a *film à clef* and a badge of honour for its survivors, Tarr's extraordinary adaptation of a László Krasznahorkai novel achieves the purest possible distillation of a particular arthouse aesthetic, and stakes some claim to being – not coincidentally – the least commercial movie ever made. Comprising seven hours of long takes photographing muddy agricultural flatlands in resolute monochrome, *Sátántangó* shouldn't be watched back-to-back with, say, *Speed*; if shock didn't kill you outright, you'd almost certainly get the moviegoer's equivalent of the bends.

As an experiment in screen time and how immersive the film experience can be, Tarr's film makes *Céline and Julie Go Boating* seem a breeze at half the length. What the director's imitators (yes, that means you, Gus Van Sant) haven't quite grasped is how these experiments don't circumscribe a satisfying telling of stories. From its chapter headings onwards, the film is unapologetically novelistic in its description of a community where nothing much happens except it rains.

Tarr takes at least 30 minutes to introduce each of the characters dancing with the devil, where a conventional film would in only one or two scenes, ten minutes tops. Here, then, are squabbling business partners Futaki (Miklos Székely B) and Schmidt (László Lugossy), one cuckolding the other. Here is the returning poet Irimiás (Mihály Vig), in whose florid turn of phrase the villagers come to place far too much trust. And here's the grumpy village doctor (Peter Berling), whose trip out to find pear brandy turns into an epic quest, and sets up the film's magnificently sardonic punchline.

Yes, it's tough-going in places – a cinema that exposes characters and viewers alike to the elements, the K2 of film – but Tarr conjures up hypnotic set-pieces from nightmarish bars and empty town squares at dusk. Though it travels great distances, its characters – cursed by fate, squabbling over money, scared and superstitious; people who, even when in groups, seem to be ploughing their own lonely furrow, waiting for God only knows what – aren't so very far removed from you or me.

THE DISCS

Only a Tarr filmography, alas, although – in the circumstances – a director's commentary would probably have been too much to ask, and it's unlikely anyone would have been buying this set for bloopers and out-takes. Transfer quality is generally good, although sporadic scratches and reel-change markers suggest it's been sourced directly from the cinema print. The real achievement here is bringing the film back within (easier) reach. (MIKE McCAHILL)

School of Rock
(USA, 2003)

Director: Richard Linklater
Label: Paramount (all territories)
Region: Any
Discs: 1

THE FILM

You could read the synopsis for *School of Rock* and wince. Jack Black plays a selfish wannabe rock star who, through the peculiarities of cinematic fate, finds himself without a band and pretending to be a teacher at a top-notch prep school, where he starts out slouching behind his desk, bitching about MTV and waiting for payday. Prof Black soon discovers that the kids he had originally dismissed as hangover-enhancing, high-pitched irritants are musical prodigies, so the self-centred sloth decides to educate the children in the mysterious and deadly ways of rock 'n' roll. Will they learn their AC from their DC before the Battle of the Band showcase hits town?

Written by co-star (and Black's former neighbour) Mike White, *School of Rock* clearly benefits from the stabilising hand of Richard Linklater, whose key ability is keeping moondog Black on the knife-edge that separates dramatic comedy from camera-hogging clowning. Drawing credible performances from half-a-dozen pre-teens is also no mean feat, and Linklater approached it in his usual style – rehearsal, rehearsal, rehearsal. It pays off: the film offers the flavour of Black's familiar ad-libbed lunacy alongside a cohesiveness that suggests nothing has been left to chance. Linklater and Black's shared love of rock music also helps, and the film's simultaneous veneration and subversion of that creed is what really carries the piece. Rock hasn't been served so well by the big screen since *This is Spinal Tap*.

THE DISC

You get a feel for the, er, unique challenge of working with the effervescent Black on *School of Rock*'s main commentary track, which largely consists of Black riffing all over Linklater's valiant attempts to explain what's going on. Black's blabbermouth is a major part of his appeal, but it does get a little wearing. Not that Linklater seems to mind. Mike White had flu on the day the commentary was recorded, sadly, but there are still some great kernels here, including mention of Linklater's fleeting cameo and some alternate plotlines. (There are no deleted scenes.)

Other extras include a good making-of documentary (called 'Lessons Learned in *School of Rock*'), Black's MTV diary and plea to Led Zeppelin to licence their 'Immigrant Song', a short film of the kids at the Toronto Film Festival, and an interactive DVD-ROM feature offering a History of Rock according to Black's character Dewey Finn. There's also a commentary track supplied by the kids, which has some cute moments but even for the dedicated could be an extra too far. (PETER WATTS)

Se7en

(USA, 1995) 2-disc Set /
New Line Platinum Edition

Director: David Fincher
Label: Entertainment in Video (UK) /
New Line Home Video (USA)
Region: 2 (PAL) /1 (NTSC)
Discs: 2

THE FILM

This writer remembers limping from a west London cinema in January 1996, dazed by the sheer darkness of the film that had just played out, but also thrilled at having witnessed something so blazingly fresh. An instant modern classic, Se7en was only the second feature by MTV alumnus David Fincher, and ten years on it's still like nothing else ever made. A buddy movie from some inner ring of hell, it spirals towards a pitch-black conclusion that reads as an eloquent up-yours to the entire test-audience phenomenon, and it also demonstrates a cunning, near-Aristotelian refusal to show any direct action.

Like detectives Mills and Somerset (Brad Pitt and Morgan Freeman), we're always a tantalising step behind the clever killer (Kevin Spacey) who emerges from the shadows in the final act – which means that, like them, we witness not murders but a succession of grisly aftermaths, one for each of the Seven Deadly Sins. (The lone exception to this rule is a ravishingly choreographed chase that erupts without warning, an hour or so in.) On first viewing, Se7en's sense of mystery grips like a crocodile's jaws, but it rewards endless rewatching: for its immaculately considered performances (including a touching contribution from Gwyneth Paltrow), for the grimly gripping methodology of the killings, and, above all, for Fincher's ruthless maintenance of stylishly dank dread. One popular, glib carp about the film has always been, 'Why the hell don't they ever turn on the lights?' Sorry guys, but this nightmare works just beautifully in the dark.

THE DISCS

Where to start? The bonus disc features an exhaustive look at the pioneeringly jittery opening credits sequence and the killer's obsessive notebooks (the former alone cost $50,000 to make, the latter a further $15,000), as well as deleted scenes and extended takes fascinating both for their content and their ultimate exclusion from the final cut. (In particular, there's an alternative opening that at last explains that small swatch of paper that Somerset lays out with his police paraphernalia at the start of the finished movie.)

There's more besides, but the meat of this gruesome banquet lies on the main disc: there are some four separate commentaries, at least two (one by Pitt, Freeman and Fincher, the other by screenwriter Kevin Walker and academic Richard Dyer) so revelatory that they're pretty much impossible to turn off once embarked upon. Walker memorably describes his script as 'my love-letter to New York City' – if *billets-doux* don't come any darker, nor do DVD releases come any more loving. (MARK MONAHAN)

Secretary

(USA, 2000)

Director: Steven Shainberg
Label: Tartan (UK)
Region: 2 (PAL)
Discs: 1

THE FILM

If ever a mainstream film demanded to be watched repeatedly in the privacy of one's own dungeon, it's this sweet comedy about two obsessive-compulsives. He organises his red pens, she cuts herself. He's E Edward Grey (James Spader), a lawyer whose overwrought yet bland name underlines his vulnerability. She's Lee Holloway (Maggie Gyllenhaal), recently released from a mental institution after an accidental suicide attempt, and in search of a job.

Lee answers Mr Grey's job ad, and finds herself answering first his phones and, soon after, his desire to put the dictator into dictation. Kinky and consensual (with an emphasis on the sensual in the rich, almost Sirkian colour of Grey's offices), the film celebrates the liberation Lee discovers in submission, as she matures from an overgrown teenage misfit tied to her mother's apron strings and awaiting Stepford entrapment with her dumb fiancé (Jeremy Davies).

Gyllenhaal plays Lee like a bent Bridget Jones whose odyssey of self-discovery involves throwing out her bright pink self-mutilation kit. Spader is Spader, only more so, his ticcy exterior brilliantly used as the carapace of a man obsessed with control. The climactic sequence in which Grey, having dismissed her, discovers he has met his match, shows Shainberg's skill as a director, moving the tone from media satire through family values to erotic reunion. Lee obtains a beatific glow that combines Dreyer's *The Passion of Joan of Arc* with the triumph of teen heroines who get their guy.

Strangely reminiscent of the Mollie Ringwald oeuvre, this is a film of secret pleasures, including the wonderful Lizzie West, whose 'Chariots Rise' soundtracks the reunion, and drove me to websearch obsession until the soundtrack, including Angelo Badalamenti's witty score, was released. Like Lee, the viewer may initially be wary of getting sucked in, but the charm of *Secretary* is the way it shows sadomasochism as something to be elected and enjoyed. And, finally, rewarded, as Edward opens up, revealing the hidden meaning of secretary – one who keeps your secrets.

THE DISC

More Gyllenhaal, who effortlessly dominates the behind-the-scenes featurette, thanks to her sheer pleasure in the role (her first lead). Unusually, there's a commentary by the writer, Erin Cressida Wilson, who adapted Mary Gaitskill's short story with Shainberg. They are a wise-cracking pair with an evident love for a project that was a hard sell, and the commentary is unusually entertaining. Tartan's disc edges the contest with a couple of extra interviews with the actors and DTS sound. No handcuffs supplied. (SOPHIE MAYER)

Sense and Sensibility

(USA, 1995) Collector's Edition / Special Edition

Director: Ang Lee
Label: Columbia TriStar (UK/USA)
Region: 2 (PAL) / 1 (NTSC)
Discs: 1

THE FILM

Ang Lee's English-language debut is a beautifully literate adaptation of Jane Austen's rather shrewish first novel, offering in its account of the Dashwood sisters, Eleanor and Marianne, a story of the interests and the passions that's as sharp as anything in David Hume or Adam Smith. A world away from Andrew Davies' clogged-up Victoriana, this is a movie rooted firmly in the eighteenth century, dividing its time between a Hogarthian London and endless rolling fields recalling Gainsborough's *Mr and Mrs Andrews*. Emma Thompson is sensible Eleanor, forever totting up the pennies and biting her tongue, with Kate Winslet as ring-locked Marianne, prettily heaving her porcelain breast and pining for dark stranger Willoughby (Greg Wise), who has a nice way with words and a nasty habit of disappearing at the wrong time. Off to the sidelines, meanwhile, Alan Rickman's anguished silence suggests that somebody knows what's *really* going on.

There's an absurd amount to enjoy here: uniformly terrific performances – particularly Imogen Stubbs' essay in bashful malice and Hugh Laurie's fruitful departure from his line in fops – a jig of a score from Patrick Doyle, and of course Emma Thompson's triumph of a screenplay, improving on Austen's original no end with a lovely scene involving Vladivostok's famed Volga river and half a dozen icy put-downs for anyone with ideas above their station in the Pump Room. But the real wonder of the thing is the way that Ang achieves a *glissando* between the two sisters' stories, shifting from Eleanor's tightly-framed scenes, all scoured in Methodist morning sunlight, to Marianne suffering against a monstrous pathetic fallacy, as *Sturm und Drang* thunderclouds glower at her travails. Both a careful film and a swoony one, it's as good as anything Ang's ever done.

THE DISC

Columbia TriStar comes up trumps with a splendid disc. Together with A+ sound and picture there's a trailer, several deleted scenes and two delightful audio commentaries, one with Ang and co-producer James Schamus and the other with Thompson and producer Lindsay Doran. Schamus and Thompson are particularly convivial raconteurs, riffing cheerfully for the movie's entire two-hour length. Schamus touches on fainting sheep, Edward Heath's prime ministerial career and scandalous theories about the origins of the National Trust, while Thompson talks about fish-eyes, Praxitelean physiognomies and eighteenth-century concepts of privacy. Put these commentaries on a loop, and they'd make for good company in your old age; listen to one after the other right now, and you'll be left in no doubt that Ang Lee is a genius. (PETER VÁSÁRY)

Seven Samurai

(Japan, 1954)

Director: Akira Kurosawa
Label: Criterion Collection (USA)
Region: 1 (NTSC)
Discs: 3

THE FILM

Few films are as thrilling as *Seven Samurai*, or as single-minded: its stakes are set in the first few minutes, and all of what follows is the working out of its eminently straightforward premise. Single-minded but far from simple-minded, or simple: in telling the story of imperilled farmers in 16th-century Japan, obliged by marauders to hire masterless samurai to protect them, Kurosawa engineers a magnificently fluent succession of tones – comic, tragic, resolute – and a rich, finely pitched cross-examination of collective and individual action, of duty and self-interest, of social justice and the law of the jungle.

All this (and more) while delivering some of the purest, most exciting action scenes in cinema, notably in the climatic battle – a whirlwind of fast cutting, flashing steel, charging horses, running men, rain, mud and blood. The actors, many of them Kurosawa regulars, are all excellent, none better than Takashi Shimura (a new man after *Ikiru*) as the samurai leader, and Toshiro Mifune as tagger-on Kikuchiyo (a role that gave Mifune ample scope to exercise his comic talent and tigerish fire). With *Ikiru*, this was the achievement Kurosawa was best pleased with, and his longest film. Two hundred minutes is indeed long – but *Seven Samurai* never, ever feels it.

THE DISCS

Criterion's new three-disc edition utterly trumps all forerunners for both transfer quality and extras. The film itself is spread over two discs for a higher detail level (although Criterion's pictureboxing – recording a surrounding black frame – spoils the intention slightly), and has never looked better, with incredible deep blacks and bright whites, and remarkably few scratches. The remastered 4.0 audio mix gives the soundtrack a commensurate depth and heft.

Then there's the battery of bonuses: two audio commentaries, one (from Criterion's original issue of the film) by Japanese film specialist Michael Jeck, the other a relay between luminaries Donald Richie, Tony Rayns, Joan Mellen, Stephen Prince and David Desser; a 50-minute documentary on the making of the film; 'My Life in Cinema', a two-hour filmed conversation between Kurosawa and Nagisa Oshima; and a new documentary, '*Seven Samurai*: Origins and Influences'. The 56 pages of liner notes include an interview with Toshiro Mifune and essays by Arthur Penn, Sidney Lumet and a clutch of critics. The word is 'magisterial'. (SIMON CROPPER)

Sex and Lucía

(Spain, 2001)

Director: Julio Medem
Label: Palm Pictures (USA)
Region: 1 (NTSC)
Discs: 1

THE FILM

Richard Kelly's 2001 release **Donnie Darko** may have pulled off some audacious storytelling coups with the aid of its time-travelling wormholes, but, in Europe, arthouse luminary Julio Medem was performing even more impressive narrative contortions in his fifth feature *Sex and Lucía*. Here, as always, Medem delights in teasingly tangled tales which pivot on shifting identities and outrageous coincidences, exposing his characters to extremes of ecstatic pleasure and heartbreaking pain; this time, though, he foregrounds the process of storytelling itself, exploring fiction's liberating qualities (all the film's main characters 're-invent' themselves) while suggesting that taking control of our own stories can carry weighty consequences. Lucía (Paz Vega), believing that her novelist boyfriend Lorenzo (Tristán Ulloa) has been killed in a traffic accident, travels from Madrid to an unnamed Mediterranean island that he often spoke of. She stays in a guesthouse run by Elena (Najwa Nimri), who unknown to Lucía spent an ecstatic night with Lorenzo on the island six years previously. As Medem whirls us between separate timeframes, we gradually learn of Lucía's passionate romance with Lorenzo, Lorenzo's discovery that he fathered a child with Elena, and his tragic attempt to forge a relationship with his lost daughter, as well as the anonymous, healing relationship he's struck up with Elena over the internet; the stage is finally set for redemptive reunions on the island's stark shorelines, and the chance for characters to rewrite their destinies for the better.

Medem wrote the film by fusing two scripts originally written independently of each other ('Lucía' and 'El sexo'), and the unresolved ambiguities and mysterious symbolism – as in his earlier *The Red Squirrel* and *The Lovers of the Arctic Circle* – follow the logic of dream and desire rather than rational schema, resonating in the mind and heart all the more effectively for it. Sex is certainly one of the film's main motors, but is seen as a precious natural force, easily corrupted into (unnatural) pornographic perversion and capable of destruction as well as creation. Several years on, though, the film is less remarkable for its explicit sexual imagery than for its ravishing, pioneering use of High-Definition digital video: just as much as the red earth fields of the Basque region in Medem's *Tierra* (1996), the bleached lunar landscape of his island (actually Formentera) provides a suitably otherworldly setting for this magical metaphysical masterpiece.

THE DISC

This Palm Pictures R1 release preserves these wonderful widescreen vistas, and has comparable picture quality to Tartan's R2 version, but boasts superior extras – including a making-of, interviews with cast and crew, and tracks from Alberto Iglesias' lyrical score. (ANDY RICHARDS)

The Shining
(USA/UK, 1980)

Director: Stanley Kubrick
Label: Warners (UK)
Region: 2 (PAL)
Discs: 1

THE FILM

Kubrick's films have an odd thing in common: they're never quite set where they're meant to be. *Lolita* decamped to the Home Counties, *Full Metal Jacket* played out in London's Docklands, and the Greenwich Village of *Eyes Wide Shut* was, infamously, a backlot at Pinewood Studios. Still, it's Kubrick's horror masterpiece *The Shining*, adapted from Stephen King's book, that takes the boldest step of really sequestering us away and having us spin in time and space. When blocked writer Jack Torrance (Jack Nicholson) takes a winter caretaker position at the Overlook, an isolated hotel in the Colorado Rockies, the words 'middle' and 'nowhere' are about all we've got for co-ordinates. The formal architecture – mazes all around – give us few clues as to how we got in or expect to exit; dismissive reviews on its release ('a cruel tease'; 'a snake swallowing its own tail') missed a trick in not recognising these as both conscious methods of disorientation and invites to viewing after mesmerised viewing.

Kubrick's vision of stir-crazed family breakdown plays out like some warped *Tom and Jerry* cartoon stuck at half-speed, pitting Nicholson's pantomime malice against rag-doll darlings Shelley Duvall and Danny Lloyd, who scurry through the Overlook's grandiose hallways with their axe-wielding hubby/daddy never far behind. By pushing its situation this far into Looney Tunes caricature, *The Shining* signals itself as a man's murderous fantasy about regaining control, dreamt up as he cradles a bourbon at the bar, envious of the special – even psychic? – bond between his wife and son, and egging himself on with the advice of phantom friends who know exactly how he feels. As the closing glimpse of a bygone ball unforgettably hints, it was ever thus.

THE DISC

You get more *Shining* for your buck on the Region 1 disc – a whole 25 minutes more – which Kubrick removed after American reviews complained the pace lagged. While the US version's worth seeing once, the brisker, more implacable European one is the real keeper. There's only one substantial extra on either disc, but it's tremendous – Vivian Kubrick's on-set 'Making of *The Shining*', originally aired by the BBC and supplemented here by her chatty and funny commentary. Only 17 at the time, Kubrick managed to get everyone's guard down except her father's: Nicholson, at least, let her into his dressing-room and excuses himself hilariously at one point to take a piss, while blow-ups between the director and Shelley Duvall are documented for all to see. Stray gaffers kept getting lost in the maze, apparently – you only hope they did a head-count when shooting wrapped. (TIM ROBEY)

Shoah

(France, 1985)

Director: Claude Lanzmann
Label: Masters of Cinema (UK)
Region: 2 (PAL)
Discs: 4

THE FILM

Whether you see Claude Lanzmann's uniquely moving Holocaust documentary on the big or small screen, surely what's most important is that you see it; and on DVD its nine and a half hours are so much more manageable (what's that in these days of *24* box sets anyway?), its wrenching testimonies and formal audacity so much easier to access.

No straightforward history lesson – for former resistance fighter and magazine editor Lanzmann, no mere set of social conditions could explain the singular, horrific reality of the Nazis' crimes – its evocation of the exterminations drifts freely around in time and space, using absolutely no archive footage or dramatic reconstructions, only the interviews with survivors, camp commandants (mostly filmed in secret) and other witnesses whom Lanzmann toiled for 12 years from 1973-85 tracking down and recording.

The details that the talking heads reveal (the silence as workers went about burning bodies, corpses tumbling out of a gas-chamber door like stone slabs), and their unpredictable facial expressions as they tell them (serene, smiling, astonished) accost your preconceptions, preventing you from filing the Holocaust neatly away, making it vividly immediate. Often accompanying their words are present-day shots of the camera roving over the places they describe (the ruins of the Treblinka, Auschwitz, Chelmo and Sobibor sites, railway routes, the Warsaw ghetto), which further heave the horrific scenes into the here and now, helping you imagine, for instance, how several thousand doomed people crammed into cattle cars would have slotted alongside the everyday.

It's this encouragement to imagine, to fill the gap between past and present, that defines *Shoah*. It's in this gap, more than in history books or Hollywood reconstructions, the film implies, where you should search for the Holocaust – and to go on searching is to honour the millions it extinguished.

THE DISCS

Though approved by Lanzmann, the transferred print is a little scratched, but certainly adequate. There are no extras, though, usefully, the film is diligently divided into plentiful well-labelled chapters. Far more impressive, however, is the accompanying 184-page book, which, as well as repeating all the chapter labels, features a photo gallery of the interviewees, a Lanzmann biography, an excellent introductory essay by *Shoah* scholar Stuart Liebman and a transcript of a seminar Lanzmann gave at Yale back in 1990, which thoughtfully offers chapter references for the three sequences he discusses. (NICK FUNNELL)

Show Me Love

(Sweden/Denmark 1998)

Director: Lukas Moodysson
Label: Strand Home Video (USA)
Region: 1 (NTSC)
Discs: 1

ORIGINAL TITLE: *Fucking Åmål*

THE FILM

Lukas Moodysson's fresh, distinctive first film was called a masterpiece by Ingmar Bergman, no less. An overstatement? Perhaps. But it's not hard to see why Bergman flipped for *Show Me Love*: girl-on-girl teen romances don't get much better than this. There's a lovely matter-of-factness, an almost documentary feel to the movie, which carefully picks its way through the adolescent heartache we look back on as comedy. The grainy, flat, fitfully luminous camerawork finds the half-formed beauty in teenage faces.

Stultifying small-town Sweden is the backdrop for the story of Agnes (Elin Olsson), a bright loner with a crush on bolshy, popular classmate Elin (Rebecca Liljeberg). The latter, who stomps around in clumpy boots and a mini-skirt, spends a lot of time slumped on furniture, belowing 'Everything's boring!', but she's a convincing object of desire: her forlorn strops are more endearing than exasperating. Pitching up unexpectedly at Agnes's botched birthday party, Elin kisses her for a bet, then scarpers. When she returns, remorseful and rather drunken, the girls go for a night-time stroll together, and it's in the back of a stranger's car that they have their first full-on snog, high on the excitement of hitching a ride out of town.

This pair, with their puffy, sensual features and wide-awake eyes, are a good match: both of them kick around in a state of fierce, frustrated longing. But after a swoony wet-dream about Agnes, Elin promptly hooks up with Johan (Mathias Rust), a 17-year-old who's been trailing after her like a clumsy puppy. Buzzing with submerged feelings, the film gives us an education of the heart: we discover the girls' passion along with them. Moodysson, who can inspire small bursts of affection for even minor characters, cuts parents and families some slack. Elin's harried mother and older sister, and Agnes's solicitous dad are well rounded. And the director's eye for teenage grooming and mating rituals is unerring. Telephones and doors are pivotal objects and, more often than not, instruments of casual torture: an anonymous girl sobs into a phone at a party; Agnes gets prank calls from her schoolmates; Elin dumps Johann over the mobile; Agnes gets locked out of her own bedroom by Elin and her sister.

THE DISC

Every bit as winning as Moodysson's hippy commune movie *Together*, also available as part of Metrodome's four-disc UK box set, *Show Me Love* hovers closer to the edge of pain, foreshadowing the bleak and acclaimed *Lilya 4-ever*. Strand's stand-alone US disc has no extras; Metrodome's UK one only has 'Talk', a creepy short so lethally predictable it only serves – beyond setting the scene for the similarly empty *A Hole in My Heart* – as a reminder of how Moodysson progressed. (MAXIE SZALWINSKA)

Singin' in the Rain

(USA, 1952) Special Edition

Directors: Stanley Donen & Gene Kelly
Label: Warners (all territories)
Region: Any
Discs: 2

THE FILM

People who expect to dislike *Singin' in the Rain* inevitably wind up loving it. Viewers who profess indifference or even annoyance with regard to film musicals are summarily converted. Meanwhile, the movie's ardent devotees always find more to see, hear, and relish in it. One is tempted to say that no work of 20th-century popular art offers a purer jolt of positive feeling – the clean, clear oxygen of exuberant imagination and creative warmth.

And the superlatives don't stop there. Gene Kelly and Donald O'Connor, unimprovably cast as a pair of 1920s vaudevillians navigating their way into talking pictures, share the sweetest friendship between two men in any American movie, and Debbie Reynolds, a twinkly charmer, becomes Kelly's sweetheart by joining into the friendship rather than more predictably disrupting it. Jean Hagen, a sultry brunette two years earlier in *The Asphalt Jungle*, reinvents herself as the definitive dumb blonde, and Betty Comden and Adolph Green's jubilant and clever screenplay is as perfectly tailored to the actors as are their Technicolor costumes. The lighting, choreography, and production design mark a perfect transition between the dreamy confections of *An American in Paris* and the sophisticated meta-theatre of *The Band Wagon*, which in fact bracketed this picture in the MGM/Arthur Freed production sequence – making *Singin' in the Rain* the undisputed jewel in a truly distinguished crown.

THE DISCS

Miracle of miracles, the two-disc special edition commissioned for the film's 50th anniversary is as gem-packed and delectable as the movie itself. On the first disc, beyond the impeccable cosmetic attention lavished on every note, colour, and line, a cocktail party of creative personnel has been gathered for a commentary track, emceed by an effusive Debbie Reynolds. Co-director Stanley Donen reminisces about the sterling pool of talent collected under Freed at MGM, but also vividly describes some of the stresses of working on such a chaotic, prolific studio lot. Donald O'Connor and Cyd Charisse, still giddy about the film after all these years, dish out delicious anecdotes, and latter-day tyro Baz Luhrmann describes the film's indelible stamp on future musicals. Meanwhile, on the second disc, viewers are treated to a buffet of short documentaries, a previously deleted scene, and, most exceptionally, a compendium of footage from other Freed-unit musicals, some of it quite rare, and all of it supported by more interviews and testimonies from on- and off-camera talent. (NICK DAVIS)

Solaris
(USA, 2003)

Director: Steven Soderbergh
Label: 20th Century Fox (all territories)
Region: Any
Discs: 1

THE FILM

After the critical and box-office bonanza of *Erin Brockovich*, *Traffic* and *Ocean's Eleven*, Steven Soderbergh proceeded to blow all his Hollywood capital in one go on this commercially disastrous Tarkovsky remake. However he persuaded Fox to finance an actionless science fiction mood-piece about love, death and the tyranny of memory, we can only be grateful they bought it, as it remains, scene for scene, his riskiest and most impressive movie. Condensing the philosophical concerns of Stanislaw Lem's source novel right back down to what matters, Soderbergh homes in on the quandary of Chris Kelvin (George Clooney), posted to a deep-space research vessel where his dead wife Rheya (Natascha McElhone), in a pattern of visitation familiar to the other crew members, keeps materialising. If she's a figment, generated in Kelvin's mind by the pulsating ocean planet outside, she's a distressingly self-aware one, cursed with both the knowledge of how their relationship played out on Earth and the infinite capacity to relive it.

Arguably, it's the shade of Kubrick rather than Tarkovsky which hangs over this interpretation – we get *The Shining*'s idea of trauma repeating itself, the framework of an *Eyes Wide Shut*-style marital autopsy, and repeated visual and thematic echoes of *2001*. But it's Kubrick re-thought and re-humanised, with career-best work from Clooney and McElhone helping us feel our way through what's essentially a relationship movie in space. Their dilemma would lack a vital animating force, it should be added, without Cliff Martinez's quite remarkable ambient score, which beeps and throbs throughout like the inner workings of a clinically curious alien intelligence.

THE DISC

Beyond the movie, pretty anomalous in its own right, this disc's USP is producer James Cameron's one and only commentary track to date, in the company of Soderbergh. While yeah-yeahing the idea that his own version would probably have had 'lots of car chases', the *Titanic* maestro is able to complement Soderbergh on the integrity of his choices without this ever devolving into a mutual back-slap: it's a conversation between two very savvy film artists bringing in all sorts of rewarding sidebar observations. Both are rightly impressed by Clooney, a genuine revelation here – it's a pity his input on the DVD is limited to a couple of cursory promo spots. The elephant in the room is *Solaris*'s grim fate at the multiplexes, but beyond berating themselves for not getting on the case with a coherent marketing strategy, the duo stifle any disappointment and shrug. The film's the thing. (Presented anamorphically here, it looks a treat.) (TIM ROBEY)

Some Like It Hot

(USA, 1959) Special Edition

Director: Billy Wilder
Label: MGM (UK)
Region: 2 (PAL)
Discs: 1

THE FILM

Set in the prohibition era, Billy Wilder's most famous film teams Jack Lemmon (Jerry/Daphne) and Tony Curtis (Joe/Josephine) as impoverished musicians who, to save their lives, dress as women and join an all-girl band after witnessing the St Valentine's Day massacre. Joe romances the band's singer, Sugar Kane Kowalczyk (Marilyn Monroe), while Jerry is pursued by a millionaire, Osgood Fielding III (Joe E Brown). Wilder's interest in role-playing and transformation is fundamental to the comedy, which casts an unsparingly ironic eye on various types of pretence (not excluding the gangsters' posturing) and confusion: Sugar seeks to break her series of unhappy relationships with saxophonists and marry a millionaire; Joe is a saxophonist pretending to be a woman as well as pretending to be a millionaire (and impersonating Cary Grant in the process); while the millionaire, instead of directing his attentions to Sugar, becomes engaged to a man – and one who intends (like Fielding's previous spouses) to marry him for the alimony.

Thus *Some Like it Hot*'s immortal final line, 'Well, nobody's perfect', spoken by Fielding after Jerry has revealed his gender, not only ridicules the conventional happy ending, but also certifies the estranged relationship between desire and reality in the film. Lemmon and Curtis, who will always be remembered for this, deliver superb performances. Monroe's Sugar – a touching portrayal combining sexiness and vulnerability – is all the more memorable for appearing to be the actress's self-portrait.

THE DISC

Leonard Maltin gives Tony Curtis a gentle quizzing in the half-hour 'Nostalgic Look Back' interview feature. Curtis recalls that he visited the set even when not working, as there was so much to be learned from Wilder. Wilder is praised for his patience and skilled handling of performers. Lemmon and Curtis insisted that their dresses, as well as Monroe's, be designed by Orry-Kelly; and, although they were helped by a female impersonator, the actors' attempts to pass themselves off as women in public did not invariably succeed (seeing Josephine as more refined than Daphne, Curtis modelled her on Grace Kelly!). The surviving members of the all-girl band Sweet Sues, evidently, still delighted with their roles in the film, are also gathered for a juicy trip down memory lane, and there are film clips, photos and soundbites arranged by performer in the 20-minute 'Virtual Hall of Memories'. There's also a gallery of the film's original press materials, and trailers for a selection of Wilder's other movies. The anamorphic 1.85:1 transfer looks excellent, while the sound is remixed to Dolby 5.1. (No original mono version, sadly.) (ADAM STREVENS)

The Sorrow and the Pity

(West Germany/Switzerland, 1969)

Director: Marcel Ophüls
Label: Arrow Films (UK)
Region: 0 (PAL)
Discs: 2

THE FILM

Modestly subtitled 'Chronicle of a French City under the German Occupation', Marcel Ophüls' legendary film is as much a study of memory and self-deception à la Resnais or Marker as the 'four-hour documentary on Nazis' famously fought over in *Annie Hall*. Intended to interrupt de Gaulle's amnesiac Alphaville with an unforgettable flashback, the film contradicted the Big Lie of post-war France, inscribed in films like Melville's *Army of Shadows*, also released in 1969, that the nation had been united in its resistance to Nazism and loyalty to de Gaulle.

Ophüls' pointed juxtaposition of contemporary newsreel and interviews with former (and not so former) supporters, contestants and all-too-passive observers of the Vichy regime and Occupation in Clermont-Ferrand reveals a society still multiply divided by its conduct a quarter of a century before, but unwilling publicly to acknowledge the fact. Interviewees are sometimes shown in profile, rehearsing often-evasive arguments, as if justifying their actions – or failure to act – to themselves.

Although there is nothing positively admirable in the conduct of those who spent the war years 'getting by', the cumulative effect of the film over four hours is to bring the war home to its viewers, challenging still-prevalent Anglo-Saxon assumptions of moral superiority and 'It Couldn't Have Happened Here' hubris. By treating its themes of occupation, resistance and collaboration with uncommon integrity and historical intelligence, *The Sorrow and the Pity* could hardly be more pertinent today.

THE DISCS

In a long interview filmed in 2004, Ophüls takes us through the twists of fate that led him reluctantly from fiction into documentary filmmaking, and then brought about the production of his most famous film by German television, where he was – reversing his father Max's journey three decades prior – in professional exile following his involvement in the May 1968 'événements' in Paris.

Ophüls explains to a London audience that he and his fellow protesters within the French state broadcaster ORTF had campaigned 'quite explicitly' for the autonomy from political control enshrined in the BBC's charter. A token of their failure was ORTF's refusal to show the film even after Ophüls had successfully picked up financing elsewhere; as he relates in the interview, it took a press campaign mounted by the likes of François Truffaut and Louis Malle to get the film its Paris debut in a small Left Bank cinema. Though Ophüls won't call it censorship, the film was not broadcast in France for a full decade. (HENRY K MILLER)

The Spirit of the Beehive

(Spain, 1973)

Director: Victor Erice
Label: Criterion Collection (USA)
Region: 1 (NTSC)
Discs: 1

THE FILM

Victor Erice's mesmerising fable stands alongside Bergman's *Fanny and Alexander* as one of the cinema's great evocations of childhood and its imaginative yearnings. Set in a remote Castilian village in the aftermath of the Spanish Civil War, the film unfolds as a sequence of haunting vignettes, depicting a community drained of its vitality and fractured into lonely individuals locked into private worlds. Following a screening of James Whale's *Frankenstein* in the village hall, eight-year-old Ana (Ana Torrent) becomes obsessed with befriending the spirit of the film's creature, which her precocious older sister Isabel (Isabel Tellería) has told her is roaming the nearby countryside. While their mother pines for her absent lover and their father broods over his bees, Ana's inchoate desire to commune with a monstrous soulmate finds an unexpected outlet when she stumbles on a fugitive Republican soldier taking refuge in an isolated barn.

Fans of socio-political subtexts and Freudian undercurrents will find plenty here to pick over, but the real strength of Erice's approach is that nothing feels forced or schematic, while the winning naturalism of the two young performers banishes all sense of contrivance. The film's most indelible sequences explore points at which a childish sense of 'play' edges into darker, crueller territory: Isabel is scratched by her cat after she idly starts to strangle it, and then – experimentally, sensually – smears the blood onto her lips; later, she feigns her own death to test out her sister's reaction. Films which sentimentalise children are two a penny, but for Erice childhood is fraught with anxieties and far from carefree. As incarnated with wide-eyed intensity by Torrent, Ana lives in a state of fearful wonderment and an almost mystically heightened consciousness, disturbingly absorbed by the junctures of life and death (dangerous train tracks, poisonous mushrooms, a potentially murderous monster stitched from corpses) – as if Eros and Thanatos are warring for possession of her soul.

THE DISC

Criterion's new anamorphic transfer is impressive, doing justice to cinematographer Luis Cuadrado's painterly tableaux and helping convey the film's masterly use of landscapes and changing natural light to set its complex moods. A touch sharper than Optimum's non-anamorphic R2 version, it's also much more generous with extras. The second disc includes two featurettes: an hour-long interview with Victor Erice in a Madrid cafe, recorded in 2000, and the fine Spanish doc 'The Footprints of a Spirit', retracing the film's locations in Hoyuelos, Castille, with the adult Ana Torrent. Cast and crew talk us through the film's themes and inspirations, which Erice suggests began with the girl-and-monster scene from *Frankenstein*: 'Everything you could say was captured in that image.' There are also shorter standalone interviews with venerable star Fernando Fernán Gómez and Erice scholar Linda C Ehrlich, and liner notes by Paul Julian Smith. (ANDY RICHARDS)

A Star is Born

(USA, 1954)

Director: George Cukor
Label: Warners (all territories)
Region: Any
Discs: 2

THE FILM

It's perverse how often Tinseltown likes to tell this archetypal story of its own fickleness and voracity, about one star rising as another plummets. George Cukor's *What Price Hollywood?* (1932) had a waitress taken under the wing of a washed-up producer; William Wellman directed the Janet Gaynor/Fredric March *A Star is Born* (1937) to seven Oscar nominations; and Cukor returned to the material for this glitzy musical remake, lavishly enjoyable to the nth degree, and fascinating for both its dark-side-of-showbiz critique and its bizarre self-congratulation for same.

The oddest thing is Judy Garland, giving the performance of her career but at quite the wrong end of it: she'd been dumped by MGM five years earlier, and though this was touted as her big comeback she wouldn't appear on screen again until *Judgment at Nuremberg* (1961). Cukor's movie, hatched by Garland's producer husband Sidney Luft to put her back in the public eye, proved both a rebirth and a farewell, at least to musical megastardom. And the ironies just keep mounting: Garland's Vicki Lester ends by delivering a eulogy in song to self-destructive other half Norman Maine (James Mason, magnificent), but her own battles with booze and amphetamines had sent Garland into irreversible Maine-like decline by this point, and Mason himself would deliver her funeral oration 15 years later.

Even without these screwy biographical parallels, Cukor's film would well know the cruel, cannibalistic appetite of celebrity, and if its three strategically placed red-carpet galas make the movie feel like one long awards ceremony for itself, it's one that rarely goes according to plan. Garland belts out the big numbers as if her life depended on it – and, in her mind, perhaps it did.

THE DISCS

Though Jack Warner threw on a huge premiere and afterparty – both shown here in newsreels – he was less kind to *A Star is Born* after its first run, hacking a good half-hour off the 181-minute running time. Not all of the original footage survives, but a 1983 reconstruction job was achieved using audio outtakes and filling in the gaps with publicity stills – a brave choice, but one you get used to, given the otherwise glistening restoration work. Disc 2's other perks include several alternate versions of Judy's first song, 'The Man Who Got Away', which suggest studio tinkering with costume and design choices until quite a late stage; and trailers, too, for the Wellman version and the much-derided 1976 Barbra Streisand/Kris Kristofferson one. (TIM ROBEY)

Starship Troopers

(USA, 1997) Special Edition

Director: Paul Verhoeven
Label: Buena Vista (USA)
Region: 1 (NTSC)
Discs: 2

THE FILM

Starship Troopers was made at a time when America – or at least Hollywood's America – had no enemies, so, like its contemporaries *Independence Day* and *Mars Attacks!*, it turned to alien evil to supply this lack. Those were both essentially Clintonian films and viewed militarism with unease bordering on disdain; and both play now like period pieces. *Starship Troopers*, however, increasingly looks like the defining motion picture of the Bush era, an aptly pre-emptive strike against neo-conservatism on the rise. Its ground troops are not defending Earth from invasion but peremptorily engaging an enemy on its home turf, panicked by WMDs, accompanied by embeds, uninterested in debate because . . . hell, there's a war on.

Based on Robert Heinlein's 1959 novel and following the educational, military and romantic progression of a group of conspicuously plastic teens, the film expertly blends elements of WWII propaganda (from Allied 'Why We Fight' films to Riefenstahlian aesthetics) with accomplished pastiches of contemporary US news media. In fact it is, as its writer Ed Neumeier notes on the DVD commentary, 'a fascist action adventure film' and director Paul Verhoeven's audacious approach was to present it entirely on its own terms, challenging audiences to recognise that sympathy to leading characters should not be granted automatically or on the basis of rousing presentation alone. The result is a spectacularly shiny shell, a triumphalist picture of a soulless world in which choice and freedom are name-checked but, on closer inspection, sex and sacrifice are cultivated as sufficient ambitions. Viewed as a relic from a future world – a promotional picture encouraging 23rd-century youth to sign up – it presents a cogent picture of a brutal society's willing self-delusion.

THE DISCS

Overarching irony not being a conventional component of the big-budget blockbuster, most critics took *Starship Troopers* at face value on its initial release. As a result, Verhoeven and Neumeier felt obliged to deliver a DVD commentary in which they repeatedly stress that yes, they are fully aware of the fascist undertones of their feature and no, they don't think audiences should simply cheer at them. Overall, the commentary offers an unusually politicised take on Hollywood aesthetics; note the opening disclaimer that the opinions expressed don't necessarily reflect those of its production company, Buena Vista, a Disney subsidiary. It's also instructive to compare the somewhat gung-ho promo film made for the film's initial release and the more sophisticated, defensive one made for this disc. Throw in a couple more commentaries – from the cast and, unusually but informatively, the composer – plus the usual storyboards and effects featurettes and it adds up to a Federation-sized package. (BEN WALTERS)

Stop Making Sense

(USA, 1984)

Director: Jonathan Demme
Label: Palm Pictures (UK/USA)
Region: 2 (PAL) / 0 (NTSC)
Discs: 1

THE FILM

There isn't a miniature Stonehenge in sight in Jonathan Demme's electrifying concert movie about Talking Heads. Recorded over three nights at Hollywood's Pantages Theater, *Stop Making Sense* unfurls with astonishing fluidity. From the moment the band's big-suited lead singer David Byrne walks onstage, accompanied by a boombox and a guitar, we witness a remarkable live performance coming together.

Byrne is soon joined by bassist Tina Weymouth, before black-clad stagehands spring from the wings to set up Chris Frantz's drumkit. And then a black curtain drops, backing musicians appear, and the entire cast is on stage at last.

According to Byrne, Demme knew 'what not to film'. Wisely, he focused on Talking Heads' enigmatic front man playing with an effects pedal or serenading a lamp, rather than waste time filming the crowd.

The music is fiercely inventive, too. From the elegant restraint of 'Heaven' and 'Naïve Melody', to the triumphant riot of 'Burning Down the House' and 'Life During Wartime', Talking Heads are at the top of their game. When *Stop Making Sense* was first released, audiences stood up and danced in the aisles. Two decades on, it dares you to do the same.

THE DISC

'Like *60 Minutes* on acid,' Byrne describes the look he wanted to give the film. His droll remarks are part of a loopy segment in which he interviews himself in various guises, one of several highlights on the Palm Pictures special edition.

As well as a Talking Heads discography and band member bios, there's an explanation of the infamous big suit – it was originally doodled on a napkin and influenced by kabuki theatre costumes – and the stylish trailer for the 15th-anniversary release of the film. The commentary track is a gem too, with Demme joining all four Heads in a lively discussion that covers everything from the title art and the lighting, to the stage design and the story behind particular songs.

Equally fascinating is Byrne's original storyboard, which illustrates how meticulously planned and theatrical the three concerts were, and provides names for each of Byrne's dances. And, as a treat, the special edition includes two bonus songs – 'Cities' and 'Big Business/I Zimbra'. (JAMES CLASPER)

Strange Days

(USA, 1995)

Director: Kathryn Bigelow
Label: Universal (UK)
Region: 2 (PAL)
Discs: 1

THE FILM

In 1995, director Kathryn Bigelow and writers James Cameron and Jay Cocks committed a prediction to celluloid. Come the turn of the century, their film *Strange Days* suggested, America would be comprehensively split along racial lines, its public distracted from harsher realities by shiny metallic discs loaded with all the sex and violence one might want to see. Not too far off the mark, as it happens.

Ralph Fiennes's Lenny Nero deals in clips: tiny fragments of other people's lives, snatched straight from the cerebral cortex. Making a life for himself as the world falls down around him – peddling amateur pornography to businessmen in strip joints – Lenny heads blithely towards New Year's Eve, 1999, until the combination of a young woman's death and the arrival of kick-ass chauffeur Mace (Angela Bassett) shakes him from his complacency.

Exhilarating, disturbing, and sometimes overwhelming, this is what *Peeping Tom* might look like replayed as a mainstream studio's big-budget action picture. It's certainly one of the few '90s action movies to interrogate, as well as satisfy, its audience's desires, fully aware that voyeurism is a drug (the clips come 'pure' and 'uncut'), while conceding its effects can be both good *and* bad.

Hold on to your *English Patients* and *Constant Gardeners*: for this writer, this remains Fiennes's finest hour, cast disarmingly against type as a knight in the most tarnished armour. Bassett, too, has never been better, as a template for an entirely different kind of action heroine, and it's hard not to underplay the significance of having women in control of this material. Male directors, from Hitchcock to Verhoeven, have tended to get as hooked on voyeurism as their leading characters, but Bigelow invests the film with something else: an understanding that spectacle is nothing without a fulfilling emotional life.

THE DISC

Region-for-region, the extras prove somewhat less visionary than the main feature. Fox's R1 disc has but a couple of negligible deleted scenes and trailers; Universal's R2 disc comes without the deleted scenes, but with a featurette detailing two of the more challenging set-pieces. Be warned, though: Bigelow's 'director's commentary' comprises a 50-minute taped lecture that runs asynchronous to the action. Worse still, the UK disc features a cut version of the film, its pivotal rape-murder scene having fallen foul of BBFC guidelines on sexual violence. (Kinowelt's 2-disc Special Edition on R2 has the most comprehensive set of extras, but they're predominantly in German.) (MIKE McCAHILL)

Stranger than Paradise

(USA, 1984)

Director: Jim Jarmusch
Label: Kinowelt (Germany)
Region: 2 (PAL)
Discs: 1

THE FILM

Jim Jarmusch's sophomore feature (after 1980's fledgling *Permanent Vacation*) blew in like a cool north wind in 1984. If John Cassavetes's DIY streak had, until then, been glossed over as a cinematic anomaly, *Stranger than Paradise*, along with the Coens' **Blood Simple**, heralded an independent wave that the mainstream could not ignore. And that title seemed to capture the serene oddness of Jarmusch's vision.

Strikingly minimalist, the film fronts its laconic study of three young drifters through Tom DiCillo's crisp monochrome images and a rhythm as languid as the characters' own, poised somewhere between identification and ironic detachment. Eva (Eszter Balint) flies in from Budapest to a New York neighbourhood seemingly paved with crumbs. Her loafer cousin Willie (John Lurie), who has shunned his Hungarian heritage, grudgingly puts her up for ten days; his sidekick Eddie (Richard Edson) even shows an interest in talking to her. A year later, they're ready to go visit Eva at her aunt's in Cleveland, from where all three make a road trip to an equally desultory Florida.

Eva is the first of a series of immigrants and outsiders in Jarmusch's art (to be followed by Roberto Benigni in *Down By Law*, Nicoletta Braschi and the Japanese couple in *Mystery Train*, and several subsequent multi-ethnic ensembles) – and for all the film's deadpan style, it's clear he's reaching for a view of grassroots American myths and realities. Willie affects a beat pose, but he's stultifying in his aimlessness and isolation; and where some of his countrymen toil for a living (there's a brief, poignant kerbside encounter between Willie and a New York factory worker, waiting for his bus), others see cheating and gambling as a way of life. Jarmusch gets the boys' cool, but he can see beyond it: with wry humour and glimmers of emotional thawing, the film is both bleak beat existentialism and an exquisitely open book.

THE DISC

Kinowelt's Region 2 German disc comes in a smooth anamorphic transfer, with a handful of Jarmusch trailers and his brother Tom's 15-minute behind-the-scenes doc 'January 1984: *Stranger than Paradise* in Cleveland', a silent Super-8 home movie that shows but doesn't tell. Don't buy the American MGM disc, which chops the latter in half and has a wretchedly noisy soundtrack. Jarmusch's follow-up, *Down by Law*, is available in a generous double-disc Criterion Collection set, with extras ranging from the director's phone calls with his cast to a Tom Waits music video – but the film doesn't cut quite as deep as *Stranger than Paradise*. (A Criterion Collection edition was in the works at the time of going to press.) (NICK BRADSHAW)

A Streetcar Named Desire

(USA, 1951) Special Edition

Director: Elia Kazan
Label: Warner (UK/USA)
Region: 2 (PAL) / 1 (NTSC)
Discs: 2

THE FILM

In an age when Hollywood rarely casts an eye to the Broadway stage for inspiration – and when wan adaptations of prizewinners like *Proof* make the plays themselves look meagre in retrospect – Kazan's magisterial transfer of *A Streetcar Named Desire* looms even more largely as a summit of realist drama on screen. Curiously, given the film's cultural stature, Kazan's *Streetcar* is by no means a definitive realisation of Tennessee Williams' text. Well beyond the usual emendations and spatial expansions required by the screen, the very upshot of the final sequence has been changed, and entire stylistic and musical registers of the script have been sacrificed to the film's emphasis on dank, tactile realism.

Still, this vision of the play has stayed iconic for very, very good reasons: the score, the ingenious blocking of the action and the sightlines, the low-contrast grayscale photography, simultaneously the dull colour of cobwebs and evocative use of incredible visual detail in every frame. And then, of course, there are the two miracles named Vivien Leigh and Marlon Brando, equal and opposite conductors of blazing electricity that invite and startle the camera's gaze without losing the element of theatrical self-creation, improvisation and expressive artifice.

THE DISCS

The two-disc version of *A Streetcar Named Desire* is an embarrassment of riches, not least for the shimmering clarity and well-preserved depth of the images. Karl Malden appears alongside two film historians for an unusually gratifying commentary track, in which he recalls key details of the filming process, such as the moveable walls that made the Kowalskis' apartment even more claustrophobic as the story unfolds. He is also generous with fond personal anecdotes about interactions with Brando, including their debates over the very different Blanches of Vivien Leigh and their Broadway co-star Jessica Tandy.

A bouquet of documentaries on the second disc illuminates the stage history of *Streetcar*, the adaptation process, the careers of Brando and Kazan, the music and the run-ins with censors. The jewel in this set for many viewers will be the rare out-takes of on-set footage and the even rarer excerpts of Brando's screen test. Finally, the film and its supplementary materials are perhaps best viewed in light of the full 'Tennessee Williams Film Collection' of which it was the centrepiece. Kazan's *Baby Doll*, from an original screenplay by Williams, takes more risks than *Streetcar* does with the playwright's humour and expressionistic style, and even the bowdlerised productions of *Sweet Bird of Youth* and *The Roman Spring of Mrs. Stone* help to place *Streetcar*'s themes and textures within the wider, weirder web of Williams' concerns. (NICK DAVIS)

Sunrise: A Song of Two Humans

(USA, 1927)

Director: FW Murnau
Label: Eureka (UK)
Region: 2 (NTSC)
Discs: 1

THE FILM

Murnau's story of a country couple renewing their love after weathering infidelity and intrigue is amongst the most beautiful films ever made. Brought to America on the back of his German successes, the *Nosferatu* director was given carte blanche at Fox, and the film shows a talented artist making hay with the resources of Hollywood. Murnau believed that a sufficiently expressive camera could 'photograph thought', and *Sunrise* treats a potentially risible story with pathos and conviction.

The impassioned performances are part and parcel of the film's lyricism. Tempted by his mistress from the city, a farmer (George O'Brien) takes his wife (Janet Gaynor) for a boat trip across the lake, meaning to drown her. Overcome by remorse at the last moment, he follows her into town, where the jazz and bustle of the modern city blows away their tensions and revives their old tenderness. Then the storm clouds gather once more . . .

Released just weeks before *The Jazz Singer* grabbed audiences by the ears, *Sunrise* stands with *The Passion of Joan of Arc* at the pinnacle of silent cinema. The sparsity of intertitles is as almost as remarkable as Murnau's fluid camera moves and dynamic use of space. The countryside photography quotes from the Dutch masters, while the exaggerated city set designs borrow from Bauhaus. Perhaps the ending is a little hokey; but if Murnau ever bettered this, it was only in his (less Manichean) later Hollywood work *City Girl*, still awaiting rediscovery . . .

THE DISC

Now reduced to one disc, Eureka's latest edition essentially replicates the Region 1 Fox disc, and both are excellent. The transfer is a progressively encoded, high-def transfer from a 2003 preservation negative; the images won't ever be immaculate, but the contrast is rich and deep. The original mono Movietone score has also been remastered; with its diegetic sound effects, it's preferable to Timothy Brock's more experimental stereo alternative, recorded with the Olympic Chamber Orchestra.

Cinematographer John Bailey, a protegé of the film's co-DP Karl Struss, provides a technically illuminating commentary on the film and ten minutes of out-takes. There's also a trailer, a PDF of Carl Mayer's original scenario and screenplay (with Murnau's hand-written annotations), and Janet Bergstrom's 40-minute documentary 'Murnau's *4 Devils*: Traces of a Lost Film', sketching Murnau's vanished follow-up to *Sunrise*. On top of that, Eureka's set adds a 40-page illustrated booklet with essays by Robin Wood, Lotte Eisner and more. (There's also an Easter egg in the disc's out-takes section: pressing Left brings up a single still of Murnau lying in his coffin.) (NICK BRADSHAW)

Sunset Boulevard

(USA, 1950)

Director: Billy Wilder
Label: Paramount (all territories)
Region: Any
Discs: 1

THE FILM

Fifty years into the cinema's lifespan, with its pioneers just beginning to die off, regular collaborators Wilder and Charles Brackett (along with entertainment journo DM Marshman Jr) came up with one of the biggest and most morbid of all Hollywood in-jokes. *Sunset Boulevard*'s punchline is almost secondary to how it's told: by the late screenwriter Joe Gillis (William Holden), introduced floating face-down in a pool belonging to reclusive diva Norma Desmond (Gloria Swanson), fallen idol of the silent screen.

It's still a remarkably transgressive film, persuading backlot legends (Cecil B DeMille, Buster Keaton, Hedda Hopper) to play not-especially-flattering versions of themselves and demoting director Erich von Stroheim to the status of a Lurch-like butler. Many scenes are simply turned over to Swanson's performance, which is amazingly stylised − it's a 1930s performance in a 1950s film, and a 1930s horror-show at that, curled hands as claws beneath a barracuda smile − but has passed into movie, not to mention drag-act, lore.

Underpinning all the baroque theatrics is an ahead-of-the-curve understanding of fame-as-commodity, and a credible relationship based on money, mutual need and outright desperation. Notice that the title appears on screen not as a roadsign, but on a kerbstone in the gutter: Wilder here gets to the bottom of a Hollywood state of mind, offering a dazzlingly articulate explanation for why so many films and careers continue to end up dead in the water.

THE DISC

Compiled just after Wilder's death in 2002, this is a respectful packaging of one of the treasures of the studio system. A smart, amiable commentary by author Ed Sikov identifies sell-outs like Gillis as central to the director's work and proves strong on the details of Swanson's performance. *Boulevard* aficionados should also be fascinated by the reconstruction of the film's bizarre morgue prologue, rejected by early test audiences.

There are as many knick-knacks here as there are in Norma Desmond's mansion: a fun location-map feature, galleries that highlight the routinely high standard of still photography of the era, the trailer ('announcing the most unusual motion picture in many years'), and substantial featurettes on costume designer Edith Head and composer Franz Waxman. In a 25-minute making-of, supporting player Nancy Olson reveals how von Stroheim used to edge his chair closer and closer to where Wilder was directing: further proof, if the film itself wasn't enough, of the spell the movie camera can cast. (MIKE McCAHILL)

Jan Svankmajer: The Complete Short Films

(Czechoslovakia, 1964–92)

Director: Jan Svankmajer
Label: BFI (UK)
Region: 2 (PAL)
Discs: 3

THE FILMS

Like a last-surviving dragon from more fanciful days of yore, Jan Svankmajer lies in his Czech lair, issuing the occasional fiery snort to remind humankind of its laughably poxy perversity. Last of the great card-carrying Surrealists, he connects us to multiple old eras – of Eastern European Communist repression, of engaged and visionary art, even of medieval magickry – that are not entirely bygone, as he endeavours to remind us. His predominantly stop-motion-animated films render puppets, putty, found objects and live actors with equal paranormal feverishness; the results are both cinematically visceral and philosophically disturbing, transcending their immediate political contexts to offer endlessly eerie and unnerving lowdowns on the human black comedy.

Since his 1988 Lewis Carroll adaptation *Alice*, and with the frosty funding climate of the market economy, Svankmajer has moved apparently exclusively towards feature-filmmaking. His short films, though, not only made his reputation but are often his most succinct and astringent pieces; 1982's *Dimensions of Dialogue*, for instance, a brief triptych of lessons in mutually assured destruction, is an excoriating masterpiece.

The BFI's new set collects all 26 of Svankmajer's shorts work over two discs, 'Early Shorts 1964–72' and 'Late Shorts 1979–92', bisected by his years of enforced filmmaking sabbatical. You can watch the films chronologically, of course, but check out the curated programmes, whose titles say it all: styles and subjects here include Human Protagonists (typically early work: *The Flat*, *A Quiet Week in the House*), Puppets and Theatre, Stones and Bones (*Historia Naturae*, *The Ossuary*), Stop-Motion Animation, Two-Dimensional Animation, Claymation, Fear and Curiosity (the Sisyphean nursery nightmare *Down to the Cellar*), Food (*Meat Love*), Gothic Literature (Poe adaptations *The Fall of the House of Usher* and *The Pendulum, the Pit and Hope*), Oppression (*The Death of Stalinism in Bohemia*) and Tactilism. There's even a rare commissioned work – a music video for Hugh Cornwell's 'Another Kind of Love', unmistakeable as everything else here.

THE DISCS

Elsewhere – i.e. on the third disc – there's a new Brothers Quay introduction with the full-length doc 'The Cabinet of Jan Svankmajer', glimpses of Svankmajer's features and work with his wife Eva in the hour-long French doc 'Les Chimères de Svankmajer', Czech TV interviews with the pair, Emil Radok's 1958 short *Johanes Doktor Faust* (Svankmajer's first screen credit), and his mid-'70s special effects work-for-hire. All the shorts are new digital remasters, in native PAL, and look quite triumphant; even the menus offer a sampler medley of the treats to come. The booklet carries a page of BFI notes, old and new, on each of the films. (NICK BRADSHAW)

Margaret Tait: Selected Films 1952-76

(UK, 1952–76)

Director: Margaret Tait
Label: Lux (UK)
Region: 0 (PAL)
Discs: 1

THE FILMS

Until recently one of the UK's most shamefully neglected but wildly talented artist filmmakers, the fiercely independent Tait worked entirely at the edges of both the industry mainstream and the geographical mainland, living between Edinburgh and the Scottish Orkney islands. The author, over five decades, of over 30 shorts and one feature (the inspirational *Blue Black Permanent*), as well as three volumes of poetry and two of short stories, she made almost all her work without any formal funding, driven, like many of her peer group in the United States, towards a recording of the heightened, phenomenal world through close observation of her immediate environment and daily life. Through her own company Ancona Films, set up after she returned from formal study in Rome at the height of the neorealist movement, she set about making what she called 'film poems', often quoting the Spanish poet Lorca's claim to be 'stalking the image' to define both her intention and method.

This idea of absolute attention to everyday objects, locations and weathers, coupled with an innate sense of seasonal and aesthetic rhythms, gives her short work the intensity of a lyric without any sacrifice of the accessibility her subject matter suggested. *Portrait of Ga* (1952), the earliest work included here, is a study of the deepest origin, a voyage around Tait's mother. In a similar vein, *Place of Work* (1976), at 30 minutes one of the longest pieces, explores the long-time family home in Orkney in the months before it had to be vacated. *Aerial* (1974) and *Colour Poems* (1974), on the other hand, deal with the elements and include some animation directly onto the filmstock. However, her masterpiece is perhaps *Where I Am Is Here* (1964), a 33-minute symphony of amplifying patterns and hues, a moving paean to the passing beauty of things that exemplifies Tait's singular approach to both film and the world.

THE DISC

A debut DVD from the London-based artists' film and video archive Lux, this no-frills disc offers no extras, but a handsome presentation of eight of Tait's restored films (those mentioned above plus *Hugh MacDiarmid, a Portrait* (1964), *John MacFayden (The Stripes in the Tartan)* (1970) and *Tailpiece* (1976)). You can also find the texts produced for the Lux's magnificent companion catalogue *Subjects and Sequences* – essays, statements, poems, stories and interviews by and about Tait – online at *lux.org.uk/margarettait*. (GARETH EVANS)

The Talented Mr Ripley
(USA, 1999)

Director: Anthony Minghella
Label: Buena Vista (UK) / Paramount (USA)
Region: 2 (PAL) / 1 (NTSC)
Discs: 1

THE FILM

Forget *The English Patient*; Minghella *al massimo* is to be found in his dark, layered adaptation of Patricia Highsmith's cracking Italian-set novel about the duplicitous and ultimately murderous Tom Ripley. With considerable help from cinematographer John Seale, Minghella lures us in with the sun-drenched hues of the Neapolitan Riviera, 1958-style. He then lets the shadowy alleyways and cavernous palazzi of Rome and Venice darken the mood as Ripley's increasingly intricate deception, and the undertones of class envy and homoeroticism, mount.

It's no surprise that Minghella, with his microscopic attention to detail, tends to draw career-best performances from his actors. Matt Damon uses his blond-bland face to considerable advantage as Ripley, presenting it as a blank canvas ready to be painted over with the bright colours of other people's lives, loves and good fortune. The *dolce vita* he particularly craves is that belonging to Dickie Greenleaf, and as this trust-fund playboy Jude Law positively gleams with health and wealth. Gwyneth Paltrow too, as Dickie's girlfriend Marge, was surely born to wear the headbands and tight-waisted skirts of the post-war American woman abroad, and there are outstanding supporting turns from the likes of Cate Blanchett, Philip Seymour Hoffman and Jack Davenport.

It's rare to find a piece that looks this gorgeous – the Italian tourist board itself couldn't have come up with a better advert for the country – while simultaneously stumping up as much searing, though subtle, social commentary. A long-term lack of money, not to mention love, can be corrosive: Minghella knows and shows this, which is why, disturbingly, thrillingly, we end up rooting for a killer.

THE DISC

No wonder Minghella takes so long over his films. 'I try to make every single moment in the movie do more than one job', he relates during an incisive audio commentary. Who would have guessed, for instance, that the bust (of Hadrian, as Minghella carefully explains) that plays a fleeting yet vital part could have such a carefully thought-out back-story?

This should be required listening for aspiring filmmakers, as Minghella elaborates on the minutiae of each frame, each scene. There are enjoyable tales from the shoot, too, of the behaviour of Ripley's most capricious player: the Italian countryside itself. 'Italy in 1998–99 had absolutely no interest in being Italy in 1958–59', Minghella says wryly of the hordes of tourists who objected to their sightseeing being interrupted by the likes of Paltrow.

The rest of the disc is more routine publicity guff, although the cast at least try to bring their smarts to bear. There are two making-of featurettes, on the film and its soundtrack, and a couple of clip montages masquerading as 'music videos'. No major complaints with the tech specs. (FIONA MOUNTFORD)

Talk to Her

(Spain, 2002)

Director: Pedro Almodóvar
Label: Sony (USA)
Region: 1 (NTSC)
Discs: 2

ORIGINAL TITLE: *Habla con Ella*

THE FILM

Judging by its outline, Almodóvar's tale might sound like a wilfully contrived piece of whimsy. Two men sit side by side at the ballet. One starts to cry; the other notices. The first is Marco (Darío Grandinetti), a journalist; the second is nurse Benigno (Javier Cámara), who cares for coma victim and dancer Alicia (Leonor Watling) with whom he is more than a little obsessed. Their paths cross again when Marco's lover, a fiery female matador (Rosario Flores), is gored by a bull and ends up comatose in Benigno's hospital. But as their analogous, but opposingly experienced situations — Marco struggling to come to terms with his now lifeless lover, Benigno deliriously fulfilled living vicariously for the sleeping Alicia — unite them in friendship, Almodóvar takes you into areas of emotion and thought that few other filmmakers could dream of.

Touching on the nature of love, obsession and identity, *Talk to Her* emerges as a gently seesawing complex of relationships that settle towards a point of poignant equilibrium in the theatre in which it opened. Propelling us there are several sensual performance pieces: routines from choreographer Pino Bausch's dancers; a sublime serenade by Brazilian Caetano Veloso, his resonant voice raising hairs not just on the characters' necks; and a surreal silent-movie pastiche in which a shrunken man climbs inside his lover's vagina, never to return. All attest to the power of art to bring people together; all attest to Almodóvar's acuity.

THE DISCS

Extras-wise, the main draw is a commentary track with Almodóvar and Geraldine Chaplin, who plays Alicia's dance teacher in the film, and a distinct second-fiddle on the commentary. Despite his intermittent threats to clam up, Almodóvar has plenty to say on the whats, hows and whys of the film, while Chaplin manages the occasional prompt or interjection. Notwithstanding that the track was recorded in Los Angeles (where Almodóvar seems to have had a cold), both talk in Spanish; hence the commentary is given subtitles in place of the film itself, which isn't ideal during the few dialogue scenes that are left to run without comment. The disc's high-definition mastering looks lovely, though. (NICK FUNNELL)

Team America: World Police
(USA, 2004) Special Collector's Edition

Director: Trey Parker
Label: Paramount (all territories)
Region: Any
Discs: 1

THE FILM

Geopolitics Trey Parker/Matt Stone-style was never going to be pretty. With *Team America: World Police*, the *South Park* creators intended to make a Jerry Bruckheimer blockbuster with puppets (and songs): that it was to be set during George W Bush's War on Terror simply offered a whole new range of targets. Team America is a freedom-loving, terrorist-hating task force whose members live inside Mount Rushmore and spend their time having feelings for each other and blowing things up. In a bid to rid the world of rogue WMDs, they embark on a wild ride of puppet sex and vomit, wholesale destruction of world heritage sites, casual racism, patriotic same-sex blow jobs, encounters with panthers, soft-rock anthem renditions and the slaughter of some of Hollywood's leading personalities.

Weapons inspector Hans Blix, North Korea's Kim Jong-Il, Osama Bin Laden and assorted anonymous Middle Eastern terrorists all take a beating, but it's the politically inclined actors of Hollywood that really bear the brunt. Rarely has pomposity been taken down with such savage glee. Explained Stone, by way of motivation, 'When Sean Penn is on CNN before the Iraq War talking about the nuclear non-proliferation treaty ... that is pure comic gold.' In between decapitating Susan Sarandon, demolishing Michael Moore and debasing Matt Damon, Parker and Stone expertly deconstruct the traditional blockbuster over an impeccable three-act curve, while simultaneously skewering American exceptionalism, European finger-pointing and the interminability of *Pearl Harbor*. The message? Don't make films about things you don't understand. Contradictory? Of course. Hilarious? Fuck, yeah!

THE DISC

Unsurprisingly, the DVD doesn't have a commentary track, Parker and Stone perhaps wisely deciding that extended exposure would remove some of the mystery surrounding their political motivations. However, it does include a batch of short films that talk through the making of the puppets and the construction and destruction of their tiny world. Here we learn that the devil is in the detail, and scrupulous use of freeze-frame will reward the viewer with evidence of the filmmakers' judicious use of cheese-graters, nail clippers, silver dollars, croissants and marijuana leaves. There's also a host of deleted scenes – including a couple of gags that really should have made the final cut – and that rarity of rarities, a puppet screen-test. If you want 60 seconds more puppet sex, you should get the 'Uncensored and Unrated Special Collector's Edition', but otherwise there's not a great deal of difference between the various discs available. Picture quality is flawless anamorphic widescreen, and the Dolby Digital 5.1 sound really helps when you're singing along to Kim Jong-Il's tearjerking ballad 'I'm So Ronery'. (PETER WATTS)

Ten & 10 on Ten

(Iran, 2002/2004)

Director: Abbas Kiarostami
Label: mk2 (France)
Region: 2 (PAL)
Discs: 2

THE FILM

The Iranian master Abbas Kiarostami had been making films, mostly for and about children, for nearly 20 years when he came to the world's attention with the Chinese-boxes Koker trilogy (*Where is the Friend's House?*, *And Life Goes On . . .*, and *Through the Olive Trees* (1987–94)), and his reconstructive 1990 documentary about a film fabulist, *Close-Up*. Mixing narrative simplicity, formal reflexivity and rich landscape photography, they are some of the most fecund films of the last 20 years (and unavailable on DVD). In *And Life Goes On . . .*, and in particular with the Beckettian lost figures of *Taste of Cherry* and *The Wind Will Carry Us*, Kiarostami also hit upon the use of cars as a correlate to the landscape – a way into it and bulwark from it.

In light of which, *Ten* is both an extension of his work and something of a new direction. Exploiting the new tool of mini-DV cameras, it's entirely confined to the cabin of a car, and consists of ten sequential dialogues between a Tehrani driver (Mania Akbari) and her passengers: her quarrelsome son Amin, the film's lone (little) man, outraged that she has divorced his father; and also her sister, an older woman going to prayer, a jilted wife, a troubled fiancée and a prostitute. The cinema has often found the car windscreen a seductive analogy for its own window on the world; *Ten* reverses the gaze, fixing its two static, dashboard-mounted cameras on the intimate dramas unfolding within its human landscapes.

Indeed, with Kiarostami the director entirely absent from the location as his non-actors improvised on his outline, the film takes neorealism to a whole new level. Most strikingly of all, though, is its trenchant humanism: it completely invests you in the lives of these modern Iranians.

THE DISCS

Like the same company's gorgeous transfer of *The Wind Will Carry Us*, the French mk2 disc is the one to choose. It includes English subtitles, but also a second disc featuring Kiarostami's video masterclass *10 on Ten*, an elucidation in ten chapters of his approach to cinema, including thoughts on cars, digital cameras and art, non-professional actors and Hollywood. That's also an extra on the Region 1 Zeitgeist disc, but compressed onto the same disc as the film (there's no quibbling to be done about transfer quality, this being a straight re-format of the DV source). Artificial Eye also includes the doc on its two-disc *Taste of Cherry* edition – but with *Ten* is where it belongs. (NICK BRADSHAW)

The Terminator

(USA, 1984) Ultimate Edition

Director: James Cameron
Label: MGM (Europe)
Region: 2 (PAL)
Discs: 2

THE FILM

Watching this seminal slam-bang sci-fi actioner now provokes multiple pangs of nostalgia: for a time when Arnold Schwarzenegger wasn't preoccupied with cultivating a wholesome image on his road to California governorship; for a time before James Cameron anointed himself 'King of the World', when he was a hungry Corman acolyte with *Piranha II: The Spawning* to live down and everything to prove; and for a pre-CGI era when resourceful SFX artists on low-budget pictures had to pull off jaw-dropping feats of ingenuity to create their illusions. The appeal of Cameron's concept lay in the way it presciently tapped into the zeitgeist's fears of our growing dependence on technology to fashion its tale of a soldier (Michael Biehn) travelling back from a post-apocalyptic future to present-day LA to save a waitress (Linda Hamilton) from an implacable cyborg (Arnie, natch) so that she can give birth to the saviour of the human race.

The provenance and originality of the film's plot was debatable (its resemblances to a Harlan Ellison-scripted episode of *The Outer Limits* resulted in an out-of-court settlement), but there's absolutely no denying the brilliance with which Cameron orchestrates proceedings – coaxing memorably intense performances from his couple-on-the-run, staging numerous exciting action set-pieces, and using Schwarzenegger's physicality and Stan Winston's stop-motion effects to create one of the all-time-great movie monsters. *Aliens* (see *The Alien Quadrilogy*) would later confirm Cameron's interest in strong, independent female characters, and here Hamilton's plucky heroine is a breeze to root for, her terrified bewilderment plausibly morphing into tough-minded resourcefulness as she grasps her historic destiny – proving that even the most humble can change the world.

THE DISCS

The Ultimate Edition pretty much lives up to its name, providing a slew of informative documentaries and featurettes describing the film's genesis and execution, as well as its lucrative afterlife as a video smash. One segment looks at the film's impact on other filmmakers as well as the wider culture, while another considers contemporary trends in automated warfare that make the film's 'Rise of the Machines' conceit sound increasingly plausible. Cameron provides a commentary for several deleted sequences (through not, unfortunately, for the film itself), and there are a whole clutch of Easter eggs squirreled away in the menus. (ANDY RICHARDS)

Tetsuo – The Iron Man

(Japan, 1988)

Director: Shinya Tsukamoto
Label: Rarovideo (Italy)
Region: 0 (PAL)
Discs: 3

THE FILM

Shinya Tsukamoto announced himself with a bang with this 67-minute techno-punk blitzkrieg, a demented fever dream of the communion of man and machine. It starts with a young salaryman pursued by ferrous scrap, sprouting iron pimples and then a raging killer-drill penis, while an industrial dervish (played by the director) rams a metal rod into his own thigh. It ends, or almost, with memories of kinky sex over a car crash, true to the spirit of future-human laureates Ballard and Cronenberg. And somewhere in the mix, the salaryman's girlfriend cops a load of that whirling tool . . .

But this isn't really a plot movie. Direct, visceral, head-banging experiential cinema, the film forges a fast and feral syntax that's like a live-action manga scored to Lou Reed's *Metal Machine Music*. Shot in grainy black-and-white 16mm, it makes regular recourse to the stop-motion/pixillation technique reminiscent of Jan Svankmajer's animation; cut in churning quick-time to a clanging industrial score by Chu Ishikawa, it also recalls the nightmarish junkyard surrealism of David Lynch's *Eraserhead*, as filtered through the eyes of Sogo Ishii, from whom Tsukamoto inherited the mantle of *enfant terrible* of Japanese cinema.

Through the years since, he's continued to refine his visions of spiritual discovery through sex and self-mutilation, but for pure cartoon sci-fi virtuosity – think *Godzilla* on poppers – *Tetsuo* really can't be beat.

THE DISCS

Go out of your way for the Italian edition from Rarovideo (*www.rarovideo.com*). Tartan's UK and US discs are fine for quality (the US version includes a DTS soundtrack) – but the Raro set includes two more Tsukamoto movies. Neither is quite *Tetsuo*'s equal, but fans and collectors should certainly turn their heads. Rare and ragged, 1987's *The Adventures of Denchu Kozo* (aka *The Adventure of Electric Rodboy*) is a 47-minute, Super-8, goth sci-fi odyssey, concerning a geek tasked with saving the future from vampires armed with menstrual-blood-powered atomic bombs. The comparatively bombastic *Tetsuo II: Body Hammer* (1992) finds our bespectacled protagonist, now with family, wound back up as a blockbusting blend of Travis Bickle, Hulk and the Terminator. All carry optional English subtitles, as well as Italian. The accompanying booklet is also bilingual; and there's an interview with Tsukamoto in an accompanying video discussion, entitled 'A Video Thing by Enrico Ghezzi'. (NICK BRADSHAW)

The Texas Chain Saw Massacre

(USA, 1974) Special Edition

Director: Tobe Hooper
Label: Universal (UK)
Region: 2 (PAL)
Discs: 1

THE FILM

A camper van full of bell-bottomed hippies revisits a family home in the Lone Star State, only to end up on the menu of a deranged cannibal clan.

Fresh out of film school in Austin, Texas, Hooper, Henkel and friends set out to create a grimly humorous snapshot of the world they saw around them. And in 1973, America, or at least Texas, was not a pretty place, being the era of Vietnam, the Manson family, Watergate, *Last House on the Left* and *Night of the Living Dead*. Hooper and Henkel drew on these already darker-than-night stimuli, wrapping them around the gruesome story of cannibal necrophile Ed Gein and the horrors visible daily on the local TV news.

Shooting over a month in the murderous July heat, the cast and crew decamped to the sticks, where production designer Robert Burns, surely the film's unsung hero, decked out a house with animal bones and human body parts shaped into grisly sculptures and freaky furniture.

The all-too-real blood, sweat and tears paid off. *Texas Chain Saw* justly deserves its legendary status as the mother of all grindhouse films, a near perfect combination of adrenaline-pumping terror, tar-black humour and not-so-subtle social comment. Thirty years later, the film remains amongst the most gruellingly intense, visceral and yet consistently rewarding horror films in history. Its gritty, fly-on-the-wall feel, unrelenting, morbid energy and memorably deranged set pieces keep it feeling as fresh as roadkill and as funny as a hammer to a clown's head.

THE DISC

Despite an impressive clean-up job, the film feels as satisfyingly grimy as ever, while the feast of extras is an example to DVD makers everywhere. Highlights include a feature-length documentary in which the cast and crew reminisce, if that's the right word, about the hellish conditions of the shoot. Commentaries come from Tobe Hooper, cinematographer Daniel Pearl (who would go on to shoot pop videos for the likes of – yikes! – Michael Jackson and Jennifer Lopez) and Gunnar Hansen, who played Leatherface, effectively condemning himself to appear in trashy horror films and *TCSM* spinoffs for the rest of his career. We're also treated to a number of deleted and alternative scenes, bloopers (!) and, best of all, a ten-minute, 8mm tour of Robert Burns's house of horrors itself. (MARK PILKINGTON)

That Obscure Object of Desire

(France, 1977)

Director: Luis Buñuel
Label: Criterion
Collection (USA)
Region: 1 (NTSC)
Discs: 1

FRENCH TITLE: *et Obsur objet du Déser*

THE FILM

Buñuel made his last film almost half a century after his first (*Un Chien Andalou*), and it brings a kind of open closure to one of the greatest bodies of work in cinema.

The movie has heritage. Pierre Louÿs's 1898 source novel *La Femme et la Pantin* ('The Woman and the Puppet') plays pyromaniac matchmaker between the archetypes of Carmen and Casanova, the wanton gypsy mantrap and the stymied would-be lothario; his heroine Conchita is paid for by her would-be sugar daddy Don Mateo, but never sells herself to him. The six movie adaptations include von Sternberg's final Dietrich vehicle *The Devil is a Woman* (1935), and Jacques de Baroncelli's more faithful 1929 version, released just as Buñuel and Dali were preparing *Andalou*. The material's a cinch for Buñuelian sex comedy; *Obscure Object* ranks with *El* (1953) and *The Criminal Life of Archibaldo de la Cruz* (1955) as one of his most gleeful satires of male sexual delusion and dementia. With the director's latter-day alter ego Fernando Rey as Don Mateo, it's also one of his most deadpan suave and discreetly charming.

Buñuel made several surrealist interventions in the text. The mystery sacks that Don Mateo intermittently grasps recall the priest-piano-donkey load that burdens *Andalou*'s lover, as well as the whatsit box in *Belle de Jour*. Most famously, Buñuel cast two actresses as Conchita, Carole Bouquet and Angela Molina, alternating in the role like Perrier and chilli oil. Is the joke on Don Mateo? Us?

Finally, he makes the violence of Mateo and Conchita's perverse relationship, with its dynamics of patriarchy and cock-tease, masochism and sadism, resonate throughout the streets in a series of unaccounted terrorist atrocities. As a young Surrealist, Buñuel had described *Un Chien Andalou* as a 'passionate call to murder', in keeping with the group's incitements to social outrage; in his late years he was struck by how eerily the political terrorism born in the '60s seemed to heed those prompts. Three decades on, the tango of such violence and its partner, repression, has become as routine and desensitizing as *That Obscure Object of Desire* prophesies. Slippery and deadly serious, the film is an uncanny object all its own.

THE DISC

Optimum (UK)'s eight-film Luis Buñuel Collection makes a good primer to the master's French films, but real fans with deep wallets will want to collect Criterion's richer individual releases. No longer state-of-the-art, this 2001 release is anamorphic-transferred and reasonably sharp. The liner notes are somewhat paltry, but the disc undersells its main extra, a comparison of three pivotal scenes in Louÿs' novel and de Baroncelli's 1929 movie. The latter looks beautiful. *That Obscure*'s trailer is amusingly offbeat, too, and there's a useful on-screen interview with Buñuel's screen-writing mainstay Jean-Claude Carrière. (NICK BRADSHAW)

The Thin Red Line
(USA, 1998)

Director: Terrence Malick
Label: 20th Century Fox (all territories)
Region: 1 (NTSC) / 2 (PAL)
Discs: 1

THE FILM

MIA since 1978's *Days of Heaven*, Malick dragged us into the wilderness with this rapt miracle of a late-career comeback, the most nakedly poetic and ruminative megabudget war epic Hollywood has ever dared fund. Nominally adapting James Jones's 1962 novel about America's WWII campaign in Guadalcanal, Malick hopscotches back to the *Iliad* for his tragic vision of earthly paradise and its despoliation, humanity and its assaults on itself, and what men come face to face with when they're cut loose from their own terrain, individuality and moral instinct.

'What's this war in the heart of nature?' drawls rebel dreamer Private Witt (Jim Caviezel, auditioning for Christ), but bear with him: few war-movie protagonists take up such a serene stand in the maelstrom, working out an honest way to live even as artillery fire rips friends' limbs apart. Like Sergeant Welsh (Sean Penn) we're both vexed and seduced by this holy fool; we may or may not know the Greek, as Lt Col Tall (Nick Nolte) does, for 'rosy-fingered dawn', but we recognise a ranting Agamemnon figure when we see one; and in sympathy with Bell (Ben Chaplin), writing home to a faithless Penelope, we can only wonder whether war's microcosmic to-do-list – does a bunker mean much more than a blade of grass? – adds up to a hill of beans if there's no home left to fight for.

Malick's film is a rangy pantheist manifesto and a marvel of democratic collaboration – no Hanks-down deployment of his star power, but almost throwaway cameos for sundry Travoltas and Clooneys while Woody Harrelson promptly blows his ass off. That it climaxes an hour before the end with a heartstopping assault on a Japanese bamboo base makes *The Thin Red Line* structurally awkward, no question, but you could see that as the surest badge of its integrity: narrative checkpoints are all well and good, but when civilisation's in tatters you've got to show the rags.

THE DISC

Adrien Brody thought he had one of the main parts until he saw Malick's finished cut. He might at least have hoped for a deleted scene or two, even if worshippers at the temple of Malick simply *hurt* at the thought of so much unused footage. Will we get a *Thin Red Line Redux*, one day? Please just stop. The R1 transfer is available either with DTS sound and no extras or Dolby 5.1 and 11 Melanesian songs. The R2 edition adds the trailer. The picture quality's more than alright. The movie is – did we mention this? – staggering. (TIM ROBEY)

The Thing

(USA, 1982) Collector's Edition

Director: John Carpenter
Label: Universal (USA)
Region: 1 (NTSC)
Discs: 1

THE FILM

Like *Blade Runner*, John Carpenter's *The Thing* had the bad luck to come out in the summer of 1982, when its downbeat and downright *ugly* extra-terrestrial visitation was no match at the box office for a boy, his bike and his leathery best pal, and the movie was chalked up as a significant flop for Universal and for Carpenter. The director's sensibility is grizzled, counter-cultural, alluringly spare, and clearly influenced as much by Hawks and Hitchcock as other horror mavericks: his *Assault on Precinct 13* was a remake of Hawks's *Rio Bravo* in all but name, whereas here he bypassed the 1951 Hawks-produced *The Thing From Another World* to deliver a more pointed, faithful rendering of John W Campbell Jr's original 1938 novella *Who Goes There?*

With its tale of a devious changeling alien assimilating members of an Antarctic research facility, Campbell's story significantly pre-dated Jack Finney's *Invasion of the Body Snatchers* and lends itself no less chameleonically to the allegories of the moment: it's hard to watch the blood tests, dangerous goo, and ever-present threat of metastatic infection here without thinking of a just-then diagnosed virus beginning to cut a swathe across west central Africa. Aptly, Rob Bottin's ever-mutating effects set a standard for body horror that even Cronenberg wouldn't top until *The Fly*, while supplying the focus for a terrifically wary gross-out managed with poker-faced wit by Carpenter, his cast, and the insinuating camerawork of Dean Cundey. Topped by a justly famous opening, as a helicopter chases a husky across the ice to the throbbing electronic heartbeat of Ennio Morricone's score, and tailed by a heroically bleak waiting game of a non-denouement, *The Thing* is a cleverly illogical movie in which we trust no-one, progressively lose track of who's what, and can only hazard a halfwit's linear guess at where they're hiding.

THE DISC

'Theirs was sweet and ours was mean', says Carpenter of *E.T.* in his laid-back commentary with Russell, but there are no regrets here, and a surprisingly comprehensive batch of extras reflects the movie's strong afterlife. We get production snaps, out-takes, storyboards and all the rest of it, but the meatiest component is the 80-minute 'Terror Takes Shape', a very good interview-led retrospective with detailed input from Carpenter and Bottin in particular, and a nice send-off for the veteran matte artist Albert Whitlock (*The Birds*), who did the ice crater. The new anamorphic R1 edition improves on the image quality of the R2 PAL disc, which carries multiple language tracks. (TIM ROBEY)

The Third Man

(UK, 1949) Special Edition

Director: Carol Reed
Label: Optimum Releasing (UK)
Region: 2 (PAL)
Discs: 2

THE FILM

The writer and director of *The Third Man* – Graham Greene and Carol Reed – came to it flush with the success of their previous collaboration, *The Fallen Idol*. Its star, Orson Welles, came to it with something else: a reputation. Having quit the US for Europe, the 32-year-old was seen by some as a has-been, by others as a king over the water, but everyone had an opinion. This, of course, made him ideal for the role of Harry Lime, the elusive charmer whose presence saturates the film despite his appearing on screen for mere minutes. Welles's old chum Joseph Cotten is Holly Martins, the hack cowboy writer summoned by Lime to post-war Vienna only to find him being mourned. His investigations reveal his pal to be a black marketeer of the most poisonously profiteering kind, yet Welles' charisma makes him impossible to hate even as he sinks into the sewer; audiences fondly remembered the privilege of being taken into his confidence rather than the rotten core that barefaced smirk concealed. The character epitomises the charmingly treacherous setting of ruined Vienna – an environment quite beyond the naïve American Martins but consummately captured by Greene, Reed and a supporting cast of local veterans. The film is ultimately a testament to a mutually beneficial collaborative process in utter opposition to the ruthless self-interest its story dissects.

THE DISC

The double-edged benefit of Welles's performance can be seen – or rather heard – on two vintage radio broadcasts included here: played by another actor in the Lux Radio Theater version of the story (made at the same time as the film and also starring Cotten), Lime is revealed as a shabby, hateful grifter; while an episode from the later BBC series 'The Lives of Harry Lime' – which does star Welles – shows how easily the character could be turned into a roguish yet conscientious hero. Disc One includes several other valuable extras: contemporary newsreel footage of the production's shooting in the city sewers; the opening minutes of the American cut of the film, in which the knowing, almost cynical opening voice-over – spoken in the British version by Reed himself – is rather incongruously delivered by the guileless Martins; and later footage of the creator of the film's unique score, Anton Karas, who – as the trailer (also included) aptly observed – 'will have you in a dither with his zither'. For their 2006 Special Edition, Optimum have thrown in Frederick Baker's excellent BBC documentary 'Shadowing the Third Man' on a second disc. (BEN WALTERS)

This is Spinal Tap

(USA, 1984) Special Edition

Directors: Rob Reiner
Label: MGM (UK/USA)
Region: 2 (PAL) / 1 (NTSC)
Discs: 2

THE FILM

In the quarter of a century since *This is Spinal Tap* first toured cinemas, it has become one of the most influential, and oft-quoted, cult movies of all time – 'None more black'; 'You can't dust for vomit'; '*This* much talent' – the lingua franca of an entire pop culture strand, not least amongst rock musicians themselves, who constituted the film's original fan base. Alongside director Rob Reiner, actors Michael McKean, Christopher Guest and Harry Shearer launched an entire genre of improvised comic documentaries – 'mockumentaries', if you will – which Guest has pursued in movies like *Waiting for Guffman*, *Best in Show* and *A Mighty Wind*. Like other cult perennials (*The Big Lebowski*, *Withnail & I*), much of the joy of *This is Spinal Tap* comes through familiarity and repetition; on first viewing, the film can seem surprisingly authentic (famously, Liam Gallagher of Oasis believed the group was real).

Spinal Tap, meanwhile, are now arguably far better known than many of the middle-ranking rock groups they spoofed in the first place; and the film has become a time-capsule, a monument to the questionable glories of heavy metal. Altogether now: 'Stonehenge! Where the demons dwell . . . '

THE DISCS

Who's in here? If there was ever a non-sci-fi movie guaranteed to appeal to the 'serious DVD collecting enthusiast' (or 'nerd'), *This is Spinal Tap* is surely it. Fortunately, the current Special Edition acknowledges this simply by being one of the best DVDs on the market. Quite apart from the 70 minutes of deleted scenes (superb), new short feature 'Catching Up with Marti DiBergi', advertisements, trailers, music videos for 'Hell Hole', 'Listen to the Flower People' et al, there is the spectacularly amusing commentary track – McKean, Guest and Shearer in character as St Hubbins, Tufnell and Smalls, criticising the film's many distortions and inaccuracies from Spinal Tap's aggrieved perspective. Until such time as someone releases the much-bootlegged four-and-a-half-hour rough cut of the movie, this is the definitive edition.

Or is it? In 1998, Criterion released a Region 1 DVD of the movie, with 79 minutes of deleted scenes, not all of which are duplicated on MGM's Special Edition. Furthermore, the Criterion version offers two alternative commentary tracks, one by the actors (as themselves) and one by Rob Reiner and the film's producers. Deleted after only two years, this DVD now commands very high prices on Internet auction sites. Nonetheless, if you love this film as so many do, you should be prepared to go up to 11 for this edition. And let's not even get started on the CD-ROM, the Laserdisc . . . (ANDY MILLER)

The Three Burials of Melquiades Estrada

(USA, 2005)

Director: Tommy Lee Jones
Label: Optimum (UK)
Region: 2 (PAL)
Discs: 1

THE FILM

'*21 Grams* meets *The Treasure Of The Sierra Madre*' is how actor Dwight Yoakam pitches this in the commentary. It's an excellent summary of Tommy Lee Jones's assured directorial debut: at heart, a terrific, old-fashioned, yet contemporary-set western about death, masculine friendship, loyalty, honour and redemption, set over the Tex-Mex border.

When his best friend Melquiades (Julio César Cedillo), an illegal alien worker, is gunned down, ranch operator Pete Perkins (Tommy Lee Jones) vows to give him a proper burial. Sensing a cover-up from the local police chief (Dwight Yoakam), grief-stricken Pete sets out to hunt the killer himself and bring him to justice. Yet the vengeance he exacts from Mike (an intense Barry Pepper), the nasty white trash border guard with blood on his hands, is more like a hard-knocks mentorship. There are delicious digs at black comedy referencing Peckinpah's *Bring Me The Head Of Alfredo Garcia*, as Pete forces Mike to grave-rob Melquiades, and the three (two men and a corpse) set off from the shallow values of mall-town US consumerism, across the Rio Grande of John Ford towards the land of 'what it takes to be a good man'.

'Ees a love story – but nothing gay' is how writer Guillermo Arriaga (*Amores Perros, 21 Grams, Babel*) sums up his trademark multi-strand narrative of deftly interwoven flashbacks and superbly-realised characters. Set deliberately on the borders of old and new, the script of this rich, humanistic western may be smart and contemporary, but the epic, rocky sweeps of two-time Oscar-winning cinematographer, Chris Menges, echo with soundings of Ennio Morricone – no surprise since that composer's young disciple, Marco Beltrami, wrote the highly charged, twanging score.

THE DISC

Dolby Digital stereo sound and anamorphic widescreen both do justice to the lush soundtrack and visuals, but the making-of featurette and interview with Jones and Arriaga are something of a disappointment. Both are essentially much of the same repeated smile-and-wave footage drawn from the 2005 Cannes Film Festival (where the movie won both Best Actor and Best Screenplay) – including what seems like the entirety of its 15-minute standing ovation. That said, though the group audio commentary by Jones, Yoakam and January Jones recalls a particularly awkward car journey, their remarks are sporadically illuminating. Understandably keen to earn his intellectual spurs after the likes of *Men In Black 2*, the *Batman Forever* star name-checks everything from Kabuki Theatre to Jean-Paul Sartre. Twenty-seven minutes of deleted scenes remain mainly memorable for a macho Tommy Lee lassoing a bull – little lost here except extra testosterone. (LARUSHKA IVAN-ZADEH)

The Three Colours Trilogy

(France/Poland/Switzerland, 1993–34)

Director: Krzystof Kieslowski
Label: Artificial Eye (UK)
Region: 2 (PAL)
Discs: 4

THE FILMS

Liberté, egalité, fraternité? As trilogies go, it sounds pretty arid, even for Slavic misery-guts Krzysztof Kieslowski. But the Ten Commandments promised to be a scholasticist's wet dream, and look how his *Dekalog* squeezed humanity into an apartment block. What, he asks in this career-crowning final testament, do the ideals underpinning the French Revolution actually mean in the context of everyday lives?

The trick is, he starts simple. A mother clambering alone from the wreckage of a car crash. A discarded husband busking on the Metro. A dog forgetting to look left and right. From these specifics KK segues gradually into the universal: can a grieving parent detach herself from the constraints of society? Might a jilted spouse get even? Is coincidence, for driver or dog-owner, an invite to share? And what about us?

The phenomenal Juliette Binoche really doesn't need the other actors, who hover on the peripheries of the moody, minimalist *Blue*. The dialogue's sparse, but Binoche is fluent in Kieslowski's visual language of submersion and withdrawal. The fact that Julie swims aggressive widths, not lengths, says more about her fractured state of mind than pages of script ever could. Irene Jacob, in *Red*, is also masterful at extracting heightened significance from seemingly mundane actions and objects.

But if this, and the iconic, *tricolore*-based images on the trilogy's posters, suggest a masterclass mainly for its leggy leads, look closer. The underrated, Everyman-type focus of *White* is Zbigniew Zamachowski, and Jean-Louis Trintignant gives *Red* its mournful undertow. Besides, stick these films on your wall and their mesmerising surfaces will only stay unscratched. You may just have to watch them.

THE DISCS

'Do you think western civilisation is coming to an end?' In the pleasingly bonkers-around-the-edges Kieslowski documentary 'I'm So-So', no topic is too large for director Krzysztof Wierzbicki. Think your subject might be illuminated by interviews with graphologists and clairvoyants? Throw them in too. Kieslowski, magnificently craggy and with a cigarette seemingly prosthetically attached to his finger, only studied film to secure admittance on a course for stage directing. This after he'd abandoned his early ambition to be a stoker. Each film is accompanied by a short Kieslowski masterclass: in *Blue*'s, he describes how he had his assistant spend hours testing the absorbency of different sugar cubes. (FIONA MOUNTFORD)

THX 1138

(USA, 1971) The George Lucas
Director's Cut

Director: George Lucas
Label: Warners (all territories)
Region: 1 (NTSC) / 2 (PAL)
Discs: 2

THE FILM

To anyone whose experience of George Lucas begins and ends with the *Star Wars*
hexalogy, his strange, experimental first feature will come as a shock. Set in a
subterranean future in which everyone's head is homogenisingly shaved, sexual
contact is outlawed and medicine cabinets prescribe a barrage of mind-numbing
sedatives, it's a fleshing out of a 15-minute short that Lucas made while golden
boy at the University of Southern California in the late '60s. It divides with
clinical precision into three acts: the first, heavy with Lalo Schifrin's doomily
atmospheric score, plunges us into this unforgiving world and the dangerously
burgeoning affection between THX 1138 (Robert Duvall) and roommate LUH
3417 (Maggie McOmie); the second, a protracted and faintly loony fusion of
dazzling white walls and impenetrable psychobabble, deals with THX's inevitable
punishment; and the third covers his escape, shot by inveterate speed-freak Lucas
in tunnels below San Francisco at a shuddering 140 mph. You may only partly
go along with Lucas's claims to the film's underlying 'irony' – if there's humour
here, it's so dry as to be desiccated, and the picture seems to take itself awfully
seriously. Yet there are tremendous passages, and *THX*'s chilly, almost Kubrickian
beauty shines through in this re-master, lending it a hypnotic power all its own.

THE DISCS

THX 1138 was not only Lucas's first feature, it was also the opening gambit of
American Zoetrope, the company formed in a frenzy of optimism by him and
his similarly brilliant counterpart at UCLA, Francis Ford Coppola. Indeed, this
upmarket two-disc set is enjoyable above all for its historical value: for the excellent, 63-minute documentary that charts the planet-like alignment of these two
chalk-and-cheese masters and what was essentially the birth of the American
New Wave, and for the film as both an early, Vietnam-era flourishing of this
movement and a foretaste of industry-changing things to come. It's arresting
just how closely Walter Murch's soundscapes here anticipate those he created
for a later Zoetrope production, *Apocalypse Now*. And, as both he and Lucas
suggest on a strong making-of doc, the preoccupations so central to *Star Wars*
are already present: Lucas's obsession with design, technology and oppressive
empires, and his shrewdest trick of all, the anticipation of a 'used' future in
which high-tech machines actually break down. Also included are the original
student short, and a rich main-feature commentary in which Lucas declares,
'This is . . . probably the kind of filmmaking I'm going to go back to some day.'
Now there's a thought.

(The 2004 'George Lucas Director's Cut' contains several updated sequences
and a number of computer-enhanced effects. The prior version is no longer available on current DVDs.) (MARK MONAHAN)

Timecode

(USA, 2000)

Director: Mike Figgis
Label: Sony (US); Optimum Releasing (UK)
Region: 1 (NTSC) /2 (PAL)
Discs: 1

THE FILM

When Aleksandr Sokurov released his single-shot museum tour *Russian Ark* in 2002, critics around the world went gaga over the stunt's logistical virtuosity, treating the endeavour as more revolutionary artifact than mere movie. Two years before, Mike Figgis pulled off the same trick in quadruplicate with the far more interesting *Timecode*, a genuinely experimental work which gets down and dirty with the guerrilla possibilities of digital video. Splitting the screen into quadrants, each of which houses an unbroken and simultaneously-shot 93-minute take, Figgis weaves together an Altmanesque narrative in and around the offices of an LA production company, where a casting session affords access to the petty vanities, paranoia and sexual intrigue which unite, among others, dyspeptic producer Alex Green (Stellan Skarsgård), his seriously depressed wife (Saffron Burrows), auditioning starlet Rose (Salma Hayek) and her jealous lover (Jeanne Tripplehorn, a revelation).

As characters criss-cross their way into each other's frames, our attention is juggled by the sound mix, which works like a selective form of eavesdropping – you feel Figgis toying with his own grid, pairing incident off against incident, and using the actors, more than locations, as his ever-present spatial reference points. Fittingly for a film set down by trial and error on sheet music, it works like a fluid fugue, constantly swapping keys and instrumentalists, coming together for moments of rhythmic punctuation (an earthquake, then its aftershocks) and achieving something close to audiovisual jazz: quite why the makers of the pseudo-real-time, sporadically splitscreen TV thriller *24* haven't handed the reins over to Figgis yet is anyone's guess.

THE DISC

If ever a movie was made to be watched on DVD this was. The theatrical sound mix was never intended as definitive – Figgis has been known to perform live ones, sitting behind his decks like the 21st-century equivalent of a silent movie organist. But the interactive capabilities of DVD allow us, Harry Caul-style (see *The Conversation*), to pick our way piecemeal through the audio tracks – listen to more of Burrows' top-right therapy sessions, should you so wish, or, directly underneath, get a load of the often hysterically funny movie-talk with Holly Hunter, Xander Berkeley, Steven Weber et al. (Me, I'll just tune into Tripplehorn's entire performance and not miss a word.) Flip to track seven and you get Figgis's typically sharp commentary, one of two he did for this disc: the other accompanies 'Version 1' of the film, whose radical differences from the theatrically released 'Version 15' give us a fascinating handle on the start and end points of this whole improvisatory project. (TIM ROBEY)

Time of the Wolf

(France/Austria/Germany, 2002)

Director: Michael Haneke
Label: Artificial Eye (UK)
Region: 2 (PAL)
Discs: 1

THE FILM

As TS Eliot wrote, this is how the world ends – not with a bang but a whimper. Intellectual Austrian auteur Michael Haneke's project of clinically dissecting the flimsy fundamentals on which we Westerners base our lives reaches its apotheosis with this post-apocalypse movie, one without bomb blasts or asteroids or grinning psychotics but with a haunting sense that this is what it will really be like at the end: isolated individuals, struggling.

The film opens in familiar Haneke terrain, with a middle-class family whose sense of security and entitlement are laid bare as possibly arrogant and certainly false. As in *Funny Games*, these bourgeois are disturbed in their country retreat by unwelcome guests, but the trajectory of the earlier film is traced here in mere moments as the father, symbolic lynchpin of the social order, is shot dead, leaving his family – tight-lipped wife (an extraordinary Isabelle Huppert), pre-teen daughter and profoundly traumatised younger son – adrift in a world whose regular infrastructure is gone. Without home, power, food, transport or communications, they meander through gaunt, empty countryside and settle alongside other refugees in a remote train station. Teasing reminders of civilisation and of narrative materialise, but nothing coheres. Much of the time is spent in genuine pitch darkness which the recurrent fires do little to brighten: though they're heavy with symbolic weight, it's impossible to determine whether they bring hope, homeliness, destruction or damnation in this structureless world. No train arrives.

A thriller without thrills, *Wolf* holds the viewer's nerves perpetually at breaking point with its calculated manipulation of expectation and demonically rigorous control. It is a superb example of Haneke's master showmanship, but, unlike his other works, his talents are pressed into proving more than that we and his protagonists are all suckers, moving beyond smart cinema to a profound humanism which makes this surely his masterpiece.

THE DISC

The trailer included here – a muddy and rather uninspiring affair – makes clear by contrast just how fine is the quality of the film's presentation, crisp and colour-perfect in both dense night-time blacks and cold, hard light of day. The making-of documentary offers critical illumination, with characteristic-ally intelligent analysis of the film from Huppert and the owlish Haneke, relaxed as he reveals his plan to bring home the end of the world to those used to watching it from a distance. On set, he generates precisely that cheery bonhomie and sense of mutual engagement so markedly absent from his finished film – a hint, perhaps, to seek hope in the 'real' world, not in the movies. (The AV Channel's Australian edition scraps the trailer and a Cannes featurette in favour of additional interviews with Haneke and Huppert.) (REBEKAH POLDING)

To Be or Not To Be

(USA, 1942)

Director: Ernst Lubitsch
Label: Warners (USA)
Region: 1 (NTSC)
Discs: 1

THE FILM

Lubitsch's WWII farce was savaged on its release for, as *New York Times* critic Bosley Crowther had it, staging 'a spy thriller of fantastic design amid the ruins and frightful oppressions of Nazi-invaded Warsaw . . . One has the strange feeling that Mr Lubitsch is a Nero, fiddling while Rome burns.' Still, it's quality fiddling. Give or take Chaplin's *The Great Dictator*, this was the first great comedy to lampoon the Third Reich as a ship of fools, and what was good for *The Producers* 25 years later was better, bolder and far more provocatively thought up (by screenwriters Melchior Lengyel and Edwin Justus Mayer) bang in the middle of hostilities.

Jack Benny and Carole Lombard play Joseph and Maria Tura, bickering members of a Polish Shakespearean theatre troupe whose anti-Nazi melodrama gets cancelled, meaning perennial ham Joseph must play the Dane again while Maria gets secretly chatted up backstage by a hunky pilot (Robert Stack). The satire kicks into high gear when the company help Stack thwart a Gestapo spy (Stanley Ridges) and his clownish commanding officer Colonel Erhardt (Sig Ruman, priceless) by arranging for Benny to impersonate both men and intercept a crucial piece of intelligence. Lombard, in her final role, is superbly controlled as the bored glamour girl faking moral corruptibility for a good cause, and Benny's great scene opposite the bug-eyed Ruman ('So zey call me Concentration Camp Erhardt!') stands out as a matchlessly played *pas de deux*. Mel Brooks would remake the movie himself in 1983 (with Charles Durning picking up the Best Supporting Actor nod Ruman deserved) but, needless to say, the Lubitsch touch beats the Brooks ham fist.

THE DISC

Two brief extras on the disc for Benny fans – one, his 1930 short 'The Rounder', a pretty tired single-reel farce in which his drunken playboy clambers up a ladder into the bedroom of a spoiled heiress (Buster Keaton's then mistress Dorothy Sebastian), who proposes marriage. 'Buy Savings Bonds! A Patriotic Drama', which lasts all of a minute and a half, does pretty much what it says on the tin, playing off Benny's skin-flint reputation as child star Carolyn Lee asks him for some change to buy stamps. Lubitsch's sublime *The Shop Around the Corner* gets similar treatment from Warners, while meatier Criterion editions are available for *Trouble in Paradise* and *Heaven Can Wait*. (TIM ROBEY)

Toy Story & Toy Story 2

(USA, 1995/1999)
10th Anniversary Edition/Special Edition

Director: John Lasseter
Label: Disney (USA)
Region: 1 (NTSC)
Discs: 4

THE FILMS

John Lasseter's *Toy Story* made movie history in 1995, and, as the first completely computer-generated feature film, it's a better fit for DVD than almost any other entry in this book. Not that it doesn't make for superb communal big-screen entertainment, but as an all-digital creation, there's no loss of film texture in the transfer to home media. Nor will it be worn out by endless viewings . . .

Riffing on the story of *The Velveteen Rabbit*, the first *Toy Story* offers sweet lessons in empathy, imagining the secret lives of toys living with the threat of redundancy as their owners grow older, or, in the case of shiny new space ranger Buzz Lightyear, facing the fact that the universe doesn't revolve around himself.

Come *Toy Story 2*, the storytelling and gag-writing becomes, if anything, even more richly hued, hand in hand with the improving technology. With Woody the trad cowboy doll abducted by a collector, and promised the toy equivalent of plastic surgery and cryogenic preservation, the film asks the biggie 'How to live?', again with the lightest touch and surest wit. Lasseter's Pixar is rightly praised for the classicism of its storytelling (in contrast to the disposable pop references of DreamWorks' *Shrek* et al), but one uproarious *Star Wars*-based routine was clearly too good to pass up. Female characters are still too sparse, but Joan Cusack's Jessie the Yodelling Cowgirl is a sassy addition to the fold.

THE DISCS

Like *The Godfather* (*Parts I* and *II*), the *Toy Story* films can be considered an entity above and besides their consituent parts. (At least, that's our excuse for this double citation.) They've also already undergone multiple incarnations on DVD. The three-disc 'Ultimate Toy Box (Collector's Edition)', released in 2000, seemed top-notch at the time, festooned with commentaries, out-takes and background features, although the Region 2 version lacked the advertised audio commentaries. Most of those items have made their way onto these two successor sets, although the Pixar shorts 'Tin Toy' and 'Luxo Jr' have been dropped, and new docs added, with the likes of Hayao Miyazaki and Peter Jackson vouching for the films' legacy. There are also new interactive games. Picture and sound are even sprucer, although only high-end connoisseurs are likely to appreciate the higher transfer bit rate. The Region 2 discs promise DTS sound, like their R1 equivalents, but it just ain't there. (NICK BRADSHAW)

Trainspotting

(UK, 1996) The Definitive Edition

Director: Danny Boyle
Label: Universal (UK)
Region: 2 (PAL)
Discs: 2

THE FILM

Overexposure tarnished its domestic reputation in the years following its release, and some of its hip trickery has been dulled by age and imitation, but Danny Boyle's take on the hit novel by Irvine Welsh remains a dynamic, catchy and oddly generous portrait of opiate-addled urban existence. Ewan McGregor set himself up for super-stardom with a turn he's never bettered, as mercurial, sensitive Edinburgh heroin addict Mark Renton; other performers launched here include Robert Carlyle as the monstrous moustachioed casual Begbie, Kevin McKidd as the (initially) clean-living Tommy, and Kelly Macdonald as schoolgirl-seductress Diane.

Based upon a book formed of separate, loosely interlinked anecdotes, the film is inevitably episodic, and its stylised stop-start aesthetic (exemplified by the now ubiquitous freeze-frame character introductions) imposes further distance. But the more emotional scenes are well handled, with Ewen Bremner's puppyish loser Spud providing a touchstone of naïve humanity in a world of self-serving scumbags. The use of music, too, is a powerful linking factor – as well as anchoring the film firmly in a historical moment shared with the explosion of Britpop, the decay of Conservative rule, and the ascent of Tony Blair. Fittingly for its period, this is a film layered in irony and bluntly aware of its own internal contradictions. Its heroic acts are crimes and betrayals, its romance is on highly dubious moral ground – and the famed exhortation to 'Choose life!' that bookends its narrative acknowledges that the 'good health, low cholesterol and dental insurance' lifestyle that its characters initially reject represents their only hope of sanity or survival.

THE DISCS

The initial 2000 DVD was bereft of extras, lacking even the deleted scenes that were included in a beefed-up VHS version released around the same time. This 2003 two-disc 'Definitive Edition' (more or less replicated by Miramax's Region 1 'Collector's Edition') belatedly rectifies the situation. Celebrating the film as both artwork and pop culture phenomenon, it provides a top-notch transfer of the film backed up by copious background materials. Disc 1 includes a cheery but informative audio commentary with director, screenwriter and star; a ten-minute featurette made at the time of shooting and featuring an interview with Irvine Welsh; and a set of deleted scenes, with the valuable option to watch them at their intended point in the film.

Disc 2 includes two documentaries on the film's visuals and two on its sound and music; a mixed set of old and new cast and crew interviews, a hectic documentary on the film's Cannes premiere, and an oddly complicated multi-camera option allowing you to view a scene with Boyle while he talks it through. There's also a trailer, cast photos, and English subtitles for those not experienced with the subtleties of Edinburgh pronunciation. (HANNAH McGILL)

Trilogy of the Dead

(USA, 1968/1978/1985)

Director: George A Romero
Label: Anchor Bay (UK)
Region: 2 (PAL)
Discs: 4

THE FILMS

Back in 1968, Romero's seminal micro-budget *Night of the Living Dead* changed the landscape of the horror genre by both raising the bar for graphic gore and introducing a new tone of nihilistic despair: both would influence the films of David Cronenberg, Tobe Hooper, Wes Craven and scores of lesser talents. It also proved that a regional (Pittsburgh), privately funded indie could make a big splash if it was scary enough – a lesson the makers of *The Blair Witch Project* clearly took to heart.

The film depicts a group of survivors who hole up in a farmhouse to escape the hordes of flesh-eating corpses roaming the countryside. But instead of presenting a united front, the characters quickly succumb to vicious in-fighting, as pragmatist Ben (Duane Jones) argues bitterly with cowardly family man Karl (Harry Cooper) over their best strategy for survival. Romero offers flashes of black humour, but his primary intention is clearly to scare us witless; to this end, the film's grainy, off-kilter black-and-white photography gives it a gripping *verité* immediacy, while the sweaty claustrophobia of the setting combined with the unrelenting shock tactics are highly effective. Reassuring conventions are mercilessly trashed: Barbara (Judith O'Dea) is initially established as the film's heroine, but then spends the rest of the film in a near-catatonic stupor until she's eaten by her brother, while Ben survives the night's onslaught only to be shot by a redneck posse; the fact that lead actor Jones is black – itself a rarity – gives his role an inevitable political dimension.

The sociological aspects of the film were developed in the first sequel, 1978's overtly satirical *Dawn of the Dead*, in which another group of survivors barricade themselves into a huge shopping mall and live out an American Dream of endless material consumption, while bloodily dispatching the zombie hordes returning there out of mindless habit ('This was an important place in their lives!'). The trilogy concluded with 1985's underrated *Day of the Dead*, which focused on a team of scientists experimenting on captured ghouls in a huge Florida bunker, supervised by an increasingly truculent military squad; as in Romero's original, the survivors manage to tear each other apart without needing much help from the living dead.

THE DISCS

The Anchor Bay set features good transfers, although the 30th Anniversary edition of *Night* contains a new synthesised score and 15 minutes of silly, redundant newly shot non-Romero footage. (Elite Entertainment's R1 Millennium and Special Collector's editions offer the best packages for that individual film.) *Dawn* exists in multiple versions (including producer Dario Argento's Italian cut) – this one is the longest, minus six seconds of BBFC trims. The *Dawn* commentary by makeup/stuntman Tom Savini is welcome, but one from Romero would doubtless have been more illuminating. (ANDY RICHARDS)

Twelve Monkeys

(USA, 1995) Special Edition

Director: Terry Gilliam
Label: Universal (USA)
Region: 1 (NTSC)
Discs: 1

THE FILM

It might be that *Twelve Monkeys* marks the high point of Terry Gilliam's career to date, a point he seems unlikely to reach again. That's not to say it's flawless, but its balance is superb: the wit and cultish quirkiness of his early career for once mesh perfectly with big-screen visuals and an A-list cast. Brad Pitt attacks his pin-up image with a weird, showy turn as an unhinged animal liberationist, both farcical and unsettling, and Madeleine Stowe is solid and credible as a psychologist investigating Bruce Willis' case. Willis, like Keanu Reaves in *The Matrix*, suits his character by looking confused: he seems such an unlikely person to be in a Gilliam film that his thuggish ex-con time-traveller gains our sympathy through his bewilderment, both brutal and childishly helpless.

But *Twelve Monkeys'* real strengths are down to Gilliam. Paul Buckmaster's jolly score helps him treat the extermination of mankind with ghoulish levity, and there are plenty of striking visuals: the steampunk machinery and snowy wastelands of the future; the disused shop where Pitt makes his plans, a WWI trench and, best of all, a dozen TV screens in a department store window reflecting Willis' paranoid, cracking face as he tries to hide.

For once with Gilliam, everything clicks. Added to this is a script, inspired by Chris Marker's legendary short *La Jetée*, almost too ingenious for its own good, which throws a second viewing into an entirely different light. It's a devious film, pulling off the rare trick of combining story, character and visuals, keeping each strong while allowing none to undermine the others.

THE DISC

Various editions (but not the UK one) carry a solid commentary track with Gilliam and producer Charles Roven; Shochiku's Japanese version comes with a book and extra featurettes on a second disc. The key extra to look for, though, is *The Hamster Factor*, a 90-minute documentary by Keith Fulton and Louis Pepe, who went on to record Gilliam's disastrous attempt to film Don Quixote in *Lost in La Mancha*. *The Hamster Factor* — the title refers to his obsession with details to the possible detriment of the overall film — recounts the making of what Gilliam describes as his 'seventh-and-a-half feature film', but it goes far beyond the usual fare. We hear about the troubled history of his earlier movies, and his difficulties with funding: it's this contrast between Gilliam the artist and basic commercial requirements that fuels the documentary, an intriguing look at the sheer awkward and sometimes miraculous struggle of filmmaking.
(TOBY FROST)

24 Hour Party People

(UK, 2002) Special Edition

Director: Michael Winterbottom
Label: Pathé (UK)
Region: 2 (PAL)
Discs: 2

THE FILM

Michael Winterbottom's film tells the story of Factory Records, the wayward independent label that dominated the Manchester music scene from the punk late '70s into the rave '90s before collapsing in a mess of bad drugs and worse debt. By casting TV comedians in the key roles, including Steve Coogan as label boss Tony Wilson, Winterbottom plays up the lighter side of the label's tragi-comic trajectory, allowing Wilson, via direct-to-camera address, to give his hindsight-laden account of the enterprise while the chaos around him hints at another, less heroic narrative.

Regardless of its fidelity to the original, Coogan's Wilson, a variation on his celebrated Alan Partridge character, is a remarkable invention, straddling the fourth wall as he attempts to convince on one side the audience, on the other his dour associates, that his chronic lack of business smarts – just about covered by the chart success of bands like Happy Mondays and New Order – is in fact a Situationist *détournement* of music-biz orthodoxy. His uncompromisingly pretentious frame of reference itself becomes a running joke: 'If you know what I mean, great; if you don't, it doesn't matter,' says Wilson – 'but you should probably read more.'

Winterbottom and cinematographer Robby Müller (veteran of Wim Wenders' similarly music-fuelled '70s work) conjure a north of England in the process of de-industrialisation, their intimate DV style making for a dynamic reinvention of this well-trodden Brit-flick backdrop.

THE DISCS

Navigating this DVD, it becomes clear that the cinema release of the same name was only the tip of a cracked iceberg, the commercially viable version of a sprawling, contradictory, collective endeavour, further traces of which make up the two-disc set. Typically deleted for good reasons, the numerous cut scenes here hint at an alternative, non-Wilson-centric film (testified to in the commentaries), possibly closer to Winterbottom's original sprawling vision, but lacking Coogan's star-pull.

Wilson himself offers a commentary, contesting much of the film ('this sequence is very funny, touching, poignant – and entirely untrue'), and getting tied up in conceptual knots, accusing Coogan of performing a 'self-parody of a parody of a self-parody'. Bluntly disputing his slant, 'From the Factory Floor' is a reverse-angle commentary, a Warholian piece in which we watch a bar full of Factory veterans, led by New Order's Peter Hook, watching the film (included as an small insert), not so much discussing it as roasting everyone involved in the production. Bakunin would have loved it. (HENRY K MILLER)

Ugetsu

(Japan, 1953)

Director: Kenji Mizoguchi
Label: Criterion Collection (USA)
Region: 1 (NTSC)
Discs: 2

THE FILM

The full title of Kenji Mizoguchi's acclaimed classic, *Ugetsu Monogatari*, translates roughly as 'Tales of the Pale and Silvery Moon After the Rain', and the
film itself is a luminous and haunting fable of greed and folly. Set amidst the
turbulence and turpitude of Japan's 16th-century civil wars, it focuses on two
neighbouring peasant families swept up in the prevailing opportunism and
derangement. Lured by the phantoms of fame and fortune, Tobei and Genjuro
venture into town to sell their pottery, deaf to their wives' pleas to mind their
riches at home. Tobei steals the trophy of a fallen general's head and attains
brief pomp as a samurai; Genjuro is seduced by the numinous Lady Wakasa,
only to learn that she is not all that she seems.

Serene and sublimely expressive, *Ugetsu* reflects Mizoguchi's abiding theme
of women's degradation at the hands of exploitative men, and offers perhaps
his clearest comment on the machismo that led Japan into WWII. Aesthetically,
the film is ravishing: Mizoguchi held the theory that cinema should follow the
form of Japanese picture scrolls, with minimal breaks (unlike the more stac-
cato style of the younger Kurosawa). But also in contrast to the static compositions of his fellow master Ozu, Mizoguchi's camera is forever moving along
with the action. His tracking shots are some of the wonders of the cinematic
world.

THE DISCS

Despite his towering reputation amongst cineastes, Mizoguchi has been all too
rarely represented on video, so Criterion's typically scholarly buff job is more
than welcome. Kazuo Miyagawa's black-and-white cinematography is resplen-
dently showcased, though some blemishes remain. The English subtitles have
also been reworked.

Disc 1's extras include an erudite and expansive commentary by Tony Rayns,
and three interviews, two new. Director Masahiro Shinoda (*Samurai Spy*) provides
an encyclopedic appreciation of Mizoguchi's style and influence; *Ugetsu*'s first
AD Tokuzo Tanaka recalls his boss's dictatorial working manner; while the
late Miyagawa elaborates on the director's visual sensibility in a 1992 interview.

Disc 2 is occupied by Kaneto Shindo's two-and-a-half hour documentary
Kenji Mizoguchi: The Life of a Film Director, tracking the subject to his birth
town of Kyoto and through interviews with friends and colleagues. The package
also comes with a 72-page booklet, featuring an excellent essay on the film by
Phillip Lopate, and the full texts of the three short stories that inspired *Ugetsu*:
Akinari Ueda's *The House in the Thicket* and *Lust of the Serpent*, and Guy de
Maupassant's *How He Got the Legion of Honour*. (NICK BRADSHAW)

The Umbrellas of Cherbourg

(France, 1964)

Director: Jacques Demy
Label: Optimum (UK)
Region: 2 (PAL)
Discs: 2

THE FILM

Candy-coloured but bitter-sweet, *The Umbrellas of Cherbourg* is first love as a film. Its world is dazzlingly hyperreal – a retouched Cherbourg, all ravishing pastels and primes, with characters in chic wallpaper-matching outfits singing their every syllable to lyrical jazz from Michel Legrand. Your heart soars, yet your feet are kept flat on the ground: lines lilt from 'I love you' to the more pedestrian 'The engine still knocks when it's cold but that's normal'; mothers may not understand but may also be right; and debts, war, and unplanned pregnancy all dampen the delights. Unlike the protagonists, style and substance are perfectly aligned: Catherine Deneuve's glowing shopgirl Geneviève and her garage-mechanic boyfriend believe their love is forever, but romance falls by the wayside when he's shipped off to fight in Algeria. Four years later, a chance meeting finds them both married to others, in a famously exquisite snow scene in a service-station forecourt.

Though its successor, the similarly musical *The Young Girls of Rochefort*, was a flop, *Umbrellas* brought director Jacques Demy critical acclaim, commercial triumph and a Palme d'Or trophy. It revealed the vivid whimsy which marks his most lasting films (and his affiliation to Jean Cocteau), and which makes him unique in the French New Wave. Though his cinephilia shines through the Gallicity of this MGM homage, and the sung script is a first, Demy is not a formal innovator *á la* Godard or Resnais; as romantic as Truffaut, he underpins his artifice with a social awareness in his depiction of petit bourgeois dreams. It is not unreasonable to see *Umbrellas'* melancholy broken fairytale alongside Pontecorvo's ***Battle of Algiers*** as one of the most moving documents of the Franco–Algerian War.

THE DISCS

Following Demy's death in 1990, his widow (filmmaker Agnès Varda) oversaw *Umbrellas'* restoration, bringing back brightness and sharpness to Cherbourg. All currently available DVDs have reaped the benefits. France Video presents the film in its ideal aspect ratio and Koch International offers the option of turning the film's original mono into surround sound, but Optimum's two-disc special edition wins out for its superb saturated colour and admirable extras. There is a warm introduction by critic Geoff Andrew; Varda's tribute documentary *The Universe of Jacques Demy* appears in full (and with subtitles); and a rare '60s short, 'L'Amérique Lunaire', for which Legrand provides the soundtrack, is a surprising treat. (REBEKAH POLDING)

Unforgiven

(USA, 1992)
10th Anniversary Edition

Director: Clint Eastwood
Label: Warners (UK)
Region: 2 (PAL) / 1 (NTSC) (2-disc Special Edition)
Discs: 2

THE FILM

Unforgiven is Clint Eastwood's farewell to the western, and it's no accident that valediction, reminiscence and summing up should be so close to its heart. This is a western about the western, an anatomy of myth-making and America's view of itself, a tale of the wild west's sunset whose anti-hero, sometime vicious outlaw William Munny (Eastwood), is haunted by the past. (Significantly, and unusually for a western, its weather is bad: late autumn storm clouds, rain and mud.)

Munny is a hard-up farmer persuaded to take part in a revenge killing for a cash reward, at first a man comically out of practice, out of time and out of countenance. Before long, though, events triggered by the initial crime – the mutilation of a prostitute – bring out his suppressed talent for mayhem, and at the final showdown he transforms, fuelled by whisky and rage, into a terrifying angel of death. Violence in *Unforgiven* is frequent and shocking, but the film never loses sight of its cost: 'It's a hell of a thing, killing a man,' says Munny in what has become a classic scene; 'You take away all he's got – and all he's ever going to have.' Eastwood's last western is a sophisticated, unforgettable masterpiece.

THE DISCS

The film has a good commentary track by *Time* critic and Eastwood biographer Richard Schickel. Schickel was present during the shoot, but steers mercifully clear of movie procedural and 'That was the day the catering truck ran out of ketchup' anecdote. Instead he gets his teeth into the moral meat of the film – the contagion and consequences of violence, the myth-making – and sizes up its complex characters, of whom he's a shrewd and fair-minded judge.

The second disc has a handful of short docs: on-set footage and a portrait of Eastwood at work; an appraisal of the film ten years on, which explains how Eastwood sat on his option to film David Webb Peoples' script until, at 62, he'd aged into the role of its protagonist, and why he liked Peoples' screenplay ('It had everything that I ever wanted to say in a western and was never able to.') There's also a one-hour biography doc, 'Eastwood on Eastwood', and an 1959 episode of TV serial *Maverick* featuring a young Eastwood some years before stardom struck. Disc 1 has a roll-call of the prizes showered on *Unforgiven*: four Oscars (including Best Film and Best Director) and umpteen others. (HD version now available.) (SIMON CROPPER)

United 93

(USA/UK, 2006)

Director: Paul Greengrass
Label: Universal (all territories)
Region: Any
Discs: 1

THE FILM

Despite widespread popular misgivings, this gripping account of the hijacked flight that crashed in Pennsylvania on September 11, 2001, was the best-reviewed American film of the year. Using the same docu-drama techniques he applied to *Bloody Sunday*, Greengrass recreates events from multiple viewpoints in something approximating real time, using a handheld camera and cutting rapidly between passengers and crew before there's any danger of slipping into hokey 'human interest' angles. It makes for a radically different kind of disaster movie.

Greengrass also shows what was going on in various control towers, in the National Air Traffic Control Center, and in a military command room, as what starts out like every other day turns into a nightmare. With a number of the cast playing themselves, these scenes are riveting, and there is an unparalleled feeling that this is what it must have been like. An extraordinary act of dramatic reconstruction, this is a sober, sensitive and intensely harrowing movie, yet its scope is necessarily narrow. In sticking strictly to the official records of events, Greengrass ducks wider questions about what September 11 was all about and ends up (as he admits in his commentary track) mythologising the heroic fight-back of the passengers against the terrorists.

THE DISC

The Region 1 Special Edition has already gone out of print, and in any case the only additional content − a 50-minute documentary in which military personnel recounted their experience of that morning − covered much the same ground as the feature. Presumably a more extensive package will be forthcoming at some point, but the principal focus of the single-disc release is to allay doubts about the film's opportunism, and honour the victims and their families.

'The Families and the Film' is an hour-long documentary in which the families talk about their hopes and fears for the film, and in many cases meet the actor who will play their loved one. It sounds like a queasy PR move − and on some level it is − but it's also moving and a reasonably dignified way to bridge the chasm between real loss and artistic interpretation. The same impulse explains the 'Memorial Pages', written remembrances of each of the 40 victims on the flight. These supplements humanise individual passengers and crew in a way the feature doesn't (the terrorists are quietly excluded). The only other extra is a commentary track from Greengrass, as thoughtful and rigorous as you would expect. (TOM CHARITY)

The Untouchables

(USA, 1987) Special Edition

Director: Brian DePalma
Label: Paramount (all territories)
Region: Any
Discs: 1

THE FILM

Every now and again, a movie comes along where every credit – from the names above the title to those assembled behind the camera – yields a yelp of delight from even hardened critics. Even more occasionally, a film of this type actually lives up to its stellar billing. A prime example of '80s Hollywood packaging (based on an old TV series, written by David Mamet, directed by Brian De Palma), *The Untouchables* is one such rarity.

De Palma's Steadicam-led recreation of Prohibition-era Chicago – with Al Capone (Robert De Niro) facing off against clean-cut Fed Eliot Ness (Kevin Costner) – is most often described as operatic in scope. Yet its high and wide extremes allow writer and director simply to get a lot more in here than the common-or-garden blockbuster: the pleasures of the ensemble drama, the western and, in its still-thrilling set-pieces, the grade-A action movie.

The playing is marked by a refreshingly uncomplicated classical heroism. Costner's ever-squareish sincerity is cleverly matched with the mischievous charms of Sean Connery's beat cop Malone, a role from the days when making good movies still mattered more to this actor than playing golf. De Niro, too, steps up to the plate, baseball bat in hand, as a truly malevolent Capone. A stirring piece of all-American myth-making, *The Untouchables* triumphs by embracing whole Ness's battle-charge philosophy: 'Let's do some good!'

THE DISC

Four decent featurettes blend retrospective interviews with on-set material featuring Costner and Connery. The first of these, 'The Script, The Cast', omits mention of Mamet's turbulent relationship with the film, but producer Art Linson does acknowledge how the writer was crucial in pulling in the opposite direction from the original television series. De Palma, meanwhile, reveals his reluctance to cast Costner, and we learn how Bob Hoskins (who bears more resemblance to Capone) was initially cast ahead of De Niro.

In 'Production Stories' the problems of finding authentic 1930s locations in 1980s Chicago come to light, and Giorgio Armani is employed to back up De Palma's assertion that 'corruption looks great'. 'Reinventing the Genre' focuses on the shoot, with the director discussing how Connery nearly walked off the film for good. A fourth, shorter featurette, 'The Classic', charts the understandably popular reaction to a film that speaks to all our best instincts. The booklet folds out into a poster of Eliot Ness, presumably for aspirant G-men to hang on their wall. (MIKE McCAHILL)

The Usual Suspects

(USA, 1995) Special Edition

Director: Bryan Singer
Label: MGM (USA)
Region: 1 (NTSC)
Discs: 2

THE FILM

'The greatest trick the devil ever pulled was convincing the world he didn't exist,' says Verbal Kint at the end of Bryan Singer's masterful movie about a bunch of small-time crooks caught in a Los Angeles bloodbath. And diabolical trickery is the name of the game in *The Usual Suspects*, an intricate thriller written by Christopher McQuarrie and starring a terrific ensemble cast. Gabriel Byrne, Benicio Del Toro, Kevin Spacey, Stephen Baldwin and Kevin Pollak all jostle for attention as five thieves herded into the same police line-up one afternoon. Pete Postlethwaite slithers around as mysterious middle-man Kobayashi, and Chazz Palminteri smoulders as Detective Kujan, a sardonic customs agent trying to figure out why there's a boatload of dead Hungarians in California and a crippled guy rabbiting on about someone called Keyser Söze.

The Usual Suspects made Spacey a household name. Sly, witty, and menacing, he typifies the movie's irreverent spirit and lurid intrigue. But it also marked an audacious effort by Singer, who then stepped up to the *X-Men* and *Superman* franchises. Handling McQuarrie's Byzantine screenplay with breathtaking aplomb, he tips his hat to Akira Kurosawa and Raymond Chandler, refuses to be cowed by his cast, and delivers one of the craftiest thrillers in years.

THE DISCS

'Lose the leather pants', sneers Kevin Pollak during one of several interviews included on Disc 2. Intended for co-star Stephen Baldwin, it's further evidence that the two of them got on like a house on fire, as well as one of several strange moments on the disc. Alongside deleted scenes and a bizarre gag reel featuring the regrettable Keyser Söze rap, there are five short documentaries.

The first features a series of interviews with the main characters. Best of all is Gabriel Byrne, who says he didn't want to appear in the film and that he'd only agreed to do it if it was shot in Los Angeles in fewer than five weeks – unaware that that was all the producers had budgeted for. And he's unwittingly amusing in a documentary called 'Keyser Söze, Fact or Fiction?' Trying to shed light on the identity of the Hungarian druglord at the heart of the movie, Byrne says he thought he was Keyser Söze right up until he saw the final cut.

Other highlights include two commentary tracks – the first by Singer and McQuarrie, the second by editor and composer John Ottman – and a segment on the sheer impenetrability of Benicio del Toro's Martian dialogue. (The Region 1 SE also includes a handful of Easter eggs, notably an interview with composer/editor John Ottman.) (JAMES CLASPER)

Uzak

(Turkey, 2002)

Director: Nuri Bilge Ceylan
Label: Artificial Eye (UK)
Region: 2 (PAL)
Discs: 1

THE FILM

Ceylan's 2003 Cannes prizewinner is a masterpiece, but a very modest masterpiece. A near-silent account of two cousins failing to communicate in a snowy, muffled Istanbul of CD stores and Ottoman backstreets, *Uzak* is emphatically *not* just an updated essay in 1960s Antoniennui and whereof-we-cannot-speak defeatism. Sure, the backdrop evokes the opening of a Pamuk novel before the first whisperings of gnosis, and there's a hint of high-art exhibitionism in the slow, stately and heavily-filtered camerawork: ignore all this, though, and the film is a beautifully *ordinary* work about people going about the practical dramas of everyday life.

Mehmet Emin Toprak gives a lovely performance as Yusuf, the country mouse hitting town in the doomed hope of finding work in the docks, only to become ever more sexually frustrated in the middle of mini-skirted Istanbullu modernity. Like Mark Ruffalo in *You Can Count On Me*, he convincingly depicts a man who knows he's making mistakes even as he makes them, yet can't stay his hand from the wrong course of action. Equally good is Muzaffer Özdemir as Yusuf's increasingly resentful host Mahmut, a first-generation city-dweller making a living on photography contracts whose pretensions to urbanity are undermined by his cousin's arrival with a fake leather holdall and a single pair of shoes. The issue here is not Turkey's (enormous) town–country divide, but the fragility of the personae we create for ourselves. Like Ceylan's own character in the rather less successful *Climates* (2006), Mahmut's got himself in the trap of appearing a better man than he is: and it's difficult to maintain this illusion if your cousin's forever eating crisps on the other side of the room.

THE DISC

Some nice features available both on a good disc from Artificial Eye and a cheaper edition released in Turkey by Palermo. No director's commentary anywhere in Turkish or English, sadly, but as compensation there's *Koza*, a heavily *Mirror*-influenced short which involves grass blowing in the wind and lots of symbolic objects on fire, plus on the Palermo disc a breathless promo piece chronicling *Uzak*'s Cannes triumph. Best of all, there's a 40-minute compilation of behind-the-scenes footage, with lots of camera assistants heroically chain-smoking their way through Istanbul blizzards, and a priceless sequence with Nuri and the boys dutifully working their way through porn movies to find a clip that'll be dramatically appropriate for a scene in the film, and sniggering. (PETER VÁSÁRY)

Van Gogh
(France, 1991)

Director: Maurice Pialat
Label: Artificial Eye (UK)
Region: 2 (PAL)
Discs: 2

THE FILM

'There's one terrible thing in this world, and that is that everyone has their reasons.' This line from Renoir became axiomatic for a certain tendency of humanist cinema, but in Pialat's films these reasons are not always knowable. *Van Gogh* follows the three months in the painter's life prior to his suicide at the age of 37, most of which were spent in an attempt at psychological recuperation – think Boudu, drowning – at the house of Dr Gachet near Paris. Where everything in Minnelli's *Lust For Life* exists to explain this final act, in Pialat's version, however tormented Van Gogh becomes, the end is never inevitable.

Instead, and arising from Pialat's characteristically rough-and-ready technique, belonging to Renoir's alfresco tradition, the film suggests lives going on between shots, outside the frame – and, matter-of-factly, after the artist's death. At its anguished heart is Jacques Dutronc's portrayal of Antonin Artaud's 'man suicided by society'. Intense, beset by inner demons that Pialat, with Artaud, does not think psychiatry can explain, disgusted by the commercial art world represented by his brother Théo, and by Gachet's bourgeois contentment, Pialat and Dutronc's Vincent is unreasonable, not wholly sympathetic and finally unfathomable. Pialat once claimed 'the case of Van Gogh was very simple: he was a guy who painted, period. I don't think that type of person really has a life.' There's no romantic artist bullshit here: this is the Van Gogh who sank without trace.

THE DISCS

At one point in the deleted scenes Van Gogh compares himself harshly with Gachet's hero Cézanne: 'I'm satisfied with a rough, easy technique.' While former painter Pialat was not easily satisfied, the line holds good for the director's own working methods – and functional madness – as explored on Artificial Eye's second disc. Introduced by Pialat's distinguished long-time editor Yann Dedet (now a regular collaborator with Pialat disciple Cédric Kahn), the deleted scenes are unusually welcome for the insight they provide into Pialat's elliptical approach to narrative. According to Dedet 'when he got fed up with a scene, we stopped it . . . editing is cutting shots when you're bored, and starting them where you want them'. What the director wanted to leave out would have made a less oblique portrait – though other cuts, such as a great sequence detailing Van Gogh's farm labourer-like working day in the wheat fields, seem to have been made simply because Pialat – according to an amusing interview with the star – detested Dutronc's manner of painting.
(HENRY K MILLER)

Vertigo
(USA, 1958)

Director: Alfred Hitchcock
Label: Universal (UK)
Region: 2 (PAL)
Discs: 1

THE FILM

Cascading violins, eyes nervously flicking left to right, a pupil dissolving into a void: *Vertigo*'s score (Bernard Herrmann) and its title sequence (Saul Bass) are enmeshed so perfectly it's nigh-impossible to imagine one without the other. Both suck us into Hitchcock's most morbid and obsessive romance, his strangest thriller, and, not coincidentally, his most critically adored film: one in which cinema's preeminent psychoterrorist has himself, and his audience, squirming on the couch.

San Fran private dick Scottie (James Stewart, never better) is scared of heights. But that's not the only thing he's scared of: the title motif seems both red herring and metaphor for his precarious sanity, setting us up continually for a fall. Hired to trail Kim Novak's daydreamy blonde, Madeleine, for a client, Scottie tumbles right into the trap that's been laid for him. It's just that no-one expected him to fall so hard, or so far . . .

Abruptly, *Vertigo* starts again. Instead of titles we get a Bass-designed dream sequence, and Herrmann serves up a deadly tarantella. Start watching the film from this point, and it has the elusive logic of a nightmare, as the events of the first half are replayed through a glass darkly. Madeleine's dead, and instead there's Judy, whom Scottie goes about turning into Madeleine. Hitchcock wanted Vera Miles for the role; he got Novak, whom he proceeded to turn into Vera Miles.

The movie's mind-boggling chromatic oppositions – red for confinement and repression, green for liberation and fantasy – indicate how in the space of four years Hitchcock had achieved a mastery of colour to rival William Egglestone. When Gus Van Sant remade *Psycho*, he took all this on board. MOTEL's done in red neon; VACANCY's in green.

THE DISC

Thanks to the bang-up restoration work of Robert Harris and James Katz, *Vertigo* looks richer and sharper than ever before, and sounds . . . different. The degraded state of the original sound elements prompted the restorers to re-dub various foley effects and use a new stereo recording of Herrmann's score, a decision which wasn't universally popular. There's an original mono option for purists (currently only on the 'Alfred Hitchcock Master's Collection' box set in R1), a half-hour featurette ('Obsessed with *Vertigo*') detailing the work done, and a commentary with the restorers. Screenwriter Samuel Taylor also pops up to describe the movie perfectly as your usual tale of 'boy meets girl, boy loses girl, boy meets girl again, boy loses girl again'. Oh, and location-spotters should scrap that visit to the tower at San Juan Batista: it hasn't got one.
(TIM ROBEY)

Videodrome
(USA, 1983)

Director: David Cronenberg
Label: Criterion Collection (USA)
Region: 1 (NTSC)
Discs: 2

THE FILM

For many the quintessential Cronenberg film, and certainly the point at which his obsessive, metaphysical body horror broke him out of the ghetto, *Videodrome* remains, paradoxically, the director's most oblique and challenging work to date.

James Woods carries the film magnificently as sleazy porno cable TV boss Max Renn, whose search for stronger kicks leads him to the enigmatic, sadistic satellite station Videodrome. As he closes in on the source of the signal, strange figures emerge from the static: video demiurge Brian O'Blivion, Debbie Harry's masochistic Nicki Brand and the sinister corporateer Barry Convex. The more he learns about Videodrome, the shakier Renn's grip on reality becomes, until his disturbing hallucinations end up indistinguishable from reality.

A powerful synthesis of sex, gore, science fiction and ontological vexation, *Videodrome* remains a potent, prescient statement about the media's role in shaping reality. Its preoccupation with the loss of personal identity and the physical manifestations of unconscious urges – a literal visualisation of Freud's often bizarre notions of libido – have been shared by nearly all Cronenberg's films, but find perhaps their fullest expression here. Despite its focus on a 20-year-old technology, and reliance on prosthetic make-up effects (most of which still look stunning), the *Videodrome* signal remains strong. So strong in fact, that Cronenberg effectively remade the film with *eXistenZ* and revisited it in *A History of Violence*.

THE DISCS

Two discs packaged in a super-cool faux-Betamax case. Disc 1 contains a great, crisp print of the film, tweaked for 16:9 widescreen TVs, along with two lively commentaries from Cronenberg and DP Mark Irwin, and James Woods and Debbie Harry. Disc 2's treats include a documentary about Rick Baker's prosthetic effects and the joys of filming gallons of pig innards for hours on end, a flood of behind-the-scenes photos, and a 25-minute discussion between Cronenberg, John Landis and John Carpenter, shot as a Universal promo film in 1982. This last item makes for particularly nostalgic viewing, especially given that Cronenberg is really the only one of the three directors to have lived out the 20th century with his reputation intact. (MARK PILKINGTON)

The Jean Vigo Collection

(France, 1930–34)

Director: Jean Vigo
Label: Artificial Eye (UK)
Region: 2 (PAL)
Discs: 2

THE FILMS

Few great directors' complete works could be compiled on a single DVD, but then few had as little time as Jean Vigo, who died of septicemia at 29. Not that there's anything vauntingly self-aggrandising about his art – on the contrary, part of what makes these films still so fresh and vital is their playful free spirits and keen feeling. The son of an anarchist journalist killed in prison during WWI, Vigo made what he called 'schoolboy's cinema', refusing conformity and cliché, so that his brief career was clouded not only by ill health but by censorship and producers' meddling.

His first film, *À Propos de Nice* (1930), co-credited to his regular collaborator, the great-cinematographer-to-be Boris Kaufman, is a city symphony with a decidedly surrealist bent, skewering the resort's picture-postcard glamour with a carnivalesque sense of the grotesque. *Taris, Champion de Natation* (1931) is a minor frolic, deconstructing the French swimming champion's various strokes in slow- and reverse-motion.

But Vigo's reputation really rests on two films, the 45-minute boarding-school rampage *Zéro de Conduite* (1933) and the floating love poem *L'Atalante* (1934). A puckish summons to subversion and revolt, *Zéro* is as coltish and cruel as the boys it depicts, cocking a snook at authority figures everywhere. Banned in France until 1945, its influence on Truffaut's *The 400 Blows* and Lindsey Anderson's *If . . .* is marked. The dream-like tone carries through into *L'Atalante*, a portrait of a newly wed couple's tugs of love on board a barge on the Seine. Handed the screenplay as a deliberately banal outline by his producer, Vigo gave the story a third leg in the form of Michel Simon's salty sailor Père Jules, added some not incidental sideswipes at urban inequity, and fashioned a subtle but rapturous paean to the confounding power of love. It's a film that never ceases to surprise and beguile.

THE DISCS

Artificial Eye's compendium boasts Gaumont's excellent digital transfers (including the 2001 revisit of the 1990 restoration of *L'Atalante*, still broken in places). The second disc carries Jacques Rozier's 1964 feature-length documentary, incorporating interviews with Vigo's friends and collaborators including actors Dita Parlo, Jean Dasté and Simon. There's also an appreciation by the Georgian auteur Otar Iosseliani, a look at *L'Atalante*'s multiple incarnations and the three sound films' audio restorations, Gaumont newsreel footage of Taris in action, and a stills and posters gallery. A rival French double-disc set features some of this and some alternate commentaries and reflections (including a short by Portuguese auteur Manoel de Oliveira), but without English subtitles. (NICK BRADSHAW)

Visions of Light

(USA/Japan, 1992)

Directors: Arnold Glassman, Todd McCarthy, Stuart Samuels
Label: BFI (UK)
Region: 2 (PAL)
Discs: 1

THE FILMS

Interviewed at the start of this American Film Institute-produced tribute to the art of the cinematographer, the late, legendary director of photography Conrad Hall (*Cool Hand Luke*, *American Beauty*) reveals he's always thought one of his jobs is to ensure the viewer could turn down the sound on any of his films, and still figure out what was going on. By extension, the same holds true for *Visions of Light* – which highlights the work of the world's greatest lensmen – but it's even better watched with the volume up.

Turning the camera on the cameramen at the very least helps put faces to those names (such as Hall, Michael Chapman and Vittorio Storaro) that have graced the credits of many of the twentieth century's most essential works. But the documentary's lines of inquiry are shaped entirely by the cinematographer's eye: the interviewees prove capable of identifying subtle shades, and distinct camera styles, in – to take one example – a set of *films noirs* that might otherwise have been lumped together.

Glassman and his collaborators strike a blow for DoPs everywhere by crediting clips of *The Magnificent Ambersons* to Stanley Cortez over Orson Welles, and those of *The Birth of a Nation* to Billy Bitzer over DW Griffith. The usual suspectacles – *Gone with the Wind*, *Lawrence of Arabia*, *Days of Heaven* – are paraded like the treasures they are, but the film shows real nous by including examples from films that don't instantly strike you as visually sophisticated: *The Cocoanuts* (see *The Marx Brothers*), *Jaws*, *Dog Day Afternoon*.

An eventual sequel might outline how digital technology, and the business of having to incorporate elements that aren't physically present in the frame, has shaped the cinematographer's art. In the meantime, though, this is as good a tribute to a very particular form of craftsmanship as the optical nerve could wish for. Pause *Visions of Light* at almost any moment in its 90 minutes and, chances are, the image wouldn't look out of place in a gallery.

THE DISC

Given that the main feature is, in its own way, the ultimate making-of, the BFI's package is sensible in adhering to a less-is-more philosophy, and letting the film speak for itself, 30 seconds' worth of camera-themed newsreel from 1922 aside. The transfer, as you'd hope from a film so concerned with *the look* of cinema, is pin-sharp; the occasional shift in aspect ratio all the better to accommodate some masterly, unforgettable images. (MIKE MCCAHILL)

The War Game & Culloden
(UK, 1965/1964)

Director: Peter Watkins
Label: New Yorker Films (USA)
Region: 1 (NTSC)
Discs: 1

THE FILMS

Peter Watkins' first films belong to the dawn of British television drama's golden age, but like the work of his contemporary Alan Clarke, they have easily outstripped both their medium and their national tradition – as well as meeting the limits of the BBC's liberalism. For *Culloden*, broadcast in December 1964, Watkins re-enacted a much-mythologised episode in British – or rather, Scottish and English – history, his only break from the record being to embed a *cinema vérité* crew on the battlefield, interviewing participants at all levels of the hierarchy on either side and getting in the thick of the action.

As a result, history in *Culloden* is not the predetermined thing of conventional cinematic reconstruction – or, pointedly, of Whig historiography, one of whose practitioners is among the cast – but something that unfolds before our eyes, or more to the point those of its helpless participants. Watkins' next film took the same approach to a more immediately contentious topic: the likely effects of a nuclear attack on the civilian population of Britain. Confronting the comforting words of the official literature on 'civil defence' with the reality of modern warfare and the known consequences of area bombing on Germany and Japan, *The War Game* (1965) is every bit as harrowing as it needed to be.

Burning through the fourth wall, Watkins once again interviews his non-pro cast, but this time without the pretence of characterisation, revealing a shocking ignorance of the effects of radioactive fall-out and, perhaps as a result, a terrifying will to vengeance among the British public. Watkins' depiction of a firestorm in Rochester, Kent, renders rhetorical the question posed at the end of the film: 'Would the survivors envy the dead?'

THE DISC

New Yorker's double A-side has commentaries from two British academics with full access both to Watkins himself and his archives, much of it hitherto unpublished. The BBC, in Watkins' words, 'violated their own Charter of Independence' by showing *The War Game* to Whitehall mandarins for (dis)approval, and Patrick Murphy's commentary, backed up with a booklet essay, contains a forensically detailed account of what amounted to the corporation's decision to invite the Home Office to suppress its own film. Though a press campaign obtained theatrical distribution for the film – eventually winning an Oscar for, surreally, Best Documentary – it was not broadcast in Britain until 1985. Dr John Cook's equally well-researched *Culloden* commentary meanwhile explores Watkins' semi-amateur m.o. as a form of political utopianism. (HENRY K MILLER)

John Wayne–John Ford Film Collection

(USA, 1939–57)

Director: John Ford
Label: Warners
Region: 1 (NTSC)
Discs: 10

FILM TITLES: *The Searchers, Stagecoach, Fort Apache, She Wore a Yellow Ribbon, The Wings of Eagles, They Were Expendable, 3 Godfathers, The Long Voyage Home*

THE FILMS

Although both men made well over 100 films in careers that stretched from the silent period through to the 1970s, the 14 titles on which John Wayne and John Ford collaborated remain indelible. Wayne had first worked on a Ford film as a prop man back in 1927, but it wasn't until 1939 that the old man cast him in a speaking role. The film was *Stagecoach*, a prestige 'New Deal' western that resuscitated the ailing genre and helped propel Duke from B-movie star to American icon. Orson Welles said he learned to direct by running the picture 30 times.

If *Stagecoach* now looks a little creaky, 1956's *The Searchers* remains a vital work. Wayne is Ethan Edwards, hunting down the Commanche who murdered his brother's family and kidnapped his niece. There is a devastating moment when we realise that if Ethan 'rescues' Debbie he means to kill her. *The Searchers* clearly confronts the latent racist anxieties and historical suppressions which agitate Wayne and the western. Shot in Technicolor, it is both Ford's most terrible and his most beautiful work.

Fort Apache (1948) and *She Wore a Yellow Ribbon* (1950) are two thirds of the popular cavalry trilogy (*Rio Grande* is MIA), the first an astute appraisal of the Custer myth with Henry Fonda as the vainglorious martinet Owen Thursday, the second a more elegiac picture with a moving performance from Wayne as Captain Nathan Brittles. *The Long Voyage Home* (1940) is a curio, a doomy Eugene O'Neill adaptation with arty cinematography by Gregg Toland and Wayne trying on a Swedish accent. *3 Godfathers* (1948) and *The Wings of Eagles* (1957) will appeal to completists, but *They Were Expendable* (1945) is another bona fide classic, one of the most honest and heartfelt pictures to come out of WWII.

THE DISCS

Both *Stagecoach* and *The Searchers* get lavish double-disc treatment as befits their status as landmarks in American film, with new transfers, commentary tracks, and above par supplementary documentaries (including Nick Redman's *A Turning of the Earth* and an appreciation for *The Searchers* featuring Martin Scorsese, John Milius and Curtis Hanson). A few more make-weight docs are spread across the other discs. These titles are also available separately, as are such key Wayne–Ford movies as *The Man Who Shot Liberty Valance*, *Rio Grande* and *The Quiet Man*. (TOM CHARITY)

The Lina Wertmüller Collection

(Italy, 1974–99)

Director: Lina Wertmüller
Label: Koch Lorber (USA)
Region: 1 (NTSC)
Discs: 6

FILM TITLES: Summer Night, The Nymph, Swept Away, Seven Beauties, Ferdinand and Carolina

THE FILMS

The one thing saving Guy Ritchie's career from complete ignominy is that his remake of the controversial 1974 thriller *Swept Away* reawakened interest in its director, Italy's Lina Wertmüller. The first woman to receive an Academy Award nomination for Best Director (for *Seven Beauties* in 1977), Wertmüller is the Brecht of sex.

Rather than economics and power, the narrative tensions in her films come down to desire – which, given her gorgeous actors and sets, is far more photogenic. While her tempestuous portraits of macho men and wilful women have been accused of misogyny and melodrama, they are hostage to neither. Her films are fascinated by power's submission to desire – and not just the desire for a person, but the desire to be desired by them. The relations between the sexes are every inch as epic, as bloody and as thrilling as war.

The sides are equally matched: whether it's communist sailor Gennarino and the wealthy socialite he desires dragging each other around a desert island by the hair in *Swept Away*, or the eponymous, voracious Neapolitan royals plotting each other's downfall in *Ferdinando and Carolina* (1999), there's a wit and daring to Wertmüller's wild scripts matched by the high drama of the performances and the outrageously lush cinematography. Like fellow Italian Bernardo Bertolucci, Wertmüller is a dazzling Technicolor artist: the depths of the Mediterranean and the interior of palaces come equally, riotously alive.

Wertmüller began her training in the theatre, and her filmmaking career with Federico Fellini, and it shows – in how far she can push her performers, in how every gesture and word illuminates the screen. At the end of an illustrious career, her costume drama *Ferdinando and Carolina* stands as an example of a master of Italian new wave cinema still in full possession of her politics, her sense of irony, and her inventive energies.

THE DISCS

In the substantial Italian television interview included on the sixth disc of extras, Wertmüller describes her filmmaking style as the ability 'to turn serious defeats into the desire to fight'. As well as offering a delirious snapshot album of the foundational years of Italian post-war cinema, she offers sage advice and canny criticism of her own work with great wit and style. An informative 16-page booklet by critic John Simon contextualises the director's long and varied career.

Koch Lorber's set is a good survey of Wertmüller's biggest American hits. The restored transfers are generally good, even if only two of the five titles are widescreen-enhanced. (SOPHIE MAYER)

When the Levees Broke: A Requiem in Four Acts
(USA, 2006)

Director: Spike Lee
Label: HBO (USA)
Region: 1 (NTSC)
Discs: 3

THE FILM

Spike Lee is the most frustrating of US filmmakers. While the eye-popping *mise-en-scène* and strong characters of *Do the Right Thing* (1989) and *25th Hour* (2002) rival anything by his peers, they're tainted by untamed elements and sledgehammered-home messages. *Levees*, on the other hand, his rapid response to New Orleans' Hurricane Katrina catastrophe, exhibits artful understatement: focused, finely drawn and furious, it's his best film to date.

Over four acts, Lee's hundred-strong line-up of victims, journalists, academics, politicians and celebrities takes us through the events of late August 2005. The hurricane itself is documented within the first half hour; the real damage was done by the resulting flood-defence breaches, which put 80 per cent of the city under water and left (mostly poor) residents drowning, stranded on rooftops and sweltering in the Superdome for five days waiting for federal government help. Then the film turns to the equally traumatic aftermath, which saw lives ruined, rubble not being cleared, evacuees not returning and The Big Easy facing an uncertain future.

'How could this happen in America?' the participants repeatedly ask, and what's perhaps most impressive about *Levees* is its tireless attempt to provide answers. As if dissatisfied with every reason proffered, it's constantly widening its scope – pointing the finger at, among other causes, local political spats, poor state–federal dialogue, the Bush government's indifference, New Orleans' long-term neglect and ecological problems.

Without a voice-over and Lee nowhere to be seen, everything's skilfully woven from the testimonies (plus footage and stills), which, chopped into bite-sized snippets, pull you through some jaw-dropping stories (looking disturbingly baffled, one young guy explains how he returned home after a few weeks to find his mum's rotting corpse wedged under the fridge).

Unsensationalist and all the more powerful for it, this adds up to a nuanced anatomy of a terrible tragedy, which, in turn, flashes light on the complacency and awry priorities of Bush-era America. Whether its commendable restraint is a sign of Lee's maturation, or speechlessness at the still-unfolding devastation, however, only time will tell.

THE DISCS

An hour and 50 minute-long fifth act, 'Next Movement', included on the DVD, is less a continuation than a consolidation, expanding stories and issues from the first four parts (including Sean Penn's self-financed rescue campaign). The odd outburst aside, Lee's commentary on the main film is mostly lackadaisical, mentioning how Katrina news reports moved him to start filming just one month after it struck, as well as how he'd like to continue following his subjects *7-Up*-style – though his yelling of 'Travis Bickle!' whenever a certain traumatised interviewee appears somewhat taints his show of concern. Completing the package is a photo gallery set to a score by New Orleans resident, and *Levees* interviewee, Terence Blanchard. (NICK FUNNELL)

Where Eagles Dare

(USA, 1968)

Director: Brian G Hutton
Label: Warners (all territories)
Region: Any
Discs: 1

THE FILM

Orson Welles famously called the cinematic apparatus 'the biggest electric train set any boy ever had'. Frequently, though, it's been more like an elaborate game of toy soldiers: Airfix model warfare on a 1:1 scale. A favourite of Quentin Tarantino, the Coen brothers, and my dad, *Where Eagles Dare* is the apotheosis of the WWII action-and-adventure yarn. Interminable, incomprehensible ('but to the British, very, very simple') and incredibly violent, it's credited to one Brian G Hutton, who went on to make another hit with the spoofy and cynical *Kelly's Heroes*. But *Eagles*, scripted by Alistair MacLean, is played straight.

The film opens and closes on a captured German aircraft carrying a team of Allied commandos through the Bavarian Alps. In the two-and-a-half hours between these two moments our guys, led by MI6 agent Major Smith (Richard Burton) and US Ranger Lieutenant Schaffer (Clint Eastwood), parachute in, get taken prisoner, escape, infiltrate the impregnable Schloss Adler – regional headquarters of German intelligence *and* the Wehrmacht Alpenkorps – rescue a captured American general, reveal that the general is *really* an actor, uncover a Nazi spy ring in Britain, kill about 500 stormtroopers, exfiltrate via cable car, and somehow get to the airfield for the trip back to Blighty. The true object of their mission remains elusive right up until the final scene, and even then you have your doubts.

If one wanted to construct a cinephile's alibi for *Where Eagles Dare*, it could be called the missing link between *Look Back in Anger*, *The Wild Bunch*, *Last Year at Marienbad* and Nicholas Ray's *Bitter Victory*. But it is perhaps a sad day when such calculations become necessary.

THE DISC

Louder, wider and longer, *Where Eagles Dare* was part of Hollywood's long rearguard action against television, when bigness was all. Four decades on, it's best known in a substandard, monaural television version as a staple of the holiday season schedules. Though no home viewing system can duplicate the full 70mm experience, the transfer on this DVD replicates the proper aspect ratio and whatnot; while the sound, which preserves the original stereo mix of Ron Goodwin's score, is awesome.

An *On Location* promotional film is mostly valuable for its hilarious voiceover ('memories of Nazi tyranny are brought to vivid life by the invasion – of a movie company'), especially the preposterous claim that the film set out 'to recreate one of World War II's most exciting adventures'. (HENRY K MILLER)

Whity

(West Germany, 1970)

Director: Rainer Werner Fassbinder
Label: Fantoma (USA)
Region: 0 (NTSC)
Discs: 1

THE FILM

Every director produces anomalies. The long-unseen *Whity*, shot in lurid, over-ripe Technicolor, is the work least readily assimilated into the canon of the erstwhile art-house darling Rainer Werner Fassbinder. As one of the director's most obscure films, *Whity* is an unorthodox proposition, but a fascinating example of genre cinema colliding with art-house.

This film is completely deranged: a western, in German, shot in a Spanish village owned by Sergio Leone, with one actor in black face, another wearing white make-up, and a prevailing atmosphere of downbeat camp. Fassbinder's then-lover, Gunther Kaufmann, plays the slave Whity, who is the illegitimate son of the black maid and the white plantation owner. The picture contains many examples of classic Fassbinder over-emphasis, in which a shot or gesture is protracted to the point of absurdity and beyond – note the agonizing, endless laughter with which a mother greets the sight of her son dressed in a Ku Klux Klan hood, or the moment when Whity and his lover Hanna (Fassbinder's muse, Hanna Schygulla) freeze during a post-coital financial trans-action. And yet it doesn't take long for our laughter to subside and the film to be revealed for what it is: a cool anthropological study of the racial and social dynamics of desire.

THE DISC

On the Fantoma DVD edition, the only extra is an audio commentary by the actor/producer Ulli Lommel (who went on to direct the creepy *Tenderness of Wolves*) and cinematographer Michael Ballhaus, who later worked with Coppola and Scorsese. There is little of the gossip surrounding the film's production, which was so traumatic that it inspired Fassbinder's hellish film-about-film-making, *Beware of a Holy Whore*. But Ballhaus is good on his relationship with Fassbinder: 'I remember my first meeting with him. He was not so friendly. Maybe he was shy. Or just not nice. Because I'd made more films than him, he felt I'd try to do things he didn't like, so it was constantly a fight between us.'

After watching dailies, the director was so blown away by Ballhaus's work that he went out and got drunk; the next day's shooting had to be cancelled. Ballhaus maintains that, even after this show of approval, he dare not unpack his luggage for three weeks because he was convinced Fassbinder would fire him. Lommel, for his part, reveals that in later years Fassbinder was averse to Spielberg movies: 'He couldn't stand them. He'd say, "They're so exciting that you forget you're in a movie. There's no time for reflection. Afterwards, you're sillier than when you went in."' (RYAN GILBEY)

The Wicker Man

(UK, 1974) 3-Disc Collector's Edition

Director: Robin Hardy
Label: Optimum (UK)
Region: 2 (PAL)
Discs: 3

THE FILM

In film, lasting cult status is something that is earned, not consciously created. And if any film deserves such a sobriquet, it's *The Wicker Man*, which for years was as swathed in legend as the fiery giant of the title.

When Christian copper Sergeant Howie (Edward Woodwood) visits Summerisle off the coast of Scotland in search of a missing child, he finds a community that has rejected Christianity in favour of something . . . older. As Howie's search intensifies, so his disgust at the island's pagan ways grows. He is literally led round the houses until he confronts the dapper Lord Summerisle himself (Lee, in what must be his finest role), and the true horror of the situation is made fatally clear.

Crammed with creepy imagery and fantastic detail, the film's eerie heathen atmosphere is bolstered by a continuous soundtrack of folk songs olde and new by Paul Giovani and Gary Carpenter, many of them so cleverly integrated into the film that it often feels like a musical. (This reviewer's dream of a stage version starring Lee and Cliff Richard as Howie has sadly never been realised.)

With its colourful depictions of rural folklore and earth magic, it's no wonder that the film has inspired its own magazine, *Nuada*, academic conferences and even occasional wicker-man-burning ceremonies. It's also probably done more to inspire successive generations of neo-pagans and wiccans than 100 books on the subject. The film was so plagued with difficulties following its production that writer Anthony Shaffer considered it cursed, and it's only thanks to the persistence of its obsessive fans, and the faith of many of its cast and crew – including Christopher Lee, who has declared it to be the best of his many films – that it survives in its original form today.

Not exactly a horror flick, but immensely spooky nonetheless, it remains one of the most unique films ever to have emerged from the UK, as its hallowed reputation suggests.

THE DISCS

This double-disc edition includes both the original theatrical version, in a great, clean print, and the Director's Cut, with the 'lost' scenes reinserted. Because the original negatives are still missing, these scenes are a little the worse for wear, but are a welcome addition nonetheless. We also get a commentary from director Hardy and stars Woodwood and Lee, two docs including Mark Kermode's 'Burnt Offering' on the film's cult, a separate interview with Lee, numerous trailers and an amazing bonus of Lee singing the 'Tinker's Song' on US television in 1979, along with a CD of the film's soundtrack. Bar an actual piece of the Wicker Man itself, what more could you ask for? (MARK PILKINGTON)

Winchester '73

(USA, 1950)

Director: Anthony Mann
Label: Universal (UK/USA)
Region: 2 (PAL) / 1 (NTSC)
Discs: 1

THE FILM

Winchester '73, a wistful revenge story set in the Wild West, marked the first collaboration between James Stewart and director Anthony Mann. The pair would go on to make a series of classic westerns together, including *The Far Country*, *Bend of the River* and *The Naked Spur*.

The story is surprisingly solemn. Stewart plays Lin McAdams, a sharp-shooter who rides into Dodge City and wins a much-coveted Winchester '73 rifle in a Fourth of July shooting competition. When the gun is stolen by Stephen McNally's snarling hoodlum Dutch, Stewart sets off in pursuit, running into Shelley Winters as the token moll, Rock Hudson as an Indian chief, and Dan Duryea as a garrulous Texan outlaw.

As impressive as the supporting roles are, it's Stewart who stands out. *Winchester '73* saw him adopt a new image – tougher, more intense, yet more vulnerable. He even called it a 'life saver', because the westerns he went on to make with Anthony Mann and John Ford revamped his Hollywood persona. But credit also goes to Mann and cinematographer William Daniels. *Winchester '73* is cleverly knit and beautifully shot – never more so than in the nailbiting final shoot-out.

THE DISC

There's only one special feature on Universal's release but it's worth treas-uring: the only commentary track James Stewart ever recorded. It's delightful to listen to Stewart reflect on his long and storied career. During the course of the movie, he discusses his work in radio, acting on Broadway during the Depression, and the Hollywood contract system, which saw him working for Universal. Stewart says he essentially had a full-time job, which required him to work out in the gym, take voice lessons, and learn the craft – a far cry from the pampered stars of Hollywood today.

There's also a touching story about the young Stewart writing and acting in a play called *To Hell with the Kaiser*, plus the obligatory anecdote about his father, who never got the acting lark and put his son's Academy Award for *The Philadelphia Story* in the window of his hardware store.

But, above all, Stewart's commentary is a unique opportunity to hear him talk about working with Mann, John Ford and Alfred Hitchcock. All of them realised that cinema is a visual art, Stewart says – and that, as much as words matter, a great story should always be told visually. (JAMES CLASPER)

Witchfinder General

(UK, 1968)

Director: Michael Reeves
Label: Prism Leisure (UK)
Region: 0 (PAL)
Discs: 1

THE FILM

From its unforgettable opening sequence of a woman being dragged screaming to a gallows and hanged as a witch, through to its despairing finale in the bowels of the earth, Michael Reeves's harrowing masterpiece spares no punches in its unflinching depiction of human savagery and moral corruptibility. Part Jacobean tragedy, part post-Hammer Gothic period horror, and part Anthony Mann/Budd Boetticher revenge western transplanted to the East Anglian countryside, Reeves's final film – more than delivering on the promise of his *Revenge of the Blood Beast* (1966) and *The Sorcerers* (1967) – proved him one of exploitation cinema's rare visionaries; and, while the cynicism of that vision doesn't appeal to all tastes, few would deny that Reeves's death from a barbiturate overdose at the age of just 25 was a significant loss for the British film industry.

Loosely based on a historical pot-boiler by Ronald Bassett, the film is set in 1645, with the chaos of the Civil War fanning the flames of superstition and allowing vicious opportunists like the Parliament-appointed 'Witchfinder' Matthew Hopkins (Vincent Price, imported at the behest of US co-producers AIP) and his brutish assistant John Stearne to stir the bloodlust of the peasantry and orchestrate the torture and execution of vulnerable outsiders. Reeves's regular star Ian Ogilvy plays Richard Marshall, a Roundhead trooper engaged to Sarah (striking ingénue Hilary Dwyer), the niece of a parish priest. After Sarah falls foul of Hopkins, Marshall becomes obsessed with tracking down his nemesis and dispensing some summary justice. For Reeves, violence is a contagion that debases everyone it touches; there is nothing ennobling in Marshall's quest for vengeance and no catharsis in his final, terrible act.

Reeves was keen to restrain Price's camp excesses (overly familiar from his Poe cycle with Roger Corman) and elicited a chillingly understated performance from the veteran star. At one point, an exasperated Price is said to have declared, 'Young man, I've been in 84 films. How many have you made?' Reeves' retort? 'Two good ones.' Reeves also gets great mileage out of his locations, juxtaposing his acts of brutality with the superficial tranquillity of the English countryside – resplendent in its autumnal beauty, but pregnant with hidden menace.

THE DISC

The disc contains a decent 16:9 transfer of the full 'Export' version of the film (with slightly extended violence for more lenient foreign markets) as well as the trimmed British version, trailers, a documentary about Reeves with contributions from his collaborators, and excellent production notes by critic Kim Newman. For good measure there's also a bizarrely atrocious music video for the track 'Matthew Hopkins' by UK 'doom metal' band Cathedral. (ANDY RICHARDS)

Withnail & I

(UK, 1987) 20th Anniversary Edition

Director: Bruce Robinson
Label: Anchor Bay (UK)
Region: 2 (PAL)
Discs: 3

THE FILM

It's odd that a film about two failed actors trudging around the Lake District should have rung so true with so many. An entire generation of 30-year-olds now knows the quotes, legends and drinking games associated with an unassuming low-budget comedy rooted in an era before their own.

The characters shamble through the film in a haze of drink and drugs; fittingly, it has episodes rather than a continual plot. Richard Griffiths has never been better than as Uncle Monty, comical, grotesque and ultimately pathetic, like a queeny Falstaff, uttering his lines with real relish. Richard E Grant is superb, both ridiculous and credible as the wretched Withnail, burnt-out and cynical before his career has begun. By turns bitter, weakly irascible and almost hysterically paranoid, he seems constantly on the verge of completely breaking down. Paul McGann, as the film's equivalent of a likeable everyman, puts in a subtle performance as the object of Withnail's contempt and Monty's lust.

Withnail & I ostensibly considers the death of '60s idealism, and has been seen as a commentary on friendship, masculinity and the countryside. Ultimately, though, it is about three characters trapped in lives that would seem miserable to the viewer were they not so funny, and about the struggle to escape to better things.

THE DISCS

Anchor Bay's anniversary set strikes a balance between explaining the film's improbable cult existence and pandering to it. Trailers and behind-the-scenes photos (taken by cartoonist Ralph Steadman) are provided, as are a Withnail drinking game and (as a hidden Easter egg) a 'Swearathon'. Bruce Robinson emerges to provide an informative if dry commentary and angrier interview, although you might prefer the sight of him in the 1999 documentary 'Withnail and Us', swilling wine and giving the worrying impression that Withnail is as much a hero to him as a figure of fun. A variety of obsessive fans also appear, quoting the film verbatim in incongruously reputable surroundings, and two make the pilgrimage to the film's Lake District locations in the featurette 'Postcards from Penrith'. There's another (older, funnier) commentary track by actors McGann and Ralph Brown. The DVD picture is sharply remastered and anamorphic (unlike even Criterion's slightly earlier version), although the Dolby 5.1 and DTS audio options are shams – nothing more than the stereo recording routed five ways. The third disc contains the film's original score (minus the songs). (TOBY FROST)

The Wizard of Oz

(USA, 1939) Special Edition

Director: Victor Fleming
Label: Warners (UK/USA)
Region: 2 (PAL) / 1 (NTSC)
Discs: 2

THE FILM

The positively, absolutely, undeniably and reliably beloved *Wizard of Oz* was far from dead on release in 1939, as legend would tell – though it was never likely to recoup its extraordinarily high production costs. Its wonderful whizness, however, was to be proved on the small screen, as it hop-skipped its ruby slippers into our hearts via ritual festive screenings on the magic box. As Dorothy said, there is no place like home.

It's a strange fate for a film so insistently cinematic, not least as this pioneer of glorious Technicolor was first broadcast in black and white. The vaudevillian turns of Lion, Tin Man and Scarecrow may be the teensiest bit theatrical, but the rest is stamped with MGM's signature insistence on the moviest movie that studio money could buy: glamorous, polished and utterly spectacular. Glowing bubbles convey pink-frocked witches, winged monkeys take to the skies and munchkins cavort in their own metropolis. We're carried away by a tornado so technically ingenious that the footage was still being borrowed in 1964, transported from our sepia lives to a world of yellow brick roads and emerald cities.

And this is not just delightful but a matter of moral worth: as the film insists, a willing suspension of disbelief brings its own rewards, and a Lion really has courage when he accepts a badge of bravery from a wizard whose powers, we know, are all smoke and mirrors. The cinemascape of Oz proffers life and liberty, though in pursuit of true happiness you must find your way home. Like *It's a Wonderful Life* and *Singin' in the Rain*, there's a tug between fantasies offered by filmic fakery and the down-to-earth decency of everyday life. But why choose? Watch the DVD, and Judy Garland will whisk you away above the chimney-pots without you setting foot beyond your own sofa.

THE DISCS

Benefiting from the film's 50th anniversary theatrical re-release, this two-disc special edition brings the hard-boiled sweetness of the film to fully restored audio-visual perfection. Though the primary-yellow packaging looks pitched at kids, the edition is all for the grown-up collector with glossy stills, premiere memorabilia, and over ten hours of extras, including now-famous deleted scenes. Of three documentaries, the tribute from contemporary technicians (including Peter Jackson) offers most illumination, while the commentary track is the best route to mining the many mythologies of Oz. (The rarer three-disc Collector's Edition box gathers an even dizzier wonderland of extras – enough that you may never leave home.) (REBEKAH POLDING)

Xiao Wu & Unknown Pleasures

(China, 1997/2002)

Director: Jia Zhang-Ke
Label: Artificial Eye (UK)
Region: 2 (PAL)
Discs: 2

ENGLISH TITLE: *Pickpocket*

THE FILMS

The films of Jia Zhang-ke, one of the leading forces of China's Sixth Generation of filmmakers, stand in stark contrast to the opulent period dramas of his predecessors. Directors like Zhang Yimou and Chen Kaige courted controversy from within the officially sanctioned film community, challenging censors with their veiled criticism of the state. Jia, like his peers Wang Xiaoshuai and Zhang Yuan, had to rely on private or foreign funding to produce their early gritty realist dramas, direct, scathing portraits of contemporary China.

In *Xiao Wu*, Jia's feature debut, the film's eponymous lead, a pickpocket, has become an embarrassment to his friends, whose lives have moved on from petty crime to something more insidious. Their trade – black marketeering and trafficking – is hardly legal, yet has the private support of local officials, willing to turn a blind eye provided their coffers are filled; Xiao Wu, by contrast, can barely stay one step ahead of the police's anti-crime sweep. Gripping in its complex characterisation, the film paints this troubled individual as a tragi-comic bit player in China's feverish embrace of capitalism and corruption. There are nods to Bresson, De Sica and, in its most comical moments, early Godard, but *Xiao Wu* still heralded a startlingly original voice.

Following the epic *Platform*, Jia moved on from his home-town of Fenyang to the more urban landscape of Datong, a depressed mining town, again in the north of China. Darker in tone than *Xiao Wu*, *Unknown Pleasures* again finds both comedy and compassion in the plight of its two leads, disaffected youths with little opportunity and no faith in the future. While Xiao Ji spends the film forlornly courting a local pop performer with bigger suitors to fry, Bin Bin resignedly watches his relationship with his studious girlfriend Qiao Qiao wither. Their only interface with the world appears to be through their consumption of mass media, but while state television may trumpet China's nomination to host the 2012 Olympics, the film itself finds more pointed prospects in the image of the half-built, half-abandoned Datong–Beijing highway, a literal road to nowhere.

THE DISCS

The grainy transfer of *Xiao Wu* is as good as could be expected from a 16mm film, and certainly suits the material. *Unknown Pleasures* is a more polished transfer, particularly in the darker nightclub scenes, which lose none of their potency. In an insightful interview, Jia expounds on the aesthetic of his work, the issues that underpin his films and how he manages to communicate his concerns whilst trying to avoid state censure. (IAN HAYDN SMITH)

Y Tu Mamá También

(Mexico, 2001)

Director: Alfonso Cuarón
Label: Icon (UK)
Region: 2 (PAL)
Discs: 1

ENGLISH TITLE: *And Your Mother Too*

THE FILM

Two best pals — though it's difficult, with one cosseted and indulged by
servants and the other nervy in a cramped little apartment (and God knows
if they even really *like* one another) — on a road trip. The aim along the way?
To bullshit their way into the knickers of a stranger they've picked up: a job
made a little tougher, of course, because each depends on his opposite not to
let slip what one friend will always know of another's little deceits. They drive,
and drink, and take turns to stomp off down the hillside in high dudgeon as
secrets are revealed and vanities laid bare; thank heavens for the kindness of
their intended, then, because these schmucks wouldn't get very far on their
own. Thus the marvellous *Sideways*, and it's no shame to Alexander Payne that
it's thus also Alfonso Cuarón's equally marvellous sex comedy pre-dating it by
two years.

Should any director aspire to that realism at which in *Sideways* Payne shows
himself adept, *Y Tu Mamá* is where s/he should turn before all else. Cuarón
has worked out the trick of the thing. Realism is not un-simulated fellatio,
sure, and it's not filming in an igloo; more relevantly, it's not the cruelty =
truth reductionism of a Todd Solondz, whose cut-out characters exist only
ever to illustrate a programmatic failing. Cuarón does realism as sympathy,
both for what we know of characters — whether Gael García Bernal's steamed-
up protagonist Julio or a beer-bellied fisherman glimpsed for a minute and
accorded a life in voice-over — and for what we shouldn't know: for fibs and
privacies and Julio's reluctance to admit that he always strikes a match after
taking a dump. It's all right, this film tells us, as we bump along the road,
occasional glimpses of labourers at the wayside setting a beautifully observed
study of fragile braggadocio within a far vaster humanistic worldview. You are
not alone.

THE DISC

There's no loneliness to be sensed in Icon's commentary, as Bernal, co-star
Diego Luna and some little-known actor who wanders through the opening
minutes of the movie in a beanie hat appear to throw packets of crisps at one
another in a recording studio, stumbling off to the loo or the vending machine
during the quieter sequences. Lots of discussion as to who has the spottier
backside, and voluble agreement that putting a Brian Eno song on the soundtrack was a serious creative error. (PETER VÁSÁRY)

Yi Yi

(Taiwan/Japan, 2000)

Director: Edward Yang
Label: Criterion Collection (USA)
Region: 1 (NTSC)
Discs: 1

ENGLISH TITLE: *A One and a Two*

THE FILM

Alongside Hou Hsiao-Hsien and the younger Tsai Ming-Liang, Edward Yang was one of the prime movers of the New Taiwanese Cinema of the 1980s and '90s, when filmmakers found rich and subtle ways to reflect on that country's turbulent history and growing pains. While his long-haul 1991 masterpiece, *A Brighter Summer Day*, couched those themes in the lives of a cluster of gang kids in the early '60s, Yang's films are mostly more urban and urbane than Hou's spare period pieces, fashioning contemporary portraits of a rapidly developing city (Taipei) exchanging traditional Confucian values for a nebulous and distended freedom. Formally elegant, they're also as gently humorous as they are complexly humane.

None, lamentably, are available on DVD in the West, with the excellent exception of *Yi Yi*, Yang's most touching film alongside *A Brighter Summer Day*. Using the simple structure of a few weeks in the life of an extended Taipei family, this intimate, impromptu epic shows and shapes more experience than most films dream of. With his elderly mother fallen into a coma, his wife Min-Min seeking sanctuary in a spiritual retreat, and his work colleagues scorning his business ethics, family head NJ is further ruffled by a chance encounter with the lover he left 30 years ago. His daughter Ting-Ting is experiencing her own first pangs of love, with a boy entangled with the mother and daughter next door, while her brother Yang-Yang (an eight-year-old proxy for the director?) busies himself taking snapshots of the backs of people's heads – the side of themselves they can't see.

As the character names suggest, Yang's perspective is kaleidoscopic, working motifs of reflections, partnerships, double-takes and second chances through the film's full fabric. And as the musical count-in of the English title connotes, it's an ensemble piece with a delightfully easy rhythm. Proceeding with the patience and insight of a fine novelist, Yang touches on everything from the present particulars of globalised urban anomie to the eternal business of transient love, finally elucidating a view on life as all-embracing as Shakespeare's 'Seven Ages of Man' speech.

THE DISC

Criterion's HD transfer is the best-looking *Yi Yi* DVD yet, certainly much improved on previous editions from Fox Lorber and the ICA. The latter's commentary track with Yang and Tony Rayns is carried over; there's a stolidly shot 15-minute to-camera interview with Rayns, 'Everyday Realities', expounding on the New Taiwanese Cinema of the 1980s and '90s; and in the liner booklet, some typically astute notes from Kent Jones, along with Yang's own on the film's title and casting. (NICK BRADSHAW)

INDEX

1978) 79; *Deren, Maya: Experimental Films* (Maya Deren [with Alexander Hammid], 1943–59) 81; *Die Hard* (John McTiernan, 1988) 83; *DodgeBall: A True Underdog Story* (Rawson Marshall Thurber, 2004) 85; *Donnie Darko* (Richard Kelly, 2001) 89; *Don't Look Back* (D.A. Pennebaker, 1967) 87; *Duck Soup* (Leo McCarey, 1933) 197; *Election* (Alexander Payne, 1999) 95; *Elf* (Jon Favreau, 2003) 96; The *Empire Strikes Back* (Irving Kirshner, 1980) 97; *The Errol Morris Collection* (1980–88) 208; *E.T.: The Extra-Terrestrial* (Steven Spielberg, 1982) 100; *Eternal Sunshine of the Spotless Mind* (Michel Gondry, 2004) 99; *The Exorcist* (William Friedkin, 1973) 101; *Far from Heaven* (Todd Haynes, 2002) 106; *Ferris Bueller's Day Off* (John Hughes, 1986) 107; *Fight Club* (David Fincher, 1999) 109; *The Film Noir Classic Collection, Vol I* (Various Directors, 1944–50) 110; *Final Destination 2* (David Ellis, 2003) 111; *Fort Apache* (John Ford, 1948) 333; *Frankenstein & Bride of Frankenstein* (James Whale, 1931 and 1935) 114; *The General* (Clyde Bruckman and Buster Keaton, 1926) 166; *Go West* (Buster Keaton, 1925) 166; *The Godfather DVD Collection* (Francis Ford Coppola, 1972–90) 120; *Gone with the Wind* (Victor Fleming, 1939) 121; *The Graduate* (Mike Nichols, 1967) 124; *Grease* (Randal Kleiser, 1978) 127; *Gremlins & Gremlins 2: The New Batch* (Joe Dante, 1984–90) 129; *Groundhog Day* (Harold Ramis, 1993) 130; *Gun Crazy* (Joseph H. Lewis, 1949) 110; *Hairspray* (John Waters, 1988) 132; *Hannah and Her Sisters* (Woody Allen, 1986) 133; *Harlan County, USA* (Barbara Kopple, 1976) 136; *Heat* (Michael Mann, 1995) 137; *Hedwig and the Angry Inch* (John Cameron Mitchell, 2001) 138; *Hellraiser Puzzle Box* (Various Directors, 1987–92) 139; *High Art* (Lisa Cholodenko, 1998) 141; *The Hired Hand* (Peter Fonda, 1971) 142; *The Hitcher* (Robert Harmon, 1986) 145; *Hoop Dreams* (Steve James, 1994) 146; *Horse Feathers* (Norman Z. MacLeod, 1932) 197; *I ♥ Huckabees* (David O. Russell, 2004) 150; *Imitation of Life* (Douglas Sirk, 1959) 152; *International House* (Edward Sutherland, 1933) 108; *Invasion of the Body Snatchers* (Philip Kaufman, 1978) 154; *The Iron Giant* (Brad Bird, 1999) 155; *It's a Gift* (Norman Z. MacLeod, 1934) 108; *iванxтс.* (Bernard Rose, 2000) 156; *Jaws* (Steven Spielberg, 1975) 157; *The Jerk* (Carl Reiner, 1979) 159; *John Wayne – John Ford Film Collection* (1939–57) 333; *Johnny Guitar* (Nicholas Ray; US, 1954) 161; *Junebug* (Phil Morrison, 2005) 164; *Kill Bill: Vols 1 & 2* (Quentin

Tarantino, 2003/4) 167; *The Killers* (Don Siegel, 1964) 168; *King Kong* (Merian C. Cooper and Ernest B. Schoedsack, 1933) 170; *The King of Comedy* (Martin Scorsese, 1983) 171; *Kiss Me Deadly* (Robert Aldrich, 1955) 173; *L.A. Confidential* (Curtis Hanson, 1997) 175; *Labyrinth* (Jim Henson, 1986) 176; *The Lady Eve* (Preston Sturges, 1941) 177; *The Last Picture Show* (Peter Bogdanovich, 1971) 178; *Laura* (Otto Preminger, 1944) 180; *Lilo and Stitch* (Dean DeBois and Chris Sanders, 2002) 183; *Little Foxes* (William Wyler, 1941) 185; *The Long Voyage Home* (John Ford, 1940) 333; *The Lord of the Rings: The Fellowship of the Rings* (Peter Jackson, 2001) 188; *Magnolia* (Paul Thomas Anderson, 1999) 190; *The Manchurian Candidate* (John Frankenheimer, 1962) 193; *Manhunter* (Michael Mann, 1986) 194; *Marathon Man* (John Schlesinger, 1976) 195; *Maria Full of Grace* (Joshua Marston, 2004) 196; *The Marx Brothers Silver Screen Collection* (Various Directors, 1929–33) 197; *Master and Commander: The Far Side of the World* (Peter Weir, 2003) 198; *The Matrix* (Larry and Andy Wachowski, 1999) 199; *Memento* (Chris Nolan, 2000) 201; *Metallica: Some Kind of Monster* (Joe Berlinger and Bruce Sinofsky, 2004) 203; *Monkey Business* (Norman Z. MacLeod, 1931) 197; *MouseHunt* (Gore Verbinski, 1998) 209; *Mrs Harris* (Phyllis Nagy, 2005) 210; *Mulholland Drive* (David Lynch, 2001) 211; *Murder, My Sweet* (Edward Dmytryk, 1944) 110; *My Little Chickadee* (Edward F. Cline, 1940) 108; *My Own Private Idaho* (Gus Van Sant, 1991) 213; *Nashville* (Robert Altman, 1975) 215; *The Navigator* (Donald Crisp and Buster Keaton, 1924) 166; *New York, New York* (Martin Scorsese, 1977) 216; *Night Moves* (Arthur Penn, 1975) 217; *The Night of the Hunter* (Charles Laughton, 1955) 219; *Night of the Living Dead* (George A. Romero, 1968) 317; *A Nightmare on Elm Street* (Wes Craven, 1984) 220; *Norman McLaren: Masters' Edition* (Various Directors, 1933–83) 200; *Once Upon a Time in the West* (Sergio Leone, 1968) 226; *The Others* (Alejandro Amenabar, 2001) 229; *Our Hospitality* (John G. Blystone and Buster Keaton, 1923) 166; *Out of the Past* (Jacques Tournier, 1947) 110; *The Passenger* (Michelangelo Antonioni, 1975) 234; *Sam Peckinpah – The Legendary Western Collection* (1961–73) 236; *Pee Wee's Big Adventure* (Tim Burton, 1985) 238; *A Personal Journey with Martin Scorsese through American Movies* (1995) 241; *Petulia* (Richard Lester, 1968) 242; *Planet of the Apes* (Franklin J. Schaffner, 1968) 245; *Point Blank*

(John Boorman, 1967) 246; *Predator* (John McTiernan, 1987) 249; *Psycho* (Alfred Hitchcock, 1960) 250; *Q: The Winged Serpent* (Larry Cohen, 1982) 252; *Raging Bull* (Martin Scorsese, 1980) 254; *Requiem for a Dream* (Darren Aronofsky, 2000) 259; *The Roaring Twenties* (Raoul Walsh, 1939) 260; *Roger & Me* (Michael Moore, 1989) 261; *The Royal Tenenbaums* (Wes Anderson, 2001) 265; *Safe* (Todd Haynes, 1995) 267; *Salesman* (Albert and David Maysles, 1969) 268; *Salvador* (Oliver Stone, 1986) 269; *School of Rock* (US, 2003) 273; *The Searchers* (John Ford, 1957) 333; *Secretary* (Steven Shainberg, 2000) 275; *Se7en* (David Fincher, 1995) 274; *Sense and Sensibility* (Ang Lee, 1995) 276; *The Set-Up* (Robert Wise, 1948) 110; *Seven Chances* (Buster Keaton, 1925) 166; *She Wore a Yellow Ribbon* (John Ford, 1950) 333; *Sherlock Junior* (Buster Keaton, 1924) 166; *The Shining* (Stanley Kubrick, 1980) 279; *Singin' in the Rain* (Stanley Donen and Gene Kelly, 1952) 282; *Solaris* (Steven Soderbergh, 2003) 283; *Some Like It Hot* (Billy Wilder, 1959) 284; *Spike Jonze, Work of* (1994–2003) 162; *Stagecoach* (John Ford, 1939) 333; *A Star is Born* (George Cukor, 1954) 287; *Starship Troopers* (Paul Verhoeven, 1997) 288; *Steamboat Bill Jr* (Charles Reisner, 1927) 166; *Stop Making Sense* (Jonathan Demme, 1984) 289; *Strange Days* (Kathryn Bigelow, 1995) 290; *Stranger than Paradise* (Jim Jarmusch, 1984) 291; *A Streetcar Named Desire* (Elia Kazan, 1951) 292; *Sunrise: A Song of Two Humans* (F.W. Murnau, 1927) 293; *Before Sunrise* (Richard Linklater, 1995) 25; *Sunset Boulevard* (Billy Wilder, 1950) 294; *Before Sunset* (Richard Linklater, 2004) 25; *The Talented Mr Ripley* (Anthony Minghella, 1999) 297; *Team America: World Police* (Trey Parker, 2004) 299; *The Terminator* (James Cameron, 1984) 301; *The Texas Chain Saw Massacre* (Tobe Hooper, 1974) 303; *The Buster Keaton Collection* (Various Directors, 1923–27) 166; *They Were Expendable* (John Ford, 1945) 333; *The Thin Red Line* (Terrence Malick, 1998) 305; *The Thing* (John Carpenter, 1982) 306; *This is Spinal Tap* (Rob Reiner, 1984) 308; *Three Ages* (Buster Keaton, 1923) 166; *The Three Burials of Melquiades Estrada* (Tommy Lee Jones, 2005) 309; *3 Godfathers* (John Ford, 1948) 333; *THX 1138* (George Lucas, 1971) 311; *Timecode* (Mike Figgis, 2000) 312; *Toy Story 2 – Special Edition* (John Lasseter, 1999) 315; *Toy Story – 10th Anniversary Edition* (John Lasseter, 1995) 315; *Twelve Monkeys* (Terry Gilliam, 1995) 318; *Unforgiven* (Clint Eastwood, 1992) 322; *United 93* (Paul Greengrass, 2006) 323; *The*

1913: *Fantômas* (Louis Feuillade, France) 105

1921–47: *Avant-Garde: Experimental Cinema of the 1920s and '30s* (Various Directors; US/France/Germany/Netherlands) 19

1923: *Our Hospitality* (John G. Blystone and Buster Keaton, US) 166; *Three Ages* (Buster Keaton, US) 166

1923–27: *The Buster Keaton Collection* (Various Directors, US) 166

1924: *The Navigator* (Donald Crisp and Buster Keaton, US) 166; *Sherlock Junior* (Buster Keaton, US) 166

1925: *Go West* (Buster Keaton, US) 166; *Seven Chances* (Buster Keaton, US) 166

1926: *Battling Butler* (Buster Keaton, US) 166; *The General* (Clyde Bruckman and Buster Keaton, US) 166; *Metropolis* (Fritz Lang, Germany) 204

1927: *College* (James W. Horne, US) 166; *Steamboat Bill Jr* (Charles Reisner, US) 166; *Sunrise: A Song of Two Humans* (F.W. Murnau, US) 293

1928: *The Passion of Joan of Arc* (Carl Th. Dreyer, France) 235

1929: *The Cocoanuts* (Robert Florey and Joseph Santley, US) 197; *Man with a Movie Camera* (Dziga Vertov, Soviet Union) 192; *Pandora's Box* (G.W. Pabst, Germany) 230

1929/1930: *Un Chien Andalou & L'Age d'Or* (Luis Buñuel and Salvador Dalí, France) 54

1929–33: *The Marx Brothers Silver Screen Collection* (Various Directors, US) 197

1930: *Animal Crackers* (Victor Heerman, US) 197; *The Blue Angel* (Josef von Sternberg, Germany) 33

1930–34: *The Jean Vigo Collection* (France) 330

1931: *City Lights* (Charlie Chaplin, US) 59; *Monkey Business* (Norman Z. MacLeod, US) 197

1931/1935: *Frankenstein & Bride of Frankenstein* (James Whale, US) 114

1932: *Horse Feathers* (Norman Z. MacLeod, US) 197

1933: *Duck Soup* (Leo McCarey, US) 197; *International House* (Edward Sutherland, US) 108; *King Kong* (Merian C. Cooper and Ernest B. Schoedsack, US) 170

1933–40: *W.C. Fields Comedy Collection* (Various Directors, US) 108

1933–83: *Norman McLaren: Masters' Edition* (Various Directors) 200

1934: *It's a Gift* (Norman Z. MacLeod, US) 108

1935: *Bride of Frankenstein* (James Whale, US) 114

1936: *Partie de Campagne* (Jean Renoir, France) 232

1937: *La Grande Illusion* (Jean Renoir, France) 125

1938: *Alexander Nevsky* (Sergei Eisenstein, Soviet Union) 94; *Bringing Up Baby* (Howard Hawks, US) 40

1938–58: *Sergei Eisenstein: The Sound Years* (Soviet Union) 94

1939: *Gone with the Wind* (Victor Fleming, US) 121; *The Roaring Twenties* (Raoul

Walsh, US) 260; *Stagecoach* (John Ford, US) 333; *The Wizard of Oz* (Victor Fleming, US) 342; *You Can't Cheat an Honest Man* (George Marshall, US) 108

1939–57: *John Wayne – John Ford Film Collection* (US) 333

1940: *The Bank Dick* (Edward F. Cline, US) 108; *The Long Voyage Home* (John Ford, US) 333; *My Little Chickadee* (Edward F. Cline, US) 108

1941: *Citizen Kane* (Orson Welles, US) 58; *The Lady Eve* (Preston Sturges, US) 177; *Little Foxes* (William Wyler, US) 185

1942: *To Be or Not To Be* (Ernst Lubitsch, US) 314; *Casablanca* (Michael Curtiz, US) 48; *Listen to Britain* (Humphrey Jennings, UK) 158

1942–46: *The Humphrey Jennings Collection* (UK) 158

1943: *Fires Were Started* (Humphrey Jennings, UK) 158; *I Was a Fireman* (Humphrey Jennings, UK) 158; *The Life and Death of Colonel Blimp* (Michael Powell and Emeric Pressburger, UK) 182

1943–59: *Deren, Maya: Experimental Films* (Maya Deren [with Alexander Hammid], US) 81

1944: *Laura* (Otto Preminger, US) 180; *Murder, My Sweet* (Edward Dmytryk, US) 110

1944–50: *The Film Noir Classic Collection, Vol I* (Various Directors, US) 110

1945: *Brief Encounter* (David Lean, UK) 39; *Les Enfants du Paradis* (Marcel Carné, France) 98; *They Were*

317; *Once Upon a Time in the West* (Sergio Leone, Italy/US) 226; *Partner* (Bernardo Bertolucci, Italy) 233; *Petulia* (Richard Lester, US) 242; *Planet of the Apes* (Franklin J. Schaffner, US) 245; *Where Eagles Dare* (Brian G. Hutton, US) 336; *Witchfinder General* (Michael Reeves, UK) 340

1968–79: *Turi Norstein – The Complete Works* (USSR) 221

1969: *On Her Majesty's Secret Service* (Peter Hunt, UK) 224; *Salesman* (Albert and David Maysles, US) 268; *The Sorrow and the Pity* (Marcel Ophüls; West Germany/ Switzerland) 285

1970: *The Conformist* (Bernardo Bertolucci, Italy) 67; *The Go-Between* (Joseph Losey, UK) 119; *Le Cercle Rouge* (Jean-Pierre Melville, France) 52; *Performance* (Donald Cammell and Nicholas Roeg, UK) 239; *Whity* (Rainer Werner Fassbinder, Germany) 337

1971: *The Hired Hand* (Peter Fonda, US) 142; *The Last Picture Show* (Peter Bogdanovich, US) 178; *THX 1138* (George Lucas, US) 311

1972: *Aguirre, the Wrath of God* (Werner Herzog, Germany) 140; *Cries and Whispers* (Ingmar Bergman, Sweden) 72

1972–90: *The Godfather DVD Collection* (Francis Ford Coppola, US) 120

1972–99: *Herzog Kinski – aka Werner Herzog Box Set I* (Germany) 140

1973: *Don't Look Now* (Nicholas Roeg, Italy/UK) 88; *The Exorcist* (William Friedkin, US) 101; *Lisa and the Devil* (Mario Bava, Italy/Germany/Spain) 184; *The Spirit of the Beehive* (Victor Erice, Spain) 286

1974: *Ali: Fear Eats the Soul* (Rainer Werner Fassbinder, Germany)) 6; *Bring Me the Head of Alfredo Garcia* (Sam

Peckinpah, US) 41; *Céline and Julie Go Boating* (Jacques Rivette, France) 50; *Chinatown* (Roman Polanski, US) 56; *The Conversation* (Francis Ford Coppola, US) 68; *F for Fake* (Orson Welles, France) 103; *Swept Away* (Lina Wertmüller, Italy) 334; *The Texas Chain Saw Massacre* (Tobe Hooper, US) 303; *The Wicker Man* (Robin Hardy, UK) 338

1974–99: *The Lina Wertmüller Collection* (Italy) 334

1975: *Jaws* (Steven Spielberg, US) 157; *The Lost Honor of Katharina Blum* (Volker Schlöndorff and Margarethe von Trotta, West Germany) 189; *Monty Python and the Holy Grail* (Terry Gilliam and Terry Jones, UK) 206; *Nashville* (Robert Altman, US) 215; *Night Moves* (Arthur Penn, US) 217; *The Passenger* (Michelangelo Antonioni, France/Italy/US/Spain) 234

1976: *Ai No Corrida* (Nagisa Oshima; Japan) 3; *Carrie* (Brian DePalma, US) 47; *Harlan County, USA* (Barbara Kopple, US) 136; *Marathon Man* (John Schlesinger, US) 195

1977: *New York, New York* (Martin Scorsese, US) 216; *That Obscure Object of Desire* (Luis Buñuel, France) 304; *Seven Beauties* (Lina Wertmüller, Italy) 334

1978: *Dawn of the Dead* (George A. Romero, US) 317; *The Deer Hunter* (Michael Cimino, US) 79; *Invasion of the Body Snatchers* (Philip Kaufman, US) 154

1979: *Alien* (Ridley Scott, US) 7; *Cannibal Holocaust* (Ruggero Deodato, Colombia/Italy) 44; *The Jerk* (Carl Reiner, US) 159; *Nosferatu* (Werner Herzog, Germany) 140

1979/2001: *Apocalypse Now: The Complete Dossier* (Francis Ford Coppola, US) 15

1979–2003: *Quay Brothers – The Short Films 1979–2003*

(Steven and Timothy Quay; UK) 253

1980: *Airplane!* (Jim Abrahams, David and Jerry Zucker, US) 4; *The Big Red One – The Reconstruction* (Sam Fuller, US) 29; *The Empire Strikes Back* (Irving Kirshner, US) 97; *Raging Bull* (Martin Scorsese, US) 254; *The Shining* (Stanley Kubrick, US/UK) 279

1980–88: *The Errol Morris Collection* (US) 208

1981: *Coup de Torchon* (Bertrand Tavernier, France) 70

1982: *The Draughtsman's Contract* (Peter Greenaway, UK) 91; *E.T.: The Extra-Terrestrial* (Steven Spielberg, US) 100; *Fanny and Alexander* (Ingmar Bergman, Sweden) 104; *Q: The Winged Serpent* (Larry Cohen, US) 252; *The Thing* (John Carpenter, US) 306

1983: *Born in Flames* (Lizzie Borden, US) 36; *The Boys from Fengkuei* (Hou Hsiao-Hsien, Taiwan) 147; *The King of Comedy* (Martin Scorsese, US) 171; *Sans Soleil* (Chris Marker, France) 160; *Videodrome* (David Cronenberg, US) 329

1983–86: *Hou Hsiao-Hsien Classic Movie Collection* (Taiwan) 147

1984: *Amadeus* (Milos Forman, US) 10; *Blood Simple* (Joel (and Ethan) Coen, US) 32; *The Company of Wolves* (Neil Jordan, UK) 65; *A Nightmare on Elm Street* (Wes Craven, US) 220; *Paris, Texas* (Wim Wenders, France/Germany) 231; *Stop Making Sense* (Jonathan Demme, US) 289; *Stranger than Paradise* (Jim Jarmusch, US) 291; *A Summer at Grandpa's* (Hou Hsiao-Hsien, Taiwan) 147; *The Terminator* (James Cameron, US) 301; *This is Spinal Tap* (Rob Reiner, US) 308

1984/1990: *Gremlins & Gremlins 2: The New Batch* (Joe Dante, US) 129

1985: *Come and See* (Elem Klimov, Belarus) 63; *Day of*

(Anthony Minghella, US) 297; *Toy Story 2 – Special Edition* (John Lasseter, US) 315

2000: *Amores Perros* (Alejandro Gonzáles Iñárritu, Mexico) 11; *Atanarjuat: The Fast Runner* (Zacharias Kunuk; Canada) 17; *The Cell* (Tarsem Singh, US) 51; *Crouching Tiger, Hidden Dragon* (Ang Lee, US/China) 73; *Dancer in the Dark* (Lars von Trier, Denmark) 75; *The House of Mirth* (Terence Davies, UK) 148; *ivansxtc.* (Bernard Rose, UK/US) 156; *Memento* (Chris Nolan, US) 201; *Requiem for a Dream* (Darren Aronofsky, US) 259; *Secretary* (Steven Shainberg, US) 275; *Timecode* (Mike Figgis, US) 312; *Ti Ti* (Edward Yang, Tiawan/Japan) 345

2001: *A.I. Artificial Intelligence* (Steven Spielberg, US) 2; *Donnie Darko* (Richard Kelly, US) 89; *Happiness of the Katakuris* (Takashi Miike, Japan) 134; *Hedwig and the Angry Inch* (John Cameron Mitchell, US) 138; *The Lord of the Rings: The Fellowship of the Rings* (Peter Jackson, New Zealand/US) 188; *Metoroporisu – Metropolis* (Rintaro, Japan) 205; *Mulholland Drive* (David Lynch, France/US) 211; *Onde Jaz O Teu Sorriso* (Pedro Costa, France/Portugal) 227; *The Others* (Alejandro Amenabar, Spain/France/US) 229; *The Royal Tenenbaums* (Wes Anderson, US) 265; *Sex and Lucía* (Julio Medem, Spain) 278; *Y Tu Mamá*

También (Alfonso Cuarón, Mexico) 344

2002: *Bus 173* (José Padilha, Brazil) 42; *demonlover* (Olivier Assayas; France) 80; *Far from Heaven* (Todd Haynes, US) 106; *Lilo and Stitch* (Dean DeBois and Chris Sanders, US) 183; *My Little Eye* (Marc Evans, UK) 212; *Talk to Her* (Pedro Almodóvar, Spain) 298; *Time of the Wolf* (Michael Haneke, France/Austria/Germany) 313; *24 Hour Party People* (Michael Winterbottom, UK) 319; *Unknown Pleasures* (Jia Zhang-Ke, China) 343; *Uzak* (Nuri Bilge Ceylan, Turkey) 326

2002/2004: *Ten & 10 on Ten* (Abbazzs Kiarostami,Iran) 300

2003: *Angels in America* (Mike Nichols, US) 13; *Capturing the Friedmans* (Andrew Jarecki, US) 45; *The Company* (Robert Altman, US) 64; *The Corporation* (Mark Achbar, Jennifer Abbott and Joel Bakan, Canada) 69; *Elf* (Jon Favreau, US) 96; *Final Destination 2* (David Ellis, US) 111; *Goodbye, Dragon Inn* (Tsai Ming-Liang, Taiwan) 122; *Master and Commander: The Far Side of the World* (Peter Weir, US) 198; *Oldboy* (Park Chan-Wook, South Korea) 223; *The Saddest Music in the World* (Guy Maddin, Canada) 266; *School of Rock* (Richard Linklater, US) 273; *Solaris* (Steven Soderbergh, US) 283

2003–04: *Kill Bill: Vols 1 & 2* (Quentin Tarantino, US) 167

2004: *The Bourne Supremacy* (Paul Greengrass, US) 37; *Directors Commentary* (TV Director, UKTV) 84; *DodgeBall: A True Underdog Story* (Rawson Marshall Thurber, US) 85; *Eternal Sunshine of the Spotless Mind* (Michel Gondry, US) 99; *I ♥ Huckabees* (David O. Russell, US) 150; *Innocence* (Lucile Hadzihalilovic, France) 153; *Kabhi Kushi Kabbie Gham* (Karan Johar, India) 165; *Kung Fu Hustle* (Stephen Chow; Hong Kong/China) 174; *Maria Full of Grace* (Joshua Marston; US/Colombia) 196; *Metallica: Some Kind of Monster* (Joe Berlinger and Bruce Sinofsky, US) 203; *Moolaadé* (Ousmane Sembene, Senegal/France/Burkina Faso) 207; *La Niña Santa* (Lucrecia Martel, Argentina) 221; *Before Sunset* (Richard Linklater, US) 25; *Team America: World Police* (Trey Parker, US) 299

2005: *Junebug* (Phil Morrison, US) 164; *Mrs Harris* (Phyllis Nagy, US) 210; *The Three Burials of Melquiades Estrada* (Tommy Lee Jones, US) 309

2006: *Borat: Cultural Learnings of America for Make Benefit Glorious Nation of Kazakhstan* (Larry Charles; US) 35; *Children of Men* (Alfonso Cuarón, US) 55; *United 93* (Paul Greengrass, US) 323; *When the Levees Broke: A Requiem in Four Acts* (Spike Lee, US) 335